DEVIANCE

THE INTERACTIONIST PERSPECTIVE

EIGHTH EDITION

EARL RUBINGTON

Northeastern University

MARTIN S. WEINBERG

Indiana University

ALLYN AND BACON

Boston   London   Toronto   Sydney   Tokyo   Singapore

Series Editor: Jennifer Jacobson
Editorial Assistant: Tom Jefferies
Marketing Manager: Judeth Hall
Production Administrator: Deborah Brown
Editorial-Production Service: P. M. Gordon Associates
Cover Administrator: Kristina Mose-Libon
Composition Buyer: Linda Cox
Manufacturing Buyer: Joanne Sweeney
Electronic Composition: Omegatype Typography, Inc.

Library of Congress Cataloging-in-Publication Data

Rubington, Earl.
    Deviance : the interactionist perspective / [compiled by] Earl Rubington,
Martin S. Weinberg. — 8th ed.
        p.   cm.
    Includes bibliographical references.
    ISBN 0-205-31908-4
    1. Deviant behavior.   2. Social interaction.   I. Weinberg, Martin S.
    II. Title.

HM811.R8 2002
302.5'42—dc21

                                                    2001018927

Printed in the United States of America
10 9 8 7 6 5 4 3 2 1   05 04 03 02 01

*To
Sara and Alex,
Barbara, Ellana, Marion, Caitlin,
Charles, Lilly, Julia, and Reilly*

Contents

PREFACE

The purpose of this book has been to present students with recent and important work in the sociology of deviance. We have, however, limited ourselves to one particular approach to this study. We call this approach the interactionist perspective.

The interactionist approach to the study of deviance is by no means new. But until the appearance of the first edition of *Deviance: The Interactionist Perspective,* students had to search for statements of the approach as well as for studies that exemplified it. The purpose of the first edition, then, was to present the interactionist approach to the study of deviance and to make readily available the excellent studies that set forth or illustrate it. In the succeeding editions, we have updated the readings and made special efforts to make our own text more readable.

We see this book as having two major uses. As a statement on the interactionist perspective on deviance and a collection of readings employing that approach, the book can be used in deviance courses that are taught from the interactionist point of view. The second use is that of adjunct to deviance courses that are organized around other points of view. Most of the papers presented in this book can very easily stand on their own merits, and even if the book does nothing more than familiarize readers with these works, it will have served its purpose.

In this edition we have incorporated twelve new readings and made some modifications in the book's organization and text. In this way, we have tried to continue to update *Deviance: The Interactionist Perspective.*

E. R.
M. S. W.

GENERAL INTRODUCTION

This book examines deviance as a social phenomenon. Central to this approach is the notion that deviance is, above all, a matter of social definition. That is, an alleged behavior or condition is "deviant" if people say it is. The social aspect of deviance becomes clear when someone perceives another person as departing from accepted norms, interprets the person to be some kind of deviant, and influences others also to regard the person as deviant and to act on the basis of that interpretation. As a *social* phenomenon, then, deviance consists of a set of interpretations and social reactions.

When people are interpreted as being deviant, they are usually regarded as being a particular *type* of deviant. These types may be general (e.g., ex-convict, mentally ill, sexually "loose," retarded), or they may be more specific (e.g., car thief, paranoid schizophrenic, call girl, Down syndrome). Whether these labels are general or specific, they usually suggest what one can expect of the so-called deviant and how one should act toward the deviant (e.g., with suspicion, avoidance, vigilance, vengeance). And in coming to terms with such labeling the "deviants" may revise their self-concepts and their actions in accordance with the way they have been labeled. For example, a child who has been typed by school authorities as having a speech problem may become self-conscious and shy, with a concomitant loss of self-esteem, because the child has been told that he or she doesn't talk properly.

At the same time, social typing does allow people to relate to one another in an organized manner. Imagine how much more complicated it would be for police officers, for example, to do their jobs if they did not have a set of categories in which to place people ("She's a hooker"; "He's a junkie"; "He looks like he might be casing that store"; "She's a teenage runaway"; "He's a derelict with no place to go").

The interactionist perspective focuses on just such issues as these—how people label one another, how they relate to one another on the basis of these labels, and the consequences of these social processes. As such, the interactionist perspective helps immensely in our understanding not only of the sociology of deviance but also of social process in general.

THE PLAN OF THE BOOK

The selections that follow spell out the interactionist perspective in greater detail. The first half of the book, which consists of Parts One and Two, deals with how people define some persons as deviant and act on the basis of these definitions. Part One shows how deviance is dealt with in primary groups and informal relations and how a person is singled out and assigned a deviant status by intimates such as family members. Part Two deals with these processes in the formal regulation of deviance. For example, it considers how agents of social control, such as the police, define persons as deviants, how they act on these definitions, and what some of the consequences of formal sanctions are.

The second half of the book (Parts Three and Four) discusses deviants themselves: how they respond to being typed by others, how they type themselves, and how they form deviant groups. Part Three examines the social organization of deviance, and how people get into a deviant group and learn its norms. Finally, this section examines the social diversity that can exist in what many people assume is a homogenous group. Part Four shows how persons may take on deviant identities through self-typing, how they manage deviant identities, and how they may eventually regain "respectability."

This book, then, focuses not on people's motivations for doing things that are regarded as deviant but rather on the *sociology* of deviance—the processes that divide society into different types of people and the social effects of these processes.

PART ONE

THE SOCIAL DEVIANT

Sociology is the study of social relations. Sociologists study how people arrive at common definitions of their situation; how they form groups based on such definitions; and how they go on to set down rules of conduct, assign social roles to each other, and enforce their rules. Sociologists examine these questions as part of the larger question: How do people attempt to produce and sustain social order?

Deviance implies an alleged breach of a social norm. By looking at deviance we can come to a better understanding of social interaction. At the same time, the study of deviance also sheds light on the way "deviant" patterns and lifestyles are themselves organized.

There are at least two ways of studying deviance as a social phenomenon. The first is to approach deviance as objectively given; the second, as subjectively problematic.

Deviance as objectively given. Sociologists who treat deviance as objectively given delineate the norms of the society under study and regard any deviation from these norms as "deviant." These sociologists generally make three assumptions. First, they assume that there is widespread consensus in the society in the realm of norms; this widespread agreement, they believe, makes it relatively easy to identify deviance. Second, they assume that deviance typically evokes negative sanctions such as gossip or legal action. Third, they assume that the punishment meted out to the deviant reaffirms for the group that it is bound by a set of common norms. The major questions raised by this approach are the following: What sociocultural conditions are most likely to produce deviance? Why do people continue to deviate despite the negative sanctions that are brought to bear on them? and How can deviance best be minimized or controlled?

From these assumptions and questions, certain procedures have evolved for studying deviants. First list the "do's" and "don'ts" of the society or group. Then study the official records kept on persons who violate these rules. Interview persons appearing in these records, and consult agents of social control such as police and judges. Try to discover the ways in which deviants differ from nondeviants (e.g., are deviants more likely than nondeviants to come from broken homes?) in order to discern the kinds of social and cultural conditions that seem to make deviant behavior more likely. Try to derive a theory to "explain" deviance, and then apply the theory for the correction and prevention of deviance.

The strength of this approach is the sharpness and simplicity with which it phrases questions. The weak points of this approach follow from its key assumptions. In the United States there are so many different groups and ways of thinking that people often do not agree on norms. Because of this lack of agreement, and also because of the fact that some people get caught whereas others avoid discovery, it is often very difficult and complex to identify who is deviant and who is not. Also, most social control agencies operate with selective enforcement, so that certain categories of people are more likely than others to be punished for their deviance. Thus the nature, causes, and consequences of deviance are neither simple nor uniform.

Deviance as subjectively problematic. Sociologists who focus on the social differentiation of deviants generally make another set of assumptions. First, they assume that when people and groups interact they communicate with one another by means of shared symbols (verbal and body language, style of dress, etc.). Through such symbolic communication, it is assumed, people are able to type one another and formulate their actions accordingly. Second, they assume that deviance can best be understood in terms of this process, that deviant labels are symbols that differentiate and stigmatize the people to whom they are applied. Finally, sociologists using this approach assume that people act on the basis of such definitions. Thus people treat the alleged deviant differently from other people. The alleged deviant, in turn, may also react to this definition. On the basis of these assumptions, sociologists using this perspective focus on social definitions and on how these influence social interaction. On the one hand, they focus on the perspective and actions of those who define a person as being deviant. They look at the circumstances under which a person is most likely to get set apart as deviant, how a person is cast into a deviant role, what actions others take on the basis of that definition of a person, and the consequences of these actions. On the other hand, these sociologists also focus on the perspective and reactions of the person adjudged to be deviant. They consider how a person reacts to being so adjudged, how a person adopts a deviant role, what changes in group memberships result, and what changes occur in the alleged deviant's self-concept.

Whereas the objectively given approach focuses primarily on the characteristics of the deviant or the conditions that give rise to deviant acts, the subjectively problematic approach focuses on the definitions and actions both of the deviants themselves and of the people who label them deviant, and on the social interaction between the two. Thus we call the latter approach the interactionist perspective.

This book adopts the interactionist perspective, approaching deviance as subjectively problematic rather than as objectively given. In this book, then, deviants are considered simply as people who are socially typed in a certain way. Such typing usually involves an attempt to make sense of seemingly aberrant acts. As people seek to make sense of such acts, they generally employ stereotypical interpretations that define the actor as a particular kind of person (a kook, a drunk, a psychopath, etc.), that include a judgment about the moral quality of the deviant or his or her motives, and that suggest how a person should act toward the deviant. The social definitions of deviance, then, consist of a *description,* an *evaluation,* and a *prescription.* For example, a "kook" is a person who is mildly eccentric (description). The term connotes that "kooks" are odd but not particularly evil or dangerous (evaluation). Thus one may display dislike or friendly disrespect toward them (prescription). A person who comes to be defined as a "psychopath," on the other hand, is considered to be both odd and severely unpredictable (description). The psychopath is often regarded as self-centered, evil, and dangerous (evaluation). And the psychopath is to be taken seriously at all times; a person who shows dislike or disrespect toward a "psychopath" does so at great personal risk (prescription). Thus the definition of a person as a particular type of deviant organizes people's responses to that person. And the more people who share the definition that a person is a particular type of deviant, the greater the consequences.

Taking the subjective approach to deviance, Part One of this book examines such phenomena more specifically. The topics treated in this part of the book include how people type, or label, others as deviants, the cultural context of typing, the accommodations people make to the so-called deviance, and how people may collaborate to exclude deviants from their midst.

THE PROCESS OF SOCIAL TYPING

Sociologically, deviance is approached here in terms of social differentiation. This differentiation arises from the perception that something is amiss. If a potential typer, or labeler, ignores or excuses the alleged aberrant quality of a person or event, it goes unlabeled as deviant. For instance, a person who works hard is expected sometimes to be tired and cranky, and in such situations people may not attach any particular importance to this behavior. Once an act or a person is typed as "deviant," however, a variety of social phenomena may come into play. These phenomena include who types whom, on what grounds, in what ways, before or after what acts (real or imputed), in front of what audience, and with what effects.

Let us for a moment consider the conditions that seem to make typing more effective. First, typing generally has the most effect when the typer, the person typed as deviant, and other people all share and understand the deviant definition in their social relationships. The typer and others act toward the "deviant" in accord with their shared understanding of the situation. Aware of having been so typed, the deviant, in turn, takes that shared understanding into account in relating to people. Thus, willingly or otherwise, all parties may subscribe to the definition. When all agree in this way, the definition of the person as a particular type of deviant is most socially effective, or confirmed. As an example, Frank Tannenbaum, one of the fathers of the interactionist perspective on deviance, has said: "The process of making the criminal…is a process of tagging, defining, identifying, segregating, describing, emphasizing, and evoking the very traits that are complained of…. The person becomes the thing he is described as being." Tannenbaum says that "the community cannot deal with people whom it cannot define" and that "the young delinquent becomes bad because he is defined as bad and because he is not believed if he is good."[1]

Second, social types are generally more apt to be accepted by other people if a high-ranking person does the typing. Effective social typing usually flows down rather than up the social structure. For example, an honor bestowed by the President of the United States is more likely to be consequential than an honor bestowed by a low-ranking official. Conversely, a denunciation by a very high-ranking person such as the president of a company will usually carry more weight, and be confirmed by more people, than a denunciation by a low-ranking person such as one of the company's janitors.

Third, deviant typing is also more apt to be effective if there is a sense that the alleged deviant is violating important norms and that the violations are extreme. For instance, if factory workers are tacitly expected to turn out only a limited amount of work, a worker who produces much more than the norm may be singled out and ostracized as a "rate-buster." On the other hand, a person who jaywalks is unlikely to be typed and treated as a deviant.

Fourth, it also seems that negative social typing is more readily accepted than positive typing. For one thing, "misery loves company"; people find comfort in learning about the frailties of others. In addition, norms seem to be highlighted more by infraction than by conformity. Also, negative typing is seen as a valuable safeguard if the type indicates an aberrant pattern that will probably continue and that has major consequences. Some police officers, for instance, expect upper-class adolescents to misbehave in their youth but later to become influential and respected citizens, while they expect slum adolescents who are vandals, troublemakers, or delinquents to become hardened criminals in adulthood; thus such police officers are more likely to negatively type slum youths than upper-class youths who break the same laws.

Fifth, typing will be accepted more readily if the audience stands to gain from the labeling. Endorsing attention to another person's deviant behavior, for example, may divert attention from one's own. It may also sustain a status difference between oneself and the so-called deviant.

When social typing is effective, there are three kinds of consequences that most often follow: self-fulfilling prophecy, typecasting, and recasting. In the self-fulfilling prophecy, typing is based on false beliefs about the alleged deviant, but the actions other people take on the basis of these false beliefs eventually make them become a reality. For example, both black and white police officers believe that it is more difficult to arrest blacks than whites. As a result, they tend to use more force in arresting blacks, and in turn they experience more resistance from blacks. In typecasting, the deviant stereotype is so widely accepted that confirmation of the typing proceeds rapidly, and typer, audience, and the person typed relate to each other in an automatic manner. For instance, if one person types another as a thief, any audience can generally predict and understand the typer's attitudes and actions. In recasting, the most complex of the three consequences, the deviant is expected to behave conventionally and is encouraged to disprove the deviant typing (e.g., to reform). Probation officers, for example, may encourage conventionality by restricting the opportunities of their probationers to continue their deviant ways. In the first two consequences of typing, the typer and audience restrict the deviant's opportunities to disprove the deviant typing. In recasting, the typer and the audience restrict the deviant's opportunities to confirm the deviant typing.

THE CULTURAL CONTEXT

The process of social typing occurs within a cultural context. Each culture, for example, has its own assortment and corresponding vocabulary of types. Thus in our own culture we no longer talk about "witches"; consequently, no one is so typed. Similarly, if we had no word for or concept of "psychopath," no one would be so typed. The culture's repertoire of deviant types and stereotypes is ordinarily created, defined, sustained, and controlled by highly valued realms of the culture (e.g., psychiatry, law, religion). In addition, it should also be noted, different categories are used in different subcultures. "Sinners," for example, are typed only in the religious sector.

Because different groups and cultures have different ideas about deviance, however, typing often has an ethnocentric bias. People in one culture or subculture may be quick to type an outsider as deviant, for instance, simply because the outsider's lifestyle is so different from their own. Among persons within the same culture or subculture, on the other hand, the risks of being typed deviant are usually smaller.

Once a person has been labeled, the question of how to relate to the deviant is more easily resolved when cultural prescriptions exist. These include the prescriptions, for example, that sick people should be treated and evil people punished. In sum, typing is easier to act on when cultural guidelines exist.

ACCOMMODATION TO DEVIANCE

As noted previously, sociologically, deviants are persons who have been effectively labeled as deviant, and *effectively* means simply that the label does in fact affect social relations. The person who has been typed as a deviant, for example, acquires a special status that carries a set of new rights and duties or changes in old ones, and a new set of expectations about future conduct. Thus when people type a certain person as deviant, they imply, "We now expect you to engage in deviant actions." In some cases, this expectation amounts to a license to deviate, as when a group may not only tolerate but actually shelter a deviant in its midst. More often, however, the expectation of deviant conduct gives other people license to treat the deviant in a demeaning way.

The pace of events in labeling is one of the critical factors in this entire process. If aberrant conduct occurs only gradually and irregularly within a small, intimate group, deviant typing may not take place at all. Even if the events place some immediate strain on relationships, members of the group may adjust to the strain without perceiving the person any differently. Eventually, though, some critical point may be reached at which the group becomes aware that things are not what they used to be. Sometimes the members of the group have long entertained suspicions of deviance, and their accommodation represents an acknowledgement that the deviation is here to stay. In other instances, though, even as they type the person as deviant, group members may be optimistic that the deviance is only temporary. In any case, the group's accommodation to the so-called deviance has usually been going on for some time before labeling actually occurs.

THE ROLE OF THIRD PARTIES

As already noted, in intimate, primary groups, people are usually slower to type one of their members as deviant than are outsiders. Such in-group labeling does happen at times, however, particularly if the deviant's aberrant behavior has begun to cause considerable strain for the rest of the group. When such strain exists, the typing of the person as deviant is often facilitated or precipitated by some outsider or outside agency—in short, by some third party.

In some cases the third party may act without solicitation. A wife, for example, may fail to recognize that her husband is involved with another woman until the community gossip (the third party) so informs her; she may then type her husband as a "son of a bitch" and may, through separation or divorce, exclude him from the family.

In other cases a member of the primary group may seek out the third party in order to validate such typing or to exclude the deviant from the group. If a man's wife is emotionally disturbed, for example, he may turn to third parties outside the family (a psychiatrist, the courts, the sheriff, etc.) in order to remove his wife from the home, officially labeling her as mentally disturbed and seeking treatment for her.

Thus we have seen some of the ways in which the social definition of deviants proceeds. A real or imputed violation of norms can activate the process of social typing, and a variety of social factors affect its success. The nature and likelihood of this typing are influenced by the cultural context. People may at first attempt to accommodate these alleged violations. Over the course of time, however, the deviant may no longer be protected. Third parties may intervene, and at that point exclusion of the deviant may take place.

NOTE

1. Frank Tannenbaum, *Crime and the Community* (New York: Columbia University Press, 1938), pp. 19–20.

CHAPTER 1

THE PROCESS OF SOCIAL TYPING

Outsiders

HOWARD S. BECKER

When people hear that a person has broken a rule, they are likely to ask, "What kind of person would do a thing like that?" What they have heard other people say in the past about deviants leads them to designate the alleged rule breaker as a certain kind of deviant social type. When researchers study the records of people who have committed crimes or who are patients in mental hospitals, they also classify the offenders or the patients into certain categories. In both instances, whether talking about or studying those thought to have broken the rules, a construction of the "kinds of people" who violate rules is supported, shared, and transmitted for use in future communication about similar actors. The result is a cultural catalog of deviant social types.

Howard S. Becker, in the following excerpt from his classic book *Outsiders: Studies in the Sociology of Deviance,* points out that the only thing all people so categorized have in common is the fact that they have been labeled deviant. Thus, his definition: Deviant behavior is behavior that people label deviant. And for labeling to take place there have to be responses of other people who may apply negative sanctions of one kind or another. He goes on to point out the variety of conditions under which labeling takes place along with the consequences of such labeling.

On the one hand, many people break rules and are never labeled. On the other hand, some are falsely accused. Time, place, the status of the rule, the person being considered, and the rule enforcer are all contingencies. And for some who have come to official attention, a deviant career can be their fate.

DEVIANCE AND THE RESPONSES OF OTHERS

[One sociological view]…defines deviance as the infraction of some agreed-upon rule. It then goes

on to ask who breaks rules, and to search for the factors in their personalities and life situations that might account for the infractions. This assumes that those who have broken a rule constitute a homogeneous category, because they have committed the same deviant act.

Such an assumption seems to me to ignore the central fact about deviance: it is created by society. I do not mean this in the way it is ordinarily understood, in which the causes of deviance are located in the social situation of the deviant or in "social factors" which prompt his action. I mean, rather, that *social groups create deviance by making the rules whose infraction constitutes deviance,* and by applying those rules to particular people and labeling them as outsiders. From this point of view, deviance is *not* a quality of the act the person commits, but rather a consequence of the application by others of rules and sanctions to an "offender." The deviant is one to whom that label has successfully been applied; deviant behavior is behavior that people so label.[1]

Since deviance is, among other things, a consequence of the responses of others to a person's act, students of deviance cannot assume that they are dealing with a homogeneous category when they study people who have been labeled deviant. That is, they cannot assume that those people have actually committed a deviant act or broken some rule, because the process of labeling may not be infallible; some people may be labeled deviant who in fact have not broken a rule. Furthermore, they cannot assume that the category of those labeled deviant will contain all those who actually have broken a rule, for many offenders may escape apprehension and thus fail to be included in the population of "deviants" they study. Insofar as the category lacks homogeneity and fails to include all the cases that belong in it, one cannot reasonably expect to find common factors of personality or life situation that will account for the supposed deviance.

What, then, do people who have been labeled deviant have in common? At the least, they share the label and the experience of being labeled as outsiders. I will begin my analysis with this basic similarity and view deviance as the product of a transaction that takes place between some social group and one who is viewed by that group as a rule-breaker. I will be less concerned with the personal and social characteristics of deviants than with the process by which they come to be thought of as outsiders and their reactions to that judgment....

The point is that the response of other people has to be regarded as problematic. Just because one has committed an infraction of a rule does not mean that others will respond as though this had happened. (Conversely, just because one has not violated a rule does not mean that he may not be treated, in some circumstances, as though he had.)

The degree to which other people will respond to a given act as deviant varies greatly. Several kinds of variation seem worth noting. First of all, there is variation over time. A person believed to have committed a given "deviant" act may at one time be responded to much more leniently than he would be at some other time. The occurrence of "drives" against various kinds of deviance illustrates this clearly. At various times, enforcement officials may decide to make an all-out attack on some particular kind of deviance, such as gambling, drug addiction, or homosexuality. It is obviously much more dangerous to engage in one of these activities when a drive is on than at any other time. (In a very interesting study of crime news in Colorado newspapers, Davis found that the amount of crime reported in Colorado newspapers showed very little association with actual changes in the amount of crime taking place in Colorado. And, further, that people's estimate of how much increase there had been in crime in Colorado was associated with the increase in the amount of crime news but not with any increase in the amount of crime.)[2]

The degree to which an act will be treated as deviant depends also on who commits the act and who feels he has been harmed by it. Rules tend to be applied more to some persons than others. Studies of juvenile delinquency make the point clearly. Boys from middle-class areas do not get as far in the legal process when they are apprehended as do boys from slum areas. The middle-class boy is less likely, when picked up by the police, to be taken to the station; less likely when taken to the station to be booked; and it is extremely unlikely that he will be convicted and sentenced.[3] This variation occurs even though the original infraction of the rule is the same in the two cases. Similarly, the law is differentially applied to Negroes and whites. It is well known that a Negro believed to have attacked a white woman is much more likely to be punished than a white man who commits the same offense; it is only slightly less well known that a Negro who murders another Negro is much less likely to be punished than a white man who commits murder.[4] This, of course, is one of the main points of Sutherland's analysis of white-collar crime: crimes committed by corporations are almost always prosecuted as civil cases, but the same crime committed by an individual is ordinarily treated as a criminal offense.[5]

Some rules are enforced only when they result in certain consequences. The unmarried mother furnishes a clear example. Vincent[6] points out that illicit sexual relations seldom result in severe punishment or social censure for the offenders. If, however, a girl becomes pregnant as a result of such activities the reaction of others is likely to be severe. (The illicit pregnancy is also an interesting example of the differential enforcement of rules on different categories of people. Vincent notes that unmarried fathers escape the severe censure visited on the mother.)

Why repeat these commonplace observations? Because, taken together, they support the proposition that deviance is not a simple quality, present in some kinds of behavior and absent in others. Rather, it is the product of a process which involves responses of other people to the behavior. The same behavior may be an infraction of the rules at one time and not at another; may be an infraction when committed by one person, but not when committed by another; some rules are broken with impunity, others are not. In short, whether a given act is deviant or not depends in part on the nature of the act (that is, whether or not it violates some rule) and in part on what other people do about it.

Some people may object that this is merely a terminological quibble, that one can, after all, define terms any way he wants to and that if some people want to speak of rule-breaking behavior as

deviant without reference to the reactions of others they are free to do so. This, of course, is true. Yet it might be worthwhile to refer to such behavior as *rule-breaking behavior* and reserve the term *deviant* for those labeled as deviant by some segment of society. I do not insist that this usage be followed. But it should be clear that insofar as a scientist uses "deviant" to refer to any rule-breaking behavior and takes as his subject of study only those who have been *labeled* deviant, he will be hampered by the disparities between the two categories.

If we take as the object of our attention behavior which comes to be labeled as deviant, we must recognize that we cannot know whether a given act will be categorized as deviant until the response of others has occurred. Deviance is not a quality that lies in behavior itself, but in the interaction between the person who commits an act and those who respond to it....

In any case, being branded as deviant has important consequences for one's further social participation and self-image. The most important consequence is a drastic change in the individual's public identity. Committing the improper act and being publicly caught at it places him in a new status. He has been revealed as a different kind of person from the kind he was supposed to be. He is labeled a "fairy," "dope fiend," "nut" or "lunatic," and treated accordingly.

In analyzing the consequences of assuming a deviant identity let us make use of Hughes' distinction between master and auxiliary status traits.[7] Hughes notes that most statuses have one key trait which serves to distinguish those who belong from those who do not. Thus the doctor, whatever else he may be, is a person who has a certificate stating that he has fulfilled certain requirements and is licensed to practice medicine; this is the master trait. As Hughes points out, in our society a doctor is also informally expected to have a number of auxiliary traits: most people expect him to be upper middle class, white, male, and Protestant. When he is not there is a sense that he has in some way failed to fill the bill. Similarly, though skin color is the master status trait determining who is Negro and who is white, Negroes are informally expected to have certain status traits and not to have others; people are surprised and find it anomalous if a Negro turns out to be a doctor or a college professor. People often have the master status trait but lack some of the auxiliary, informally expected characteristics; for example, one may be a doctor but be female or Negro.

Hughes deals with this phenomenon in regard to statuses that are well thought of, desired and desirable (noting that one may have the formal qualifications for entry into a status but be denied full entry because of lack of the proper auxiliary traits), but the same process occurs in the case of deviant statuses. Possession of one deviant trait may have a generalized symbolic value, so that people automatically assume that its bearer possesses other undesirable traits allegedly associated with it.

To be labeled a criminal one need only commit a single criminal offense, and this is all the term formally refers to. Yet the word carries a number of connotations specifying auxiliary traits characteristic of anyone bearing the label. A man who has been convicted of housebreaking and thereby labeled criminal is presumed to be a person likely to break into other houses; the police, in rounding up known offenders for investigation after a crime has been committed, operate on this premise. Further, he is considered likely to commit other kinds of crimes as well, because he has shown himself to be a person without "respect for the law." Thus, apprehension for one deviant act exposes a person to the likelihood that he will be regarded as deviant or undesirable in other respects.

There is one other element in Hughes' analysis we can borrow with profit: the distinction between master and subordinate statuses.[8] Some statuses, in our society as in others, override all other statuses and have a certain priority. Race is one of these. Membership in the Negro race, as socially defined, will override most other status considerations in most other situations; the fact that one is a physician or middle-class or female will not protect one from being treated as a Negro first and any of these other things second. The status of deviant (depending on the kind of deviance) is this kind of master status. One receives the status as a result of breaking a rule, and the identification proves to be more important than most others. One will be identified as a deviant first, before other identifications are made....

NOTES

1. The most important earlier statements of this view can be found in Frank Tannenbaum, *Crime and the Community* (New York: Columbia University Press, 1938), and E. M. Lemert, *Social Pathology* (New York: McGraw–Hill Book Co., Inc., 1951). A recent article stating a position very similar to mine is John Kitsuse, "Societal Reaction to Deviance: Problems of Theory and Method," *Social Problems,* 9 (Winter, 1962), 247–256.

2. F. James Davis, "Crime News in Colorado Newspapers," *American Journal of Sociology,* LVII (January, 1952), 325–330.

3. See Albert K. Cohen and James F. Short, Jr., "Juvenile Delinquency," in Robert K. Merton and Robert A. Nisbet, eds., *Contemporary Social Problems* (New York: Harcourt, Brace, and World, 1961), p. 87.

4. See Harold Garfinkel, "Research Notes on Inter- and Intra-Racial Homicides," *Social Forces,* 27 (May, 1949), 369–381.

5. Edwin H. Sutherland, "White Collar Criminality," *American Sociological Review,* V (February, 1940), 1–12.

6. Clark Vincent, *Unmarried Mothers* (New York: The Free Press of Glencoe, 1961), pp. 3–5.

7. Everett C. Hughes, "Dilemmas and Contradictions of Status," *American Journal of Sociology,* L (March, 1945), 353–359.

8. *Ibid.*

Careers in Deviance

DAVID F. LUCKENBILL and JOEL BEST

Criminologists have long studied the processes by which persons move from being juvenile delinquents to becoming adult criminals. And since the publication of Howard S. Becker's *Outsiders: Studies in the Sociology of Deviance,* sociologists of deviance have studied the stages in deviant careers. In both the criminological and deviance traditions, the focus has been on orderly, unilinear careers in deviance. The general assumption has been that people first experiment with deviant behavior, go on to occasional deviant practices, and then move on to regular violations of the norms.

David F. Luckenbill and Joel Best caution against too readily operating on the assumption of orderly careers in deviance. If anything, they argue that most deviant careers are disorderly. They point out that where careers in respectability are characterized by few choices and considerable certainty, careers in deviance are more often characterized by many choices and considerable uncertainty. Similarly, the risk-profit ratios are more often in favor of respectable rather than deviant careers. And where respectable careers are more often slow and regular, moving onward and upward, deviant careers are more often rapid, intermittent, episodic, and likely to move in any direction—up, down, sideways, and in and out of both deviance and respectability.

One of the central topics in the sociology of deviance is the deviant career, an individual's movement through the deviant experience. In general, studies of deviant careers assume that deviant and respectable careers are, for the most part, analogous. For example, Becker (1963:24) argues:

> Originally developed in studies of occupations, the concept [of career] refers to the sequence of movements from one position to another in an occupational system made by any individual who works in that system.... The model can easily be transformed for use in the study of deviant careers.

While the concept of deviant career rests on the analogy with respectable careers, there has been little effort to critically assess the analogy's validity.

Reprinted from "Careers in Deviance and Respectability: The Analogy's Limitations," *Social Problems,* Vol. 29, No. 2 (December 1981), pp. 197–206, by permission of the Society for the Study of Social Problems and the authors. Copyright © 1981 by the Society for the Study of Social Problems.

This failure to examine the analogy may be due to sociologists' concentration on the initial phases of the deviant career. Most researchers focus on career entry, the process of becoming deviant. This concern is reflected in theoretical statements that identify conditions facilitating entry, such as labeling, association with other deviants, and the acquisition of a deviant ideology (Becker, 1963: 22–39; Lofland, 1969:39–205; Matza, 1969: 81–197; Sutherland and Cressey, 1978:77–98). Further, empirical studies usually focus on the initial stages of specific deviant careers (Becker, 1963: 41–58; Bryan, 1965; Buckner, 1970; Dank, 1971; Goffman, 1961; Gray, 1973; Heyl, 1979; Skipper and McCaghy, 1970; Weinberg, 1966; Werthman, 1967). There are relatively few studies that examine career departure, the pathways out of deviance (Harris, 1973:113–126; Irwin, 1970; Livingston, 1974; Lofland, 1969:109–195; Ray, 1961; Stebbins, 1971). With some notable exceptions (Klockars, 1975; Lesieur, 1977), there is almost no research on the deviant career's intermediate stages, between entry and departure.

In several respects, entering a deviant career resembles entering a respectable career; the individual acquires the knowledge and skill needed to perform central roles, makes contacts with others, and so on. However, the intermediate and final career stages feature some important differences between deviant and respectable experiences. Respectable careers—particularly occupational careers in formal organizations—develop within a relatively stable institutional environment. Organizational rules spell out the career's positions, pathways for mobility, and rewards, while authorities enforce these rules and ensure the career's security. In contrast, deviants usually cannot draw on institutional resources; they risk social control sanctions and exploitation by deviant associates and their rewards from deviance are precarious. Thus, deviant careers develop within a non-institutional environment. This is important. Faced with high risks and precarious rewards, deviants' careers tend to be less structured and less stable than their respectable counterparts, requiring special strategies for career management.

By critically examining the analogy between deviant and respectable careers, this paper refines the concept of deviant career. It begins with an examination of respectable careers, followed by a comparison with deviant careers. This comparison reveals some important differences, challenging the analogy between deviance and respectability.

RESPECTABLE CAREERS

Sociological research on respectable careers typically focuses on occupational careers within legitimate formal organizations (Becker and Strauss, 1956; Blankenship, 1973; Glaser, 1968; Hughes, 1958; Miller and Form, 1964; Stebbins, 1970). In their well-known analysis of organizational careers, Becker and Strauss (1956) use the metaphor of a multi-storied building. Each floor represents a position in the organizational structure, and members ride escalators from one floor to the next. This metaphor suggests several definitive features of respectable organizational careers. First, the organizational structure through which individuals move contains a set of formally defined positions. Written rules articulate the qualifications, responsibilities, benefits, and privileges associated with specific positions. Organizational codes also regulate the relationships among positions, specifying relative ranks and appropriate claims and obligations. Second, individuals move from one position to another along established pathways. Members cannot move wherever or whenever they choose. Rather, organizational rules prescribe the sequences of positions through which members must move, so that an individual usually cannot reach one position without having served in certain other positions. Third, the expected career path involves upward movement through the organization's ranks. Progress depends on acquiring certain competencies or serving a specified period of time at a particular rank; members who fail to meet the standards for upward mobility may be forced out of the organization. Often, progress is a public matter; promotions may be formally announced and affirmed through new status symbols. Fourth, as members move upward, they receive greater rewards, including more money and fringe benefits. Increased rewards generally are coupled with greater security; promotion may bring tenure, for instance. Organizational rules that articulate reward scales, as well as a career's positions and pathways, are enforced by recognized authorities. Finally, the organizational career is a central involvement in the individual's life. Simultaneous involvement in another occupation (moonlighting) may be discouraged; the individual should view other, part-time jobs as less important than the organizational career. Furthermore, the career should extend over the individual's working life; members are expected to spend years within the organization.

The escalator metaphor implies that organizational careers involve a well-defined structure, established pathways, and progress with increased rewards and security. Admittedly, this characterization is ideal–typical; many respectable careers do not fit this pattern. Contingencies can make organizational careers problematic; individuals may face ambiguous career routes, limited access to established pathways, insufficient sponsorship, and so forth (Blankenship, 1973). They may change paths in the course of movement, move from one organization to another, or change occupations and begin new careers. But overall, the respectable careers studied by sociologists occur within well-defined organizational environments. As a consequence, the career concept implies movement through a relatively clear, stable structure.

DEVIANT CAREERS

In contrast, deviant careers develop within a relatively unstructured environment; the features characterizing respectable careers do not fit deviant careers. Deviant careers do not occur within a hierarchy of well-defined positions. Many deviants learn codes of conduct that specify the actions expected of them in particular situations and their relationships with other deviants. For instance, road hustlers learn to work together when cheating people and to divide their profits equally (Prus and Sharper, 1977). However, because their activities make them eligible for social control efforts, deviants cannot commit their positions, relationships, and codes to a written record. Deviants also lack the institutional supports available to respectable people; deviants cannot turn to social control agents to enforce their rules and mediate their disputes (McIntosh, 1973). Consequently, the positions and relationships within a deviant scene are relatively ambiguous, subject to interpretation and negotiation among deviants. For example, it is customary for fences to pay thieves one-third the value for stolen goods, but the actual price generally is negotiable (Klockars, 1975). Negotiation is possible because most deviant networks are small enough for members to deal with one another through face-to-face interaction and most relationships between members of a deviant scene are informal (Best and Luckenbill, 1980).

Except in deviant formal organizations which supply illicit goods and services, deviants rarely occupy formal positions of authority over one another. A delinquent gang's president is an informal leader; authority resides in the person, not the office. Deviants' relationships are governed by custom but, lacking institutional supports, individuals are vulnerable to betrayal or exploitation by deviant associates. Without well-defined positions and institutional supports, a deviant scene becomes an arena where strength and intention are problematic and risks are high.

Without a formal hierarchy, most deviant scenes have few well-defined sequences for career mobility. Studies of the initial stages of deviant careers typically argue that newcomers share a set of cognitive experiences analogous to those of individuals beginning respectable organizational careers. Yet most deviant careers lack a regular, established sequence of positions through which individuals move; there are multiple pathways into, through, and out of deviant scenes. For instance, women entered nineteenth-century brothels for many reasons: some were pregnant, abandoned by their lovers; others were tricked or forced into prostitution; a few grew up in brothels with mothers who were prostitutes or madams; and many chose prostitution because it offered better economic prospects than the respectable jobs available to them. After entering a brothel, most women were geographically mobile, moving from one city to another or from brothel to brothel within the same city. Some brothel prostitutes became madams, others turned to streetwalking. Similarly, death, marriage, reform, and retirement offered different pathways out of vice (Best, 1982a). Rather than following a standard sequence, deviant careers vary in their contours. Variation is affected by career contingencies, including the individual's objectives, resources, and opportunities. These contingencies shape the nature, order, and timing of the deviant's experiences. In the absence of a clear organizational structure, career contingencies become particularly important.

Deviants' career pathways do not always lead upward. In fact, some descriptions of deviance emphasize downward mobility; prostitutes supposedly move downward, making less money as they grow older and less attractive (Winick and Kinsie, 1971). But it is often difficult to determine the direction of mobility in a deviant scene, or to know where an individual stands at a given moment (Stebbins, 1971:32). If a marijuana user begins to experiment with other illicit drugs, the deviant career takes a new turn, but it is not necessarily upward or downward. Models of respectable career progress share an assumption that upward mobility can be measured against some standard. However, deviant scenes usually lack established standards. Respectable organizational careers move through positions of known rank, so that advancement can be measured, but many deviant careers feature diverse involvements—with different scenes, different associates, and so on. For instance, male prostitutes can be ranked according to income and prestige, ranging from the call boy through the bar hustler to the street-hustler. But boys move continuously among these ranks; a boy who finds few customers in a bar may turn to the street, and if the street fails to produce customers, he may return to a bar or call a steady customer (Luckenbill, 1981). Mobility in a deviant career is often of uncertain direction.

The rewards of deviance are equally uncertain. Whereas upward mobility in respectable careers brings greater rewards and more security, the fruits of deviance are precarious, subject to career contingencies. Deviant operations generally offer an uncertain return; a pickpocket cannot be sure how much money the next mark will have. Moreover, deviants lack the institutional supports that insure the security of respectable careers. They routinely face the risk of apprehension and sanctioning by social control agents, as well as the danger of betrayal or exploitation by their associates. Nor do these risks diminish as the deviant career proceeds; they may even increase, making the career more insecure. As individuals become more deeply involved in deviance, their reputations spread, making it more likely that they will attract the attention of the authorities or other, predatory deviants.

Because publicity increases the deviant's risks, career advancement cannot be made public. Secrecy is an important theme in the deviant experience. Individuals adopt various tactics to maintain secrecy: they commit deviant acts in private whenever possible; they limit contacts to those associates who can be trusted; and they control information which social control agents might use to identify and apprehend them. Ideally, their deviance remains secret; they pass as respectable (Goffman, 1963). Even those who know about an individual's deviance may not comprehend the full extent of his or her illicit involvements. While secrecy minimizes the deviant's risks, it adds to the ambiguity of career progress.

Deviant careers differ from their respectable counterparts in another important respect. Ideally, respectable organizational careers remain a central involvement throughout the individual's working life. In contrast, many careers in deviance are short-lived. In some cases, a single episode comprises the deviant career, as when a woman obtains an illegal abortion. More often, the individual's deviant involvement lasts only a few years; delinquency is confined to adolescence, for example. When deviance requires youthful qualities, such as physical attractiveness, agility, or strength, most people find it increasingly difficult to maintain their illicit activities, and they eventually leave deviance. Moreover, deviant careers often include several deviant involvements. Unlike a respectable worker's central commitment to an organizational career, deviants often combine deviant involvements. For instance, some drug addicts steal and others sell drugs. While these diverse involvements can be distinguished analytically, they blend together in the individual's deviant experience.

In summary, deviant and respectable careers display very different characteristics. Deviant careers are less likely to develop within a well-defined organizational hierarchy and they are less likely to follow standard career pathways leading upward. Rewards and security are less likely to increase as the deviant career continues and career progress is less often public. Finally, deviant careers are more likely to feature multiple, short-term involvements. These comparisons reveal limitations in the analogy between deviant and respectable careers; deviant careers develop within a relatively ambiguous and unstable structural context.

OCCUPATIONAL AND NON-OCCUPATIONAL CAREERS

The differences between deviant and respectable careers reflect, in part, researchers' choices of topics. Because analyses of respectable careers developed as part of the sociology of work, they concentrated on occupational careers (Hughes, 1958). Although some studies of deviance also use the sociology of work perspective (Inciardi, 1975; Letkemann, 1973; Miller, 1978), most research on deviance removes the career concept from the context of occupational sociology. The most familiar studies of deviant careers focus on drug use, mental illness, homosexuality, and other non-occupational involvements. Just as respectable activities can be divided into work and leisure, deviance can be classified into occupational and non-occupational forms. This has consequences for careers; occupational involvements are more likely to involve careers in well-structured organizations. To the degree that studies of respectable careers focus on the world of work and studies of deviant careers examine non-occupational deviance, they exaggerate the differences between deviance and respectability.

Yet the distinction between occupational and non-occupational careers cannot account for all of the differences between deviant and respectable careers. Among those with occupational careers, deviants are less likely to belong to formal organizations with established pathways for upward mobility, to receive greater rewards and security as their careers progress, to have public careers, or to

have long-term, central career involvements. Similarly, respectable non-occupational careers are more likely to have these features than their deviant counterparts. For instance, those who enjoy respectable leisure careers in hobbies are more likely to develop voluntary associations with other enthusiasts, attend conventions, compete for prizes, subscribe to magazines about the topic, and so on (cf. Dannefer, 1980). In leisure as in work, respectable careers develop in a more clearly structured context than deviant careers.

CAREER SHIFTS IN DEVIANCE

The analysis of deviant careers requires a framework which recognizes the ambiguous and unstable structure of the deviant experience. Riding escalators between floors may be an effective metaphor for respectable organizational careers, but it fails to capture the character of deviant careers. A more appropriate image is a walk in the woods. Here, some people take the pathways marked by their predecessors, while others strike out on their own. Some walk slowly, exploring before moving further, but others run, caught up in the action. Some have a destination in mind and proceed purposefully; others view the trip as an experience and enjoy it for its own sake. Even those intent on reaching a destination may stray from the path; they may try a shortcut or they may lose sight of familiar landmarks, get lost, and find it necessary to backtrack. Without a rigid organizational structure, deviant careers can develop in many different ways (Lemert, 1967:50–51; Sagarin, 1975:137–138).

Movement through deviant careers can be described in terms of one or more career shifts. Career shifts can take any of the following forms: (1) A deviant can shift laterally within a deviant scene, as when a professional dice mechanic becomes a shoot-up man. (2) A deviant can shift vertically within a deviant scene, as when a numbers runner becomes the manager of the regional office. (3) A deviant can shift to a new deviant scene but perform the same activity, as when a call girl later works as a streetwalker. (4) A deviant can shift to an entirely different scene, as when a safecracker turns to check forgery as a source of income. (5) A deviant can undertake additional activities within additional scenes, as when a compulsive gambler steals. With each career shift, the deviant begins a new deviant involvement. A given involvement can range from short-term to long-term, depending on career contingencies. Further, the sequence of involvements varies from one deviant to the next; some prostitutes begin to use illicit drugs for recreation or solace, while some female addicts turn to prostitution to support their habits (Goldstein, 1979). This example also suggests that deviant involvements need not occur in discrete stages; a person may have several, simultaneous involvements during the career. The concept of career shift emphasizes the fluidity of deviant careers. Deviant careers lack a prescribed sequence of career shifts; they stand in contrast to respectable organizational careers with their orderly pathways.

A deviant career shift involves several stages. In the *preliminary* stage, the deviant assembles the knowledge, skills, motives, equipment, and contacts needed to make the shift. For instance, the experienced marijuana user may get a sample of another illicit drug, such as LSD, as well as advice and encouragement from other users. During *commission,* the actor carries out the new line of action, sometimes in a tentative, experimental fashion. Thus, feeling sufficiently prepared, the marijuana user tries LSD for the first time. *Assessment* follows commission; the actor interprets the new experience. The deviant may evaluate the risks involved in the career shift, the prospects for success, the quality of the potential rewards, and so forth. The reactions of others, including deviant associates and social control agents, can help the deviant assess the shift. For example, through interaction with other LSD users, the novice compares the drug's effects to those of marijuana. Some deviants may decide not to pursue the shift, but others continue, entering the stage of *routine.* Here, deviants become familiar with the new in-

volvement, improving their skills with practice and developing an integrated framework for interpreting the experience. Thus, experienced LSD users develop a practical pharmacology of drug lore (Stoddart, 1974). With this immersion into the now familiar experience, the actor may become aware of additional *options.* These include opportunities for shifts into new positions or scenes. The LSD user may consider trying new drugs or selling LSD, for instance. Therefore, the final stage in one shift can signal the start of another shift in the deviant's career.

The deviant can abandon the process at any stage in the career shift. In the preliminary stage, the individual may assemble the needed resources but then decide not to continue, perhaps believing that the risks are too great. Similarly, deviants may back out in the midst of commission or, after assessing the new experience, choose not to repeat it. Members of respectable organizations often find it difficult to change their career pathways; refusing a promotion may threaten their careers as well as their prospects within the organization (Becker and Strauss, 1956). But the less structured pathways taken by deviants offer a wide range of choices. Some deviants experiment through career shifts, exploring the limits of their deviant involvements. Others become involved in a wide range of deviant activities, sometimes simultaneously. Still others choose to restrict their deviance, refusing to make career shifts. Deviants, unlike their respectable counterparts, can choose or refuse a career shift or interrupt a shift without endangering their deviant involvements.

Career shifts often are tentative, and deviant careers which feature one or more shifts may evolve in an uncertain direction. Individuals whose respectable organizational careers follow standard, upwardly mobile pathways can assess their own career progress, and others familiar with the organization's practices also can evaluate the pace and direction of members' careers. However, deviant careers, with their minimal structure, secrecy, and diverse career shifts, are more difficult to interpret. In retrospect, it may be possible to chart the direction of a deviant career; but while the career is in progress, both the deviant and others observing the career may be uncertain about its direction and outcome.

MANAGING DEVIANT CAREERS

The differences between deviant and respectable careers are consequential for deviants. Developing within a less clearly structured context, with comparatively few institutional supports, deviant careers feature individualized career shifts, rather than standard sequences of positions. Decisions to make career shifts reflect special career contingencies: deviants risk apprehension and sanctioning by the authorities; they face betrayal or exploitation by deviant associates; the rewards from deviant activities are unstable and irregular; and the supply of resources needed for deviance is difficult to control. These contingencies contribute to the uncertainty of the deviant experience. Deviants respond by leaving deviance or devising tactics for managing uncertainty and insuring career security.

Some choose to leave deviance. Whereas respectable careers generally extend over the individual's working life, deviant careers vary in length. Some people quit deviance after a single episode, and others leave after a few years; relatively few make it a lifelong commitment. Most studies of leaving deviance emphasize the role of the authorities or associations of ex-deviants in individuals' decisions to reform (Livingston, 1974; Lofland, 1969; Volkman and Cressey, 1963). Less is known about those who find their own paths out of deviance. Yet some deviants leave voluntarily, without the intervention of authorities or former deviants; they tire of coping with the uncertainty of the experience, with social control efforts, exploitation by other deviants, and irregular rewards (Allen, 1977; Carey, 1968; Harris, 1973). Those who remain in deviance must find ways of managing the major sources of uncertainty.

Because threats to deviants are a principal source of uncertainty, protection becomes a central concern. Obviously, deviants face the threat of social control sanctions, but deviant associates also present dangers. In respectable organizations, formal rules regulate competition among members. In contrast, deviants' relationships typically are unregulated; they may betray one another to social control agents, blackmail each other, cheat in their dealings, or attack one another. The dangers posed by officials and deviant associates jeopardize deviants' security. To protect themselves, deviants adopt various tactics. First, they attempt to neutralize social control efforts. They may gather information about social control agencies' resources and tactics, the identities of their undercover agents, and the areas where enforcement is intense and weak, and use such information to avoid apprehension and sanctioning. Deviants may corrupt social control agents, bribing officials to let them operate without interference, or paying others to fix cases when they are caught. Second, deviants attempt to protect their deviant operations. Whenever possible, deviants keep their activities secret, choosing private, secluded settings and associates who will be discreet about their illicit involvements. Some deviants may even erect respectable fronts to disguise their deviant operations, as when a fence buys and sells stolen property behind a respectable business front. Deviants also try to control their deviant transactions. Those who sell illicit goods or services seek to control their customers, setting the time and place as well as the terms for the exchange. Deviants who exploit others attempt to control their operations by disguising their personal identities, so as to avoid identification, and using force, stealth, or deception to manipulate victims and insure compliance. Third, deviants try to regulate their relationships with one another. Most deviants restrict their dealings to trustworthy associates, those with a record or reputation for honesty. Deviants develop informal codes of conduct, backed by sanctions, emphasizing loyalty and fairness; for instance, it is customary for thieves to divide their earnings evenly. Deviants sometimes negotiate their conflicting interests;

fences and thieves bargain over prices, for example. Where other arrangements fail, deviants may settle their disputes and regulate their relations through force. The uncertainty of deviance demands many tactics for insuring security, and much of the subcultural knowledge passed along to novices describes techniques for protecting deviant operations.

The irregularity of rewards from deviance also renders deviant careers uncertain. Deviants gain various gratifications from deviance, but they often cannot predict the degree to which their operations will be rewarding. Social control efforts and exploitation by deviant associates can disrupt deviants' operations and block their rewards. In addition, the sources of deviants' rewards are difficult to maintain. The nature of these sources varies with deviants' rewards; they may be suppliers (e.g., a drug addict's dealer), customers (e.g., a prostitute's client), or targets (e.g., an armed robber's victim). In any case, officials disrupt deviants' relations with sources; suppliers and customers are subject to social control and targets are protected from exploitation. Deviants depend on their sources for rewards, and they adopt various tactics to maintain sources and regularize rewards. The selection of tactics reflects the nature of the deviance. First, deviants must gain access to sources. Because deviant activities are secret, deviants must learn how to locate sources; drug addicts must learn how to contact dealers and prostitutes must learn to find customers. Second, deviants try to maintain regular contacts with sources to avoid further problems of gaining access. For instance, those who buy and sell illicit goods or services may establish a record of fair dealing to satisfy their sources and insure further contact. Third, deviants try to protect regular sources by being discreet about sources' identities and locations, or by assisting sources who are apprehended. Fourth, deviants may control their sources. Racketeers use threats of force to maintain relationships with their targets (Best, 1982b). Monopolizing a source's contacts is another method of control; drug dealers with distribution mo-

nopolies have substantial control over their customers. Finally, when sources are meager or cannot be protected or controlled, deviants may devise tactics for continually locating new sources. For example, some exploitative deviants, such as pickpockets, are geographically mobile in order to find new targets. The choice of tactics reflects the nature of the deviance, but most deviants need some method for regularizing rewards.

Some types of career shifts reduce uncertainty. First, deviants can shift to forms of deviance that pose fewer risks and offer more regular rewards. Social organization affects the uncertainty of deviance. Deviant transactions vary in organizational complexity (Best and Luckenbill, 1981). Deviant exploitation, where an offender uses force, stealth, or deception to exploit a target, is more complex than deviant exchange, where two or more deviants exchange illicit goods or services. In exploitation, uncertainty is high; deviants' targets often complain to the authorities or resist the offender. In contrast, exchange features cooperation; as long as the participants are discreet, they can minimize the risks of social control. Consequently, career shifts may involve moving from exploitation to exchange. For example, drug addicts may shift from theft to drug dealing as a means of financing their habits (Smith and Stephans, 1976). This type of career shift can reduce uncertainty by increasing security—exchange runs less risk of coming to the attention of control agents—and regularizing rewards—exchange more often produces regular profits. Thus, career shifts toward involvement in less complex deviant transactions reduce uncertainty.

Second, deviants can shift to forms of deviant organization involving fewer risks and regularized rewards. The social organization of deviants mediates the uncertainty of the deviant experience. Deviants organize in patterns of varying sophistication, ranging from loners to deviant formal organizations (Best and Luckenbill, 1980). The greater the sophistication of the deviants' organization, the lower their career uncertainty. More sophisticated forms of organization have extensive resources to protect their members' operations; their sources of information, codes of conduct, punitive capacity, and linkages to corrupted authorities reduce the risks of exploitation by associates and apprehension by officials. Similarly, more sophisticated forms have organizational resources for assuring regular rewards: their economic resources can protect and control their reward sources; their punitive capacity lets them negotiate with rivals and exact major concessions from them; and they can undertake systematic deviant operations, such as supplying illicit markets. In order to reduce uncertainty, individuals may make career shifts toward more sophisticated forms of organization. For instance, delinquents may leave their peer groups to join more sophisticated mobs of career thieves (Letkemann, 1973). The mob's code of conduct, its contacts with corrupt authorities, and its well-planned, well-coordinated operations insure a relatively secure and profitable experience. In such cases, shifts into more sophisticated organizational forms minimize uncertainty.

With multiple pathways through deviance, not all shifts are in the direction of less complexly organized transactions or more sophisticated forms of deviant organization. Individuals' career shifts reflect other contingencies as well. But those who seek to maintain extended deviant careers are likely to make career shifts which reduce the uncertainty of the deviant experience.

CONCLUSION

Sociologists of deviance borrow the concept of career from studies of respectable occupations. In using the concept, they draw an analogy between respectable careers, particularly in formal organizations, and the deviant experience. The two have analogous properties, but there are important differences between careers in deviance and respectability. Deviant careers do not involve movement along standard pathways leading upward; they lack prescribed sequences of career shifts. Deviant careers are fluid; they develop in many differ-

ent directions, depending on such contingencies as the individual's objectives, resources, abilities, and opportunities. The uncertainty of the deviant experience encourages deviants to adopt tactics which foster security and regular rewards. In particular, deviants with strong commitments to their careers may make career shifts which reduce uncertainty. In short, deviant and respectable careers differ in several important respects, and the career concept must be used carefully so that these differences are not ignored.

This analysis reminds sociologists that deviance and respectability are very different. Labeling theory argues that deviant behavior is not qualitatively different from respectable behavior; the attribution of a deviant label is all that sets the two apart. The use of the career concept emphasizes the arbitrary nature of the distinction between deviance and respectability. Yet, identifying and labeling some behavior as deviant has consequences. Those who commit deviant acts become liable to social control sanctions, and deviants cannot turn to the authorities when they are exploited by their associates. To avoid sanctioning and exploitation, deviants must conceal their operations and restrict their dealings to those who can be trusted. Thus, secrecy and trust become central themes in the deviant experience. The designation of some behavior as deviant may be arbitrary, but it has real consequences for individuals' lives, reflected in the differences between deviant and respectable careers.

REFERENCES

Allen, John. 1977. *Assault with a Deadly Weapon.* New York: McGraw-Hill.

Becker, Howard S. 1963. *Outsiders.* New York: Free Press.

Becker, Howard S. and Anselm L. Strauss. 1956. "Careers, personality, and adult socialization." *American Journal of Sociology* 62:253–263.

Best, Joel. 1982a. "Careers in brothel prostitution." *Journal of Interdisciplinary History* 12:597–619.

———. 1982b. "Crime as strategic interaction." *Urban Life* 11.

Best, Joel and David F. Luckenbill. 1980. "The social organization of deviants." *Social Problems* 28:14–31.

———. 1981. "The social organization of deviance." *Deviant Behavior* 2:231–259.

Blankenship, Ralph L. 1973. "Organizational careers." *Sociological Quarterly* 14:88–98.

Bryan, James H. 1965. "Apprenticeships in prostitution." *Social Problems* 12:287–297.

Buckner, H. Taylor. 1970. "The transvestic career path." *Psychiatry* 33:381–389.

Carey, James T. 1968. *The College Drug Scene.* Englewood Cliffs, N.J.: Prentice-Hall.

Dank, Barry M. 1971. "Coming out in the gay world." *Psychiatry* 34:180–197.

Dannefer, Dale. 1980. "Rationality and passion in private experience." *Social Problems* 27:392–412.

Glaser, Barney G. (ed.). 1968. *Organizational Careers.* Chicago: Aldine.

Goffman, Erving. 1961. *Asylums.* Garden City, N.Y.: Anchor.

———. 1963. *Stigma.* Englewood Cliffs, N.J.: Prentice-Hall.

Goldstein, Paul J. 1979. *Prostitution and Drugs.* Lexington, Mass.: Lexington.

Gray, Diana. 1973. "Turning out." *Urban Life and Culture* 1:401–425.

Harris, Mervyn. 1973. *The Dilly Boys.* Rockville, Md.: New Perspectives.

Heyl, Barbara Sherman. 1979. *The Madam as Entrepreneur.* New Brunswick, N.J.: Transaction.

Hughes, Everett C. 1958. *Men and Their Work.* New York: Free Press.

Inciardi, James A. 1975. *Careers in Crime.* Chicago: Rand McNally.

Irwin, John. 1970. *The Felon.* Englewood Cliffs, N.J.: Prentice-Hall.

Klockars, Carl B. 1975. *The Professional Fence.* New York: Free Press.

Lemert, Edwin M. 1967. *Human Deviance, Social Problems, and Social Control.* Englewood Cliffs, N.J.: Prentice-Hall.

Lesieur, Henry R. 1977. *The Chase.* Garden City, N.Y.: Anchor.

Letkemann, Peter. 1973. *Crime as Work.* Englewood Cliffs, N.J.: Prentice-Hall.

Livingston, Jay. 1974. *Compulsive Gamblers.* New York: Harper and Row.

Lofland, John. 1969. *Deviance and Identity.* Englewood Cliffs, N.J.: Prentice-Hall.

Luckenbill, David F. 1981. "Careers in male prostitution." Unpublished paper.

Matza, David. 1969. *Becoming Deviant.* Englewood Cliffs, N.J.: Prentice-Hall.

McIntosh, Mary. 1973. "The growth of racketeering." *Economy and Society* 2:35–69.

Miller, Delbert C. and William H. Form. 1964. *Industrial Sociology,* 2nd edition. New York: Harper and Row.

Miller, Gale. 1978. *Odd Jobs.* Englewood Cliffs, N.J.: Prentice-Hall.

Prus, Robert C. and C. R. D. Sharper. 1977. *Road Hustler.* Lexington, Mass.: Lexington.

Ray, Marsh. 1961. "The cycle of abstinence and relapse among heroin addicts." *Social Problems* 9:132–140.

Sagarin, Edward. 1975. *Deviants and Deviance.* New York: Praeger.

Skipper, James K., Jr. and Charles H. McCaghy. 1970. "Stripteasers: The anatomy and career contingencies of a deviant occupation." *Social Problems* 17:391–405.

Smith, R. B. and Richard C. Stephans. 1976. "Drug use and 'hustling': A study of their interrelationships." *Criminology* 14:155–176.

Stebbins, Robert A. 1970. "Career: The subjective approach." *Sociological Quarterly* 11:32–49.

———. 1971. *Commitment to Deviance.* Westport, Conn.: Greenwood.

Stoddart, Kenneth. 1974. "The facts of life about dope." *Urban Life and Culture* 3:179–204.

Sutherland, Edwin H. and Donald R. Cressey. 1978. *Criminology,* 10th edition. Philadelphia: Lippincott.

Volkman, Rita and Donald R. Cressey. 1963. "Differential association and the rehabilitation of drug addicts." *American Journal of Sociology* 69:129–142.

Weinberg, Martin S. 1966. "Becoming a nudist." *Psychiatry* 29:15–24.

Werthman, Carl. 1967. "The functions of social definitions in the development of delinquent careers." Pp. 155–170 in *President's Commission on Law Enforcement and Administration of Justice, Task Force Report: Juvenile Delinquency and Youth Crime.* Washington, D.C.: U.S. Government Printing Office.

Winick, Charles and Paul M. Kinsie. 1971. *The Lively Commerce.* Chicago: Quadrangle.

Active Responses to Labeling

KAROLYNN SIEGEL, HOWARD LANE, and ILAN H. MEYER

The interactionist tradition in the study of deviance draws heavily on the ideas of George Herbert Mead. Mead argued that one's sense of self arises in the course of social interaction with other people, through a process he described as "taking the role of the other." Early on, during the *play stage,* for example, children learn to take the role of a particular significant individual, like their mother, toward themselves. Later, in the *game stage,* children become able to take the role of the *generalized other* toward themselves—to take the point of view of the group or community and to anticipate the response to a possible course of action. The approach in this book simply extends Mead's idea to the development of a deviant self-conception.

For example, Edwin M. Lemert's concept of *secondary deviation* refers to persons who have been socially defined and reacted to as deviants. As a result, such persons adapt in certain ways to the societal reaction, for example, by elaborating an even more deviant role for themselves. Secondary deviants now define themselves as social deviants. On the other hand, John I. Kitsuse coined the term *tertiary deviance* to describe the conditions under which overt social deviants not only reject their social definition as deviant but actually seek to gain acceptance on their own terms as human beings.

In the introduction to their study of the various ways that gay and bisexual men with HIV/AIDS cope with the social stigma of their condition, Karolynn Siegel, Howard Lane, and Ilan H. Meyer list categories of social deviants who have rejected degrading characterizations. Their summary of these struggles for acceptance and redefinition serves to broaden the understanding of the development of various adaptations by deviant social types. It also points to a number of general conclusions. Perhaps the most important one may be that the transformation of the meaning of one's social type is more likely to come about with the support of like-minded deviant others.

…Stigmatized persons have been described as experiencing a number of negative sequelae including social exclusion, anxiety, alienation, loss of self-esteem, discrimination, and social disenfranchisement (Allport 1954; Goffman 1963; Rosenberg 1979; Jones et al. 1984; Alonzo & Reynolds 1995; Whiteford & Gonzalez 1995). The anticipated liabilities of being labeled as deviant create sufficient motivation for most potentially discreditable individuals to try to manage (i.e., avoid or minimize) stigmatization.

Reprinted from "Stigma Management Among Gay and Bisexual Men," *Qualitative Sociology,* Vol. 21 (1998), pp. 4–6, by permission of Plenum Publishing and K. Siegel. Copyright © 1998 by Plenum Publishing.

Goffman's (1963) seminal work on stigma is almost certainly the most important contribution to this field of inquiry to date and has strongly influenced much of the subsequent writing in this field. Yet his writings, and much derivative work, can and has been criticized as heavily biased toward seeing individual responses to stigma as primarily defensive and aimed at reducing or avoiding the private experience of stigmatization (Anspach 1979; Gussow & Tracey 1968). Gussow and Tracey (1968: 317), for example, contend that "Goffman's people are both other- and self-stigmatized and forever doomed" to feeling discredited because ultimately they "concur with the norms and therefore view themselves as failures."

Similarly, Anspach (1979) points out that while Goffman (1963: 767–8) sees stigmatized persons as "strategists and con artists" rather than merely passive victims, he nevertheless depicts them as ultimately accepting the prevailing definitions of normals and thus "deriving their identity reactively, in response to the imputations of the wider society." Anspach's (1979: 767) criticism, however, is not limited to Goffman. She writes, "most studies of deviance generated by the labeling perspective portray the deviant as powerless, passive and relatively uninvolved in the labeling process."…

While early sociological writing may have been biased toward emphasizing the passivity of deviants in the face of societal stigmatization, more recent work has emphasized that stigmatized individuals are not passive recipients of stigma and prejudice, but rather may reject prevalent constructions and seek to influence "normals" to do so as well. Gussow and Tracey (1968: 317), for example, discussed attempts by stigmatized groups to develop theories or ideologies "to counter the ones that discredit them" and "disavow their imputed inferiority or danger."…

In reviewing the dominant theoretical orientations to stigma, Anspach (1979: 768) contended that "the sociology of deviance must revise its conceptions to account for active attempts on the part of those labeled as deviant to mold their own identities." As an example, she described how handicapped individuals and former mental patients used political activism to counter the prevailing negative societal beliefs and assumptions about them, and in so doing enhanced their own self-conceptions. Jones et al. (1984: 153) wrote that such collective action by stigmatized groups to repudiate the norms that render them discreditable "may take the form of banding together with fellow targets,… withdrawing from one social environment and embracing another, and redefining an attribute of the self that was previously considered to be negative as positive." Crocker and Major (1989) noted that by uniting, stigmatized individuals may be able to affirm and validate their minority culture and values, and to discredit stigmatizing norms and values of dominant culture. Active responses to managing stigma often involve attempts to confront stigma in the hope of "breaking through" societal prejudice (c.f., Jones et al. 1984; Crocker & Major 1989) and altering the assumptions by which a condition is treated as discrediting. As an example, with the "Black is Beautiful" campaigns of the 1960s African Americans challenged stigma by reappropriating the discrediting trait as a source of pride. Whittaker (1992), studying "resistance by [HIV] positive people" in Australia, identified similar reappropriation processes as "the inversion of AIDS metaphors."…

REFERENCES

Allport G. W. (1954). *The Nature of Prejudice*. Addison-Wesley Publishing Company; Reading, MA.

Alonzo A. and Reynolds N. (1995). An exploration and elaboration of a stigma trajectory. *Social Science & Medicine*, 41, 303–315.

Anspach R. (1979). From stigma to identity politics: political activism among the physically disabled and former mental patients. *Social Science & Medicine*, 13A, 765–773.

Crocker J. and Major B. (1989). Social stigma and self-esteem: the self protective properties of stigma. *Psychological Review*, 96, 608–630.

Goffman E. (1963). *Stigma: Notes on the Management of Spoiled Identity*. Prentice-Hall, Englewood Cliffs, NJ.

Gussow Z. and Tracey G. S. (1968). Status, ideology and adaption to stigmatized illness: a study of leprosy. *Human Organization*, 27, 316–325.

Jones E., Farina A., Hastorf A., Markus H., Miller D., and Scott R. (1984). *Social Stigma: The Psychology of Marked Relationships*. W. H. Freeman: New York.

Rosenberg M. (1979). *Conceiving the Self*. Basic Books, New York.

Whiteford L. M. and Gonzalez L. (1995). Stigma: The hidden burden of infertility. *Social Science and Medicine*, 40, 27–36.

Whittaker Andrea M. (1992). Living with HIV: resistance by positive people. *Medical Anthropology Quarterly*, 6(4), 385–390.

CHAPTER 2

THE CULTURAL CONTEXT

Gendered Rules on Alcohol Use

MARJA HOLMILA

Cultural expectations, and conformity to them, confer predictability on everyday life, shore up social order, and induce trust. One essential condition of deviance then becomes the violation of a cultural rule.

Age and gender are two important sources of both expectations and their variations. Until they reach a particular age, children are not deemed responsible for their conduct. They are not thought either to understand or to know the difference between right and wrong. And when old people commit wrongful acts, the punishment they receive is usually milder than what a younger adult would receive for the same deviant act. Similarly, a culture often allows more leeway in behavior for one gender than for another. What is acceptable for men to do is not always acceptable for women to do. Thus, cultural rules are sometimes gendered rules.

One social act that exemplifies these gender variations in cultural expectations and reactions to their violations is the use of alcohol: what and how much someone drinks, and with what effects. As a result of these expectations, women are more likely to order white wine, more likely to drink less, and less likely to get drunk than men are. Women who drink straight hard liquor, who drink heavily, and who get drunk are breaching cultural rules to a greater extent than men who act the same way, and are subsequently responded to more negatively.

Examining a cultural context that has gendered rules, Marja Holmila describes how such rules regarding alcohol use are linked to the culture's broader expectations with respect to gender. She reports on the Finnish women she studied who have been placed in the category of "problem drinkers" because of the character of their alcohol use, the popular cultural images of women who are deviant, the degree to which heavy-drinking women subscribe to these images and/or are haunted by them, the patterns of external control imposed on these women, and how they feel about these controls.

GENDER ROLES

...Alcohol seems to have an important position in the ideological and practical bargaining that takes place between the genders. The family is central to the regulation of society's gender order and is the primary institution for the articulation of that order with other features of the social structure (Morgan, 1985). This regulation and articulation entails a continuous process of bargaining between the two genders in order to adapt men's and women's goals and interests to each other.

Reprinted from "Social Control Experienced by Heavily Drinking Women," *Contemporary Drug Problems,* Vol. 18 (Winter 1991), pp. 547–571, by permission of Federal Legal Publications, Inc. Copyright © 1992 by Federal Legal Publications, Inc.

Within the family, symbolic struggles over the norms for alcohol use may serve the purpose of delineating the statuses of the worlds of men and women.

Family ideology stresses that continuity, security, and an orderly everyday life are important for the upbringing of healthy children and for the well-being of everyone. And since women's work is largely tied to reproduction, family ideology looks on these values as "feminine." Conversely, the courage to undertake risks, and the importance of male sociability in order to dominate the public life, are designated "masculine." To some extent drinking can be a mode of expression here. It is "manly" to venture into the unknown, to take risks, to have fun, and to prioritize male networks instead of the family. Heroically boozing men may seem to achieve something that women with their never-finished bottles of liqueur know nothing about. Only women always control themselves and worry about tomorrow.

The role of a wife has traditionally been connected to controlling the husband's drinking. This activity can be seen as caring work (Holmila, 1988). Paying attention to another person's behavior and attempting to direct it certainly is work. Time and energy are demanded, as are planning and reflection. It is work also in the sense that the wider society expects it, and strong ideological forces bind women to this task. This work is performed in all kinds of families, not just in the alcoholic family.

Breaking the traditional pattern and becoming the drinker thus entails various adjustments for a woman in her relationships to men and in her conception of her feminine role. To what extent that really does happen is a question to be looked at. It is also possible that heavily drinking women maintain their traditional role of the one who drinks less and who controls and worries over others' even heavier drinking. Studies on alcoholic women and their partners indicate that these women often live with men who also misuse alcohol (Bjerver, 1983; Dahlgren, 1979; Koistinen and Wiman, 1985).

INTERNALIZED CONTROL AND "PRIVATE TALKS"

It seems particularly important to look at the interplay of internalized and externalized forms of control in women's lives. Very often the forms of social control of women's behavior do not take the form of other people's acts or remarks. Women's behavior is led by their own contemplation and "private talks" about what a particular act or series of acts would mean to their role in the eyes of others and how it would shape their social existence.

According to symbolic interactionism, deviance is held to be a kind of description used in the conversations that order social life (Downes and Rock, 1988, 169–191). Interactionists do not take conversation to be confined entirely to activities outside the self. Any action requires an appraisal of one's capacities and of the action's implications for oneself. Monitoring and assessment of the self are indispensable to any intelligent social strategy. A mind must scan itself just as it scans other objects in its environment. This happens also when a person is involved in an action that is not along the norms of conformist behavior, but is more towards deviance. The process of recognizing and negotiating deviance is thus importantly merged with the inner world of the self. Decisions about future conduct turn on readings of the meaning of deviance and the acceptability of deviant identity, the significance of particular acts, and the possible responses of others. Thus an early and important article by Becker traces some of the stages of one such private conversation (Becker, 1963). It discusses the manner in which the marijuana user came to terms with known and likely definitions of drugs. The prospective user was obliged to consider what kind of person he might become. His management of the problem had little to do with social control emanating from direct confrontations with other people, the police and the courts. But it did center on the social control embedded in the meanings of deviation and the self.

EXTERNAL CONSTRAINTS

Some writers maintain, however, that the constraints created by women's active part in maintaining societal control pales beside the complex but enormously limiting external forces that operate upon women's lives and their leisure. Such constraints are to be felt in all areas of women's lives. In the *domestic setting*, women's use of time is often strictly constrained and is sometimes effectuated with economic dependency or the threat or use of violence (Heidensohn, 1985, 174–200). Green, Hebron and Woodward argue that women living with male partners experience particular forms of control over their leisure and over substantial areas of their daily lives, and that this control has historically been understood as legitimate or even desirable. It has been pointed out that the dictum "Woman's place is in the home" does not so much mean that she shall not go out to work, but that she should not go out to play (see Green, Hebron and Woodward, 1987, 81).

In the context of everyday life, women make individual choices and enter into negotiations about appropriate ways to conduct themselves. These negotiations are most typically experienced with individual men in the private sphere (*ibid.*, p. 79). The actors of control are thus often individual men, typically partners. It seems that male disapproval and displeasure are particularly marked in relation to women's drinking.

The control over women's leisure that is exercised at an individual level within households cannot be separated from the ways in which women's social behavior is regulated in the *public field*. A significant aspect of the social control of women's leisure is still their access to public places and their behavior in such places. Many leisure venues are male dominated, and women are either made unwelcome there or are welcome only on specific terms. This is particularly true of public places where alcohol is served. Women without a male escort often feel discomfort when entering a pub and are disturbed by male customers' ridicule or sexual harassment (Hey, 1986, 6–7). According to

a study on women in Sheffield, 84% of the respondents felt uncomfortable about going to a pub on their own, and 93% felt uncomfortable on their own in working men's clubs (Green, Hebron, and Woodward, 1990, 132). Women's practices of buying drinks may be limited by pointing out that their behavior is "unfeminine" (Hunt and Satterlee, 1987, 10) or somehow "amateurish" (Spradley and Mann, 1975).

Ideologies about appropriate feminine behavior reinforce the popular assumption that respectable women have no place in certain areas of public life. Unaccompanied single women or women in groups are therefore considered to be potentially sexually "available." Underlying the strategies of making women aware of these constraints is the threat of physical violence. Many women are afraid to use public transport or walk alone late at night, especially if intoxicated. Men have the quasi-monopoly of force and violence in public places (Heidensohn, 1985, 174–200).

Women's leisure can be constrained also by their position in work life. Women less often than men occupy posts with flexible and uncontrolled working patterns, are under stricter surveillance, and are at the bottom end of the work hierarchy. Thus their work allows women less liberty, time and space to pursue excessive or unaccepted forms of leisure.

PUBLIC IMAGES

The differences in male and female deviance have been explained in the light of differences in the public images of deviant men and women. Many deviant and also criminal male roles either receive public approval—"Boys will be boys"—or are at least positively portrayed. Almost no films or books romanticize the female tramp or hobo; such women really do not excite anyone's fantasies or envy. This is in contrast with the "noble savage" portrayal of the male alcoholic (Otto, 1984, 163; Heidensohn, 1985, 98).

According to Heidensohn, the public images of female deviance fall into three main categories.

First there is the witch, the evil woman. Second is the whore, which is quite a complex and distorting image or set of images; in particular it means sexualizing of many other, sometimes all, types of nonconforming female behavior (Heidensohn, 1985, 93). Third, deviant women are often portrayed as "non-women," as masculine women. If their behavior is deviant in one area of life, this is connected to a loss or distortion of their entire gender-identity. To Heidensohn's three categories of female deviance one could add that of a sick woman. A woman can perhaps be more easily characterized as mad than as bad. This characterization does not, however, fit very well with the interview data of heavily drinking women. They did not describe many situations where the environment would have controlled them by labeling them as sick.

DATA COLLECTION

The project has two stages.... First a large representative postal survey was conducted in the Helsinki area. The data were gathered between January and May 1990. The sample, 6,000 women 20–64 years old, was taken from the central census register. It was designed to be as large as 6,000 in order to include an adequate number of heavily drinking women....

The last page of the postal survey was a separate sheet asking if the respondent would be willing to take part in an interview. If she wanted to take part, she was asked to write down her first name and her telephone number or address. Among those responding to the postal survey, 34% were willing to take part in the interview....

RESULTS

IMAGES OF DRINKING WOMEN

The stigmatized image of a drinking woman is held not only by men or by those women who drink moderately but seems to be haunting the minds of heavily drinking women themselves.

Gomberg found that both alcoholic women in treatment and a matched group of nonalcoholic women felt that social attitudes are more negative toward female intoxication and problem drinking than toward male intoxication and drinking problems. Alcoholic women themselves reported significantly more negative attitudes, both social and personal, than did the nonalcoholic women. Fifty-one percent of the alcoholic women and 36% of the other women agreed with the statement "A woman who is drunk is more obnoxious and disgusting than a man who is drunk." The older group of alcoholic women was consistently harsher than the younger group in its judgments (Gomberg, 1988, 507–510).

The images held by the women interviewed here can be presented using Heidensohn's (1988) description of public images of deviant women.

The women themselves had internalized the images of evil woman and non-feminine woman. Sexual promiscuity was, however, an image felt to be imposed on them by others, and no woman thought that this image corresponded with reality.

The evil woman is a threat to the whole society, and her downfall is worse than a man's downfall. Sometimes this was seen to be age-specific, so that young women were allowed more liberties than older women, women in "mother's age group."

I think that women should be the moral supporter of the family.... Men are weaker by nature, and one does not expect so much from them. It is of course wrong to say this, it is not equalitarian, but if women fall, the whole society falls. (54-year-old bank officer...)

I find it easier to tolerate alcoholic men than women. They are unpleasant. Maybe I have old-fashioned gender role attitudes, I don't know. A woman should take care of herself. (29-year-old travel agent...)

It is different, being a woman or being a mother. One should condemn a drinking mother. (26-year-old social worker...)

The ugliness or non-femininity of a woman's drinking was an often mentioned image.

A woman is worse than a man, or is it because one is more used to men's drunkenness. But a woman does look awful. Eyes popping out and hardly standing up and shouting horribly. (27-year-old sales secretary...)

Women's drinking, especially in public places, is often connected to *sexual promiscuity.* Although some women pointed out that in Finland women are freer than in southern Europe to go out on their own, it was common to feel that one had to challenge some norms and to tolerate harassment of various kinds when doing so. Restaurants are not really for women on their own. One has to defend one's right to be interested only in having a drink and maybe a chat with someone, especially other women. Pubs that one attends regularly are most relaxing.

Men do not mind if a woman has a beer in a restaurant, but they think one is there to find a man. (43-year-old trade union official...)

EXTERNAL CONTROL

The main agents for active informal control of drinking are family members and sometimes friends. The data obtained in the postal survey allow us to look at the frequency of such control in the group of [heavily drinking] women....

Nearly half of the heavily drinking women who had a partner recalled his having tried to limit her drinking. This is considerably more than in average families. Roles in the male-female relationship can turn around, or controlling can be mutual, if the woman's drinking exceeds certain limits. However, women still reported many fewer control experiences than frequently drinking men (Holmila, 1988).

...[There are several] reasons why women are not objects of control more often than they are. Only 18% of these women said they drank more than their partners, and nearly half thought they drank less than he did. Thus one reason for the

partner's passivity in control probably is the fact that he drinks more himself.

Women also very commonly drink together with their partners. Only 12% said they mostly drank separately from their partner, and half drank mostly together with him. Being away from home or drinking apart from the spouse's company is one of the major reasons for disagreements about drinking (Holmila, 1988). Lack of control may reflect the partner's satisfaction with the situation if she shares the drinking with him, he has nothing to complain about....

FORMS OR METHODS OF CONTROL

...[P]artners are the most important agents of control. Friends and relatives are important, too. Children's impact is probably stronger than the...[data show], as their methods are not as varied as those of the adults. Employers' role is not very great.

Children's and parents' reactions to the respondents' drinking had often created *feelings of guilt.* Children do not need to say much for their mothers to register their negativeness about their drinking.

I saw in the children's eyes that they noticed something, so I had to drink more at once, because I already felt so guilty. (41-year-old storage worker...)

The girl always said that you become so stupid.... And my son said that I turn into the opposite from what I am when sober. That drinking changes me so much. (57-year-old cleaning woman...)

The guilt inflicted by parents is often connected to the parents' own drinking problems.

My father goes on saying that he knows what it is like to drink. And he is sad, he always says he is super-sad and worried about me.... He has good reasons, too. Luckily he does not know how worried he should be. (31-year-old clerk...)

Referring to moral rules consists almost solely of attempts to remind the woman of her duties as a mother. The reminders are members of the nuclear family.

Patronizing or nagging is often done by men, but sometimes by female friends, too. A partner may talk to her as if she "was a naughty child." Young girls can be disciplined by their male acquaintances about proper feminine behavior by, for instance, use of mocking names.

Various kinds of people had *given advice* or *suggested a change.* Giving advice often presupposed long discussions and also listening.

Experiences of being *prevented from going out* were restricted to relationships with men. This was also one of the most common methods used by the partner. Usually the partner did not want her to go out if he was not going with her. Sometimes he had negative feelings about her habit of drinking alone at home, too, maintaining that drinking should be shared.

> *If I have been out with other girls he thinks I am too drunk.... He then goes out with his friends; sort of revenge. (21-year-old student...)*

> *We have quarreled with my husband about drinking if I have been drinking in somebody else's company. (47-year-old editor...)*

Quarreling was closely linked with trying to stop her from going out alone, as the reason for quarrels was not so much drinking itself as jealousy and the frustration of not knowing where she had been.

The partners' *nonverbal methods of control* consist of various acts of covering, caring, fetching home, keeping some of the drinks for himself, and making sure she has to drive the car. Friends sometimes act as controllers by refusing to share a drink with a person whom they find cumbersome, or by excluding her from the circle of friends.

> *Sometimes we have talked about how to help her.... But our group of friends does not accept someone behaving badly, and she will be quickly excluded, not asked along any more.... Drinking together is supposed to be a happy occasion and the people in the group should drink in a similar fashion. (38-year-old advertisement manager...)*

Statements about strangers' nonverbal control described sexual harassment in restaurants or in the streets.

Threats as nonverbal acts of control finally meant a threat of losing the custody of one's children, of losing one's apartment or job, or of physical violence in the streets.

> *I have lost my job twice because of drinking, but I have been in so many jobs anyway. (57-year-old cleaning woman...)*

> *This man made a false statement against me in the court...about my drinking;...the children's father definitely drank more... but he wanted the children. (42-year-old cleaning woman...)*

INTERPLAY BETWEEN INTERNAL AND EXTERNAL CONTROL

Informal control can be effective only if the receiver accepts it and agrees that there is need for it. One of the questions in the postal survey asked if the respondent felt she drank more than she actually wanted to. There seemed to be a close relationship between outside control and one's own thoughts about drinking too much....

A majority of those who often felt that they were drinking more than they actually wanted to had been limited by their spouses. Very often, although not quite as often, someone else had also expressed concern about their drinking. Only a small group (about 10 respondents...) had been in a clear conflict; they never felt that they drank more than they wanted to, and yet someone had tried to set limits on them.

The respondents had usually agreed with their friends and partners that there was a need to limit the respondent's drinking. Controlling or being worried had not been considered uncalled for. This does not, however, necessarily mean that the reactions from others had been felt to be totally positive.

It is possible to look at the reactions in more detail on the basis of the qualitative interviews.

APPROVAL AND DISAPPROVAL OF CONTROL

The interviewees expressed various feelings and thoughts about the reactions they had received from their surroundings.

1 Hopes for more control were expressed by women who felt that they could not cope alone. Mostly this hope or wish was directed to their partners.

> *They have not been interested enough to listen [to my problems].…. I have never had a man who cared enough about me to think about my problems. (27-year-old cook…)*

> *I am not happy about my relationship with my husband because he does not care about my drinking. I can drink myself to death and it means nothing, nothing, to him. I wish he would express his opinion in some way. (41-year-old free-lance teacher…)*

> *He wants to live with me, and says I can go out as much as I ever want. I don't want that, I think it is shocking. I wish he would say, "Stop drinking now!" But to say, "Do what you want, just tell me where you are and I will come and get you home"—I cannot stand it! (31-year-old invoicer…)*

One woman expressed her wish for better formal control: she had always been able to buy alcohol in the liquor store, even if she was drunk. She felt it would be better if that was not the case, even though her feelings after the only time the salesperson had said something, and yet sold to her, were very confused and she had felt terribly ashamed.

2 Approval of control was often expressed, when the intervention had actually prevented a woman from acting in a shameful way. Women's working morale was very high; they hardly ever stayed at home during work days, however bad they felt after a night out.

> *Naturally we have tried to keep our drinking problems inside these four walls. Once he actually dragged me home from our neighbors'. I am very happy that he saw I was in that state. (47-year-old editor…)*

Approval could also be caused by empathy, seeing the situation with the controller's eyes. This was usually the case with children, and sometimes with partners. Friends had a special role, being able to say things straight in a not too emotional or complicated way.

> *I have started to drink a lot less because we are so much together with my husband and I simply don't have the nerve to hurt him, he feels enormously sad. He has psychosomatic symptoms…he already had them when we got married…but my drinking does make them worse, I cannot deny that. (64-year-old nurse…)*

> *When my son is going to stay overnight with his friends or cousins, he asks me not to go out to drink. And I think then: do I really have to go, why do I go? (35-year-old cashier…)*

A few women had developed a system of mutual assistance with their partners. Attempts to control were approved, because they were reciprocal and served the interests of both of them.

> *He has come to take me home. Either I telephone him or he comes on his own. He knows the places I go to, so he comes and takes me home.… It feels fine. I like him to come and get me, so that my drinking will not go on. I feel ashamed.… He says, "Come on, Eeva, let us go home now," and then we go.… I have gone to get him home, too. We get each other home, yes. (42-year-old cleaning woman…)*

3 Conflicting feelings were created by control that was felt to limit one's freedom or access to places. In public, in private, and at work, women had experienced this, and even if the exclusion or surveillance was partly understood, it could not be received positively. The respondents also felt that men and women were not treated in an equal manner. The partner's control had created conflicting feelings if it seemed that he was trying to keep her quiet and nice for his own convenience or to avoid some underlying problems she felt like dwelling on.

> *It is not so much about drinking but about the consequences. He says he does not dare to go any-*

where with me because he doesn't know what will happen...we start digging up the things of the past. (26-year-old assistant lawyer...)

4 *Opposition and criticism* were caused by the environment's tendency to connect women's drinking with sexual behavior and by the strong stigma attached to mothers who use alcohol. Often the partner's and also relatives' *own* drinking made control attempts seem false and thus aroused opposition. Disagreements about drinking in a relationship also seemed to be very closely interlinked with both partners' feelings of jealousy, bargaining about individual rights and household duties, and general emotional insecurity.

Well, he has had some fits of jealousy. He is jealous all the time, but he shows it when we are drinking. (30-year-old recorder...)

Sometimes when we have been drinking together his criticism of my drinking has been justified. But mostly it is because he feels bad about his own drinking and wants to find a co-sinner. He has had blackouts and has tried to gain his self-respect by blaming me. (43-year-old trade union official...)

Even if it was considered natural to go to work every day whatever shape one is in, and that employers have the right to expect that, it was felt that sometimes women were forgiven less than men.

When the men come to work at midday with a hangover, they are easily forgiven. We have often talked with the girls about that—-if we did the same, we would certainly be fired or something. (31-year-old secretary...)

CONCLUSIONS AND DISCUSSION

The goal of this paper was to look at the social control of drinking experienced by heavily drinking women. It is difficult to make simple definitions as to what kind of drinking is to be considered heavy or problematic. There is plenty of social and individual variation. In this study a screening instrument for harmful or hazardous drinking was used to define the group of women to be studied. It was then assumed that these women represented the heavy and rebellious drinking style.

Most of the interviewed women thought their drinking was at least to some extent a problem, but only a few of them defined themselves as alcoholics.

A lot of the social control imposed on women's behavior is so internalized that it is hard to see it or to question it. Women are often the most active social group to maintain social order and control. Consequently, those women who break the rules keep on thinking the same way as the controllers, not as the controlled. There are no positive images of drinking women or myths of rebellion to reflect upon.

The approach of symbolic interactionism seems useful here. According to that approach, the process of recognizing and negotiating deviance is importantly merged with the inner world of the self. The way the interviewed women described the control they had felt, and how they had reacted to it, can be seen as a way of negotiating their own deviance as women. Thus the interviews may tell us as much about women as controllers of themselves as about the way other people control them.

It may be that the close link between internalized values and control of others explains why control was so often approved and considered appropriate. The ethics of motherhood and also of conscientious work habits were not questioned; the respondents felt that mothers could not be excused and that one must go to work every day. Neither did they particularly fight for a right to be drunk in public the same was as men, but they felt that it would be better if they could avoid the loss of dignity and the shame of being in that "ugly" condition.

Women are nowadays free to enter public places to drink and they earn enough to buy their own alcohol. But the gender-specific mechanisms of control still exist in the form of sexualizing women's behavior. The modern independent women we interviewed often reported the difficulty they had with the sexual images of a lonely woman in a restaurant.

The most controversial and conflict-loaded area of social control reported by the respondents was, however, the one taking place in private, between partners or spouses. Marital conflicts, jealousy, and bargaining over the equality of rights for individual leisure were interwoven into the descriptions of partners' efforts to control. The control was opposed, as it was seen to be motivated by something other than concern over the respondent's well-being. Its effectiveness was also weakened by the partner's own heavy drinking, which was common. Similarly, when parents were mentioned as controllers, this was often seen to be caused by their own drinking problems. There were, however, some women who gave credit to their partners for keeping the drinking within some limits, and children were very often mentioned as the "best reason" for not drinking.

Many of those who had admitted to themselves that they had lost their ability to control themselves would have liked someone else, usually the partner, to control their behavior. Partners were criticized for not caring enough or not understanding the seriousness of the problem. Some, but not all, of these women had also attempted to get help from treatment institutions. Difficulties in getting help and making someone else take over the control could then be interpreted as loneliness and lack of love and become additional reasons for drinking.

The social control of drinking is a very complex mixture of norms, attitudes, feelings, interaction and direct violence. It is also a mixture of an individual's own monitoring and the acts of others. At one end of the continuum it represents repression and stigmatization; at the other end it can be seen as a sign of love and caring. It seems that studying women's experiences of social control of drinking can be particularly illuminating because they are so much involved in it and are unable to see themselves as mere objects of control.

REFERENCES

Becker, H.: *Outsiders*. Free Press, New York, 1963.

Bjerver, Tom: Erfarenheter från EWA—projektet för kvinnor med tidligt missbruk (Experiences from EWA—a project for women in the early stage of alcohol misuse). *Alkohol och Narkotika*, 5, 1983, 24–28.

Dahlgren, Lena: Female alcoholics. IV. Marital situation and husbands. *Acta psychiatrica scandinavica* 1979, 59–69.

Downes, David and Rock, Paul: *Understanding deviance: A guide to the sociology of crime and rule breaking*. Clarendon Press, Oxford, 1988.

Gomberg, Edith S.: Alcoholic women in treatment: The question of stigma and age. *Alcohol and Alcoholism*, Vol. 23, No. 6, 1988, 507–514.

Green, Eileen, Hebron, Sandra and Woodward, Diana: Women, leisure and social control. *In*: Hanmer, Jalna and Maynard, Mary (eds.): *Women, violence and social control*. Macmillan Press, London, 1987, 75–92.

_____: *Women's leisure, what leisure?* Macmillan, Hong Kong, 1990.

Heidensohn, Frances: *Women and crime*. Macmillan, Hong Kong, 1985.

Hey, V.: *Patriarchy and pub culture*. Tavistock, London, 1986.

Holmila, Marja: Wives, husbands and alcohol: A study of informal drinking control within the family. The Finnish Foundation for Alcohol Studies, Helsinki, Vol. 36, 1988.

Hunt, Geoffrey and Satterlee, Saundra: Darts, drink and the pub: The culture of female drinking. *Sociological Review*, Vol. 35, No. 3, 1987, 575–601.

Koistinen, Paavo and Wiman, Rolf: Psychodynamical and social aspects of the relationship between life cycle events and alcohol abuse of women. *Proceedings of the 34th International Congress on Alcoholism and Drug Dependence*. Calgary, August 4–10, 1985, 391–393.

Morgan, D. H. J.: *The family, politics, and social theory*. Routledge and Kegan Paul, London, 1985.

Otto, Shirley: Women, alcohol and social control. *In*: Hutter, Bridget and Williams, Gillian: *Controlling women: The normal and the deviant*. Croom Helm, London. 1984, 154–167.

Spradley, James and Mann, Brenda: *The cocktail waitress: Woman's work in a man's world*. Wiley, New York, 1975.

The Culture's Drug Addict Imagery

CRAIG REINARMAN and CERES DUSKIN

Our culture maintains the image that drinking or using drugs inevitably leads to a downward spiral of increased intake, loss of control, addiction, illness, crime, dependency, insanity, early death, and so on. Media images of "drunks" and "dope fiends" helped to create and aid in sustaining this cultural fiction. Newspapers, for example, selectively attend to any and all events centering on what can be alleged to be a loss of self-control. And, in accord with their need to be simple, dramatic, and direct, they develop and convey oversimplified stereotypes of various kinds of offenders. A key example through the years has been the standard accounts of people who have gotten into some kind of trouble apparently because of their use of alcohol or drugs.

Craig Reinarman and Ceres Duskin's case study exemplifies the conditions under which erroneous beliefs about drugs are accepted as fact. A "good story" draws attention, sells newspapers, and rewards the reporter, the editor, and the paper. The "good story" that is presented in this article, although extreme and rare in many ways, can be seen as a logical extension of the pictures of the addicted found in the heads of newspaper people. And the story seems all the more credible because its author is an African American who is deemed, on the face of it, to be more knowledgeable about drug addiction because of her assumed easier access to lower-class black people living in the inner city. Acceptance of the story as true seemed to be the result of the image of "dope fiends" established and constantly repeated in media reports of drug addicts. In effect, the producers become consumers of their own tales.

Jimmy is 8 years-old and a third-generation heroin addict, a precocious little boy with sandy hair, velvety brown eyes and needle marks freckling the baby-smooth skin of his thin brown arms.

So began a front-page feature in the *Washington Post* on Sunday, September 28, 1980. The reporter, Janet Cooke, claimed that Jimmy had "been an addict since the age of 5." She told of how Jimmy "doesn't usually go to school, preferring instead to hang with older boys." When he did go, Cooke wrote, it was "to learn more about his favorite subject—math," which he planned to use in his drug-dealing career. She noted the

Reprinted from "Dominant Ideology and Drugs in the Media," *International Journal on Drug Policy,* Vol. 3 (1992), by permission of Elsevier Science.

"cherubic expression" on Jimmy's face when he spoke about "hard drugs, fast money and the good life he believes both can bring." He sported "fancy running shoes" and an "Izod shirt." "Bad, ain't it, I got me six of these," the child reportedly told Cooke.

She described Jimmy's house in detail. There were addicts "casually" buying heroin every day from Ron, Jimmy's mother's "live-in lover," cooking it, and then firing up in the bedrooms. "People of all shapes and sizes," a "human collage" including teenagers, "drift into the dwelling…some jittery, uptight and anxious for a fix, others calm and serene after they finally 'get off.'" These things were, Cooke wrote, "normal occurrences in Jimmy's world."

"And every day, Ron or someone else fires up Jimmy, plunging a needle into his bony arm, sending the fourth grader into a hypnotic nod." Cooke then quoted Ron on how he first "turned Jimmy one": "He'd been buggin' me all the time about what the shots were and what people was doin' and one day he said, 'When can I get off?'" She described Ron as "learning against a wall in a narcotic haze, his eyes half-closed, yet piercing," and quoted him as answering Jimmy, "'Well, s—, you can have some now.' I let him snort a little and, damn, the little dude really did get off."

"Six months later," Cooke wrote, the five-year-old "was hooked." She quoted the boy as saying, "I felt like I was part of what was goin' down.... It [heroin] be real different from herb [marijuana]. That's baby s—."

Cooke also quoted Jimmy's mother: "I don't really like to see him fire up. But, you know, I think he would have got into it one day, anyway. Everybody does. When you live in the ghetto, it's all a matter of survival.... Drugs and black folk been together for a very long time."

The mother had been routinely raped, Cooke wrote, by her mother's boyfriend, one such instance leading to Jimmy's birth and then to heroin use to blot out her growing pain. When her drug sources dried up after a bust, she turned to prostitution to support further heroin use. Cooke quoted the mother as saying that she wasn't alarmed by her son's dealing ambitions "because drugs are as much a part of her world as they are of her son's."

Cooke made the more general point that heroin use had "become part of life" among people in poor neighborhoods—people who "feel cut off from the world around them"—often "filtering down to untold numbers of children like Jimmy who are bored with school and battered by life." Many kids "no older than 10," Cooke claimed, could "relate with uncanny accuracy" dealer names and drug nomenclature.

Cooke's story then offered a familiar litany of quotes to bolster and contextualize her story. Drug Enforcement Agency officials noted the influx of "Golden Crescent heroin." Local medical experts spoke of the "epidemic" of heroin deaths in Washington. Social workers observed how the lack of

"male authority figures" and peer pressure combine to make such childhood tragedies common.

"At the end of an evening of strange questions about his life," Cooke concluded, "the calm and self-assured little man recedes" to reveal a "jittery and ill-behaved boy" who was "going into withdrawal." Ron then left the room, according to Cooke, and returned with "syringe in hand, and calls the little boy over to his chair." He grabbed Jimmy's "left arm just above the elbow, his massive hand tightly encircling the child's small limb. The needle slides into the boy's soft skin like a straw pushed into the center of a freshly baked cake. Liquid ebbs out of the syringe, replaced by bright red blood. The blood is then reinjected into the child." The final scene in Cooke's drama depicted little Jimmy "looking quickly around the room" and climbing into a rocking chair, "his head dipping and snapping upright again in what addicts call 'the nod.'"

THE STORY BECOMES THE STORY

Two days after Cooke's story appeared, the *Washington Post* ran a fascinating follow-up article entitled, "D.C. Authorities Seek Identity of Heroin Addict, 8" (*Washington Post,* 30 September 1980). Such a tragic tale of a young life lost to drugs, so compellingly conveyed by Cooke and so prominently published by the *Post,* had led to hundreds of outraged calls and letters to the paper and to local officials.

The then-mayor Marion Barry was "incensed" by the story and assigned a task force of hundreds of police and social workers to find Jimmy. It was later learned that the police intensively combed the city for nearly three weeks. Teachers throughout Washington checked the arms of thousands of young students for needle marks. Citizens from housing projects called in offering to help. A $10,000 reward was offered. The police, supported by the mayor and the U.S. attorney, threatened to subpoena Cooke in an effort to find and "save" the boy. The *Post* refused to identify Jimmy, citing First Amendment rights to protect confidential sources (*New York Times,* 16 April 1981).

The *Post* assigned an eleven-member reporting team to cover all this, six of whom were told to search for another Jimmy, "on the theory that if there is one, there must be others" (Green 1981). Cooke and one of her editors searched for Jimmy's house for seven hours. For some unexplained reason, they never found it. Neither the police nor anyone else found Jimmy either. And, neither the other *Post* reporters nor anyone else ever found any other child addict.

Meanwhile, *Post* publisher Donald Graham congratulated Cooke. Bob Woodward, a senior editor who eight years earlier had broken the Watergate scandal, promoted her. The *Post* went on with its normal coverage of drug issues.

Six months later, on April 13, 1981, "Jimmy's World" resurfaced in a ceremony at Columbia University in New York, where it was announced that Janet Cooke had won the Pulitzer Prize in Feature Writing for her story. The next day, the *Post* published a piece proudly announcing Cooke's Prize and reprinted "Jimmy's World" in honor of the occasion (*Washington Post,* 14 April 1981). The story noted that "Jimmy's World" had first met with shock and disbelief. But despite the fact that none of the massive follow-up efforts had ever turned up Jimmy or anyone like him, the *Post* asserted that experts had confirmed the fact that heroin addicts of Jimmy's age were common.

For any American reporter, winning a Pulitzer—the journalist's equivalent of a Nobel Prize—is as good as it gets. Such prizes make careers, catapult[ing] people out of the grind of routine reportage into prestigious positions, often to fame and fortune. Journalism students fantasize about such feats. Competitive cub reporters across the country covet chances for front-page stories that might get noticed and nominated. Janet Cooke should have been ecstatic. As the world would soon learn, she wasn't.

Two days later, on April 16, the *Washington Post* published another front page piece on "Jimmy's World": "The Pulitzer Prize Committee withdrew its feature-writing prize from Washington Post reporter Janet Cooke yesterday after she admitted that her award-winning story was a fabrication.... It was said to be based on interviews with the boy, his mother and his mother's boyfriend. Cooke now acknowledges that she never met or interviewed any of those people and that she made up the story of Jimmy" (*Washington Post,* 16 April 1981).

The *Post*'s lead editorial that day, "The End of the 'Jimmy' Story," began with an unusual phrase for papers of the *Post*'s stature: "We apologize." It went on to say, "This newspaper, which printed Janet Cooke's false account of a meeting with an 8-year-old heroin addict and his family, was itself the victim of a hoax—which we then passed along in a prominent page-one story, taking in the readers as we ourselves had been taken in. How could this have happened?"

To find out, Executive Editor Ben Bradlee invited the *Post*'s ombudsman, Bill Green, to conduct an independent, "full disclosure" investigation. Green learned that the *Post* had been running many more routine stories about drug problems in Washington, and that Cooke had been researching the local heroin problem for some time. She took extensive notes to City Editor Milton Coleman. In describing her material she mentioned in passing an eight-year-old addict. Recognizing the print media equivalent of "dramatic footage," Coleman stopped her right there and said, "That's the story. Go after it. It's a front-page story."

Green discovered that when Cooke followed Coleman's instructions she was unable to come up with the young addict. Coleman sent her back out to find him. Again she could not. A week later Cooke told him that she had found *another* eight-year-old addict, "Jimmy," by going to elementary school playgrounds and passing out her cards. She told her editor that one of her cards found its way to a mother, who called and angrily asked, "Why are you looking for my boy?"

Cooke said she then extracted promises of confidentiality for "Jimmy's" mother and told her editors that she had visited the child's home, according to Green's report. She soon turned in a thirteen-page draft of the story. She rendered the furnishings and other aspects of the home and "Jimmy's" life in such delicious detail, Green found, that no editor had ever asked for "Jimmy's" or his mother's identity. Editor Coleman later told Green that he went over the story carefully: "I wanted it to read like John Coltrane's music. Strong. It was a great story, and it never occurred to me that she could make it up. There was too much distance between Janet and the streets."[1]

Green came to feel that the *Post* had been blinded by its ambition for a dramatic feature and by the fine prose of a reporter who was African-American and thus assumed trustworthy on such matters. Editors dismissed doubts and decided to run "Jimmy's World." It was not until Cooke was awarded the Pulitzer that the story started to unravel. Even then, questions centered on her background, not her story.

The first clue emerged when Cooke's earlier employer, the *Toledo Blade*, wanted to run the prize-winning story. In setting up a sidebar on Cooke's Toledo roots, *Blade* editors discovered that the biographical information they had received over the Associated Press wire "did not jibe" with what they knew of Cooke's background. Her "official" resume—sent in by the *Post*, released by the Pulitzer Committee, and carried with the AP story—had Cooke graduating from Vassar magna cum laude, studying at the Sorbonne, earning a master's degree from the University of Toledo, speaking four languages, and winning half a dozen Ohio newspaper awards.[2] When the editors at the *Blade* called AP to check on the discrepancies, AP editors began to ask questions of their own. They discovered other discrepancies. No Sorbonne. No master's degree. They called Cooke. She asserted that her official resume was correct. AP knew at this point that "something was wrong."

Prompted by the AP inquiry, Green discovered, the *Post*'s editors compared her personnel file and the Pulitzer biography form she filled out.

After discovering that the two did not match in several respects, Bradlee told Coleman to "take her to the woodshed." Coleman took Cooke for a walk and grilled her. Cooke eventually admitted she had not graduated from Vassar, but continued to insist that everything else, especially the Jimmy story, was true.

Coleman phoned his superiors with these answers, according to Green's report. Bradlee told him to bring Cooke back to the *Post* via a side entrance "to avoid being conspicuous" and to sequester her in a vacant office three stories above the newsroom. Bradlee came up and grilled her. He asked about the foreign language skills she had listed on her resume: "Say two words to me in Portuguese," Green quoted Bradlee as saying. She couldn't. Her French wasn't much better. He asked about her journalism prizes. Her answers were inconclusive. Bradlee said, "You're like Richard Nixon, you're trying to cover up."

In another office, Assistant Managing Editor Bob Woodward joined Deputy Metro Editor David Maraniss and another editor to go over the 145 pages of Cooke's notes and two hours of tape-recorded interviews. According to Green's report, they found "echoes" of the "Jimmy" story, but no evidence that she had actually spoken with a child addict.

Meanwhile, under pressure of intense questioning, Cooke gave Coleman what she claimed were the real names of Jimmy, his mother, and her boyfriend, as well as their address. Coleman and Cooke went there, but, as had been the case six months before, she somehow could not find the house. (Forgotten at this point in the investigation was the fact that in the immediate aftermath of her story, Cooke had been unable to find the house, returning the next day claiming to have found it but that the family had moved.)

It was nearly midnight when they got back to the *Post*. By this point, according to Green, each of the editors who had bought the story all along had become convinced that she was lying. Woodward then confronted Cooke: "It's all over. You've gotta come clean. The notes show us the story is wrong. We know it. We can show you point by point how you concocted it." Cooke continued to deny it. The more Woodward yelled, the more stubbornly she stuck to her story.

Exhausted from failed interrogations, they left Cooke in the room with only her closest colleague, Maraniss. Cooke knew that he knew, according to Green. They talked quietly for an hour about how tough it was to succeed at a national newspaper (Bradlee called it "major-league journalism" or "hardball") and how far they had come. After she had tiptoed all around a confession, Maraniss gently pushed Cooke by asking her what he should tell the others.

She broke down. "Jimmy's World" was, she finally admitted, "a fabrication." "There was no Jimmy and no family.... I want to give the prize back," Green quoted her as saying. Maraniss told the others. Bradlee asked him to get a written admission and a resignation. Cooke complied.

THE LESSONS LEARNED

The ombudsman's report (Green 1981) was the second longest article ever published in the *Post*. Its conclusions were that warning signals were ignored, that senior editors were uninformed, that competition for prizes had pushed an ambitious young reporter too hard, and that the result was "a temporary lapse." The majority of the *Post* editors and reporters interviewed agreed, interpreting this lapse in terms of ambition and competition.

The *Post* editorial accompanying the first admission of the fraud framed the whole affair in terms of the breakdown of normal journalistic editing procedures—"quality control," Green later dubbed it. The writers thus implied that this was the ultimate cause of fraud and expressed the hope that it would be seen as the aberration it was, thereby leaving intact the *Post*'s "prized credibility" (*Washington Post*, 16 April 1981).

Other newspapers, of course, closely covered the scandal and offered similar interpretations. The *San Francisco Chronicle* (19 April 1981) blamed the *Post* editors for trusting their reporters

too much. The *Los Angeles Times* (19 April 1981) blamed the fraud on the growing use of unnamed sources, a practice it claimed arose during the Vietnam and Watergate debacles. A few days later a *Los Angeles Times* columnist went further to opine that the lesson of the Cooke fraud was that the Watergate-era spirit of "gung-ho press investigators" needed to be reversed (23 April 1981).

According to the *New York Times* (23 April 1981), the six hundred editors who attended the annual convention of the American Society of Newspaper Editors a week after the scandal broke talked of little else. They expressed a variety of concerns about the "loss of credibility for all newspapers." But almost all supported the ombudsman's principal conclusions that the scandal stemmed from "internal pressures" to "produce sensational articles and to win prizes" and from the failure to use the editing and checking "system that should have detected the fraud." Some editors added that the scandal had "forced them to re-examine" the procedures for checking the background of new reporters and the use of unidentified sources.

The *Post* itself (18 April 1981) published a summary of what other papers said about the Cooke affair. The core themes were the same: failure to check confidential sources and the risks of putting sensationalism above editorial judgment. The *Post* story also quoted a *Wall Street Journal* piece, which asked whether in all of these investigations "the hard questions" would be raised, but did not say what those questions were. The *Post*'s summary closed with a *Chicago Tribune* editor's rotten apple theory—like many others, he blamed the whole affair on "one highly unethical person."

Strangely, none of these accounts mentioned anything about the media's general assumptions and beliefs about drugs and drug users, which ultimately allowed Cooke's concoction to slip into print. For us, this is the hardest question, and it was neither asked nor answered in any of the press postmortems.

What of the Pulitzer Prize jury? Surely, if the *Post*'s editors could suffer a "temporary lapse," at least one of the esteemed editors and journalists selected to serve on the prestigious Pulitzer jury should have detected some flaw in Cooke's story. As it turns out, a few of the jurors were concerned. One questioned Cooke's guarantee of confidentiality when a child's life seemed at stake. A second was troubled by the lack of attribution, but accepted Cooke's piece "on faith" because "it had gone through the editing process on a reputable newspaper." A third overcame her doubts because she felt the article "spoke to a very compelling problem of our time. We did not suspect that it was not what it seemed to be. *We had no reason to*" (*Los Angeles Times* 1981a; emphasis added).

Still other jurors expressed doubts after the fact, but these centered largely on the unusual procedure by which Cooke's article had won. The *Post* had submitted it in the "general local reporting" category. The local reporting jury picked "Jimmy's World" second. The Pulitzer Board agreed with the jury, awarding that prize to another reporter. However, several board members felt that the Cooke piece belonged in the feature category. After discussion, board member Joseph Pulitzer suggested that it be reconsidered later in that category (Green 1981).

Meanwhile, the jury for the feature-writing prize had selected three finalists and submitted them to the board. None had ever seen the Cooke article. When the board discussed overruling the jury in favor of "Jimmy's World," some members raised the familiar question about the article. Their opposition "evaporated," however, when one member, distinguished African-American journalist Roger Wilkins, "eloquently" argued "that he could easily find child addicts within 10 blocks" of where the board was meeting at Columbia University (*Los Angeles Times* 1981a). Just as no one at the *Post* had challenged an articulate African-American reporter six months earlier, no juror challenged Wilkins's assertions about addiction in the inner city. Whatever questions they may have had about "Jimmy's World" were quickly dropped. The board overruled the jury and unanimously awarded Janet Cooke the Pulitzer Prize in Feature Writing.[3]

THE LESSONS NOT LEARNED

In all of this, no one ever turned up any concrete evidence that a child addict such as "Jimmy" existed. It is, of course, statistically possible that America's inner cities may somewhere contain a few eight-year-old addicts whose mothers' boyfriends shoot them full of heroin every day. But it is a virtual certainty that if such child addicts exist at all they are exceedingly rare. So for us, the most curious part of the Cooke scandal is that in the ensuing decade and throughout the dozens of press accounts we analyzed, no one has yet critically examined the ideology that allowed her bizarre claim that such child addicts are common to pass unnoticed into publication and on to a Pulitzer.

No one doubts that Janet Cooke was a talented writer. No one disputes that the "Jimmy" story was compelling. And certainly no one questions that tragic drug problems persist across the United States, particularly in inner cities. Was it not reasonable, then, for the *Post*'s editors to have been "taken in," and for even the prestigious Pulitzer jury to have become "victims of a hoax"? Who could have seen through a fraud perpetrated by an otherwise fine reporter whose pathological ambition led her to such thorough deceit?

We wish to suggest that the "Jimmy" story was, in fact, rather unreasonable on its face, and that the media would not have been "taken in" by it had they not been blinded by bias. We think that the *Post* editors and Pulitzer jurors—and virtually all the others in the news business who interpreted the scandal—*missed the point*.

The "hoax" to which the American media became "victim'" was one they played a central role in making. Drug scares have been a recurring feature of American history. From the early nineteenth century until Prohibition passed in 1919, many in the press were willing handmaidens to the zealous moral entrepreneurs in the Temperance crusade. Newspapers and magazines often uncritically repeated wild claims that alcohol was the primary cause of crime, insanity, poverty, divorce, "illegitimacy," business failure, and virtually all other social problems afflicting America at the time of its industrialization (Levine 1984).

Throughout the twentieth century the media helped foment a series of drug scares, each magnifying drug menaces well beyond their objective dimensions. From the turn of the century into the 1920s, the yellow journalism of the Hearst newspapers, for example, offered a steady stream of ruin and redemption melodramas. These depicted one or another chemical villain, typically in the hands of a "dangerous class" or racial minority, as responsible for the end of Western civilization (see Musto 1973; Mark 1975; Morgan 1978). In the 1930s, newspapers repeated unsubstantiated claims that marijuana, "the killer weed," led users, Mexicans in particular, to violence (Becker 1963). In the 1950s, the media spread a story of two teenagers in Colorado who had gotten high accidentally by inhaling model airplane glue. This led to nationwide hysteria, which in turn spread the practice of glue-sniffing (Brecher 1972).

In the 1960s, the press somehow remade "killer weed" into "the drop-out drug" (Himmelstein 1983), and spread other misleading reports that LSD broke chromosomes and yielded two-headed babies (Weil 1972; Becker 1967). The media that might have served as a source of credible warnings about the risks of drug abuse were dismissed with derision by the very users they needed to reach. In the 1970s, the press again falsely reported that "angel dust" or PCP gave users such superhuman strength that the police needed new stun guns to subdue them (Feldman, Agar, and Beschner 1979). In 1986, the press and politicians once again joined forces on crack use among the black underclass. The drug was unknown outside a few neighborhoods in three cities until newspapers, magazines, and TV networks blanketed the nation with horror stories that described the crack high (Reinarman and Levine 1989).

In each of these drug scares the media has consistently erred on the side of the sensational and dutifully repeated the self-serving scare stories of politicians in search of safe issues on which to take strong stands. And in each scare, including the current "war on drugs," reporters and editors have engaged in the *routinization of caricature*—rhetorically recrafting worst cases into typical cases, and profoundly distorting the nature of drug problems in the interest of dramatic stories.

A century from now historians may ponder this construction of drug demons just as they now ponder the burning of witches and heretics.[4] But what is already clear is that a century's worth of scapegoating chemical bogeymen left even the best journalists quite prepared to believe the very worst about drug users, especially inner-city addicts. Given the deep structure of bias prevailing within media institutions, it is little wonder that Janet Cooke's story elicited so little of the press's vaunted skepticism.

Thus, her immediate editor, Milton Coleman, told the *Post*'s investigating ombudsman that he "had no doubts" about "Jimmy's World" and that "it never occurred to me that she could make it up." Assistant managing editor and former Pulitzer winner Bob Woodward admitted similarly that "my skepticism left me," that his "alarm bells simply did not go off," and that "we never really debated whether or not it was true." The few doubts of the distinguished Pulitzer jury were washed away when one African-American voice asserted that "Jimmys" were everywhere in the ghetto. Even after the scandal broke wide open, ombudsman Green's thoroughly detailed report never really asked *why,* as he put it, "None of the *Post*'s senior editors subjected Cooke's story to close questioning."

These things were possible, we contend, precisely because America's guardians of truth had no touchstone of truth on drug problems apart from their own scare stories. In this the *Washington Post* was no worse than most media institutions in the United States. When seen as part of the historical pattern of news "coverage" of drug issues, the Pulitzer Prize–winning fraud was less a "lapse" than part of a long tradition. On almost any other subject, editors' "crap detectors" would have signaled that something was amiss.

The evidence for this contention oozed from every pore of Cooke's tale and was bolstered at every turn in the follow-up investigations. First, there were the shaky assumptions about addiction. Cooke alleged that "Jimmy" was "addicted" to heroin at age five and that he smoked marijuana before that. Children are curious creatures, so it is theoretically possible that a four- or five-year-old might push himself to learn to inhale foul-tasting smoke and hold it deep in his lungs repeatedly. It is even possible, although even less likely, that a five-year-old could learn to enjoy snorting heroin powder into his nostrils day after day. What is hardly possible and highly unlikely is that a five-year-old would ask to have a needle stuck in his "thin brown arms" more than once a day for the weeks it would take him to become addicted. One needn't be a drug expert for such claims to set off "alarm bells"; one need only have seen a doctor try to vaccinate a child.

All this aside, if any journalists had checked, they would have found that most heroin users experience serious nausea the first few times they use. In addition to the difficulties posed by needles and nausea, a mildly skeptical editor easily could have discovered that drug effects are rarely unambiguously pleasurable early on. Drug "highs" are in many important respects acquired tastes that are learned over time through processes that five- or eight-year-olds are exceedingly unlikely to endure (Becker 1953; Zinberg 1984). Yet, after all of journalism had put this story-scandal under its microscopes, no one had even asked about such things.

Cooke's fiction contained a second set of "red flags" having to do with assumptions about addicts. How moronic would addicts have to be (even crass "junkie" sterotypes depict them as shrewd) to allow a reporter from a top newspaper to witness them "firing up"? Even if paranoia were not an occupational hazard, there is no evidence that addicts are proud of their habits. And in a home Cooke herself described as a dealing den and shooting gallery full of other addicts, no known drug is capable of inducing the magnitude

or stupidity necessary for adult addicts to show a reporter how they inject heroin into their small child.

Let us leave this aside, too, and examine a third set of "red flags." Neither *Post* editors nor Pulitzer jurors nor any of the other editors who both reprinted Cooke's article and later dissected the scandal ever seemed to question Cooke's claims that "Ron" routinely injected "Jimmy" and that his "mother" tacitly approved of this. Not even the tallest tales of Temperance crusaders gave us such villainous villains. What sort of people would knowingly and repeatedly inject heroin into a child that they clothed, fed, and bathed?

There is nothing in the scientific literature to suggest that addicts recommend addiction to anyone, much less their own kids. The media apparently knew so little about heroin that they could simply assume it induced depravity and transformed users into the sort of vile subhumans who think nothing of doing such things. Thus the media smuggled into their stories a simplistic sort of pharmacological determinism. Clearly heroin can be powerfully addicting, but even if it were capable of morally lobotomizing all addicts, why would such addicts *give* away the very expensive stuff for which they reputedly lie, cheat, and steal?[5]

Almost any street junkie could have served as an expert informant (a "Deep Throat," if you will) and saved the *Post* from scandal. If the editors had picked ten addicts at random and asked them if a junkie would give away precious junk to a child, nine would have thought it absurd, moral qualms aside. Asked to read the Cooke story, most addicts could have told the *Post* immediately that it was concocted. Even if one accepted all of the other demonstrably dubious assumptions upon which the story rested, it made no sense even according to the perverse logic attributed to addicts.

A final set of red flags shot up immediately after "Jimmy's World" was published. According to the *Post*'s own follow-up stories, hundreds of police officers and social workers scoured the city looking for "Jimmy." Elementary school teachers inspected thousands of small student arms. Aroused citizens from housing projects in neighborhoods like "Jimmy's" all over Washington hunted for him. As Green's (1981) report put it, "The intense police search continued for 17 days. The city had been finely combed. Nothing." Half a dozen *Post* reporters also searched in vain for any other child addict. Our point here is not merely that none of these myriad searchers turned up so much as a clue as to "Jimmy's" specific whereabouts. More significant is that with everyone so certain that "untold numbers of children like Jimmy" existed, no one found *any* child addict—not an eight-year-old, not a ten-year old, not a twelve-year-old.

For some reason these journalistic findings were not considered newsworthy. Presented with the choice of publishing the recalcitrant facts uncovered by their reporters or what they wanted to believe, the *Post* editors and their print brethren chose to print the more ideologically compliant assertion that eight-year-old heroin addicts are "common" in America's inner cities. The Cooke affair thus suggests that the *Post* had more in common with President Reagan than it likes to believe. Reagan was, for example, fond of attacking "welfare chiselers" for buying vodka with their food stamps. No matter how many times his own experts told him this was untrue due to food stamp redemption rules, he continued to tell the tale because it suited his ideological purposes. Lies uttered as political demagogy are one thing, but we expect more from the great newspapers on which we rely to expose such lies. In continuing to insist that "Jimmys" were everywhere in the face of their own evidence to the contrary, the *Post* seemed to be saying that if "Jimmy's World" doesn't exist in reality, then it can be made to exist in ideology.

Unfortunately, the nonfictional lives of African-Americans in our inner cities and of growing numbers of other poor Americans are sufficiently harsh that some of them seek solace, comfort, and meaning in drugs. But editors seem to believe that readers don't like to be reminded that there is something fundamentally wrong with the social

system from which most of them benefit. Editors and readers alike, it seems, feel more comfortable believing that the worsening horrors of our inner cities are caused by evil individuals from a different gene pool—"addicts." Thus, a story about how crushing poverty and racism give rise to despair that sometimes leads to drug use, abuse, or addiction is not considered "newsworthy." Stories that simply depict addicts as complicated, troubled human beings would be neither comforting enough for readers nor dramatic enough for prizes. To us, this sin of omission is more the real pity of this story than Janet Cooke's sin of commission.

About a week after the story first appeared and months before the scandal broke, *Post* publisher Donald Graham sent Cooke a congratulatory note on her "very fine story" (Green 1981). It said, in part, that "the *Post* has no more important and tougher job than explaining life in the black community in Washington." Here he was as close to the ideal of journalism as Cooke's tale was distant from it.

Graham went on to praise the struggle of "black reporters who try to see life through their own eyes instead of seeing it the way they're told they should." In calling attention to the importance of independent reporting, Graham again articulated an important ideal. Ironically, Cooke had so internalized the way reporters in general "are told they should" see drug users that she gave a whole new meaning to the idea of seeing things through her "own eyes."

Finally, Graham wrote of how Cooke's article displayed the "gift" of "explaining" how the world works. "If there's any long-term justification for what we do," he wrote, it is that "people will act a bit differently and think a bit differently if we help them understand the world even slightly better. Much of what we write fails that first test because we don't understand what we're writing about ourselves." Here Graham displayed unintended prescience. For what he took to be an exception turned out to be a glaring example of his rule.

Cooke's concoction led readers to misunderstand the lives of addicts "in the black community." But hers was only an egregious case of the press's cultivated incapacity for understanding drug problems. If the *Post* scandal has value, it inheres in the accidental glimpse it affords into the normally hidden process by which media institutions force the untidy facts of social life through the sieve of dominant ideology (Molotch and Lester 1974). We submit that it is this process that allowed Cooke's tale to sail undetected past *Post* editors, Pulitzer jurors, and the hundreds of other journalists who analyzed the fraud. And we suggest that this process continues to camouflage the ways our world produces drug problems in the first place, and thereby helps to forge a public prepared to swallow the next junkie stereotype and to enlist in the next drug war.

NOTES

1. By all accounts in Ombudsman Green's investigation, Janet Cooke was not streetwise. She was middle-class and upwardly mobile. Her immediate supervisor told Green that Cooke "was not really street-savvy— She was Gucci and Cardin and Yves St. Laurent— She didn't know the kinds of people she was dealing with, but she was tenacious and talented" (Green 1981).
2. The Vassar degree had caught Editor-in-Chief Ben Bradlee's eye, causing him to sift Cooke's resume from the hundreds he receives each week and to set in motion the hiring process that brought her to the *Post* (Green 1981).
3. The Pulitzer Board drew its own lesson from the Cooke scandal. Seven months later it adopted new procedures to guard against such problems. Pulitzer juries would henceforth deliberate for two days instead of one (*New York Times*, 22 November 1981).
4. The authors are indebted to Dr. Peter Cohen for the analogy to witches and heretics (personal communication, 1991).
5. To be fair, we did find one article (*New York Times,* 16 April 1981) that mentioned the idea that addicts might not want to give away their heroin, but this lead was not pursued. Also, Mayor Marion Barry told the *Post* after the citywide search that he doubted "the mother or the pusher would allow a reporter to see them shoot up" (Green 1981).

REFERENCES

Becker, Howard S. 1953. "Becoming a Marijuana User." *American Journal of Sociology* 59:235–43.

Becker, Howard S. 1963. *Outsiders: Studies in the Sociology of Deviance.* New York: Free Press.

Becker, Howard S. 1967. "History, Culture, and Subjective Experience: An Exploration of the Social Bases of Drug-Induced Experiences." *Journal of Health and Social Behavior* 8:162–76.

Brecher, Edward M. 1972. *Licit and Illicit Drugs.* Boston: Little, Brown.

Cooke, Janet. 1980. "Jimmy's World—8-Year-Old Heroin Addict Lives for a Fix." *Washington Post*, 28 September, p. A1

Feldman, Harvey, Michael Agar, and George Beschner. 1979. *Angel Dust* Lexington, MA: D.C. Heath.

Green, Bill. 1981. "Janet's World—The Story of a Child Who Never Existed—How and Why It Came to Be Published." *Washington Post*, 19 April, p. A1.

Himmelstein, Jerome. 1983. *The Strange Career of Marihuana.* Westport, CT: Greenwood.

Levine, Harry Gene. 1984. "The Alcohol Problem in America: From Temperance to Prohibition." *British Journal of Addiction* 79:109–19.

Los Angeles Times. 1981a. "Story That Was Fabricated Found a Friend on Pulitzer Board." 17 April, Section I, p. 9.

Los Angeles Times. 1981b. "A Matter of Confidence." 19 April, p. 1V5.

Los Angeles Times. 1981c. "Finally, the Watergate Spirit Is Dead in America." 23 April, Section II, p. 11.

Mark, Gregory. 1975. "Racial, Economics, and Political Factors in the Development of America's First Drug Laws." *Issues in Criminology* 10:56–75.

Molotch, Harvey and Marilyn Lester. 1974. "News as Purposive Behavior: On the Strategic Uses of Routine Events, Accidents, and Scandals." *American Sociological Review* 39:101–12.

Morgan, Patricia. 1978. "The Legislation of Drug Law." *Journal of Drug Issues* 8:53–62.

Musto, David. 1973. *The American Disease: Origins of Narcotic Control.* Oxford: Oxford University Press.

New York Times. 1981a. "Washington Post Gives Up Pulitzer, Calling Article on Addict, 8, Fiction." 16 April, p. A1.

New York Times. 1981b. "Paper's False Article Is a Major Topic at Convention of Newspaper Editors." 23 April, p. A16.

New York Times. 1981c. "Pulitzer Prize Board Adopts New Procedures." 22 November, p. A38.

Reinarman, Craig and Harry G. Levine. 1989. "Crack in Context: Politics and Media in the Making of a Drug Scare." *Contemporary Drug Problems* 16:535–77.

San Francisco Chronicle. 1981 "Washington Post Blames Its Editors for Pulitzer Fiasco." 19 April, p. A6.

Washington Post. 1980. "D.C. Authorities Seek Identity of Heroin Addict, 8." 30 September, p. A11.

Washington Post. 1981a. "Post Writer Wins Pulitzer for Story on Child Addict." 14 April, p. A1.

Washington Post. 1981b. "The End of the 'Jimmy' Story." 16 April, p. A8.

Washington Post. 1981c. "Post Reporter's Pulitzer Prize Is Withdrawn." 16 April, p. A1.

Washington Post. 1981d. "'Jimmy' Episode Evokes Outrage, Sadness." 17 April, p. C13.

Washington Post. 1981e. "The District Line—The Problem Is All Too Real." 17 April, p. C13.

Washington Post. 1981f. "Nation's Editors Plumb 'Jimmy's World.'" 18 April, p. A3.

Washington Post. 1981g. "Putting the Creator of 'Jimmy's World' in Context." 19 April, p. D1.

Weil, Andrew. 1972. *The Natural Mind: An Investigation of Drugs and the Higher Consciousness.* Boston: Houghton Mifflin.

Zinberg, Norman. 1984. *Drug, Set, and Setting: The Basis for Controlled Intoxicant Use.* New Haven, CT: Yale University Press.

Labeling the Mentally Retarded

JANE R. MERCER

Two viewpoints seem to prevail when it comes to thinking about deviance. Laymen, as well as students of the subject, blame deviant behavior either on the person or on the social environment. The medical model locates the sources of deviance in characteristics of the person. A number of sociological theories of deviant behavior locate the sources of deviance in the characteristics of people's social environments. The interactionist perspective can combine both viewpoints by arguing that deviance turns out to be the result of transactions between an individual and persons in the individual's social environment.

The interactionist perspective focuses on the official definitions of deviance that are current in different social situations, the agents of control who apply those definitions, and the responses of those who are implicated in these labels of deviance. Jane R. Mercer compares and contrasts the ways in which high-status and low-status families respond to their children if they have a low "IQ." The findings lend support to the "relativity of deviance" generalization. Thus, some families suspect that a child is "different" and seek confirmation of their suspicions from specialists. Others perceive that agents of control are imposing an official definition of deviance. These are less likely than the first set of families to accept the official definition.

The clinical perspective is the frame of reference most commonly adopted in studies of mental defi-

Reprinted from "Social System Perspective and Clinical Perspective: Frames of Reference for Understanding Career Patterns of People Labeled as Mentally Retarded," *Social Problems,* Vol. 13, No. 1 (Summer 1965), pp. 21–30, 33–34, by permission of the Society for the Study of Social Problems and the author. Copyright © 1965 by the Society for the Study of Social Problems.

ciency, mental illness, drug addiction, and other areas which the students of deviance choose to investigate.[1,2] This viewpoint is readily identified by several distinguishing characteristics.

First, the investigator accepts as the focus for study those individuals who have been labeled deviant. In so doing, he adopts the values of whatever social system has defined the person as deviant and assumes that its judgments are the valid measure of deviance.... Groups in the social structure sharing the values of the core culture tend to accept the labels attached as a consequence of the application of these values without serious questioning....

A second distinguishing characteristic of the clinical perspective is the tendency to perceive deviance as an attribute of the person, as a meaning inherent in his behavior, appearance, or performance. Mental retardation, for example, is viewed as a characteristic of the person, a lack to be explained. This viewpoint results in a quest for etiology. Thus, the clinical perspective is essentially a medical frame of reference, for it sees deviance as individual pathology requiring diagnostic classification and etiological analysis for the purpose of determining proper treatment procedures and probable prognosis.

Three additional characteristics of the clinical perspective are the development of a diagnostic nomenclature, the creation of diagnostic instruments, and the professionalization of the diagnostic function.

When the investigator begins his research with the diagnostic designations assigned by official defining agents, he tends to assume that all individuals placed in a given category are essentially equivalent in respect to their deviance.... Individuals assigned to different categories of deviance are compared with each other or with a "normal" population consisting of persons who, for whatever reason, have escaped being labeled. The focus is on the individual.

Another characteristic of the clinical perspective is its assumption that the official definition is somehow the "right" definition....

Finally, when deviance is perceived as individual pathology, social action tends to center upon changing the individual or, that failing, removing him from participation in society. Prevention and cure become the primary social goals....

The social system [labeling] perspective, on the other hand, attempts to see the definition of an individual's behavior as a function of the values of the social system within which he is being evaluated. The professional definers are studied as one of the most important of the evaluating social systems but within the context of other social systems which may or may not concur with official definitions.

Defining an individual as mentally ill, delinquent, or mentally retarded is viewed as an interpersonal process in which the definer makes a value judgment about the behavior of the persons being defined.... Deviation is not seen as a characteristic of the individual or as a meaning inherent in his behavior, but as a socially derived label which may be attached to his behavior by some social systems and not by others.[3]

...Thus, it follows that a person may be mentally retarded in one system and not mentally retarded in another. He may change his label by changing his social group. This viewpoint frees us from the necessity of seeing the person as permanently stigmatized by a deviant label and makes it possible to understand otherwise obscure patterns in the life careers of individuals.... The research reported in this paper attempts to answer these questions about a group of persons who shared the common experience of having been labeled retarded by official defining agencies and placed in a public institution for the retarded....

The specific question which this study seeks to investigate within the above framework is: "Why do the families of some individuals take them back home after a period of institutionalization in a hospital for the retarded while other families do not, when, according to official evaluations, these individuals show similar degrees of deviance, that is, have comparable intelligence test scores, and are of equivalent age, sex, ethnic status, and length of hospitalization?"...

METHOD

Two groups of labeled retardates were studied. One group consisted of patients who had been released to their families from a state hospital for the retarded and the other group consisted of a matched group of patients still resident in the hospital at the time of the study.[4]...

FINDINGS

SOCIAL STATUS OF RELEASED PATIENTS

Several indices were used to measure the socio-economic level of the family of each retardate. A socioeconomic index score based on the occupation and education of the head of the household, weighted according to Hollingshead's system, was used as the basic measure. In addition, the interviewer rated the economic status of the street on which the patient's home was located, rated the physical condition of the housing unit, and completed a checklist of equipment present in the household.... [T]he families of the released patients rated significantly lower than the families of the resident patients on every measure. The heads of the households in the families of released patients had less education and lower level jobs, the family residence was located among less affluent dwellings, the housing unit was in a poorer state of repair, and the dwelling was less elaborately furnished and equipped. Contrary to the pattern found in studies of those placed as mentally ill,[5] it is the "retardate" from lower socioeconomic background who is most likely to be released to his family while higher status "retardates" are more likely to remain in the hospital.

From the clinical perspective, several explanations may be proposed for these differences. It has been found in hospital populations that patients with an I.Q. below 50 are more likely to come from families which represent a cross-section of social levels, while those with an I.Q. between 50 and 70 are more likely to come from low status families.[6] Since persons with higher I.Q.'s have a higher probability of release, this could account for higher rates of release for low status persons. However, in the present study, the tested level of intelligence was equal for both groups, and this hypothesis cannot be used as an explanation.

A second possible explanation from a clinical perspective might be based on the fact that persons who have more physical handicaps tend to be institutionalized for longer periods of time than persons with few handicaps.[7] Should it be found

that high status patients have more physical handicaps than low status patients, then this could account for the latter's shorter hospitalization. Data from the present sample were analyzed to determine whether there was a significant relationship between physical handicap and social status. Although released patients tended to have fewer physical handicaps than resident patients, this was irrespective of social status. When high status patients were compared with low status patients, 50% of the high status and 56% of the low status patients had no physical handicaps....

A third explanation from the clinical perspective may hinge on differences in the diagnostic categories to which retardates of different social status were assigned.... A diagnostic label of "familial" or "undifferentiated" ordinarily indicates that the individual has few or no physical stigmata and is essentially normal in body structure. All other categories ordinarily indicate that he has some type of physical symptomatology. Although released patients were more likely to be diagnosed as familial or undifferentiated than resident patients...this, like physical handicap, was irrespective of social status. Fifty-seven per cent of the high status retardates and 69% of the low status retardates were classified as either undifferentiated or familial, a difference which could be accounted for by chance....

DIVERGENT DEFINITIONS

In analyzing social status, four types of situations were identified. The modal category for resident patients was high social status with a smaller number of resident patients coming from low status families. The modal category for released patients was low status with a smaller number of released patients coming from higher status families. If we are correct in our hypothesis (that higher release rates for low status patients are related to the fact that the family social system [labeling] is structurally more distant from the core culture and that its style of life, values, and definitions of the patient are more divergent from official definitions than that of high status families), we could expect the largest differences to occur when high status resident families are compared to low status released families....

[T]hree questions [were] asked to determine the extent to which family members concurred in the official label of "retardation," the extent to which they believed the patient's condition amenable to change, and the extent to which they anticipated that the individual could live outside the hospital and, perhaps, fill adult roles. The patterns of the divergent definitions of the situation which emerged for each group are illuminating.

When asked whether *he* believed the patient to be retarded, the high status parent more frequently concurred with the definitions of the official defining agencies while the low status parent was more prone to disagree outright or to be uncertain. This tendency is especially marked when the two modal categories are compared. While 33.3% of the parents of the low status released patients stated that they did not think the patient was retarded and 25.6% were uncertain whether he was retarded, only 4.6% of the parents of high status resident patients felt he was not retarded and 20.9% were uncertain.

When parents were asked whether they believed anything could change the patient's condition, the differences between all groups were significant at the .02 level or beyond. The high status parent was most likely to believe that nothing could change his child's condition, and this was significantly more characteristic of parents whose children were still in the hospital than those who had taken their child from the hospital on both status levels.

When asked what they saw in the future for their child, all groups again differed significantly in the expected direction. The modal, high status group was least optimistic and the modal, low status group, most optimistic about the future. Fully 46% of the parents of the latter group expressed the expectation that their child would get a job, marry, and fulfill the usual adult roles while only 6.9% of the modal, high status group responded in

this fashion. High status parents, as a group, more frequently see their child playing dependent roles. It is interesting to note that, although a large percentage of parents of released patients believe the patient will be dependent, they demonstrate their willingness to accept responsibility for the retarded child themselves by their responding that they foresee him having a future in which he is dependent at home. Only 9.3% of the high status and 22.2% of the low status parents of the resident patients see this as a future prospect. Release to the family clearly appears to be contingent upon the willingness of the family to accept the patient's dependency, if they do not foresee him assuming independent adult roles.

FACTORS IN THE LABELING PROCESS

From the social system [labeling] perspective, retardation is viewed as a label placed upon an individual after someone has evaluated his behavior within a specific set of norms. Retardation is not a meaning necessarily inherent in the behavior of the individual. We have seen that the parents of low status, released patients tend to reject the label of retardation and to be optimistic about the future. We surmised that this divergent definition could well be related to factors in the process by which the child was first categorized as subnormal, such as his age at the time, the type of behavior which was used as a basis for making the evaluation, and the persons doing the labeling. Consequently, parents were asked specifically about these factors....

Children from lower status families were labeled as mentally subnormal at a significantly later age than children from high status families. Seventy-nine per cent of the patients in the high status, modal group were classified as retarded by the age of six while only 36.1% of those in the low status, modal group were identified at such an early age. The largest percentage of low status retardates were first classified after they reached public school age. This indicates that relatives and friends, who are the individuals most likely to observe and evaluate the behavior of young children, seldom saw anything deviant in the early development of lower status children later labeled retarded, but that the primary groups of higher status children did perceive early deviation.

This is related to the responses made when parents were asked what first prompted someone to believe the patient retarded. The modal, high status group reported slow development in 48.8% of the cases and various types of physical symptoms in an additional 20.9%, while only 14.7% and 11.8% of the modal, low status parents gave these responses. On the other hand, 55.9% of the modal, low status group were first labeled because they had problems learning in school, while this was true of only 9.3% of the modal high status group.

When parents were asked who was the most important person influencing them in placing the child in the hospital, a parallel pattern emerged. Medical persons are the most important single group for the modal, high status persons while the police and welfare agencies loom very significant in 64.1% of the cases in the modal, low status group. These findings are similar to those of Hollingshead and Redlich in their study of paths of the hospital for the mentally ill.[8] Of additional interest is the fact that the person important in placement differentiates the low status released from the low status resident patient at the .01 level. The resident low status patient's path to the hospital is similar to that of the high status patient and markedly different from released low status persons. When authoritative figures such as police and welfare are primary forces in placement, the patient is more likely to return home.

We interpret these findings to mean that when the family—or persons whose advice is solicited by the family, i.e., medical persons—is "most important" in placing a person in a hospital for the retarded, the primary groups have themselves first defined the individual as a deviant and sought professional counsel. When their own suspicions are supported by official definitions, they are most likely to leave the patient in an institution.

Conversely, when a person is labeled retarded by an authoritative, government agency whose advice is not solicited and who, in the case of the police, may be perceived as a punishing agent, the family frequently rejects the official definition of the child as retarded and withdraws him from the institution at the first opportunity. This attitude was clearly exemplified by one mother who, when asked why the family had taken the child from the hospital, replied, "Why not? He had served his time."

The police [are more of] a factor in labeling the low status person as retarded.... Fifty per cent of the low status retardates had some type of police record while only 23% of the high status subnormals were known to the police....

DISCUSSION AND CONCLUSIONS

The life space of the individual may be viewed as a vast network of interlocking social systems [labeling] through which the person moves during the course of his lifetime. Those systems which exist close to one another in the social structure tend, because of overlapping memberships and frequent communication, to evolve similar patterns of norms. Most individuals are born and live out their lives in a relatively limited segment of this social network and tend to contact mainly social systems which share common norms. When an individual's contacts are restricted to a circumscribed segment of the structure, this gives some stability to the evaluations which are made of his behavior and to the labels which are attached to him.

However, when the person's life career takes him into segments of the social network which are located at a distance from his point of origin, as when a Mexican-American child enters the public school or a black child gets picked up by police, he is then judged by a new and different set of norms. Behavior which was perfectly acceptable in his primary social systems [labeling] may now be judged as evidence of "mental retardation." At this point, he is caught up in the web of official definitions. However, because he has primary social systems [labeling] which may not agree with these official labels, he may be able to return to that segment of the social structure which does not label him as deviant after he has fulfilled the minimal requirements of the official system. That is, he can drop out of school or he can "serve his time" in the state hospital and then go home. By changing his location in social space, he can change his label from "retarded" to "not much different from the rest of us." For example, the mother of a Mexican-American, male, adult patient who had been released from the hospital after being committed following an incident in which he allegedly made sexual advances to a young girl, told the author, "There is nothing wrong with Benny. He just can't read or write." Since the mother spoke only broken English, had no formal schooling, and could not read or write, Benny did not appear deviant to her. From her perspective, he didn't have anything wrong with him.

The child from a high status family has no such recourse. His primary social systems [labeling] lie structurally close to the official social systems and tend to concur on what is acceptable. Definitions of his subnormality appear early in his life and are more universal in all his social groups. He cannot escape the retarded label because all his associates agree that he is a deviant.[9]

In conclusion, tentative answers may be given to the three questions raised earlier in this discussion. "Who sees whom as retarded?" Within the social system perspective, it becomes clear that persons who are clinically similar may be defined quite differently by their primary social systems. The person from lower status social systems is less likely to be perceived as mentally subnormal.

"What impact does this differential definition have on the life career of the person?" Apparently, these differential definitions do make a difference because the group which diverges most widely from official definitions is the group in which the most individuals are released from the institution to their families.

Finally, "What are the characteristics of the social systems [labeling] which diverge most widely from official definitions?" These social systems [labeling] seem to be characterized by low educational achievement, high levels of dependency, and high concentrations of ethnic minorities.

A social system [labeling] perspective adds a useful dimension to the label "mental retardation" by its focus on the varied definitions which may be applied to behavior by different groups in society. For those interested in the care and treatment of persons officially labeled as mentally subnormal, it may be beneficial in some cases to seek systematically to relocate such individuals in the social structure in groups which will not define them as deviant. Rather than insisting that family members adopt official definitions of abnormality, we may frequently find it advisable to permit them to continue to view the patient within their own frame of reference and thus make it easier for them to accept him.

NOTES

1. August B. Hollingshead and Frederick C. Redlich, *Social Class and Mental Illness,* New York: John Wiley and Sons, 1958, Chapter 11.

2. H. E. Freeman and O. G. Simmons, "Social Class and Posthospital Performance Levels," *American Sociological Review,* 2 (June, 1959), p. 348.

3. Howard S. Becker, editor, *The Other Side: Perspectives on Deviance,* New York: The Free Press, 1964.

4. Pacific State Hospital, Pomona, California, is a state-supported hospital for the mentally retarded with a population of approximately 3,000 patients.

5. August B. Hollingshead and Frederick C. Redlich, 1958, *op. cit.,* Chapter 11.

6. Georges Sabagh, Harvey F. Dingman, George Tarjan, and Stanley W. Wright, "Social Class and Ethnic Status of Patients Admitted to a State Hospital for the Retarded," *Pacific Sociological Review,* 2 (Fall, 1959), pp. 76–80.

7. G. Tarjan, S. W. Wright, M. Kramer, R. H. Person, Jr., and R. Morgan, "The Natural History of Mental Deficiency in a State Hospital. I: Probabilities of Release and Death by Age, Intelligence Quotients, and Diagnosis," *AMA J. Dis. Childr.,* 96 (1958) pp. 64–70.

8. August B. Hollingshead and Frederick C. Redlich, 1958, *op. cit.,* Chapter 11.

9. Lewis Anthony Dexter, "On the Politics and Sociology of Stupidity in Our Society" in *The Other Side: Perspectives on Deviance,* edited by Howard S. Becker, New York: The Free Press, 1964, pp. 37–49.

CHAPTER 3

ACCOMMODATION TO DEVIANCE

How Women Experience Battering

KATHLEEN J. FERRARO and JOHN M. JOHNSON

Conduct depends upon social definitions. Before people can take some action, they have to have some ideas about what kind of action to take and with whom. Some general questions the sociology of deviance asks are the following: Who creates the definitions of deviance? Who applies those definitions? What are the consequences of applying definitions? Applications of definitions and their consequences vary considerably according to the kinds of groups in which labeling and responses to deviance occur. If in some groups there is a lapse of time between repeated violations and labeling, in others there is a history of repeated violations without labeling.

Battered women are a case in point. For example, Kathleen J. Ferraro and John M. Johnson note that the general question asked about battered women is "Why do they stay with their partners?" People outside the situation of battering are quick to define the batterer as the deviant. By contrast, battered women in the early stages of the relationship may not see the batterer's actions as deviant or may define themselves as the deviant ones. In time, over a long series of stages, some battered women are able to see the batterer as the one who is the deviant. And some are able to end the relationship with their partner when others assist them in redefining their situation.

...Marriages and their unofficial counterparts develop through the efforts of each partner to maintain feelings of love and intimacy. In modern, Western cultures, the value placed on marriage is high; individuals invest a great amount of emotion in their spouses, and expect a return on that investment. The majority of women who marry still adopt the roles of wives and mothers as primary identities, even when they work outside the home, and thus have a strong motivation to succeed in their domestic roles. Married women remain economically dependent on their husbands. In 1978, married men in the United States earned an average of $293 a week, while married women earned $167 a week (U.S. Department of Labor, 1980). Given these high expectations and dependencies, the costs of recognizing failures and dissolving marriages are significant. Divorce is an increasingly common phenomenon in the United States, but it is still labeled a social problem and is seldom undertaken without serious deliberations and emotional upheavals (Bohannan, 1971). Levels of

Reprinted from "How Women Experience Battering: The Process of Victimization," *Social Problems,* Vol. 39, No. 3 (February 1983), pp. 325–335, by permission of the Society for the Study of Social Problems and the authors. Copyright © 1983 by the Society for the Study of Social Problems.

commitment vary widely, but some degree of commitment is implicit in the marriage contract.

When marital conflicts emerge there is usually some effort to negotiate an agreement or bargain, to ensure the continuity of the relationship (Scanzoni, 1972). Couples employ a variety of strategies, depending on the nature and extent of resources available to them, to resolve conflicts without dissolving relationships. It is thus possible for marriages to continue for years, surviving the inevitable conflicts that occur (Sprey, 1971).

In describing conflict-management, Spiegel (1968) distinguishes between "role induction" and "role modification." Role induction refers to conflict in which "one or the other parties to the conflict agrees, submits, goes along with, becomes convinced, or is persuaded in some way" (1968: 402). Role modification, on the other hand, involves adaptations by both partners. Role induction seems particularly applicable to battered women who accommodate their husbands' abuse. Rather than seeking help or escaping, as people typically do when attacked by strangers, battered women often rationalize violence from their husbands, at least initially. Although remaining with a violent man does not indicate that a woman views violence as an acceptable aspect of the relationship, the length of time that a woman stays in the marriage after abuse begins is a rough index of her efforts to accommodate the situation. In a U.S. study of 350 battered women, Pagelow (1981) found the median length of stay after violence began was four years; some left in less than one year, others stayed as long as 42 years.

Battered women have good reasons to rationalize violence. There are few institutional, legal, or cultural supports for women fleeing violent marriages. In Roy's (1977:32) survey of 150 battered women, 90 percent said they "thought of leaving and would have done so had the resources been available to them." Eighty percent of Pagelow's (1981) sample indicated previous, failed attempts to leave their husbands. Despite the development of the international shelter movement, changes in police practices, and legislation to protect battered

women since 1975, it remains extraordinarily difficult for a battered woman to escape a violent husband determined to maintain his control. At least one woman, Mary Parziale, has been murdered by an abusive husband while residing in a shelter (Beverly, 1978); others have been murdered after leaving shelters to establish new, independent homes (Garcia, 1978). When these practical and social constraints are combined with love for and commitment to an abuser, it is obvious that there is a strong incentive—often a practical necessity—to rationalize violence.

Previous research on the rationalizations of deviant offenders has revealed a typology of "techniques of neutralization," which allow offenders to view their actions as normal, acceptable, or at least justifiable (Sykes and Matza, 1957). A similar typology can be constructed for victims. Extending the concepts developed by Sykes and Matza, we assigned the responses of battered women we interviewed to one of six categories of rationalization: (1) the appeal to the salvation ethic; (2) the denial of the victimizer; (3) the denial of injury; (4) the denial of victimization; (5) the denial of options; and (6) the appeal to higher loyalties. The women usually employed at least one of these techniques to make sense of their situations; often they employed two or more, simultaneously or over time.

1. *The appeal to the salvation ethic:* This rationalization is grounded in a woman's desire to be of service to others. Abusing husbands are viewed as deeply troubled, perhaps "sick," individuals, dependent on their wives' nurturance for survival. Battered women place their own safety and happiness below their commitment to "saving my man" from whatever malady they perceive as the source of their husbands' problems (Ferraro, 1979a). The appeal to the salvation ethic is a common response to an alcoholic or drug-dependent abuser. The battered partners of substance-abusers frequently describe the charming, charismatic personality of their sober mates, viewing this appealing personality as the "real man" being destroyed by disease.

They then assume responsibility for helping their partners to overcome their problems, viewing the batterings they receive as an index of their partners' pathology. Abuse must be endured while helping the man return to his "normal" self. One woman said:

> I thought I was going to be Florence Nightingale. He had so much potential; I could see how good he really was, and I was going to "save" him. I thought I was the only thing keeping him going, and that if I left he'd lose his job and wind up in jail. I'd make excuses to everybody for him. I'd call work and lie when he was drunk, saying he was sick. I never criticized him, because he needed my approval.

2. *The denial of the victimizer:* This technique is similar to the salvation ethic, except that victims do not assume responsibility for solving their abusers' problems. Women perceive battering as an event beyond the control of both spouses, and blame it on some external force. The violence is judged situational and temporary, because it is linked to unusual circumstances or a sickness which can be cured. Pressures at work, the loss of a job, or legal problems are all situations which battered women assume as the causes of their partners' violence. Mental illness, alcoholism, and drug addiction are also viewed as external, uncontrollable afflictions by many battered women who accept the medical perspective on such problems. By focusing on factors beyond the control of their abuser, women deny their husbands' intent to do them harm, and thus rationalize violent episodes.

> He's sick. He didn't used to be this way, but he can't handle alcohol. It's really like a disease, being an alcoholic.... I think too that this is what he saw at home, his father is a very violent man, and alcoholic too, so it's really not his fault, because this is all he has ever known.

3. *The denial of injury:* For some women, the experience of being battered by a spouse is so discordant with their expectations that they simply refuse to acknowledge it. When hospitalization is not required—and it seldom is for most cases of battering[1]—routines quickly return to normal. Meals are served, jobs and schools are attended, and daily chores completed. Even with lingering pain, bruises, and cuts, the normality of everyday life overrides the strange, confusing memory of the attack. When husbands refuse to discuss or acknowledge the event, in some cases even accusing their wives of insanity, women sometimes come to believe the violence never occurred. The denial of injury does not mean that women feel no pain. They know they are hurt, but define the hurt as tolerable or normal. Just as individuals tolerate a wide range of physical discomfort before seeking medical help, battered women tolerate a wide range of physical abuse before defining it as an injurious assault. One woman explained her disbelief at her first battering:

> I laid in bed and cried all night. I could not believe it had happened, and I didn't want to believe it. We had only been married a year, and I was pregnant and excited about starting a family. Then all of a sudden, this! The next morning he told me he was sorry and it wouldn't happen again, and I gladly kissed and made up. I wanted to forget the whole thing, and wouldn't let myself worry about what it meant for us.

4. *The denial of victimization:* Victims often blame themselves for the violence, thereby neutralizing the responsibility of the spouse. Pagelow (1981) found that 99.4 percent of battered women felt they did not deserve to be beaten, and 51 percent said they had done nothing to provoke an attack. The battered women in our sample did not believe violence against them was justified, but some felt it could have been avoided if they had been more passive and conciliatory. Both Pagelow's and our samples are biased in this area, because they were made up almost entirely of women who had already left their abusers, and thus would have been unlikely to feel major responsibility for the abuse they received. Retrospective accounts of victimization in our sample, however, did reveal evidence that some women believed their right to leave violent men was restricted by their participation in the conflicts. One subject said:

> Well, I couldn't really do anything about it, because I did ask for it. I knew how to get at him, and I'd keep after it and keep after it until he got fed up and knocked me right out. I can't say I like it, but I shouldn't have nagged him like I did.

As Pagelow (1981) noted, there is a difference between provocation and justification A battered woman's belief that her actions angered her spouse to the point of violence is not synonymous with the belief that violence was therefore *justified*. But belief in provocation may diminish a woman's capacity for retaliation or self-defense, because it blurs her concept of responsibility. A woman's acceptance of responsibility for the violent incident is encouraged by an abuser who continually denigrates her and makes unrealistic demands. Depending on the social supports available, and the personality of the battered woman, the man's accusations of inadequacy may assume the status of truth. Such beliefs of inferiority inhibit the development of a notion of victimization.

5. *The denial of options:* This technique is composed of two elements: practical options and emotional options. Practical options, including alternative housing, source of income, and protection from an abuser, are clearly limited by the patriarchal structure of Western society. However, there are differences in the ways battered women respond to these obstacles, ranging from determined struggle to acquiescence. For a variety of reasons, some battered women do not take full advantage of the practical opportunities which are available to escape, and some return to abusers voluntarily even after establishing an independent lifestyle. Others ignore the most severe constraints in their efforts to escape their relationships. For example, one resident of the shelter we observed walked 30 miles in her bedroom slippers to get to the shelter, and required medical attention for blisters and cuts to her feet. On the other hand, a woman who had a full-time job, had rented an apartment, and had been given by the shelter all the clothes, furniture, and basics necessary to set up housekeeping, returned to her husband two weeks after leaving the shelter. Other women refused to go to job interviews, keep appointments with social workers, or move out of the state for their own protection (Ferraro, 1981b). Such actions are frightening for women who have led relatively isolated or protected lives, but failure to take action leaves few alternatives to a violent marriage. The belief of battered women that they will not be able to make it on their own—a belief often fueled by years of abuse and oppression—is a major impediment to [acknowledgment] that one is a victim and taking action.

The denial of *emotional* options imposes still further restrictions. Battered women may feel that no one else can provide intimacy and companionship. While physical beating is painful and dangerous, the prospect of a lonely, celibate existence is often too frightening to risk. It is not uncommon for battered women to express the belief that their abuser is the only man they could love, thus severely limiting their opportunities to discover new, more supportive relationships. One woman said:

> He's all I've got. My dad's gone, and my mother disowned me when I married him. And he's really special. He understands me, and I understand him. Nobody could take his place.

6. *The appeal to higher loyalties:* This appeal involves enduring battering for the sake of some higher commitment, either religious or traditional. The Christian belief that women should serve their husbands as men serve God is invoked as a rationalization to endure a husband's violence for later rewards in the afterlife. Clergy may support this view by advising women to pray and try harder to please their husbands (Davidson, 1978; McGlinchey, 1981). Other women have a strong commitment to the nuclear family, and find divorce repugnant. They may believe that for their children's sake, any marriage is better than no marriage. One woman we interviewed divorced her husband of 35 years after her last child left home. More commonly women who have survived violent relationships for that long do not have the desire or strength to divorce and begin a new life. When the appeal to higher loyalties is employed as a strategy to cope with battering, commitment to and involvement with an ideal overshadows the mundane reality of violence.

CATALYSTS FOR CHANGE

Rationalization is a way of coping with a situation in which, for either practical or emotional reasons, or both, a battered woman is stuck. For some women, the situation and the beliefs that rationalize it, may continue for a lifetime. For others, changes may occur within the relationship, within individuals, or in available resources which serve as catalysts for redefining the violence. When battered women reject prior rationalizations and begin to view themselves as true victims of abuse, the victimization process begins.[2]

There are a variety of catalysts for redefining abuse; we discuss six: (1) a change in the level of violence; (2) a change in resources; (3) a change in the relationship; (4) despair; (5) a change in the visibility of violence; and (6) external definitions of the relationship.

1. *A change in the level of violence:* Although Gelles (1976) reports that the severity of abuse is an important factor in women's decisions to leave violent situations, Pagelow (1981) found no significant correlation between the number of years spent cohabiting with an abuser and the severity of abuse. On the contrary: the longer women lived with an abuser, the more severe the violence they endured, since violence increased in severity over time. What does seem to serve as a catalyst is a sudden change in the relative level of violence. Women who suddenly realize that battering may be fatal may reject rationalizations in order to save their lives. One woman who had been severely beaten by an alcoholic husband for many years

explained her decision to leave on the basis of a direct threat to her life:

> *It was like a pendulum. He'd swing to the extremes both ways. He'd get drunk and beat me up, then he'd get sober and treat me like a queen. One day he put a gun to my head and pulled the trigger. It wasn't loaded. But that's when I decided I'd had it. I sued for separation of property. I knew what was coming again, so I got out. I didn't want to. I still loved the guy, but I knew I had to for my own sanity.*

There are, of course, many cases of homicide in which women did not escape soon enough. In 1979, 7.6 percent of all murders in the United States where the relationship between the victim and the offender was known were murders of wives by husbands (Flanagan *et al.*, 1982). Increases in severity do not guarantee a reinterpretation of the situation, but may play a part in the process.

2. *A change in resources:* Although some women rationalize cohabiting with an abuser by claiming they have no options, others begin reinterpreting violence when the resources necessary for escape become available. The emergence of safe homes or shelters since 1970 has produced a new resource for battered women. While not completely adequate or satisfactory, the mere existence of a place to go alters the situation in which battering is experienced (Johnson, 1981). Public support of shelters is a statement to battered women that abuse need not be tolerated. Conversely, political trends which limit resources available to women, such as cutbacks in government funding to social programs, increase fears that life outside a violent marriage is economically impossible. One 55-year-old woman discussed this catalyst:

> *I stayed with him because I didn't want my kids to have the same life I did. My parents were divorced, and I was always so ashamed of that.... Yes, they're all on their own now, so there's no reason left to stay.*

3. *A change in the relationship:* Walker (1979), in discussing the stages of a battering relationship, notes that violent incidents are usually followed by periods of remorse and solicitude. Such phases deepen the emotional bonds, and make rejection of an abuser more difficult. But as battering progresses, periods of remorse may shorten, or disappear, eliminating the basis for maintaining a positive outlook on the marriage. After a number of episodes of violence, a man may realize that his victim will not retaliate or escape, and thus feel no need to express remorse. Extended periods devoid of kindness or love may alter a woman's feelings toward her partner so much so that she eventually begins to define herself as a victim of abuse. One woman recalled:

> *At first, you know, we used to have so much fun together. He has kind've, you know, a magnetic personality; he can be really charming. But it isn't fun anymore. Since the baby came, it's changed completely. He just wants me to stay at home, while he goes out with his friends. He doesn't even talk to me, most of the time.… No, I don't really love him anymore, not like I did.*

4. *Despair:* Changes in the relationship may result in a loss of hope that "things will get better." When hope is destroyed and replaced by despair, rationalizations of violence may give way to the recognition of victimization. Feelings of hopelessness or despair are the basis for some efforts to assist battered women, such as Al-Anon.[3] The director of an Al-Anon organized shelter explained the concept of "hitting bottom":

> *Before the Al-Anon program can really be of benefit, a woman has to hit bottom. When you hit bottom, you realize that all of your own efforts to control the situation have failed; you feel helpless and lost and worthless and completely disenchanted with the world. Women can't really be helped unless they're ready for it and want it. Some women come here when things get bad, but they aren't really ready to be committed to Al-Anon. Things haven't gotten bad enough for them, and they go right back. We see this all the time.*

5. *A change in the visibility of violence:* Creating a web of rationalizations to overlook violence is accomplished more easily if no intruders are present to question their validity. Since most violence between couples occurs in private, there are seldom conflicting interpretations of the event from outsiders. Only 7 percent of the respondents in Gelles' (1974) study who discussed spatial location of violence indicated events which took place outside the home, but all reported incidents within the home. Others report similar findings (Pittman and Handy, 1964; Pokorny, 1965; Wolfgang, 1958). If violence does occur in the presence of others, it may trigger a reinterpretation process. Battering in private is degrading, but battering in public is humiliating, for it is a statement of subordination and powerlessness. Having others witness abuse may create intolerable feelings of shame which undermine prior rationalizations.

> *He never hit me in public before—it was always at home. But the Saturday I got back (returned to husband from shelter), we went Christmas shopping and he slapped me in the store because of some stupid joke I made. People saw it, I know, I felt so stupid, like, they must all think what a jerk I am, what a sick couple, and I thought, "God, I must be crazy to let him do this."*

6. *External definitions of the relationship:* A change in visibility is usually accomplished by the interjection of external definitions of abuse. External definitions vary depending on their source and the situation; they either reinforce or undermine rationalizations. Battered women who request help frequently find others—and especially officials—don't believe their story or are unsympathetic (Pagelow, 1981; Pizzey, 1974). Experimental research by Shotland and Straw (1976) supports these reports. Observers usually fail to respond when a woman is attacked by a man, and justify nonintervention on the grounds that they assumed the victim and offender were married. One young woman discussed how lack of support from her family left her without hope:

It wouldn't be so bad if my own family gave a damn about me.... Yeah, they know I'm here, and they don't care. They didn't care about me when I was a kid, so why should they care now? I got raped and beat as a kid, and now I get beat as an adult. Life is a big joke.

Clearly, such responses from family members contribute to the belief among battered women that there are no alternatives and that they must tolerate the abuse. However, when outsiders respond with unqualified support of the victim and condemnation of violent men, their definitions can be a potent catalyst toward victimization. Friends and relatives who show genuine concern for a woman's well-being may initiate an awareness of danger which contradicts previous rationalizations.

My mother-in-law knew what was going on, but she wouldn't admit it.... I said, "Mom, what do you think these bruises are?" and she said, "Well, some people just bruise easy. I do it all the time, bumping into things."...And he just denied it, pretended like nothing happened, and if I'd said I wanted to talk about it, he'd say, "Life goes on, you can't just dwell on things."...But this time, my neighbor knew what happened, she saw it, and when he denied it, she said, "I can't believe it! You know that's not true!"...and I was so happy that finally, somebody else saw what was goin' on, and I just told him then that this time I wasn't gonna come home!

Shelters for battered women serve not only as material resources, but as sources of external definitions which contribute to the victimization process. They offer refuge from a violent situation in which a woman may contemplate her circumstances and what she wants to do about them. Within a shelter, women meet counselors and other battered women who are familiar with rationalizations of violence and the reluctance to give up commitment to a spouse. In counseling sessions, and informal conversations with other residents, women hear horror stories from others who have already defined themselves as victims. They are supported for expressing anger and re-

jecting responsibility for their abuse (Ferraro, 1981a). The goal of many shelters is to overcome feelings of guilt and inadequacy so that women can make choices in their best interests. In this atmosphere, violent incidents are reexamined and redefined as assaults in which the woman was victimized.

How others respond to a battered woman's situation is critical. The closer the relationship of others, the more significant their response is to a woman's perception of the situation. Thus, children can either help or hinder the victim. Pizzey (1974) found adolescent boys at a shelter in Chiswick, England, often assumed the role of the abusing father and themselves abused their mothers, both verbally and physically. On the other hand, children at the shelter we observed often became extremely protective and nurturing toward their mothers. This phenomenon has been thoroughly described elsewhere (Ferraro, 1981a). Children who have been abused by fathers who also beat their mothers experience high levels of anxiety, and rarely want to be reunited with their fathers. A 13-year-old, abused daughter of a shelter resident wrote the following message to her stepfather:

I am going to be honest and not lie. No, I don't want you to come back. It's not that I am jealous because mom loves you. It is [I] am afraid I won't live to see 18. I did care about you a long time ago, but now I can't care, for the simple reason you['re] always calling us names, even my friends. And another reason is, I am tired of seeing mom hurt. She has been hurt enough in her life, and I don't want her to be hurt any more.

No systematic research has been conducted on the influence children exert on their battered mothers, but it seems obvious that the willingness of children to leave a violent father would be an important factor in a woman's desire to leave.

The relevance of these catalysts to a woman's interpretation of violence vary with her own situation and personality. The process of rejecting rationalizations and becoming a victim is ambiguous, confusing, and emotional. We now turn to the feelings involved in a victimization.

THE EMOTIONAL CAREER
OF VICTIMIZATION

As rationalizations give way to perceptions of victimization, a woman's feelings about herself, her spouse, and her situation change. These feelings are imbedded in a cultural, political, and interactional structure. Initially, abuse is contrary to a woman's cultural expectations of behavior between intimates, and therefore engenders feelings of betrayal. The husband has violated his wife's expectations of love and protection, and thus betrayed her confidence in him. The feeling of betrayal, however, is balanced by the husband's efforts to explain his behavior, and by the woman's reluctance to abandon faith. Additionally, the political dominance of men within and outside the family mediate women's ability to question the validity of their husband's actions.

At the interpersonal level, psychological abuse accompanying violence often invokes feelings of guilt and shame in the battered victim. Men define violence as a response to their wives' inadequacies or provocations, which leads battered women to feel that they have failed. Such character assaults are devastating, and create long-lasting feelings of inferiority (Ferraro, 1979b):

> I've been verbally abused as well. It takes you a long time to…you may say you feel good and you may…but inside, you know what's been said to you and it hurts for a long time. You need to build up your self-image and make yourself feel like you're a useful person, that you're valuable, and that you're a good parent. You might think these things, and you may say them.… I'm gonna prove it to myself.

Psychologists working with battered women consistently report that self-confidence wanes over years of ridicule and criticism (Hilberman and Munson, 1978; Walker, 1979).

Feelings of guilt and shame are also mixed with a hope that things will get better, at least in the early stages of battering. Even the most violent man is nonviolent much of the time, so there is always a basis for believing that violence is exceptional and the "real man" is not a threat. The vacillation between violence and fear on the one hand, and nonviolence and affection on the other was described by a shelter resident:

> First of all, the first beatings—you can't believe it yourself. I'd go to bed, and I'd cry, and I just couldn't believe this was happening. And I'd wake up the next morning thinking that couldn't of happened, or maybe it was my fault. It's so unbelievable that this person that you're married to and you love would do that to you but yet you can't leave either because, ya' know, for the other 29 days of the month that person loves you and is with you.

Hope wanes as periods of love and remorse dwindle. Feelings of love and intimacy are gradually replaced with loneliness and pessimism. Battered women who no longer feel love for their husbands but remain in their marriages enter a period of emotional dormancy. They survive each day, performing necessary tasks, with a dull depression and lack of enthusiasm. While some battered women live out their lives in this emotional desert, others are spurred by catalysts to feel either the total despair or mortal fear which leads them to seek help.

Battered women who perceive their husbands' actions as life-threatening experience a penetrating fear that consumes all their thoughts and energies. The awareness of murderous intent by a presumed ally who is a central figure in all aspects of her life destroys all bases for safety. There is a feeling that death is imminent, and that there is nowhere to hide. Prior rationalizations and beliefs about a "good marriage" are exploded, leaving the woman in a crisis of ambiguity (Ridington, 1978).

Feelings of fear are experienced physiologically as well as emotionally. Battered women experience aches and fatigue, stomach pains, diarrhea or constipation, tension headaches, shakes, chills, loss of appetite, and insomnia. Sometimes, fear is expressed as a numbed shock, similar to rape trauma syndrome (Burgess and Holmstrom, 1974), in which little is felt or communicated.

If attempts to seek help succeed, overwhelming feelings of fear subside, and a rush of new emotions are felt: the original sense of betrayal re-emerges, creating strong feelings of anger. For women socialized to reject angry feelings as unfeminine, coping with anger is difficult. Unless the expression of anger is encouraged in a supportive environment, such women may suppress anger and feel only depression (Ball and Wyman, 1978). When anger is expressed, it often leads to feelings of strength and exhilaration. Freedom from threats of violence, the possibility of a new life, and the unburdening of anger create feelings of joy. The simple pleasures of going shopping, taking children to the park, or talking with other women without fear of criticism or punishment from a husband, constitute amazing freedoms. One middle-aged woman expressed her joy over her newly acquired freedom this way:

> *Boy, tomorrow I'm goin' downtown, and I've got my whole day planned out, and I'm gonna do what I wanna do, and if somebody doesn't like it, to hell with them! You know, I'm having so much fun, I should've done this years ago!*

Probably the most typical feeling expressed by women in shelters is confusion. They feel both sad and happy, excited and apprehensive, independent, yet in need of love. Most continue to feel attachment to their husbands, and feel ambivalent about divorce. There is grief over the loss of an intimate, which must be acknowledged and mourned. Although shelters usually discourage women from contacting their abusers while staying at the shelter, most women do communicate with their husbands—and most receive desperate pleas for forgiveness and reconciliation. If there is not strong emotional support and potential material support, such encouragement by husbands

often rekindles hope for the relationship. Some marriages can be revitalized through counseling, but most experts agree that long-term batterers are unlikely to change (Pagelow, 1981; Walker, 1979). Whether they seek refuge in shelters or with friends, battered women must decide relatively quickly what actions to take. Usually, a tentative commitment is made, either to independence or working on the relationship, but such commitments are usually ambivalent. As one woman wrote to her counselor:

> *My feelings are so mixed up sometimes. Right now I feel my husband is really trying to change. But I know that takes time. I still feel for him some. I don't know how much. My mind still doesn't know what it wants. I would really like when I leave here to see him once in a while, get my apartment, and sort of like start over with our relationship for me and my baby and him, to try and make it work. It might. It kind of scares me. I guess I am afraid it won't.... I can only hope this works out. There's no telling what could happen. No one knows.*

The emotional career of battered women consists of movement from guilt, shame, and depression to fear and despair, to anger, exhilaration, and confusion. Women who escape violent relationships must deal with strong, sometimes conflicting, feelings in attempting to build new lives for themselves free of violence. The kind of response women receive when they seek help largely determines the effects these feelings have on subsequent decisions.

NOTES

1. National crime survey data for 1973–76 show that 17 percent of persons who sought medical attention for injuries inflicted by an intimate were hospitalized. Eighty-seven percent of injuries inflicted by a spouse or ex-spouse were bruises, black eyes, cuts, scratches, or swelling (National Crime Survey Report, 1980).
2. Explanation of why and how some women arrive at these feelings is beyond the scope of this paper. Our goal is to describe feelings at various stages of the victimization process.

3. Al-Anon is the spouse's counterpart to Alcoholics Anonymous. It is based on the same self-help, 12-step program that A.A. is founded on.

REFERENCES

Ball, Patricia G., and Elizabeth Wyman. 1978. "Battered wives and powerlessness: What can counselors do?" *Victimology* 2(3–4):545–552.

Beverly. 1978. "Shelter resident murdered by husband." *Aegis,* September/October:13.

Bohannan, Paul (ed.). 1971. *Divorce and After.* Garden City, New York: Anchor.

Burgess, Ann W., and Linda Lytle Holmstrom. 1974. *Rape: Victims of Crisis.* Bowie, Maryland: Brady.

Davidson, Terry. 1978. *Conjugal Crime.* New York: Hawthorn.

Ferraro, Kathleen J. 1979a. "Hard love: Letting go of an abusive husband." *Frontiers* 4(2):16–18.

———. 1979b. "Physical and emotional battering: Aspects of managing hurt." *California Sociologist* 2(2):134–149.

———. 1981a. "Battered women and the shelter movement." Unpublished Ph.D. dissertation, Arizona State University.

———. 1981b. "Processing battered women." *Journal of Family Issues* 2(4):415–438.

Flanagan, Timothy J., David J. van Alstyne, and Michael R. Gottfredson (eds.). 1982. *Sourcebook of Criminal Justice Statistics: 1981.* U.S. Department of Justice, Bureau of Justice Statistics, Washington, D.C.: U.S. Government Printing Office.

Garcia, Dick. 1978. "Slain women 'lived in fear.'" *The Times* (Erie, Pa.) June 14:B1.

Gelles, Richard J. 1974. *The Violent Home.* Beverly Hills: Sage.

———. 1976. "Abused wives: Why do they stay?" *Journal of Marriage and the Family* 38(4):659–668.

Hilberman, Elaine, and Kit Munson. 1978. "Sixty battered women." *Victimology* 2(3–4):460–470.

Johnson, John M. 1981. "Program enterprise and official cooptation of the battered women's shelter movement." *American Behavioral Scientist* 24(6):827–842.

McGlinchey, Anne. 1981. "Woman battering and the church's response." Pp. 133–140 in Albert R. Roberts (ed.), *Sheltering Battered Women.* New York: Springer.

National Crime Survey Report. 1980. *Intimate Victims.* Washington, D.C.: U.S. Department of Justice.

Pagelow, Mildred Daley. 1981. *Woman-Battering.* Beverly Hills: Sage.

Pittman, D. J., and W. Handy. 1964. "Patterns in criminal aggravated assault." *Journal of Criminal Law, Criminology, and Police Science* 55(4):462–470.

Pizzey, Erin. 1974. *Scream Quietly or the Neighbors Will Hear.* Baltimore: Penguin.

Pokorny, Alex D. 1965. "Human violence: A comparison of homicide, aggravated assault, suicide, and attempted suicide." *Journal of Criminal Law, Criminology, and Police Science* 56 (December):488–497.

Ridington, Jillian. 1978. "The transition process: A feminist environment as reconstitutive milieu." *Victimology* 2(3–4):563–576.

Roy, Maria (ed.). 1977. *Battered Women.* New York: Van Nostrand.

Scanzoni, John. 1972. *Sexual Bargaining.* Englewood Cliffs, N.J.: Prentice-Hall.

Shotland, R. Lance, and Margret K. Straw. 1976. "Bystander response to an assault: When a man attacks a woman." *Journal of Personality and Social Psychology* 34(5):990–999.

Spiegel, John P. 1968. "The resolution of role conflict within the family." Pp. 391–411 in N. W. Bell and E. F. Vogel (eds.), *A Modern Introduction to the Family.* New York: Free Press.

Sprey, Jetse. 1971. "On the management of conflict in families." *Journal of Marriage and the Family* 33(4):699–706.

Sykes, Gresham M., and David Matza. 1957. "Techniques of neutralization: A theory of delinquency." *American Sociological Review* 22(6):667–670.

U.S. Department of Labor. 1980. *Handbook of Labor Statistics.* Washington, D.C.: U.S. Government Printing Office.

Walker, Lenore E. 1979. *The Battered Woman.* New York: Harper & Row.

Wolfgang, Marvin E. 1958. *Patterns in Criminal Homicide.* New York: John Wiley.

Accommodation to Madness

MICHAEL LYNCH

A general conception held by laypeople as well as sociologists is that deviance creates the need for social control. One textbook definition, for example, says deviance is a violation of norms likely to elicit negative sanctions. Such a definition, however, takes for granted a consensus on both rules and sanctions. Interactionists assume that deviance is subjectively problematic rather than objectively given. If so, then sociologists must research what happens when rules are allegedly broken.

The objectively given definition of deviance arrives at generalizations by studying people who have been apprehended and processed by the various formal agencies of social control. Michael Lynch asks a different question: How do people who are not police officers or psychiatrists deal with "difficult persons" who disrupt social order? Analyzing student papers on how people they knew dealt with makers of interpersonal troubles, Lynch shows that few of their responses could be classified as negative sanctions.

The variety of responses he describes all have the effect of protecting the selves of people in face-to-face contact with these "difficult persons," the group, and its reputation—and, in some instances, even to save the troublemaker's self. Lynch finds the common factor in these various responses to be socially organized attempts to preserve the appearance of normality for all concerned. All these efforts are intended to repair and retain the appearance of orderly social interaction.

People are committed to mental hospitals after informal efforts to accommodate them in society fail. Studies report that spouses of prospective mental patients (Cumming and Cumming, 1957; Mayo *et al.*, 1971; Sampson *et al.*, 1962; Spitzer *et al.*, 1971; Yarrow *et al.*, 1955), co-workers (Lemert, 1962), and police officers (Bittner, 1967) claim that they contact psychiatric authorities only as a last resort, when informal methods of "care" are unavailable or are overwhelmed by the extremity of the person's disorder. There is widespread reluctance, especially in lower-class families (Hollingshead and Redlich, 1958:172–179; Myers and Roberts, 1959:213–220), to take a perspective on relational disorders which supports professional

Reprinted from "Accommodation Practices: Vernacular Treatments of Madness," *Social Problems,* Vol. 31, No. 2 (December 1983), pp. 152–164, by permission of the Society for the Study of Social Problems and the author. Copyright © 1983 by the Society for the Study of Social Problems.

intervention and hospitalization. As a result, the population of potential mental patients is said to vastly outnumber the population of professionally treated patients (Srole *et al.,* 1962). Accommodating families can hide potential patients from official scrutiny by placing few demands upon them and allowing them to "exist as if in a one-person chronic ward, insulated from all but those in a highly tolerant household" (Freeman and Simmons, 1958:148).

Such observations suggest that a massive program of community care exists independently of formally established programs of inpatient and outpatient treatment. Countless numbers of undiagnosed, but troublesome, individuals, as well as an increasing number of diagnosed outpatients, are consigned by default to the informal care of family and community. Although the social characteristics of professionally administered mental health care institutions have been exhaustively analyzed, the practices that make up ordinary lay-operated "institutions" of care remain largely unexamined. In this study I call attention to such accommodation practices, elaborate upon previous descriptions of the practices, and present some conjectures on the social construction of the individual.

Accommodation practices are interactional techniques that people use to manage persons they view as persistent sources of trouble. Accommodation implies attempts to "live with" persistent and ineradicable troubles.[1] Previous studies mention a number of accommodation practices. Lemert (1962) describes how people exclude distrusted individuals from their organization's covert activities by employing methods of "spurious interaction." Such forms of interaction are:

> ...distinguished by patronizing, evasion, "humoring," guiding conversation onto selected topics, underreaction, and silence, all calculated either to prevent intense interaction or to protect individual and group values by restricting access to them. When the interaction is between two or more persons in the individual's presence it is cued by a whole repertoire of subtle expressive signs which are meaningful only to them. (1962:8)

Other methods for managing perceived "troublemakers" include: isolation and avoidance (Lemert, 1962; Sampson et al., 1962), relieving an individual of ordinary responsibilities associated with their roles (Sampson et al., 1962); hiding liquor bottles from a heavily drinking spouse (Jackson, 1954); and "babying" (Jackson, 1954).

Some studies (Yarrow et al., 1955) treat accommodation practices as sources of delay in the recognition and treatment of mental illness; others (Goffman, 1961, 1969; Lemert, 1962) portray them as primary constituents of "illness." Whether the studies assume a realist or a societal reaction perspective on the nature of mental illness, they attempt to explain how persons become mental patients by reconstructing the social backgrounds of hospitalized patients. As Emerson and Messinger (1977:131) point out, retrospective analyses of the "careers" of diagnosed mental patients presuppose

a specific pathological outcome to the "prepatient's" biography. To avoid this problem, social scientists need to abandon retrospective methods and analyze contemporary situations where troublesome individuals are accommodated. Such people are not yet patients, and may never attain that status. Therefore, institutional records cannot be used to locate cases for study. An appropriate way to find them is to use vernacular accounts of madness or mental illness, and to document the patterns of accommodation that others use to control such troublesome people.

THE STUDY

This study is an analysis of the results of an assignment which I gave to students in classes on the sociology of mental illness in 1981 and 1982. I instructed students to locate someone in a familiar social environment who was identified by others (and perhaps by themselves) as "crazy"; the subject need not appear "mentally ill," but need only be a *personal* and *persistent* source of trouble for others. The vast majority of the students had little trouble finding such subjects. I instructed them to interview persons who consistently dealt with the troublemaker in a living or work situation. The interviews were to focus on the practices used by others to "live with" the troublemaker from day to day. Students who were personally acquainted with the troublemaker were encouraged to refer to their own recollections and observations in addition to their interviews. They were instructed not to interview or otherwise disturb the troublemakers. Each student wrote a 5–7 page paper on accommodation practices with an appendix of notes from their interview....

I have organized accommodation practices under three thematic headings: (1) practices which *isolate* the troublemaker within the group; (2) practices which *manipulate* the troublemaker's behavior, perception, and understanding; and (3) practices which members use to influence how others react to the troublemaker. The first set of practices defines and limits the troublemaker's chances for interaction, expression, and feedback within the group. The second set directs the details of the troublemaker's actions and establishes the discrepant meanings of those actions for "self" and "other." The third set includes attempts to make the troublemaker's public identity into a covert communal project.

MINIMIZING CONTACT WITH THE TROUBLEMAKER

Avoiding and *ignoring* were the two accommodation practices mentioned most often by students. Both were methods for minimizing contact with the troublemaker, and had the effect of isolating the troublemaker within the organizational network. While both were negative methods of behavior control, attenuating the troublemaker's actual and possible occasions of interaction, they worked quite differently. Avoiding limited the gross *possibility* of interaction, while ignoring worked *within* ongoing occasions of interaction to limit the interactional *reality* of the encounter. Where avoiding created an absence of encounter, ignoring created a dim semblance to ordinary interaction.

AVOIDING

In virtually every student's account, one or more of the members they interviewed mentioned that they actively avoided the troublemaker. Avoidance created an interactional vacuum around the troublemaker. Members managed to stay out of the way of the troublemaker without actually requesting or commanding the troublemaker to stay away from them. Methods of avoidance included individual and joint tactics such as "ducking into restrooms," "keeping a lookout for her at all times," and "hiding behind a newspaper or book."

Some members were better placed than others within the structure of the organization to avoid the troublemaker. In larger organizations like fraternities and sororities, persons could stake out positions which minimized contact with the troublemaker. In more intimate circles avoidance ran more of a risk of calling attention to the *absence* of usual interactional involvement. Avoidance *did* occur in such intimate groups as families (Sampson *et al.,* 1962), but only at the cost of threatening the very integrity of the group.

IGNORING/NOT TAKING SERIOUSLY

Ignoring differed from avoiding because it entailed at least some interaction, though of an attenuated and inauthentic kind. One account described conversations with the troublemaker as being "reduced to superficial 'hellos,' most of which are directed at her feet; there is an obvious lack of eye contact." Many accounts mentioned the superficiality of interactions with troublemakers. In some cases this was accomplished by what one student called "rehearsed and phony responses" to limit the openness of their conversations to a few stock sequences.[2]

Although ignoring entailed interaction, it was like avoidance in that it circumscribed the troublemaker's interactional possibilities. Where avoidance operated to limit, in a gross way, the intersection of pathways between troublemaker and other members, ignoring operated intensively to trivialize the troublemaker's apparent involvements in group activities.[3] Bids for positive notice were ignored, and had little effect on the troublemaker's position within the group.

DIRECTLY MANAGING THE TROUBLEMAKER'S ACTIONS

Members used a number of more direct interventions to control and limit the troublemaker's behavior, including humoring, screening, taking over, orienting to local prospects of normality, and practical jokes and retaliations. While such methods had little hope of permanently modifying the behavior, they were used to curtail episodic disruptions by the troublemaker.

HUMORING

Members often used the term humoring to describe attempts to manage the troublemaker by maintaining a veneer of agreement and geniality in the face of actions which would ordinarily evoke protest or disgust. For example, in the case of "an obnoxiously argumentative person," members offered superficial tokens of agreement in response to even the most outlandish pronouncements for the sake of avoiding more extreme disruptions.

Humoring was often made possible through insight into recurrent features of the troublemaker's behavior. Members recognized recurrent situations in ordinary interactions which triggered peculiar reactions by the troublemaker. They developed a heightened awareness of ordinary and seemingly innocuous details of interaction which could touch off an explosive reaction. One student described how her parents managed a "crazy aunt," who she said was prone to sudden and violent verbal assaults:

> My parents avoided discussing specific topics and persons that they knew distressed her. Whenever she began talking about an arousable [sic] event or person, my parents and her husband attempted to change the subject.[4]

Although members rationalized humoring as a way "to make it easy for everybody," they did not always find it easy to withhold their reactions to interactional offenses. A student wrote about her efforts to prepare her fiancé for a first encounter with her grandmother, said to be suffering from senile dementia, Alzheimer type:

> I attempted to explain to him that he should not say anything controversial, agree with whatever she says, and generally stay quiet as much as possible. [He assured her that everything would be okay, but when he was confronted with the actual grandmother, the assurance proved quite fragile.] That encounter proved to be quite an experience for Charles—we left Grandma's house with Charles screaming back at her for his self-worth.

Other accounts mentioned the strain and difficulty of trying to humor troublemakers. They described an exceedingly fragile interactional situation which was prone to break down at any moment:

> You don't want to set him off, so you're very careful about what you do and say. You become tense trying to keep everything calm, and then something happens to screw it up anyway: The car won't start, or a light bulb blows. It's all my fault because I'm a rotten wife and mother.

Humoring often entailed obedience or deference to what members claimed (when not within earshot of the troublemaker) were outrageous or absurd demands:

> Everyone did what she asked in order to please her and not cause any bad scenes.

In some cases, members exerted special efforts or underwent severe inconvenience for the sake of a person they secretly despised. Not surprisingly, such efforts often, though not always, were exerted by persons over whom the troublemaker had formal authority. In one case the members of a crew traveling with a rock and roll band would set up the troublesome member's equipment before that of the others and set up daily meetings with him to discuss his "technical needs," while at the same time they believed it was foolish of him to demand such special attention. They described the special meetings and favors as a "bogus accommodation." In every case, whether correlated with formal divisions of authority or not, humoring contributed to the troublemaker's sense of interactional power over others.

Humoring always included a degree of duplicity in which members "kept a straight face" when interacting with the troublemaker or acted in complicity with the troublemaker's premises—premises which members otherwise discounted as delusional or absurd:

> We played along with her fantasy of a boyfriend, "John." We never said what a complete fool she was for waiting for him.

Commonly, members practiced *serial du-plicity* by waiting until the troublemaker was out of earshot to display for one another's appreciation the "real" understanding they had previously suppressed:

> They pretend to know what she is talking about, they act as if they are interested…they make remarks when she is gone.

At other times they practiced *simultaneous duplicity* by showing interest and serious engagement to the troublemaker's face while expressing detachment and sarcasm to one another through furtive glances, gestures, and double entendres (Lemert, 1962:8):

> Those employees who she is not facing will make distorted faces and roll their eyes around to reaffirm the fact that she is a little slow. All the time this occurs Susan is totally oblivious to it, or at least she pretends to be.

In one fraternity, members devised a specific hand gesture (described as "wing flapping") which they displayed for one another when interacting with a troublemaker they called "the bird."

Members occasionally rationalized their duplicity by describing the troublemaker as a self-absorbed and "dense" person, whose lack of orientation to others provided ample opportunity for their play:

> People speak sarcastically to him, and Joe, so wrapped up in himself, believes what they are saying and hears only what he wants to hear.

SCREENING

Jackson (1954:572) reported that alcoholics' wives attempted to manage their husbands' heavy drinking by hiding or emptying liquor bottles in the house and curtailing their husbands' funds. One student described a similar practice used by friends of a person who they feared had suicidal tendencies. They systematically removed from the person's environment any objects that could be used to commit suicide.

Screening and monitoring of troublemakers' surroundings also occurred in the interactional realm. A few accounts mentioned attempts to monitor the moods of a troublemaker, and to screen the person's potential interactions on the basis of attributed mood. When one sorority's troublemaker was perceived to be especially volatile, members acted as her covert receptionists by turning away her visitors, explaining that she was not in or was ill. In this case members were concerned not only to control the potential actions of the individual, but also to conceal those actions from others, and by doing so to protect the collective "image" of their sorority from contamination.

TAKING OVER

A number of accounts mentioned efforts by members to do activities which ordinarily would be done by someone in the troublemaker's social position. Like published accounts of cases in which husbands or mothers take over the household duties of a wife (Sampson *et al.*, 1962), the apartment mates of a troublemaker washed dishes and paid bills for her "as if she wasn't there." A circle of friends insisted on driving the automobile of a man they considered dangerously impulsive. Fraternity members gradually and unofficially took over the duties of their social chairman in fear of the consequences of his erratic actions and inappropriate attire. Taking over sometimes included such intimate personal functions as grooming and dressing, as when the spouse of a drunk diligently prepared her husband for necessary public appearances.

ORIENTING TO LOCAL PROSPECTS OF NORMALITY

Yarrow *et al.* (1955) mention that wives of mental patients sustained efforts to live with their husbands by treating interludes between episodes as the beginnings of "recovery" rather than as periods of calm before the inevitable storms. By keeping tabs on the latest developments in the troublemaker's behavior, members were often able to determine when it was "safe" to treat the troublemaker as a "normal" person. This method was not always as unrealistic as one would be led to believe from Yarrow *et al.* (1955). Since most troublemakers were viewed as persons whose difficulties, though inherent, were intermittent, living with them required knowing what to expect in the immediate interactional future:

> I have observed the occasion when a friend at the fraternity house entered the television room and remained in the rear of the room, totally quiet, watching Danny, waiting for a signal telling him how to act. When Danny turned and spoke to him in a friendly, jovial manner, the young man enthusiastically pulled his chair up to sit next to Danny and began speaking freely.

Members described many troublemakers as persons with likeable and even admirable qualities, whose friendship was valued during their "good times." When a member anticipated an encounter with a troublemaker, he or she wanted most of all to avoid touching off a "bad scene." The local culture of gossip surrounding a troublemaker tended to facilitate such an aim by providing a running file on the current state of his or her moods. By using the latest news members could decide when to avoid encounters and when they could approach the troublemaker without undue wariness.

PRACTICAL JOKES AND RETALIATIONS

Although direct expressions of hostility toward troublemakers were rarely mentioned, it is possible that they occurred more frequently than was admitted. Practical jokes and other forms of retaliation were designed not to reveal their authors. The troublemaker would be "clued in" that *somebody* despised him or was otherwise "out to get" him, but he would be left to imagine just who it was. Some jokes were particularly cruel, and were aimed at the troublemaker's particular vulnerabilities. A member of a touring rock and roll band was known to have difficulty forming relationships with women:

> They would get girls to call his room and make dates they would never keep. Apparently, the spot-

light operator was the author of a series of hot love letters of a mythical girl who was following Moog [a pseudonym for the troublemaker] from town to town and would soon appear in his bedroom. The crew must have been laughing their heads off for days. Moog was reading the letters out loud in the dressing room.

INFLUENCING THE REACTION TO THE TROUBLEMAKER

A group of practices, instead of focusing solely on the troublemaker's interactional behavior, attempted to control others' *reactions to* and *interpretations of* that behavior. These accommodations recognized that there could be serious consequences in the reactions of outsiders—non-members—to the troublemaker. Such practices included efforts by members to control the reactions of persons outside the group; and to control assessments not only of the individual troublemaker, but of the group as well. The responsibilities for, and social consequences of, the individual's behavior were thus adopted by members as a collective project.

TURNING THE TROUBLEMAKER INTO A NOTORIOUS CHARACTER

In stories to outsiders as well as others in the group, members were sometimes able to turn the troublemaker into a fascinating and almost admirable character. A classic case was the fraternity "animal." Although litanies of crude, offensive, and assaultive actions were recounted, the character's antics were also portrayed with evident delight. Such descriptions incorporated elements of heroism, the prowess of the brawler, or the fearlessness and outrageousness of a prankster. In one case a student reported that the fraternity troublemaker, nicknamed "the deviant," was supported and encouraged by a minority faction who claimed to an outsider that he was merely "a little wild," and that nothing was wrong with him. This faction seemed unembarrassed by, and perhaps a bit proud of, the troublemaker's "animal" qualities that others might ascribe to the fraternity as well. The quasi-heroic or comical repute of the troublemaker did not overshadow many members' distaste for the disruptions, but it did constitute a supportive moral counterpoint.

SHADOWING

In one instance a group of students living in a dorm arranged covertly to escort their troublemaker on his frequent trips to local bars. He had a reputation for drinking more than his capacity and then challenging all comers to fights. To inhibit such adventures members of the group volunteered to accompany him under various pretexts, and to quell any disputes he precipitated during the drinking sessions. In the case of the member of the rock and roll band, other members chaperoned him during interviews with media critics. When he said something potentially offensive, his chaperon attempted to turn his statement into a joke. Another account described efforts by a group to spy on a member who they believed was likely to do something rash or violent.

ADVANCE NOTICES

As Lemert (1962) points out, members often build a legacy of apocryphal stories about their troublemaker. Stories told by one member to another about the troublemaker's latest antics provided a common source of entertainment, and perhaps solidarity. Some members admitted that they could not imagine what they would talk about with one another if not the troublemaker's behavior:

> The highlight of the day is hearing the latest story about Joanie.

Such gleeful renditions helped to prepare non-members for first encounters with the troublemaker.

A few students mentioned that the troublemakers they studied appeared normal or even charming during initial encounters, but that members soon warned them to be careful about getting involved with the person. Subsequent experience confirmed the warnings, although it was difficult to discern whether this was a result of their accuracy or of the wariness they engendered.

Members of a group that included a persistently troublesome character "apologized for him beforehand" to persons who shortly would be doing business with him. They also warned women he approached that he was "a jerk." In addition to preparing such persons for upcoming encounters, the apologies and warnings carried the tacit claim that "we're not like him." This mitigated any potential contamination of the group's moral reputation.

HIDING AND DILUTING THE TROUBLEMAKER

Some fraternities and sororities institutionalized a "station" for hiding troublemakers during parties and teas where new members were recruited. Troublemakers were assigned out-of-the-way positions in social gatherings and, in some cases, were accompanied at all times by other members whose job it was to cut off the troublemaker's interaction with prospective members.

The methods used for hiding and diluting were especially artful when they included pretexts to conceal from the troublemakers that their role had been diminished. The troublemaker in the rock and roll band was said to embarrass other members with "distasteful ego tripping" on stage during public concerts. Such "ego trips" were characterized by loud and "awful" playing on his instrument and extravagant posturing in attempts to draw the audience's attention to himself. These displays were countered by the sound and light men in the crew:

> On those nights the sound man would turn up the monitors on stage so Moog sounded loud to himself and would turn down Moog in the [concert] hall and on the radio.

Simultaneously, the lighting director would "bathe him in darkness" by dimming the spotlights on him. These practices, in effect, technically created a delusional experience for the troublemaker. They produced a systematic distortion of his perception of the world and simultaneously diminished his public place in that world.

COVERING FOR/COVERING UP

Friends and intimates sometimes went to great lengths to smooth over the damages and insults done to others by the troublemaker. The husband of a "crazy woman" monitored his wife's offenses during her "episodes" and followed in the wake of the destruction with apologies and sometimes monetary reparations to offended neighbors. Similar efforts at restoring normality also occurred in immediate interactional contexts:

> *Before she will even tell you her name, she is telling you how one day she was hitchhiking and was gang raped by the five men who picked her up. This caused so many problems for her that she ended up in a mental hospital and is now a lesbian. The look on people's faces is complete shock.... Those hearing this story for the first time will sit in shock as if in a catatonic stupor, with wide eyes and their mouths dropped open, absolutely speechless. Someone who has already heard this story will break the silence by continuing with the previous conversation,...putting it on extinction by ignoring it as if she never said anything.*

Members sometimes conspired, ostensibly on behalf of the troublemaker, to prevent the relevant authorities from detecting the existence and extent of the troubles. One group of girls in a freshman dorm deliberately lied to hide the fact that one of their members was having great difficulty and, in their estimation, was potentially suicidal. When her parents asked how she was doing the students responded that she was doing "fine." Members tried to contain her problems and to create a "blockade" around any appearances of her problems that might attract the attentions of university authorities. Once underway, such coverups gained momentum, since the prospect of exposure increasingly threatened to make members culpable for not bringing the matter to the attention of remedial agents.

DISCUSSION

A prevailing theme in the students' accounts of accommodation practices was the avoidance of confrontation. They described confrontation as potentially "unpleasant," to be avoided even when considerable damage and hardship had been suffered:

> *When students' money began disappearing from their rooms, we had a group meeting to discuss our mode of intervention. Although we all believed Chris was responsible, we did not confront her. Instead, we simply decided to make sure we locked our bedroom doors when not in our rooms.*

In general, a number of reasons for avoiding confrontation were given, including the anticipation of denial by the troublemaker, fear that the troublemaker would create a "bad scene," and the belief that confrontation would make no difference in the long run.

Less direct methods were used to communicate the group's opinions to the troublemaker. Instead of telling the troublemaker in so many words, members employed a peculiar sort of gamesmanship. Systematic "leaks" were used to *barely* and *ambiguously* expose the duplicity and conspiracy, so that the troublemaker would realize something was going on, but would be unable or unwilling to accuse specific offenders. Duplicitous gestures or comments which operated *just* on the fringes of the troublemaker's awareness produced maximum impact.

The successful operation of these practices relied, in part, on the troublemaker's complicity in the conspiracy of silence:

> *Once I was in the room next door to her and the girls were imitating her. Two minutes later she walked in asking [us] to be quiet because she was trying to sleep. I thought I was going to die. Obviously Tammy realized what was going on as the walls are extremely thin; however, Tammy seems to be conspiring on the side of her "friends" to prevent any confrontation of the actual situation.*

Hostilities were therefore expressed, and retaliations achieved, often with rather specific reference to the particular offenses and their presumed source. At the same time, they remained "submerged" in a peculiar way. They were not submerged in a psychological "unconscious," since both members and troublemakers were aware of what was going on. Instead, both members and troublemakers made every effort to [ensure] that the trouble did not disturb the overtly normal interaction. "Business as usual" was preserved at the cost of keeping secret deep hostilities within the organization.

A few accounts did mention instances of explicit confrontation. However, members claimed that such confrontations did not alter troublemakers' subsequent behaviors; instead they resulted in misunderstandings or were received by troublemakers in a defensive or unresponsive way.

Efforts to remove troublemakers from organizations were rarely described, though members of the rock band eventually expelled their troublemaker after he hired a lawyer to redress his grievances against the group. In another case a fraternity "de-pledged" a new recruit who had not yet been fully initiated. In no other case was an established member removed, although numerous dramatic offenses were recounted and widespread dislike for troublemakers was commonly reported.

Taken as a whole, accommodation practices reveal *the organizational construction of the normal individual.* The individual is relied upon both in commonsense reasoning and social theory as a source of compliance with the standards of the larger society. The normal individual successfully adapts to the constraints imposed by social structure. Troublemakers were viewed as persons who, for various reasons, could not be given full *responsibility* for maintaining normality. Instead, the burden of maintaining the individual's normal behavior and appearance was taken up by others. Troublemakers were not overtly sanctioned; instead, they were shaped and guided through the superficial performances of ordinary action. Their integration into society was not a cumulative mastery learned "from inside"; it was a constant project executed by others from the "outside."

Accommodation practices allow us to glimpse the project of the self as a practical struggle. A semblance of normal individuality for troublemakers was a carefully constructed artifact produced by members. When the responsibility for normality is assumed as an individual birthright, it appears inevitable that conformity or defiance proceeds "from inside" the individual, just as it appears in common sense that gender is a natural inheritance. In the latter instance, a transsexual's unusual experience indicates the extent to which the ordinary behavior and appearance of being female is detachable from the individual's birthright, and can be explicated as a practical accomplishment (Garfinkel, 1967). Similarly, for the organizational colleagues of a troublemaker, the elements of normal individuality cannot be relied upon, but must be achieved through deliberate practice. Members together performed the work of minding the troublemaker's business, of guiding the troublemaker through normal interactional pathways, and of filling the responsibilities and appearances associated with the troublemaker's presence for others.[5]

Of course, such projects were less than successful; members complained of the undue burden, disruptions occurred despite their efforts, and the troublemaker was provided with a diminished self and a distorted reality. Perhaps all would have been better off had they "left the self inside where it belongs." Nevertheless, accommodation practices enable us to see the extent to which the division between self and other is permeable, and subject to negotiation and manipulation. We can see that individual responsibility for the conduct of affairs is separable from the actual performance of those affairs. Troublemakers were manipulated into a tenuous conformity by members who relied upon the fact that such conformity would be attributed to the individual's responsibility. The individual was thus reduced to the subject of an informal code of responsibility, separable from any substantive source of action (Goffman, 1969:357)....

NOTES

1. The equally interesting topic of how patients accommodate to their own disorders (Critchley, 1971:290; O. Sacks, 1974:227) is not included in this discussion of interactional practices.

2. A topic needing further study is how members use greetings and other conversational "adjacency pairs" (Sacks *et al.*, 1974) to foreclose conversation with troublemakers at the earliest convenient point, but in such a way as not to call attention to their action as a snub.

3. See Wulbert (n.d.) for a poignant discussion of trivializing practices.

4. Jefferson and Lee (1980) characterize some of the detailed ways in which participants in ordinary conversations head off "troubles talk" and transform it to "business as usual." Such procedures are much more varied and intricate than can adequately be described by such phrases as "changing the subject."

5. My discussion of the social production of the individual is heavily indebted to Pollner and Wikler's (1981) treatment of that theme. Pollner and Wikler (1981) discuss a family's efforts to construct the appearance of normality for their (officially diagnosed) profoundly retarded daughter. Not only does *normality* become a communal project in these cases, *abnormality* becomes shared as well. One student in my research described an alcoholic's family as "three characters revolving around a central theme—alcoholism." The preoccupation with alcohol was shared along with the *denial* that the man's drinking was an official problem.

REFERENCES

Bittner, Egon. 1967. "Police Discretion in Emergency Apprehension of Mentally Ill Persons." *Social Problems,* 14(3):278–292.

Critchley, MacDonald. 1971. *The Parietal Lobes.* New York: Hafner Publishing Co.

Cumming, Elaine and John Cumming. 1957. *Closed Ranks.* Cambridge, MA: Harvard University Press.

Emerson, Robert and Sheldon Messinger. 1977. "The Micro-politics of Trouble." *Social Problems,* 25(2):121–134.

Freeman, Howard and Ozzie Simmons. 1958. "Mental Patients in the Community: Family Settings and Performance Levels." *American Sociological Review,* 23(2):147–154.

Garfinkel, Harold. 1967. *Studies in Ethnomethodology.* Englewood Cliffs, NJ: Prentice-Hall.

Goffman, Erving. 1961. *Asylums.* Garden City, NY: Doubleday.

———. 1969. "The Insanity of Place." *Psychiatry,* 32(4):352–388.

Hollingshead, August and Frederick Redlich. 1958. *Social Class and Mental Illness.* New York: Wiley.

Jackson, Joan. 1954. "The Adjustment of the Family to the Crisis of Alcoholism." *Quarterly Journal of Studies on Alcohol,* 15(4):562–586.

Jefferson, Gail and John Lee. 1980. "The Analysis of Conversations in Which Anxieties and Troubles Are Expressed." Unpublished report for the Social Science Research Counsel, University of Manchester, England.

Lemert, Edwin. 1962. "Paranoia and the Dynamics of Exclusion." *Sociometry,* 25(1):2–20.

Mayo, Clara, Ronald Havelock, and Diane Lear Simpson. 1971. "Attitudes Towards Mental Illness among Psychiatric Patients and Their Wives." *Journal of Clinical Psychology,* 27(1):128–132.

Myers, Jerome and Bertram Roberts. 1959. *Family and Class Dynamics.* New York: Wiley.

Pollner, Melvin and Lynn Wikler. 1981. "The Social Construction of Unreality: A Case Study of the Practices of Family Sham and Delusion." Unpublished paper, Department of Sociology, University of California, Los Angeles.

Sacks, Harvey, Emanuel Schegloff, and Gail Jefferson. 1974. "A Simplest Systematics for the Organization of Turn Taking in Conversation." *Language,* 50(4): 696–735.

Sacks, Oliver. 1974. *Awakenings.* New York: Doubleday.

Sampson, Harold, Sheldon Messinger, and Robert Towne. 1962. "Family Processes and Becoming a Mental Patient." *American Journal of Sociology,* 68(1):88–98.

Spitzer, Stephan, Patricia Morgan, and Robert Swanson. 1971. "Determinants of the Psychiatric Patient Career: Family Reaction Patterns and Social Work Intervention." *Social Service Review,* 45(1):74–85.

Srole, Leo, Thomas Langer, Stanley Michael, Marvin Opler, and Thomas Rennie. 1962. *Mental Health in the Metropolis: The Midtown Manhattan Study.* New York: McGraw-Hill.

Wulbert, Roland. n.d. "Second Thoughts about Commonplaces." Unpublished paper, Department of Sociology, Columbia University (circa 1974).

Yarrow, Marian, Charlotte Schwartz, Harriet Murphy, and Leila Deasy. 1955. "The Psychological Meaning of Mental Illness in the Family." *Journal of Social Issues,* 11(4):12–24.

The Adjustment of the Family to Alcoholism

JOAN K. JACKSON

In order for interaction to take place, people have to define and interpret what they see before them, and then take action on their interpretations. Their actions hold meaning both for themselves and for other persons as well. And this is the case whether the situation stays within the limits of conformity or strays over the boundaries into deviance. If in some social situations, definition-interpretation-action take place immediately (as when police in patrol cars respond to a "robbery in progress" report over their radio), in others there may be a considerable time lag between definition, interpretation, and action (as when a wife begins to call into question the meaning of her husband's actions with alcoholic beverages). For, as Howard Becker has noted, deviance is both process and product of social interaction. For the most part, the process turns out to be considerably slower in primary groups, the product less clear-cut.

Joan K. Jackson, in her classic study of how wives come to terms with their husbands' alcoholism, demonstrates that the process in the family has its own natural history. Labeling the husband as an alcoholic and then acting on that interpretation, rather than being an instance of simultaneity, is the outcome of seven stages that she has charted. Her work suggests the generalization that the more intimate the relationship, the slower the pace of the process.

…Over a 3-year period, the present investigator has been an active participant in the Alcoholics Anonymous Auxiliary in Seattle. This group is composed partly of women whose husbands are or were members of Alcoholics Anonymous, and partly of women whose husbands are excessive drinkers but have never contacted Alcoholics Anonymous. At a typical meeting one-fifth would be the wives of Alcoholics Anonymous members who have been sober for some time; the husbands of another fifth would have recently joined the fellowship; the remainder would be equally divided between those whose husbands were "on and off" the Alcoholics Anonymous program and those whose husbands had as yet not had any contact with Alcoholics Anonymous.

At least an hour and a half of each formal meeting of this group is taken up with a frank

Reprinted from "The Adjustment of the Family to the Crisis of Alcoholism," *Quarterly Journal of Studies on Alcohol,* Vol. 15 (December 1954), pp. 564–586, by permission.

discussion of the current family problems of the members. As in other meetings of Alcoholics Anonymous the questions are posed by describing the situation which gives rise to the problem and the answers are a narration of the personal experiences of other wives who have had a similar problem, rather than direct advice. Verbatim shorthand notes have been taken of all discussions, at the request of the group, who also make use of the notes for the group's purposes. Informal contact has been maintained with past and present members. In the past three years 50 women have been members of this group.

The families represented by these women are at present in many different stages of adjustment and have passed through several stages during the past few years. The continuous contact over a prolonged period permits generalizations about processes and changes in family adjustments.

In addition, in connection with research on hospitalized alcoholics, many of their wives have been interviewed. The interviews with the hospitalized alcoholics, as with male members of Alcoholics Anonymous, have also provided information on family interactions. Further information has been derived from another group of wives, not connected with Alcoholics Anonymous, and from probation officers, social workers and court officials....

The families represented in this study are from the middle and lower classes. The occupations of the husbands prior to excessive drinking include small business owners, salesmen, business executives, skilled and semiskilled workers. Prior to marriage the wives have been nurses, secretaries, teachers, saleswomen, cooks or waitresses. The economic status of the childhood families of these husbands and wives ranged from very wealthy to very poor....

The similarities in the process of adjustment to an alcoholic family member are presented here as stages of variable duration. It should be stressed that only the similarities are dealt with. Although the wives have shared the patterns dealt with here, there have been marked differences in the length of time between stages, in the number of stages passed through up to the present time, and in the relative importance to the family constellation of any one type of behavior. For example, all admitted nagging but the amount of nagging was variable....

STATEMENT OF THE PROBLEM

For purposes of this presentation, the family is seen as involved in a cumulative crisis. All family members behave in a manner which they hope will resolve the crisis and permit a return to stability. Each member's action is influenced by his previous personality structure, by his previous role and status in the family group, and by the history of the crisis and its effects on his personality, roles and status up to that point. Action is also influenced by the past effectiveness of that particular action as a means of social control before and during the crisis. The behavior of family members in each phase of the crisis contributes to the form which the crisis takes in the following stages and sets limits on possible behavior in subsequent stages.

Family members are influenced, in addition, by the cultural definitions of alcoholism as evidence of weakness, inadequacy or sinfulness; by the cultural prescriptions for the roles of family members; and by the cultural values of family solidarity, sanctity and self-sufficiency. Alcoholism in the family poses a situation defined by the culture as shameful but for the handling of which there are no prescriptions which are effective or which permit direct action not in conflict with other cultural prescriptions. While in crises such as illness or death the family members can draw on cultural definitions of appropriate behavior for procedures which will terminate the crisis, this is not the case with alcoholism in the family. The cultural view has been that alcoholism is shameful and should not occur. Only recently has any information been offered to guide families in their behavior toward their alcoholic member and, as yet, this information resides more in technical journals than in the media of mass communication. Thus, in facing alcoholism, the family is in an unstructured situation and must find the techniques for handling it through trial and error.

STAGES IN FAMILY ADJUSTMENT TO AN ALCOHOLIC MEMBER

The Beginning of the Marriage. At the time marriage was considered, the drinking of most of the men was within socially acceptable limits. In a few cases the men were already alcoholics but managed to hide this from their fiancées. They drank only moderately or not at all when on dates and often avoided friends and relatives who might expose their excessive drinking. The relatives and friends who were introduced to the fiancée were those who had hopes that "marriage would straighten him out" and thus said nothing about the drinking. In a small number of cases the men spoke with their fiancées of their alcoholism. The women had no conception of what alcoholism meant, other than that it involved more than the usual frequency of drinking, and they entered the marriage with little more preparation than if they had known nothing about it.

Stage 1. Incidents of excessive drinking begin and, although they are sporadic, place strains on the husband-wife interaction. In attempts to minimize drinking, problems in marital adjustment not related to the drinking are avoided.

Stage 2. Social isolation of the family begins as incidents of excessive drinking multiply. The increasing isolation magnifies the importance of family interactions and events. Behavior and thought become drinking-centered. Husband–wife adjustment deteriorates and tension rises. The wife begins to feel self-pity and to lose her self-confidence as her behavior fails to stabilize her husband's drinking. There is an attempt still to maintain the original family structure, which is disrupted anew with each episode of drinking, and as a result the children begin to show emotional disturbance.

Stage 3. The family gives up attempts to control the drinking and begins to behave in a manner geared to relieve tension rather than achieve long-term ends. The disturbance of the children becomes more marked. There is no longer an attempt to support the alcoholic in his roles as husband and father. The wife begins to worry about her own sanity and about her inability to make decisions or act to change the situation.

Stage 4. The wife takes over control of the family and the husband is seen as a recalcitrant child. Pity and strong protective feelings largely replace the earlier resentment and hostility. The family becomes more stable and organized in a manner to minimize the disruptive behavior of the husband. The self-confidence of the wife begins to be rebuilt.

Stage 5. The wife separates from her husband if she can resolve the problems and conflicts surrounding this action.

Stage 6. The wife and children reorganize as a family without the husband.

Stage 7. The husband achieves sobriety and the family, which had become organized around an alcoholic husband, reorganizes to include a sober father and experiences problems in reinstating him in his former roles.

STAGE 1. ATTEMPTS TO DENY THE PROBLEM

Usually the first experience with drinking as a problem arises in a social situation. The husband drinks in a manner which is inappropriate to the social setting and the expectations of others present. The wife feels embarrassed on the first occasion and humiliated as it occurs more frequently. After several such incidents she and her husband talk over his behavior. The husband either formulates an explanation for the episode and assures her that such behavior will not occur again; or he refuses to discuss it at all. For a time afterward he drinks appropriately and drinking seems to be a problem no longer. The wife looks back on the incidents and feels that she has exaggerated them, feels ashamed of herself for her disloyalty and for her behavior. The husband, in evaluating the incident, feels shame also and vows such episodes will not recur. As a result, both husband and wife attempt to make it up to the other and, for a time, try to play their conceptions of the ideal husband and wife roles, minimizing or avoiding other difficulties which arise in the marriage. They thus create the illusion of a "perfect" marriage.

Eventually another inappropriate drinking episode occurs and the pattern is repeated. The wife worries but takes action only in the situations in which inappropriate drinking occurs, as each long intervening period of acceptable drinking behavior convinces her that a recurrence is unlikely. As time goes on, in attempting to cope with individual episodes, she runs the gamut of possible trial-and-error behaviors, learning that none is permanently effective.

If she speaks to other people about her husband's drinking, she is usually assured that there is no need for concern, that her husband can control his drinking and that her fears are exaggerated. Some friends possibly admit that his drinking is too heavy and give advice on how they handled similar situations with their husbands. These friends convince her that her problem will be solved as soon as she hits upon the right formula for dealing with her husband's drinking.

During this stage the husband-wife interaction is in no way "abnormal." In a society in which a large proportion of the men drink, most wives have at some time had occasion to be concerned, even though only briefly, with an episode of drinking which they considered inappropriate (1). In a society in which the status of the family depends on that of the husband, the wife feels threatened by any behavior on his part which might lower it. Inappropriate drinking is regarded by her as a threat to the family's reputation and standing in the community. The wife attempts to exert control and often finds herself blocked by the sacredness of drinking behavior to men in America. Drinking is a private matter and not any business of the wife's. On the whole, a man reacts to his wife's suggestion that he has not adequately controlled his drinking with resentment, rebelliousness and a display of emotion which makes rational discussion difficult. The type of husband-wife interaction outlined in this stage has occurred in many American families in which the husband never became an excessive drinker.

STAGE 2. ATTEMPTS TO ELIMINATE THE PROBLEM

Stage 2 begins when the family experiences social isolation because of the husband's drinking. Invitations to the homes of friends become less frequent. When the couple does visit friends, drinks are not served or are limited, thus emphasizing the reason for exclusion from other social activities of the friendship group. Discussions of drinking begin to be side-stepped awkwardly by friends, the wife and the husband.

By this time the periods of socially acceptable drinking are becoming shorter. The wife, fearing that the full extent of her husband's drinking will become known, begins to withdraw from social participation, hoping to reduce the visibility of his behavior, and thus the threat to family status.

Isolation is further intensified because the family usually acts in accordance with the cultural dictate that it should be self-sufficient and manage to resolve its own problems without recourse to outside aid. Any experiences which they have had with well-meaning outsiders, usually relatives, have tended to strengthen this conviction. The husband has defined such relatives as interfering and the situation has deteriorated rather than improved.

With increasing isolation, the family members begin to lose perspective on their interaction and on their problems. Thrown into closer contact with one another as outside contacts diminish, the behavior of each member assumes exaggerated importance. The drinking behavior becomes the focus of anxiety. Gradually all family difficulties become attributed to it. (For example, the mother who is cross with her children will feel that, if her husband had not been drinking, she would not have been so tense and would not have been angry.) The fear that the full extent of drinking may be discovered mounts steadily; the conceptualization of the consequences of such a discovery becomes increasingly vague and, as a result, more anxiety-provoking. The family feels different from others and alone with its shameful secret.

Attempts to cover up increase. The employer who calls to inquire about the husband's absence from work is given excuses. The wife is afraid to face the consequences of loss of the husband's pay check in addition to her other concerns. Questions from the children are evaded or they are told that their father is ill. The wife lives in terror of the day when the children will be told by others of the nature of the "illness." She is also afraid that the children may describe their father's symptoms to teachers or neighbors. Still feeling that the family must solve its own problems, she keeps her troubles to herself and hesitates to seek outside help. If her husband beats her, she will bear it rather than call in the police. (Indeed, often she has no idea that this is even a possibility.) Her increased isolation has left her without the advice of others as to sources of help in the community. If she knows of them, an agency contact means to her an admission of the complete failure of her family as an independent unit. For the middle-class woman particularly, recourse to social agencies and law-enforcement agencies means a terrifying admission of loss of status.

During this stage, husband and wife are drawing further apart. Each feels resentful of the behavior of the other. When this resentment is expressed, further drinking occurs. When it is not, tension mounts and the next drinking episode is that much more destructive of family relationships. The reasons for drinking are explored frantically. Both husband and wife feel that if only they could discover the reason, all members of the family could gear their behavior to making drinking unnecessary. The discussions become increasingly unproductive, as it is the husband's growing conviction that his wife does not and cannot understand him.

On her part, the wife begins to feel that she is a failure, that she has been unable to fulfill the major cultural obligations of a wife to meet her husband's needs. With her increasing isolation, her sense of worth derives almost entirely from her roles as wife and mother. Each failure to help her husband gnaws away at her sense of adequacy as a person.

Periods of sobriety or socially acceptable drinking still occur. These periods keep the wife from making a permanent or stable adjustment. During them her husband, in his guilt, treats her like a queen. His behavior renews her hope and rekindles positive feelings toward him. Her sense of worth is bolstered temporarily and she grasps desperately at her husband's reassurance that she is really a fine person and not a failure and an unlovable shrew. The periods of sobriety also keep her family from facing the inability of the husband to control his drinking. The inaccuracies of the cultural stereotype of the alcoholic—particularly that he is in a constant state of inebriation—also contribute to the family's rejection of the idea of alcoholism, as the husband seems to demonstrate from time to time that he can control his drinking.

Family efforts to control the husband become desperate. There are no culturally prescribed behavior patterns for handling such a situation and the family is forced to evolve its own techniques. Many different types of behavior are tried but none brings consistent results; there seems to be no way of predicting the consequences of any action that may be taken. All attempts to stabilize or structure the situation to permit consistent behavior fail. Threats of leaving, hiding his liquor away, emptying the bottles down the drain, curtailing his money, are tried in rapid succession, but none is effective. Less punitive methods, such as discussing the situation when he is sober, babying him during hangovers, and trying to drink with him to keep him in the home, are attempted and fail. All behavior becomes oriented around the drinking, and the thought of family members becomes obsessive on this subject. As no action seems to be successful in achieving its goal, the wife persists in trial-and-error behavior with mounting frustration. Long-term goals recede into the background and become secondary to just keeping the husband from drinking today.

There is still an attempt to maintain the illusion of husband-wife-children roles. When father is sober, the children are expected to give him respect and obedience. The wife also defers to him in his role as head of the household. Each drinking event thus disrupts family functioning anew. The children begin to show emotional disturbances as a result of the inconsistencies of parental behavior. During periods when the husband is drinking the wife tries to shield them from the knowledge and effects of his behavior, at the same time drawing them closer to herself and deriving emotional support from them. In sober periods, the father tries to regain their favor. Due to experiencing directly only pleasant interactions with their father, considerable affection is often felt for him by the children. This affection becomes increasingly difficult for the isolated wife to tolerate, and an additional source of conflict. She feels that she needs and deserves the love and support of her children and, at the same time, she feels it important to maintain the children's picture of their father. She counts on the husband's affection for the children to motivate a cessation of drinking as he comes to realize the effects of his behavior on them.

In this stage, self-pity begins to be felt by the wife, if it has not entered previously. It continues in various degrees throughout the succeeding stages. In an attempt to handle her deepening sense of inadequacy, the wife often tries to convince herself that she is right and her husband wrong, and this also continues through the following stages. At this point the wife often resembles what Whalen (2) describes as "The Sufferer."

STAGE 3. DISORGANIZATION

The wife begins to adopt a "What's the use?" attitude and to accept her husband's drinking as a problem likely to be permanent. Attempts to understand one another become less frequent. Sober periods still engender hope, but hope qualified by skepticism; they bring about a lessening of anxiety and this is defined as happiness.

By this time some customary patterns of husband-wife-children interaction have evolved. Techniques which have had some effectiveness in controlling the husband in the past or in relieving pent-up frustration are used by the wife. She nags, berates or retreats into silence. Husband and wife are both on the alert, the wife watching for increasing irritability and restlessness which mean a recurrence of drinking, and the husband for veiled aspersions on his behavior or character.

The children are increasingly torn in their loyalties as they become tools in the struggle between mother and father. If the children are at an age of comprehension, they have usually learned the true nature of their family situation, either from outsiders or from their mother, who has given up attempts to bolster her husband's position as father. The children are often bewildered, but questioning their parents brings no satisfactory answers as the parents themselves do not understand what is happening. Some children become terrified; some have increasing behavior problems within and outside the home; others seem on the surface to accept the situation calmly.[1]

During periods of the husband's drinking, the hostility, resentment and frustrations felt by the couple are allowed expression. Both may resort to violence—the wife in self-defense or because she can find no other outlet for her feelings. In those cases in which the wife retaliates to violence in kind, she feels a mixture of relief and intense shame at having deviated so far from what she conceives to be "the behavior of a normal woman."

When the wife looks at her present behavior, she worries about her "normality." In comparing the person she was in the early years of her marriage with the person she has become, she is frightened. She finds herself nagging and unable to control herself. She resolves to stand up to her husband when he is belligerent but instead finds herself cringing in terror and then despises herself for her lack of courage. If she retaliates with violence, she is filled with self-loathing at behaving in an "unwomanly" manner. She finds herself compulsively searching for bottles, knowing full well that finding them will change nothing, and is worried because she engages in such senseless behavior. She worries about her inability to take constructive action of any kind. She is confused about where her loyalty lies, whether with her husband or her children. She feels she is a failure as a wife, mother and person. She believes she should be strong in the face of adversity and instead feels herself weak.

The wife begins to find herself avoiding sexual contact with her husband when he has been drinking. Sex under these circumstances, she feels, is sex for its own sake rather than an indication of affection for her. Her husband's lack of consideration of her needs to be satisfied leaves her feeling frustrated. The lack of sexual responsiveness reflects her emotional withdrawal from him in other areas of family life. Her husband, on his part, feels frustrated and rejected; he accuses her of frigidity and this adds to her concern about her adequacy as a woman.[2]

By this time the opening wedge has been inserted into the self-sufficiency of the family. The husband has often been in difficulty with the police and the wife has learned that police protection is available. An emergency has occurred in which the seeking of outside help was the only possible action to take; subsequent calls for aid from outsiders do not require the same degree of urgency before they can be undertaken. However, guilt and a lessening of self-respect and self-confidence accompany this method of resolving emergencies. The husband intensifies these feelings by speaking of the interference of outsiders, or of his night in jail.

In Stage 3 all is chaos. Few problems are met constructively. The husband and wife both feel trapped in an intolerable, unstructured situation which offers no way out. The wife's self-assurance is almost completely gone. She is afraid to take action and afraid to let things remain as they are. Fear is one of the major characteristics of this stage: fear of violence, fear of personality damage to the children, fear for her own sanity, fear that relatives will interfere, and fear that they will not help in an emergency. Added to this, the family feels alone in the world and helpless. The problems, and the behavior of family members in attempting to cope with them, seem so shameful that help from others is unthinkable. They feel that attempts to get help would meet only with rebuff, and that communication of the situation will engender disgust.

At this point the clinical picture which the wife presents is very similar to what Whalen (2) has described as "The Waverer."

STAGE 4. ATTEMPTS TO REORGANIZE IN SPITE OF THE PROBLEM

Stage 4 begins when a crisis occurs which necessitates that action be taken. There may be no money or food in the house; the husband may have been violent to the children; or life on the level of Stage 3 may have become intolerable. At this point some wives leave, thus entering directly into Stage 5.

The wife who passes through Stage 4 usually begins to ease her husband out of his family roles. She assumes husband and father roles. This involves strengthening her role as mother and putting aside her role as wife. She becomes the manager of the home, the discipliner of the chil-

dren, the decision-maker; she becomes somewhat like Whalen's (2) "Controller." She either ignores her husband as much as possible or treats him as her most recalcitrant child. Techniques are worked out for getting control of his pay check, if there still is one, and money is doled out to her husband on the condition of his good behavior. When he drinks, she threatens to leave him, locks him out of the house, refuses to pay his taxi bills, leaves him in jail overnight rather than pay his bail. Where her obligations to her husband conflict with those to her children, she decides in favor of the latter. As she views her husband increasingly as a child, pity and a sense of being desperately needed by him enter. Her inconsistent behavior toward him deriving from the lack of predictability inherent in the situation up to now, becomes reinforced by her mixed feelings toward him.

In this stage the husband often tries to set his will against hers in decisions about the children. If the children have been permitted to stay with a friend overnight, he may threaten to create a scene unless they return immediately. He may make almost desperate efforts to gain their affection and respect, his behavior ranging from getting them up in the middle of the night to fondle them, to giving them stiff lectures on children's obligations to fathers. Sometimes he will attempt to align the males of the family with him against the females. He may openly express resentment of the children and become belligerent toward them physically or verbally.

Much of the husband's behavior can be conceptualized as resulting from an increasing awareness of his isolation from the other members of the family and their steady withdrawal of respect and affection. It seems to be a desperate effort to regain what he has lost, but without any clear idea of how this can be accomplished—an effort to change a situation in which everyone is seen as against him; and, in reality, this is becoming more and more true. As the wife has taken over control of the family with some degree of success, he feels, and becomes, less and less necessary to the ongoing activity of the family. There are fewer and fewer roles left for him to play. He becomes aware that members of the family enjoy each other's company without him. When he is home he tries to enter this circle of warmth or to smash it. Either way he isolates himself further. He finds that the children discuss with the mother how to manage him and he sees the children acting on the basis of their mother's idea of him. The children refuse to pay attention to his demands: they talk back to him in the same way that they talk back to one another, adding pressure on him to assume the role of just another child. All this leaves him frustrated and, as a result, often aggressive or increasingly absent from home.

The children, on the whole, become more settled in their behavior as the wife takes over the family responsibilities. Decisions are made by her and upheld in the face of their father's attempts to interfere. Participation in activities outside the home is encouraged. Their patterns of interaction with their father are supported by the mother. Whereas in earlier stages the children often felt that there were causal connections between their actions and their father's drinking, they now accept his unpredictability. "Well," says a 6-year-old, "I'll just have to get used to it. I have a drunken father."

The family is more stabilized in one way but in other ways insecurities are multiplied. Pay checks are received less and less regularly. The violence or withdrawal of the father increases. When he is away the wife worries about automobile accidents or injury in fights, which become more and more probable as time passes. The husband may begin to be seriously ill from time to time; his behavior may become quite bizarre. Both of these signs of increasing illness arouse anxiety in the family.

During this stage hopes may rise high for father's "reform" when he begins to verbalize wishes to stop drinking, admits off and on his inability to stop, and sounds desperate for doing something about his drinking. Now may begin the trek to sanitariums for the middle-class alcoholic, to doctors, or to Alcoholics Anonymous. Where just the promise to stop drinking has failed to revive hope, sobriety through outside agencies has the ability to rekindle it brightly. There is the feeling that at last he is "taking really constructive action." In failure the discouragement is deeper. Here another wedge has been inserted into the self-sufficiency of the family.

By this time the wedges are many. The wife, finding she has managed to bring some semblance of order and stability to her family, while not exactly becoming a self-assured person, has regained some sense of worth which grows a little with each crisis she meets successfully. In addition, the very fact of taking action to stabilize the situation brings relief. On some occasion she may be able to approach social agencies for financial help, often during a period when the husband has temporarily deserted or is incarcerated. She may have gone to the family court; she may have consulted a lawyer about getting a restraining order when the husband was in a particularly belligerent state. She has begun to learn her way around among the many agencies which offer help.

Often she has had a talk with an Alcoholics Anonymous member and has begun to look into what is known about alcoholism. If she has attended a few Alcoholics Anonymous meetings, her sense of shame has been greatly alleviated as she finds so many others in the same boat. Her hopes rise as she meets alcoholics who have stopped drinking, and she feels relieved at being able to discuss her problems openly for the first time with an audience which understands fully. She begins to gain perspective on her problem and learns that she herself is involved in what happens to her husband, and that she must change. She exchanges techniques of management with other wives and receives their support in her decisions.

She learns that her husband is ill rather than merely "ornery," and this often serves to quell for the time being thoughts about leaving him which have begun to germinate as she has gained more self-confidence. She learns that help is available but also that her efforts to push him into help are unavailing. She is not only supported in her recently evolved behavior of thinking first of her family, but now this course also emerges from the realm of the unconceptualized and is set in an accepted rationale. She feels more secure in having a reason and a certainty that the group accepts her as "doing the right thing." When she reports deviations from what the group thinks is the "right way," her reasons are understood; she receives solid support but there is also pressure on her to alter her behavior again toward the acceptable. Blaming and self-pity are actively discouraged. In group discussions she still admits to such feelings but learns to recognize them as they arise and to go beyond them to more productive thinking.

How much her altered behavior changes the family situation is uncertain, but it helps her and gives her security from which to venture forth to further actions of a consistent and constructive type, constructive at least from the point of view of keeping her family on as even a keel as possible in the face of the disruptive influence of the husband. With new friends whom she can use as a sounding board for plans, and with her growing acquaintance with the alternatives and possible patterns of behavior, her thinking ceases to be circular and unproductive. Her anxiety about her own sanity is alleviated as she is reassured by others that they have experienced the same concern and that the remedy is to get her own life and her family under better control. As she accomplishes this, the difference in her feelings about herself convinces her that this is so.

Whether or not she has had a contact with wives of Alcoholics Anonymous members or other wives who have been through a similar experience and have emerged successfully, the very fact of taking hold of her situation and gradually making it more manageable adds to her self-confidence. As her husband is less and less able to care for himself or his family, she begins to feel that he needs her and that without her he would be destroyed. Such a feeling makes it difficult for her to think of leaving him. His almost complete social isolation at this point and his cries for help reinforce this conviction of being needed.

The drinking behavior is no longer hidden. Others obviously know about it, and this becomes accepted by the wife and children. Already isolated and insulated against possible rejection, the wife is often surprised to find that she has exaggerated her fears of what would happen were the situation known. However, the unpredictability of her husband's behavior makes her reluctant to form social relationships which could be violently disrupted or to involve others in the possible consequences of his behavior.

STAGE 5. EFFORTS TO ESCAPE THE PROBLEM

Stage 5 may be the terminal one for the marriage. In this stage the wife separates from her husband. Sometimes the marriage is reestablished after a period of sobriety, when it appears certain that the husband will not drink again. If he does revert to drinking, the marriage is sometimes finally terminated but with less emotional stress than the first time. If the husband deserts, being no longer able to tolerate his lack of status in his family, Stage 6 may be entered abruptly.

The events precipitating the decision to terminate the marriage may be near-catastrophic, as when there is an attempt by the husband to kill the wife or children, or they may appear trivial to outsiders, being only the last straw to an accumulation of years.

The problems in coming to the decision to terminate the marriage cannot be underestimated. Some of these problems derive from emotional conflicts; some are related to very practical circumstances in the situation; some are precipitated by the conflicting advice of outsiders. With several children dependent on her, the wife must decide whether the present situation is more detrimental to them than future situations she can see arising if she should leave her husband. The question of where the money to live on will come from must be thought out. If she can get a job, will there be enough to provide for child care also while she is away from home? Should the children, who have already experienced such an unsettled life, be separated from her to be cared for by others? If the family still owns its own home, how can she retain control of it? If she leaves, where can she go? What can be done to tide the family over until her first earnings come in? How can she ensure her husband's continued absence from the home and thus be certain of the safety of individuals and property in her absence? These are only a small sample of the practical issues that must be dealt with in trying to think her way through to a decision to terminate the marriage.

Other pressures act on her to impede the decision-making process. "If he would only stay drunk till I carry out what I intend to do," is a frequent statement. When the husband realizes that his wife really means to leave, he frequently sobers up, watches his behavior in the home, plays on her latent and sometimes conscious feelings of her responsibility for the situation, stresses his need for her and that without her he is lost, tears away at any confidence she has that she will be able to manage by herself, and threatens her and the children with injury or with his own suicide if she carries out her intention.

The children, in the meantime, are pulling and pushing on her emotions. They think she is "spineless" to stay but unfair to father's chances for ultimate recovery if she leaves. Relatives, who were earlier alienated in her attempts to shield her family but now know of the situation, do not believe in its full ramifications. They often feel she is exaggerating and persuade her to stay with him, Especially is this true in the case of a "solitary drinker." His drinking has been so well concealed that the relatives have no way of knowing the true nature of the situation. Other relatives, afraid that they will be called on for support, exert pressure to keep the marriage intact and the husband thereby responsible for debts. Relatives who feel she should leave him overplay their hands by berating the husband in such a manner as to evoke her defense of him. This makes conscious the positive aspects of her relationship with him, causing her to waver in her decision. If she consults organized agencies, she often gets conflicting advice. The agencies concerned with the well-being of the family may counsel leaving; those concerned with rehabilitating the husband may press her to stay. In addition, help from public organizations almost always involves delay and is frequently not forthcoming at the point where she needs it most.

The wife must come to terms with her own mixed feelings about her husband, her marriage and herself before she can decide on such a step as breaking up the marriage. She must give up hope that she can be of any help to her husband. She must command enough self-confidence, after years of having it eroded, to be able to face an unknown future and leave the security of an unpalatable but familiar past and present. She must accept that she has failed in her marriage, not an easy thing to do after having devoted years to stopping up the cracks in the family structure as they appeared. Breaking up the marriage involves a complete alteration in the life goals toward which all her behavior has been oriented. It is hard for her to rid herself of the feeling that she married him and he is her responsibility. Having thought and planned for so long on a day-to-day basis, it is difficult to plan for a long-term future.

Her taking over of the family raises her self-confidence, but failure to carry through on decisions undermines the new gains that she has made. Vacillation in her decisions tends to exasperate the agencies trying to help her, and she begins to feel that help from them may not be forthcoming if she finally decides to leave.

Some events, however, help her to arrive at a decision. During the absences of her husband she has seen how manageable life can be and how smoothly her family can run. She finds that life goes on without him. The wife who is working comes to feel that "my husband is a luxury I can no longer afford." After a few short-term separations in which she tries out her wings successfully, leaving comes to look more possible. Another step on the path to leaving is the acceptance of the idea that, although she cannot help her husband, she can help her family. She often reaches a state of such emotional isolation from her husband that his behavior no longer disturbs her emotionally but is only something annoying which upsets daily routines and plans.

STAGE 6. REORGANIZATION OF PART OF THE FAMILY

The wife is without her husband and must reorganize her family on this basis. Substantially the process is similar to that in other divorced families, but with some additions. The divorce rarely cuts her relationship to her husband. Unless she and her family disappear, her husband may make attempts to come back. When drunk, he may endanger her job by calls at her place of work. He may attempt violence against members of the family, or he may contact the children and work to gain their loyalty so that pressure is put on the mother to accept him again. Looking back on her marriage, she forgets the full impact of the problem situation on her and on the children and feels more warmly toward her husband, and these feelings can still be manipulated by him. The wide circulation of information on alcoholism as an illness engenders guilt about having deserted a sick man. Gradually, however, the family becomes reorganized.

STAGE 7. RECOVERY AND REORGANIZATION OF THE WHOLE FAMILY

Stage 7 is entered if the husband achieves sobriety, whether or not separation has preceded. It was pointed out that in earlier stages most of the problems in the marriage were attributed to the alcoholism of the husband, and thus problems in adjustment not related directly to the drinking were unrecognized and unmet. Also, the "sober personality" of the husband was thought of as the "real" personality, with a resulting lack of recognition of other factors involved in his sober behavior, such as remorse and guilt over his actions, leading him to act to the best of his ability like "the ideal husband" when sober. Irritation or other signs of growing tension were viewed as indicators of further drinking, and hence the problems giving rise to them were walked around gingerly

rather than faced and resolved. Lack of conflict and lack of drinking were defined as indicating a perfect adjustment. For the wife and husband facing a sober marriage after many years of an alcoholic marriage, the expectations of what marriage without alcoholism will be are unrealistically idealistic, and the reality of marriage almost inevitably brings disillusionments. The expectation that all would go well and that all problems be resolved with the cessation of the husband's drinking cannot be met and this threatens the marriage from time to time.

The beginning of sobriety for the husband does not bring too great hope to the family at first. They have been through this before but are willing to help him along and stand by him in the new attempt. As the length of sobriety increases, so do the hopes for its permanence and efforts to be of help. The wife at first finds it difficult to think more than in terms of today, waking each morning with fear of what the day will bring and sighing with relief at the end of each sober day.

With the continuation of sobriety, many problems begin to crop up. Mother has for years managed the family, and now father again wishes to be reinstated in his former roles. Usually the first role reestablished is that of breadwinner, and the economic problems of the family begin to be alleviated as debts are gradually paid and there is enough left over for current needs. With the resumption of this role, the husband feels that the family should also accept him at least as a partner in the management of the family. Even if the wife is willing to hand over some of the control of the children, for example, the children often are not able to accept this change easily. Their mother has been both parents for so long that it takes time to get used to the idea of consulting their father on problems and asking for his decisions. Often the father tries too hard to manage this change overnight, and the very pressure put on the children toward this end defeats him. In addition, he is unable to meet many of the demands the children make on him because he has never really become acquainted with them or learned to understand them and is lacking in much necessary background knowledge of their lives.

The wife, who finds it difficult to conceive of her husband as permanently sober, feels an unwillingness to let control slip from her hands. At the same time she realizes that reinstatement of her husband in his family roles is necessary to his sobriety. She also realizes that the closer his involvement in the family the greater the probability of his remaining sober. Yet she remembers events in the past in which his failure to handle his responsibilities was catastrophic to the family. Used to avoiding anything which might upset him, the wife often hesitates to discuss problems openly. At times, if she is successful in helping him to regain his roles as father, she feels resentful of his intrusion into territory she has come to regard as hers. If he makes errors in judgment which affect the family adversely, her former feelings of being his superior may come to the fore and affect her interaction with him. If the children begin to turn to him, she may feel a resurgence of self-pity at being left out and find herself attempting to swing the children back toward herself. Above all, however, she finds herself feeling resentful that some other agency achieved what she and the children could not.

Often the husband makes demands for obedience, for consideration and for pampering which members of the family feel unable to meet. He may become rather euphoric as his sobriety continues and feel superior for a time.

Gradually, however, the drinking problem sinks into the past and marital adjustment at some level is achieved. Even when this has occurred, the drinking problem crops up occasionally, as when the time comes for a decision about whether the children should be permitted to drink. The mother at such times becomes anxious, sees in the child traits which remind her of her husband, worries whether these are the traits which mean future alcoholism. At parties, at first, she is watchful and concerned about whether her husband will take a drink or not. Relatives and friends may, in a party mood, make the husband the center of attention by emphasizing his nondrinking. They may unwittingly cast aspersions on his character by trying to convince him that he can now "drink like a man." Some relatives and friends have gone so far as secretly to "spike" a non-alcoholic drink and then cry "bottoms up!" without realizing the risk of reactivating patterns from the past.

If sobriety has come through Alcoholics Anonymous [A.A.], the husband frequently throws himself so wholeheartedly into A.A. activities that his wife sees little of him and feels neglected. As she worries less about his drinking, she may press him to cut down on these activities. That this is dangerous, since A.A. activity is correlated with success in Alcoholics Anonymous, has been shown by Lahey (4). Also, the wife discovers that, though she has a sober husband, she is by no means free of alcoholics. In his Twelfth Step work, he may keep the house filled with men he is helping. In the past her husband has avoided self-searching; and now he may become excessively introspective, and it may be difficult for her to deal with this.

If the husband becomes sober through Alcoholics Anonymous and the wife participates actively in groups open to her, the thoughts of what is happening to her, to her husband and to her family will be verbalized and interpreted within the framework of the Alcoholics Anonymous philosophy and the situation will probably be more tolerable and more easily worked out....

SUMMARY

The onset of alcoholism in a family member has been viewed as precipitating a cumulative crisis for the family. Seven critical stages have been delineated. Each stage affects the form which the following one will take. The family finds itself in an unstructured situation which is undefined by the culture. Thus it is forced to evolve techniques of adjustment by trial and error. The unpredictability of the situation, added to its lack of structure, engenders anxiety in family members which gives rise to personality difficulties. Factors in the culture, in the environment and within the family situation prolong the crisis and deter the working out of permanent adjustment patterns. With the arrest of the alcoholism, the crisis enters its final stage. The family attempts to reorganize to include the ex-alcoholic and makes adjustments to the changes which have occurred in him.

It has been suggested that the clinical picture presented by the wife to helping agencies is not only indicative of a type of basic personality structure but also of the stage in family adjustment to an alcoholic. That the wives of alcoholics represent a rather limited number of personality types can be interpreted in two ways, which are not mutually exclusive.

(a) That women with certain personality attributes tend to select alcoholics or potential alcoholics as husbands in order to satisfy unconscious personality needs;

(b) That women undergoing similar experiences of stress, within similarly unstructured situations, defined by the culture and reacted to by members of the society in such a manner as to place limits on the range of possible behavior, will emerge from this experience showing many similar neurotic personality traits. As the situation evolves some of these personality traits will also change. Changes have been observed in the women studied which correlate with altered family interaction patterns. This hypothesis is supported also by observations on the behavior of individuals in other unstructured situations, in situations in which they were isolated from supporting group interaction. It is congruent also with the theory of reactions to increased and decreased stress.

NOTES

1. Some effects of alcoholism of the father on children have been discussed by Newell (3).
2. It is of interest here that marriage counselors and students of marital adjustment are of the opinion that unhappy marriage results in poor sexual adjustment more often than poor sexual adjustment leads to unhappy marriage. If this proves to be true, it would be expected that most wives of alcoholics would find sex distasteful while their husbands are drinking. The wives of the inactive alcoholics report that their sexual adjustments with their husbands are currently satisfactory; many of those whose husbands are still drinking state that they enjoyed sexual relationships before the alcoholism was established.

REFERENCES

1. Club and Educational Bureaus of Newsweek. 1950. "Is Alcoholism Everyone's Problem?" Platform, N.Y., p. 3 (January).
2. Whalen, T. 1953. "Wives of Alcoholics: Four Types Observed in a Family Service Agency." *Quarterly Journal of Studies on Alcohol,* 14:632–641.
3. Newell, N. 1950. "Alcoholism and the Father-Image." *Quarterly Journal of Studies on Alcohol,* 11:92–96.
4. Lahey, W. W. 1950. *A Comparison of Social and Personal Factors Identified with Selected Members of Alcoholics Anonymous.* Master's thesis: University of Southern California.

CHAPTER 4

THE ROLE OF THIRD PARTIES

The Enforcement of College Alcohol Policy

EARL RUBINGTON

Although violations of rules may be brought to anyone's attention at times, only some people are officially required to respond to them. Examples of these formal agents of social control are police and corrections officers, schoolteachers, mental hospital attendants, and supervisors in various workplaces. The situation of enforcement in which an agent comes in contact with someone thought to be a "rule breaker" can mark the beginning of a deviant social career. And so a key question for students of deviance is, What happens when a rule is assumed to have been broken? Under what conditions do negative sanctions take place?

Unlike most official agents of social control, residence-hall assistants live where they also do their work. And one important part of their work is enforcement of the college's "no-drinking rule." Earl Rubington examines how residence-hall assistants manage the complexities of their relations with fellow students when enforcing the college's alcohol policy. His findings support the tentative generalization that the more frequent the contact of control agents with persons under surveillance, the less likely the enforcement of the rules. And so, at least in college residence halls, familiarity breeds leniency rather than contempt.

When law and custom are in conflict, "patterned evasion" often follows (Williams 1970). As community support for a law wanes, official enforcement becomes selective, lax, or even nonexistent. The years from 1920 to 1933, when Prohibition was the law of the land, are generally considered to provide the classic example of patterned evasion (Merz 1970). Yet since repeal of Prohibition,

Reprinted from "The Ethic of 'Responsible Drinking,'" *Deviant Behavior,* Vol. 17 (1996), pp. 319–335. Taylor & Francis, Inc., Washington, DC. Reproduced with permission. All rights reserved.

age-specific prohibition and patterned evasion have long coexisted.

Despite laws enjoining sales, purchase, possession, or consumption of alcoholic beverages by minors, more underage youth drink today, and more of them are "binge drinkers." The law causes youth to drink, and the lack of enforcement only makes underage drinkers indifferent to or contemptuous of the law (Mosher 1980; Engs and Hanson 1989a). Since 1987, when all 50 states raised the drinking age to 21, although teenage drinking and driving has declined, teenage drinking remains at high levels.

Whether alcohol problems on campus are more prevalent than a generation ago, college administrators seem more concerned (Engs 1977). They seek to eliminate underage drinking on campus through formulating more detailed alcohol policies, more stringent sanctions, or a combination of both. As a consequence, freshman residence halls have become the focal point for the kinds of problems that contradiction between law and its enforcement can create. The vast majority of entering 1st-year students not only are already drinking but are also quite well accustomed to obtaining alcoholic beverages with impunity (O'Hare 1990). Thus, when they enter residence halls in the fall, they experience culture shock when they learn that the college forbids them to drink on campus. Most 1st-year students believe that they have been denied their "right to drink" (Engs and Hanson 1989b) and face a conflict between how they define drinking and how their college does.

It falls to residential assistants (RAs) to enforce the policies administrators have formulated. Documenting and reporting infractions of residence hall rules are an important part of RAs' duties (Blimling and Miltenberger 1990; Upcraft 1982). Unlike other agents of control such as police officers, prison guards, mental hospital attendants, and elementary school teachers, RAs live, work, and associate with the people whom they may have to report for infractions of residence hall rules (Becker 1952; Reiss 1971; Perrucci 1974; Zimmer 1986; Lombardo 1989). Thus, the complexity of RAs' social situation makes study of their enforcement role theoretically significant.

Police officers, prison guards, mental hospital attendants, and elementary school teachers, for example, have more community support and institutional authority than RAs. Their "clients" are all subordinate to them by reason of deviant or age status. Similarly, they are socially distant from them and share few cultural values with them. And, perhaps most important, these enforcers' chances of experiencing role conflict in their work with clients are considerably less than those of RAs (Merton 1957; Goode 1960).

Unlike the above-mentioned agents, RAs live and work in the same building with freshman residents. Like them, they are also students. They share many facilities both on and off campus, are not that far apart in age, share many values, and more or less share the same drinking culture (Berkowitz and Perkins 1986). Often, they meet one another in off-campus drinking parties or when they patronize the same drinking establishments. Thus, RAs can come into frequent contact with residents in a variety of social contexts including enforcement over the course of the academic years. That the kinds of relationships that emerge out of such contacts may have some bearing on how they enforce the no-drinking rule seems reasonable. But just what kinds of influence these contacts and relationships have had on enforcement of age-specific prohibition in freshman residence halls has not drawn a lot of research attention.

Three studies give some indication of the conditions under which enforcement of college alcohol policy varies. Moffatt (1989) studied a Rutgers University residence hall floor where upperclass students lived. He found that the RA went from being a lax to a strict enforcer of the no-drinking rule when the state raised the legal drinking age to 21 (Moffatt 1989). Cohn and White carried out a field experiment at the University of New Hampshire. Comparing three kinds of disciplinary policies, they found more violations of all residence hall rules in those residence halls where residents rather than administrators formulated alcohol policy (Cohn and White 1990). Concentrating on freshman residence halls, I studied RA–resident relations when the legal drinking age was 20. Comparing two residence halls, I found that floor layout as well as RAs' own drinking patterns influenced the way RAs enforced City University's (CU's) policy (Rubington 1993a).

After the drinking age was raised to 21, I compared the frequency of alcohol violations in three CU freshman residence halls for three consecutive years (1989 to 1992). These studies yielded the following uniformities: RAs recorded most alcohol violations in the fall quarter, with 30% of those violations coming in the week before the start of classes; most alcohol violators, whether one-time or repeat, were male; and male RAs reported four males for every single female violator, whereas for female RAs the sex ratio of reported violators was three males for every two females (Rubington 1991, 1993a, 1993b).

The present paper, pooling qualitative interview data from the three previous studies, seeks to account for variations in RAs' performance as prohibition agents.

RAs' job description mandates enforcement of residence hall rules. The contradiction between drinking age laws and their enforcement makes role problems for RAs. They are well aware of the ease with which residents can obtain alcoholic beverages off campus. Such easy access to alcoholic beverages, coupled with CU's ban on alcohol in the residence halls requires a cultural compromise. Just as residents have interests in violating the no-drinking rule, so do RAs have interests in its enforcement. What those interests are and how they may be best served comes out of their work experience. Through a process of mutual socialization, they adopt enforcement styles that best serve their interests. We turn now to an examination of those experiences, the enforcement roles they adopted, and their consequences.

The Student Handbook and CU's Housing Handbook, issued to all residents of university housing, spells out the university's policy on drinking: no possession, service, sale, or consumption of alcoholic beverages by students under 21; and students of legal age may drink only in their rooms. As part of their police function, RAs report most violations during those times when they are "on duty" and have to "make rounds" of the entire building. During the year a single RA is "on duty" on weekdays (Monday, Tuesday, and Wednesday); on weekends (defined as Thursday, Friday, Saturday, and Sunday), two RAs do "double duty." RAs are on duty for approximately 10 weekdays and 3 weekends dur-

ing each of the three academic quarters. On weekdays, they make rounds at 8:00, 10:00, and 12:00 at night; weekends, they add a fourth round at 1:00 a.m. On rounds, they check up on the building and its residents, and document any violations of residence hall rules. After each round, they record infractions on "discipline cards" and make more detailed entries in a staff log. Discipline card entries contain resident's name, date, time, place, and kind of infraction; resident's attitude (cooperative or uncooperative); and the RA's initials.

The three categories of infractions (sometimes occurring in combination) are alcohol, noise, and all others. Alcohol violations include being in the presence of alcohol; underage drinking (in the lobby, corridor, bathroom, stairway, elevator, or room); alcohol possession; drunkenness; attempting to smuggle alcohol into the building; residents' guest drinking; and the like. Noise violations include loud voices, stereos, radios, or musical instruments. Other violations include hallway sports, vandalism, throwing objects out of room windows, insubordination, suspicion of marijuana use, burning incense, and the like. Over the course of a year, alcohol and noise usually account for about two-thirds of all recorded violations.

SETTING AND METHOD

These studies took place in South, East, and West Halls, three CU freshman residence halls. (Names of the persons and places, including "City University," are fictitious.) The three residence halls housed men and women on alternate floors. An upper-class student of the same gender had a single room on each floor and served as the RA. Data for the three studies came from tabulation and analysis of all infractions RAs recorded on discipline cards, examination of residence hall staff logs, some participant observation, and interviews with resident directors (RDs), graduate assistants (GAs), and RAs in each of the three study years. The analysis and interpretation in this paper [are] based primarily on interviews with RAs. In the interview quotes that follow, R = residential assistant, D = residence director, and G = graduate assistant.

BECOMING A RESIDENTIAL ASSISTANT

RAs constitute the first line of defense of college alcohol policy. In the course of making rounds, RAs confront residents in situations that may require action on their part. In time, they develop their own style, a term RAs use when discussing their work as prohibition agents. Stages in RA careers and development of their styles follow below.

RAs AS RESIDENTS

CU requires that RAs have some prior experience as residents in a college residence hall. Most had been residents in one of CU's freshman residence halls. RAs who drank as freshmen reported a variety of experiences with their floor RAs. Most reported that their RAs were quite lax in enforcement of the no-drinking rule. Some reported RAs' collusion in alcohol violations.

A few recalled being "written up" for alcohol violations when they were freshmen, but most reported that they drank in the residence hall with impunity. One male said he got drunk once a week throughout the year without ever being written up. Others recalled their RAs inviting them into their room for a drink, or joining in a drinking party already going on in the informant's room. Still others noted that when the RA on rounds came upon them drinking in their rooms, he or she simply closed the door. One informant noted that the RA simply had them "dump" the beer (pour contents in sink or toilet bowl). And one female said that her RA used to call up on the phone to warn them when the RA on duty was making rounds. Thus RAs as freshmen were socialized to a number of ideas about drinking in the residence halls. Their freshman experiences showed them that drinking was ubiquitous, its enforcement lax.

FORMAL AND INFORMAL TRAINING

Both in the week before freshmen arrive and then later throughout the academic year, RAs attend training sessions, mainly lectures on a variety of subjects. The closest thing to "hands-on" experience that participants recalled was role-playing, which took place the week before classes started. It involved new RAs getting some idea of what went on behind closed doors. They had to knock on a resident's door, identify themselves as the RA, and request permission to enter. Once inside, they confronted veteran RAs acting as residents of the room and simulating one of the many kinds of situations they could expect to deal with once the fall quarter started. Underage drinking, domestic disputes, insubordination, suicidal residents, and the smell of marijuana were but a few of the surprises veteran RAs had in store for them. After the new RA responded to the situation, the veterans suggested other ways he or she could have handled the situation or commended the new RA for what he or she did.

In the early weeks of the quarter, veteran RAs sometimes accompany 1st-year RAs when they are making rounds. One source of informal training comes from observing how veterans manage confrontations with residents. Discussion with them after the fact also provides information for novice RAs on how to act should they come upon similar situations. In time, RAs fashion their own particular style by blending or avoiding techniques veteran RAs employ. Being matter-of-fact or strictly business, using humor to defuse situations, and taking charge more quickly are only some of the points RAs made in interviews. Some noted that with experience they managed confrontations with less time and effort.

THE FIRST FLOOR MEETING

In the first week of the fall quarter, RDs meet with all residents of the building and orient them to Big Town, CU, and residence hall rules. They point out that underage students cannot have alcohol in their rooms and cannot drink; and they tell them that anyone who breaks the rules will be subject to sanctions. Later, RAs hold their own first floor meetings. After mutual introductions, they also inform their residents about CU's alcohol policy.

At these meetings, RAs present their views about alcohol policy in one of four ways: tacit, proscriptive, conditional, or prescriptive. The few RAs who take the tacit route say nothing at all about the subject. Presumably, they believe that the RD has said all that needs to be said on the subject. A somewhat larger number of RAs are proscriptive. On the subject of alcohol and other drugs, they are both succinct and specific: They simply say: "Don't do it here." Most RAs, however, are conditional in their alcohol policy orientations. The way R-4 stated alcohol policy to her floor was typical. She said: "I don't see it, smell it, or hear it. [Hear it?] Quarters [a drinking game played with quarters], opening cans. The implied message is if I don't see it, smell it, or hear it, there's nothing I can do about it." First-year RAs were more apt to be prescriptive. Some wondered if they had sent mixed messages to their residents. For example, R-2 said: "'I know you're gonna be drinking. It's gonna happen. Be quiet. Be in control. Don't let it get out of hand.' Some may have thought that validated drinking. Some took it that way."

RAs have notions on how to present themselves as rule enforcers at the start of the fall quarter. At the outset, some present themselves as sticklers. R-7 pointed out: "I decided to tell them that I was going to be strict, sort of scare them. Common sense says it's easier to go from hard to soft than from soft to hard. It's harder to get tough.... I'm majoring in marketing. It's only common sense to start with a higher price, then mark it down."

But, on the whole, RAs have a different relationship with the residents of their own floors than with residents of the other floors in the building. For one thing, they live on their own floors. They do not make scheduled rounds on their floor except when on duty. Although they do write up residents of their own floor, they are more lenient when disciplining them; they are more apt to use informal rather than formal means of social control. But, at the same time, they have to be somewhat concerned about the behavior of their own residents. For instance, RAs are subject to periodic performance reviews and evaluation by their RDs. "Problem floors" as well as "troublemakers" get labeled quickly after just a few rounds. Disorder, vandalism, noise, trash in the hallways, and numerous write-ups reflect on the floor RA's competence and affect his or her performance evaluation as well as reputation with fellow RAs. A "wild floor" makes for considerable work for all the other RAs when they have to make rounds. These RAs sometimes let the RA who has made extra work for them know how they feel; through direct comments or indirectly, in the staff log.

MAKING ROUNDS

RAs are most likely to come upon alcohol violations when making rounds. If they see people drinking in hallways or in their rooms, or if they hear loud voices or stereos coming from a room, they confront residents. Confrontation requires them to knock on the door, identify themselves as the RA, and request permission to enter. Once inside, if they see open cans of beer, people holding cans, or people drinking from containers, they ask all present for their IDs. After restoring order, they go downstairs to fill out discipline cards. They enter all names from the IDs on the cards along with the violations, and they enter the same information in the staff log.

The first time RAs make rounds, they experience some anxiety; but in a very short time it becomes, as one of them described it, "second nature." Confrontations with residents, of course, are not always matters of routine. RAs are expected to remain cool, assertive, and in control of the situation rather than become angry or excited. However, numerous contingencies attend RA–resident confrontations. As G-1 said: "You never know what you'll find once they open the door." A number of RAs have pointed out that residents become upset simply because RAs have intervened in their activities. These enforcement encounters generate understanding on not only how residents feel about being written up, but also how RAs themselves feel about writing up residents.

Thus, enforcement can be problematic for RAs. It soon becomes incumbent on them to fashion their own personal solutions to problems of their identity as RAs, situation control, and exercise of authority.

RAs expressed dislike about having to write up residents, having to document violations in accordance with Housing Office requirements. In addition to disliking the idea in general, some said they really didn't enjoy "getting people in trouble." Many residents, for example, took being written up quite personally and claimed that the RA was "out to get them." RAs reported that they often went out of their way the following morning to say hello to residents they had written up the night before. Greeting them as if nothing had happened, they sought to communicate that they had been "only doing their job." Whereas some residents came to understand, others did not. They showed their animosity by refusing to return the greeting.

DEVELOPMENT OF A STYLE

Over time, RAs solve problems of confrontation by developing what they call their "style." As experience with enforcing rules becomes routine, RAs opt for one of three styles: strict ("by-the-book"), moderate ("in between"), or lenient ("laid-back").

RAs who are "by-the-book" approach all encounters as if the matter were "cut and dried." They have a no-nonsense, matter-of-fact approach; take command of a situation immediately; collect IDs rapidly; are strictly business, quick, and cool. For the most part, they are rule-oriented. RAs who are "laid-back" are more apt to give residents the benefit of the doubt. More often situation-oriented, they will find a way to restore order without having to write residents up if possible. RAs who are

"in between" are more often person-oriented. If residents are cooperative in a confrontation and do not give them a "hard time," they may manage a situation without necessarily documenting a violation of residence hall rules. But, as is generally the case with police-citizen contacts, disrespect guarantees being written up (Westley 1970; Reiss 1971; Black 1978). D-1 summarized the three types of RA styles when she said that "there are RAs who write up everything they see, RAs who will give a person a chance, and RAs who ignore everything."

RAs evolve their own styles out of a combination of observation, experience, and discussion with other RAs. R-2, for example, blended the styles of the two other veteran RAs, becoming an "in between." He said: "I hang around more with R-10 and R-11. R-10 gives more leeway, he deals personally, he's a humanist, he's friends with his residents, he's a fun guy. R-11, he's by-the-book: This is the policy, that's it. I learned from them. I relied on them. I found a middle ground." But here R-2 was talking about developing a style for dealing with his own floor.

Making rounds, however, brings RAs into more fleeting contacts with residents of a whole building on the dozen or more times they make rounds in the course of a quarter. These contacts necessarily turn on whether there has been a violation of the rules, which requires RAs to assert their authority, take charge, and alter the situation. Breaking up drinking parties, getting people in a room to leave, quieting residents, and getting them to dump the beer are just some examples. What is quite clear is that most RAs handle residents of their own floors differently. As R-12 said: "You use your discretion. I treat guys on my floor different from the rest of the building."

As previously noted, what makes RAs different from other control agents is that they live and work in the same place with people they may have to report for violating rules. During the course of an academic year they can make contact with residents of the whole building, but they are much more likely to come into frequent contact with residents of their own floor. The more frequent the contact between people, the more likely that something like friendship may develop (Homans 1951). Some RAs commented, for example, that visiting residents in their room and accepting a slice of pizza may set up expectations for special consideration at some later time. R-14 dropped in to visit a friend on her floor. Her friend's boyfriend was present, drinking a beer. R-14 had the boyfriend dump the beer, which upset her friend. Some RAs are aware of the need, as they put it, to "walk the line" between being a friend and being an RA. The friend–RA or cop-counselor conflict has been a problem for RAs ever since the establishment of the position (Upcraft 1982).

But if all RAs work in the same building, particularly when they are "on duty," they live on their home floors. As R-24 said: "I have to live with these guys for the rest of the year." And so variation in violation sites can make for variations in enforcement styles. RAs enforce rules on their home floors as well as on all floors and locations within the building, but once home floor versus all other floors is taken into account the site of enforcement makes for variations in styles of enforcement.

First, there are RAs who are "by-the-book" on all floors, their own as well as others. They know the rules, and when in the presence of a violation they write up the violator no matter who he or she is or where the violation took place. These sticklers can be generalists or specialists. R-15 considered making noise a more serious violation than drinking in one's room; he specialized in writing up residents for noise violations. Most violators he cited were residents of his floor. R-3 and R-16, both former problem drinkers, on the other hand, were specialists in writing up residents for alcohol violations whether on their home floors or on any of the others. But whether generalists or specialists, pure "by-the-book" RAs are paragons of consistency in the enforcement of residence hall rules. Most pure "by-the-book" RAs in this study were either seniors or veteran RAs, and more of them were women.

Next are those RAs who are "laid-back" with respect to their home floors but "by-the-book"

when dealing with residents of any of the other floors. D-2 said: "R-17 is most lax enforcing rules on his floor. He loves his floor; they can do no wrong: But he's very consistent when enforcing rules off his floor." Other residence hall staff agreed that RAs are less strict with residents of their own floor. R-18 exemplified reluctance to document infractions on one's own floor. She acknowledged that when making "double-duty" rounds, she always stayed in the background when they got to her floor and let the other RA write up any of her residents. Being "laid-back" with one's own floor and "by-the-book" with all other floors is probably the typical enforcement style.

RAs who are "laid-back" on all floors are least frequent but most notorious. There are three degrees of "laid-backness": lenient, lax, and absent. Generally, the overly lenient lean more in the direction of friend rather than RA when it comes to confrontations with residents, irrespective of floors. This means that most of the time such an RA gives the resident the benefit of the doubt. Walking by an open door and seeing a student drinking, the RA may just close the door. Coming upon a student standing or walking in the corridor with an open beer in his or her hand, the RA may suggest that the person go to his or her room and close the door. On occasion, such an RA may ask the resident to dump a beer without later recording the incident on a discipline card and noting it on the staff log. The distinction between the lenient and the lax is that lenient RAs see the violation but do not treat it as such, whereas lax RAs go out of their way not to see any violations that require documenting. G-1 once accompanied R-5 on rounds. He was amazed at R-5's selective inattention. R-5 was a master at "looking the other way."

Laxity on the home floor can also come about when RAs have "lost control" of their floor. Over-identification with residents, coupled with an inability to accept identity as an RA and to exercise the authority that goes with the position, produces loss of control. D-1 pointed out R-19 as a good example of an RA who had lost control of his floor. Residents of his floor were written up for numerous trash, vandalism, noise, and alcohol violations. When I interviewed R-19 later, he said that his first two alcohol write-ups had made him most uncomfortable. He went on to say: "I was a freshman once. How do I get off getting them in trouble when I did the same things?" And later in that same interview he acknowledged that "I am more lax on my own floor."

Absence produces the third degree of "laid-backness." Occasionally RAs are off their floors for extended periods if they are holding another job, or are spending much of their time with a boyfriend or girlfriend. Extended absence produces the situation of "when the cat's away, the mice will play," as R-20 put it. A classic example of absence was R-21: Although he served as RA for an entire academic year, he wrote only one violation for that year. In turn, his floor was known as the wildest. The other seven RAs all wrote up a considerable number of violations whenever they made rounds on R-21's floor.

The last category consisted of RAs who were "in betweens." RAs who called themselves "in betweens" were most conscious of what they called "gray areas." They said that all RAs varied in their personal tolerances for alcohol and for noise. And some "in betweens" acknowledged that their mood sometimes influenced whether they wrote up a resident for a violation. The few "in betweens" were most apt to be women who made fine distinctions about incidents that came to their attention. These few were usually seniors and/or veteran RAs.

After a while, both residents and RAs become aware of these varied styles of enforcement among RAs. Consistency in rule enforcement can well become an issue, as it was in East Hall in the 1989–1990 academic year, when the "by-the-books" lined up against the "laid-backs" and the "in betweens."

"LIGHTENING UP"

During interviews, RAs either volunteered information or answered questions on how they as well as residents may have changed over the course of the academic year. On changes in residents' drinking, RAs gave one of four answers: Most drinking took place during the fall quarter (the "rite of passage" argument), during winter quarter (the "cabin fever" argument), during spring quarter (the "spring fever" argument), or at the beginning and end of each quarter (the "tension release" argument).

RAs said their own behavior changed with the quarters for one of three reasons: They "lightened up," they became apathetic, or they "burned out." Typically, they complained of "living in a fishbowl," of lacking privacy. Although part of their job was surveillance, they deplored the fact that they "were always being watched." Informants often said that, whereas they had lightened up, it was usually the other RAs who had become apathetic or were burnouts. Over time, costs of rule enforcement began to outweigh its benefits. Yet despite variations in enforcement styles as well as lightening up as the year went on, in serving their own particular enforcement interests, RAs managed to collaborate in fashioning a common understanding of what the term "responsible drinking" came to mean in residence hall life.

THE ETHIC OF "RESPONSIBLE DRINKING"

Keeping the peace in CU residence halls depends on the ethic of "responsible drinking." For alcohol educators, responsible drinking means persons understand the action of alcohol, know their limits, make informed choices when they drink, and are prepared to take the consequences of their drinking, whatever they may be (Weisheit 1990). Responsible drinking means something entirely different to residence hall staff.

They take it as inevitable that freshmen are going to drink, that there is no stopping them. They claim that most freshmen drink, that many of them have fake IDs. They see empty cans and bottles in the trash cans. Many residents tell them about their drinking experiences. They overhear conversations in the building about parties, escapades, incidents, and hangovers. They see or hear residents vomiting in the bathroom at night or early in the morning. They come to know those rare residents who do not get out of bed until midafternoon. They know of vandalism, verbal or physical assaults that sometimes follow drinking, and occasions when they or other RAs have had to call campus police to deal with unruly, insubordinate residents. They know of cases of alcohol poisoning.

For RAs, drinking is a problem only if it makes trouble for them. Thus, those residents who drink behind closed doors, with few people in the room and voices or stereos lowered, have learned how to "drink responsibly." They are not, in D-1's words, "calling attention to themselves." G-4 said that when having an administrative meeting with residents she sometimes asked them why they hadn't considered "closing the door and turning it down."

At the beginning of the fall quarter, RAs are "gung ho," eager, enthusiastic. In line with Housing Office's suggestion that they start out tough as top sergeants, they come on in early confrontations as "hard-asses." They employ more aggressive tactics on rounds. They intimidate residents who try to sneak alcohol into the building. Since the development of the student rights movement, staff are not permitted to examine gym, duffel, or hockey bags, or to open the refrigerators that many students have in their rooms, or to enter rooms without residents' permission. Nevertheless, in the beginning of the year, they ask students if they may see what's in their bags or in their refrigerators. They always catch naive 1st-year students who are unaware of their rights. Once caught with unopened bottles or cans, residents must either remove them from the building or dump them while RAs watch.

The aggressive drive in the early weeks of the fall quarter probably discourages some residents from drinking in the residence halls. These early weeks also constitute a mutual testing period; residents and RAs alike negotiate over the definition and enforcement of the no-drinking rule. Over time, RAs spell out their definition of the rule.

Agreement with their terms constitutes the ethic of "responsible drinking." "Responsible drinking" means drinking that goes on behind closed doors and makes no public trouble. Drinking that is not disorderly, disruptive, or destructive is considered responsible. For example, although the Housing Handbook lists public drunkenness as a violation, RAs don't write up residents who return to the residence hall intoxicated after a night's drinking if they can make it to their rooms without making a disturbance.

RAs interviewed attributed the marked decline in alcohol violations to the workings of the agreement. RAs said residents learned what they could and could not get away with. If for many this meant not drinking in the building, for others it meant learning the best times and places for sneaking alcohol in, adjusting their drinking to the RAs' cycle of rounds, finding out which RAs were hard on alcohol violations and which were not, becoming aware that they did not have to say what was in bags or refrigerators, and opening doors slowly when RAs knocked so as to conceal open containers. For most, it meant becoming more discreet when they did drink in the residence hall. And the reciprocal of the exercise of residents' discretion was the gradual relaxation of strict enforcement of the no-drinking rule by the RAs.

The ratio of actual to reported alcohol violations, of course, can never be known. Some RAs exaggerate the frequency of clandestine drinking. R-23 estimated that "we only catch about 30% of them." R-24 said that if she were to write up all the violations that came to her attention, they would probably total around 30 after all of her three rounds. Exaggerated or not, these estimates suggest that RAs' compliance with the terms of the unwritten agreement, that is, the ethic of "responsible drinking," keeps the peace in CU's freshman residence halls.

DISCUSSION

RAs face a particular role problem. On the one hand, the university asks them to enforce a rule inside the residence hall that is violated regularly outside. On the other hand, RAs live, work, and study among the very people who are subject to the rule they are required to enforce. Central to their dilemma is the social fact that those who enforce an unpopular rule can become as unpopular as, if not more so than, the rule itself. Enforcement of the rule creates the friend–RA role conflict endemic to the position of RA.

RAs' styles evolve out of the interests they believe enforcement will best serve. Those interests come to shape the stance they take in resolving the friend–RA conflict. Thus, those RAs who are "by-the-book" when making rounds on all floors as well as enforcing rules on their home floor resolve conflict by being strictly RAs. Their strict and regular enforcement symbolizes the relational distance they keep between themselves and all residents.

Those RAs who are "laid-back" with their own floors while being "by-the-book" on all the other floors tailor their enforcement efforts to the degree of social distance between them and residents: formal control for "strangers" (residents of the other floors), informal control for residents of their own floor. They "walk the line" between being the RA and being a friend because they believe they know their residents better than the pure "by-the-book" RAs know theirs. Informal control does the least damage to their relations with their residents. It takes two to make a role conflict. Although their residents would prefer them as friends, they teach their residents that they can be friends who also can be RAs when circumstances require it.

"Laid-back" RAs, whether on home floors or others, seek to be friends to everyone, authorities to none. Finally, those RAs who are neither friend nor RA to anyone are that way because they are rarely around. RAs of all degrees of "laid-backness" lose control of their floors, only making more enforcement work for all the other RAs when they make rounds.

The failure of the "laid-backs" to comply with the ethic of "responsible drinking" becomes a special residence hall form of patterned evasion. Then the other RAs have to redefine the situation by their more consistent enforcement of the residence hall drinking norm when they make their rounds. Residents with interests in defying the rules are left with two choices: drink outside the building or drink only when strict RAs are not making rounds. And to the extent that they don't call attention to themselves, they too are complying with the ethic of responsible drinking.

REFERENCES

Becker, Howard S. 1952. "The Career of the Chicago Public School Teacher." *American Journal of Sociology* 57:470–477.

Berkowitz, Alan D., and H. Wesley Perkins. 1986. "Resident Advisers as Role Models: A Comparison of Drinking Patterns of Resident Advisers and Their Peers." *Journal of College Student Personnel* 27:146–153.

Black, Donald J. 1978. "The Social Organization of Arrest." Pp. 154–160 in *Deviance: The Interactionist Perspective*, 2nd ed., edited by Earl Rubington and Martin S. Weinberg. New York: Macmillan.

Blimling, Gregory S., and Lawrence J. Miltenberger. 1990. *The Resident Assistant*. Dubuque, IA: Kendall/Hunt.

Cohn, Ellen, and Susan White. 1990. *Legal Socialization: A Study of Norms and Roles*. New York: Springer-Verlag.

Engs, Ruth C. 1977. "The Drinking Patterns and Problems of College Students." *Journal of Studies on Alcohol* 38:2144–2156.

Engs, Ruth C., and David J. Hanson. 1989a. "University Students' Drinking Patterns and Problems: Examining the Effects of Raising the Purchase Age." *Public Health Reports* 103:667–673.

Engs, Ruth C., and David J. Hanson. 1989b. "Reactance Theory: A Test with Collegiate Drinking." *Psychological Reports* 64:1083–1086.

Goode, William J. 1960. "A Theory of Role Strain." *American Sociological Review* 25:483–496.

Homans, George C. 1951. *The Human Group*. New York: Harcourt Brace.

Lombardo, Lucien X. 1989. *Guards Imprisoned: Correctional Officers at Work*. Cincinnati: Anderson.

Merton, Robert K. 1957 "The Role-Set: Problems in Sociological Theory." *British Journal of Sociology* 8:106–120.

Merz, Charles. 1970. *The Dry Decade.* Seattle, WA: University of Washington Press.

Moffatt, Michael. 1989. *Coming of Age in New Jersey: College and American Culture.* New Brunswick, NJ: Rutgers University Press.

Mosher, James F. 1980. "The History of Youthful-Drinking Laws: Implications for Current Policy." Pp. 11–38 in *Minimum Drinking-Age Laws,* edited by Henry Wechsler. Lexington, MA: Lexington Books.

O'Hare, T. M. 1990. "Drinking in College: Consumption Patterns, Problems, Sex Differences and Legal Drinking Age." *Journal of Studies on Alcohol* 51: 536–541.

Perrucci, Robert. 1974. *Circle of Madness.* Englewood Cliffs, NJ: Prentice-Hall.

Reiss, Albert J. 1971. *The Police and the Public.* Chicago: University of Chicago Press.

Rubington, Earl. 1990. "Drinking in the Dorms: The Etiquette of RA–Resident Relations." *Journal of Drug Issues* 20:451–461.

Rubington, Earl. 1991. "Drinking Sanctions and Freshman Residence Halls: An Exploratory Case Study." *Contemporary Drug Problems* 18:373–387.

Rubington, Earl. 1993a, August. "Drinking Sanctions and Freshman Residence Halls, 1989–1992." Paper delivered at the annual meeting of the Society for the Study of Social Problems, Arlington, VA.

Rubington, Earl. 1993b. "College Drinking and Social Control." *Journal of Alcohol and Drug Education* 39:56–65.

Upcraft, Lee. 1982. *Residence Hall Assistants in College.* San Francisco: Jossey-Bass.

Weisheit, Richard A. 1990. "Contemporary Issues in the Prevention of Adolescent Alcohol Abuse." Pp. 194–207 in *Alcoholism: Introduction to Theory and Treatment,* edited by David A. Ward. Dubuque, IA: Kendall/Hunt.

Westley, William. 1970. *Violence and the Police.* Cambridge, MA: MIT Press.

Williams, Robin M. 1970. *American Society.* New York: Alfred A. Knopf.

Zimmer, Lynn. 1986. *Women Guarding Men.* Chicago: University of Chicago Press.

Paranoia and the Dynamics of Exclusion

EDWIN M. LEMERT

One of the core values of American culture is individualism. Related to this is the value placed on effort. Thus, people succeed or fail on the basis of their individual efforts. In accounting for deviance, the individualist scheme of interpretation spills over: Deviance is seen to stem from the person's character rather than from a complex pattern of interactions with other people.

A familiar example of the individualist scheme of interpretation is the popular application of the psychiatric term "paranoid" in everyday life. Paranoids, it is said, are typically extremely suspicious persons who view the social world as a great conspiracy with everybody plotting against them. And the consensus is that this is a completely distorted view of the real world and by itself sufficient proof that the problem is "in their head" rather than in their social circle.

Edwin M. Lemert, after interviewing a number of mental patients who had been classified as paranoids and then studying the history of their exclusion in the workplace, developed an interactionist account for the circumstances under which the definition, interpretation, and actions against them occurred. He found the paranoids were not deluded.

People in fact had conspired against them. In all cases, groups in the workplace, after collectively defining them as "difficult persons," formed coalitions to exclude them from membership in their social circle. In responding to this process of mutual alienation and estrangement, these patients had assumed the role and status of the "paranoid."

The paranoid process begins with persistent interpersonal difficulties between the individual and his family, or his work associates and superiors, or neighbors, or other persons in the community. These frequently or even typically arise out of bona fide or recognizable issues centering upon some actual or threatened loss of status for the individual. This is related to such things as the death of relatives, loss of a position, loss of professional certification, failure to be promoted, age and physiological life cycle changes, mutilations, and changes in family and marital relationships. The status changes are distinguished by the fact that they leave no alternative acceptable to the individual, from whence comes their "intolerable" or "unendurable" quality. For example: the man trained to be a teacher who loses his certificate, which means he can never teach; or the man of 50 years of age who is faced with loss of promotion which is a regular order of upward mobility in an organization, who knows that he can't "start over"; or the wife undergoing hysterectomy, which mutilates her image as a woman.

In cases where no dramatic status loss can be discovered, a series of failures often is present, failures which may have been accepted or adjusted to, but with progressive tension as each new status situation is entered. The unendurability of the current status loss, which may appear unimportant to others, is a function of an intensified commitment, in some cases born of an awareness that there is a quota placed on failures in our society. Under some such circumstances, failures have followed the person, and his reputation as a "diffi-

cult person" has preceded him. This means that he often has the status of a stranger on trial in each new group he enters, and that the groups or organizations willing to take a chance on him are marginal from the standpoint of their probable tolerance for his actions.

The behavior of the individual—arrogance, insults, presumption of privilege and exploitation of weaknesses in others—initially has a segmental or checkered pattern in that it is confined to status-committing interactions. Outside of these, the person's behavior may be quite acceptable—courteous, considerate, kind, even indulgent. Likewise, other persons and members of groups vary considerably in their tolerance for the relevant behavior, depending on the extent to which it threatens individual and organizational values, impedes functions, or sets in motion embarrassing sequences of social actions. In the early generic period, tolerance by others for the individual's aggressive behavior generally speaking is broad, and it is very likely to be interpreted as a variation of normal behavior, particularly in the absence of biographical knowledge of the person. At most, people observe that "there is something odd about him," or "he must be upset," or "he is just ornery," or "I don't quite understand him" [1].

At some point in the chain of interactions, a new configuration takes place in perceptions others have of the individual, with shifts in figure-ground relations. The individual, as we have already indicated, is an ambiguous figure, comparable to textbook figures of stairs or outlined cubes which reverse themselves when studied intently. From a normal variant the person becomes "unreliable," "untrustworthy," "dangerous," or someone with whom others "do not wish to be involved." An illustration nicely apropos of this came out in

Reprinted from "Paranoia and the Dynamics of Exclusion," *Sociometry,* Vol. 25, No. 1 (March 1962), pp. 7–15, by permission of the author and the American Sociological Association.

the reaction of the head of a music department in a university when he granted an interview to a man who had worked for years on a theory to compose music mathematically:

> *When he asked to be placed on the staff so that he could use the electronic computers of the University I shifted my ground…when I offered an objection to his theory, he became disturbed, so I changed my reaction to "yes and no."*

As is clear from this, once the perceptual reorientation takes place, either as the outcome of continuous interaction or through the receipt of biographical information, interaction changes qualitatively. In our words it becomes *spurious,* distinguished by patronizing, evasion, "humoring," guiding conversation onto selected topics, underreaction, and silence, all calculated either to prevent intense interaction or to protect individual and group values by restricting access to them. When the interaction is between two or more persons it is cued by a whole repertoire of subtle expressive signs which are meaningful only to them.

The net effects of spurious interaction are to:

1. stop the flow of information to ego;
2. create a discrepancy between expressed ideas and affect among those with whom he interacts;
3. make the situation or the group image an ambiguous one for ego, much as he is for others.

Needless to say this kind of spurious interaction is one of the most difficult for an adult in our society to cope with, because it complicates or makes decisions impossible for him and also because it is morally invidious.[1]

The process from inclusion to exclusion is by no means an even one. Both individuals and members of groups change their perceptions and reactions, and vacillation is common, depending upon the interplay of values, anxieties and guilt on both sides. Members of an excluding group may decide they have been unfair and seek to bring the individual back into their confidence. This overture may be rejected or used by ego as a means of further attack. We have also found that ego may capitulate, sometimes abjectly, to others and seek group reentry, only to be rejected. In some cases compromises are struck and a partial reintegration of ego into informal social relations is achieved. The direction which informal exclusion takes depends upon ego's reactions, the degree of communication between his interactors, the composition and structure of the informal groups, and the perceptions of "key others" at points of interaction which directly affect ego's status.

ORGANIZATIONAL CRISIS AND FORMAL EXCLUSION

Thus far we have discussed exclusion as an informal process. Informal exclusion may take place but leave ego's formal status in an organization intact. So long as this status is preserved and rewards are sufficient to validate it on his terms, an uneasy peace between him and others may prevail. Yet ego's social isolation and his strong commitments make him an unpredictable factor; furthermore the rate of change and internal power struggles, especially in large and complex organizations, means that preconditions of stability may be short-lived.

Organizational crises involving a paranoid relationship arise in several ways. The individual may act in ways which arouse intolerable anxieties in others, who demand that "something be done." Again, by going to higher authority or making appeals outside the organization, he may set in motion procedures which leave those in power no other choice than to take action. In some situations ego remains relatively quiescent and does not openly attack the organization. Action against him is set off by growing anxieties or calculated motives of associates—in some cases his immediate superiors. Finally, regular organizational procedures incidental to promotion, retirement or reassignment may precipitate the crisis.

Assuming a critical situation in which the conflict between the individual and members of the organization leads to action to formally exclude him, several possibilities exist. One is the transfer of ego from one department, branch or division of the organization to another, a device frequently resorted to in the armed services or in large corporations. This requires that the individual be persuaded to make the change and that some department will accept him. While this may be accomplished in different ways, not infrequently artifice, withholding information, bribery, or thinly disguised threats figure conspicuously among the means by which the transfer is brought about. Needless to say, there is a limit to which transfers can be employed as a solution to the problem, contingent upon the size of the organization and the previous diffusion of knowledge about the transferee.

Solution number two we call encapsulation, which, in brief, is a reorganization and redefinition of ego's status. This has the effect of isolating him from the organization and making him directly responsible to one or two superiors who act as his intermediators. The change is often made palatable to ego by enhancing some of the material rewards of his status. He may be nominally promoted or "kicked upstairs," given a larger office, or a separate secretary, or relieved of onerous duties. Sometimes a special status is created for him.

This type of solution often works because it is a kind of formal recognition by the organization of ego's intense commitment to his status and in part a victory for him over his enemies. It bypasses them and puts him into direct communication with higher authority who may communicate with him in a more direct manner. It also relieves his associates of further need to connive against him. This solution is sometimes used to dispose of troublesome corporation executives, high-ranking military officers, and academic *personae non gratae* in universities.

A third variety of solutions to the problem of paranoia in an organization is outright discharge, forced resignation or non-renewal of appointment. Finally, there may be an organized move to have the individual in the paranoid relationship placed on sick leave, or to compel him to take psychiatric treatment. The extreme expression of this is pressure (as on the family) or direct action to have the person committed to a mental hospital.

The order of the enumerated solutions to the paranoid problem in a rough way reflects the amount of risk associated with the alternatives, both as to the probabilities of failure and of damaging repercussions to the organization. Generally, organizations seem to show a good deal of resistance to making or carrying out decisions which require expulsion of the individual or forcing hospitalization, regardless of his mental condition. One reason for this is that the person may have power within the organization, based upon his position, or monopolized skills and information,[2] and unless there is a strong coalition against him the general conservatism of administrative judgments will run in his favor. Herman Wouk's novel of *The Caine Mutiny* dramatizes some of the difficulties of cashiering a person from a position of power in an essentially conservative military organization. An extreme of this conservatism is illustrated by one case in which we found a department head retained in his position in an organization even though he was actively hallucinating as well as expressing paranoid delusions. Another factor working on the individual's side is that discharge of a person in a position of power reflects unfavorably upon those who placed him there. Ingroup solidarity of administrators may be involved, and the methods of the opposition may create sympathy for ego at higher levels.

Even when the person is almost totally excluded and informally isolated within an organization, he may have power outside. This weighs heavily when the external power can be invoked in some way, or when it automatically leads to raising questions as to the internal workings of the organization. This touches upon the more salient reason for reluctance to eject an uncooperative and retaliatory person, even when he is relatively unimportant to the organization. We refer to a kind of negative power derived from the vulnerability of organizations to unfavorable publicity and exposure of their private lives that are likely if the crisis proceeds to formal hearings, case review or litigation. This is an imminent possibility where paranoia exists. If hospital commitment is attempted, there is a possibility that a jury trial will be demanded, which will force leaders of the organization to defend their actions. If the crisis turns into a legal contest of this sort, it is not easy to prove insanity, and there may be damage suits. Even if the facts heavily support the petitioners, such contests can only throw unfavorable light upon the organization.

THE CONSPIRATORIAL NATURE OF EXCLUSION

A conclusion from the foregoing is that organizational vulnerability as well as anticipations of retaliations from the paranoid person lay a functional basis for conspiracy among those seeking to contain or oust him. Probabilities are strong that a coalition will appear within the organization, integrated by a common commitment to oppose the paranoid person. This, the exclusionist group, demands loyalty, solidarity and secrecy from its members; it acts in accord with a common scheme and in varying degrees utilizes techniques of manipulation and misrepresentation.

Conspiracy in rudimentary form can be detected in informal exclusion apart from an organizational crisis. This was illustrated in an office research team in which staff members huddled around a water cooler to discuss the unwanted associate. They also used office telephones to arrange coffee breaks without him and employed symbolic cues in his presence, such as humming the Dragnet theme song when he approached the group. An office rule against extraneous conversation was introduced with the collusion of supervisors, ostensibly for everyone, actually to restrict the behavior of the isolated worker. In another case an interview schedule designed by a researcher was changed at a conference arranged without him. When he sought an explanation at a subsequent conference, his associates pretended to have no knowledge of the changes.

Conspiratorial behavior comes into sharpest focus during organizational crises in which the exclusionists who initiate action become an embattled group. There is a concerted effort to gain consensus for this view, to solidify the group and to halt close interaction with those unwilling to completely join the coalition. Efforts are also made to neutralize those who remain uncommitted but who can't be kept ignorant of the plans afoot. Thus an external appearance of unanimity is given even if it doesn't exist.

Much of the behavior of the group at this time is strategic in nature, with determined calculations as to "what we will do if he does this or that." In one of our cases, a member on a board of trustees spoke of the "game being played" with the person in controversy with them. Planned action may be carried to the length of agreeing upon the exact words to be used when confronted or challenged by the paranoid individual. Above all there is continuous, precise communication among exclusionists, exemplified in one case by mutual exchanging of copies of all letters sent and received from ego.

Concern about secrecy in such groups is revealed by such things as carefully closing doors and lowering of voices when ego is brought under discussion. Meeting places and times may be varied from normal procedures; documents may be filed in unusual places and certain telephones may not be used during a paranoid crisis.

The visibility of the individual's behavior is greatly magnified during this period; often he is the main topic of conversation among the exclusionists, while rumors of the difficulties spread to other groups, which in some cases may be drawn into the controversy. At a certain juncture steps are taken to keep the members of the ingroup continually informed of the individual's movements and, if possible, of his plans. In effect, if not in form, this amounts to spying. Members of one embattled group, for example, hired an outside person unknown to their accuser to take notes on a speech he delivered to enlist a community organization on his side. In another case, a person having an office opening onto that of a department head was persuaded to act as an informant for the nucleus of persons working to depose the head from his position of authority. This group also seriously debated placing an all-night watch in front of their perceived malefactor's house.

Concomitant with the magnified visibility of the paranoid individual come distortions of his image, most pronounced in the inner coterie of exclusionists. His size, physical strength, cunning, and anecdotes of his outrages are exaggerated, with a central thematic emphasis on the fact that he is dangerous. Some individuals give cause for such beliefs in that previously they have engaged in violence or threats, others do not. One encounters characteristic contradictions in interviews on this point, such as: "No, he has never struck anyone around here—just fought with the policemen at the State Capitol," or "No, I am not afraid of him, but one of these days he will explode."

It can be said parenthetically that the alleged dangerousness of paranoid persons storied in fiction and drama has never been systematically demonstrated. As a matter of fact, the only substantial data on this, from a study of delayed admissions, largely paranoid, to a mental hospital in Norway, disclosed that "neither the paranoiacs nor paranoids have been dangerous, and most not particularly troublesome" [4]. Our interpretation of this, as suggested earlier, is that the imputed dangerousness of the paranoid individual does not come from physical fear but from the organizational threat he presents and the need to justify collective action against him.

However, this is not entirely tactical behavior—as is demonstrated by anxieties and tensions which mount among those in the coalition during the more critical phases of their interaction. Participants may develop fears quite analogous to those of classic conspirators. One leader in such a group spoke of the period of the paranoid crisis as a "week of terror," during which he was wracked with insomnia and "had to take his stomach pills." Projection was revealed by a trustee who, during a school crisis occasioned by discharge of an aggressive teacher, stated that he "watched his shadows," and "wondered if all would be well when he returned home at night." Such tensional states, working along with a kind of closure of communication within the group, are both a cause and an effect of amplified group interaction which distorts or symbolically rearranges the image of the person against whom they act.

Once the battle is won by the exclusionists, their version of the individual as dangerous becomes a crystallized rationale for official action. At this point misrepresentation becomes part of a more deliberate manipulation of ego. Gross misstatements, most frequently called "pretexts," become justifiable ways of getting his cooperation, for example, to get him to submit to psychiatric examination or detention preliminary to hospital commitment. This aspect of the process has been effectively detailed by Goffman, with his concept of a "betrayal funnel" through which a patient enters a hospital [5]. We need not elaborate on this, other than to confirm its occurrence in the exclusion process, complicated in our cases by legal strictures and the ubiquitous risk of litigation.

THE GROWTH OF DELUSION

The general idea that the paranoid person symbolically fabricates the conspiracy against him is in our estimation incorrect or incomplete. Nor can we agree that he lacks insight, as is so frequently claimed. To the contrary, many paranoid persons properly realize that they are being isolated and excluded by concerted interaction, or that they are being manipulated. However, they are at a loss to estimate accurately or realistically the dimensions and form of the coalition arrayed against them.

As channels of communication are closed to the paranoid person, he has no means of getting feedback on consequences of his behavior, which is essential for correcting his interpretations of the social relationships and organization which he must rely on to define his status and give him identity. He can only read overt behavior without the informal context. Although he may properly infer that people are organized against him, he can only use confrontation or formal inquisitorial procedures to try to prove this. The paranoid person must provoke strong feelings in order to receive any kind of meaningful communication from others—hence his accusations, his bluntness, his insults. Ordinarily this is non-deliberate; nevertheless, in one complex case we found the person consciously provoking discussions to get readings from others on his behavior. This man said of himself: "Some people would describe me as very perceptive, others would describe me as very imperceptive."

The need for communication and the identity which goes with it does a good deal to explain the preference of paranoid persons for formal, legalistic, written communications, and the care with which many of them preserve records of their contracts with others. In some ways the resort to litigation is best interpreted as the effort of the individual to compel selected others to interact directly with him as equals, to engineer a situation in which evasion is impossible. The fact that the person is seldom satisfied with the outcome of his letters, his petitions, complaints and writs testifies to their function as devices for establishing contact and interaction with others, as well as "setting the record straight." The wide professional tolerance of lawyers for aggressive behavior in court and the nature of Anglo-Saxon legal institutions, which grew out of a revolt against conspiratorial or star-chamber justice, mean that the individual

will be heard. Furthermore his charges must be answered; otherwise he wins by default. Sometimes he wins small victories, even if he loses the big ones. He may earn grudging respect as an adversary, and sometimes shares a kind of legal camaraderie with others in the courts. He gains an identity through notoriety....

NOTES

1. The interaction in some ways is similar to that used with children, particularly the *"enfant terrible."* The function of language in such interactions was studied by Sapir [2] years ago.
2. For a systematic analysis of the organizational difficulties in removing an "unpromotable" person from a position see [3].

REFERENCES

1. Cumming, E. and J. Cumming. 1957. *Closed Ranks.* Cambridge, Mass.: Harvard Press, Ch. 6.
2. Sapir, E. 1915. "Abnormal Types of Speech in Nootka." *Canada Department of Mines, Memoir 62* (5).
3. Levenson, B. 1961. "Bureaucratic Succession." In A. Etzioni (ed.), *Complex Organizations.* New York: Holt, Rinehart and Winston, pp. 362–395.
4. Ödegard, Ö. 1958. "A Clinical Study of Delayed Admissions to a Mental Hospital." *Mental Hygiene,* 42:66–67.
5. Goffman, E. 1959. "The Moral Career of the Mental Patient." *Psychiatry,* 22:127 ff.

The Moral Career of the Mental Patient

ERVING GOFFMAN

Textbooks on psychiatry distinguish neurosis from psychosis. Generally, neurotics make much trouble for themselves but little or none for others, are not dangerous to others, and can function in daily life. Generally, psychotics make as much trouble for others as they do for themselves, are often a danger to themselves as well as to others, and are less able to take care of themselves. Public opinion concurs with professional judgment but adds to it the important dimensions of fear, anxiety, and ambivalence. Lay and expert judgment concur that the most severely impaired are rightly confined to mental hospitals.

Erving Goffman counters this view with his own conception of three stages a person goes through as a "mental patient"—prepatient, patient, and ex-patient. Some degree of impairment in everyday life may be a condition for becoming a mental patient. But the sufficient condition according to him is the marshalling together of a team of laypersons as well as professional agents of social control who in concert facilitate the person's entry into the mental hospital. Hence, severity of impairment is of considerably less importance than the social organization of what he calls an *alienative coalition.* Once again, the social reaction to a pattern of behavior assumes considerably more importance than the pattern of behavior in its own right when a person becomes socially constructed as a deviant.

Traditionally the term *career* has been reserved for those who expect to enjoy the rises laid out within a respectable profession. The term is coming to be used, however, in a broadened sense to refer to any social strand of any person's course through life. The perspective of natural history is taken: unique outcomes are neglected in favor of such changes over time as are basic and common to the members of a social category, although occurring independently to each of them. Such a career is not a thing that can be brilliant or disappointing; it can no more be a success than a failure. In this light, I want to consider the mental patient, drawing mainly upon data collected during a year's participant observation of patient social life in a public mental hospital,[1] wherein an attempt was made to take the patient's point of view.

One value of the concept of career is its two-sidedness. One side is linked to internal matters held dearly and closely, such as image of self and felt identity; the other side concerns official position, jural relations, and style of life, and is part of a publicly accessible institutional complex. The concept of career, then, allows one to move back and forth between the personal and the public, between the self and its significant society, without having overly to rely for data upon what the person says he thinks he imagines himself to be.

This paper, then, is an exercise in the institutional approach to the study of self. The main concern will be with the *moral* aspects of career— that is, the regular sequence of changes that career entails in the person's self and in his framework of imagery for judging himself and others.[2]

Reprinted from "The Moral Career of the Mental Patient," *Psychiatry: Journal for the Study of Interpersonal Processes,* Vol. 22 (May 1959), pp. 123–135, by special permission of the author and The William Alanson White Psychiatric Foundation, Inc. Copyright © 1959 by The William Alanson White Psychiatric Foundation, Inc.

The category "mental patient" itself will be understood in one strictly sociological sense. In this perspective, the psychiatric view of a person becomes significant only insofar as this view itself alters his social fate—an alteration which seems to become fundamental in our society when, and only when, the person is put through the process of hospitalization.[3] I therefore exclude certain neighboring categories: the undiscovered candidates who would be judged "sick" by psychiatric standards but who never come to be viewed as such by themselves or others, although they may cause everyone a great deal of trouble;[4] the office patient whom a psychiatrist feels he can handle with drugs or shock on the outside; the mental client who engages in psychotherapeutic relationships. And I include anyone, however robust in temperament, who somehow gets caught up in the heavy machinery of mental hospital servicing. In this way the effects of being treated as a mental patient can be kept quite distinct from the effects upon a person's life of traits a clinician would view as psychopathological.[5] Persons who become mental hospital patients vary widely in the kind and degree of illness that a psychiatrist would impute to them, and in the attributes by which laymen would describe them. But once started on the way, they are confronted by some importantly similar circumstances and respond to these in some importantly similar ways. Since these similarities do not come from mental illness, they would seem to occur in spite of it. It is thus a tribute to the power of social forces that the uniform status of mental patient cannot only assure an aggregate of persons a common fate and eventually, because of this, a common character, but that this social reworking can be done upon what is perhaps the most obstinate diversity of human materials that can be brought together by society....[6]

The career of the mental patient falls popularly and naturalistically into three main phases: the period prior to entering the hospital, which I shall call the *prepatient phase;* the period in the hospital, the *inpatient phase;* the period after discharge from the hospital, should this occur, namely, the *ex-patient phase.*[7] This paper will deal only with the first...[phase].

THE PREPATIENT PHASE

A relatively small group of prepatients come into the mental hospital willingly, because of their own idea of what will be good for them, or because of wholehearted agreement with the relevant members of their family. Presumably these recruits have found themselves acting in a way which is evidence to them that they are losing their minds or losing control of themselves. This view of oneself would seem to be one of the most pervasively threatening things that can happen to the self in our society, especially since it is likely to occur at a time when the person is in any case sufficiently troubled to exhibit the kind of symptom which he himself can see. As Sullivan described it,

> What we discover in the self-system of a person undergoing schizophrenic changes or schizophrenic processes, is then, in its simplest form, an extremely fear-marked puzzlement, consisting of the use of rather generalized and anything but exquisitely refined referential processes in an attempt to cope with what is essentially a failure at being human—a failure at being anything that one could respect as worth being.[8]

Coupled with the person's disintegrative re-evaluation of himself will be the new, almost equally pervasive circumstance of attempting to conceal from others what he takes to be the new fundamental facts about himself, and attempting to discover whether others too have discovered them.[9] Here I want to stress that perception of losing one's mind is based on culturally derived and socially engrained stereotypes as to the significance of symptoms such as hearing voices, losing temporal and spatial orientation, and sensing that one is being followed, and that many of the most spectacular and convincing of these symptoms in some instances psychiatrically signify merely a temporary emotional upset in a stressful situation, however terrifying to the person at the time. Similarly, the anxiety consequent upon this perception of oneself, and the strategies devised to reduce this anxiety, are not a product of abnormal psychology, but would be exhibited by any person socialized into our culture who came to conceive of himself as someone losing his mind. Interestingly, subcultures in American society apparently differ in the amount of ready imagery and encouragement they supply for such self-views, leading to differential rates of *self*-referral; the capacity to take this disintegrative view of oneself without psychiatric prompting seems to be one of the questionable cultural privileges of the upper classes.[10]

For the person who has come to see himself—with whatever justification—as mentally unbalanced, entrance to the mental hospital can sometimes bring relief, perhaps in part because of the sudden transformation in the structure of his basic social situations; instead of being to himself a questionable person trying to maintain a role as a full one, he can become an officially questioned person known to himself to be not so questionable as that. In other cases, hospitalization can make matters worse for the willing patient, confirming by the objective situation what has theretofore been a matter of the private experience of self.

Once the willing prepatient enters the hospital, he may go through the same routine of experiences as do those who enter unwillingly. In any case, it is the latter that I mainly want to consider, since in America at present these are by far the more numerous kind.[11] Their approach to the institution takes one of three classic forms: they come because they have been implored by their family or threatened with the abrogation of family ties unless they go "willingly"; they come by force under police escort; they come under misapprehension purposely induced by others, this last restricted mainly to youthful prepatients.

The prepatient's career may be seen in terms of an extrusory model; he starts out with relationships and rights, and ends up, at the beginning of his hospital stay, with hardly any of either. The moral aspects of this career, then, typically begin with the experience of abandonment, disloyalty, and embitterment. This is the case even though to others it may be obvious that he was in need of treatment, and even though in the hospital he may soon come to agree.

The case histories of most mental patients document offense against some arrangement for face-to-face living—a domestic establishment, a work place, a semipublic organization such as a church or store, a public region such as a street or park. Often there is also a record of some *complainant,* some figure who takes that action against the offender which eventually leads to his hospitalization. This may not be the person who makes the first move, but it is the person who makes what turns out to be the first effective move. Here is the *social* beginning of the patient's career, regardless of where one might locate the psychological beginning of his mental illness.

The kinds of offenses which lead to hospitalization are felt to differ in nature from those which lead to other extrusory consequences—to imprisonment, divorce, loss of job, disownment, regional exile, noninstitutional psychiatric treatment, and so forth. But little seems known about these differentiating factors; and when one studies actual commitments, alternate outcomes frequently appear to have been possible. It seems true, moreover, that for every offense that leads to an effective complaint, there are many psychiatrically similar ones that never do. No action is taken; or action is taken which leads to other extrusory outcomes; or ineffective action is taken, leading to the mere pacifying or putting off of the person who complains. Thus, as Clausen and Yarrow have nicely shown, even offenders who are eventually hospitalized are likely to have had a long series of ineffective actions taken against them.[12]

Separating those offenses which could have been used as grounds for hospitalizing the offender from those that are so used, one finds a vast number of what students of occupation call career contingencies.[13] Some of these contingencies in the mental patient's career have been suggested, if not explored, such as socioeconomic status, visibility of the offense, proximity to a mental hospital, amount of treatment facilities available, community regard for the type of treatment given in available hospitals, and so on.[14] For information about other contingencies one must rely on atrocity tales: a psychotic man is tolerated by his wife until she finds herself a boyfriend, or by his adult children until they move from a house to an apartment; an alcoholic is sent to a mental hospital because the jail is full, and a drug addict because he declines to avail himself of psychiatric treatment on the outside; a rebellious adolescent daughter can no longer be managed at home because she now threatens to have an open affair with an unsuitable companion; and so on. Correspondingly there is an equally important set of contingencies causing the person to bypass this fate. And should the person enter the hospital, still another set of contingencies will help determine when he is to obtain a discharge—such as the desire of his family for his return, the availability of a "manageable" job, and so on. The society's official view is that inmates of mental hospitals are there primarily because they are suffering from mental illness. However, in the degree that the "mentally ill" outside hospitals numerically approach or surpass those inside hospitals, one could say that mental patients *distinctively* suffer not from mental illness, but from contingencies.

Career contingencies occur in conjunction with a second feature of the prepatient's career—*the circuit of agents*—and agencies—that participate fatefully in his passage from civilian to patient status.[15] Here is an instance of that increasingly important class of social system whose elements are agents and agencies, which are brought into systemic connection through having to take up and send on the same persons. Some of these agent-roles will be cited now, with the understanding that in any concrete circuit a role may be filled more than once, and a single person may fill more than one of them.

First is the *next-of-relation*—the person whom the prepatient sees as the most available of those upon whom he should be able to most depend in times of trouble; in this instance the last to doubt his sanity and the first to have done everything to save him from the fate which, it transpires, he has been approaching. The patient's next-of-relation is usually his next of kin; the special term is introduced because he need not be. Second is the *complainant*—the person who retrospectively appears to have started the person on his way to the hospital. Third are the *mediators*—the sequence of agents and agencies to which the prepatient is referred and through which he is relayed and processed on his way to the hospital. Here are included police, clergy, general medical practitioners, office psychiatrists, personnel in public clinics, lawyers, social service workers, school teachers, and so on. One of these agents will have the legal mandate to sanction commitment and will exercise it, and so those agents who precede him in the process will be involved in something whose outcome is not yet settled. When the mediators retire from the scene, the prepatient has become an inpatient, and the significant agent has become the hospital administrator.

While the complainant usually takes action in a lay capacity as a citizen, an employer, a neighbor, or a kinsman, mediators tend to be specialists and differ from those they serve in significant ways. They have experience in handling trouble, and some professional distance from what they handle. Except in the case of policemen, and perhaps some clergy, they tend to be more psychiatrically oriented than the lay public, and will see the need for treatment at times when the public does not.[16]

An interesting feature of these roles is the functional effects of their interdigitation. For example, the feelings of the patient will be influenced by whether or not the person who fills the role of complainant also has the role of next-of-relation—an embarrassing combination more prevalent, apparently, in the higher classes than in the lower.[17] Some of these emergent effects will be considered now.[18]

In the prepatient's progress from home to the hospital he may participate as a third person in what he may come to experience as a kind of *alienative coalition.* His next-of-relation presses him into coming to "talk things over" with a medical practitioner, an office psychiatrist, or some other counselor. Disinclination on his part may be met by threatening him with desertion, disownment, or other legal action, or by stressing the joint and explorative nature of the interview. But typically the next-of-relation will have set the interview up, in the sense of selecting the professional, arranging for time, telling the professional something about the case, and so on. This move effectively tends to establish the next-of-relation as the responsible person to whom pertinent findings can be divulged, while effectively establishing the other as the patient. The prepatient often goes to the interview with the understanding that he is going as an equal of someone who is so bound together with him that a third person could not come between them in fundamental matters; this after all, is one way in which close relationships are defined in our society. Upon arrival at the office the prepatient suddenly finds that he and his next-of-relation have not been accorded the same roles, and apparently that a prior understanding between the professional and the next-of-relation has been put in operation against him. In the extreme but common case the professional first sees the prepatient alone, in the role of advisor, while carefully avoiding talking things over seriously with them both together.[19] And even in those nonconsultative cases where public officials must forcibly extract a person from a family that wants to tolerate him, the next-of-relation is likely to be induced to "go along" with the official action, so that even here the prepatient may feel that an alienative coalition has been formed against him.

The moral experience of being third man in such a coalition is likely to embitter the prepatient, especially since his troubles have already probably led to some estrangement from his next-of-relation. After he enters the hospital, continued visits by his next-of-relation can give the patient the "insight" that his own best interests were being served. But the initial visits may temporarily strengthen his feeling of abandonment; he is likely to beg his visitor to get him out or at least to get him more privileges and to sympathize with the monstrousness of his plight—to which the visitor ordinarily can respond only by trying to maintain a hopeful note, by not "hearing" the requests, or by assuring the patient that the medical authorities know about these things and are doing what is medically best. The visitor then nonchalantly goes back into a world that the patient has learned is incredibly thick with freedom and privileges, causing the patient to feel that his next-of-relation is merely adding a pious gloss to a clear case of traitorous desertion.

The depth to which the patient may feel betrayed by his next-of-relation seems to be increased by the fact that another witnesses his betrayal—a factor which is apparently significant in many three-party situations. An offended person may well act forbearantly and accommodatively toward an offender when the two are alone, choosing peace ahead of justice. The presence of a witness, however, seems to add something to the implications of the offense. For then it is beyond the power of the offended and offender to forget about, erase, or suppress what has happened; the offense has become a public social fact.[20] When the witness is a mental health commission as is sometimes the case, the witnessed betrayal can verge on a "degradation ceremony."[21] In such circumstances, the offended patient may feel that some kind of extensive reparative action is required before witnesses, if his honor and social weight are to be restored.

Two other aspects of sensed betrayal should be mentioned. First, those who suggest the possibility of another's entering a mental hospital are not likely to provide a realistic picture of how in fact it may strike him when he arrives. Often he is told that he will get required medical treatment and a rest, and may well be out in a few months or so. In some cases they may thus be concealing what they know, but I think, in general, they will be telling what they see as the truth. For here there is a quite relevant difference between patients and me-diating professionals; mediators, more so than the public at large, may conceive of mental hospitals as short-term medical establishments where re-quired rest and attention can be voluntarily ob-tained, and not as places of coerced exile. When the prepatient finally arrives he is likely to learn quite quickly, quite differently. He then finds that the information given him about life in the hospital has had the effect of his having put up less resis-tance to entering than he now sees he would have put up had he known the facts. Whatever the inten-tions of those who participated in his transition from person to patient, he may sense they have in effect "conned" him into his present predicament.

I am suggesting that the prepatient starts out with at least a portion of the rights, liberties, and satisfactions of the civilian and ends up on a psy-chiatric ward stripped of almost everything. The question here is *how* this stripping is managed. This is the second aspect of betrayal I want to consider.

As the prepatient may see it, the circuit of significant figures can function as a kind of *be-trayal funnel.* Passage from person to patient may be effected through a series of linked stages, each managed by a different agent. While each stage tends to bring a sharp decrease in adult free status, each agent may try to maintain the fiction that no further decrease will occur. He may even manage to turn the prepatient over to the next agent while sustaining this note. Further, through words, cues, and gestures, the prepatient is implicitly asked by the current agent to join with him in sustaining a running line of polite small talk that tactfully avoids the administrative facts of the situation, be-coming, with each stage, progressively more at odds with these facts. The spouse would rather not have to cry to get the prepatient to visit a psychia-trist; psychiatrists would rather not have a scene when the prepatient learns that he and his spouse are being seen separately and in different ways; the police infrequently bring a prepatient to the hospital in a strait jacket, finding it much easier all

around to give him a cigarette, some kindly words, and freedom to relax in the back seat of the patrol car; and finally, the admitting psychiatrist finds he can do his work better in the relative quiet and luxury of the "admission suite" where, as an incidental consequence, the notion can survive that a mental hospital is indeed a comforting place. If the prepatient heeds all of these implied requests and is reasonably decent about the whole thing, he can travel the whole circuit from home to hospital without forcing anyone to look directly at what is happening or to deal with the raw emo-tion that his situation might well cause him to ex-press. His showing consideration for those who are moving him toward the hospital allows them to show consideration for him, with the joint re-sult that these interactions can be sustained with some of the protective harmony characteristic of ordinary face-to-face dealings. But should the new patient cast his mind back over the sequence of steps leading to hospitalization, he may feel that everyone's *current* comfort was being busily sus-tained while his long-range welfare was being un-dermined. This realization may constitute a moral experience that further separates him for the time from the people on the outside.[22]

I would now like to look at the circuit of ca-reer agents from the point of view of the agents themselves. Mediators in the person's transition from civil to patient status—as well as his keep-ers, once he is in the hospital—have an interest in establishing a responsible next-of-relation as the patient's deputy or *guardian;* should there be no obvious candidate for the role, someone may be sought out and pressed into it. Thus while a per-son is gradually being transformed into a patient, a next-of-relation is gradually being transformed into a guardian. With a guardian on the scene, the whole transition process can be kept tidy. He is likely to be familiar with the prepatient's civil in-volvements and business, and can tie up loose ends that might otherwise be left to entangle the hospital. Some of the prepatient's abrogated civil rights can be transferred to him, thus helping to sustain the legal fiction that while the prepatient does not actually have his rights he somehow actually has not lost them.

Inpatients commonly sense, at least for a time, that hospitalization is a massive unjust deprivation, and sometimes succeed in convincing a few persons on the outside that this is the case. It often turns out to be useful, then, for those identified with inflicting these deprivations, however justifiably, to be able to point to the cooperation and agreement of someone whose relationship to the patient places him above suspicion, firmly defining him as the person most likely to have the patient's personal interest at heart. If the guardian is satisfied with what is happening to the new inpatient, the world ought to be.[23]

Now it would seem that the greater the legitimate personal stake one party has in another, the better he can take the role of guardian to the other. But the structural arrangements in society which lead to the acknowledged merging of two persons' interests lead to additional consequences. For the person to whom the patient turns for help—for protection against such threats as involuntary commitment—is just the person to whom the mediators and hospital administrators logically turn for authorization. It is understandable, then, that some patients will come to sense, at least for a time, that the closeness of a relationship tells nothing of its trustworthiness.

There are still other functional effects emerging from this complement of roles. If and when the next-of-relation appeals to mediators for help in the trouble he is having with the prepatient, hospitalization may not, in fact, be in his mind. He may not even perceive the prepatient as mentally sick, or, if he does, he may not consistently hold to this view.[24] It is the circuit of mediators, with their great psychiatric sophistication and their belief in the medical character of mental hospitals, that will often define the situation for the next-of-relation, assuring him that hospitalization is a possible solution and a good one, that it involves no betrayal, but is rather a medical action taken in the best interests of the prepatient. Here the next-of-relation

may learn that doing his duty to the prepatient may cause the prepatient to distrust and even hate him for the time. But the fact that this course of action may have had to be pointed out and prescribed by professionals, and be defined by them as a moral duty, relieves the next-of-relation of some of the guilt he may feel.[25] It is a poignant fact that an adult son or daughter may be pressed into the role of mediator, so that the hostility that might otherwise be directed against the spouse is passed on to the child.[26]

Once the prepatient is in the hospital, the same guilt-carrying function may become a significant part of the staff's job in regard to the next-of-relation.[27] These reasons for feeling that he himself has not betrayed the patient, even though the patient may then think so, can later provide the next-of-relation with a defensible line to take when visiting the patient in the hospital and a basis for hoping that the relationship can be reestablished after its hospital moratorium. And of course this position, when sensed by the patient, can provide him with excuses for the next-of-relation, when and if he comes to look for them.[28]

Thus while the next-of-relation can perform important functions for the mediators and hospital administrators, they in turn can perform important functions for him. One finds, then, an emergent unintended exchange or reciprocation of functions, these functions themselves being often unintended.

The final point I want to consider about the prepatient's moral career is its peculiarly *retroactive* character. Until a person actually arrives at the hospital there usually seems no way of knowing for sure that he is destined to do so, given the determinative role of career contingencies. And until the point of hospitalization is reached, he or others may not conceive of him as a person who is becoming a mental patient. However, since he will be held against his will in the hospital, his next-of-relation and the hospital staff will be in great need of a rationale for the hardships they are sponsoring. The medical elements of the staff will also need evidence that they are still in the trade they were trained for. These problems are eased, no doubt unintentionally, by the case-history construction that is placed on the patient's past life, this having the effect of demonstrating that all along he had been becoming sick, that he finally became very sick, and that if he had not been hospitalized much worse things would have happened to him—all of which, of course, may be true. Incidentally, if the patient wants to make sense out of his stay in the hospital, and, as already suggested, keep alive the possibility of once again conceiving of his next-of-relation as a decent, well-meaning person, then he too will have reason to believe some of this psychiatric workup of his past.

Here is a very ticklish point for the sociology of careers. An important aspect of every career is the view the person constructs when he looks backward over his progress; in a sense, however, the whole of the prepatient career derives from this reconstruction. The fact of having had a prepatient career, starting with an effective complaint, becomes an important part of the mental patient's orientation, but this part can begin to be played only after hospitalization proves that what he had been having, but no longer has, is a career as a prepatient....

NOTES

1. The study was conducted during 1955–56 under the auspices of the Laboratory of Socio-environmental Studies of the National Institute of Mental Health. I am grateful to the Laboratory Chief, John A. Clausen, and to Dr. Winfred Overholser, Superintendent, and the late Dr. Jay Hoffman, then First Assistant Physician of Saint Elizabeth's Hospital, Washington, D.C., for the ideal cooperation they freely provided. A preliminary report is contained in Goffman, "Interpersonal Persuasion," pp. 117–193; in *Group Processes: Transactions of the Third Conference,* edited by Bertram Schaffner; New York, Josiah Macy, Jr. Foundation, 1957. A shorter version of this paper was presented at the Annual Meeting of the American Sociological Society, Washington, D.C., August, 1957.

2. Material on moral career can be found in early social anthropological work on ceremonies of status transition, and in classic social psychological descriptions

of those spectacular changes in one's view of self that can accompany participation in social movements and sects. Recently new kinds of relevant data have been suggested by psychiatric interest in the problem of "identity" and sociological studies of work careers and "adult socialization."

3. This point has recently been made by Elaine and John Cumming, *Closed Ranks;* Cambridge, Commonwealth Fund, Harvard Univ. Press, 1957; pp. 101–102. "Clinical experience supports the impression that many people define mental illness as 'That condition for which a person is treated in a mental hospital.'...Mental illness, it seems, is a condition which afflicts people who must go to a mental institution, but until they do almost anything they do is normal." Leila Deasy has pointed out to me the correspondence here with the situation in white-collar crime. Of those who are detected in this activity, only the ones who do not manage to avoid going to prison find themselves accorded the social role of the criminal.

4. Case records in mental hospitals are just now coming to be exploited to show the incredible amount of trouble a person may cause for himself and others before anyone begins to think about him psychiatrically, let alone take psychiatric action against him. See John A. Clausen and Marian Radke Yarrow, "Paths to the Mental Hospital," *J. Social Issues* (1955) 11:25–32; August B. Hollingshead and Frederick C. Redlich, *Social Class and Mental Illness;* New York, Wiley, 1958; pp. 173–174.

5. An illustration of how this perspective may be taken to all forms of deviancy may be found in Edwin Lemert, *Social Pathology;* New York, McGraw-Hill, 1951; see especially pp. 74–76. A specific application to mental defectives may be found in Stewart E. Perry, "Some Theoretic Problems of Mental Deficiency and Their Action Implications," *Psychiatry* (1954) 17:45–73; see especially p. 68.

6. [Goffman developed this point more fully as follows.] Whatever...the various patient's psychiatric diagnoses, and whatever the special ways in which social life on the "inside" is unique, the researcher can find that he is participating in a community not significantly different from any other he has studied. Conscientious objectors who voluntarily went to jail sometimes arrived at the same conclusion regarding criminal inmates. See, for example, Alfred Hassler, *Diary of a Self-made Convict;* Chicago, Regnery, 1954; p. 74.

7. This simple picture is complicated by the somewhat special experience of roughly a third of ex-patients—

namely, readmission to the hospital, this being the recidivist or "repatient" phase.

8. Harry Stack Sullivan, *Clinical Studies in Psychiatry,* edited by Helen Swick Perry, Mary Ladd Gavel, and Martha Gibbon; New York, Norton, 1956; pp. 184–185.

9. This moral experience can be contrasted with that of a person learning to become a marihuana…[user], whose discovery that he can be "high" and still "op" effectively without being detected apparently leads to a new level of use. See Howard S. Becker, "Marihuana Use and Social Control," *Social Problems* (1955) 3:35–44; see especially pp. 40–41.

10. See Hollingshead and Redlich, *op. cit.,* p. 187, Table 6, where relative frequency is given of self-referral by social class grouping.

11. The distinction employed here between willing and unwilling patients cuts across the legal one, of voluntary and committed, since some persons who are glad to come to the mental hospital may be legally committed, and of those who come only because of strong familial pressure, some may sign themselves in as voluntary patients.

12. Clausen and Yarrow, *op. cit.*

13. An explicit application of this notion to the field of mental health may be found in Edwin M. Lemert, "Legal Commitment and Social Control," *Sociology and Social Research* (1946) 30:370–378.

14. For example, Jerome K. Meyers and Leslie Schaffer, "Social Stratification and Psychiatric Practice: A Study of an Outpatient Clinic," *Amer. Sociological Rev.* (1954) 19:307–310. Lemert, see footnote 5; pp. 402–403. *Patients in Mental Institutions, 1941;* Washington, D.C., Department of Commerce, Bureau of the Census, 1941; p. 2.

15. For one circuit of agents and its bearing on career contingencies, see Oswald Hall, "The Stages of a Medical Career," *Amer. J. Sociology* (1948) 53:327–336.

16. See Cumming and Cumming, *op. cit.;* p. 92.

17. Hollingshead and Redlich, *op. cit.;* p. 187.

18. For an analysis of some of these circuit implications for the inpatient, see Leila C. Deasy and Olive W. Quinn, "The Wife of the Mental Patient and the Hospital Psychiatrist," *J. Social Issues* (1955) 11:49–60. An interesting illustration of this kind of analysis may also be found in Alan G. Gowman, "Blindness and the Role of Companion," *Social Problems* (1956) 4:68–75. A general statement may be found in Robert Merton, "The Role Set: Problems in Sociological Theory," *British J. Sociology* (1957) 8:106–120.

19. I have one case record of a man who claims he thought *he* was taking his wife to see the psychiatrist, not realizing until too late that his wife had made the arrangements.

20. A paraphrase from Kurt Riezler, "The Social Psychology of Shame," *Amer. J. Sociology* (1943) 48:458.

21. See Harold Garfinkel, "Conditions of Successful Degradation Ceremonies," *Amer. J. Sociology* (1956) 61:420–424.

22. Concentration camp practices provide a good example of the function of the betrayal funnel in inducing cooperation and reducing struggle and fuss, although here the mediators could not be said to be acting in the best interests of the inmates. Police picking up persons from their homes would sometimes joke good-naturedly and offer to wait while coffee was being served. Gas chambers were fitted out like delousing rooms, and victims taking off their clothes were told to note where they were leaving them. The sick, aged, weak, or insane who were selected for extermination were sometimes driven away in Red Cross ambulances to camps referred to by terms such as "observation hospital." See David Boder, *I Did Not Interview the Dead;* Urbana, Univ. of Illinois Press, 1949; p. 81; and Elie A. Cohen, *Human Behavior in the Concentration Camp;* London, Cape, 1954; pp. 32, 37, 107.

23. Interviews collected by the Clausen group at NIMH suggest that when a wife comes to be a guardian the responsibility may disrupt previous distance from in-laws, leading either to a new supportive coalition with them or to a marked withdrawal from them.

24. For an analysis of these nonpsychiatric kinds of perception, see Marian Radke Yarrow, Charlotte Green Schwartz, Harriet S. Murphy, and Leila Calhoun Deasy, "The Psychological Meaning of Mental Illness in the Family," *J. Social Issues* (1955) 11:12–24; Charlotte Green Schwartz, "Perspectives on Deviance—Wives' Definitions of Their Husbands' Mental Illness," *Psychiatry* (1957) 20:275–291.

25. This guilt-carrying function is found, of course, in other role-complexes. Thus, when a middle-class couple engages in the process of legal separation or divorce, each of their lawyers usually takes the position that his job is to acquaint his client with all of the potential claims and rights, pressing his client into demanding these, in spite of any nicety of feelings about the rights and honorableness of the ex-partner. The client, in all good faith, can then say to self and to the ex-partner that the de-

mands are being made only because the lawyer insists it is best to do so.

26. Recorded in the Clausen data.

27. This point is made by Cumming and Cumming, see *op. cit.;* p. 129.

28. There is an interesting contrast here with the moral career of the tuberculosis patient. I am told by Julius Roth that tuberculous patients are likely to come to the hospital willingly, agreeing with their next-of-relation about treatment. Later in their hospital career, when they learn how long they yet have to stay and how depriving and irrational some of the hospital rulings are, they may seek to leave, be advised against this by the staff and by relatives, and only then begin to feel betrayed.

PART TWO

THE FORMAL REGULATION OF DEVIANCE

In addition to typing on an informal, interpersonal level, much typing of deviants occurs on a formal or official level. In fact, complex societies such as ours invariably include formal agencies whose role it is to seek out, identify, and regulate deviance. Such agencies include the police, the courts, the federal Drug Enforcement Administration, the Department of the Treasury (whose agents deal with smuggling), county and state health and welfare agencies—the list could go on and on. When these agencies of social control take action against someone adjudged deviant, the effects can be dramatic. These may include a formal confirmation of deviant typing, induction into a deviant role, and launching on a deviant career. This turning point in the deviant's life can also bring about a radical redefinition of self. What the deviant may experience as a unique personal crisis, however, is usually merely organizational routine for the agent and the agency.

The controls that such agents and agencies can impose differ significantly from those available to lay people. In terms of power, for example, the political state stands behind many agencies, while informal labelers may be no more powerful than the deviant. Likewise, the agents' control is usually legitimized by the state, whereas labeling by other people may simply represent an opposing set of norms. Finally, agents of social control usually operate according to an elaborate set of rules that provide standardized ways of dealing with deviants; other people's actions against the deviant need not be based on any plan at all.

AGENCIES AND THEIR THEORIES

A special perspective, composed of rules, beliefs, and practices, underlies the formal processing of deviants. In the course of their work with deviant clients, agents of social control come to adopt this perspective. As they become more familiar with the agency's perspective, agents find that they can process their deviant clients more efficiently. And, as these conceptions become routine for agents, so does their processing of deviants take on a routine character.

Agencies of control also put forth claims as to why they should be the sole organization to handle deviance and how they would go about regulating the social deviants who come to their official attention. Common to all of these agencies and organizations is their ideology. All of these special ideologies have three major ideas: etiology, or how people become deviants; treatment rationale, or how the agency processes its deviant clientele; and justification, or the basis of the agency's claim for expertise in regulating deviance.

The growth and expansion of agents and agencies within the institutions of religion, criminal justice, and medicine have only added to the relativization of deviance. In addition, they have fueled increasing conflicts between agencies concerning jurisdiction over and theories about particular types of deviance. In addition to professional specialization, there are two other developments adding to the complexity of organized responses to deviance. One is the privatization of police and corrections. The other is the spread of numerous mutual-help movements that have fashioned themselves after the model of Alcoholics Anonymous.

ORGANIZATIONAL PROCESSING OF DEVIANTS

Once persons have been socially designated as deviants, they can be subject to two kinds of organizational processing. In the first instance, they have allegedly violated the law or breached taken-for-granted rules of interpersonal conduct. They can come to the attention of the formal agencies of criminal justice or institutions of mental health. In the second instance, they have broken the rules of some complex organization in which they are an employer, employee, member, student, or client. Complex organizations, such as colleges, corporations, and schools, have their own internal agencies of control, primarily to respond to organizational troublemakers.

Despite the differences in the degrees of deviance and the ways in which deviants come to be clients of these two types of agencies, both kinds of agencies face similar kinds of problems. Hard-pressed to perform their work, often because of the number of clients, agents of control devise a shared perspective. This perspective evolves primarily through close and frequent interaction with colleagues. Not only does the agent's perspective help in categorizing the people who have come to the attention of the agency, but it also helps in specifying which agent should do what and when, and how and why action should be taken in the course of the client's contact with the agency. Perhaps most important of all are those unwritten rules, derived from the perspective, that prescribe the kinds of treatment the clients may or may not receive. In effect an etiquette of agency-client relations obtains. In addition, the fusion of agent's and agency goals often plays a major part in the organizational processing of clients through intake, screening, and agency action, as well as after discharge. As a consequence, the variety of agency labels of deviance go a long way toward simplifying the work of agents at the same time that they are fixating clients into deviant roles.

THE EFFECTS OF CONTACT WITH CONTROL AGENTS

When a person comes into contact with an agency of social control, the agency may view the person solely in terms of a deviant label. Initial contact with such an agency may suffice to call into question the person's "good name." Additional contact may give the person a definitely bad reputation.

Thus deviant typing may not end with the person's experience with a given agency. When meeting a stranger, for example, people look for information to help them type the stranger. If they find out that a person has been in a prison or mental hospital, they may type the person primarily on the basis of that past experience, assuming that a person who has had contact with an agency of social control is likely to repeat the behavior that originally led to that contact. Accordingly, laypeople feel less inclined to trust such a person. The agency perspective is so powerful that a deviant label, once formally applied, can long outlive any evidentiary basis. Once formally labeled, the so-called deviant becomes defined as the kind of person who probably did perform the imputed behaviors, or at least would if given a chance. Both the deviant and others may then organize their social relations around this belief.

CHAPTER 5

AGENCIES AND THEIR THEORIES

Case Routinization in Investigative Police Work

WILLIAM B. WAEGEL

In everyday life people sometimes come into contact with specific instances of deviance. Some but not necessarily all of these contacts may be crises for them. By contrast, what may be a crisis for laypeople in everyday life turns out to be routine for agents of social control. Their official task is to process cases of deviant behavior that come before them. The sheer number of clients with whom agents come into frequent contact generates a need for classification. Agents classify the cases that come before them in accordance with organizational requirements, informal work norms, and status concerns. In order to manage the many cases they have to deal with, they devise a set of constructions that give rise to recipes for handling cases in the most efficient manner for themselves as well as for the agency in which they work.

William B. Waegel shows how detectives produce reports and arrests that meet supervisors' demands and enhance their own chances for promotion. They classify cases in accordance with the chances that arrests are likely or unlikely to be made. According to detectives' routine conceptions, 10 percent of burglary cases are likely to produce an arrest, while 90 percent are unlikely to. Thus, in the absence of solid information, detectives frequently suspend cases because they are unlikely to produce arrests. They fit these cases to the constructed stereotypes they have fashioned (often without any basis in fact) to expedite their goals and the agency's.

...In the police department studied,[1] detectives face two practical problems which substantially shape the manner in which cases are handled. They must satisfy the paperwork demands of the

Reprinted from "Case Routinization in Investigative Police Work," *Social Problems,* Vol. 28, No. 3 (February 1981), pp. 263–275, by permission of the Society for the Study of Social Problems and the author. Copyright © 1981 by the Society for the Study of Social Problems.

organization (referred to as "keeping the red numbers down") by classifying each case and producing a formal investigative report within two weeks after the case is assigned. Sanctions may be applied to those who fail to meet deadlines and who thus accumulate too many "red numbers." At the same time, the detectives are under the same pressure as other employees: they must produce. Specifically, detectives believe they must produce an acceptable level of arrests which will enhance their chances of remaining in the detective division and gaining promotion. While no arrest quota is formalized in the division, there is a shared belief that one should produce roughly two to three lock-ups per week. This arrest level is a practical concern for the detective because most wish to remain in the division and avoid transfer "back to the pit" (i.e., back into uniform in the patrol division). Moreover, the position of detective holds the highest status of any assignment in the department, and a transfer, therefore, generally entails a loss of status.

For the vast majority of cases handled, no explicit procedures exist to indicate what must be done on the case and how to go about doing it. As detectives go about the ordinary business of investigating and processing cases, they can select strategies ranging from a *pro forma* victim interview comprising the total investigative activity devoted to the case, to a full-scale investigation involving extensive interviewing, physical evidence, the use of informants, interrogation, surveillance, and other activities. The selection of a particular handling strategy in most cases is an informal process and not the direct result of formal organizational policy or procedure. This process of selection is grounded in practical solutions to concrete problems faced by the detective; it consists of an assignment of meaning to persons and events in ways that are regarded as proper because they have "worked" in previous cases.

A great deal of actual detective work may thus be seen as a process of mapping the features of a particular case onto a more general and commonly recognized *type* of case. The present work suggests that a detective's interpretation, classification, and handling of cases is guided by a set of occupationally shared typifications. The categorization schemes used by detectives center around specific configurations of information regarding the victim, the offense, and possible suspects. Information pertaining to these three elements constitutes the meaningful unit that detectives deal with: the case.

The most basic dimension of case categorization is that of the routine versus the nonroutine. Where a particular configuration of information regarding the victim, the offense, and possible suspects appears, the competent detective understands the case as a routine one—as an instance of a familiar type—and particular handling strategies are deemed appropriate. Such cases contrast with those which are viewed as nonroutine: that is, where no general type is available to which the case reasonably corresponds, and where the case is vigorously investigated and the detective attends to the unique features of the case. Case routinization is most characteristic for burglaries, which comprise the bulk of cases handled by detectives, but it is also exhibited in the handling of many assault, robbery, rape, and homicide cases.

The categorization schemes used by detectives are derived from concrete experiences in working cases and are continually assessed for their relevance, adequacy, and effectiveness in handling one's caseload. It is because typificatory schemes serve as a solution to practical problems commonly faced by all detectives that they learn to share most of the content of these schemes. Both through direct experience in working cases and through interaction with other members, the detective learns to categorize and handle cases in ways that are regarded as proper by other detectives.

Routine case imageries serve as resources upon which detectives may draw to construct a solution to their problem of interpreting, investigating, and resolving their cases. The features of a specific case are compared with routine case imagery in a process of interpretive interplay. In some instances a correspondence is readily apparent, in others a fit is forced by the detective, and in still others the features of a specific case render the use of the typical imagery inappropriate. The interpretation and handling of a case may also change over the case's history; a routine case may come to be treated as nonroutine upon the receipt of additional information, and vice versa.

THE ORGANIZATIONAL CONTEXT
OF CASE ROUTINIZATION

In the department studied, detectives have no formal guidelines for allocating time and effort to different cases and there is little effective monitoring of daily activities by supervisors.[2] In conducting their work, detectives are, however, guided and constrained by two organizational imperatives: 1) the requirement to submit investigative reports, and 2) the requirement to produce arrests. In other words, the work is not organized by formal rules, but rather by the kinds of outcomes that are expected. Both of these expected outcomes generate practical problems leading to routinized solutions.

An investigative report must be produced for each case assigned, and its submission within the prescribed time limit is viewed as a fundamental constraint on how vigorously different cases can be investigated. Departmental policy indicates that each investigative report submitted must be reviewed and signed by a supervisory lieutenant. However, in practice, these reports are often given only a cursory glance, and seldom is the content of a report questioned or challenged by a lieutenant. The primary concern of the supervisor is that the submission of reports comply with time deadlines.

The potential a case appears to hold for producing an arrest also has an important impact on how the case will be handled. Most detectives believe that the number of arrests they produce will be used as a basis for evaluating performance and, therefore, will affect decisions regarding promotions and transfers. Attempts to cope with the practical problems of meeting paperwork demands, while at the same time producing a satisfactory number of arrests, creates a situation in which one burglary case involving a $75 loss may receive less than five minutes' investigative effort, yet another case with an identical loss may be worked on exclusively for two or three full days. These two concerns constitute central features of the work setting which structure case handling.

PAPERWORK

Formal organizational procedure demands that a case be investigated, classified, and a report produced within a specified time period after it is assigned. Detectives experience paperwork requirements and deadlines as central sources of pressure and tension in their job, and stories abound concerning former detectives who "could handle the job but couldn't handle the paperwork."

Most cases are assigned during the daily roll-call sessions. At this point, the information about the incident consists of an original report written by a patrol officer and any supplemental reports submitted by personnel in the evidence detection unit. Each case is stamped with a "red number" which supervisors use to monitor compliance with report deadlines.

Ordinary cases require the submission of two reports within specific time periods. A brief first-day report, consisting essentially of an interview with the victim, is formally required the day after the case is assigned. However, this deadline is generally ignored by supervisors and first-day reports are seldom submitted. The more meaningful deadline for detectives is the fourteen-day limit for the submission of an investigative report. Here, the detective must provide a detailed accounting of the activities undertaken in investigating the incident and assign an investigative status to the case. Compliance with this second deadline is closely monitored; every Sunday a lieutenant draws up a list of each detective's overdue red numbers, and this list is read at the next roll call along with a caution to keep up with one's paperwork.

In the investigative report, the detective must classify the status of the investigation as suspended, closed arrest, or open. The ability to manipulate information about cases to fit them into these categories is of the utmost importance to detectives, for it is through such strategic manipulations that they are able to manage their caseloads effectively.

Of the total cases handled by a detective, a substantial majority are classified as suspended.

This means that the steps already taken in the investigation (which may consist merely of a telephone interview with the victim) have not uncovered sufficient information to warrant continued investigation of the incident. Any number of acceptable reasons for suspending a case may be offered, ranging from a simple statement that the victim declines to prosecute up to a fairly elaborate report detailing contacts with the victim, the entry of serial numbers of stolen articles into the computerized crime files, the usefulness of evidence obtained from the scene, and a conclusion that the case must be suspended because there are no further investigative leads. Over 80 percent of the burglary cases assigned in the city are suspended; this percentage drops considerably for robbery cases and even more for assault, rape, and homicide cases.[3]

An investigation is classified as closed when one or more arrests have been made pertaining to the incident and the detective anticipates no additional arrests. A case is classified as open when an investigation extends beyond the fourteen-day limit but it is expected that an arrest eventually will be made. Generally, only major cases may remain classified as open after the fourteen-day investigative period.

PRODUCING ARRESTS

As organizations become more bureaucratized and their procedures more formalized, there evolves a general tendency to develop quantitative indices or measures of individual performance. In the department studied, most detectives believe that the crude number of lock-ups they make is used as a basis for assessing their performance and competence in doing investigative work. Every arrest a detective makes is entered into a logbook, which is available for inspection by superiors and from which they can compare each detective's arrest level with that of others.

Ambitious detectives in particular are very conscious of producing a steady stream of arrests, feeling that this is an effective way to achieve recognition and promotion. One young detective boasted:

> *I've made over forty lock-ups since the beginning of the year and eleven in April alone. Since I don't really have a godfather in here, I gotta depend on making good lock-ups if I'm gonna make sergeant.*

This detective's use of the term "godfather" reveals a widely shared belief that some individuals are promoted not because of their performance but because they have a friend or relative in a position of power within the department.

Skimming off selected cases from one's workload is widely practiced as a means of achieving a steady stream of arrests. The practice of skimming refers to 1) selectively working only those cases that appear potentially solvable from information contained in the original report, and 2) summarily suspending the remainder of one's ordinary cases. Supervisors are certainly aware of both aspects of this practice, but they recognize its practical value in producing arrests. Moreover, supervisors, to a greater extent than working detectives, find their performance assessed in crude quantitative terms, and they are likely to be questioned by superiors if arrest levels begin to drop sharply. Supervisors support the practice of skimming even though they recognize that it ensures that a majority of ordinary cases will never receive a thorough investigation. The pragmatic work orientation of detectives is further revealed in the lack of attention given to conviction rates by both detectives and supervisors. Competence and productivity are judged by the arrests made, not by the proportion of cases which survive the scrutiny of the judicial process.

The recognition of potentially productive cases and of their utility in effectively managing one's caseload is among the earliest skills taught to the neophyte in the detective division. Moreover, newcomers are taught that their work on burglary cases is the primary basis upon which their performance will be judged. In a sizeable percentage of crimes against persons, the perpetrator is readily identified from information provided by the victim. Since no great investigative effort or acumen is involved, the same credit is not accorded an arrest in this type of case as in burglary cases. Detectives are expected to produce a steady flow of "quality" arrests: that is, arrests involving some effort and skill on the part of the investigator. Straightforward assault cases involving acquainted parties, for example, are often handed out by supervisors along with a remark such as "Here's an easy one for you."

INTERPRETING CASES

The preceding observations have suggested that detectives are constrained in their conception and handling of cases not by the formal organization of their work or by supervisory surveillance, but rather by the bureaucratic pressure of writing reports and producing the proper number and quality of arrests. The process of interpreting cases in accordance with these pragmatic concerns may now be considered.

Data derived from observation of detective-victim interviews and from written case reports provide a basis for examining the interpretive schemes used by detectives. In the victim interview, the kinds of questions asked and the pieces of information sought out reveal the case patterns recognized as routine for the different offenses commonly encountered.[4] However, in attempting to make sense of the incident at hand, detectives attend to much more than is revealed in their explicit communications with the victim. Interpretation of the case is also based upon understanding of the victim's lifestyle, racial or ethnic membership group, class position, and possible clout or connections—especially as these factors bear upon such concerns as the likelihood of the victim inquiring into the progress of the investigation, the victim's intentions regarding prosecution, and the victim's competence and quality as a source of information.

The interpretive schemes employed also receive partial expression in the written investiga-

tive reports which must be produced for each case. These reports contain a selective accounting of the meaning assigned to a case, the information and understandings upon which this interpretation is based, and the reasonableness of the linkage between this particular interpretation of the case and the handling strategy employed.[5]

Several important features of the process of interpreting cases as routine or nonroutine may be seen in the following incidents.

CASE 1: ATTEMPTED HOMICIDE

A radio call was broadcast that a shooting had just occurred on the street in a working-class residential area. The victim, a white male, was still conscious when the detectives arrived, although he had been severely wounded in the face by a shotgun blast. He indicated that he had been robbed and shot by three black males, and provided a vague description of their appearance and clothing. This description was broadcast, an area search was initiated, the crime scene was cordoned off, and a major investigation was begun.

The following morning, the victim's employer brought into question the account of the incident that had been provided. He indicated his belief that the incident involved a "lover's triangle" situation between the victim, a male acquaintance of the victim, and a woman. All three were described as "hillbillies." The three parties were interviewed separately and each denied this version of the incident. After further questioning, the victim finally admitted that the story concerning three black males was false, but would say nothing more about the incident. Articles of the woman's clothing believed to show bloodstains and a weapon believed to have been used were obtained, but crime lab analysis would take at least three weeks. The case was now interpreted as a routine "domestic shooting" and little additional effort was devoted to it.

CASE 2: BURGLARY

A detective parked his car in front of an address in a public housing project and pulled out the original burglary report. A new member of the prosecutor's office was riding along to observe how detectives work. The detective read over the report, and after hesitating for awhile decided to go into the residence. He explained to the prosecutor that the loss was an inexpensive record player and added, "This one's a pork chop, like most of the burglaries we get. But we gotta go and interview the victim before suspending it." The detective asked the victim if she knew who might have committed the burglary or if she had heard about anyone committing burglaries in the area. Negative replies followed both questions. The entire encounter with the victim lasted less than two minutes.

CASE 3: ASSAULT AND ROBBERY

A robbery squad detective was waiting for two victims to come in the hall to be interviewed. Both were black, middle-aged, center-city residents who were described by the detective as "dead-end alcoholics." They had been robbed in their residence by a young male who had forced his way in, taken $20 from the pair, and cut the female victim on the hand with a knife. The victims were able to provide the detective with the name of their assailant, and they both picked his photograph out of a number of pictures they were shown. Several minutes later the detective handed them a photograph of a different individual, asking, "Are you sure this is the guy who robbed you?" After inspecting the picture they replied that they knew this person as well but he had not been the one who robbed them. At this point, the detective sat down and took a formal statement from the victims.

When the victims had left, the detective explained his views and usual handling of such "ghetto robberies": "In a case like this, what can we do? To tell you the truth, the only way this kind of thing is going to stop is for the victims or somebody they know to kill this guy off. My involvement in this case is minimal. If the two victims, those two old drunks, if they sober up and if

they show up in court, we'll see how they do there. It's up to them here and not up to me."

CASE 4: BURGLARY

A detective entered the center-city residence of a burglary victim in a block where about one-fourth of the row houses were vacant. He examined a large hole in a basement wall that had been made to gain entry, and then sat down to compile a list of articles that had been stolen. The victim had literally been cleaned out, losing every easily transportable item of value she had owned. The woman explained that she worked during the day, that this was the fifth time she had been burglarized in the past four years, and that her coverage had been dropped by the insurance company. She added that she lived in the house for 21 years and was not about to move, and then asked, "What can I do to keep this from happening again?" The detective replied: "Ma'am, I don't know what to tell you. You're the only white family on this block. Most of the people around here work during the daytime, and a lot of these people, even if they saw somebody coming out of your house with some of your stuff, they're not going to call the cops anyhow. That's the way it is around here. It's a shame, but that's the way it is." The detective entered the serial numbers of some of the stolen articles into the computerized stolen property files, "to cover myself, just in case." The written report indicated that the pawn shop sheets had been checked but in fact this step was not taken. When the report deadline approached, the case was suspended.

CASE 5: HOMICIDES

Two homicides had occurred over the weekend. On Monday morning two detectives who were working on the different cases were discussing the status of their investigations. One detective, who was investigating a shooting death that occurred in a crowded bar in the presence of 100 persons noted that he was on the verge of making a lockup even though none of the witnesses present had voluntarily come forward. The other detective was investigating the bludgeoning death of a male homosexual whose body had been found by firemen called to extinguish a small fire in the victim's residence. There were as yet no suspects in the case. The second detective took offense to remarks made by the other comparing the lack of progress in the second case to the nearly completed investigation in the barroom case. The second detective remarked, "Anybody can handle a killing like you've got. What we've got here is a murder, not a killing."

The above incidents illustrate detectives' use of a body of accumulated knowledge, beliefs, and assumptions which lead to the interpretation of certain case patterns as common, typical, and routine. Cases are interpreted primarily using conceptions of 1) how identifiable the perpetrators seem to be; 2) the normal social characteristics of the victims; and 3) the settings involved, and behavior seen as typical in such settings. A detective's initial efforts on a case tend to focus on these three aspects, in the process of assigning meaning to the case and selecting an appropriate strategy for handling it.

1. Conceptions of how different kinds of offenses are typically committed—especially how identifiable the perpetrators seem to be—are routinely used in interpreting incidents. These imageries are specifically relevant to a detective's practical concerns. The ordinary burglary (Cases 2 and 4) is seen as involving a crude forced entry at a time of day or at a location where it is unlikely that anyone will witness the perpetrator entering or exiting. A burglary victim's ability or inability to provide information identifying a probable perpetrator constitutes the single feature of burglary cases which is given greatest interpretive significance. In roughly 10 percent of these cases, the victim provides the name of a suspected perpetrator (commonly an ex-boyfriend, a relative, or a neighboring resident), and vigorous effort is devoted to the case. For the remaining burglary

cases, the initial inclination is to treat them as routine incidents deserving of only minimal investigative effort. In these routine cases the victim's race and class position have a decisive impact on whether the case will be summarily suspended or whether some minor investigative activities will be undertaken to impress the victim that "something is being done."

On the other hand, assault, rape, and homicide cases commonly occur in a face-to-face situation which affords the victim an opportunity to observe the assailant. Further, detectives recognize that many personal assault offenses involve acquainted parties. The earliest piece of information sought out and the feature of such cases given the greatest interpretive significance is whether the offense occurred between parties who were in some way known to one another prior to the incident. The interpretation and handling of the shooting incident in Case 1 changed markedly when it was learned that the victim and suspect were acquainted parties and that the offense reasonably conformed to a familiar pattern of domestic assaults. Where the victim and perpetrator are acquainted in assault, rape, and homicide cases, the incident is seen as containing the core feature of the routine offense pattern for these cases. In such incidents a perfunctory investigation is usually made, for the identity of the perpetrator generally is easily learned from the victim or from persons close to the victim.

The barroom homicide in Case 5 was termed a "killing" and viewed as a routine case because the victim and perpetrator were previously acquainted and information linking the perpetrator to the crime could be easily obtained. The term "murder" is reserved for those homicides which do not correspond to a typical pattern.

A somewhat different pattern follows in the category of incidents which detectives refer to as "suspect rapes." Victims having certain social characteristics (females from lower-class backgrounds who are viewed as having low intelligence or as displaying some type of mental or emotional abnormality) are viewed as most likely to make a false allegation of rape. Where a victim so perceived reports a sexual assault by a person with whom she had some prior acquaintance, the initial orientation of the detective is to obtain information which either negates the crime of rape (the complainant actually consented) or warrants reducing the charge to a lesser offense. Where the victim and assailant were not previously acquainted, the case receives a vigorous investigative effort. The level of police resources devoted to the case varies according to the race and social standing of the victim.

2. Conceptions of the normal social characteristics of victims are also central to case routinization. Victims having different social characteristics are regarded as being more or less likely to desire or follow through with prosecution in the case, to be reliable sources of information about it, and to inquire as to the outcome of the investigation.

The treatment of the assault and robbery in Case 3 illustrates how a case may be interpreted and handled primarily in terms of the victim's class position, race, and presumed lifestyle and competencies. The case was cleared by arrest on the basis of information provided by the victims, but the handling of this "ghetto robbery" involved little actual police effort. No attempt was made to locate witnesses, gather evidence from the crime scene, or otherwise strengthen the case against the accused.

Poor and working-class people who are regarded as unlikely to make inquiries regarding the handling and disposition of the case are seen as typical of victims in the category of routine burglaries. Case 2 illustrates how the interpretation of an incident may be accomplished solely on the basis of information contained in the patrol report and prior to an actual interview with the victim. The interview was structured in this case by the detective's expectation of its outcome.

Case 4 illustrates how inconsistent elements in an otherwise routine pattern (in this instance the victim's social status and apparent interest in

the handling of the case) are managed to suit the purposes of the detective. Detectives speak of a case "coming back on them" if a respectable victim contacts superiors regarding progress in the case when the incident has received little or no investigative effort. Informing the victim that the case was not solvable largely because of her neighbor's attitudes enabled the detective to suspend the case with minimal problems.

3. Routinization formulas, finally, contain conceptions of the settings in which different kinds of offenses normally occur and the expected behavior of inhabitants of those settings. While assumptions about victims and perpetrators are derived in part from the nature of the offense involved, the physical and social setting where the incident occurred also contributes to a detective's understanding of these parties. The fact that the burglary in Case 2 occurred in a particular public housing project told the detective much of what he felt he had to know about the case. It should be noted that none of these perceptions were communicated to the prosecutor observing the detective work; they were part of the taken-for-granted background upon which the detective based his handling of the case.

With regard to actual and potential *witnesses,* however, a detective's assumptions and beliefs are based primarily on the offense setting, if the witness is seen as a normal inhabitant of that setting. (This latter qualification simply recognizes that detectives attribute different inclinations and sentiments to social workers or salesmen who may have witnessed an incident than to residents of the area who may have witnessed a crime.)

The impact of territorial conceptions may be seen in the handling of Case 4. Routine burglaries occur mainly in low-income housing projects, residences in deteriorating center-city areas or, less frequently, in commercial establishments in or near these locations. Residents of these areas are considered unlikely to volunteer that they have witnessed a crime. Although official investigative procedure dictates that neighboring residents be interviewed to determine whether they saw or heard anything that might be of value to the investigation, this step was not undertaken in Cases 2 or 4 because it was assumed that the residents would be uncooperative.

Routine cases, then, may be seen as having two components, one at the level of consciousness and cognition, and the other at the level of observable behavior. A detective's interpretation of a case as routine involves an assessment of whether sufficient correspondence exists between the current case and some typical pattern to warrant handling it in the normal way. The criterion of sufficient correspondence implies that not all the elements of the typical pattern need be present for a detective to regard a case as a routine one. Common elements are viewed and used as resources which may be drawn upon selectively in accordance with one's practical concerns and objectives. Further, when certain elements in a case appear inconsistent with the typical pattern, there is a tendency to force and manage a sufficient fit between the particular and the typical in ways that help detectives deal with their caseload management problems and constraints.

These features of the interpretation process mean that the assessments of the routine or nonroutine nature of a case take on more of the character of a dichotomy than a continuum. Once an assessment is made, the case will be handled by means of prescribed formulas unless additional information changes the interpretation. It must be emphasized that the routinization process is not a matter of automatic or unreflective mapping of case features onto more general conceptions of criminal incidents. The interpretation of any particular case is shaped by a detective's understandings of what is required and expected and of how to manage these concerns effectively.

CASE HANDLING

Case handling normally proceeds in accordance with informal understandings shared among detectives. Routine case patterns are associated with prescribed handling recipes. It is critical to an understanding of investigative police work that interpretation of criminal incidents as routine or nonroutine largely determines which cases will be summarily suspended, which will be investigated, and how vigorous or extensive that investigation will be.

The characteristic behavioral element of a routine case is an absence of vigorous or thorough investigative effort. Two distinct sets of circumstances are ordinarily encountered in routine cases which lead to such a superficial or cursory investigative effort. The first, most common in burglary and robbery cases, is that the available information concerning the incident is seen as so meager or of so little utility that the possibility of making a quick arrest is virtually nonexistent. Viewing the case as nonproductive, and not wishing to expend effort on cases for which there are no formal rewards, the detective produces a brief investigative report detailing the routine features of the incident, concludes the case summary with "N.I.L." (no investigative leads were found), and classifies it as a suspended case.

The second set of circumstances associated with an absence of vigorous investigative effort involves assault, rape, and homicide cases which require some investigation because of their seriousness and the possibility of scrutiny by the judicial process. However, in many such incidents the facts of the case are so obvious and straightforward that little actual investigative work needs to be done. In these three types of offenses the victim and perpetrator are often known to one another, and it is not at all uncommon for the victim to name the assailant as soon as the police arrive. Cases in which a spouse or lover is still standing by the victim with weapon in hand when the police arrive, or in which the victim names the perpetrator before expiring, are not unusual. In essence, such cases are solved without any substantial police investigation. The detective is obligated to produce a comprehensive report on the incident, and the investigation is generally classified as closed in this report if the perpetrator has been apprehended. Indeed, in such obvious and straightforward cases the detective's only difficult task may be that of locating the perpetrator.[6]

Handling recipes associated with routine cases have a practical and instrumental character, reflecting the objective circumstances surrounding the investigation of many criminal events. After all, in the great majority of burglary cases the probability of ascertaining the identity of the perpetrator is rather small. Yet, handling recipes reflect certain *beliefs* and *assumptions* on the part of detectives concerning such matters as a victim's willingness to cooperate fully in the case, whether persons in particular sections of the city are likely to volunteer information about a crime, or the kind of impression a victim or witness would make in court. Such beliefs and assumptions constitute integral features in the construction of cases as routine or nonroutine, and they represent a pivotal linkage between specific features of cases and particular handling recipes.

The following incident illustrates the extent to which case handling may be guided by the detective's beliefs and assumptions about the nature of an incident and the parties involved:

CASE 6:

A detective was assigned a case in which a man had stabbed his common-law wife in the arm with a kitchen knife. The patrol report on the incident indicated that the woman had been taken to City Hall to sign an arrest warrant, while the man had been arrested by patrol officers on the charge of felony assault and released on his own recognizance. Nominally, the detective was required to collect additional information and evidence relating to the incident and to write a detailed and comprehensive report which would be used in prosecuting the case. However, the detective's interpretation of the incident, based on his understanding of the area in which it occurred and the lifestyles of the persons involved, led him to view any further investigative effort on his part as futile. He remarked: "These drunks, they're always stabbing one another over

here. Then you see 'em the next day and they're right back together again. She won't show up in court anyhow. Why waste my time and everybody else's on it." The handling of the case involved only the production of a brief report which concluded: "The victim in this complaint wishes no further investigation by the police department. This complaint is to be classified as closed."

The interpretive schemes used by detectives are not based solely on their experiences as police investigators, but also on their accumulated experiences as everyday social actors; they thus reflect commonsense social knowledge. Categorizations made by detectives about race, class, ethnicity, sex, and territory parallel wider cultural evaluations of morality and worth. None of the features of the formal organization of detective work substantially reduces this reliance on commonsense knowledge and its typical biases, prejudices, and interpretations.

SUMMARY AND IMPLICATIONS

Some general features of case routinization may now be noted in an attempt to clarify the interpretive activities through which detectives achieve order and predictability in their handling of cases and their encounters with victims and other relevant actors.

1. Shortly after receipt of a case, specific pieces of information are sought out and attended to for use in assessing the typicality of the incident. That is, the fundamental case-working orientation of detectives involves an attempt to establish commonalities between an actual case and typical case patterns. Incidents having typical features are interpreted and constructed as some variety of routine case. The orientation to typify and routinize cases is partly traceable to bureaucratic pressures and constraints to meet paperwork deadlines and produce a certain quantity and quality not of convictions but of arrests.

2. The interpretation of an incident is accomplished by attending to case features having commonly recognized utility as indicators of the type of case at hand. Detectives use such routinization schemes unless some problematic feature of an actual case brings into question their applicability and appropriateness. The interpretation of a case as routine or nonroutine essentially determines whether the case will be quickly closed or suspended or whether it will receive a more vigorous and extensive investigation. However, this initial assignment of meaning is provisional and subject to revision or modification upon receipt of additional information. Most importantly, the handling of cases is directed by these informal categorization schemes and is not the result of formal organizational policy or procedures. These schemes constitute a taken-for-granted background of decision making.

3. The interpretive schemes shared by detectives represent "successful" solutions to common practical problems, based on experience and shared understandings about the nature of urban crime and about types of urban residents, lifestyles, and territories. These understandings are rooted in socially distributed as well as role-specific knowledge, for both provide a basis for constructing solutions to work problems. Occupationally specific knowledge provides a set of instructions for interpreting case patterns in ways which enable a detective to successfully manage organizational constraints and demands. Commonsense social knowledge provides an understanding of the typical characteristics, attitudes, and action patterns of persons encountered. Identities may be readily assigned to persons by drawing on this stock of knowledge. Such identity assignments structure case handling along race, class, age, sex, and territorial lines in ways that are intended to minimize case handling problems. Because of this reliance on general social knowledge, the treatment of different types of urban residents tends to reflect wider cultural evaluations of social worth.

4. The essential nature of these interpretive processes is phenomenological rather than mechanical or rule-guided. In formulating a particular case, the operative process involves a determination of whether sufficient correspondence exists between the actual case and the paradigmatic case to warrant handling the incident in routine, low-effort ways. Sufficient correspondence assessments are accomplished in ways that serve the practical purposes of detectives, especially those of paperwork compliance and productivity.

5. Accordingly, routine cases are not constituted as a single determinant pattern. A variety of combinations of case features may result in routine handling of the case. For each offense, a core feature or set of features gets maximum interpretive significance. When a core feature is recognized in a particular case, other features which are ambiguous or even contradictory tend to be interpreted in a manner consistent with the identified core feature. Additional interpretive features, particularly the social status of the victim, are used as resources in selecting a safe and workable handling strategy.

6. In highly routinized case patterns, there is a tendency to squeeze great indicativeness out of a few case features. Detectives often rely upon assumptions to add detail to a case rather than actually gather information to further specify the type of case at hand. In other words, it is frequently taken for granted that certain investigative procedures will have predictable outcomes. Frequently, this process manifests itself in the fudging, doctoring, and manipulation of formal organizational reports.

It is likely that interpretive schemes having similar features will be found in all bureaucratically organized enterprises where large numbers of clients or cases are processed (e.g., social service centers, public hospitals, and other agencies in the criminal justice system). Whenever we find an organizational setting where members deal with similar events time and again, and where there are no features in the formal organization of the work which act to counter stereotyping, we may expect to find routinization schemes in use. These schemes will be used to categorize the population and apply standard patterns of treatment to each category.

These observations have significant implications for the study of decision making by legal agents. Decision making by bureaucratic agents inevitably involves discretion on the part of the agent who must fit general rules to particular cases. This discretionary latitude will be reflected in different forms of decision making in different kinds of organizational settings. The work of Roth (1977), Scheff (1978), Sudnow (1965), and others suggests that caseload size, amount of information readily available about the person or event, the nature of the body of knowledge used, and the expectation of future interaction with the person are crucial features governing the nature of the decision-making process. Where caseloads are high, continued interaction is not anticipated, minimal information is available, and the body of knowledge used by the agent is imprecise—stereotypes tend to become the operative and binding basis for decision making. Accordingly, detective work, presentence casework, public defender work, and medical practice in clinics or emergency rooms may be seen as lying toward the end of a continuum where typifications act as essentially final judgments.

At the other end of the continuum are settings where caseload sizes are smaller, more detailed information about the person is available, future interaction is anticipated, and decision making is grounded in a more substantial body of knowledge. In such settings, typificatory schemes are likely to be used only as provisional hypotheses, to be amplified and modified over the course of the encounter. Thus in probation work, some types of social service work, and the practice of general medicine, we might expect to find interaction only tentatively structured by stereotypic understandings. As interaction proceeds in these latter settings, typifications will begin to fade in importance as the basis for decision making.

NOTES

1. The description and the analysis presented here are based on nine months of participant observation field work in a city police detective division. Further information about access agreements, characteristics of the city and department, the field role adopted, and problems encountered during the research is available from the author.

2. An exception to this general observation occurs where a supervisor imposes a "major case" definition on an incident. In highly publicized or nonroutine homicide or rape cases, especially those involving higher status victims, a supervisor frequently takes an active part in the investigation and more closely monitors and directs the activities of detectives. With regard to the influence of the victim's social status on case handling, see Wilson's (1968:27) analysis of police perceptions of the legitimacy of complaints made by middle-class versus lower-class victims.

3. Official nationwide clearance rates are listed as 17.6% for burglary, 27.3% for robbery, 63.4% for felonious assault, 51.1% for rape, and 79.9% for homicide (Hindelang *et al.*, 1977).

4. Cf. Sudnow's (1965) argument that public defenders use their first interview with a client to gain an initial sense of the defendant's place in the social structure as well as the typicality or lack thereof of the offense with which the person has been charged.

5. Garfinkel (1967:186–207) argues that organizational records are not to be treated as accurate or mirror reflections of the actual handling of a client or case by organizational members. However, these records can be employed to examine how members go about constructing a meaningful conception of a client or case and use it for their own practical purposes. Any valid sociological use of such records requires detailed knowledge on the part of the researcher regarding the context in which the records are produced, background understandings of members, and organizationally relevant purposes and routines.

6. Reiss (1971) makes a similar observation. He found that a great deal of detective work in the department studied merely involves attempting to locate identified perpetrators. The Rand survey of investigative practices in 153 police departments draws conclusions similar to those presented here. It was found that substantially more than half of all serious reported crimes receive no more than superficial attention from investigators (Greenwood and Petersilia, 1975).

REFERENCES

Garfinkel, Harold. 1967. *Studies in Ethnomethodology.* Englewood Cliffs, N.J.: Prentice-Hall.

Greenwood, Peter W. and Joan Petersilia. 1975. The *Criminal Investigation Process,* Volume I. Santa Monica, Calif.: The Rand Corporation.

Hindelang, M., M. Gottfredson, C. Dunn and N. Parisi. 1977. *Sourcebook of Criminal Justice Statistics.* Washington, D.C.: National Criminal Justice Information and Statistics Service.

Reiss, Albert. 1971. *Police and the Public.* New Haven: Yale University Press.

Roth, Julius. 1977. "Some contingencies of the moral evaluation and control of clients." *American Journal of Sociology* 77 (October):830–856.

Scheff, Thomas. 1978. "Typification in rehabilitation agencies." Pp. 172–175 in E. Rubington and M. S. Weinberg (eds.), *Deviance: The Interactionist Perspective.* New York: Macmillan.

Sudnow, David. 1965. "Normal crimes: Sociological features of the penal code in a public defender's office." *Social Problems* 12 (3):255–276.

Wilson, James Q. 1968. *Varieties of Police Behavior.* Cambridge, Mass.: Harvard University Press.

Control Agents and the Creation of Deviant Types

KATHRYN J. FOX

A division of labor specifies what institution of social control will respond to an alleged violation of norms. The nature of the control that is anticipated as being the necessary one determines the institution to which it is assigned. Criminal justice takes charge when it is assumed that an offender could have controlled his or her conduct but chose not to. Health agencies assume responsibility when offenders are assumed to be unable to control their conduct. Social welfare agencies respond when offenders are assumed to have had neither choice nor control. Subsequently, the criminal justice system confines and punishes the persons found guilty of crimes. Health agencies treat offenders whose putative illness is believed to have caused their violations. Social welfare agencies help or support those seen as having been victimized by social or natural disasters. These social definitions regarding personal control further shape the production and use of constructions of the deviance by control agents within these institutions of social control.

Kathryn J. Fox studied a treatment unit for violent offenders in a Vermont prison. She spells out some of the conditions and consequences of a particular construction of deviance. Caseworkers held that errors in thinking always preceded violent behavior. In twice-weekly group meetings, two caseworkers and eight inmates met to go over inmates' past and present instances of rule-breaking. Workers had inmates search in both talk and writing for their errors in thought. Many inmates saw this search as an attempt to cram many varieties of behavior into one narrow category. When they resisted the workers' interpretation of their actions, workers simply interpreted their resistance as but another instance of errors in their thinking. And whenever inmates became angry in the group meetings, workers took their anger as evidence confirming their overarching conception of a "criminal type." Fox's study calls attention to an irony of formal social control: Agency staff tend to induce behavior in their interactions with inmates, patients, or clients that can confirm their stereotypes of deviants.

The institutional production of social types and identities has been studied extensively throughout various parts of the criminal justice system by early ethnomethodologists and others (Cicourel 1968; Quinney 1970; Skolnick 1966; Sudnow 1965). In other institutional settings, researchers have documented the significance of interactional dynamics between "expert" (or official) agents and clients. Agents rely on representations of particular types and, in turn, interpret clients' actions as evidence of the veracity of the construction (Frohmann 1991; Garfinkel 1967; Goffman 1961; Holstein 1992, 1993; Loseke 1989; Maynard 1984; Miller 1991, 1992; Pfohl 1978). These studies share an interest in the ways in which "collective representations" (Durkheim 1953) of particular "types" of people influence officials' and helping professionals' actions and, as such, have power in producing realities. These representations can help to manufacture a "social type"—a reductionist characterization that subsumes diverse client experiences into a narrow interpretation of those experiences (Holstein 1992; Loseke 1989, 1992; Miller 1992). Often these typologies are built into the institutional rhetoric, having "political consequences" insofar as they express the intersection of power and knowledge (Edelman 1977, p. 59)....

I observed the construction of criminal "types" in a cognitive therapy program for violent offenders in prison. The Cognitive Self-Change (CSC) program, which is in operation in several Vermont correctional facilities, maintains that violent offenders' "cognitive distortions" explain their criminality. The program works with violent offenders to reorient their "thinking" about or perceptions of their own lives and selves....

METHODS

I observed CSC group meetings for approximately eight months, conducted formal and infor-

Reprinted from *The Sociological Quarterly*, Vol. 40, No. 3 (Summer 1999), pp. 435–453, by permission. Copyright © 1999 by The Midwest Sociological Society.

mal interviews with inmates and facilitators, and participated in CSC training sessions. In addition, I formally interviewed two administrators in the Vermont Department of Corrections and informally interviewed several program facilitators. The majority of the findings presented here come from observation of group sessions, focusing on dialogue among facilitators and participants in the CSC program....

THE TALK OF CSC

The CSC groups I attended were held in a regional correctional facility that housed both men and women at various security levels. Each group consisted of eight inmate participants and two cofacilitators. A few facilitators were subcontractors who worked in mental health fields. However, most CSC facilitators were correctional caseworkers and probation/parole officers. According to a program designer, the "use of authority is the keystone piece"—a concept that reveals the function of employing correctional workers as group facilitators.

Participation in the CSC program was voluntary, yet an inmate would not be eligible for early release without completing the program, so nearly all chose to participate. This paradox of voluntary coercion (Peyrot 1985) created a situation in which, as the program designer said, "They're going to try to please us and they're going to show their resentment at the same time." This context allowed anger to fester and find expression, and, in turn, reinforced an interpretation of criminals as having distinctively derelict, aggressive thought processes.

Meetings were held twice a week and lasted for an hour and a half each. In each group, inmates reflected upon their criminal histories and current, as well as past, situations that put them "at risk" for violence. Every session began with a "check-in" in which each inmate reported a recent risky situation that either could have or did prompt an angry or aggressive response. The inmates were asked to report the situation "objectively"; thus, the requisite format insisted that they refrain from evaluative language. For example, an inmate phrased a situation "someone snapped at me for no reason" and was informed that her phrasing included an unnecessary judgment. The group analyzed each situation for the thoughts, feelings, attitudes, and beliefs that surrounded it. Inmates were asked to report several different thoughts and feelings to learn how to identify the ones that preceded and motivated anger and/or violence. Thoughts were often "fuck this" or "I can't believe this shit." Feelings were usually reported as "anger, frustration, irritation, upset," and so on. A "good" check-in identified the "risk" for "going off on someone" that may be involved in particular ways of thinking, as well as some intervention thoughts to help deescalate a situation. Intervention thoughts were often of the variety "it's not worth doing more time."

Some meeting sessions focused exclusively on check-ins, depending upon how long they took and the extent to which other matters arose. Check-ins might fill the entire meeting if facilitators challenged participants' characterization of the situation. For example, if a report of a "situation" involved a lengthy explanation of what others were doing "to" the inmate, facilitators would be prompted to point out the error in that kind of thinking. Usually, after check-ins, a particular individual might post a thinking report (similar to a written check-in on a risky situation or crime) for the group to help analyze for life patterns or to question the integrity of the account. The facilitators might challenge the objectivity of the account if, for example, the report focused heavily on the inmate's own victimization. Or perhaps one inmate might present his or her "Fearless Criminal Inventory" (FCI), which is supposed to be an honest and thoughtful history of one's rule-breaking behaviors, beginning with the earliest one and including rule breaking in prison. FCIs included the reasons behind their actions and the consequences of them in hopes of finding a similar theme or pattern that motivated a particular individual's criminal impulses. In sum, the CSC program concentrated exclu-

sively on the connection between thoughts (and their relationship to feelings, attitudes, and beliefs) and actions; as such, reports of rule-breaking behaviors by inmates were decontextualized from situations and rearticulated as the product of thinking errors characteristic of criminals.

In the group sessions, facilitators instructed participants in the language of the CSC program. Inmates needed to recast their crimes within the sanctioned interpretive and linguistic framework (Pollner and Stein 1994). For example, inmates selected "patterns" from a list that best explained their personal thought processes. The list described the typical "thinking errors" of criminal personalities; for instance, among the most popular ones were "victim stance" (feeling victimized by others), "justification," "power thrust" (needing power and control over others), and "failure to consider others." Intervention thoughts for avoiding future crimes, especially violent ones, were designed based upon inmates' understandings of their life patterns.

The CSC program literature stressed that the program did not insist that inmates change, rather that they demonstrate that they know *how* to change—which meant that they must explain how they *could* intervene in their thought process. One facilitator confided: "I'm saying, 'I'm not trying to tell you how you should think and feel'—at least that's my disclaimer. I'm not sure if it'll hold up or not." Some facilitators believed strongly that the CSC program was merely an educational tool to provide skills that inmates either chose to employ or not; others stated that the program indeed insisted that inmates' beliefs were wrong and must be changed, at least superficially to meet the "competencies" of the program. Another facilitator explained, "You can't just *say* certain thoughts—you gotta say what we want."

Participants were evaluated on their performance according to the program standards and must have completed the competencies (identifying and intervening in risky thoughts) that were measured by in-group participation, written assignments, and the adequacy of their "relapse prevention" plans. In this sense, true rehabilitation was not forced, but some recognized effort toward that end was required for positive evaluation. As one facilitator explained, "There are no wrong beliefs—there *are* wrong ones for making it through the program." In fact, one participant was suspended from the group because "he's not buying it." In this respect, "buying" the CSC rhetoric was demanded; rejection of the dictated moral standard reflected pathology and reproduced it (Henry and Milovanovic 1996; Miller and Rose 1994)....

CREATING CRIMINAL TYPES

The CSC program was designed to treat violent offenders by targeting their distinctive thought patterns. The rhetoric drew heavily upon Samuel Yochelson and Stanton E. Samenow's (1976) research on criminal personalities. Thus, CSC reduced inmates' experiences into ideal-typical criminal patterns by interpreting their actions and words according to a particular schematic representation of criminals. Although a recent move has attempted to eliminate the terms "error" and "distortion" from the program's language, pathology was implied (and the terms are still used). In asking inmates to reflect upon their "core patterns" of thought that precede violent actions and asking explicitly that they devise new ways of thinking, program participation informed inmates that their *thinking* was different and troubling. In this respect, the CSC program relied on and reinforced a construction of a type of person—criminal type—that was evident in the interactions of group meetings.

Group thinking reports and journal assignments focused on "mind-sets" or particular ways of seeing the world that led to a cycle of violence. Many thinking reports concentrated on the ways in which their thoughts motivated feelings of anger and how beliefs and attitudes supported such thoughts. Yet often the inmates' thoughts were about how their victims deserved what they got or that correctional personnel victimized them. Facilitators insisted that inmates' complaints about

mistreatment in prison or unfair prosecution or sentencing were reflective of their "thinking patterns." For example, in one group, inmates complained about the behavior of prison guards and the facilitator suggested this kind of sentiment reflected a "mind-set." An inmate responded: "If you have so many inmates telling you that guards are out to get them, how can that be a mind-set?" After the facilitator explained how this same mind-set shared by inmates was what landed them all in prison, the inmate joked, "I guess the mind is a terrible thing."

In another example, an inmate was asked to consider: "When I have these thoughts, someone gets hurt." He responded, "There isn't anything in my life that goes like that," continuing that his thoughts do not explain his violence. He was eventually given a negative evaluation for program performance because he could not meet the basic competency, which was to connect *thoughts* to risk for violence. Insofar as inmates' counterclaims were treated as illegitimate by facilitators, they referred to a representation of criminal thinking as a particular variety of thought: "distorted concrete thinking." In reality contests such as these, inmates' versions could not be sustained, but were, rather, co-opted in the process of recontextualization. The simplicity of the CSC program's premises was regarded as one of its strengths—it was relatively easy to implement. However, as one facilitator lamented to me, "[CSC] doesn't consider the forces outside the person—it assumes that thinking alone causes behavior—there's more to it than that!"

In reducing the complexity of inmates' life situations to a simple equation between malleable thoughts and actions, the program depended upon the judgments handed down by the courts. As one facilitator said, "I start with the premise that they're a lying sack of shit because I can't retry the case." In this sense, then, the assumption of pathology (or immorality) was built into the program—after all, it was a correctional treatment program. Pathology was reproduced by eliminating other possible explanations.

DECONTEXTUALIZING CRIMINALITY

In order to construct criminality as evidence of a "type," situational explanations for crimes had to be dismissed. Most of the time, inmates claimed that their violence was provoked or somehow prompted by circumstances beyond their control. Such accounts echo Sykes and Matza's (1957) "techniques of neutralization" used by delinquents to deflect a deviant identity. For instance, inmates' claims that someone else started a fight represented "denial of responsibility," and claims that their victims deserved what they got exemplified "denial of the victim." Their techniques of neutralization were social explanations that conflicted with the notion of a criminal personality. Deviance was situational, according to inmates. Yet, in order for CSC to work, criminal acts must be disembodied from their circumstances and be considered outside of contexts. As an administrator said: "There's a difference between the *reason* for what they did and what they did." He went on to say that CSC was only interested in what the offenders did. In this sense, the group process could be seen as one that *de*contextualized inmates' behaviors and treated them as objectively deviant.

A sample exchange in a group meeting illustrated this point. Pete was discussing a written thinking report (for which he had been evaluated negatively) on a violent situation. He was supposed to describe the situation "objectively":

PETE: The situation was: I had been drinking, getting drunk, with my girlfriend and she pissed me off so I went to bed. I was sleeping and my girlfriend punched me in the balls so I broke her jaw. Then you said I didn't need to put so much here.

FACILITATOR: We don't need an explanation—like this getting drunk and all that—just what you did: you broke her jaw.

PETE: I was sleeping and my girlfriend punched me in the balls and I broke her jaw. Is that acceptable?

FACILITATOR: I don't know if I'd use the word acceptable....

The negotiation of reality that took place in this incident reflected Pete's subtle attempt to "minimize" his violence (Potter 1996, p. 187). Pete's reluctance to exclude explanatory information from his description demonstrated his efforts to "soften" the violence (Potter 1996, p. 191). A major goal of the CSC program was to make offenders accountable for their crimes—thus, these attempts to minimize were thwarted.

Also striking in this example is the way in which the facilitator asked Pete to eliminate from the discussion the context in which the act took place. Pete was then asked to reduce the situation more, excluding the part about his being attacked first. In this sense, the only aspect of the situation of interest in the group process was the act of breaking a woman's jaw. Insofar as the act was discussed, dissected, and analyzed out of context, the actor was reconfigured in another context—that of his own violent nature. In a delicate way, the description of violence was maximized. Out of context, it seemed that Pete broke a woman's jaw for no apparent reason—as such, he fit neatly into a descriptive type of a violent person. This is not meant to suggest that Pete's violence was justified in or out of context but rather to highlight the process by which criminal acts of all kinds were viewed in a vacuum in CSC.

Interestingly, the inmates' accounts were often somewhat sociological. Inmates reported acting out in school after being labeled "stupid" because of a learning disability; they explained their stealing as a result of poor employment opportunities and their violent episodes as consequences of inadequate verbal skills. In this respect, inmates stressed the social (structural) context of their criminality. Yet their discourse of social causation was a target for treatment in CSC and served as proof of extreme criminal thinking: claiming victimization. The institutional discourse of CSC needed a construction of inmates as pathological; incarceration could not be justified and rehabilitation makes no sense without such a construction. The program itself could not be validated or sustained without manufacturing evidence of criminal thinking.

REPRODUCING ERRONEOUS THINKING

The construction of criminal thinking as erroneous was the fulcrum of the CSC program. Thus, errors in thinking were the cornerstone of interpretations of inmates' thoughts. These distortions in thought were tied into the ideology of moral autonomy: any claims inmates might make about the ways they were constrained or compelled by others in their actions were treated as distortions. As a facilitator explained: "Bare bones: you gotta take responsibility for [your] offense." In addition, regardless of others' actions, inmates needed to fit their own actions and thoughts into a pattern suggestive of pathology. For example, Todd was discussing a recent situation in jail: another inmate failed to refill the coffeepot after emptying it. Todd stated that this incident fit the thinking error paraphrased as "failure to consider others." A facilitator responded:

FACILITATOR: Does that pattern fit?
TODD: It fits the person who emptied the coffeepot and didn't fill it back up.
FACILITATOR: Could it ever fit you?
TODD: Now that I think about it, it could be, like when I steal from someone else.
FACILITATOR: Then write that down for your relapse plan.

This is not to imply that stealing represented something other than a "failure to consider others." But the interactions between facilitators and inmates were devised to reorient inmates' interpretations, to examine their own responsibility for their actions, to shift the blame onto themselves.

Inmates' counterclaims in reality contests were regarded as indicative of how entrenched their thought patterns were. In this sense, claims as to one's "change" or rehabilitation actually reinforced the rhetorical claims of the facilitators. In other words, extreme resistance represented typical criminal thinking, as did ready capitulation. Because criminal thinking was the target, some resistance was expected, and was targeted as well. In an exchange with two facilitators, Todd stated:

TODD: I have a dilemma because my way[s] of thinking's changed and I know I gotta show you that but I don't get into beefs anymore—I'm above all that.
FACILITATOR: Don't show us that you've changed your thinking, show us that you have interventions.
COFACILITATOR: [incredulously] Yeah, how did you change your thinking?
TODD: You're saying someone can't change their thinking?
COFACILITATOR: Well, we think you may *respond* differently now.

In this exchange, Todd's suggestion that he thought "differently" than he did before was greeted with suspicion. In this sense, the program's discourse assumed that criminals retained their core thinking patterns—which were distorted—but that they could train themselves to intervene with some new thoughts. The rhetoric seemed contradictory: inmates could not change their thinking but they may devise *new* thinking.

Yet even interventions that inmates devised were often deemed characteristic of criminal thinking. In an exchange with a facilitator, Jens recounted an incident he had with a prison guard:

FACILITATOR: What thoughts did you have?
JENS: I start to get irritated because it's my pattern—I gotta be in control.
FACILITATOR: What are your thoughts becoming next [in the situation]?
JENS: Dehumanizing thoughts, you know, I can't say because there's a lady present [referring to me]. I start formulating plans for getting even, for revenge. For me, I always gotta get my words in, so walking away for me is a big intervention.
FACILITATOR: Walking away and getting the last word—are they similar?
JENS: Yeah, failure to consider others, to look at their side of the story.
FACILITATOR: You're thinking what now? [referring to the time of the incident]
JENS: "F—— off."

FACILITATOR: So you get the final word?

JENS: For me, I've always been drawn to confrontation.

FACILITATOR: Walking away—is it at all high risk?

JENS: Well, it's payback for his behavior, you know, like pride. I take pride in what I do.

FACILITATOR: So it *is* risky. It's getting even. So is that an intervention?

JENS: No, intervention was nowhere on my mind I guess when I walked out.

Implicit in this exchange was the presumption that even when inmates believed they were devising "real" interventions—and even when the intervention "worked" in averting violence—their intervening behaviors emanated from the criminal thought patterns that were so much a part of them. They were responsible for getting angry in the first place.

In another example, an inmate was upset over a meeting with his caseworker, and he intervened in his anger by working on his relapse plan:

FACILITATOR: Intervention should be working on the angry part. It's supposed to help you deal with the anger, not the caseworker. It's about *you*.

COFACILITATOR: "Cognitive" means thinking, changing your thinking so you're less risky. It's not a problem-solving course, it's about how can you change your thinking.

Regardless of others' actions toward participants, the "problem" and target of intervention was their response: their angry thoughts. Thus, anger was never justified for inmates, but was a normal emotion for others—inmate anger was evidence of faulty, pathological thinking. The inherent tautology in this model helped to sustain and (re)produce angry criminal "types."

REPRODUCING ANGRY CRIMINALS

CSC discourse incorporated and reified cultural conceptions of criminality. According to Alison Young (1996, pp. 1–2), the popular imagery of crime is comprised of a "binary logic of representation." Thus, crime is reduced to opposing poles: rational/irrational, responsible/irresponsible, victims/victimizers, prosocial/antisocial, and so on. In such a scheme, this reductionist logic played out in globalizing identities; in other words, a person was constructed as either one ideal type or another (see also Best 1997).

Stuart Henry and Dragan Milovanovic (1996, p. 178) stated that, "the dichotomous separation between law-abiding and law-breaking behavior is an artifact of the conventional criminologist." Indeed, the Cognitive Self-Change program was adapted from social scientific research on criminal personalities. Within the rhetoric of CSC, dichotomies of erroneous/correct thinking and anger/rationality were enforced and, in that sense, had a disciplinary effect (Foucault 1977; Rose 1988). The dichotomies became ideological, disciplining tools with a reflexive relationship to the larger system of social control. They may be cultural artifacts of an established psychological paradigm, but they were animated in microinteractions that again provided fuel for the legitimacy of the ideology of social control.

Let us look at anger as our illustration. Within CSC, inmates were regarded as victimizers, never victims. In addition, inmates' opposition to the representations of criminality in the program was interpreted as evidence of their extreme anger that motivated their violent behavior. Angel complained that his probation officer requested more "thinking reports" on his convicted crime. Angel reported this "high-risk situation" during check-in since he was angry—he was certain she had several copies in her file already,

FACILITATOR: What were your thoughts?

ANGEL: My risky thoughts were "fuck her, fuck this. I don't f'ing care. It's a buncha BS." Then, "Well, I better do it or else I ain't getting out. I gotta satisfy them. Don't do it and I stay here or do it and get out." But I was trying to figure out why she was doing this to me.

FACILITATOR: Why she's doing it to you? Do you think she would have asked that of anyone or just you?

ANGEL: Well, I don't know. I just know she has [the thinking reports].

FACILITATOR: What are your core patterns?

ANGEL: Anger, power thrust....

FACILITATOR: Your core pattern is anger—it seems you got there pretty quickly.

ANGEL: Yeah, but I didn't express it. I went to my bunk and sorted it out in my head.

FACILITATOR: But inside your head would have been an interesting thing to see. It probably would have been X-rated.

ANGEL: Yeah.

In this complex example, the facilitator initially probed to see if the inmate was grasping onto a belief that he was being "singled out" or victimized, as this was regarded as the most typical pattern. In addition, Angel described how his interventions worked to calm him down. Yet the facilitator seized upon the fact that he questioned his parole officer's motives. Although Angel explained that he did not express his anger, he was still responsible for his "criminal" thinking. Being angry was associated with erroneous thought patterns or "core" patterns that globally defined the inmate. As such, Angel's anger was of a fundamentally different nature than that of other noncriminal types: his anger was illegitimate and pathological.

In private discussions about inmate resistance to the discourse of CSC, facilitators would dismiss prisoners' complaints as "typical criminal kind of thinking." Particularly obstinate inmates were regarded as embodiments of "the culture" of prison in their antagonism toward corrections (Irwin 1987; Wieder 1974). There were several occasions in which inmates complained about the rigid requirements, for example, for expressing their beliefs in short "bumper sticker" phrases and the like. Each time, facilitators relied upon a characterization of inmates as angry or resistant to authority to marginalize their protests. For example, in one exchange, Calhoun suggested that "I don't

need a piece of paper to tell me I can drive" was an appropriate intervention for the times he felt tempted to drive without a license. The facilitator challenged him:

FACILITATOR: That's more of a belief, isn't it?

CALHOUN: Whatever.

FACILITATOR: See, I am thinking of you in Phase 3 [aftercare group for released inmates], the providers don't know a thing about your past.

CALHOUN: So? This is for us, not for you!

FACILITATOR: Well, you'll need to demonstrate that you can intervene.

CALHOUN: Oh man! That's what I'm doing! [Then Calhoun suggested alternative interventions, such as "my freedom is more important."]

FACILITATOR: Those are goals. Maybe the intervention [thought] would look like "remember past."

CALHOUN: You can't get that from what I just said? You mean to tell me you guys are that fucking stupid? All right then, I'll need another page eight to write this so you people can understand.

Calhoun's intervention thoughts were of dubious quality based on the standards required. Interestingly, though, his resistance was mostly centered on the arbitrary format requirements the facilitator enforced. However, after the meeting, the facilitators discussed Calhoun's bad "attitude" and chalked up his complaints to his "anger." Thus, his objections were dismissed as illegitimate because they were simply indicative of his criminal anger.

In another example, an inmate argued that since his return to prison was for a nonviolent offense, he should not be required to complete the CSC program (which was explicitly designed for violent offenders). The lengthy exchange between Doug and a facilitator was instructive:

FACILITATOR: It's not just a violent offender program—it's for criminal thinking—like "I can break this rule."

DOUG: But if it's all that, why would I have to take a separate drug and alcohol program?

FACILITATOR: Did you recently get some bad news?

DOUG: No, it's just that....

FACILITATOR: Did you recently get some bad news?

DOUG: [angrily] No! I see what you're getting at!

FACILITATOR: What is it you're really saying?

DOUG: I just don't see why I am in a violent offender program....

FACILITATOR: What is it you're really saying?

DOUG: Look, I did some drinking. I didn't do a violent offense!

FACILITATOR: That's only part of it. The other part is that we make decisions, like the decision to drink, based on what's going on up here [points to head]. So part of it is to teach you not to be violent by developing an awareness of how you're thinking about things so you can catch yourself. Like the decision you made to drink again: something was behind that.

DOUG: It wasn't violent though.

FACILITATOR: But your body gives you signals about your patterns.

In this interaction, Doug's concern about his forced participation in a drug and alcohol program was ignored and interpreted as evidence of his anger. He then became angry at the suggestion that his complaint was "about" something else. He was later characterized as "an angry dude" by the facilitators. This example demonstrates the reproductive aspect of the rhetoric of CSC. Built upon assumptions of violent criminals as essentially angry, the insistence on that interpretation produced anger that reinforced the representation (Young 1995). In fact, during one meeting, Doug seemed unusually happy, and the facilitator said later that he must have been smoking marijuana.

When inmates expressed resentment over their treatment by individuals in the Department of Corrections, these claims were marginalized as well. In another exchange with Doug, the facilitator asked:

FACILITATOR: When your P.O. [parole officer] gave you a negative recommendation [for parole], what were you thinking about her?

DOUG: I know her game. I knew it right off. I always thought she was a piece of shit and I planned to tell her that when I saw her.

FACILITATOR: Was that high risk [of violence] for you?

DOUG: No. I wasn't going to do anything except tell her off.

FACILITATOR: [pause] I notice your shirt says "Slap-a-[whore] tribe." Somebody that would wear a shirt like that—that's quite a statement. What did you think of [your P.O.]?

DOUG: Nothing.

FACILITATOR: You were just this calm, cool, and collected guy?

DOUG: Well, what am I gonna do—call her a bunch of names?

FACILITATOR: You said you were.

DOUG: Look, I told her I drank and she picked up the telephone and called parole.... Maybe it was something just to give her something to do, to make her book of work on me look good, like she's doing something.

FACILITATOR: It wouldn't have anything to do with the way you present yourself?

DOUG: No! Fuck it. Screw it. You got everything you need to know. What do you want to pick at?

FACILITATOR: You're angry today.

DOUG: I am just sick of everything—this revolving door into here.

One could argue that the message on the inmate's shirt spoke volumes about his perspective toward women. In addition, he seemed confused about whether or not he was planning to behave aggressively toward his parole officer. However, through a series of pointed questions, the facilitator implied that the inmate was angry, aggressive toward women, and responsible for his probation officer's decision to "violate" him for transgressing—all of which may well have been true. However, through a discursive technique, Doug was constructed interactionally. The representation of "calm, cool, collected guy" was used as a "contrast structure" (Smith 1990) to shore up the absurdity of this image of the inmate, discursively constructing him as essentially angry.

In addition, the path that the questions took led the inmate to become angry, which would later be interpreted as a sign that the facilitator had "touched a nerve." Touching a nerve meant that the core truth had been probed. In this sense, then, expressions of anger toward the line of reasoning a facilitator pursued were regarded as evidence of the righteousness of that reasoning. As such, reality was not negotiated so much as persuaded and enforced.

DEMANDING REALIGNMENT

Clearly, facilitators' assumptions about the essential anger of inmates helped to arouse sufficient anger among participants to bolster the construction. In addition, facilitators subtly demanded realignment to the program's representation of them as "angry criminals" by insisting that there was more anger than inmates admitted. In this exchange, an inmate described her thoughts about a situation in which a prison official reneged on a promise to let her daughter visit:

ANNIE: I did my end of the bargain. [She's] not doing hers.
FACILITATOR: Something else is going on in that head of yours—those are awfully tame [thoughts]. If I couldn't see my kid for three weeks, I'd be thinking, "This is bullshit. The bitch isn't keeping her end of the bargain."
ANNIE: I was thinking that in the unit.

This seemed to satisfy the facilitator. Interestingly, the facilitator admitted to having similar thoughts as those that would be classified as distorted. However, her anger was normalized, while the inmate's was pathological. In another exchange, again the facilitator insisted the inmate's thoughts were too "tame." When Annie replied that she was trying to suppress her angry thoughts, which

would be considered "prosocial" behavior, her strategy was regarded as evidence of her simmering anger.

In a different example of realignment, a facilitator was trying to persuade an inmate to see himself in the thinking errors list. One thinking error stated, "The criminal believes that he is a good and decent person. He rejects the thought that he is a criminal." An inmate had referred to this error in a thinking report, describing how he was, in fact, a good person and was not what he considered a "criminal." He said that a criminal was "a thief who steals for drugs." He was told that he misunderstood the point of the assignment—that he should have reflected upon "hurtful, destructive" things he'd done. Todd became frustrated because he was trying to do what he understood the assignment to be:

TODD: What do you want me to put here?
FACILITATOR: Whatever you want.
TODD: Obviously not.

They discussed the crime for which he was convicted.

FACILITATOR: Do you think that's criminal?
TODD: Yeah, I guess. But what do you want [for the assignment]?
FACILITATOR: "A thief" is someone else, it's not you. It's supposed to be about you.
COFACILITATOR: How are *you* criminal?
TODD: I reject the thought of being a criminal. That's what it says [on the thinking errors list]. That's what I do.

In this instance, the inmate thought he was supposed to write down the patterns that apply to his thoughts—he believed he was a good person. However, he did not perceive this to be an error. Later, when he again insisted that he was not a criminal because he had only one conviction, a facilitator replied, "It does make it difficult when your view is that you're innocent." In this sense, he was asked to internalize a "criminal" identity, to accept that his thoughts were merely "typical" criminal ones, thereby adopting his essential criminality as "master status" (Becker 1963). Acknowledging the criminality of his act was the first step in the process of talking him into being a criminal *person;* his resistance to the label was seen as a rejection of a criminal identity. Clinging to the belief that he was essentially a decent person was deemed erroneous and further evidence of how deeply ingrained his criminal thinking was.

In another important way, the inmate was asked to align himself externally with the ideology of the program. Although ostensibly the target of intervention was the inmate's "mind," the only resources available for making change in group sessions were interactional devices such as writing and speaking (Young 1995). A facilitator said, "You gotta fake it till you make it," meaning that inmates had to try using the terms and concepts to demonstrate that they "know *how* to change"—in hopes that eventually inmates would realize it works. Because this interpretive lens shaped the interactions between facilitators and inmates and was built into the rhetoric of "thinking errors," resistance was regarded as extreme criminal thinking (or "concrete thinking"). If an inmate refused to cooperate even after being sanctioned on occasion, his or her cognitive ability may be questioned; one inmate was so resistant to the concepts endorsed in the program that his mental capacity became suspect. The facilitators could not comprehend why he would choose not to "fake it" and become an "expedient confessor" (Scott 1969), given the potential consequence of suspension from the group and a stalled prison release. An exchange in a group meeting demonstrated this point:

FACILITATOR: You gotta get past this, "This isn't gonna work" stuff.

LEE: So what you're saying is that I shouldn't be honest. I should tell you what you wanna hear?

FACILITATOR: Well, by telling us what we want to hear, you're gonna *know* what we want....

LEE: I don't have a clue what you want!

In this example, the facilitator suggested that a demonstrated ability to provide the facilitators with "what they want to hear" would show competency in understanding the program. Resistance, or a reluctance to "try," was perceived as extreme willfulness—a typical criminal pattern. "Trying" was measured by attempts to utilize the terms and complete the assignments properly. Whenever inmates would ask about the possibility of failing the program, they were told that "it's not like school, no pass or fail." An inmate responded: "You say it's not like school, but why does our R.P. [relapse prevention plan] have to be accepted by you, by whoever? What standard do you use? If it's our thinking, there's no way you can grade it." At times like these, when arguments between inmates and facilitators became circular, facilitators would refer to "the program" and its requirements. Occasionally when inmates objected to the language of "thinking errors" or "criminal personalities," a facilitator would say something like "it's from a book by some psychologists!" in order to reify the program's relevance.

OBJECTIFYING DISCOURSE

Using an "objectifying discourse" (Smith 1990, p. 4) to silence resistance, CSC rhetoric reinforced its own scientistic frame. The objectivist language of "cognitive distortions," "criminal personalities," and the like rhetorically produced angry types of criminals. Thus, the taken-for-granted social facts of criminality were constituted through practices of rehabilitation (Pollner 1987). Anger was evidence of subjectivity, whereas inmates were asked to read their lives objectively. Objectivity was presumed to be the property of facilitators in their abilities to see inmates' deluded criminal thinking. In a training session for CSC facilitators, an instructor insisted "You're the experts, not them," and:

We're a step ahead of the game, right? That we can see their risk more clearly than they do. And that's not surprising because we're more objective about it and they've got, they're more close to this and defensive and the rest of that stuff.

It is clear that objectivity and rationality were preferred interpretive frames, and "criminal" anger was irrational and overly subjective. Thus, anger was a fundamental ingredient in constructing criminals as "other" types with inappropriate thoughts.

Objectivity was measured by the degree to which inmates conformed to the paradigm of the CSC program. Inmates who resisted continually, charging that the program was "bullshit" and that their thinking was undistorted, were not evaluated positively for release. In time, most inmates recognized their "choice" to serve their maximum sentence and began to adopt the language of the program. In this sense, participants in CSC were "talked into being" (Heritage 1984, p. 290) pathological types by conforming their interpretations and rearticulating their lives to fit the "narrative map" (Pollner and Stein 1994) provided.

Donileen R. Loseke (1989) argued that the production of people as types places them "within particular moral universes, which simultaneously constructs such persons as residing within particular universes of 'sympathy-worthiness' or 'condemnation-worthiness.'" Insofar as inmates inhabited a "condemnation-worthy" category, CSC imposed this moral order through rhetorical strategies and interpretations. Moral universes were mystified by the objectivist language of "cognition." For instance, the program literature emphasized that the logic of CSC eschews moral judgment and privileges an objective approach to treatment. However, in an argument with a facilitator, an inmate claimed that his crime was the result of self-defense, which he said was "the nature of human beings." The facilitator responded, "No, we've progressed past that—maybe not in your world, maybe that's the problem." In this example, the inmate's entire "world" was indicted as being regressive. Interestingly, the facilitator acknowledged the distinction between subcultural values and those endorsed by the CSC program, yet the "problem" was in reconciling the inmate's values—indeed, his view, of human nature—with those of the program. This is part of what was implied by the concept of "cognitive self-change"—borrowing from the 1960s film *Cool Hand Luke*—inmates had to "get their minds right." Within CSC, fundamental change was invisible; rather, change was measured in "verbal behavior" that reinforced criminal typification (Young 1995, p. 187).

DISCUSSION

Although other studies have documented the interactional production of types in human service settings, analyzing CSC unearths greater implications in several respects. First, CSC represents but one theory about the nature of criminality—that of a distinct criminal "personality." The specific nature of inmate pathology may vary in therapeutic approaches, but correctional ideology regards inmates as some version of immoral, irrational, irresponsible, or ill. Incarceration cannot be rationalized without some accompanying ideology of the "otherness" of inmates (Foucault 1977, 1980a; Irwin 1987; Sloop 1996). Thus, the institution relies upon the enforcement and support of its underlying premises one way or another. Whatever the construct of the essence of criminality, the "type" is constructed and reified, in part, out of institutional necessity.

Second, the creation and reproduction of types is an animating process. This is not meant to suggest that typologies or knowledges determine social practices—rather that the facilitators' activities (derived from legitimated knowledge) build and fortify existing ideologies (Garfinkel 1967). The process is interactive and dynamic. Sue Fischer and Alexandra Dundas Todd (1986, p. xiii) describe a "contextual web" in which interactions occur in the center and spread out to the organizational structure that shapes them. The larger context is refined by the microinteractions and "folds back again to shape interactions and communication." Insofar as resistant interactions solidify the "truth" of the institution's intervention paradigm, the creative and interactive relationship between the institution and its many actors is evident.

Third, intervention into socially problematic behavior is justified by an ideology of pathology, one that may be supported by social scientistic theories (Rose 1988, 1996). The CSC program is an example of the use of criminological research on criminal types. Criminology, by virtue of its focus on the study of criminals' alleged distinctiveness, can be used as an "alibi" to sustain social control ideologies (Foucault 1980b, p. 47). Thus, the ideology of pathology is enforced in a "disciplinary discourse" (Henry and Milovanovic 1996, p. 197) that merges criminology and crime control in ways of talk.

In micropolitical exchanges in CSC, the nature of the individual criminal self is negotiated and contested. Inmates are enjoined to take part in this reproductive project. In this sense, their subjectivity is constituted by an *inter*subjective process (Foucault 1983, 1988; Garland 1997). Not only are convicted violent offenders sentenced to incarceration, they are subject to a rhetorical process in which their minds are penetrated and treated as objects for intervention. As a professional discursive technology, CSC incites "troubles talk" and, as such, manufactures criminality, by constructing criminals as objects of power (Miller and Silverman 1995). Through such talk, not only are inmates' actions challenged, but their inner selves (or their "will" as the program literature puts it) as well.

Thus, as an example of cognitive social control, the CSC program powerfully represents how an interpretation of inmates as pathological is impervious to contrary evidence—inmates' actions are reinterpreted to fit the category of deviant (Fox 1999). An overt context of control shapes the interactions such that counterrhetorics are marginalized; the institution sets the parameters within which new selves can be created. Insofar as power is accomplished through discourse, the micropolitics of CSC groups reveal larger processes embodied in the rehabilitative "talk" about criminal types (Foucault 1980a, 1980b).

Finally, inmates employ rhetorical devices to try to "normalize" their activities, formulating their accountability in particular ways (Potter 1996). A construction of individuals as determined by external forces would undermine the CSC program's logic; thus, lay sociological accounts by inmates are refuted. In essence, external causation discourses are silenced by individualistic, pathologizing ones. Indeed, CSC engages in a process that actively delegitimates social explanations. The implications for sociological perspectives in crime control/talk are obvious—sociology's influence may be limited in institutions charged with regulating human behavior. Correctional philosophy has been characterized of late by a psychologistic paradigm, presumably reflecting the cultural dominance of those disciplines (Rose 1996; Simon and Feeley 1995). However, for agencies involved in the management of human behavior, the benefit of relying on "psy" disciplines may be that pathological types continue to be (re)produced.

REFERENCES

Becker, Howard. 1963. *Outsiders: Studies in the Sociology of Deviance.* New York: Free Press.

Best, Joel. 1997. "Victimization and the Victim Industry." *Society* 34:9–17.

Cicourel, Aaron V. 1968. *The Social Organization of Juvenile Justice.* London: Heinemann.

Durkheim, Emile. 1953. *Sociology and Philosophy.* Translated by D. F. Pocock. Glencoe, IL: Free Press.

Edelman, Murray. 1977. *Political Language: Words That Succeed and Policies That Fail.* New York: Academic Press.

Fischer, Sue, and Alexandra Dundas Todd. 1986. "Introduction: Communication in Institutional Contexts: Social Interaction and Social Structure." Pp. ix–xviii in *Discourse and Institutional Authority: Medicine, Education, and Law,* edited by Sue Fischer and Alexandra Dundas Todd. Norwood, NJ: Ablex.

Foucault, Michel. 1977. *Discipline and Punish: The Birth of the Prison.* New York: Vintage.

———. 1980a. *The History of Sexuality Vol I.* New York: Vintage/Random House.

———. 1980b. *Power/Knowledge.* New York: Pantheon Books.

———. 1983. "The Subject and Power." Pp. 208–226 in *Michel Foucault,* 2nd ed., edited by Hubert L. Dreyfus and Paul Rabinow. Chicago: University of Chicago Press.

———. 1988. "Technologies of the Self." Pp. 16–49 in *Technologies of the Self,* edited by Luther H. Martin, Huck Gutman, and Patrick H. Hutton. Amherst: University of Massachusetts Press.

Fox, Kathryn J. 1999. "Changing Violent Minds: Discursive Correction and Resistance in the Cognitive Treatment of Violent Offenders in Prison." *Social Problems* 46:88–103.

Frohmann, Lisa. 1991. "Discrediting Victims' Allegations of Sexual Assault: Prosecutorial Accounts of Case Rejections." *Social Problems* 38:213–226.

Garfinkel, Harold. 1967. *Studies in Ethnomethodology.* Englewood Cliffs, NJ: Prentice-Hall.

Garland, David. 1997. "'Governmentality' and the Problem of Crime: Foucault, Criminology, Sociology." *Theoretical Criminology* 1:173–214.

Goffman, Erving. 1961. *Asylums.* Garden City, NY: Anchor Books.

Henry, Stuart, and Dragan Milovanovic. 1996. *Constitutive Criminology: Beyond Postmodernism.* London: Sage.

Heritage, John C. 1984. *Garfinkel and Ethnomethodology.* Cambridge, MA: Polity Press.

Holstein, James A. 1992. "Producing People: Descriptive Practices in Human Service Work." Pp. 23–40 in *Current Research on Occupations and Professions,* edited by Gale Miller. Greenwich, CT: JAI Press.

———. 1993. *Court-Ordered Insanity: Interpretive Practice and Involuntary Commitment.* Hawthorne, NY: Aldine de Gruyter.

Irwin, John. 1987. *The Felon.* Berkeley: University of California Press.

Loseke, Donileen R. 1989. "Creating Clients." Pp. 173–193 in *Perspectives on Social Problems Vol. 1.* Edited by James A. Holstein and Gale Miller. Greenwich, CT: JAI Press.

———. 1992. *The Battered Woman and Shelters: The Social Construction of Wife Abuse.* Albany: State University of New York Press.

Maynard, Douglas. 1984. *Inside Plea Bargaining.* New York: Plenum Press.

Miller, Gale. 1991. *Enforcing the Work Ethic.* Albany: State University of New York Press.

———. 1992. "Human Service Practice as Social Problems Work." *Current Research on Occupations and Professions* 7:3–21.

Miller, Gale, and David Silverman. 1995. "Troubles Talk and Counseling Discourse: A Comparative Study." *The Sociological Quarterly* 36:725–747.

Miller, Peter, and Nikolas Rose. 1994. "On Therapeutic Authority: Psychoanalytic Expertise under Advanced Liberalism." *History of the Human Sciences* 7:29–64.

Peyrot, Mark. 1985. "Coerced Voluntarism: The Micropolitics of Drug Treatment." *Urban Life* 13:343–365.

Pfohl, Stephen J. 1978. *Predicting Dangerousness.* Lexington, MA: Lexington Books.

Pollner, Melvin. 1987. *Mundane Reason: Reality in Everyday and Sociological Discourse.* Cambridge: Cambridge University Press.

Pollner, Melvin, and Jill Stein. 1994. "Narrative Maps of Social Worlds: The Voice of Experience in Alcoholics Anonymous." *Symbolic Interaction* 19:203–223.

Potter, Jonathan. 1996. *Representing Reality: Discourse, Rhetoric, and Social Construction.* London: Sage.

Quinney, Richard. 1970. *The Social Reality of Crime.* Boston: Little, Brown.

Rose, Nikolas. 1988. "Calculable Minds and Manageable Individuals." *History of the Human Sciences* 1:179–200.

———. 1996. *Inventing Our Selves: Psychology, Power, and Personhood.* Cambridge: Cambridge University Press.

Scott, Robert A. 1969. *The Making of Blind Men: A Study of Adult Socialization.* New York: Russell Sage Foundation.

Simon, Jonathan and Malcolm M. Feeley. 1995. "True Crime: The New Penology and Public Discourse on Crime." Pp. 147–180 in *Punishment and Social Control: Essays in Honor of Sheldon L. Messinger,* edited by Thomas G. Blomberg and Stanley Cohen. Hawthorne, NY: Aldine de Gruyter.

Skolnick, Jerome H. 1966. *Justice without Trial: Law Enforcement in Democratic Society.* New York: Wiley.

Sloop, John M. 1996. *The Cultural Prison: Discourse, Prisoners, and Punishment.* Tuscaloosa: University of Alabama Press.

Smith, Dorothy E. 1990. *The Conceptual Practices of Power: A Feminist Sociology of Knowledge.* Boston: Northeastern University Press.

Sudnow, David. 1965. "Normal Crimes: Sociological Features of the Penal Code in a Public Defender's Office." *Social Problems* 12:255–276.

Sykes, Gresham M., and David Matza. 1957. "Techniques of Neutralization: A Theory of Delinquency." *American Sociological Review* 22:664–670.

Wieder, D. Lawrence. 1974. *Language and Social Reality: The Case of Telling the Convict Code.* The Hague: Mouton.

Yochelson, Samuel, and Stanton E. Samenow. 1976. *The Criminal Personality.* New York: J. Aronson.

Young, Alison. 1996. *Imagining Crime: Textual Outlaws and Criminal Conversations.* London: Sage.

Young, Allan. 1995. *The Harmony of Illusions: Inventing Post-Traumatic Stress Disorder.* Princeton, NJ: Princeton University Press.

Experts on Battered Women

DONILEEN R. LOSEKE and SPENCER E. CAHILL

People create deviant categories and theories about the people to whom they apply them. These categorizations and conceptualizations can vary in different cultures and historical periods. The rise, fall, and re-creation of deviant categories and perspectives turn out to be increasingly characteristic. More often than not, these new deviant categories are the work of social movements, which are coalitions of people and organizations that seek to produce social change. Sometimes such movements have an interest in defining a pattern of social behavior as deviant and requiring the intervention of "experts" to understand and change the behavior.

A paradox of the work of such social movements is the emergence of a social construction that, on the one hand, simplifies the complexity of the behavior under review, and, on the other hand, claims that only the "experts" they designate are capable of changing the behavior the movement has reconceptualized. The movement may disregard diversity among the persons categorized by their deviant category or the fact that, for many of these people, the behavior is not most correctly characterized as being pathological.

Donileen R. Loseke and Spencer E. Cahill show how the rebirth of feminism as a social movement gave rise to a new construction of the victims of domestic violence. In essence a new deviant social type emerged—"battered women who remain with their mates." Such a decision on the part of battered women was viewed by the "experts" as an unreasonable one. A theory was constructed that suggested that what could be considered pathological traits on the part of the women is what explained the continuation of their relationships with these men. Loseke and Cahill view this conceptualization by the "experts" as based on folklore rather than empirical evidence, and as being one that created a new clientele for their services. In its place, the authors present a theory that does not characterize battered women who remain with their mates as being pathological, unusual, or deviant.

During the 1970s, women's movement activists succeeded in focusing public attention on the topic of wife assault.[1] While the phenomenon itself was not new, contemporary feminists were the first to argue that wife assault was not merely a private trouble but a social issue as well. They asserted that public attention and resources were required in order to assist the immediate victims of this social malaise, "battered women."

While the feminist ideals underlying the movement for battered women suggested that victims of wife assault could be the only "experts" regarding their problems (Ridington, 1977–78; Segovia-Ashley, 1978; Warrior, 1978),[2] ironically, but not surprisingly, the movement was accompanied by the emergence of experts on battered women.[3] By the late 1970s, these self-identified experts were speaking on behalf of battered women to the media, in government hearings (U.S. Commission on Civil Rights, 1978; U.S. House of Representatives, 1978), and in legal proceedings (Jones, 1980:296). A diverse group, these experts share neither a common vocabulary of discourse nor a common ideological perspective; some but not all explicitly state an allegiance to the feminist ideals underlying the movement for battered women.[4] They include academics (sociologists, psychologists, legal scholars), social service providers (social workers, nurses, lawyers, shelter workers), political activists, and journalists. Their claims to expertise are based on either intellectual study (Bass and Rice, 1979; Dobash and Dobash, 1979; Gelles, 1976; Ferraro and Johnson, 1983; Hofeller, 1982; Langley and Levy, 1977; Morgan, 1982; Pagelow, 1981a,b; Roy, 1977; Truninger, 1971), practical experience in social service provision (Fleming, 1979; Hendrix *et al.*, 1978; Pizzey, 1979; Rounsaville, 1978; Shainess, 1977), or both (Hilberman, 1980; McShane, 1979; Walker, 1979, 1983).

Reprinted from "The Social Construction of Deviance: Experts on Battered Women," *Social Problems*, Vol. 31, No. 3 (February 1984), pp. 296–310, by permission of the Society for the Study of Social Problems and the authors. Copyright © 1984 by the Society for the Study of Social Problems.

Despite this diversity, the experts on battered women share a fundamentally important belief. As members of what Berger and Berger (1983:38) call the "knowledge class," these experts believe that their understandings should be used to educate and assist those who are less knowledgeable and fortunate. Among experts on battered women, this belief in the necessity of expert intervention in others' everyday matters is reflected in their common, overriding concern with a particular issue: Why do battered women remain in relationships with abusive mates? This question has been the explicit and almost sole concern of two books (Pagelow, 1981a; Walker, 1979), four academic journal articles (Bass and Rice, 1979; Ferraro and Johnson, 1983; Gelles, 1976; Pagelow, 1981b), and five chapters in larger works or edited volumes (Davidson, 1978; Dobash and Dobash, 1979; Langley and Levy, 1977; Martin, 1976, 1979).

This paper also considers the question "why do they stay?" However, we focus not on the behaviors of battered women *per se,* but on the experts. We look at how, by both asking and answering this question, the experts have constructed a new category of deviance: battered women who remain with their mates.[5] Three interrelated questions are also addressed. First, we analyze the question itself to see what asking it implies about battered women. Second, we examine the general character of the experts' responses to this question. Third, we consider the quality of the evidence offered by the experts in support of these responses. Initially, we suggest an alternative vocabulary for battered women's motives.

SOCIOLOGICAL IMPLICATIONS OF THE QUESTION

The question "why do they stay?" implicitly defines the parameters of the social problem of battered women. By asking this question, the experts imply that assaulted wives are of two basic types: those who leave their mates and those who do not. Not only are possible distinctions among assaulted wives who remain with their mates implicitly ignored, but so too are the unknown number of assaulted wives who quickly terminate such relationships. By focusing attention on those who stay, the experts imply that assaulted wives who remain with their mates are more needy and deserving of public and expert concern than those who do not. In fact, some of the experts have explicitly defined battered women as women who *remain* in relationships containing violence (Ferraro and Johnson, 1983; Pizzey, 1979; Scott, 1974; Walker, 1979).

Moreover, the experts' common and overriding concern with the question of why assaulted wives stay reveals their shared definition of the normatively expected response to the experience of battering. To ask why assaulted wives remain with their mates is to imply that doing so requires explanation. In general, as Scott and Lyman (1968) have noted, normatively expected behavior does not require explanation. It is normatively unanticipated, untoward acts which require what Scott and Lyman term an "account." By asking why battered women stay, therefore, the experts implicitly define leaving one's mate as the normatively expected response to the experience of wife assault. Staying, on the other hand, is implicitly defined as deviant, an act "which is perceived (i.e., recognized) as violating expectations" (Hawkins and Tiedeman, 1975:59).

In other words, once the experts identify a woman as battered, normative expectations regarding marital stability are reversed. After all, separated and divorced persons are commonly called upon to explain why their relationships "didn't work out" (Weiss, 1975). It is typically marital stability, "staying," which is normatively expected and marital instability, "leaving," which requires an account. However, as far as the experts on battered women are concerned, once wife assault occurs, it is marital stability which requires explanation.

In view of the experts' typifications of relationships within which wife assault occurs, this reversal of normative expectations seems only logical. Although research indicates that the severity and frequency of wife assault varies considerably across couples (Straus *et al.,* 1980), the experts stress that, *on the average,* wife assault is more dangerous for victims than is assault by a stranger (U.S. Department of Justice, 1980). Moreover, most experts maintain that once wife assault has occurred within a relationship it will become more frequent and severe over time (Dobash and Dobash, 1979), and few believe that this pattern of escalating violence can be broken without terminating the relationship.[6] It is hardly surprising, therefore, that the experts on battered women define "leaving" as the expected, reasonable, and desirable response to the experience of wife assault.[7] Staying, in contrast, is described as "maladaptive choice behavior" (Waites, 1977–78), "self-destruction through inactivity" (Rounsaville, 1978), or, most concisely, "deviant" (Ferraro and Johnson, 1983). For the experts, battered women who remain with their mates pose an intellectual puzzle: Why are they so unreasonable? Why do they stay?

To ask such a question is to request an account. Experts who provide answers to this question are, therefore, offering accounts on behalf of battered women who remain with their mates. According to Scott and Lyman (1968), two general types of accounts are possible: justifications and excuses. A justification is an account which acknowledges the actor's responsibility for the behavior in question but challenges the imputation of deviance ("I did it, but I didn't do anything wrong"). An excuse, on the other hand, acknowledges the deviance of the behavior in question but relieves the actor of responsibility for it ("I did something wrong, but it wasn't my fault").

Clearly, these different types of accounts elicit different kinds of responses. If the behavior in question is socially justifiable, then the actor was behaving reasonably, as normatively expected. The actor's ability or competence to manage everyday affairs without interference is not called into question (Garfinkel, 1967:57). In contrast, excusing behavior implies that the actor cannot manage everyday affairs without interference. Although the behavior is due to circumstances beyond the actor's control, it is admittedly deviant. By implication, assistance from others may be required if the actor is to avoid behaving similarly in the future. In order to fully understand the experts' responses to battered women who remain with their mates it is necessary, therefore, to determine which type of account they typically offer on behalf of such women.

THE EXPERTS' ACCOUNTS

Experts on battered women are a diverse group. This diversity is reflected in the emphasis each expert places on various accounts, in the number of accounts offered, and in how series of accounts are combined to produce complex theoretical explanations. Despite such diversity, however, there is a sociologically important similarity among the experts' accounts. None of the experts argues that "staying" is justifiable. "Staying" is either explicitly or implicitly defined as unreasonable, normatively unexpected, and, therefore, deviant. By implication, the accounts offered by the experts are excuses for women's deviant behavior, and they offer two basic types.[8] Battered women are said to remain with their mates because of external constraints on their behavior or because of internal constraints. In either case, the accounts offered by the experts acknowledge the deviance of staying but relieve battered women of responsibility for doing so.

EXTERNAL CONSTRAINTS

Almost all contemporary experts on battered women maintain that staying is excusable due to external constraints on women's behavior (Dobash and Dobash, 1979; Freeman, 1979; Langley and Levy, 1977; Martin, 1976; Pagelow, 1981a,b; Pizzey, 1979; Ridington, 1977–78; Roy, 1977; Shainess, 1977).

> Why does she not leave? The answer is simple. If she has children but no money and no place to go, she has no choice. (Fleming, 1979:83)

Clearly, such accounts are based on the assumption that battered women who stay are economically dependent upon their mates. If a woman has no money and no place to go, she cannot be held responsible for the unreasonable act of staying. She has no choice.

Although this excuse is the most prevalent in the literature on battered women, further elaboration is necessary. In its simplest form, such an account can be easily challenged: What about friends, family, the welfare system, and other social service agencies? In response to such challenges, experts must offer accounts which will excuse women for not taking advantage of such assistance. Experts meet these challenges with at least two further accounts of external constraints. First, experts claim that most battered women are interpersonally isolated. Even if they are not, family and friends are said to typically blame women for their problems instead of providing assistance (Carlson, 1977; Dobash and Dobash, 1971; Fleming, 1979; Hilberman and Munson, 1977–78; Truninger, 1971). Second, experts claim that social service agencies typically provide little, if any, assistance. In fact, experts maintain that the organization of agencies (bureaucratic procedures and agency mandates to preserve family stability) and the behavior of agency personnel (sexism) discourage battered women who attempt to leave (Bass and Rice, 1979; Davidson, 1978; Dobash and Dobash, 1970, Higgins, 1978; Martin, 1976, 1978; McShane, 1979; Pizzey, 1979; Prescott and Letko, 1977; Truninger, 1971). In other words, the experts maintain that battered women can expect little assistance in overcoming their economic dependency. According to the experts, the excuse of economic dependency should be honored given the additional excuses of unresponsive friends, family, and social service agencies.

Although the external constraint type of excuse acknowledges that staying is unreasonable, it relieves battered women of the responsibility for doing so. Battered women who remain with their mates are portrayed as "more acted upon than acting" (Sykes and Matza, 1957:667). The implication, of course, is that women would leave (i.e., they would be reasonable) if external constraints could be overcome. The experts provide a warrant, therefore, for intervention in battered women's everyday affairs. In order to act reasonably and leave, battered women must overcome the external constraint of economic dependency which they cannot do without the assistance of specialized experts.

Despite the prevalence of external constraint accounts in the literature on battered women, most experts consider such excuses insufficient. Instead of, or in addition to, such accounts, the experts maintain that battered women face a second type of constraint on their behavior. Although few contemporary experts argue that women stay because they enjoy being the objects of abuse, that they are masochistic, the experts do maintain that battered women face various "internal constraints."[9]

INTERNAL CONSTRAINTS

Some experts have proposed that biographically accumulated experiences may lead women to define violence as "normal" and "natural" (Ball, 1977; Gelles, 1976; Langley and Levy, 1977; Lion, 1977). Likewise, according to some experts, women define violence as a problem only if it becomes severe and/or frequent "enough" (Carlson, 1977; Gelles, 1976; Moore, 1979; Rounsaville and Weissman, 1977–78).[10] If violence is not subjectively defined as a "problem," then women have no reason to consider leaving.

For the most part, experts have focused their attention on documenting internal constraints which are said to prevent women from leaving their mates *even when* violence is subjectively defined as a problem. Experts suggest two major sources of such internal constraints: femininity and the experience of victimization.

To many experts, the primary source of internal constraints is the femininity of battered women. Attributes commonly regarded as "feminine" are automatically attributed to battered women, especially when these characteristics can conceiv-

ably account for why such women might remain with their mates. For example, women who stay are said to be emotionally dependent upon their mates (Dobash and Dobash, 1979; Fleming, 1979; Freeman, 1979; Langley and Levy, 1977; Moore, 1979; Pizzey, 1979: Roy, 1977); to have a poor self-image or low self-esteem (Carlson, 1977; Freeman, 1979; Langley and Levy, 1977; Lieberknecht, 1978; Martin, 1976; Morgan, 1982; Ridington, 1977–78; Star *et al.,* 1979; Truninger, 1971); and to have traditional ideas about women's "proper place."[11] In isolation or in combination, these so-called feminine characteristics are said to internally constrain women's behavior. According to the experts, women find it subjectively difficult to leave their mates even when violence is defined as a problem.

Internal constraints are also said to follow from the process of victimization itself. According to the experts, battered women not only display typically feminine characteristics, but they also develop unique characteristics due to the victimization process. For example, some experts have argued that once a woman is assaulted she will fear physical reprisal if she leaves (Lieberknecht, 1978; Martin, 1979; Melville, 1978). Other physical, emotional, and psychological after-effects of assault are also said to discourage battered women from leaving their mates (Moore, 1979; Roy, 1977). Indeed, battered women are sometimes said to develop complex psychological problems from their victimization. These include the "stress-response syndrome" (Hilberman, 1980), "enforced restriction of choice" (Waites, 1977–78), "learned helplessness" (Walker, 1979), or responses similar to those of the "rape trauma syndrome" (Hilberman and Munson, 1977–78). A symptom common to all such diagnostic categories is that sufferers find it subjectively difficult to leave their mates.

As with external constraint excuses, these internal constraint accounts also acknowledge the deviance of remaining in a relationship containing violence while, at the same time, relieving battered women of responsibility for doing so. They function in this way, as excuses, because the various internal constraints attributed to battered women are identified as beyond their personal control. Clearly, battered women are not responsible for their gender socialization or for the physical violence they have suffered. In other words, both external and internal constraint accounts portray battered women who stay with their mates as more acted upon than acting. What women require, "for their own good," is assistance in overcoming the various barriers which prevent them from acting reasonably. Thus, both types of accounts offered by the experts on behalf of battered women who stay provide grounds for expert intervention in these women's everyday affairs.

As Scott and Lyman (1968) have pointed out, the criteria in terms of which accounts are evaluated vary in relation to the situation in which they are offered, the characteristics of the audience, and the identity of the account provider. In the present context, the identity of the account provider is of particular interest. When experts provide accounts which implicitly serve to promote their right to intervene in others' affairs, an important evaluative criterion is the quality of supportive evidence they offer. Experts who speak on behalf of others are expected to do so on the basis of uncommon knowledge. If, therefore, the evidence which the experts offer in support of their accounts for why battered women stay fails to confirm the expectation of uncommon knowledge, then their claim to be speaking and acting on such women's behalf is open to question.

THE EVIDENCE FOR EXPERTS' ACCOUNTS

How do experts obtain their knowledge about the experiences and behavior of battered women? In order to explore the experts' claim to uncommon knowledge, we address three questions: From whom is evidence obtained (the issue of generalizability)? By what means is evidence obtained (the issue of validity)? How consistently does the evidence support the accounts offered (the issue of reliability)?

1) GENERALIZABILITY

Experts on battered women claim to have knowledge of the experiences and behavior of women who remain in relationships containing violence. Yet, while there is general agreement that many battered women suffer in silence, with few exceptions the experts have studied only those assaulted wives who have come to the attention of social service agencies, many of whom have already left their mates.[12] Women who contact social service agencies have decided that they require expert intervention in their private affairs, and there is good reason to believe that such women differ from women who have *not* sought assistance.

The decision to seek professional help is typically preceded by a complex process of problem definition, and this process is invariably more difficult and of longer duration when the problem involves the behavior of a family member (Goffman, 1969; Schwartz, 1957; Weiss, 1975; Yarrow *et al.,* 1955). Regardless of the nature of the problem, this definitional process seems to follow a fairly predictable pattern. Only as a last resort are professional helpers contacted (Emerson and Messinger, 1977; Kadushin, 1969; Mechanic, 1975). Since it is primarily the experiences of women who have reached the end of this help-seeking process which provide evidence for experts' accounts, the generalizability of this evidence is questionable.

2) VALIDITY

When not simply stating their own perceptions of battered women, experts obtain their evidence in one of two ways. They sometimes question other experts and they sometimes directly question women. Clearly, others' perceptions, whether expert or not, are of uncertain validity. However, even the evidence based on battered women's responses to the question "why do you stay?" is of doubtful validity.

To ask a battered woman to respond to this question is to request that she explain her apparently deviant behavior. This leaves her two alternatives. She can either justify her staying ("I love him"; "he's not all bad"; "the kids need him") or she can excuse her behavior. Since experts have predefined staying as undeniably deviant, it is unlikely that they will honor a justification. Indeed, some experts on battered women have explicitly characterized justifications for staying as "rationalizations," accounts which are self-serving and inaccurate (Ferraro and Johnson, 1983; Waites, 1977–78). Given the experts' presuppositions about the behavior of "staying" and the typical desire of persons to maintain "face" (Goffman, 1955), it is likely that the only accounts the experts will honor—excuses—are subtly elicited by the experts who question battered women. If this is so, then the experts, by asking women why they remain with their mates, have merely constructed an interactional situation which will produce evidence confirming the accounts they offer on women's behalf.[13]

It is hardly surprising, therefore, that the experts on battered women offer remarkably similar accounts of why women stay. This is particularly visible in the evidence which supports the external constraint accounts. By almost exclusively interviewing women who turn to inexpensive or free social service agencies and then constructing an interactional situation which is likely to elicit a particular type of account, experts practically ensure that their presuppositions about external constraints are confirmed.[14] In brief, the validity of the experts' evidence is doubtful.

3) RELIABILITY

Relying primarily on evidence from interviewing and observation, the experts on battered women offer amazingly similar accounts of why women remain. There are, however, many ways to obtain evidence. The question at hand is whether evidence gained from interviewing and observation is similar to evidence obtained using other methods.

If the economic dependency (external constraint) excuse is to avoid challenge, it must be supplemented by the additional excuses of unresponsive friends, family members, and social service agencies. Yet, evidence to support these supplementary external constraint excuses is less than overwhelming. In fact, some evidence undermines the excuse that social service agencies and providers discourage battered women from leaving their mates. Pagelow (1981a) found little relationship between her measures of "agency response" and the amount of time battered women had remained with their mates. Hofeller (1982) found that many battered women self-reported being either "completely" or "somewhat" satisfied with the efforts of social service agencies on their behalf.[15]

As with the excuse of unresponsive social service agencies, available evidence conflicts with various internal constraint accounts offered by the experts. For example, available evidence does not support assertions that battered women hold traditional beliefs about "women's proper place," or that these beliefs internally constrain women from leaving their mates. Walker (1983) reports that battered women perceive themselves to be *less* traditional than "other women," and the results of experimental studies conducted by Hofeller (1982) and Rosenbaum and O'Leary (1981) indicate that women who have *not* been victims of wife assault hold more traditional attitudes than women who are victims. Moreover, Pagelow (1981a) reports that her measures of "traditional ideology" did not help explain the length of time battered women remained with their mates.

The experts have also maintained that the low self-esteem assumed to be common to women in general is exacerbated by the process of victimization, producing a powerful internal constraint on the behavior of battered women. Yet in their now classic review of research evidence regarding sex differences in self-esteem, Maccoby and Jacklin (1974:15) labelled as a popular myth the commonsense deduction that "women, knowing that they belong to a sex that is devalued,...must have a poor opinion of themselves." Contrary to this commonsense deduction, sex differences in self-esteem have rarely been found in experimental studies, and when they have, women's self-esteem is often higher than men's. In addition, at least two studies contained in the literature on battered women refute the statement that battered women have lower self-esteem than women who have not experienced assault. Walker (1983) found that battered women reported their self-esteem as higher than that of "other women," and Star (1978) found that shelter residents who had *not* experienced wife assault scored lower on an "ego-strength" scale than residents who had been assaulted.

In short, the evidence provided to support expert claims about battered women is, by scientific standards, less than convincing. In fact, it appears as if the experts' accounts are presupposed and then implicitly guide both the gathering and interpretation of evidence. In constructing their accounts, the experts have employed the commonsense practice of automatically attributing to individual women (in this case, battered women) sets of traits based on their sex. As females, battered women are automatically assumed to be economically and emotionally dependent upon their mates, to have low self-esteem, and to hold traditional attitudes and beliefs. Methodologies which might yield conflicting evidence are seldom used, and when seemingly conflicting evidence is uncovered it is often explained away. For example, Walker (1983:40) implicitly argues that battered women have an inaccurate perception of themselves. She interprets the finding that battered women consider themselves to be in control of their own behavior as a "lack of acknowledgement that her batterer *really* is in control" (emphasis added). Likewise, Pagelow (1981a) discredits seemingly conflicting evidence by challenging her own measures; the presupposed accounts are not questioned. In other words, the interpretive force of the "master status" of sex "overpowers" evidence to the contrary (Hughes, 1945:357). What the experts on battered women offer in support of their accounts for why women remain is not uncommon knowledge, therefore, but professional "folklore" which, however sophisticated, remains folklore (Zimmerman and Pollner, 1970:44).

This does not mean that evidence which conflicts with the experts' accounts is itself above question. On the contrary, the generalizability, reliability, and validity of conflicting evidence are also problematic. For example, both Pagelow (1981a) and Star (1978) used paper and pencil tests, and both studies were primarily concerned with residents of shelters in urban southern California. Likewise, Walker's (1979, 1983) findings are based primarily on clinical records of an unrepresentative group of women, and evidence regarding self-esteem is primarily derived from experimental studies involving only college students.

The sociologically intriguing issue is not, however, the "truthfulness" of accounts. In a diverse society, a variety of different vocabularies of motive (Mills, 1940) are available for making sense out of the complex interrelationships between actor, biography, situation, and behavior. Under such circumstances, "what is reason for one man is mere rationalization for another" (Mills, 1940:910). Any attempt to ascertain battered women's "true" motives would therefore be an exercise in what Mills termed "motive-mongering." What is of sociological interest is that the experts' accounts are not based upon uncommon knowledge but upon commonsense deductions best described as folklore. Clearly, this should raise questions about both the experts' claim to be speaking on battered women's behalf and their claim to have the right to intervene in such women's private affairs.

Given the experts' claim to be speaking and acting in battered women's "best interests," the sociologically important issue is the relative plausibility of the particular vocabulary of motive used by the experts. According to the experts, their primary concerns are the condemnation and elimination of wife assault, tasks which are likely to require specialized expertise. The vocabulary of motive which supports this agenda is one of highlighting "constraints" on women's behavior which must be overcome in order for them to behave reasonably—that is, in order for them to leave. But such a vocabulary is not the only plausible way to make sense of women's behavior.

AN ALTERNATIVE VOCABULARY OF MOTIVE

Prior to the 1970s, the problems of battered women received little attention. In contrast, the contemporary experts have portrayed women as little more than victims. The tendency has been to define both battered women and their relationships with their mates almost exclusively in terms of the occurrence and effects of physical and emotional assault. Battered women are simply defined as assaulted wives who remain with assaultive mates (Ferraro and Johnson, 1983; Pizzey, 1979; Scott, 1974; Walker, 1979), and their relationships are portrayed as no more than victimizing processes. Such a focus leads to what Barry (1979) has termed "victimism," knowing a person only as a victim. One effect of the victimism practiced by the experts on battered women is that possible experiential and behavioral similarities between battered women and other persons are overlooked. It is simply assumed that the occurrence and experience of assault clearly distinguish battered women and their relationships from individuals in cross-sex relationships which do not contain violence. However, even a cursory review of the sociological literature on marital stability and instability suggests that, at least in regard to their reluctance to leave their mates, battered women are quite similar to both other women and to men.

This literature consistently indicates that marital stability often outlives marital quality. Goode (1956) found that such stability was only sometimes due to the obvious, objective costs of terminating the relationship ("external constraints"). Contrary to predictions that relationships will terminate when apparent "costs" outweigh apparent "benefits," it is not at all unusual for relationships to be sustained even when outsiders perceive costs to be greater than benefits. Although experts on battered women have argued that leaving a relationship means that a woman's status will change

from "wife" to "divorcee" (Dobash and Dobash, 1979; Truninger, 1971), a variety of family sociologists have noted that terminating a relationship is far more complex than is suggested by the concept of "status change." Over time, marital partners develop an "attachment" to one another (Weiss, 1975), a "crescive bond" (Turner, 1970), a "shared biography" (McLain and Weigert, 1979). As a result, each becomes uniquely irreplaceable in the eyes of the other. Such a personal commitment to a specific mate has been found to persist despite decreases in marital partners' liking, admiration, and/or respect for one another (Rosenblatt, 1977; Weiss, 1975). Battered women who remain in relationships which outsiders consider costly are not, therefore, particularly unusual or deviant.

Moreover, the sociological literature on marital stability and instability suggests that the process of separation and divorce, what Vaughan (1979) terms "uncoupling," is typically difficult. One indication of the difficulty of this process is the considerable time uncoupling often takes (Cherlin, 1981; Goode, 1956, Weiss, 1975). It is also typical for a series of temporary separations to precede a permanent separation (Lewis and Spanier, 1979; Weiss, 1975; Vaughan, 1979). In brief, the lengthy "leaving and returning" cycle said to be characteristic of battered women is a typical feature of the uncoupling process. Further, the guilt, concern, regret, bitterness, disappointment, depression, and lowered perception of self attributed to battered women are labels for emotions often reported by women and men in the process of uncoupling (Spanier and Castro, 1979; Weiss, 1975).

Although the experts attribute unusual characteristics and circumstances to battered women who remain with their mates, the reluctance of battered women to leave can be adequately and commonsensically expressed in the lyrics of a popular song: "Breaking up is hard to do." It can also be expressed in the more sophisticated vocabulary of sociological psychology: Individuals who are terminating intimate relationships "die one of the deaths that is possible" for them (Goffman,

1952). The sociological literature on marital stability and instability does suggest, therefore, an alternative to the vocabulary of battered women's motives provided by the experts on battered women. Because a large portion of an adult's self is typically invested in their relationship with their mate, persons become committed and attached to this mate as a uniquely irreplaceable individual. Despite problems, "internal constraints" are experienced when contemplating the possibility of terminating the relationship with the seemingly irreplaceable other. Again, if this is the case, then women who remain in relationships containing violence are not unusual or deviant; they are typical.

Some experts on battered women have reported evidence which supports this alternative characterization of the motives of women who remain. Gayford (1975) reports that half of his sample of battered women claimed to be satisfied with their relationships, and Dobash and Dobash (1979) note that, apart from the violence, battered women often express positive feelings toward their mates. Moreover, Ferraro and Johnson (1983) report that battered women typically believe that their mates are the only person they could love, and Walker (1979) reports that battered women often describe their mates as playful, attentive, exciting, sensitive, and affectionate. Yet, because of the victimism they practice, experts on battered women often fail to recognize that such findings demonstrate the multi-dimensionality of battered women's relationships with their mates. Indeed, some of these experts have explicitly advised that battered women's expressions of attachment and commitment to their mates not be believed:

> The statement that abused wives love their husbands need not be taken at face value. It may represent merely a denial of ambivalence or even unmitigated hatred. (Waites, 1977–78:542)

> The only reasons the woman does not end the marriage are dependence—emotional or practical—and fear of change and the unknown. These are often masked as love or so the woman deludes herself. (Shainess, 1977:118)

Such expressions of commitment and attachment are *justifications* for why a person might remain with their mate. To honor such a justification would be to acknowledge that staying in a relationship which contains violence is not necessarily deviant. In order to sustain their claim to expertise, therefore, the experts on battered women cannot acknowledge the possible validity of this alternative, "justifying" vocabulary of motive even when it is offered by battered women themselves. In other words, the experts discredit battered women's interpretations of their own experiences. The justifications offered by battered women are reinterpreted by the experts as merely "symptoms" of the Stockholm Syndrome (Ochlberg, 1980), of an "addiction" which "must be overcome" (Waites, 1977–78), or as the "miracle glue" which "binds a battered woman to her batterer" (Walker, 1979:xvi). By reinterpreting the justifications of battered women in these ways, the experts sustain their claim that such women require the assistance of specialized experts.

CONCLUSIONS

This case study of the social construction of deviance by a group of experts illustrates how members of the knowledge class create a new clientele for their services. In effect, experts discredit the ability of a category of persons to manage their own affairs without interference. The actors in question are portrayed as incapable of either understanding or controlling the factors which govern their behavior. In order for them to understand their experiences and gain control over their behavior, by implication, they require the assistance of specialized experts. Because the category of actors which compose such a clientele are characterized as unreasonable and incompetent, any resistance they offer to the experts' definitions and intervention is easily discredited. For example, battered women's attempts to justify staying with their mates are often interpreted by the experts as further evidence of such women's unreasonableness and incompetence. Experts are able to sustain their claims to be speaking and acting on others' behalf, therefore, despite the protests of those on whose behalf they claim to be speaking and acting.

We do not mean to suggest that experts' potential clientele do not benefit from experts' efforts. For example, the experts on battered women have played a major role in focusing public attention on the plight of the victims of wife assault. In doing so, they have helped to dispel the popular myth that these women somehow deserved to be assaulted. In turn, this has undoubtedly encouraged the general public, the police, the courts, and various social service agencies to be more responsive and sensitive to the needs of such women. Yet, battered women may pay a high price for this assistance.

The experts on battered women define leaving one's mate as the normatively expected, reasonable response to the experience of wife assault. By implication, staying with one's mate after such an experience requires explanation. In order to explain this unreasonable response, the experts have provided accounts, that is, ascribed motives to battered women which excuse such deviance. As Blum and McHugh (1971:106) have noted, "observer's ascription of motive serves to formulate …persons." In offering accounts on behalf of battered women who stay, the experts propose a formulation of the type of persons such women are. For example, the experts characterize this type of person as "oversocialized into feminine identity" (Ball and Wyman 1977–78), "bewildered and helpless" (Ball, 1977), "immature" and lacking clear self-identities (Star *et al.,* 1979), "overwhelmingly passive" and unable to act on their own behalf" (Hilberman and Munson, 1977–79), and cognitively, emotionally, and motivationally "deficient" (Walker, 1977–78). Moreover, these women are described as suffering from either the "battered wife syndrome" (Morgan, 1982; Walker, 1983) or the "adult maltreatment syndrome" in Section 995.8 of the International Classification of Diseases. They are "society's problem" (Martin, 1978). Clearly, the categorical identity of battered women is a deeply discrediting one. As

Hawkins and Tiedeman (1975) have noted, such typifications of persons by experts often have significant, practical consequences. The experts' descriptions of such "types" often serve as "processing stereotypes" which influence the perceptions and responses of social service providers. Indeed, Loseke (1982) documented how the experts' typifications of battered women served as a processing stereotype which influenced workers' perceptions and service provision at a shelter for battered women.

In summary, once a woman admits that she is a victim of wife assault, her competence is called into question if she does not leave. She is defined as a type of person who requires assistance, a person who is unable to manage her own affairs. As a result, the experts on battered women have constructed a situation where victims of wife assault may lose control over their self-definitions, interpretations of experience, and, in some cases, control over their private affairs. In a sense, battered women may now be victimized twice, first by their mates and then by the experts who claim to speak on their behalf.

NOTES

1. Consistent with the literature under review, we use the terms *marriage* and *wife* in a purely sociological, rather than legal, sense. *Marriage* refers to any continuing, cross-sex relationship and *wife* to a female participant in such a relationship.
2. For a history of the feminist-identified battered women's movement see Schechter (1983).
3. Straus (1974) has argued that three social factors combined in the 1970s to bring the topic of family violence to the attention of academics: the emergence of a politically vocal women's movement, public concern about all forms of violence, and the decline of consensus models of society.
4. See Wardell *et al.* (1983) for a discussion of disagreements among those who state an allegiance to feminist ideals.
5. See Morgan (1981), Wardell *et al.* (1983), and Stark and Flitcraft (1983) for discussions of how experts have shaped public understandings of the phenomenon of wife assault.

6. There has been little systematic study of the possibility of change in relationships. Walker (1979) reports that her pessimism is based on clinical experience. See Coleman (1980) for a more optimistic prognosis.

7. Of course, this commonsense deduction is also based on the common, although often unspoken, assumption that humans are "rational actors." If the basis of human motivation is a desire to maximize rewards and minimize costs, then why would a battered woman remain in such an obviously "costly" relationship?

8. A third type of explanation for why victims of wife assault remain with their mates is seldom found in the literature on battered women and, therefore, will not be reviewed here. This type of explanation is based on a systems theory analysis of family interactions. Straus (1974) suggests the empirical applicability of such an approach, and Denzin (1983) provides a phenomenological foundation. Erchak (1981) used this approach to explain the maintenance of child abuse, and Giles-Sims (1983) has used this to explain the behavior of battered women.

9. Theories focusing on feminine masochism have been proposed by Snell *et al.* (1964) and Gayford (1975). Waites (1977–78) suggested that the "appearance" of masochism results from "enforced restriction of choice." Most experts argue that the concept of masochism is not applicable to battered women (Breines and Gordon, 1983).

10. Empirical testing of the association between leaving and childhood experiences has not confirmed this theory (Pagelow, 1981a; Star, 1978; Walker, 1977–78). Likewise, empirical testing of the association between leaving and "severity/frequency" has also not supported theory. See Pagelow (1981b) for a complete discussion.

11. "Traditional ideology" includes such beliefs as: divorce is a stigma (Dobash and Dobash, 1979; Langley and Levy, 1977; Moore, 1979; Roy, 1977); the children need their father (Dobash and Dobash, 1979); the woman assumes responsibility for the actions of her mate (Fleming, 1979; Langley and Levy, 1977; Martin, 1976); or feels embarrassed about the family situation (Ball and Wyman, 1977–78; Fleming, 1979; Hendrix *et al.*, 1978).

12. Exceptions are Gelles (1976), Hofeller (1982), and Rosenbaum and O'Leary (1981), who included matched samples of persons not receiving services, and Prescott and Letko (1977), who used information from women who responded to an advertisement in *Ms.* magazine.

13. The situation is more complicated when women who have left are asked why *did* you stay? Or, as Dobash and Dobash (1979:147) asked: "why do you think you stayed with him as long as you did?" In such situations, the question asks women to retrospectively reconstruct their personal biographies based on their current circumstances and understandings.

14. However, Rounsaville (1978) found that "lack of resources" did not distinguish between women who had left and women who had not left.

15. The "satisfaction" of victims with social services varies considerably by the type of agency (Hofeller, 1982; Prescott and Letko, 1977).

REFERENCES

Ball, Margaret. 1977. "Issues of violence in family casework." *Social Casework* 58(1):3–12.

Ball, Patricia G., and Elizabeth Wyman. 1977–78. "Battered wives and powerlessness: What can counselors do?" *Victimology* 2(3,4):545–552.

Barry, Kathleen. 1979. *Female Sexual Slavery.* New York: Avon.

Bass, David, and Janet Rice. 1979. "Agency responses to the abused wife." *Social Casework* 60 (June):338–342.

Berger, Brigitte, and Peter L. Berger. 1983. *The War Over the Family.* New York: Anchor.

Blum, Alan F., and Peter McHugh. 1971. "The social ascription of motives." *American Sociological Review* 36 (February):98–109.

Breines, Wini, and Linda Gordon. 1983. "The new scholarship on family violence." *Signs* 8 (Spring):490–531.

Carlson, Bonnie E. 1977. "Battered women and their assailants." *Social Work* 22 (November):455–460.

Cherlin, Andrew J. 1981. *Marriage, Divorce, Remarriage.* Cambridge, MA: Harvard University Press.

Coleman, Karen Howes. 1980. "Conjugal violence: What 33 men report." *Journal of Marital and Family Therapy* 6 (April): 207–214.

Davidson, Terry. 1978. *Conjugal Crime.* New York: Hawthorne.

Denzin, Norman K. 1983. "Towards a phenomenology of family violence." *Paper presented at the meetings of the American Sociological Association.* Detroit, August.

Dobash, R. Emerson, and Russell Dobash. 1979. *Violence Against Wives: A Case Against the Patriarchy.* New York: Free Press.

Emerson, Robert M., and Sheldon L. Messinger. 1977. "The micro-politics of trouble." *Social Problems* 25 (December):121–134.

Erchak, Gerald M. 1981. "The escalation and maintenance of child abuse: A cybernetic model." *Child Abuse and Neglect* 5:153–157.

Ferraro, Kathleen J., and John M. Johnson. 1983. "How women experience battering: The process of victimization." *Social Problems* 30 (February):325–339.

Fleming, Jennifer Baker. 1979. *Stopping Wife Abuse.* New York: Anchor Books.

Freeman, M. D. A. 1979. *Violence in the Home.* Westmead, England: Saxon House.

Garfinkel, Harold. 1967. *Studies in Ethnomethodology.* Englewood Cliffs, NJ: Prentice-Hall.

Gayford, J. J. 1975. "Wife battering: A preliminary survey of 100 cases." *British Medical Journal* 1:194–197.

Gelles, Richard J. 1976. "Abused wives: Why do they stay?" *Journal of Marriage and the Family* 38(4):659–668.

Giles-Sims, Jean. 1983. *Wife Battering: A Systems Approach.* New York: Guilford Press.

Goffman, Erving. 1952. "On cooling the mark out: Some aspects of adaptation to failure." *Psychiatry* 15 (November): 451–463.

———. 1955. "On face-work: An analysis of ritual elements in social interaction." *Psychiatry* 18 (August): 213–231.

———. 1969. "Insanity of place." *Psychiatry* 32 (November):352–388.

Goode, William J. 1956. *After Divorce.* Glencoe, IL: Free Press.

Hawkins, Richard, and Gary Tiedeman. 1975. *The Creation of Deviance: Interpersonal and Organizational Determinants.* Columbus, OH: Charles E. Merrill.

Hendrix, Melva Jo, Gretchen E. LaGodna, and Cynthia A. Bohen. 1978. "The battered wife." *American Journal of Nursing* 78 (April):650–653.

Higgins, John G. 1978. "Social services for abused wives." *Social Casework* 59 (May):266–271.

Hilberman, Elaine. 1980. "Overview: The 'Wife-beater's wife' reconsidered." *American Journal of Psychiatry* 137 (November):1336–1346.

Hilberman, Elaine, and Kit Munson. 1977–78. "Sixty battered women." *Victimology* 2(3,4):460–470.

Hofeller, Kathleen H. 1982. *Social, Psychological, and Situational Factors in Wife Abuse.* Palo Alto, CA: R. and E. Associates.

Hughes, Everett. 1945. "Dilemmas and contradictions of status." *American Journal of Sociology* 50 (March):353–359.

Jones, Ann. 1980. *Women Who Kill.* New York: Holt, Rinehart and Winston.

Kadushin, Charles. 1969. *Why People Go to Psychiatrists.* New York: Atherton.

Langley, Roger, and Richard C. Levy. 1977. *Wife Beating: The Silent Crisis.* New York: Pocket Books.

Lewis, Robert A., and Graham B. Spanier. 1979. "Theorizing about the quality and stability of marriage." Pp. 268–294 in Wesley R. Burr, Reuben Hill, F. Ivan Nye, and Ira L. Reiss (eds.), *Contemporary Theories About the Family,* Volume 1. New York: Free Press.

Lieberknecht, Kay. 1978. "Helping the battered wife." *American Journal of Nursing* 78 (April):654–656.

Lion, John R. 1977. "Clinical aspects of wifebattering." Pp. 126–136 in Maria Roy (ed.), *Battered Women: A Psychosociological Study of Domestic Violence.* New York: Van Nostrand.

Loseke, Donileen R. 1982. "Social movement theory in practice: A shelter for battered women." Unpublished Ph.D. dissertation, University of California, Santa Barbara.

Maccoby, Eleanor Emmons, and Carol Nagy Jacklin. 1974. *The Psychology of Sex Differences.* Stanford, CA: Stanford University Press.

McLain, Raymond, and Andrew Weigert. 1979. "Toward a phenomenological sociology of family: A programmatic essay." Pp. 160–205 in Wesley R. Burr, Reuben Hill, F. Ivan Nye, and Ira L. Reiss (eds.), *Contemporary Theories About the Family,* Volume 2. New York: Free Press.

McShane, Claudette. 1979. "Community services for battered women." *Social Work* 24 (January):34–39.

Martin, Del. 1976. *Battered Wives.* San Francisco: Glide Publications.

———. 1978. "Battered women: Society's problem." Pp. 111–142 in Jane Roberts Chapman and Margaret Gates (eds.), *The Victimization of Women.* Beverly Hills, CA: Sage.

———. 1979. "What keeps a woman captive in a violent relationship? The social context of battering." Pp. 33–58 in Donna M. Moore (ed.), *Battered Women.* Beverly Hills, CA: Sage.

Mechanic, David. 1975. "Sociocultural and social-psychological factors affecting personal responses to psychological disorder." *Journal of Health and Social Behavior* 16(4):393–404.

Melville, Joy. 1978. "Women in refuges." Pp. 293–310 in J. P. Martin (ed.), *Violence and the Family.* New York: John Wiley.

Mills, C. Wright. 1940. "Situated actions and vocabularies of motive." *American Sociological Review* 5 (December): 904–913.

Moore, Donna M. 1979. "An overview of the problem." Pp. 7–32 in Donna M. Moore (ed.), *Battered Women.* Beverly Hills, CA: Sage.

Morgan, Patricia A. 1981. "From battered wife to program client: The state's shaping of social problems." *Kapitalistate* 9:17–40.

Morgan, Steven M. 1982. *Conjugal Terrorism: A Psychological and Community Treatment Model of Wife Abuse.* Palo Alto, CA: R. and E. Associations.

Ochberg, F. M. 1980. "Victims of terrorism." *Journal of Clinical Psychiatry* 41:73–74.

Pagelow, Mildred Daley. 1981a. *Woman-Battering: Victims and Their Experiences.* Beverly Hills, CA: Sage.

———. 1981b. "Factors affecting women's decisions to leave violent relationships." *Journal of Family Issues* 2 (December):391–414.

Pizzey, Erin. 1979. "Victimology interview: A refuge for battered women." *Victimology* 4(1):100–112.

Prescott, Suzanne, and Carolyn Letko. 1977. "Battered women: A social psychological perspective." Pp. 72–96 in Maria Roy (ed.), *Battered Women: A Psychosociological Study of Domestic Violence.* New York: Van Nostrand.

Ridington, Jillian. 1977–78. "The transition process: A feminist environment as reconstructive milieu." *Victimology* 2(3,4): 563–575.

Rosenbaum, Alan, and K. Daniel O'Leary. 1981. "Marital violence: Characteristics of abusive couples." *Journal of Consulting and Clinical Psychology* 49(1):63–71.

Rosenblatt, Paul C. 1977. "Needed research on commitment in marriage." Pp. 73–86 in George Levinger and Harold L. Raush (eds.), *Close Relationships: Perspectives on the Meaning of Intimacy.* Amherst: University of Massachusetts.

Rounsaville, Bruce J. 1978. "Theories in marital violence: Evidence from a study of battered women." *Victimology* 2(1,2): 11–31.

Rounsaville, Bruce, and Myrna M. Weissman. 1977–78. "Battered women: A medical problem requiring detection." *International Journal of Psychiatry in Medicine* 8(2):191–202.

Roy, Maria. 1977. "A current survey of 150 cases." Pp. 25–44 in Maria Roy (ed.), *Battered Women: A Psychosociological Study of Domestic Violence.* New York: Van Nostrand.

Schechter, Susan. 1983. *Women and Male Violence.* Boston: South End Press.

Schwartz, Charlotte Green. 1957. "Perspectives on deviance: Wives' definitions of their husbands' mental illness." *Psychiatry* 20(3):275–291.

Scott, Marvin B., and Stanford M. Lyman. 1968. "Accounts." *American Sociological Review* 33 (December):46–62.

Scott, P. D. 1974. "Battered wives." *British Journal of Psychiatry* 125 (November):433–441.

Segovia-Ashley, Marta. 1978. "Presentation of Marta Segovia-Ashley." Pp. 98–107 in U.S. Commission on Civil Rights (ed.), *Battered Women: Issues, of Public Policy.* Washington, DC: U.S. Commission on Civil Rights.

Shainess, Natalie. 1977. "Psychological aspects of wife-battering." Pp. 111–118 in Maria Roy (ed.), *Battered Women: A Psychosociological Study of Domestic Violence.* New York: Van Nostrand.

Snell, John E., M. D. Richard, J. Rosenwald, and Ames Robe. 1964. "The wifebeater's wife." *Archives of General Psychiatry* 11 (August):107–112.

Spanier, Graham, and Robert F Castro. 1979. "Adjustment to separation and divorce: An analysis of 50 case studies." *Journal of Divorce* 2 (Spring):241–253.

Star, Barbara. 1978. "Comparing battered and non-battered women." *Victimology* 3(1,2):32–44.

Star, Barbara, Carol G. Clark, Karen M. Goetz, and Linda O'Malia. 1979. "Psychosocial aspects of wife battering." *Social Casework* 60 (October): 479–487.

Stark, Evan, and Anne Flitcraft. 1983. "Social knowledge, social policy, and the abuse of women: The case against patriarchal benevolence." Pp. 330–348 in David Finkelhor, Richard J. Gelles, Gerald T. Hotaling, and Murray A. Straus (eds.), *The Dark Side of Families.* Beverly Hills, CA: Sage.

Straus, Murray A. 1974. "Forward." Pp. 13–17 in Richard J. Gelles. *The Violent Home.* Beverly Hills, CA: Sage.

Straus, Murray A., Richard J. Gelles, and Suzanne Stein-metz. 1980. *Behind Closed Doors: Violence in the American Home.* New York: Anchor.

Sykes, Gresham, and David Matza. 1957. "Techniques of neutralization: A theory of delinquency." *American Sociological Review* 22 (December):664–669.

Truninger, Elizabeth. 1971. "Marital violence: The legal solutions." *Hastings Law Journal* 23 (November):259–276.

Turner, Ralph. 1970. *Family Interaction.* New York: John Wiley.

U.S. Commission on Civil Rights (ed.). 1978. *Battered Women: Issues of Public Policy.* Washington, DC: U.S. Commission on Civil Rights.

U.S. Congress: House of Representatives. 1978. *Research into Violent Behavior: Domestic Violence.* Hearings Before the Sub-Committee on Domestic and International Scientific Planning, Analysis and Cooperation of the Committee on Science and Technology. 95th Congress, 2nd Session. January 10–12. Washington, DC: U.S. Government Printing Office.

U.S. Department of Justice. 1980. *Intimate Victims: A Study of Violence Among Friends and Relatives.* Washington, DC: U.S. Government Printing Office.

Vaughan, Diane. 1979. "Uncoupling: The process of moving from one lifestyle to another." *Alternative Lifestyles* 2 (November):415–442.

Waites, Elizabeth A. 1977–78. "Female masochism and the enforced restriction of choice." *Victimology* 2(3,4):535–544.

Walker, Lenore E. 1977–78. "Battered women and learned helplessness." Victimology 2(3,4):525–534.

———. 1979. *The Battered Woman.* New York: Harper and Row.

———. 1983. "The battered woman syndrome study." Pp. 31–48 in David Finkelhor, Richard J. Gelles, Gerald T. Hotaling, and Murray A. Straus (eds.), *The Dark Side of Families.* Beverly Hills, CA: Sage.

Wardell, Laurie, Dair L. Gillespie, and Ann Leffler. 1983. "Science and violence against wives." Pp. 69–84 in David Finkelhor, Richard J. Gelles, Gerald T. Hotaling, and Murray A. Straus (eds.), *The Dark Side of Families.* Beverly Hills, CA: Sage.

Warrior, Betsy. 1978. *Working on Wife Abuse.* 46 Pleasant Street, Cambridge, MA: privately published manual.

Weiss, Robert. 1975. *Marital Separation.* New York: Basic Books.

Yarrow, Marian Radke, Charlotte Green Schwartz, Harriet S. Murphy, and Leila Calhoun Desy. 1955. "The psychological meaning of mental illness in the family." *Journal of Social Issues* 11(4):12–24.

Zimmerman, Don, and Melvin Pollner. 1970. "The everyday world as a phenomenon." Pp. 80–104 in Jack Douglas (ed.), *Understanding Everyday Life.* Chicago: Aldine.

CHAPTER 6

ORGANIZATIONAL PROCESSING OF DEVIANTS

Getting Rid of Troublemakers in High School

CHRISTINE BOWDITCH

A variety of formal organizations process clients in modern society. Some, such as police departments and psychiatric hospitals, typically process people who were defined as deviant prior to their current situation. Others, like schools and workplaces, process more clients who have no prior definition as deviant. In the first instance, people have a chance to either live up to or live down their prior reputations. In the second instance, people have a chance to achieve a reputation as a "good person" or to be designated a "troublemaker." In both instances, organizational personnel have to devise ways of dealing with the kinds of trouble they make.

Christine Bowditch describes how agents of social control in the high school's discipline office process students who have been sent to them by classroom teachers. These disciplinarians have many categories of misconduct for classifying their involuntary clients. In performing their work, they must take into account official school rules and different groups of people, including the school and their own office as well as the students. Given the great demands on their time and the limits on resources, they give priority to reducing trouble for their own office and for the school. In doing so, they fit more students to the "troublemaker" category. Thus, they produce a high rate of school dropouts, reduce their own troubles, and maintain school authority. Their work rules eliminate performing services for students.

...DuBois High was a troubled, inner-city school. Its all-black student body[1] came from an area of a highly segregated northern city where half of the adults never completed high school, almost half of the school's students lived in poverty, and more

Reprinted from "Getting Rid of Troublemakers: High School Disciplinary Procedures and the Production of Dropouts," *Social Problems,* Vol. 40, No. 4 (November 1993), pp. 493–509, by permission of the Society for the Study of Social Problems and the author. Copyright © 1993 by the Society for the Study of Social Problems.

than 60 percent had only one parent or guardian at home (school figures 1984).[2] Many of the teenage girls had children of their own and most of the boys belonged to one of the area's five or six corner groups or neighborhood gangs.

In the decade before my study, enrollment at DuBois had declined steadily as many students in its catchment area found their way to city magnet schools or private or parochial high schools. Of the more than 1,600 students still on the school's roll, many came late, cut classes, or just did not attend. While I was there, as many as 400 missed school daily. Another 100 or more students arrived late. Two hundred or more students cut certain classes on a regular basis; perhaps as many or more skipped some of their classes on occasion.

Most of the students worked substantially below grade level. California Achievement Test scores for 1983 showed that while no student scored above the 85th percentile in reading, 53 percent scored below the 16th percentile and another 40 percent scored between the 16th and 49th percentiles. Records of school grades provided additional evidence of low achievement. Figures from the math department for the 1984/85 school year, for instance, showed that 74 percent of all tenth graders failed math. As a consequence of the widespread academic failure, each year the school retained in grade approximately a quarter of all its tenth graders.

Student disorder and disobedience figured prominently both in the public's perception of the school and in the school's self-assessment. DuBois frequently suspended a half dozen or more students each day; by the end of the year, more than a quarter of its students were suspended at least once, and many had multiple or serial suspensions.

Despite these facts, I did not encounter scenes of violence or chaos. Teachers did not complain of belligerence or open hostility; instead they talked about apathy, silliness, inattention, and poor attendance. During my months of fieldwork, I witnessed daily the essentially familiar scenes of high school life.

Students sent from class; picked up in the halls; or brought in by the police for truancy, misbehavior, or more serious misconduct all went to the discipline office, a crowded, first floor office divided into a small waiting area and four inner offices. Although they shared a physical space, girls' and boys' discipline was administered separately. Three disciplinarians handled cases involving boys and two disciplinarians dealt with girls.

The discipline office could go from complete quiet to the confusion of three or four cases without notice. In addition to the discipline staff, three

or four nonteaching assistants [NTAs], two district security officers assigned to the school, two city police officers assigned to the school, various teachers, one or two of the school's counselors, twenty or thirty students, and five to ten parents moved in and out of the office in the course of a day. The design of the office ensured little privacy or protection from the noise and confusion of other cases. Just inside the door to the office, a half dozen mismatched classroom chairs placed between a couple of battered file cabinets and a table scattered with outdated school notices formed a waiting area. But, since the partitions that separated the disciplinarians' offices from that area did not rise completely to the ceiling and were fitted with opaque glass, waiting parents and students could monitor much of the "private" conversation and activity; shouted comments or angry remarks made in one conference often intruded upon other conferences.[3]

DISCIPLINARY WORK

Within the school's bureaucratic organization, the discipline office staff's specialized tasks were to maintain files on the documented misbehavior of DuBois students, confer with students charged with rule violations, determine punitive actions to be taken against students, contact the parents of students who had violated school rules, and process the forms documenting disciplinary actions and protecting due process. Specific and extensive rules from the school district defined misconduct and outlined policies, procedures, and proper documentation for disciplinary actions.

The disciplinarian's responsibility, when a student entered the office, was to determine what the student had done, assess the seriousness of the offense, and take the appropriate disciplinary action. Most of the routine work involved either dealing with students who were late for class, caught cutting class, or accused of disrupting class or meeting with students and their parents for the required conference following a suspension. Less routine, but still fairly common work involved determining punishments for students who were caught fighting; found in possession of marijuana; accused of theft, vandalism, or wall-writing; caught drinking alcohol; or charged with threatening a teacher. In rare instances, the disciplinary office handled cases involving a weapon, the sale of drugs, or violence directed against a teacher.[4]

Neither the formal description of disciplinary activities nor the rules and procedures governing the discipline office fully captured its operational practice. Disciplinary practice reflected the negotiated definitions, routines, and expectations developed among co-workers, and ongoing contests over work, authority, and responsibility within the school and between the school and parents. Disciplinarians relied on informally developed understandings about the discipline office's goals, the typical forms of student misconduct the office should handle, the types of students who normally caused trouble, and the standard strategies for dealing with misconduct (cf. Sudnow 1965, see also Waegel 1981). Within this context, official rules became a resource for workers to regulate the conditions of their work and to pursue informally identified goals (see Lipsky 1980).

To complete its work, the discipline staff interacted with teachers, NTAs, security personnel, administrators, parents, and students. Although school workers' jobs were formally coordinated, they frequently contested the boundaries of their authority and responsibility. Teachers, for example, negotiated their own strategies of classroom control—some taking a "hard line" allowing no deviation from formal rules, some using rules selectively to "contain problems" rather than to enforce obedience—and therefore made different demands on the discipline office (cf. Bittner 1967; Rubinstein 1973). Each student a teacher sent to the discipline office was, in essence, a test case of that teacher's authority. The discipline office's handling of the student determined whether the school's coercive power endorsed the teacher's definition of the situation or refuted it.

The nature of the disciplinarians' work meant the student's behavior was not interpreted in terms of its threat to one teacher's struggle for authority and classroom control. Instead, a student's behavior was judged in relation to the other students processed through the office. The staff was concerned with regulating and controlling its work, protecting its authority, and, most important, maintaining the institution's authority.

Because disciplinarians judged student misconduct with reference to the concerns of the school as a whole, they sometimes disagreed with teachers over what types of problems required the intervention of their office, complaining "this is something the teacher should have handled." In those instances, they typically took no action or very limited action against a student. In other cases, where the disciplinarian agreed with the teacher's assessment, punitive actions, especially severe punitive actions, were occasionally blocked by the principal. The principal shared their concern for the school's interests, but nonetheless had to evaluate both student behavior and staff authority within the context of complaints or pressures from parents and the district, or with regard to the school's public image.

DISCIPLINARY PENALTIES

The sanctions available to the disciplinary staff were few. Beyond talking to students, and short of transferring or expelling them, disciplinarians could hold students out of class, contact their parents, or enforce one- to five-day suspensions. Disciplinarians rarely, if ever, contacted parents outside the context of a suspension. Official responses to misbehavior were, thus, limited in practice to either a simple reprimand, holding the student in the office until the next class period, or a suspension.

The district's "Code Prohibiting Serious Student Misconduct" identified and defined the nine categories of misconduct that warranted suspension: (1) disruption of the school, (2) damage, destruction, or theft of school property, (3) damage, destruction, or theft of private property, (4) assault on a school employee, (5) physical abuse of a student or other person not employed by the school, (6) possession of weapons and dangerous instruments, (7) possession or use of narcotics, alcoholic beverages, and stimulant drugs, (8) repeated school violations, and (9) disruptive and/or offensive use of language (District manual on policies and procedures 1984).[5]

At DuBois High, an estimated 35.2 percent of the boys' suspensions were for "repeated school violations."[6] That figure jumped to 63 percent with the inclusion of suspensions for which no specific reason was listed. Presumably, most unspecified cases were repeated school violations rather than some more specific and serious violation. A full 81.4 percent of the suspensions could be accounted for by adding the category "disruptive and offensive use of language." These figures demonstrate how heavily the discipline staff at DuBois, in accord with national patterns (see note 4), relied on suspensions to punish behaviors that threatened the school's authority rather than its safety. The figures also emphasize the amount of discretion called for in disciplinary work. The issue of "labeling" enters when we examine how disciplinarians determine the definition of "repeated" violations and the instances when profane or obscene language warrants punishment.

The procedural instructions in the district manual for "repeated school violations" explained that the rule "basically...is aimed at those students whose conduct is consistently at odds with normal school discipline"; these were the students disciplinarians defined as "troublemakers." The instructions went on to caution that a pupil should be suspended only when unacceptable behavior continued after all available school resources and services were tried or when an exceptionally serious act that warranted such action was committed.

Since the instructions did not define "available school resources and services," the discipline staff, in practice, operated as if any "legitimate" case entering their office came there either because it was "an exceptionally serious act," or because previous efforts by teachers, or perhaps counselors, had failed. Thus, beyond assessing

whether "a teacher should have handled this," disciplinarians made little or no effort to consider other school services.[7]

THE SOCIAL CONSTRUCTION OF A TROUBLEMAKER

Conflicts over disciplinary practice arose because the definition of what constituted misconduct was itself problematic. Although the authors of the school's rules identified the categories of punishable student behavior, they realized judgments about the meaning and seriousness of any particular behavior depended upon its specific social setting, the student's intent, and the responses of others present. Understandably, some categories of misconduct, such as "disrupting class," were necessarily vague or ambiguous. The immediate context of a student's actions distinguished silliness or immaturity from insubordination or disruptiveness. Situational factors such as intent or provocation changed the meaning of an act. For that very reason, district regulations allowed disciplinarians considerable discretion.

In practice, disciplinarians rarely questioned students about the details of their misbehavior or the reasons behind them. Instead, after identifying the charge against the student, they moved on to a series of questions about grades, attendance, previous suspensions, and, in some instances, the student's year in school, age, or plans for employment. A student's answers, rather than the particular circumstances of his actions, identified the misconduct's meaning to the disciplinarians. Only when a student's academic profile seemed to violate the disciplinarian's expectations would he or she inquire further about the charges against the student. They sought to punish "types of students" more than "types of behavior."

Whereas most students occasionally violated school rules, the proper role of the discipline office, as its staff understood it, was to deal with troublemakers who persistently disregarded the institution's authority. Information on grades, attendance, and prior disciplinary problems created a profile of the student's relationship to the school used to interpret the meaning of misconduct and the appropriateness of disciplinary intervention.[8] Students who failed classes, played hookey, used drugs, or frequently troubled teachers with disruptive behavior were students who, in the minds of most school workers, did not belong in school.

The following example illustrates the use of questions to interpret the significance of a student's behavior:

Mr. Leary picked up the next file on his desk and called out, "Is Kenneth Watson out there?" Kenneth stood up and walked over to Mr. Leary's doorway.

LEARY: "Kenneth?"

KENNETH: "Yeah."

LEARY: "Sit down." Kenneth slumped into the chair in front of Mr. Leary's desk. In a combative voice: "I've got a pink slip here that says you were disrupting class. Talking. I thought we had this straightened out. Wasn't this straightened out?"

KENNETH: Muttering, "Yeah, I guess so."

LEARY: "What do you mean, 'I guess so'? If it was straightened out, you wouldn't be here." He paused, looking down at the pink slip. "It says here you were talking in class. So what is this? *I've got three others here for the same thing.* Now what's the problem?"

KENNETH: "I don't know."

LEARY: "Well, we already brought your mother in, didn't we?" Kenneth shook his head slightly, looking puzzled. "Yeah, you were present at the meeting." Mr. Leary looked again at the file. "What class is it?"

KENNETH: "Math."

LEARY: "How are you doing in it?" Kenneth shrugged. "Well, *did you pass math in the last report?*" Kenneth nodded. "What grade did you get, then?" Mr. Leary shouted, clearly exasperated.

KENNETH: After a slight hesitation, "Two As and a B. I think I had an 89 for the last report and As for the ones before."

LEARY: Visibly surprised, "You have As and Bs in math?" Slight pause, then, "You're in what, general math?"

KENNETH: "Algebra."

LEARY: *"Are you passing all your classes?"*

KENNETH: "Yeah."

LEARY: "Were you on the honor roll?"

KENNETH: "I don't know," still mumbling, still sullen.

LEARY: "What do you mean you don't know! Were you in the lottery?"

KENNETH: He gestured over his shoulder in the direction of the main hallway, "That attendance thing?"

LEARY: "No! We have one for grades, too. Didn't you go to the awards assembly?"

KENNETH: "Oh, yeah. I went to that. I got a slip…said to report…I didn't know."

LEARY: Quite frustrated, "Yeah, well I was there. I gave out the certificate and prize." He paused and looked down at the file again. *"What does this mean, 'talking in class'?"*

KENNETH: Still mumbling, "We have these pre-class exercises on the board. When I got that done, I end up talking."

LEARY: "What, you have a problem to do when you get to class?"

KENNETH: "Yeah."

LEARY: In a reasoning tone, "Well, if you finish up early can't you help out someone who isn't as bright as you, who has trouble in math?"

KENNETH: "He wants us to do our own work."

LEARY: "Yeah, well, ok. That doesn't mean you have to talk. You make it sound like you can't control yourself. Why don't you do some studying for another class? *A bright boy like you shouldn't have to go through all this.* So what's the solution to this problem?"

KENNETH: "I guess I shouldn't talk in class."

LEARY: "All right. *This is Mickey Mouse stuff.*" He paused, "You wait outside until the next period." After Kenneth left the office, Mr. Leary turned to me and explained, *"Clearly a classroom problem. A kid like that can understand if you reason with him. It's not like some of the barely educable kids we see in here. The teacher—I don't know what the problem is— just wants to pass along the problem to us. We get a lot of that here. This teacher should just take him aside and talk to him, even if he has to do it every week."* (April 1984, emphasis added)

During my observation, three pink slips for disrupting class, a prior interview with a parent, and a sullen and uncooperative demeanor normally led to a student's suspension, a significant act in the creation of an official record. Disciplinarians typically did not ask students, "What does this mean?" Instead, they took "talking in class" as a known and unproblematic form of disruption.

In the case above, Mr. Leary began with the assumption that Kenneth, a student repeatedly sent to the office for disrupting class, must be a troublemaker. In the course of their interaction, however, Kenneth became a kid you could reason with; the talking in class became "Mickey Mouse stuff"; the whole problem became something the teacher should have dealt with. Each of these reconstructions occurred because Kenneth's grades altered the meaning of his behavior.

In most school workers' minds, students who received high grades demonstrated that they accepted the school's requirements and, presumably, acknowledged the value of the school's work. According to this reasoning, Kenneth obviously posed no challenge to the school's aims or operation—and indeed was one of its few success stories. Therefore, his talking in class, even if it recurred weekly, represented not a "repeated violation of school rules" but a problem with the teacher's ability to control the class.

PARENTAL INVOLVEMENT

A student's vulnerability to suspension, and to identification as a "troublemaker," may also depend upon his or her parents' ability to influence the actions of school personnel. As one NTA observed, "The only time you ever see a parent is when the kid is suspended and they have to come in." Indeed, according to district policy, "The primary purpose for the use of suspension is for the involvement of parents in the remediation of a problem."[9] In interviews, disciplinarians confirmed this objective. Ms. Gordon, an NTA working as a disciplinarian, told me: "Suspension is strictly for communication. Not to hurt the student or punish the student." Both she and the others did, however, qualify that objective with conditions such as "unless we can't keep the kid in school because it was something serious or he completely defies authority."

Although all agreed that suspensions served to bring parents into the school, the understanding among most school workers about what constituted "involvement of the parent in the remediation of a problem" challenged the claim that suspensions had no punitive intent. School workers expected parents to accept the school's authority and to support its goals and practices. They expected parents to force their children to comply with the school's rules. If parents suggested, through their words and demeanor, that they accepted the school's authority and shared its judgment of their child, then disciplinarians interpreted "involvement" as "notification." They informed the parents of the student's misbehavior and, frequently, suggested strategies for controlling the student's actions. However, if a parent either challenged the disciplinarian's version of events or argued that the student was responsible for him or herself, "involvement" became more punitive in intent. One teacher explained how a student's suspension would punish the parent and thereby encourage her to support the school's efforts:

If you got to take a day off from work because of something your child has done, that's going to make you put more pressure on him. If you can't come up here, then you keep him home until you can come up here. He becomes your problem for four or five days. You got to worry about what he's doing in your apartment or your house while you're at work. Now you're a little more concerned about this. (Mr. Fisk, May 1987)

The relatively disadvantaged status of most parents *vis-à-vis* school workers meant that many parents received disrespectful and dismissive treatment.[10] Parents had few, if any, social or political resources with which to challenge a disciplinarian's actions. Freed from the constraints more powerful, higher status parents might have imposed, disciplinarians reverted to three tactics when they faced opposition from students and parents: (1) they denigrated the parenting skills of the mother or father; (2) they threatened the student with failure, arrest, or expulsion—frequently without the power or intent to make good their threat; (3) they explicitly denied any personal responsibility or concern for resolving the problem.

In the course of a reinstatement conference, Carl told Mr. Weis, "She [the teacher] seen me, I was coming out of the bathroom, but she closed the door and wouldn't let me in." His mother characterized this as an "involuntary cut." Weis countered by repeating the rule, "If you're late to class, you're not allowed in class. It's a cut." The mother muttered something about knowing all about it since she'd gone to school, too.

WEIS: *"Perhaps if you talked to your son—"*
MOTHER: "I talk to Carl every day…but I have to go to work, and sleep, I can't watch him every minute. And he is sixteen…."
WEIS (TO CARL): *"You want to go to disciplinary school? Or drop out?"* (To mother): "Cuz that's where he's headed. *We won't take him for a third year in tenth grade. Not at seventeen.* (Mother mutters something.) You have a complaint that you're not getting serviced properly, there's a principal….I really have a problem that you didn't insist on getting his second report [card]. *How important is education to you? I know if I had kids, I wouldn't let them get away with that…*unless you're going to support him for the rest of your life." (March 1987, emphasis added)

Mr. Weis told Carl's mother that he needed more responsibility and discipline at home. She claimed that her son acted responsibly at home, it was only when he came to school that he "acted like a fool." During the course of this discussion, someone delivered Carl's grades to Mr. Weis, which showed he was failing all of his classes. After a few minutes of berating Carl for his grades, Mr. Weis said, *"I have no time for this. I am writing here, 'to be dropped from school at age seventeen if there is no improvement in grades and attendance.'* So you'll receive a letter this summer, when we make our review." As they left the office, Mr. Weis turned to me and said, "All bluff." I asked, "You can't drop him?" Weis said, "Naw." "Will he get a letter?" I asked. He answered, "No."

Mr. Weis admitted to me that he was bluffing; but in such an example his threat's impact came less from his actual power to expel the student—which, informally, he could and had done—than from his presentation of the school as unforgiving and unconcerned. It was not, in fact, unusual to hear him say to a parent: "This is your problem. You'll have to deal with it. I'll readmit him, but— I don't mind, I'll keep suspending him. It's not my problem" (April 1984).

This posture by a school official seems likely to affect "secondary deviance," that is, the student's continued violation of the school's expectations. Mr. Weis has emphasized to Carl that the school has little stake in his success and a primarily negative vision of his social value and personal worth—the very conditions which may strengthen his hostility toward the school and to foster his commitment to the troublemaker role.[11] Even if Carl does not want to adopt the troublemaker identity, Mr. Weis has made it clear that he will be treated as one, in any case.[12] Moreover, as I have suggested above, it seems likely that Mr. Weis's easy rejection of Carl and his mother, and his willingness to push Carl out of school, is connected to their social position. A higher status mother might have been successful in her efforts to define Carl's behavior as an "involuntary cut" and to forestall his classification as a troublemaker.

GETTING RID OF TROUBLEMAKERS

The discipline office had two strategies to get rid of students identified as troublemakers. One was to transfer the student; the other to drop the student from the roll. Transfers were of two types: "regular" transfers, arranged when students moved out of the school's catchment area; and "disciplinary transfers," known by their code as "21s." Dropping a student from the roll required that the student be 17 years old. At that age, schooling was no longer compulsory and the discipline office interpreted this to mean the school no longer had to keep the student.

Typically, if a disciplinarian sought a regular transfer for a troublesome student, arrangements were made for the student to shift his or her legal residence to the address of a relative in another part of the district. This procedure avoided the paperwork and legal proceedings of a disciplinary transfer. In the following incident, however, Mr. Weis discovered he could get rid of a troublemaker who already lived outside the normal bounds of the school. Mr. Weis began a conference with John, a boy I had seen in the office on two previous occasions, by asking, "What's your address?" After questioning, Weis discovered John's address put him in another school's catchment area. Weis called John's house:

> *Hello, Mrs. Preston?…well you'll have to wake her up. This is DuBois High School calling…Mrs. Preston, this is Carl Weis. John has been acting up again. He refused to take off his hat and has been disruptive. I have five pink slips on him. Look, I don't know why he's here and not at Northern Heights to start with.… Yeah, well, I'm going to write up a transfer for him and get all his records together. You'll have to come down tomorrow and take him over there and enroll him.*

After John left the office, Weis turned to me and said:

> We didn't solve anything. We just sent the problem along to Northern Heights. But we have to look out for ourselves. That's the way it is—crazy system. *(April 1984, emphasis added)*

Although this case was unusual in that the student already lived in another school's catchment area, it was absolutely standard in intent. The goal of the discipline office, as Mr. Weis explained, was not to solve any problems a student might have, but to protect the school's operation. Thus, in the case of another transfer, Mr. Leary confirmed Mr. Weis's assessment of their goals. Mr. Leary escorted a boy and his mother out of the office and then sat down next to me. He explained:

> *Now that mother came in here, her son was suspended weeks ago for having a weapon, marijuana. Now she wants him transferred to Washington High. You know, for us, that's fine. We get rid of one.*

I asked if 21 transfers helped. He said:

> They help this school. They don't help the kid. But then, you can't do anything with those kids, anyway. *(March 1986, emphasis added)*

Transfers were, thus, seen as an important resource for the discipline office. If they could build a sufficiently strong case, they could get rid of a troublemaker, even if he wanted to remain in the school, through the use of a disciplinary transfer. Because district rules prohibited the use of 21s on students whose only offenses were cutting class or missing school, the disciplinarians took pains to document all other forms of misconduct on potential or identified troublemakers. Since they would be used for a 21, Mr. Leary stressed the importance of being detailed and complete when making out "pink slips."

> *You don't just write, "picked up for cutting class." You write, "cutting class, ran away from officer, used abusive language," all of which is true, but if you don't write it down—or if there's a disturbance in class, you write down, "shoved desks, said 'fuck you' to teacher"—you know, we're not squeamish. We write down just what they say, "fuck you" or "fuck you white mother."*

Since the projected future or "career" of the forms influenced their form and content,[13] the pink slips represent an important point at which discretion or "bias" can enter into the construction of an official disciplinary record.

Once disciplinarians filed the paperwork on a 21, a parent had to come in for a conference. The parent has the right to a hearing in the district superintendent's office. If a parent does not want a hearing, he or she can sign a form during the conference transferring the child. The discipline staff and the principal work toward that goal, since all the paperwork goes to the district superintendent's office for review when the parent wants a hearing. As Mr. Leary complained: "Then they mostly do nothing. Send the kid back. Decide he needs another chance."

Student transfers were not the only means available to get rid of troublemakers. Another option used by the school was the informal expulsion of overage students. Although the state granted all students the right to attend public school until the age of twenty-one, it did not require attendance past the age of sixteen. At DuBois, school workers understood that to mean that they were not required to keep a student in school once he or she turned seventeen.[14] It was not unusual, therefore, for disciplinarians to reason: "Look, he's already eighteen and only in tenth grade. You know he can only stay in school 'til he's twenty-one. I don't want him here. I'm going to talk to [the principal]." That logic also permitted the following scene. A police officer escorted four boys into the discipline office. The officer stopped at Weis's door. Weis sent the boys into Leary's office.

THE OFFICER: Two with, two without IDs.
WEIS: This one I don't know. He might be an adult. I don't know if he's a juvenile. This one's a student. Doesn't come in very often.

Weis asked the boy he didn't recognize how old he was. The boy said he was seventeen, went to DuBois, and was in tenth grade.

WEIS: You don't go to DuBois. I just dropped you as of now. *I'm not suspending you. I'm dropping you from school.*

Weis said to the officer, in reference to the other boy who was younger:

You're going to leave the building right now.

OLDER BOY: How many days' suspension?
WEIS: I just told him. Two months, three months, 'til his mother comes in. (April 1986)

Although in this example the student demonstrated little interest in attending school,[15] other students who did want to attend but who ran into problems with the discipline office were also subject to the informal expulsion of an "overage drop." In the following instance, Nicholas had missed most of his first period math classes because of familial responsibilities.

WEIS: What're you in for?
NICHOLAS: Mr. Fisk suspended me cuz I missed his class.
WEIS: Let me get your folder.

He left the office and returned with the folder. To Nicholas's stepfather he said:

As you are aware, sir, Nicholas was out of school and then let back in school. When he was readmitted, he signed a contract that he would attend school and behave himself. *Right now, he's overage, still in tenth grade, not passing* [one class]. *I recommend dropping him.*

NICHOLAS: That's only one class!
WEIS: But that's enough. You are overage in tenth grade. You have to pass....
NICHOLAS: Don't you want to know why I missed—
WEIS: No reason is—you signed a contract.
NICHOLAS: I had to do something for my mother.
WEIS: *You're eighteen years old, third year in tenth grade, you have to set priorities. If that's to do something for your mother—you signed a contract that you would obey all the rules and attend all your classes.* You know, we wanted to transfer you before. Do you have a relative

in another neighborhood? (March 1987, emphasis added)

The conference established that Nicholas was a classic troublemaker. He had previously been dropped from school, and was overage, behind in grade, and failing a class. Mr. Weis wanted him out of the school. Since he could not initiate a disciplinary transfer on the grounds of cutting class, Mr. Weis explored his two other options: an "overage" drop pressed on Nicholas because he had violated the terms of his readmission contract, and a regular transfer based on the pretense that Nicholas had changed residence.

It is important to note that because he did not conform to all of the school's demands, the school workers focused on how to exclude Nicholas rather than on how to solve his problems or to work around them. As I learned from lengthy interviews with both Nicholas and his stepfather, Nicholas had tried to work within the system. As he told me:

I have this first period class and I'm supposed to be there at five minutes before eight. And I have to take my nieces to day care in the morning.... They live with me, and there's no one else there, you know, that could take them. It's inconvenient for my mother cuz she leaves so early. And their mom is in Florida. So I was the only one that could take them. So I was taking them, and I wasn't making the class. But I was bringing notes and stuff in to show them.... Mr. Fisk wouldn't contact my mother or nothing. He just kept on telling me the notes aren't going to do no good.... I talked to my mother at one time. And that's when she told me she was going to try to work something out [about taking the girls to day care]. But at the moment to keep taking them.... You know, so that's when I went to see the counselor. She told me to see [someone else]...he was absent two days I brought in the note.... Probably if I went to see [the counselor] earlier, I would have probably got help. But I didn't know who to go see. I thought he was the teacher, I was supposed to give the notes and all that to him.... [When I did see the counselor], she was saying there's not much you can do, and everything. I could have got a roster change if it was like the beginning.

The school workers blamed his mother for putting Nicholas in the position of having to care for his sister's daughters and blamed him for accepting that responsibility. Mr. Fisk explained:

Why should that responsibility become his? The parent has to take more active—why would you thrust that responsibility on your offspring if it's creating problems in the school?...If he's thrust into this situation and he knows it's threatening his possibilities for graduation, for promotion, for passing this class, if he's truly serious about passing, he has to lighten the load. And there's only one load he can lighten. And that's the supervision of [the nieces]. So that means sitting down with whomever.

Mr. Fisk assumed that the solution to the problem involved "sitting down" with someone. Nicholas, therefore, was penalized for his mother's inability or unwillingness to make his education the family's priority.

Nicholas confronted a system which his parents had little skill in handling or power to influence, and which rejected his own efforts. Had he come from a middle-income family, it is likely he would have fared better. Not only would it have been less likely for such a family/school conflict to arise, but a middle-income parent would have had greater success in manipulating the bureaucratic requirements of the school system. As it was, Nicholas's family circumstances allowed—one might even argue, encouraged—both Mr. Fisk and Mr. Weis to dismiss him as another troublemaker who did not value education.

BEING "AT RISK"

When I spoke to Ms. Riley, the vice principal of DuBois High, she was not "amazed" that 335 of her students had "dropped out" in the previous year. Instead, citing how many kids faced problems at home or on the streets, she was amazed that so many of them "made it." DuBois High students who faced disruption, violence, substance abuse, or conflicting obligations to school and family were understandably distracted, uncooperative, or truant.

Manifesting those symptoms of broader social ills, however, brought them into contact with the discipline office. There troubled students were rather easily reconceptualized as troublemakers. And troublemakers were readily seen as undeserving of the school's services. This process is all the more disturbing when we consider that inner-city African Americans and Hispanics are disproportionately likely to suffer from such social ills. The activities of the discipline office, which routinely identified "troublemakers" and "got rid of" them through suspensions and involuntary drops, may be one important but largely unacknowledged mechanism through which schools perpetuate the racial and class stratification of the larger society.

Ironically, educational research has served to legitimate the actions of the disciplinarians. In a conference to reinstate a student following his suspension for poor attendance, Mr. Leary remarked:

> I'm talking to you like a man...this is a turning point in your life. You can go either way: follow the rules and graduate, or drop out of the whole school system. *You signed this contract. I'm going to reinstate you. But I tell you quite frankly, you got to get up, whatever you got to do, and get to school. I know, there's no doubt in my mind, [the principal]* is going to want to drop you. Not because be wants to be mean, but statistics prove it out. *(March 1986, emphasis added)*

Indeed, the statistics prove that students are most likely to "drop out" of high school if they come from a low-income background, are frequently absent or truant, have a record of school suspensions, are failing classes, and are overage in grade (Hahn and Danzberger 1987; Natriello 1986). But what is proven? Those factors are the very indicators that disciplinarians used to define troublemakers and that led to suspensions, disciplinary transfers, and involuntary drops. Although it is unwise to generalize from the findings of one case study, we can nevertheless ask: are "risk factors" correlated with "dropping out" because they are used routinely by school workers to expel students? If that is the

case, then disciplinarians' daily activities play an important role in regulating social mobility.

NOTES

1. Although all of the students were African Americans, the faculty's racial composition reflected the metropolitan area's labor pool and thus included many whites.
2. These figures come from a report prepared by the school for the visiting committee of the association charged with evaluating the school for accreditation. For reasons of confidentiality, I cannot give the full name of this publication or of other reports issued by the school or the school district.
3. The irregular tempo of activity in the discipline office made it difficult to gather accurate, quantifiable data on the number, type, and disposition of cases. Although I solicited staff members' help at one point, asking each of them to mark on a chart the type and disposition of each case they handled, I found their recordkeeping unreliable. Moreover, such records masked the very assumptions and decisions I sought to investigate.
4. National studies report that most high school suspensions are for nonthreatening behavior—defying authority, chronic tardiness, chronic absence, and use of profanity and vulgarity. Black students are suspended three times as often as whites (Hahn and Danzberger 1987:19).
5. The physical education department also suspended students who were unprepared for gym class on three occasions. Those "one day" suspensions were not processed through the discipline office and are not a part of my report.
6. These figures come from the suspension reports compiled by one of the disciplinarians for the district. I selected three months, at random, from the 1986/87 school year and computed the percentages. These figures are compatible with my observations in the discipline office. The total number of boys suspended in those three months was 244.
7. Students had extremely limited access to any form of counseling. The few "guidance counselors" in the school each had responsibility for hundreds of students and seemed to limit their "guidance" to brief conferences on scheduling or attendance problems. The only other counselor I was aware of was a part-time drug counselor from a private agency.

8. McCarthy and Hoge (1987) found that school disciplinary sanctions were influenced by the student's past official record, grades, and "general demeanor in school." These findings suggest that the practices of the discipline staff at DuBois conform to those at other schools.

9. The other purposes of suspension noted in the district's guidelines were: removing the student from the scene of difficulty, diffusing a situation when the final outcome is not yet assured, and displaying the school's dissatisfaction with the student's behavior.

10. The relatively homogeneous background of DuBois students prohibited a comparative assessment of how a parent's race and class affected her or his treatment by disciplinarians.

11. Crespo (1974) found that a school's disciplinary responses to "skippers" (truants) did indeed lead to the amplification of deviance and, in many cases, encouraged students to drop out.

12. See Anderson's discussion of how "social selves" are constructed in social interaction; as he states, "a person is somebody because others allow him to be" (1976:38).

13. See Meehan (1986) for a discussion of how the projected use of police records shapes their form and content as well as for a discussion of how police officers infer the meaning or accuracy of a record.

14. In the official statistics for the 1985/86 school year, all but six of the 335 dropouts were categorized as "overage."

15. Crespo noted, "students who do not find school rewarding are more prepared to consider missing it. In this sense, the tracking system provides the invitational edge to the activity of skipping" (1974:133). Students in lower tracks are offered less stimulating and less valuable educational experiences (Oakes 1985). We must remember, therefore, that the school bears some responsibility for its students' attitudes and behaviors.

REFERENCES

Anderson, Elijah. 1976. *A Place on the Corner.* Chicago: University of Chicago Press.

Bittner, Egon. 1967. "The police on skid-row: A 'study of peace keeping.'" *American Sociological Review* 32:699–715.

Crespo, Manuel. 1974. "The career of the school skipper." In *Decency and Deviance: Studies in Deviant Behavior,* ed. Jack Haas, 129–145. Toronto: McClelland and Stewart.

Hahn, Andrew, and Jacqueline Danzberger. 1987. *Dropouts in America: Enough Is Known for Action.* Washington, D.C.: Institute for Educational Leadership.

Lipsky, Michael. 1980. *Street-Level Bureaucracy: Dilemmas of the Individual in Public Services.* New York: Russell Sage.

McCarthy, John, and Dean Hoge. 1987. "The social construction of school punishment: Racial disadvantage out of universalistic process." *Social Forces* 65: 1101–1120.

Meehan, Albert J. 1986. "Record-keeping practices in the policing of juveniles." *Urban Life* 15:70–102.

Natriello, Gary, ed. 1986. *School Dropouts: Patterns and Policies.* New York: Teachers College Press.

Oakes, Jeannie. 1985. *Keeping Track: How Schools Structure Inequality.* New Haven, Conn.: Yale University Press.

Rubinstein, Jonathan. 1973. *City Police.* Farrar, Straus & Giroux.

Sudnow, David. 1965. "Normal crimes: Sociological features of the penal code in a public defender's office." *Social Problems* 12:255–276.

Waegel, William B. 1981. "Case routinization in investigative police work." *Social Problems* 28:263–275.

Sexual Assault

LISA FROHMANN

Whether cases that come to a prosecutor's attention ever get to trial depends on how prosecutors define the situation. If defendants wish they could drop out of the system of criminal justice, prosecutors seek not only to remain in the system but also to move up in it. To achieve personal as well as organizational goals, prosecutors have to take into account what detectives have told them as well as to anticipate how judge or jury will respond to the cases they bring to court. To achieve both personal and organizational goals of reducing the number of cases brought to trial and of moving cases brought to successful conclusion requires considerable discretion in evaluating the evidence in potential cases.

Lisa Frohmann shows that prosecutors rise or fall in accordance with bureaucratic measures of performance: the number of cases not brought to trial and the conviction rates of those cases that have been brought to trial. To meet these goals, prosecutors develop an interpretive scheme that classifies complainants according to the degree of consistency in their reported complaint and their social character. Only those sexual assault cases brought by women whom they consider "good witnesses" will be brought to trial, for only "good witnesses" will make a good impression on judges or juries.

Case screening is the gateway to the criminal court system. Prosecutors, acting as gatekeepers, decide which instances of alleged victimization will be passed on for adjudication by the courts. A recent study by the Department of Justice (Boland et al. 1990) suggests that a significant percentage of felony cases never get beyond this point, with only cases characterized as "solid" or "convictable" being filed (Mather 1979; Stanko 1981, 1982). This paper examines how prosecutors account for the decision to reject sexual assault cases for prosecution and looks at the centrality of discrediting victims' rape allegations in this justification.

A number of studies on sexual assault have found that victim credibility is important in police decisions to investigate and make arrests in sexual assault cases (LaFree 1981; Rose and Randall

Reprinted from "Discrediting Victims' Allegations of Sexual Assault: Prosecutorial Accounts of Case Rejections," *Social Problems*, Vol. 38, No. 2 (May 1991), pp. 213–226, by permission of the Society for the Study of Social Problems and the author. Copyright © 1991 by the Society for the Study of Social Problems.

1982; Kerstetter 1990; Kerstetter and Van Winkle 1990). Similarly, victim credibility has been shown to influence prosecutors' decisions at a number of stages in the handling of sexual assault cases (LaFree 1980, 1989; Chandler and Torney 1981; Kerstetter 1990).

Much of this prior research has assumed, to varying degrees, that victim credibility is a phenomenon that exists independently of prosecutors' interpretations and assessments of such credibility. Particularly when operationalized in terms of quantitative variables, victim credibility is treated statistically as a series of fixed, objective features of cases. Such approaches neglect the processes whereby prosecutors actively assess and negotiate victim credibility in actual, ongoing case processing.

An alternative view examines victim credibility as a phenomenon constructed and maintained through interaction (Stanko 1980). Several qualitative studies have begun to identify and analyze these processes. For example, Holmstrom and Burgess's (1983) analysis of a victim's experience with the institutional handling of sexual assault cases discusses the importance of victim credibility through the prosecutor's evaluation of a complainant as a "good witness." A "good witness" is someone who, through her appearance and demeanor, can convince a jury to accept her account of "what happened." Her testimony is "consistent," her behavior "sincere," and she cooperates in case preparation. Stanko's (1981, 1982) study of felony case filing decisions similarly emphasizes prosecutors' reliance on the notion of the "stand-up" witness—someone who can appear to the judge and jury as articulate and credible. Her work emphasizes the centrality of victim credibility in complaint-filing decisions.

In this article I extend these approaches by systematically analyzing the kinds of accounts prosecutors offer in sexual assault cases to support their complaint-filing decisions. Examining the justifications for decisions provides an understanding of how these decisions appear rational, necessary, and appropriate to decision-makers as they do the work of case screening. It allows us to uncover the inner, indigenous logic of prosecutors' decisions and the organizational structures in which those decisions are embedded (Garfinkel 1984).

I focus on prosecutorial accounting for case rejection for three reasons. First, since a significant percentage of cases are not filed, an important component of the case-screening process involves case rejection. Second, the organization of case filing requires prosecutors to justify case rejection, not case acceptance, to superiors and fellow deputies. By examining deputy district attorneys' (DDAs') reasons for case rejection, we can gain access to what they consider "solid" cases, providing further insight into the case-filing process. Third, in case screening, prosecutors orient to the rule—when in doubt, reject. Their behavior is organized more to avoiding the error of filing cases that are not likely to result in conviction than to avoiding the error of rejecting cases that will probably end in conviction (Scheff 1966). Thus, I suggest that prosecutors are actively looking for "holes" or problems that will make the victim's version of "what happened" unbelievable or not convincing beyond a reasonable doubt, hence unconvictable (see Miller 1970; Neubauer 1974; and Stanko 1980, 1981 for the importance of conviction in prosecutors' decisions to file cases). This bias is grounded within the organizational context of complaint filing.

DATA AND METHODS

The research was part of an ethnographic field study of the prosecution of sexual assault crimes by deputy district attorneys in the sexual assault units of two branch offices of the district attorney's offices in a metropolitan area on the West Coast.[1]...

THE ORGANIZATIONAL CONTEXT OF COMPLAINT FILING

Several features of the court setting that I studied provided the context for prosecutors' decisions. These features are prosecutorial concern with maintaining a high conviction rate to promote an image of the "community's legal protector," and prosecutorial and court procedures for processing sexual assault cases.

The promotion policy of the county district attorney's (DA) office encourages prosecutors to accept only "strong" or "winnable" cases for prosecution by using conviction rates as a measure of prosecutorial performance. In the DA's office, guilty verdicts carry more weight than a conviction by case settlement. The stronger the case, the greater likelihood of a guilty verdict, the better the "stats" for promotion considerations. The inducement to take risks—to take cases to court that might not result in conviction—is tempered in three ways: First, a pattern of not-guilty verdicts is used by the DA's office as an indicator of prosecutorial incompetency. Second, prosecutors are given credit for the number of cases they reject as a recognition of their commitment to the organizational concern of reducing the case load of an already overcrowded court system. Third, to continually pursue cases that should have been rejected outright may lead judges to question the prosecutor's competence as a member of the court.

Sexual assault cases are among those crimes that have been deemed by the state legislature to be priority prosecution cases. That is, in instances where both "sex" and "nonsex" cases are trailing (waiting for a court date to open), sexual assault cases are given priority for court time. Judges become annoyed when they feel that court time is being "wasted" with cases that "should" have been negotiated or rejected in the first place, especially when those cases have been given priority over other cases. Procedurally, the prosecutor's office handles sexual assault crimes differently from other felony crimes. Other felonies are handled by a referral system; they are handed from one DDA to another at each stage in the prosecution of the case. But sexual assault cases are vertically prosecuted; the deputy who files the case remains with it until its disposition, and therefore is closely connected with the case outcome.

ACCOUNTING FOR REJECTION BECAUSE OF "DISCREPANCIES"

Within the organizational context, a central feature of prosecutorial accounts of case rejection is the discrediting of victims' allegations of sexual assault. Below I examine two techniques used by prosecutors to discredit victim's complaints: discrepant accounts and ulterior motives.

USING OFFICIAL REPORTS AND RECORDS TO DETECT DISCREPANCIES

In the course of reporting a rape, victims recount their story to several criminal justice officials. Prosecutors treat consistent accounts of the incident over time as an indicator of a victim's credibility. In the first example two prosecutors are discussing a case brought in for filing the previous day.

> *DDA TAMARA JACOBS: In the police report she said all three men were kissing the victim. Later in the interview she said that was wrong. It seems strange because there are things wrong on major events like oral copulation and intercourse…, for example whether she had John's penis in her mouth. Another thing wrong is whether he forced her into the bedroom immediately after they got to his room or, as the police report said, they all sat on the couch and watched TV. This is something a cop isn't going to get wrong, how the report started. (Bay City)*

The prosecutor questions the credibility of the victim's allegation by finding "inconsistencies" between the complainant's account given to the police and the account given to the prosecutor. The prosecutor formulates differences in these accounts as "discrepancies" by noting that they involve "major events"—events so significant no one would confuse them, forget them, or get them wrong. This is in contrast to some differences that may involve acceptable, "normal inconsistencies" in victims' accounts of sexual assault. By "normal inconsistencies," I mean those that are expected and explainable because the victim is confused, upset, or shaken after the assault.

The DDA also discredited the victim's account by referring to a typification of police work. She assumes that the inconsistencies in the accounts could not be attributed to the incorrect writing of the report by the police officer on the grounds that they "wouldn't get wrong how the report started." Similarly, in the following example, a typification of police work is invoked to discredit the victim's account. Below the DDA and IO [investigating officer] are discussing the case immediately after the victim interview.

> *DDA SABRINA JOHNSON: [T]he police report doesn't say anything about her face being swollen, only her hand. If they took pictures of her hand, wouldn't the police have taken a picture of her face if it was swollen? (Bay City)*

The prosecutor calls the credibility of the victim's complaint into question by pointing to a discrepancy between her subsequent account of injuries received during the incident and the notation of injuries on the police reports taken at the time the incident was reported. Suspicion of the complainant's account is also expressed in the prosecutor's inference that if the police went to the trouble of photographing the victim's injured hand they would have taken pictures of her face had it also shown signs of injury.

In the next case the prosecutor cites two types of inconsistencies between accounts. The first set of inconsistencies is the victim's accounts to the prosecutor and to the police. The second set is between the account the victim gave to the prosecutor and the statements the defendants gave to the police. This excerpt was obtained during an interview.

> DDA TRACY TIMMERTON: *The reason I did not believe her [the victim] was, I get the police report first and I'll read that, so I have read the police report which recounts her version of the facts but it also has the statement of both defendants. Both defendants were arrested at separate times and give separate independent statements that were virtually the same. Her story when I had her recount it to me in the DA's office, the number of acts changed, the chronological order of how they happened has changed. (Bay City)*

When the prosecutor compared the suspects' accounts with the victim's account, she interpreted the suspects' accounts as credible because both of their accounts, given separately to police, were similar. This rests on the assumption that if suspects give similar accounts when arrested together, they are presumed to have colluded on the story, but if they give similar accounts independent of the knowledge of the other's arrest, there is presumed to be a degree of truth to the story. This stands in contrast to the discrepant accounts the complainant gave to law enforcement officials and the prosecutor.

USING OFFICIAL TYPIFICATIONS
OF RAPE-RELEVANT BEHAVIOR

In the routine handling of sexual assault cases prosecutors develop a repertoire of knowledge about the features of these crimes.[2] This knowledge includes how particular kinds of rape are committed, post-incident interaction between the parties in an acquaintance situation, and victims' emotional and psychological reactions to rape and their effects on victims' behavior. The typifications of rape-relevant behavior are another resource for discrediting a victim's account of "what happened."

Typifications of Rape Scenarios

Prosecutors distinguish between different types of sexual assault. They characterize these types by the sex acts that occur, the situation in which the incident occurred, and the relationship between the parties. In the following excerpt the prosecutor discredits the victim's version of events by focusing on incongruities between the victim's description of the sex acts and the prosecutor's knowledge of the typical features of kidnap-rape. During an interview a DDA described the following:

> DDA TRACY TIMMERTON: *[T]he only act she complained of was intercourse, and my experience has been that when a rapist has a victim cornered for a long period of time, they engage in multiple acts and different types of sexual acts and very rarely do just intercourse. (Bay City)*

The victim's account is questioned by noting that she did not complain about or describe other sex acts considered "typical" of kidnap-rape situations. She only complained of intercourse. In the next example the DDA and IO are talking about a case involving the molestation of a teenage girl.

> DDA WILLIAM NELSON: *Something bothers me, all three acts are the same. She's on her stomach and has her clothes on and he has a "hard and long penis." All three times he is grinding his penis into her butt. It seems to me he should be trying to do more than that by the third time. (Center Heights)*

Here the prosecutor is challenging the credibility of the victim's account by comparing her version of "what happened" with his typification of the way these crimes usually occur. His experience suggests there should be an escalation of sex acts over time, not repetition of the same act.

Often the typification invoked by the prosecutor is highly situational and local. In discussion a drug-sex-related rape in Center Heights, for example, the prosecutor draws on his knowledge of street activity in that community and the types of rapes that occur there to question whether the victim's version of events is what "really" happened. The prosecutor is describing a case he received the day before to an investigating officer there on another matter.

> DDA KENT FERNOME: *I really feel guilty about this case I got yesterday. The girl is 20 going on 65. She is real skinny and gangly. Looks like a cluckhead [crack addict]—they cut off her hair. She went to her uncle's house, left her clothes there, drinks some beers and said she was going to visit a friend in Center Heights who she said she met at a drug rehab program. She is not sure where this friend Cathy lives. Why she went to Center Heights after midnight, God knows? It isn't clear what she was doing between 12 and 4 a.m. Some gang bangers came by and offered her a ride. They picked her up on the corner of Main and Lincoln. I think she was turning a trick, or looking for a rock, but she wouldn't budge from her story.... There are lots of conflicts between what she told the police and what she told me. The sequence of events, the sex acts performed, who ejaculates. She doesn't say who is who.... She's beat up, bruises on face and a laceration on her neck. The cop and doctor say there is no trauma—she's done by six guys. That concerns me. There is no semen that they see. It looks like this to me—maybe she is a strawberry, she's hooking or looking for a rock, but somewhere along the line it is not consensual.... She is [a] real street-worn woman. She's not leveling with me—visiting a woman with an unknown address on a bus in Center Heights—I don't buy it.... (Center Heights)*

The prosecutor questioned the complainant's reason for being in Center Heights because, based on his knowledge of the area, he found it unlikely that a woman would come to this community at

midnight to visit a friend at an unknown address. The deputy proposed an alternative account of the victim's action based on his knowledge of activities in the community—specifically, prostitution and drug dealing—and questioned elements of the victim's account, particularly her insufficiently accounted for activity between 12 and 4 a.m., coming to Center Heights late at night to visit a friend at an unknown address, and "hanging out" on the corner.

The DDA uses "person-descriptions" (Maynard 1984) to construct part of the account, describing the complainant's appearance as a "cluckhead" and "street-worn." These descriptions suggest she was a drug user, did not have a "stable" residence or employment, and was probably in Center Heights in search of drugs. This description is filled in by her previous participation in "a drug rehab program," the description of her activity as "hanging out" and being "picked up" by gang bangers, and a medical report which states that no trauma or semen was found when she was "done by six guys." Each of these features of the account suggests that the complainant is a prostitute or "strawberry" who came to Center Heights to trade sex or money for drugs. This alternative scenario combined with "conflicts between what she told the police and what she told me" justify case rejection because it is unlikely that the prosecutor could get a conviction.

The prosecutor acknowledges the distinction between the violation of women's sexual/physical integrity—"somewhere along the line it is not consensual"—and prosecutable actions. The organizational concern with "downstream consequences" (Emerson and Paley, 1992) mitigate against the case being filed.

Typifications of Post-incident Interaction

In an acquaintance rape, the interaction between the parties after the incident is a critical element in assessing the validity of a rape complaint. As implied below by the prosecutors, the typical interaction pattern between victim and suspect after a rape incident is not to see one another. In the following cases the prosecutor challenges the validity of the victims' allegations by suggesting that the complainants' behavior runs counter to a typical rape victim's behavior. In the first instance the parties involved in the incident had a previous relationship and were planning to live together. The DDA is talking to me about the case prior to her decision to reject.

> DDA SABRINA JOHNSON: *I am going to reject the case. She is making it very difficult to try the case. She told me she let him into her apartment last night because she is easily influenced. The week before this happened [the alleged rape] she agreed to have sex with him. Also, first she says "he raped me" and then she lets him into her apartment. (Bay City)*

Here the prosecutor raises doubt about the veracity of the victim's rape allegation by contrasting it to her willingness to allow the suspect into her apartment after the incident. This "atypical" behavior is used to discredit the complainant's allegation.

In the next excerpt the prosecutor was talking about two cases. In both instances the parties knew each other prior to the rape incident as well as having had sexual relations after the incident. As in the previous instance, the victims' allegations are discredited by referring to their atypical behavior.

> DDA SABRINA JOHNSON: *I can't take either case because of the women's behavior after the fact. By seeing these guys again and having sex with them they are absolving them of their guilt. (Bay City)*

In each instance the "downstream" concern with convictability is indicated in the prosecutor's talk—"She is making it very difficult to try the case" and "By seeing these guys again and having sex with them they are absolving them of their guilt." This concern is informed by a series of common-sense assumptions about normal heterosexual relations that the prosecutors assume judges and juries use to assess the believability of the victim: First, appropriate behavior within ongoing relationships is noncoercive and nonviolent. Second, sex that occurs within the context of ongoing relationships is consensual. Third, if coer-

cion or violence occurs, the appropriate response is to sever the relationship, at least for a time. When complainants allege they have been raped by their partner within a continuing relationship, they challenge the taken-for-granted assumptions of normal heterosexual relationships. The prosecutors anticipate that their challenge will create problems for the successful prosecution of a case because they think that judges and jurors will use this typification to question the credibility of the victim's allegation. They assume that the triers of fact will assume that if there is "evidence" of ongoing normal heterosexual relations—she didn't leave and the sexual relationship continued—then there was no coercive sex. Thus the certitude that a crime originally occurred can be retrospectively undermined by the interaction between complainant and suspect after the alleged incident. Implicit in this is the assumed primacy of the normal heterosexual relations typification as the standard on which to assess the victim's credibility even though an allegation of rape has been made.

Typifications of Rape Reporting

An important feature of sexual assault cases is the timeliness in which they are reported to the police (see Torrey, forthcoming). Prosecutors expect rape victims to report the incident relatively promptly: "She didn't call the police until four hours later. That isn't consistent with someone who has been raped." If a woman reports "late," her motives for reporting and the sincerity of her allegation are questioned if they fall outside the typification of officially recognizable/explainable reasons for late reporting. The typification is characterized by the features that can be explained by Rape Trauma Syndrome (RTS). In the first excerpt the victim's credibility is not challenged as a result of her delayed reporting. The prosecutor describes her behavior and motives as characteristic of RTS. The DDA is describing a case to me that came in that morning.

> DDA TAMARA JACOBS: *Charlene was in the car with her three assailants after the rape. John (the*

driver) was pulled over by the CHP [California Highway Patrol] for erratic driving behavior. The victim did not tell the officers that she had just been raped by these three men. When she arrived home, she didn't tell anyone what happened for approximately 24 hours. When her best friend found out from the assailants (who were mutual friends) and confronted the victim, Charlene told her what happened. She then reported it to the police. When asked why she didn't report the crime earlier, she said that she was embarrassed and afraid they would hurt her more if she reported it to the police. The DDA went on to say that the victim's behavior and reasons for delayed reporting were symptomatic of RTS. During the trial an expert in Rape Trauma Syndrome was called by the prosecution to explain the "normality" and commonness of the victim's reaction. (Bay City)

Other typical motives include "wanting to return home first and get family support" or "wanting to talk the decision to report over with family and friends." In all these examples, the victims sustained injuries of varying degrees in addition to the trauma of the rape itself, and they reported the crime within 24 hours. At the time the victims reported the incident, their injuries were still visible, providing corroboration for their accounts of what happened.

In the next excerpt we see the connection between atypical motives for delayed reporting and ulterior motives for reporting a rape allegation. At this point I focus on the prosecutors' use of typification as a resource for discrediting the victim's account. I will examine ulterior motives as a technique of discrediting in a later section. The deputy is telling me about a case she recently rejected.

DDA SABRINA JOHNSON: She doesn't tell anyone after the rape. Soon after this happened she met him in a public place to talk business. Her car doesn't start, he drives her home and starts to attack her. She jumps from the car and runs home. Again she doesn't tell anyone. She said she didn't tell anyone because she didn't want to lose his business. Then the check bounces, and she ends up with VD. She has to tell her fiancé so he can be treated. He insists she tell the police. It is three weeks after the

incident. I have to look at what the defense would say about the cases. Looks like she consented, and told only when she had to because of the infection and because he made a fool out of her by having the check bounce. (Bay City)

The victim's account is discredited because her motives for delayed reporting—not wanting to jeopardize a business deal—fall outside those considered officially recognizable and explicable.

Typifications of Victim's Demeanor

In the course of interviewing hundreds of victims, prosecutors develop a notion of a victim's comportment when she tells what happened. They distinguish between behavior that signifies "lying" versus "discomfort." In the first two exchanges the DDA and IO cite the victim's behavior as an indication of lying. Below, the deputy and IO are discussing the case immediately after the intake interview.

IO NANCY FAUTECK: I think something happened. There was an exchange of body language that makes me question what she was doing. She was yawning, hedging, fudging something.

DDA SABRINA JOHNSON: Yawning is a sign of stress and nervousness.

IO NANCY FAUTECK: She started yawning when I talked to her about her record earlier, and she stopped when we finished talking about it. (Bay City)

The prosecutor and the investigating officer collaboratively draw on their common-sense knowledge and practical work experience to interpret the yawns, nervousness, and demeanor of the complainant as running counter to behavior they expect from one who is "telling the whole truth." They interpret the victim's behavior as a continuum of interaction first with the investigating officer and then with the district attorney. The investigating officer refers to the victim's recurrent behavior (yawning) as an indication that something other than what the victim is reporting actually occurred.

In the next excerpt the prosecutor and IO discredit the victim's account by referencing two typifications—demeanor and appropriate rape-victim behavior. The IO and prosecutor are telling me about the case immediately after they finished the screening interview.

IO DINA ALVAREZ: One on one, no corroboration.

DDA WILLIAM NELSON: She's a poor witness, though that doesn't mean she wasn't raped. I won't file a one-on-one case.

IO DINA ALVAREZ: I don't like her body language.

DDA WILLIAM NELSON: She's timid, shy, naive, virginal, and she didn't do all the right things. I'm not convinced she is even telling the truth. She's not even angry about what happened.…

DDA WILLIAM NELSON: Before a jury if we have a one on one, he denies it, no witnesses, no physical evidence or medical corroboration they won't vote guilty.

IO DINA ALVAREZ: I agree, and I didn't believe her because of her body language. She looks down, mumbles, crosses her arms, and twists her hands.

DDA WILLIAM NELSON: …She has the same mannerisms and demeanor as a person who is lying. A jury just won't believe her. She has low self-esteem and self-confidence.… (Center Heights)

The prosecutor and IO account for case rejection by characterizing the victim as unbelievable and the case as unconvictable. They establish their disbelief in the victim's account by citing the victim's actions that fall outside the typified notions of believable and expected behavior—"she has the same mannerisms and demeanor as a person who is lying," and "I'm not convinced she is even telling the truth. She's not even angry about what happened." They assume that potential jurors will also find the victim's demeanor and post-incident behavior problematic. They demonstrate the unconvictability of the case by citing the "holes" in the case—a combination of a "poor witness" whom the "jury just won't believe" and "one on

one," with no "corroboration" and a defense in which the defendant denies anything happened or denies it was nonconsensual sex.

Prosecutors and investigating officers do not routinely provide explicit accounts of "expected/honest" demeanor. Explicit accounts of victim demeanor tend to occur when DDAs are providing grounds for discrediting a rape allegation. When as a researcher I pushed for an account of expected behavior, the following exchange occurred. The DDA had just concluded the interview and asked the victim to wait in the lobby.[3]

IO NANCY FAUTECK: Don't you think he's credible?

DDA SABRINA JOHNSON: Yes.

LF: What seems funny to me is that someone who said he was so unwilling to do this talked about it pretty easily.

IO NANCY FAUTECK: Didn't you see his eyes, they were like saucers.

DDA SABRINA JOHNSON: And [he] was shaking too. (Bay City)

This provides evidence that DDAs and IOs are orienting to victims' comportment and could provide accounts of "expected/honest" demeanor if necessary. Other behaviors that might be included in this typification are the switch from looking at to looking away from the prosecutor when the victim begins to discuss the specific details of the rape itself; a stiffening of the body and tightening of the face as though to hold in tears when the victim begins to tell about the particulars of the incident; shaking of the body and crying when describing the details of the incident; and a lowering of the voice and long pauses when the victim tells the specifics of the sexual assault incident.

Prosecutors have a number of resources they call on to develop typification related to rape scenarios and reporting. These include how sexual assaults are committed, community residents and activities, interactions between suspect and defendants after a rape incident, and the way victims' emotional and psychological responses to rape influence their behavior. These typifications highlight discrepancies between prosecutors' knowledge and victims' accounts. They are used to discredit the victims' allegation of events, justifying case rejection.

As we have seen, one technique used by prosecutors to discredit a victim's allegations of rape as a justification of case rejection is the detection of discrepancies. The resources for this are official documents and records and typifications of rape scenarios and rape reporting. A second technique prosecutors use is the identification of ulterior motives for the victim's rape allegation.

ACCOUNTING FOR REJECTION BY "ULTERIOR MOTIVE"

Ulterior motives rest on the assumption that a woman consented to sexual activity and for some reason needed to deny it afterwards. These motives are drawn from the prosecutor's knowledge of the victim's personal history and the community in which the incident occurred. They are elaborated and supported by other techniques and knowledge prosecutors use in the accounting process.

I identify two types of ulterior motives prosecutors use to justify rejection: The first type suggests the victim has a reason to file a false rape complaint. The second type acknowledges the legitimacy of the rape allegation, framing the motives as an organizational concern with convictability.

KNOWLEDGE OF VICTIM'S CURRENT CIRCUMSTANCES

Prosecutors accumulate the details of victims' lives from police interviews, official documents, and filing interviews. They may identify ulterior motives by drawing on this information. Note that unlike the court trial itself, where the rape incident is often taken out of the context of the victim's life, here the DDAs call on the texture of a victim's life to justify case rejection. In an excerpt previously discussed, the DDA uses her knowledge of the victim's personal relationship and business transactions as a resource for formulating

ulterior motives for the rape allegation—disclosure to her fiancé about the need to treat a sexually transmitted disease, and anger and embarrassment about the bounced check. Both of these are motives for making a false complaint. The ulterior motives are supported by the typification for case reporting. Twice unreported sexual assault incidents with the same suspect, a three-week delay in reporting, and reporting only after the fiancé insisted she do so are not within the typified behavior and reasons for late reporting. Her atypical behavior provides plausibility to the alternative version of the events—the interaction was consensual and only reported as a rape because the victim needed to explain a potentially explosive matter (how she contracted venereal disease) to her fiancé. In addition she felt duped on a business deal.

Resources for imputing ulterior motives also come from the specifics of the rape incident. Below, the prosecutor's knowledge of the residents and activities in Center Heights supply the reason: the type of activity the victim wanted to cover up from her boyfriend. The justification for rejection is strengthened by conflicting accounts between the victim and witness on the purpose for being in Center Heights. The DDA and IO are talking about the case before they interview the complainant.

DDA WILLIAM NELSON: A white girl from Addison comes to buy dope. She gets kidnapped and raped.

IO BRANDON PALMER: She tells her boyfriend and he beats her up for being so stupid for going to Center Heights.... The drug dealer positively ID's the two suspects, but she's got a credibility problem because she said she wasn't selling dope, but the other two witnesses say they bought dope from her....

LF: I see you have a blue sheet [a sheet used to write up case rejections] already written up.

IO BRANDON PALMER: Oh yes. But there was no doubt in my mind that she was raped. But do you see the problems?

DDA WILLIAM NELSON: Too bad because these guys really messed her up.... She has a credibility problem. I don't think she is telling the truth about the drugs. It would be better if she said she did come to buy drugs. The defense is going to rip her up because of the drugs. He is going to say, isn't it true you had sex with these guys but didn't want to tell your boyfriend, so you lied about the rape like you did about the drugs, or that she had sex for drugs.... (Center Heights)

The prosecutor expresses doubt about the victim's account because it conflicts with his knowledge of the community. He uses this knowledge to formulate the ulterior motive for the victim's complaint—to hide from her boyfriend the "fact" that she was trading sex for drugs. The victim, "a white girl from Addison," alleges she drove to Center Heights "in the middle of the night" as a favor to a friend. She asserted that she did not come to purchase drugs. The DDA "knows" that white people don't live in Center Heights. He assumes that whites who come to Center Heights, especially in the middle of the night, are there to buy drugs or trade sex for drugs. The prosecutor's scenario is strengthened by the statements of the victim's two friends who accompanied her to Center Heights, were present at the scene, and admitted buying drugs. The prosecutor frames the ulterior motives as an organizational concern with defense arguments and convictability. This concern is reinforced by citing conflicting accounts between witnesses and the victim. He does not suggest that the victim's allegation was false— "there was no doubt in my mind that she was raped"; rather, the case isn't convictable—"she has a credibility problem" and "the defense is going to rip her up."

CRIMINAL CONNECTIONS

The presence of criminal connections can also be used as a resource for identifying ulterior motives. Knowledge of a victim's criminal activity enables prosecutors to "find" ulterior motives for her allegation. In the first excerpt the complainant's presence in an area known by police as "where prostitutes bring their clients" is used to formulate an ulterior motive for her rape complaint. This excerpt is from an exchange in which the DDA was telling me about a case he had just rejected.

> *DDA WILLIAM NELSON: Young female is raped under questionable circumstances. One on one. The guy states it is consensual sex. There is no corroboration, no medicals. We ran the woman's rap sheet, and she has a series of prostitution arrests. She's with this guy in the car in a dark alley having sex. The police know this is where prostitutes bring their customers, so she knew she had better do something fast unless she is going to be busted for prostitution, so, lo and behold, she comes running out of the car yelling "he's raped me." He says no. He picked her up on Long Beach Boulevard, paid her $25 and this is "where she brought me." He's real scared, he has no record. (Center Heights)*

Above, the prosecutor, relying on police knowledge of a particular location, assumes the woman is a prostitute. Her presence in the location places her in a "suspicious" category, triggering a check on her criminal history. Her record of prostitution arrests is used as the resource for developing an ulterior motive for her complaint: To avoid being busted for prostitution again, she made a false allegation of rape. Here the woman's record of prostitution and the imminent possibility of arrest are used to provide the ulterior motive to discredit her account. The woman's account is further discredited by comparing her criminal history—"a series of prostitution arrests" with that of the suspect, who "has no record," thus suggesting that he is the more credible of the two parties.

Prosecutors and investigating officers often decide to run a rap sheet (a chronicle of a person's arrests and convictions) on a rape victim. These decisions are triggered when a victim falls into certain "suspicious" categories, categories that have a class/race bias. Rap sheets are not run on women who live in the wealthier parts of town (the majority of whom are white) or have professional careers. They are run on women who live in Center Heights (who are black and Latina), who are homeless, or who are involved in illegal activities that could be related to the incident.

In the next case the prosecutor's knowledge of the victim's criminal conviction for narcotics is the resource for formulating an ulterior motive. This excerpt was obtained during an interview.

> DDA TRACY TIMMERTON: *I had one woman who had claimed that she had been kidnapped off the street after she had car trouble by these two gentlemen who locked her in a room all night and had repeated intercourse with her. Now she was on a cocaine diversion [a drug treatment program where the court places persons convicted of cocaine possession instead of prison], and these two guys' stories essentially were that the one guy picked her up, they went down and got some cocaine, had sex in exchange for the cocaine, and the other guy comes along and they are all having sex and all doing cocaine. She has real reason to lie, she was doing cocaine, and because she has then violated the terms of her diversion and is now subject to criminal prosecution for her possession of cocaine charge. She is also supposed to be in a drug program which she has really violated, so this is her excuse and her explanation to explain why she has fallen off her program. (Bay City)*

The prosecutor used the victim's previous criminal conviction for cocaine and her probation conditions to provide ulterior motives for her rape allegation—the need to avoid being violated on probation for the possession of cocaine and her absence from a drug diversion program. She suggests that the allegation made by the victim was false.

Prosecutors develop the basis for ulterior motives from the knowledge they have of the victim's personal life and criminal connections. They create two types of ulterior motives, those that suggest the victim made a false rape complaint and those that acknowledge the legitimacy of the complaint but discredit the account because of its unconvictability. In the accounts prosecutors give, ulterior motives for case rejection are supported with discrepancies in victims' accounts and other practitioners' knowledge.

CONCLUSION

Case filing is a critical stage in the prosecutorial process. It is here that prosecutors decide which instances of alleged victimization will be forwarded for adjudication by the courts. A significant percentage of sexual assault cases are rejected at this stage. This research has examined prosecutorial accounts for case rejection and the centrality of victim discreditability in those accounts. I have elucidated the techniques of case rejection (discrepant accounts and ulterior motives), the resources prosecutors use to develop these techniques (official reports and records, typifications of rape-relevant behavior, criminal connections, and knowledge of a victim's personal life), and how these resources are used to discredit victims' allegations of sexual assault.

This examination has also provided the beginnings of an investigation into the logic and organization of prosecutors' decisions to reject/accept cases for prosecution. The research suggests that prosecutors are orienting to a "downstream" concern with convictability. They are constantly "in dialogue with" anticipated defense arguments and anticipated judge and juror responses to case testimony. These dialogues illustrate the intricacy of prosecutorial decision-making. They make visible how prosecutors rely on assumptions about relationships, gender, and sexuality (implicit in this analysis, but critical and requiring of specific and explicit attention) in complaint filing of sexual assault cases. They also make evident how the processes of distinguishing truths from untruths and the practical concerns of trying cases are central to these decisions. Each of these issues, in all its complexity, needs to be examined if we are to understand the logic and organization of filing sexual assault cases.

The organizational logic unveiled by these accounts has political implications for the prosecution of sexual assault crimes. These implications are particularly acute for acquaintance rape situations. As I have shown, the typification of normal heterosexual relations plays an important role in assessing these cases, and case conviction is key to filing cases. As noted by DDA William Nelson: "There is a difference between believing a woman was assaulted and being able to get a conviction in court." Unless we are able to challenge the assumptions on which these typifications are based, many cases of rape will never get beyond the filing process because of unconvictability.

NOTES

1. To protect the confidentiality of the people and places studied, pseudonyms are used throughout this article.
2. The use of practitioners' knowledge to inform decision making is not unique to prosecutors. For example, such practices are found among police (Bittner 1967; Rubinstein 1973), public defenders (Sudnow 1965), and juvenile court officials (Emerson 1969).
3. Unlike the majority of rape cases I observed, this case had a male victim. Due to lack of data, I am unable to tell if this made him more or less credible in the eyes of the prosecutor and police.

REFERENCES

Bittner, Egon A. 1967. "The police on skid-row: A study of peace keeping." *American Sociological Review* 32:699–715.

Boland, Barbara, Catherine H. Conly, Paul Mahanna, Lynn Warner, and Ronald Sones. 1990. *The Prosecution of Felony Arrests, 1987.* Washington, D.C.: Bureau of Justice Statistics, U.S. Department of Justice.

Chandler, Susan M., and Martha Torney. 1981. "The decision and the processing of rape victims through the criminal justice system." *California Sociologist* 4:155–69.

Emerson, Robert M. 1969. *Judging Delinquents: Context and Process in Juvenile Court.* Chicago: Aldine Publishing Co.

Emerson, Robert M., and Blair Paley. 1992. "Organizational horizons and complaint-filing." In *The Uses of Discretion,* ed. Keith Hawkins. Oxford: Oxford University Press.

Garfinkel, Harold. 1984. *Studies in Ethnomethodology.* Cambridge, Eng.: Polity Press.

Holmstrom, Lynda Lytle, and Ann Wolbert Burgess. 1983. *The Victim of Rape: Institutional Reactions.* New Brunswick, N.J.: Transaction Books.

Kerstetter, Wayne A. 1990. "Gateway to justice: Police and prosecutorial response to sexual assaults against women." *Journal of Criminal Law and Criminology* 81:267–313.

Kerstetter, Wayne A., and Barrik Van Winkle. 1990. "Who decides? A study of the complainant's decision to prosecute in rape cases." *Criminal Justice and Behavior* 17:268–83.

LaFree, Gary D. 1980. "Variables affecting guilty pleas and convictions in rape cases: Toward a social theory of rape processing." *Social Forces* 58:833–50.

———. 1981. "Official reactions to social problems: Police decisions in sexual assault cases." *Social Problems* 28:582–94.

———. 1989. *Rape and Criminal Justice: The Social Construction of Sexual Assault.* Belmont, Calif.: Wadsworth Publishing Co.

Mather, Lynn M. 1979. *Plea Bargaining or Trial? The Process of Criminal-Case Disposition.* Lexington, Mass.: Lexington Books.

Maynard, Douglas W. 1984. *Inside Plea Bargaining: The Language of Negotiation.* New York: Plenum Press.

Miller, Frank. 1970. *Prosecution: The Decision to Charge a Suspect with a Crime.* Boston: Little, Brown.

Neubauer, David. 1974. *Criminal Justice in Middle America.* Morristown, N.J.: General Learning Press.

Rose, Vicki M., and Susan C. Randall. 1982. "The impact of investigator perceptions of victim legitimacy on the processing of rape/sexual assault cases." *Symbolic Interaction* 5:23–36.

Rubinstein, Jonathan. 1973. *City Police.* New York: Farrar, Straus & Giroux.

Scheff, Thomas. 1966. *Being Mentally Ill: A Sociological Theory.* Chicago: Aldine Publishing Co.

Stanko, Elizabeth A. 1980. "These are the cases that try themselves: An examination of the extra-legal criteria in felony case processing." Presented at the Annual Meetings of the North Central Sociological Association, December. Buffalo, N.Y.

———. 1981. "The impact of victim assessment on prosecutor's screening decisions: The case of the New York District Attorney's Office." *Law and Society Review* 16:225–39.

———. 1982. "Would you believe this woman? Prosecutorial screening for "credible" witnesses and a

problem of justice." In *Judge, Lawyer, Victim, Thief,*
ed. Nicole Hahn Rafter and Elizabeth A. Stanko,
63–82. Boston: Northeastern University Press.

Sudnow, David. 1965. "Normal crimes: Sociological features of the penal code in a public defenders office."
Social Problems 12:255–76.

Torrey, Morrison. Forthcoming. "When will we be believed? Rape myths and the idea coming of a fair
trial in rape prosecutions." U.C. Davis Law Review.

Mental Illness Assumptions in Commitment Hearings

JAMES A. HOLSTEIN

Agents of social control—for example, court personnel—have to decide what to do with the cases that are brought before them. Information on which to base their decisions stems from a number of sources: the "record" that candidates for commitment bring in, what other people have done about them to get to the point of this decision, what people say about them, and how these patients answer the questions the decision maker puts to them. Over time, personnel have considerable experience with a range of cases. In the end, how-ever, the set of background assumptions that they make about typical cases frames the kinds of interpretations they make and the decisions they reach.

James A. Holstein shows that judges in civil commitment hearings believe that peo-ple brought before them for possible commitment at a mental hospital are in fact mentally ill. Although courts generally depend upon independent, objective evidence in order to make decisions, judges in these hearings interpret all answers to their questions as symp-toms of illness rather than making an unbiased judgment. Because of the presumption of incompetence, they commit to institutions those candidate-patients who have no one to take care of them, while discharging those who have people who can care for them. In ei-ther instance, their decisions sustain dependence and are more apt to train people to play the role of mental patient than to train them to be independent and self-reliant citizens.

Challenges to the assumption that a candidate mental patient's[1] psychiatric condition is the ba-sis for involuntary mental hospitalization have commanded considerable sociological attention for more than two decades. Indeed, a persistent controversy (see Scheff, 1974; Gove, 1980, 1982; Horwitz, 1979) has revolved around the "societal

James A. Holstein, *Journal of Contemporary Ethnography,*
Vol. 16, No. 2, pp. 147–175. Copyright © 1987 by Sage Pub-
lications, Inc. Reprinted by permission of Sage Publications,
Inc.

reaction" or "labeling theory" argument that in-voluntary hospitalization depends upon condi-tions external to the individual rather than on a person's *intrapersonal* mental disorders. From this perspective, involuntary commitment is bet-ter explained by contingencies affecting societal response to those seen as deviant than by the pu-tative deviant's mental condition (Scheff, 1964, 1966, 1974; Wilde, 1968; Wenger and Fletcher, 1969). Proponents of the opposing "psychiatric" or "medical" model of mental illness have stead-fastly argued that commitment is a response to the genuine presence of mental disorder; they hold that psychiatric disturbance more than social contingencies determines hospitalization (Gove, 1970, 1980).

A sociological understanding of the involuntary commitment process does not require a resolution to this debate. Indeed, it may be rendered moot if one takes seriously a more analytically promising mandate to study how *imputations* of deviance are central to the process through which putative deviants are progressively identified, differentiated, and sanctioned (Kitsuse, 1980). This approach treats forms of behavior (or psychiatric conditions) per se as meaningless and sociologically irrelevant. Rather, it seeks to discover how relevant actors formulate, utilize, and accomplish imputations, depictions, and other representations of these behaviors and conditions in dealing with and talking about candidate deviants.

From the earliest (Scheff, 1964) to more contemporary studies of civil commitment (Warren, 1982; Hiday, 1983; Holstein, 1984, forthcoming), observers have consistently noted that authorized decision makers presume that candidate mental patients are *in fact* mentally ill. Psychiatrists called to testify routinely offer diagnoses of mental illness, and decision makers form their own commonsense opinions of candidate patients' mental condition, often guided (if not dictated) by these diagnoses. It has been less appreciated, however, that for those making commitment decisions these assessments of mental illness are experienced as objective, literal, factual (if occasionally problematic) descriptions. In this respect then it is analytically irrelevant whether or not mental illness "really exists" in any specific case; decision makers take its factual status for granted *for all practical purposes.* "Mental illness" thus has an experientially consequential place in the commitment process, its impact deriving from decision makers' *belief* in its existence and not from any necessarily "factual" conditions.

In this article I will analyze how such assumptions and imputations—that candidate patients are in fact mentally ill—are used in and affect decisions about whether or not to hospitalize. This analytic task requires specific examination of the ways in which these attributions are incorporated into the practical work and commonsense procedures (Garfinkel, 1967) of relevant decision makers. Such an approach thus both reaffirms and advances the fundamental mandate of the societal reaction perspective to investigate the *processes* by which persons come to be identified, defined, and consequentially reacted to as deviant (Kitsuse, 1962).[2]

BACKGROUND AND SETTINGS

This study is based on fieldwork in several mental health and legal settings. Extensive observations and interviews were conducted in Metropolitan Court[3] in California from 1982 to 1984, focusing on habeas corpus hearings through which persons hospitalized on an initial 14-day commitment seek their release (see Holstein, 1984, and Warren, 1982, for further details of this court and the organization of its activities). This court hears only mental health–related cases. More limited observations and formal interviews were conducted in four other jurisdictions across the United States from 1983 through 1986.[4] Laws and procedures in these five sites were generally similar, with several consequential exceptions to be noted below.

Candidate patients in Metropolitan Court are represented by legal counsel—nearly always a public defender—while the county district attorney's office argues for commitment. Hearings, conducted in a public courtroom, vary in length and typically include testimony by the certifying doctor[5] (with cross-examination) and the candidate patient (with cross-examination). Rarely are other witnesses called. Judges freely interact with witnesses and attorneys, commenting and questioning to elicit whatever information they need to resolve a case. The other settings were generally similar, although several hearings I observed were closed to the public and a few were conducted very informally in noncourtroom settings. Regardless of physical setting, hearing interactions followed the same general format.

The civil commitment laws in the five study sites varied somewhat in their literal wording, but were similar in actual use. California's Lanterman-Petris-Short Act requires that both mental illness and danger to self or others or grave disability be established in order to commit someone involuntarily. A person is gravely disabled if as a result of mental disorder he or she is unable to provide for basic personal needs of food, clothing, and/or shelter. Two other jurisdictions have essentially the same commitment requirements, but the terminology *grave disability* is not a formal legal designation. The remaining jurisdictions make no provision for grave disability as a legal basis for commitment; danger to self or others are the only formally recognized grounds. In actual practice, however, someone considered unable to provide necessary food, clothing, shelter, or medical care due to mental illness would be judged a danger to self. Consequently, these communities can and do hospitalize persons based on a de facto grave disability provision as well.[6]

Cases concerned with grave disability or its practical equivalent are by far the most common commitment cases. Warren (1977), for example, reported that 74% of the cases she studied were adjudicated on this basis. During my own observations, over 90% of the candidate patients appearing in jurisdictions maintaining an explicit grave disability provision had been certified as gravely disabled by the doctor requesting hospitalization. In the other jurisdictions the large majority of cases observed also revolved around grave disability-type issues. My discussion, therefore, focuses mainly on hearings concerned with grave disability-type issues due to their sheer frequency and the clear importance of disability judgments to the commitment process.

In grave disability hearings, the most consequential issue is typically the "tenability" of candidate patients' living situations in the community (Holstein, 1984). Judges generally orient their decision making to the answers they assemble to the following question: Can the candidate patient establish a community living situation that can contain the intra- and interpersonal havoc that is believed to be associated with mental illness? Grave disability is not established simply by reference to a person's psychiatric symptoms or even general incompetencies in caring for himself or herself. Rather, it is a characterization of the condition of a person who is judged incapable of managing a life in some imaginable community living context that might contain, accommodate, and shelter a mentally disturbed person. As such, the living situation—its tenability—is of as much concern as is the candidate patient himself or herself.

In part this orientation is due to the adoption of reformed commitment laws that promote non-institutional remedies for problems seen as mental illness. New statutes explicitly introduce hospitalization criteria beyond psychiatric diagnosis to promote treatment in the least restrictive environment available. Commitment thus requires evidence of both mental problems and inability to function as competent community members. But it would oversimplify the commitment decision-making process to conceptualize it as the *separate* resolution of the issues of candidate patients' mental health or illness, on the one hand, and their disability or dangerousness on the other. Rather, assessments of candidate patients' mental condition and appraisals of their competence and/or dangerousness are *reflexively* related so that each is practically established only in light of the other.

JUDGES' MENTAL ILLNESS ASSUMPTIONS

Judges—indeed most courtroom personnel involved in commitment cases—anticipate that nearly everyone brought before the court is severely disturbed. In part this anticipation recognizes the requisite diagnoses of pathology that must accompany recommendations to hospitalize. Routine relations between courts that handle mental health–related cases and doctors providing psychiatric evaluations develop so that it is rare to find a person advancing to candidacy for involuntary hospitalization without a psychiatric diagnosis of severe mental illness. These diagnoses are seldom challenged; rarely does a candidate patient or his or her counsel argue that a psychiatric *diagnosis* is incorrect, although they frequently question the *implications* that doctors draw from the diagnoses they reach. This tendency continually reaffirms judges' notion that civil commitment cases *always* involve persons with psychiatric troubles.

Perhaps as important as psychiatric input are judges' direct encounters with candidate patients. Those who frequently hear civil commitment cases are convinced that their experience cultivates a certain diagnostic acuity. One judge from a rural jurisdiction indicated that he "could tell if a person is mentally unbalanced—or if he should be in a hospital—as well as any psychiatrist after all the years I've been doing these hearings." And judges' experiences convince them that candidate patients brought before them are truly disturbed. One Metropolitan Court judge stated that "I know all these people, every one of them have problems. That's why they're here. Most of them are very, very sick." A judge from another jurisdiction somewhat less tactfully summarized a generally held opinion that "every one of them that comes through here is crazy in one way or another." While it is possible that comparison of the instant case with the typically experienced "case stream" (Emerson, 1983) of mental health cases may produce a sense that the candidate patient being evaluated is not a "normal" case and may not be as mentally impaired as most, the imputation of mental illness is seldom overthrown in its entirety.[7] The condition may be seen as less severe or less "case relevant" but it is rarely converted to a judgment of "not mentally ill."

Judges also assume that candidate patients' illness is chronic and view their lives as ongoing mental illness "careers." They believe that a candidate patient has a history of hospitalization and/or contact with other agents in the mental health care system, and are thoroughly convinced that a

person will not be involved in a civil commitment hearing the first time he or she experiences psychological distress or encounters mental health authorities. Judges thus assume that people who appear before them are *severely* ill, that this illness has been repeatedly confirmed elsewhere, and a number of other less coercive and restrictive interventions have been tried and have failed.

While these assumptions exist almost apart from the evidence provided about any particular candidate patient, they should not be understood as mere personal bias or prejudgment toward the mentally ill. Judges' evaluations reflect an organizational practice of responding not to individuals per se, but to *cases* within a "case set" (Emerson, 1983, 1985). As in a variety of social control settings (Dingwall et al., 1983; Emerson, 1985), prior screening is assumed, presumably at several decision points, so judges feel confident that any case sent forward merits serious attention. Indeed, much research has shown that both law enforcement and mental health personnel employ a justificatory decision logic that frames civil commitment as a remedy of "last resort" (Emerson, 1981; Emerson and Pollner, 1976; Warren, 1982; Bittner, 1967). Judges appear keenly aware of this and assume that the court is, in a sense, insulated by several layers of organizational procedures to which apparently disturbed persons are subjected before involuntary commitment is sought. This use of organizationally embedded (Gubrium, forthcoming) background knowledge leads judges to focus on candidate patients not in terms of the more particularistic qualities of individual candidate patients' *minds* but as *cases with known organizational backgrounds.*

In typifying persons as cases of mental illness, however, judges in no way yield responsibility for deciding the commitment issue. Mental status may be largely "taken for granted," but judges vigorously assert their warrant to determine its meaning within the context of tenability assessments and commitment decisions.

Beyond assuming mental illness, judges also feel there is little chance for a candidate patient's recovery or cure. They believe symptoms arise and abate in a cycle of acute psychological disturbance, temporary remission, then relapse. While judges' prognoses are rather pessimistic, they nonetheless believe that various psychiatric treatments and therapies can be beneficial, if only in containing symptoms of distress. But they are also aware of the shortcomings and side effects of most conventional treatments. In particular, most judges feel that psychotropic medications can stabilize behavior in a variety of acute episodes and also prolong periods of remission. Still, most believe that medications do not cure symptoms but merely control them temporarily. Therefore, judges are extremely concerned that the mentally ill regularly take their medications, and typically seek assurance that reliable assistance is available to maintain an effective chemotherapy regimen.

ASSUMPTION OF MENTAL ILLNESS AS A PERVASIVE INTERPRETIVE SCHEME

In insisting that judges routinely presume that candidate patients are mentally ill, I am calling attention to the fact that judges in these circumstances do not view the presence of mental illness as problematic, as an issue that must be focused on, explicitly inquired into, and conclusively established during the court hearing. Psychiatric condition is *not* a matter of *foreground* attention in these respects; rather, the imputation of psychiatric disorder provides a distinctive and pervasive *background* against which all other assessments and evaluations are made. The assumption of mental illness thus serves as a scheme of interpretation (Schutz, 1962) that imposes a particular *context* upon all other information regarding the candidate patient, embedding knowledge of and judgments about the person and his or her behavior in a particular body of commonsense knowledge about mentally ill persons.

As judges impute mental illness, they implicitly structure how they interpret candidate patients' behavior generally. "Mental illness" becomes an organizing framework through which

candidate patients' behavior comes to be meaningfully construed. That behavior, viewed as a product of mental illness, then serves further to document the presence of the illness itself. Thus descriptions of candidate patients as mentally ill and subsequent interpretations of their behavior are reflexively related, standing in a fundamentally dialectical relation to one another. The underlying pattern or structure—mental illness—provides the basis for interpreting actions in a meaningful, distinctive way. These actions, so interpreted, in turn serve to document, substantiate, and sustain the underlying pattern (Garfinkel, 1967).

Judges' commitment decisions are always made within the context that ascriptions of mental illness provide. Candidate patients and their behavior are seen against this background so that anything said or done is viewed as the claim or behavior of a "crazy person." Cast in this light, their testimony and behavior is always suspect. Their credibility is constantly challenged and their claimed capabilities discounted. Behavior that might pass for "normal" or "competent" is regarded as artificial or transitory. And, of special consequences, the assumption of mental illness fundamentally shapes judges' evaluations of the tenability of living situations—the issue on which most commitment hearings center. Indirectly, then, the candidate patient's imputed mental status has a strong bearing on how judges make commitment decisions, as the following sections demonstrate.

CANDIDATE PATIENT CREDIBILITY

Perhaps the greatest consequence of judges' assumption that candidate patients are mentally ill is the manner in which this belief consistently undermines candidate patients' credibility. As a Metropolitan Court judge related, "You have to be very careful about what you believe and what you don't. It's not that they're lying. They just don't know what the truth is. They aren't too keen on reality, if you know what I mean." Of course, this handicaps candidate patients when they are called upon to testify because all their accounts and explanations are suspect as claims made by crazy people, claims not to be trusted or believed. Even candidate patients' statements regarding "factual" information are more likely to be disbelieved, suspected, or discounted than statements made by other witnesses.

Harris Charles, for example, indicated under cross-examination that he lived in the Marriott Plaza hotel. He said that a friend had been paying for his room for the past few months. When asked the friend's name, Mr. Charles declined to reveal it, claiming that his friend was a "philanthropist" who wanted to remain anonymous: "He doesn't want to be exposed to all those people who would be begging for his help."

In explaining his subsequent finding of grave disability, the judge noted that Mr. Charles would benefit from hospitalization because "he has no place to stay on a consistent basis." The judge's inquiry into the factual status of these claims involved asking the certifying psychiatrist where Mr. Charles lived, to which the psychiatrist replied, "Apparently nowhere that we can establish." The judge continued, "He could give you no address?" to which the psychiatrist replied, "Nothing whatsoever, except the Marriott Plaza." "That story about the hotel and the philanthropist was just too crazy," the judge explained later. The judge contended he had no reason to believe such a "wild story": "There's no way in the world a guy like that could live there. If that's the best story he can come up with, I've got to assume he's got no place to go. The psychiatrist says the same thing. It's a fabrication of a disturbed mind." This example makes clear the relative credibility attributed to so-called mentally ill candidate patients and another witness. Judges' assumption of mental illness makes the evaluation of such instances of conflicting testimony a choice between honoring the claims of a "sane" person (who is frequently a psychiatric professional) or those of a "madman." While the choice is not automatic, the mere imputation of mental disturbance severely disadvantages the candidate patient.

The manner in which Mr. Charles's testimony was discounted reveals another subtle conse-

quence of judges' assumption of psychiatric disorder. Rather than viewing Charles's claim as a *report*—albeit fraudulent—about his place of residence, this testimony was understood as a *symptom* of Charles's illness, "a fabrication of a disturbed mind." This practical distinction between report and symptom casts candidate patients' talk and behavior as outward signs of their "known" underlying trouble. In this case, what might otherwise pass for rationally motivated (but deceitful) action or description comes to be seen as a sign revealing the condition such action or description attempts to dismiss. Taken to the extreme, any claim of normalcy or mental health may be apprehended as a symptom rather than a report, and thus be discounted, because it reveals the candidate patient's failure to comprehend and acknowledge the fact of his or her illness—actions clearly symptomatic of that very illness.

This situation is not unlike those mental patients encounter elsewhere in the mental health care system. There is ample documentation, for example, of the extent to which their claims are routinely discounted in a variety of treatment settings (Goffman, 1961; Rosenhan, 1973). A significant difference here is that this is allegedly a legal setting in which matters of fact are to be impartially and concretely established. All witnesses, including candidate patients, are sworn to tell the truth, yet it is uniquely assumed that these persons are incapable of valid testimony. But their assumed misrepresentation of the facts is not punished through contempt citations (as one presumably should be punished for lying while under oath), because such false claims are treated as symptoms of illness, not rationally calculated deceit. So, while candidate patients have their testimony automatically discredited and their freedom jeopardized as a result, their assumed mental illness does protect them from the consequences of willful violation of legal constraints.

CANDIDATE PATIENT PERFORMANCE

During the courtroom hearing judges typically assess candidate patients' social and interactional competence. They look beyond the mere content of official testimony to all other observable behavior that they treat as relevant decision-making data. Thus how the candidate patients comport themselves, how they respond to questioning and conduct themselves while being examined by counsel, and even how they act when not directly involved in the courtroom proceedings are matters of practical interest for judges as they consider not so much what persons claim about themselves, but rather what they reveal through their current behavior. Indeed, candidate patients are "on trial" the entire day in court, not just the few minutes spent on the witness stand, and are seldom "off-stage" because any observable behavior is treated as somehow indicative of their mental or interactional competence.[8]

In a sense, commitment proceedings orient as much to what candidate patients do *in the hearing setting* as they do to information concerning prior incidents or behaviors that mobilized commitment actions. Judges are not evaluating "sanity" per se, because they are certain that candidate patients are "insane," but they do want to establish firsthand how well candidate patients respond to the demands of community living. An Eastern Court judge indicated that he thought that formal courtroom hearings were essential to the commitment process, not just for legal reasons, but because they provided the opportunity to "check out" and "test" the candidate patient's ability to function outside the sheltered world of the mental hospital or community mental health center. "We give them a chance to prove themselves," he noted, "by letting them defend themselves. If they can't manage to show me that they can handle themselves, then I'm not gonna release them."

Much of the so-called testing takes the form of apparent checks on "reality orientation," a practice argued to be common in civil commitment proceedings (Scheff, 1964; Warren, 1982). In Metropolitan Court, in particular, judges repeatedly ask questions that demand factual information from the candidate patient: "What day is it?" "Where are you right now?" "How do you get

to your mother's house from Southpark?" "What is 50 plus 35?" One might argue, however, that many of these questions are not asked to evaluate a candidate patient's "reality orientation" as much as they are intended to reveal the person's current ability to locate himself or herself in the community, proceed to intended destinations, and conduct the routine transactions of everyday life required by release into the community. These may be conceived as very practical questions, their importance deriving from a mundane or literal interpretation of their significance. Correct answers document a sort of competence in community living; incorrect responses indicate that the person would have difficulty negotiating life outside an institution and not *necessarily* a faulty grasp of "reality."[9]

Such evaluations of responses to these questions are dictated by the presumption of mental illness, which demands locating the cause of any displayed incompetence *within* the candidate patient and his or her *psychiatric condition*. An incorrect answer will be cited as a symptom, both a product and a document of a disturbed mind; other possible reasons for a wrong answer go unconsidered. For example, a Metropolitan Court judge refused to consider the possibility that Jefferson Smith's inability to state his mother's address might be due to his recent arrival in town, or his recent 10-day hospitalization in which he was heavily medicated, or even his nervousness about appearing in court—all possible explanations suggested by Smith's attorney. Instead the judge offered the following: "This man's mental condition interferes with his ability to do the day-to-day functions that he has to do if he wants to live with his family. His psychosis has impaired his memory....He's lost. He can't look out for himself." The assumption that Smith was mentally ill precludes assigning other cause (including simple ignorance) for his misstatement of the address. Thus those *situational* explanations that relieve the "normal" actor from responsibility for many minor transgressions in the course of everyday life are invalid when evaluating the meaning of a "mentally ill" person's mistakes. The assumption of mental illness insinuates that good cause for perceived incompetence can be found in the candidate patient's "sick" mind. External causes need not be seriously considered.

Despite assuming that persons sought to be committed are mentally disturbed, judges believe that most candidate patients are conscious of their courtroom demeanor. "Let's face it," noted an Eastern Court judge, "they're on their best behavior. They're doing everything they can to hide their condition." They are viewed as intentionally concealing or containing the symptoms that judges assume lurk just below any facade of normalcy that may be temporarily sustained. Composed, situationally appropriate demeanor and organized, articulate testimony are routinely discounted, if not disregarded, as valid indicators of competence because judges assume they are little more than "acting" or "performances" that quickly evaporate once the candidate patient lets down his or her guard. Judges reveal their belief that candidate patients' courtroom behavior is often deceiving through statements such as, "That one almost slipped right by us," or "He was really trying hard to hold his act together, but he just couldn't keep it up." Marie Albeck, for example, testified in an articulate and rational manner, giving every indication of interactional competence, even by the admission of the judge who ruled her gravely disabled. Yet her composed demeanor was seen as ephemeral, merely a temporary departure from, or disguise for, the chaotic behavior of the mentally ill person she was "known" to be. Said the judge, "She's really disturbed, but she doesn't always show it. She's so sick that she tries to hide her illness even when people just want to help her. We know it can't last." Even her "good behavior"— interpreted as a calculated yet pathological departure from the typical—was used to document her psychiatric disturbance. Once assumed, mental illness remains an almost incorrigible (Pollner, 1974) description of persons sought to be committed.

Conversely, any behavior that might be interpreted as symptomatic of mental illness is readily viewed as indicative of the candidate patient's true condition. Indeed, any slipup may be viewed as the mere "tip of the iceberg" of deranged behavior that can be caused by mental illness. Judges, then, consider much behavior to be motivated, manipulative self-presentation (Goffman, 1959), while also believing that they must see beneath mere appearance to the "true" nature and condition of the persons brought before them.

Medication and Performance

The fact that most involuntary commitment hearings are held while candidate patients are undergoing institutional evaluation and treatment further colors judges' interpretations of what these persons say and do. Most candidate patients are receiving psychotropic medications at the time of their hearings. While judges clearly do not believe such medications cure mental illness, they do believe such medications can be effective in containing or suppressing symptoms. Whatever rational, composed, "appropriate" behavior candidate patients might display is often attributed to their medications. And because they are assumed to be mentally ill and mental illness is assumed to have visible symptoms, any absence of symptoms is attributed to the drugs. As one judge noted:

> These people are very, very sick. And without their medications they don't stand a chance. Usually the medications give them a chance to pull themselves together, get things under control. But they need to stay on them. It's the only way they can maintain. This last fellow today seemed very together, but take him off meds and he's in his own world again. He can do just fine—like today—if he'll just take his meds.

Thus candidate patients find themselves in the precarious position of receiving causal credit for all "inappropriate" behavior, but "appropriate" or "competent" behavior is attributed to medications. Under such circumstances, it is sometimes difficult to convince a judge that hospitalization is unnecessary because, even when no symptoms are apparent or when visible symptoms seem innocuous, one's fundamental competence is continually suspect.

Negative Cases

There are, of course, instances when candidate patients' testimony or performances are not discounted. While these may be due to extraordinary displays of competence by candidate patients, they are more likely to result from some violation of organizational procedure or expectation by the *sponsors* of commitment. For example, in Metropolitan Court, psychiatrists (or occasionally representatives of the district attorney's office) who are inexperienced with commitment cases may seek hospitalization in violation of either explicit or implicit commitment criteria. They may believe that a candidate patient's florid symptoms or disturbed behavior so warrants hospitalization that less restrictive treatment alternatives are not pursued before commitment proceedings are initiated. If this becomes apparent to a judge, all assumptions about the case—and hence the candidate patient—may be suspended. The usual attribution of mental illness may be tentative or problematic, thus allowing testimony and behavior to be seen against a new background, through a different interpretive framework.

Consider the case of Janet Conrad, a 22-year-old white female whose family had engaged a psychiatrist in private practice, Dr. Ryan, to involuntarily hospitalize her. According to her family, Janet had been very depressed, then had become delusional and agitated. In response to commands "from inside her head," Janet had tried to kill the family dog and threatened some neighborhood children. The family also claimed that Janet had repeatedly been uncontrollable in public places and finally had to be physically removed from a local shopping mall and transported to a psychiatric facility by the police due to bizarre and threatening behavior. She had been held there over the weekend, and after a psychiatric evaluation the Conrad parents asked Dr. Ryan to pursue more extended hospitalization.

At the hearing, his first in Metropolitan Court, Dr. Ryan sought Janet's involuntary commitment, arguing that he had diagnosed her as "schizophrenic" and that she was gravely disabled as well as dangerous to herself and others. After seeking some clarifications regarding Ryan's recommendation, the judge asked how long Janet had been under Ryan's care and what her history of outpatient psychiatric treatment had been. He was somewhat surprised to hear that Ryan had been brought onto the case only recently and that Janet had no treatment history. She had previously seen the Conrad family physician to discuss her feelings of "agitation" but he had done nothing more than prescribe a mild sedative. At this point the judge launched a rather extended lecture on the mandate of community mental health care, then aggressively requestioned Dr. Ryan regarding his commitment recommendation when so many alternatives had not been explored. Ryan reiterated his belief that Janet's symptoms were so bad and her behavior so bizarre and uncontrollable that institutional control and monitoring [were] clearly indicated, especially in light of her parents' request.

Janet Conrad's testimony was agitated but coherent. She admitted to hearing voices but claimed that she was not going to listen to them in the future. She repeatedly denied the need for psychiatric care but acknowledged that she could use some help "to make her feel better." The judge asked her if she would be willing to see a counselor at a community mental health center, if she would agree to take medications if they were prescribed for her, and if she would move in with her parents "until she was feeling like herself again." She reluctantly agreed to all three stipulations, although she claimed she didn't want to live at home and continued to assert that she was not the only one that needed help: "This whole mess is crazy. I'll go to the shrink if you say so, but why are you just picking on me?"

The judge released Janet Conrad with the following explanation:

> *This woman obviously needs help, but I think she can get it without hospitalizing her at this time.*

She says she can keep her act together on her own, so I'll trust her to keep her promise to get the kind of care she needs and give her a chance.... If this doesn't work out, we can always bring you back here, young lady. Let's not let your emotional problems get out of hand. You get help, so we don't have to force it on you.

Later, the judge indicated that he was ambivalent about releasing a woman whose family sought her hospitalization but felt there was insufficient evidence to warrant Janet's commitment: "She's got troubles, no doubt about that, but it's not clear that she can't overcome them. Sometimes we have to find out if they can really manage or not."

Janet Conrad's case was uncharacteristic in that a violation of the court's expectation of prior processing dislodged the typical interpretive framework through which candidate patients are evaluated. While the judge still thought that Janet was mentally ill, he apparently bracketed this assumption because it was not supported by a typical organizational and remedial history. Consequently, the judge was willing to honor Janet's claims to a much greater extent than usual. Her promises regarding management of her life in the community were not immediately dismissed because her credibility was not completely undermined by assumed psychiatric disorder. It is not that the judge doubted the psychiatric diagnosis so much as he was not yet convinced that the disorder was socially disabling, Janet's case having already departed from the ordinary.

Typical assumptions about a case are apparently rendered problematic to the extent that features of the instant case cannot be articulated with the "normal case." Thus judges' commitment decisions are not shaped so much by a predisposition to hospitalize as much as they are by their assumption about the typical course of psychiatric disturbance and its treatment, coupled with a practical understanding of its effects on one's ability to function in community settings. When that assumption is altered, the ensuing interpretation of matters at hand may change, as might the contingent decision.

TENABLE LIVING ARRANGEMENTS

Concern for a candidate patient's ability to function in the community focuses commitment decision making on *both* psychiatric disturbance and the person's proposed community living circumstances. In assessing grave disability judges try to establish whether or not the person released will maintain reliable access to basic necessities such as food, clothing, and shelter, be supervised by a competent "caretaker," and participate in an ongoing treatment regime (Holstein, 1984). Such tenability assessments are distinctively shaped by judges' assumption that a living situation must be proven viable *for a mentally ill person,* thus merging evaluation of personal capabilities and the adequacy of proposed living situations. As a result judges tend to view as problematic a variety of situations and living arrangements that might otherwise be seen as tenable. In their practical decision making, judges presume a tenable living situation must accommodate, contain, and control the havoc that is assumed to accompany mental illness. They consequently may attend to the situation's ability to deal with instability, vulnerability, irresponsibility, dangerousness, and erratic or bizarre behavior even if the candidate patient in question has given no concrete evidence of acting in these ways.

As noted earlier, when viewed against the assumption of mental illness, candidate patients' claims regarding viable living arrangements are viewed with suspicion. In addition to skepticism toward the very existence of such situations, judges are also reluctant to concede their adequacy for accommodating released patients assumed to be still "mentally ill." The practicalities of how candidate patients will support themselves are always a concern because it is assumed that mental illness renders its victims too unstable, unreliable, and incompetent to make and manage money. Judges assume the mentally ill behave erratically and are likely to lose jobs, even those marginal and menial jobs that they might most likely fill. Consequently, financial support based on employment is considered highly vulnerable, and living arrangements dependent upon holding a job are clearly untenable. Conversely, candidate patients who claim to support themselves on some sort of entitlement assistance (for example, social security, Supplemental Security Income, Social Security Disability Insurance, unemployment insurance, veteran's benefits, and so on) are considered more financially stable; their living situations are more viable because they are, in a sense, financially protected from the uncertainties that accompany mental illness.

Consider the Eastern Court case of Ned Yost, a 27-year-old white male who had been hospitalized after being arrested for causing a public disturbance in an all-night doughnut shop. At his commitment hearing Yost testified that he had been supporting himself by working as a busboy. The restaurant had agreed to participate in a locally sponsored vocational rehabilitation program and hired Yost upon his completion of the program's job training. Yost gave the judge the name and address of the restaurant and said that his supervisor could be called to verify his employment. Yost indicated that he had the job for almost three months and previously held several jobs of this nature. He was making the minimum wage, but was working enough hours to earn over $100 weekly, after taxes. This was enough to live on, he claimed, because he paid only $276 a month for rent and received free meals on the job.

At the hearing, no attempt was made to contact Yost's employer or anyone from the vocational rehabilitation program. Yost was committed, with the explanation that his financial situation was too precarious to be considered viable. The judge argued:

> The option of living outside [of the hospital] at the present time isn't very realistic. He is in no condition to fend for himself, support himself. If I release Mr. Yost, he will surely lose his job, just go out and do something to get fired. His behavior is too unpredictable. And when he loses the job, where will he be? Nowhere. I just can't release him to face that prospect. He's better off getting the help he needs in the hospital.

In contrast, the same judge released several candidate patients whose only claim of support was that they received SSI or veteran's benefits. In all the jurisdictions studied, judges regularly cited dependable income from such sources in justification of returning persons to the community, but I never observed the release of a person who claimed that he or she would hold a job as his or her source of support.

The assumption of mental illness also colors the way in which judges evaluate the adequacy of other basic necessities. The sources of such necessities were considered vulnerable to the extent that the candidate patient's assumed mental illness might be able to affect them. Living arrangements, for example, are untenable if seen as easily disrupted by disturbed or erratic behavior. Thus persons who rent apartments on their own (even if they can document their ability to pay rent) are more likely to be committed than are persons who live in some structured or institutionalized setting over which they exercise no responsibility or control. Renting, judges believe, requires meeting financial obligations and observing both formal and informal rules of apartment life. Judges feel these seemingly mundane and minimal obligations are likely to pose major difficulties for mentally ill persons. They suspect that candidate patients will almost certainly disrupt the situation, thus jeopardizing their living arrangements and effectively depriving themselves of the adequate shelter required for their release. Thus it is not the living situation per se that is judged appropriate or deficient. Rather, judges base tenability assessments on how well a housing situation can provide for the very special needs of persons presumed to be mentally ill. This presumption, then, imposes evaluative criteria upon judges' tenability assessments that render many "conventional" housing arrangements untenable.

Other aspects of tenability assessments are similarly influenced. The adequacy of a caretaker, for example, is judged in terms of those capabilities required to deal with a potentially erratic, disruptive, violent person—even though no formal psychiatric prognosis suggests that such behavior is likely. Or a candidate patient's pledge to adhere to a program of psychiatric care will be treated as a worthless promise due to the person's impaired mental capacity. Robert Castillo's case illustrates these processes. Castillo, a 37-year-old Chicano, was judged gravely disabled in Metropolitan Court after he repeatedly came to the attention of the police for "threatening and harassing" people in his neighborhood. The judge's account for his ruling emphasized the lack of a competent caretaker to monitor Castillo's daily activities or ensure his continued outpatient treatment. While the judge indicated that Castillo's wife tried her best to keep track of him, he also noted that she was away from home at her job a good portion of the day:

> *A guy like this may seem to be just fine one minute, then go off the deep end the next. If there's no one there watching all the time, who's gonna step in and take over when he loses his senses? Somebody has got to be constantly on guard.*

The judge assumed that Castillo was mentally ill and prone to unpredictable swings that called for especially rigorous supervision; these assumptions, not direct testimony about his psychological state, supported the characterization of Castillo as gravely disabled.

The assumption of mental illness also caused the judge to question Castillo's commitment to getting psychiatric care:

> *He needs treatment—regular medication—but he doesn't recognize that. In his mental state, he doesn't think he needs help. So he can't be trusted, and if she's [Mrs. Castillo] not around, who's gonna get him to the clinic? Who's gonna give him his meds? He says he'll take them now, but what about next week when he says he's better, when his delusions make him think that he feels ok and doesn't need them?*

By assuming Castillo is psychiatrically disturbed, and characterizing the symptoms of that disturbance as he does, the judge sees no hope for community treatment in the present circumstances. When one believes that mental illness causes its victims to be oblivious to their own needs, one can never trust such a person to seek psychiatric help. And when an individual is assumed to be mentally ill, others (especially judges) are likely to interpret any report by that person of a subjective sense of well-being, improvement, or remission as misapprehension, delusion, or irrationality—one further symptom of psychiatric disorder.

Certainly not all candidate patients are committed, even though they are assumed to be mentally ill. Release merely requires convincing a judge that an appropriate situation is available for the "mentally ill" person in question. In a sense, this calls for producing a match between candidate patient needs and the accommodations a situation provides (Holstein, forthcoming). This match is an accomplishment of the persons arguing the case at hand, so the demands of a particular person and the capabilities of a particular caretaker or household may be explicitly contested and negotiated as the "facts" of the case are established. Whereas Mrs. Castillo was depicted as an inadequate match to her husband's supervisorial needs, other cases may produce descriptions of household settings that can better accommodate the demands of candidate patients who wish to reside there. For example, "family rhetoric" (Gubrium and Lynott, 1985; Gubrium and Holstein, forthcoming) may depict a household composed of capable and loving caretakers for a person characterized as placing few demands on their management abilities. Release might be forthcoming in such a case. Commitment, then, is never a foregone conclusion, even though mental illness ascriptions dictate stringent criteria for determining a living situation's tenability.

CONCLUSION: THE IRONY OF COMMITMENT CRITERIA

Judges routinely ascribe mental illness to those whose hospitalization is sought through involuntary commitment. I have not questioned the validity or warrant of this imputation because members of the decision-making setting treat it as valid and correct. By focusing on *members'* use of and orientation to practical psychiatric assessments, the "actuality" of mental illness is rendered inconsequential in light of its experiential reality. Mental illness ascriptions implicitly structure judges' evaluations of candidate patients' testimony, behavior, and community living arrangements, and in many respects "straitjacket" candidate patients' attempts to establish their own competence or the tenability of their proposed living situations. Commitment decisions are thus profoundly responsive to the background assumption of mental illness.

Since hospitalization is forestalled only with a convincing argument that a candidate patient will live in a community situation that can accommodate and contain a person *who is mentally ill,* a tenable living situation, for judges' practical decision-making purposes, becomes one that approximates in many ways the structured and encompassing institutionalized setting represented by the mental hospital. This tendency ironically twists the logic and implementation of "deinstitutionalized" mental health care that undergirds most reformed commitment legislation. In place of dehumanizing total institutions (Goffman, 1961) that isolate mental patients from nearly all social contact and reinforce passive and dependent behavior patterns, the community mental health movement promotes treatment of mental patients in more natural community settings. Such placement seeks to capitalize on a wide range of healthful influences thought to be inherent in community living, influences that might render mental patients better able to manage themselves and approach some minimal level of normal functioning (Kirk and Thierren, 1975).

But when judges' involuntary commitment decisions are premised on a distinctive set of assumptions about mental illness and a derived set of assumptions about tenability, candidate patients who claim living arrangements apparently most consonant with those mandated by deinstitutionalization become those *least likely to be released.*

Specifically, persons wishing to live in community circumstances that might require independent living skills or normal social functioning are unlikely to be released because such circumstances would be viewed as *untenable* "for mentally ill persons." In contrast, candidate patients who appear more willingly dependent upon other persons and institutions to supervise all aspects of their daily lives are *more likely to avoid commitment.* Judges' persistent belief in candidate patients' mental illness thus minimizes the likelihood that a person with the desire and opportunity to live in more "conventional" circumstances requiring initiative, responsibility, and control will be allowed to do so. In this respect reformed commitment procedures within the community mental health care movement promote the hospitalization of many persons who are among the most willing and perhaps the most capable of living independently in community settings, while those released are typically the ones most willing to accept virtual custodial treatment in an alternative setting.

In effect, contemporary commitment decision making promotes a system of "community custody" (Scull, 1981). This no doubt contributes to what Warren (1981) has labeled the "transinstitutionalism" of both treatment and social control by requiring that community settings housing released candidate patients still be required to constrain and control the havoc-wreaking symptoms of mental illness that are assumed to follow these persons into their lives beyond the hospital. Release from commitment thus takes on the same character that Kirk and Thierren (1975: 212) note in the deinstitutionalization movement in general, where "the return of patients to the community has, in many ways, extended the philosophy of custodialism into the community rather than ending it at the gates of the state hospital."

NOTES

1. All persons whose commitment is being considered in the proceedings studied here will be called *candidate patients,* although in most cases they are already

patients who have been hospitalized and are now seeking their release. For example, in California's habeas corpus proceedings, their status is technically that of petitioner because they have been hospitalized and now seek their release through legal review. I use this convention to minimize the terminological confusion of these persons with "petitioners" who file petitions seeking the involuntary hospitalization of others.

2. At the same time, it might also help us better understand the findings Gove (1982) cites as the "undoing of labeling theory" in such a way as to acknowledge the apparently strong correlation between psychiatric diagnoses and hospitalizations, yet maintain the integrity of the societal reaction point of view.

3. Names of all persons and places have been fictionalized.

4. See Holstein (1984) for further descriptions of the settings studied here.

5. Generally this person is a psychiatrist, although occasionally a psychologist or medical doctor (M.D.) will be called to testify. In the other jurisdictions, psychiatrists were also the most commonly called as expert witness, but psychologists and M.D.s testified in a greater percentage of cases. Since their testimony appears to be similarly received, I will, for the sake of convenience, refer to this group as "psychiatrists," even though this may not literally be the case.

6. As a matter of convenience, I will extend the use of the term *grave disability* to all other settings.

7. In sites other than Metropolitan Court, judges hear non–mental health cases as the majority of their caseloads. For them, the case stream of all cases seen may make it seem even more apparent that candidate mental patients are mentally ill because they stand out in greater contrast to the non–mentally ill persons who more regularly appear in courts. Thus judges in these courts may develop a great deal of confidence in their "diagnostic capabilities" (that is, their ability to differentiate the sane from the insane) even though they have less experience dealing with mental health matters than do Metropolitan Court judges.

8. This is especially true of Metropolitan Court, where most candidate patients are bussed in from distant psychiatric wards between 8 and 10 a.m. and remain in the court building until the end of the day's hearings, when they are returned to their wards if they have not been released.

9. While judges may hear these answers very pragmatically, psychiatrists are still inclined to use them as evidence of underlying mental disorientation. Thus the "reality testing" that Scheff (1964) has described may in part be a product of professional and organizational location.

REFERENCES

Bittner, E. (1967) "Police discretion in apprehending the mentally ill." *Social Problems* 14: 278–292.

Dingwall, R., J. M. Eekelaar, and T. Murray (1983) *The Protection of Children: State Intervention and Family Life.* Oxford, England: Basil Blackwell.

Emerson, R. M. (1981) "On last resorts." *Amer. J. of Sociology* 87: 1–22.

Emerson, R. M. (1983) "Holistic effects in social control decision-making." *Law and Society Rev.* 17: 425–455.

Emerson, R. M. (1985) "Detecting the 'real reason' for referrals." Presented at the annual meetings of the Law and Society Association, San Diego.

Emerson, R. M. and M. Pollner (1976) "Mental hospitalization and assessments of untenability." Presented at the annual meeting of the Society for the Study of Social Problems, New York.

Garfinkel, H. (1967) *Studies in Ethnomethodology.* Englewood Cliffs, NJ: Prentice-Hall.

Goffman, E. (1959) *The Presentation of Self in Everyday Life.* Garden City, NY: Doubleday.

Goffman, E. (1961) *Asylums.* Garden City, NY: Doubleday.

Gove, W. R. (1970) "Societal reaction as an explanation of mental illness: an evaluation." *Amer. Soc. Rev.* 35: 863–884.

Gove, W. R. [ed.] (1980) "Labelling and mental illness: a critique," in *The Labeling of Deviance: Evaluating a Perspective.* Newbury Park, CA: Sage.

Gove, W. R. [ed.] (1982) "The current status of the labelling theory of mental illness," in *Deviance and Mental Illness.* Newbury Park, CA: Sage.

Gubrium, J. (forthcoming) "Organizational embeddedness and family life," in T. Brubaker (ed.) *Older Families and Long-Term Care.* Newbury Park, CA: Sage.

Gubrium, J. and J. A. Holstein (1988) "Experiential location and method in family studies." *J. of Marriage and the Family.*

Gubrium, J. and R. J. Lynott (1985) "Family rhetoric as social order." *J. of Family Issues* 6: 129–152.

Hiday, V. A. (1983) "Judicial decisions in civil commitment: facts, attitudes and psychiatric recommendations." *Law and Society Rev.* 17: 517–530.

Holstein, J. A. (1984) "The placement of insanity: assessments of grave disability and involuntary commitment decisions." *Urban Life* 13: 35–62.

Holstein, J. A. (forthcoming) "Producing gender effects: gender depictions and accommodations in the involuntary mental hospitalization process." *Social Problems.*

Horwitz, A. V. (1979) "Models, muddles, and mental illness labelling." *J. of Health and Social Behavior* 20: 296–300.

Kirk, S. and M. E. Thierren (1975) "Community mental health myths and the fate of former hospitalized patients." *Psychiatry* 38: 209–217.

Kitsuse, J. I. (1962) "Societal reactions to deviant behavior: problems of theory and method." *Social Problems* 9: 247–256.

Kitsuse, J. I. (1980) "The 'new conception of deviance' and its critics," in W. Gove (ed.) *The Labeling of Deviance.* Newbury Park, CA: Sage.

Pollner, M. (1974) "Mundane reasoning." *Philosophy of the Social Sciences* 4: 35–54.

Rosenhan, D. L. (1973) "On being sane in insane places." *Science* 179: 250–258.

Scheff, T. J. (1964) "The societal reaction to deviance: ascriptive elements in the psychiatric screening of mental patients in a midwestern state." *Social Problems* 11: 401–413.

Scheff, T. J. (1966) *Being Mentally Ill: A Sociological Theory.* Chicago: Aldine.

Scheff, T. J. (1974) "The labelling theory of mental illness." *Amer. Soc. Rev.* 39: 444–452.

Schutz, A. (1962) *The Problem of Social Reality.* The Hague: Martinus Nijhoff.

Scull, A. (1981) "A new trade in lunacy." *Amer. Behavioral Scientist* 24: 741–754.

Warren, C. A. B. (1977) "Involuntary commitment for mental disorder: the application of California's Lanterman-Petris-Short Act." *Law and Society Rev.* 11: 629–649.

Warren, C. A. B. (1981) "New forms of social control: the myth of deinstitutionalization." *Amer. Behavioral Scientist* 24: 724–740.

Warren, C. A. B. (1982) *The Court of Last Resort.* Chicago: Univ. of Chicago Press.

Wenger, D. and C. R. Fletcher (1969) "The effect of legal counsel on admissions to a state mental hospital: a confrontation of professions." *J. of Health and Social Behavior* 10: 66–72.

Wilde, W. (1968) "Decision-making in a psychiatric screening agency." *J. of Health and Social Behavior* 9: 215–221.

CHAPTER 7

THE EFFECTS OF CONTACT WITH CONTROL AGENTS

The Saints and the Roughnecks

WILLIAM J. CHAMBLISS

Organizational processing, whether in the criminal justice or health care systems, tends to produce some taken-for-granted assumptions about all of the people processed. These assumptions are frequently held just as often by laypeople as by professionals. It is believed that persons processed by these systems share a set of common characteristics. They are alike, not only in the offenses they have committed, but in other significant social respects as well. And, in turn, they are markedly dissimilar from all members of conventional society.

William J. Chambliss, in a study of two different high school gangs, finds variations in social responses to deviance that attest to the power and consequences of social reputation. Reputation is made up of one's past of alleged performance, social responses, and expectations for future performance. Although both of the gangs studied engaged in the same frequency of deviance, one gang received considerable official social control attention while the other one did not. In time, members of the two gangs lived up to the community's differential predictions about their future after graduation from high school. In this case study, the subsequent careers of both gangs turned out to be examples of a self-fulfilling prophecy—what people believe to be real will be real in its consequences.

Eight promising young men—children of good, stable, white upper-middle-class families, active in school affairs, good pre-college students—were some of the most delinquent boys at Hanibal High School. While community residents and parents knew that these boys occasionally sowed a few wild oats, they were totally unaware that sowing wild oats completely occupied the daily routine of these young men. The Saints were constantly oc-

cupied with truancy, drinking, wild driving, petty theft and vandalism. Yet not one was officially arrested for any misdeed during the two years I observed them.

This record was particularly surprising in light of my observations during the same two years of another gang of Hanibal High School students, six lower-class white boys known as the Roughnecks. The Roughnecks were constantly in trouble with police and community even though their rate of delinquency was about equal with that of the Saints. What was the cause of this disparity? The result? The following consideration of the activities, social class and community perceptions of both gangs may provide some answers.

THE SAINTS FROM MONDAY TO FRIDAY

The Saints' principal daily concern was with getting out of school as early as possible. The boys managed to get out of school with minimum danger that they would be accused of playing hookey through an elaborate procedure for obtaining "legitimate" release from class. The most common procedure was for one boy to obtain the release of another by fabricating a meeting of some committee, program or recognized club. Charles might raise his hand in his 9:00 chemistry class and ask to be excused—a euphemism for going to the bathroom. Charles would go to Ed's math class and inform the teacher that Ed was needed for a 9:30 rehearsal of the drama club play. The math teacher would recognize Ed and Charles as "good students" involved in numerous school activities and would permit Ed to leave at 9:30. Charles would return to his class, and Ed would go to Tom's English class to obtain his release. Tom would engineer Charles' escape. The strategy would continue until as many of the Saints as possible were freed. After a stealthy trip to the car (which had been parked in a strategic spot), the boys were off for a day of fun.

Over the two years I observed the Saints, this pattern was repeated nearly every day. There were variations on the theme, but in one form or another, the boys used this procedure for getting out of class and then off the school grounds. Rarely did all eight of the Saints manage to leave school at the same time. The average number avoiding school on the days I observed them was five.

Having escaped from the concrete corridors the boys usually went either to a pool hall on the other (lower-class) side of town or to a cafe in the suburbs. Both places were out of the way of people the boys were likely to know (family or school officials), and both provided a source of entertainment. The pool hall entertainment was the generally rough atmosphere, the occasional hustler, the

sometimes drunk proprietor and, of course, the game of pool. The cafe's entertainment was provided by the owner. The boys would "accidentally" knock a glass on the floor or spill cola on the counter—not all the time, but enough to be sporting. They would also bend spoons, put salt in sugar bowls and generally tease whoever was working in the cafe. The owner had opened the cafe recently and was dependent on the boys' business which was, in fact, substantial since between the horsing around and the teasing they bought food and drinks.

THE SAINTS ON WEEKENDS

On weekends, the automobile was even more critical than during the week, for on weekends the Saints went to Big Town—a large city with a population of over a million, 25 miles from Hanibal. Every Friday and Saturday night most of the Saints would meet between 8:00 and 8:30 and would go into Big Town. Big Town activities included drinking heavily in taverns or nightclubs, driving drunkenly through the streets, and committing acts of vandalism and playing pranks.

By midnight on Fridays and Saturdays the Saints were usually thoroughly high, and one or two of them were often so drunk they had to be carried to the cars. Then the boys drove around town, calling obscenities to women and girls; occasionally trying (unsuccessfully so far as I could tell) to pick girls up; and driving recklessly through red lights and at high speeds with their lights out. Occasionally they played "chicken." One boy would climb out the back window of the car and across the roof to the driver's side of the car while the car was moving at high speed (between 40 and 50 miles an hour); then the driver would move over and the boy who had just crawled across the car roof would take the driver's seat.

Searching for "fair game" for a prank was the boys' principal activity after they left the tavern. The boys would drive alongside a foot patrolman and ask directions to some street. If the policeman leaned on the car in the course of answering the question, the driver would speed away, causing him to lose his balance. The Saints were careful to play this prank only in an area where they were not going to spend much time and where they could quickly disappear around a corner to avoid having their license plate number taken.

Construction sites and road repair areas were the special province of the Saints' mischief. A soon-to-be-repaired hole in the road inevitably invited the Saints to remove lanterns and wooden barricades and put them in the car, leaving the hole unprotected. The boys would find a safe vantage point and wait for an unsuspecting motorist to drive into the hole. Often, though not always, the boys would go up to the motorist and commiserate with him about the dreadful way the city protected its citizenry.

Leaving the scene of the open hole and the motorist, the boys would then go searching for an appropriate place to erect the stolen barricade. An "appropriate place" was often a spot on a highway near a curve in the road where the barricade would not be seen by an oncoming motorist. The boys would wait to watch an unsuspecting motorist attempt to stop and (usually) crash into the wooden barricade. With saintly bearing the boys might offer help and understanding.

A stolen lantern might well find its way onto the back of a police car or hang from a street lamp. Once a lantern served as a prop for a reenactment of the "midnight ride of Paul Revere" until the "play," which was taking place at 2:00 A.M. in the center of a main street of Big Town, was interrupted by a police car several blocks away. The boys ran, leaving the lantern on the street, and managed to avoid being apprehended.

Abandoned houses, especially if they were located in out-of-the-way places, were fair game for destruction and spontaneous vandalism. The boys would break windows, remove furniture to the yard and tear it apart, urinate on the walls and scrawl obscenities inside.

Through all the pranks, drinking and reckless driving the boys managed miraculously to avoid being stopped by police. Only twice in two years was I aware that they had been stopped by a Big City policeman. Once was for speeding (which they did every time they drove whether they were drunk or sober), and the driver managed to convince the policeman that it was simply an error. The second time they were stopped they had just left a nightclub and were walking through an alley. Aaron stopped to urinate and the boys began making obscene remarks. A foot patrolman came into the alley, lectured the boys and sent them home. Before the boys got to the car one began talking in a loud voice again. The policeman, who had followed them down the alley, arrested this boy for disturbing the peace and took him to the police station, where the other Saints gathered. After paying a $5.00 fine, and with the assurance that there would be no permanent record of the arrest, the boy was released.

The boys had a spirit of frivolity and fun about their escapades. They did not view what they were engaged in as "delinquency," though it surely was by any reasonable definition of that word. They simply viewed themselves as having a little fun and who, they would ask, was really hurt by it? The answer had to be no one, although this fact remains one of the most difficult things to explain about the gang's behavior. Unlikely though it seems, in two years of drinking, driving, carousing and vandalism no one was seriously injured as a result of the Saints' activities.

THE SAINTS IN SCHOOL

The Saints were highly successful in school. The average grade for the group was "B," with two of the boys having close to a straight "A" average. Almost all of the boys were popular and many of them held offices in the school. One of the boys was vice-president of the student body one year. Six of the boys played on athletic teams.

At the end of their senior year, the student body selected ten seniors for special recognition as the "school wheels"; four of the ten were

Saints. Teachers and school officials saw no problem with any of these boys and anticipated that they would all "make something of themselves."

How the boys managed to maintain this impression is surprising in view of their actual behavior while in school. Their technique for covering truancy was so successful that teachers did not even realize that the boys were absent from school much of the time. Occasionally, of course, the system would backfire and then the boy was on his own. A boy who was caught would be most contrite, would plead guilty and ask for mercy. He inevitably got the mercy he sought.

Cheating on examinations was rampant, even to the point of orally communicating answers to exams as well as looking at one another's papers. Since none of the group studied, and since they were primarily dependent on one another for help, it is surprising that grades were so high. Teachers contributed to the deception in their admitted inclination to give these boys (and presumably others like them) the benefit of the doubt. When asked how the boys did in school, and when pressed on specific examinations, teachers might admit that they were disappointed in John's performance, but would quickly add that they "knew he was capable of doing better," so John was given a higher grade than he had actually earned. How often this happened is impossible to know. During the time that I observed the group, I never saw any of the boys take homework home. Teachers may have been "understanding" very regularly.

One exception to the gang's generally good performance was Jerry, who had a "C" average in his junior year, experienced disaster the next year and failed to graduate. Jerry had always been a little more nonchalant than the others about the liberties he took in school. Rather than wait for someone to come get him from class, he would offer his own excuse and leave. Although he probably did not miss any more classes than most of the others in the group, he did not take the requisite pains to cover his absences. Jerry was the only Saint whom I ever heard talk back to a teacher. Although teachers often called him a "cut up" or a

"smart kid," they never referred to him as a troublemaker or as a kid headed for trouble. It seems likely, then, that Jerry's failure his senior year and his mediocre performance his junior year were consequences of his not playing the game the proper way (possibly because he was disturbed by his parents' divorce). His teachers regarded him as "immature" and not quite ready to get out of high school.

THE POLICE AND THE SAINTS

The local police saw the Saints as good boys who were among the leaders of the youth in the community. Rarely, the boys might be stopped in town for speeding or for running a stop sign. When this happened the boys were always polite, contrite and pled for mercy. As in school, they received the mercy they asked for. None ever received a ticket or was taken into the precinct by the local police.

The situation in Big City, where the boys engaged in most of their delinquency, was only slightly different. The police there did not know the boys at all, although occasionally the boys were stopped by a patrolman. Once they were caught taking a lantern from a construction site. Another time they were stopped for running a stop sign, and on several occasions they were stopped for speeding. Their behavior was as before: contrite, polite and penitent. The urban police, like the local police, accepted their demeanor as sincere. More important, the urban police were convinced that these were good boys just out for a lark.

THE ROUGHNECKS

Hanibal townspeople never perceived the Saints' high level of delinquency. The Saints were good boys who just went in for an occasional prank. After all, they were well dressed, well mannered and had nice cars. The Roughnecks were a different story. Although the two gangs of boys were the same age, and both groups engaged in an equal amount of wild-oat sowing, everyone agreed that the not-so-well-dressed, not-so-well-mannered, not-so-rich boys were heading for trouble. Townspeople would say, "You can see the gang members at the drugstore night after night, leaning against the storefront (sometimes drunk) or slouching around inside buying cokes, reading magazines, and probably stealing old Mr. Wall blind. When they are outside and girls walk by, even respectable girls, these boys make suggestive remarks. Sometimes their remarks are downright lewd."

From the community's viewpoint, the real indication that these kids were in for trouble was that they were constantly involved with the police. Some of them had been picked up for stealing, mostly small stuff, of course, "but still it's stealing small stuff that leads to big time crimes." "Too bad," people said. "Too bad that these boys couldn't behave like the other kids in town; stay out of trouble, be polite to adults, and look to their future."

The community's impression of the degree to which this group of six boys (ranging in age from 16 to 19) engaged in delinquency was somewhat distorted. In some ways the gang was more delinquent than the community thought; in other ways they were less.

The fighting activities of the group were fairly readily and accurately perceived by almost everyone. At least once a month, the boys would get into some sort of fight, although most fights were scraps between members of the group or involved only one member of the group and some peripheral hanger-on. Only three times in the period of observation did the group fight together: once against a gang from across town, once against two blacks and once against a group of boys from another school. For the first two fights the group went out "looking for trouble"—and they found it both times. The third fight followed a football game and began spontaneously with an argument on the football field between one of the Roughnecks and a member of the opposition's football team.

Jack had a particular propensity for fighting and was involved in most of the brawls. He was a prime mover of the escalation of arguments into fights.

More serious than fighting, had the community been aware of it, was theft. Although almost everyone was aware that the boys occasionally stole things, they did not realize the extent of the activity. Petty stealing was a frequent event for the Roughnecks. Sometimes they stole as a group and coordinated their efforts; other times they stole in pairs. Rarely did they steal alone.

The thefts ranged from very small things like paperback books, comics and ballpoint pens to expensive items like watches. The nature of the thefts varied from time to time. The gang would go through a period of systematically lifting items from automobiles or school lockers. Types of thievery varied with the whim of the gang. Some forms of thievery were more profitable than others, but all thefts were for profit, not just thrills.

Roughnecks siphoned gasoline from cars as often as they had access to an automobile, which was not very often. Unlike the Saints, who owned their own cars, the Roughnecks would have to borrow their parents' cars, an event which occurred only eight or nine times a year. The boys claimed to have stolen cars for joy rides from time to time.

Ron committed the most serious of the group's offenses. With an unidentified associate the boy attempted to burglarize a gasoline station. Although this station had been robbed twice previously in the same month, Ron denied any involvement in either of the other thefts. When Ron and his accomplice approached the station, the owner was hiding in the bushes beside the station. He fired both barrels of a double-barreled shotgun at the boys. Ron was severely injured; the other boy ran away and was never caught. Though he remained in critical condition for several months, Ron finally recovered and served six months of the following year in reform school. Upon release from reform school, Ron was put back a grade in school, and began running around with a different gang of boys. The Roughnecks considered the new gang less delinquent than themselves, and during the following year Ron had no more trouble with the police.

The Roughnecks, then, engaged mainly in three types of delinquency: theft, drinking and fighting. Although community members perceived that this gang of kids was delinquent, they mistakenly believed that their illegal activities were primarily drinking, fighting and being a nuisance to passersby. Drinking was limited among the gang members, although it did occur, and theft was much more prevalent than anyone realized.

Drinking would doubtless have been more prevalent had the boys had ready access to liquor. Since they rarely had automobiles at their disposal, they could not travel very far, and the bars in town would not serve them. Most of the boys had little money, and this, too, inhibited their purchase of alcohol. Their major source of liquor was a local drunk who would buy them a fifth if they would give him enough extra to buy himself a pint of whiskey or a bottle of wine.

The community's perception of drinking as prevalent stemmed from the fact that it was the most obvious delinquency the boys engaged in. When one of the boys had been drinking, even a casual observer seeing him on the corner would suspect that he was high.

There was a high level of mutual distrust and dislike between the Roughnecks and the police. The boys felt very strongly that the police were unfair and corrupt. Some evidence existed that the boys were correct in their perception.

The main source of the boys' dislike for the police undoubtedly stemmed from the fact that the police would sporadically harass the group. From the standpoint of the boys, these acts of occasional enforcement of the law were whimsical and uncalled for. It made no sense to them, for example, that the police would come to the corner occasionally and threaten them with arrest for loitering when the night before the boys had been out siphoning gasoline from cars and the police had been nowhere in sight. To the boys, the police were stupid on the one hand, for not being where they should have been and catching the boys in a serious offense, and unfair on the other hand, for trumping up "loitering" charges against them.

From the viewpoint of the police, the situation was quite different. They knew, with all the confidence necessary to be a policeman, that these boys were engaged in criminal activities. They knew this partly from occasionally catching them, mostly from circumstantial evidence ("the boys were around when those tires were slashed"), and partly because the police shared the view of the community in general that this was a bad bunch of boys. The best the police could hope to do was to be sensitive to the fact that these boys were engaged in illegal acts and arrest them whenever there was some evidence that they had been involved. Whether or not the boys had in fact committed a particular act in a particular way was not especially important. The police had a broader view: their job was to stamp out these kids' crimes; the tactics were not as important as the end result.

Over the period that the group was under observation, each member was arrested at least once. Several of the boys were arrested a number of times and spent at least one night in jail. While most were never taken to court, two of the boys were sentenced to six months incarceration in boys' schools.

THE ROUGHNECKS IN SCHOOL

The Roughnecks' behavior in school was not particularly disruptive. During school hours they did not all hang around together, but tended instead to spend most of their time with one or two other members of the gang who were their special buddies. Although every member of the gang attempted to avoid school as much as possible, they were not particularly successful and most of them attended school with surprising regularity. They considered school a burden—something to be gotten through with a minimum of conflict. If they were "bugged" by a particular teacher, it could lead to trouble. One of the boys, Al, once threatened to beat up a teacher and, according to the other boys, the teacher hid under a desk to escape him.

Teachers saw the boys the way the general community did, as heading for trouble, as being uninterested in making something of themselves. Some were also seen as being incapable of meeting the academic standards of the school. Most of the teachers expressed concern for this group of boys and were willing to pass them despite poor performance, in the belief that failing them would only aggravate the problem.

The group of boys had a grade point average just slightly above "C." No one in the group failed either grade, and no one had better than a "C" average. They were very consistent in their achievement or, at least, the teachers were consistent in their perception of the boys' achievement.

Two of the boys were good football players. Herb was acknowledged to be the best player in the school and Jack was almost as good. Both boys were criticized for their failure to abide by training rules, for refusing to come to practice as often as they should, and for not playing their best during practice. What they lacked in sportsmanship they made up for in skill, apparently, and played every game no matter how poorly they had performed in practice or how many practice sessions they had missed.

TWO QUESTIONS

Why did the community, the school and the police react to the Saints as though they were good, upstanding, nondelinquent youths with bright futures but to the Roughnecks as though they were tough, young criminals who were headed for trouble? Why did the Roughnecks and the Saints in fact have quite different careers after high school—careers which, by and large, lived up to the expectations of the community?

The most obvious explanation for the differences in the community's and law enforcement agencies' reactions to the two gangs is that one group of boys was "more delinquent" than the other. Which group *was* more delinquent? The answer to this question will determine in part how we explain the differential responses to these groups by the members of the community and, particularly, by law enforcement and school officials.

In sheer number of illegal acts, the Saints were the more delinquent. They were truant from school for at least part of the day almost every day of the week. In addition, their drinking and vandalism occurred with surprising regularity. The Roughnecks, in contrast, engaged sporadically in delinquent episodes. While these episodes were frequent, they certainly did not occur on a daily or even a weekly basis.

The difference in frequency of offenses was probably caused by the Roughnecks' inability to obtain liquor and to manipulate legitimate excuses from school. Since the Roughnecks had less money than the Saints, and teachers carefully supervised their school activities, the Roughnecks' hearts may have been as black as the Saints', but their misdeeds were not nearly as frequent.

There are really no clear-cut criteria by which to measure qualitative differences in antisocial behavior. The most important dimension of the difference is generally referred to as the "seriousness" of the offenses.

If seriousness encompasses the relative economic costs of delinquent acts, then some assessment can be made. The Roughnecks probably stole an average of about $5.00 worth of goods a week. Some weeks the figure was considerably higher, but these times must be balanced against long periods when almost nothing was stolen.

The Saints were more continuously engaged in delinquency but their acts were not for the most part costly to property. Only their vandalism and occasional theft of gasoline would so qualify. Perhaps once or twice a month they would siphon a tankful of gas. The other costly items were street signs, construction lanterns and the like. All of these acts combined probably did not quite average $5.00 a week, partly because much of the stolen equipment was abandoned and presumably could be recovered. The difference in cost of stolen property between the two groups was trivial, but the Roughnecks probably had a slightly more expensive set of activities than did the Saints.

Another meaning of seriousness is the potential threat of physical harm to members of the community and to the boys themselves. The Roughnecks were more prone to physical violence; they not only welcomed an opportunity to fight; they went seeking it. In addition, they fought among themselves frequently. Although the fighting never included deadly weapons, it was still a menace, however minor, to the physical safety of those involved.

The Saints never fought. They avoided physical conflict both inside and outside the group. At the same time, though, the Saints frequently endangered their own and other people's lives. They did so almost every time they drove a car, especially if they had been drinking. Sober, their driving was risky; under the influence of alcohol it was horrendous. In addition, the Saints endangered the lives of others with their pranks. Street excavations left unmarked were a very serious hazard.

Evaluating the relative seriousness of the two gangs' activities is difficult. The community reacted as though the behavior of the Roughnecks was a problem, and they reacted as though the behavior of the Saints was not. But the members of the community were ignorant of the array of delinquent acts that characterized the Saints' behavior. Although concerned citizens were unaware of much of the Roughnecks' behavior as well, they were much better informed about the Roughnecks' involvement in delinquency than they were about the Saints'.

VISIBILITY

Differential treatment of the two gangs resulted in part because one gang was infinitely more visible than the other. This differential visibility was a direct function of the economic standing of the families. The Saints had access to automobiles and were able to remove themselves from the sight of the community. In as routine a decision as where to go to have a milkshake after school, the Saints stayed away from the mainstream of community life. Lacking transporta-

tion, the Roughnecks could not make it to the edge of town. The center of town was the only practical place for them to meet since their homes were scattered throughout the town and any non-central meeting place put an undue hardship on some members. Through necessity the Roughnecks congregated in a crowded area where everyone in the community passed frequently, including teachers and law enforcement officers. They could easily see the Roughnecks hanging around the drugstore.

The Roughnecks, of course, made themselves even more visible by making remarks to passersby and by occasionally getting into fights on the corner. Meanwhile, just as regularly, the Saints were either at the cafe on one edge of town or in the pool hall at the other edge of town. Without any particular realization that they were making themselves inconspicuous, the Saints were able to hide their time-wasting. Not only were they removed from the mainstream of traffic, but they were almost always inside a building.

On their escapades the Saints were also relatively invisible, since they left Hanibal and travelled to Big City. Here, too, they were mobile, roaming the city, rarely going to the same area twice.

DEMEANOR

To the notion of visibility must be added the difference in the responses of group members to outside intervention with their activities. If one of the Saints was confronted with an accusing policeman, even if he felt he was truly innocent of a wrongdoing, his demeanor was apologetic and penitent. A Roughneck's attitude was almost the polar opposite. When confronted with a threatening adult authority, even one who tried to be pleasant, the Roughneck's hostility and disdain were clearly observable. Sometimes he might attempt to put up a veneer of respect, but it was thin and was not accepted as sincere by the authority.

School was no different from the community at large. The Saints could manipulate the system by feigning compliance with the school norms. The availability of cars at school meant that once free from the immediate sight of the teacher, the boys could disappear rapidly. And this escape was well enough planned that no administrator or teacher was nearby when the boys left. A Roughneck who wished to escape for a few hours was in a bind. If it were possible to get free from class, downtown was still a mile away, and even if he arrived there, he was still very visible. Truancy for the Roughnecks meant almost certain detection, while the Saints enjoyed almost complete immunity from sanctions.

BIAS

Community members were not aware of the transgressions of the Saints. Even if the Saints had been less discreet, their favorite delinquencies would have been perceived as less serious than those of the Roughnecks.

In the eyes of the police and school officials, a boy who drinks in an alley and stands intoxicated on the street corner is committing a more serious offense than is a boy who drinks to inebriation in a nightclub or a tavern and drives around afterwards in a car. Similarly, a boy who steals a wallet from a store will be viewed as having committed a more serious offense than a boy who steals a lantern from a construction site.

Perceptual bias also operates with respect to the demeanor of the boys in the two groups when they are confronted by adults. It is not simply that adults dislike the posture affected by boys of the Roughneck ilk; more important is the conviction that the posture adopted by the Roughnecks is an indication of their devotion and commitment to deviance as a way of life. The posture becomes a cue, just as the type of the offense is a cue, to the degree to which the known transgressions are indicators of the youths' potential for other problems.

Visibility, demeanor and bias are surface variables which explain the day-to-day operations of the police. Why do these surface variables operate as they do? Why did the police choose to disregard the Saints' delinquencies while breathing down the backs of the Roughnecks?

The answer lies in the class structure of American society and the control of legal institutions by those at the top of the class structure. Obviously, no representative of the upper class drew up the operational chart for the police which led them to look in the ghettos and on streetcorners—which led them to see the demeanor of lower-class youth as troublesome and that of upper-middle-class youth as tolerable. Rather, the procedures simply developed from experience—experience with irate and influential upper-middle-class parents insisting that their son's vandalism was simply a prank and his drunkenness only a momentary "sowing of wild oats"—experience with cooperative or indifferent, powerless, lower-class parents who acquiesced to the laws' definition of their son's behavior.

ADULT CAREERS OF THE SAINTS AND THE ROUGHNECKS

The community's confidence in the potential of the Saints and the Roughnecks apparently was justified. If anything, the community members underestimated the degree to which these youngsters would turn out "good" or "bad."

Seven of the eight members of the Saints went on to college immediately after high school. Five of the boys graduated from college in four years. The sixth one finished college after two years in the army, and the seventh spent four years in the air force before returning to college and receiving a B.A. degree. Of these seven college graduates, three went on for advanced degrees. One finished law school and is now active in state politics, one finished medical school and is practicing near Hanibal, and one boy is now working for a Ph.D. The other four college graduates entered submanagerial, managerial or executive training positions with larger firms.

The only Saint who did not complete college was Jerry. Jerry had failed to graduate from high school with the other Saints. During his second senior year, after the other Saints had gone on to college, Jerry began to hang around with what several teachers described as a "rough crowd"—the gang that was heir apparent to the Roughnecks. At the end of his second senior year, when he did graduate from high school, Jerry took a job as a used-car salesman, got married and quickly had a child. Although he made several abortive attempts to go to college by attending night school, when I last saw him (ten years after high school) Jerry was unemployed and had been living on unemployment for almost a year. His wife worked as a waitress.

Some of the Roughnecks have lived up to community expectations. A number of them were headed for trouble. A few were not.

Jack and Herb were the athletes among the Roughnecks and their athletic prowess paid off handsomely. Both boys received unsolicited athletic scholarships to college. After Herb received his scholarship (near the end of his senior year), he apparently did an about-face. His demeanor became very similar to that of the Saints. Although he remained a member in good standing of the Roughnecks, he stopped participating in most activities and did not hang on the corner as often.

Jack did not change. If anything, he became more prone to fighting. He even made excuses for accepting the scholarship. He told the other gang members that the school had guaranteed him a "C" average if he would come to play football—an idea that seems far-fetched, even in this day of highly competitive recruiting.

During the summer after graduation from high school, Jack attempted suicide by jumping from a tall building. The jump would certainly have killed most people trying it, but Jack survived. He entered college in the fall and played four years of football. He and Herb graduated in four years, and both are teaching and coaching in high schools. They are married and have stable families. If anything, Jack appears to have a more prestigious position in the community than does Herb, though both are well respected and secure in their positions.

Two of the boys never finished high school. Tommy left at the end of his junior year and went to another state. That summer he was arrested and placed on probation on a manslaughter charge. Three years later he was arrested for murder; he pleaded guilty to second degree murder and is serving a 30-year sentence in the state penitentiary.

Al, the other boy who did not finish high school, also left the state in his senior year. He is serving a life sentence in a state penitentiary for first degree murder.

Wes is a small-time gambler. He finished high school and "bummed around." After several years he made contact with a bookmaker who employed him as a runner. Later he acquired his own area and has been working it ever since. His position among the bookmakers is almost identical to the position he had in the gang; he is always around but no one is really aware of him. He makes no trouble and he does not get into any. Steady, reliable, capable of keeping his mouth closed, he plays the game by the rules, even though the game is an illegal one.

That leaves only Ron. Some of his former friends reported that they had heard he was "driving a truck up north," but no one could provide any concrete information.

REINFORCEMENT

The community responded to the Roughnecks as boys in trouble, and the boys agreed with that perception. Their pattern of deviancy was reinforced, and breaking away from it became increasingly unlikely. *Once the boys acquired an image of themselves as deviants* [italics added], they selected new friends who affirmed that self-image. As that self-conception became more firmly entrenched, they also became willing to try new and more extreme deviances. With their growing alienation came freer expression of disrespect and hostility for representatives of the legitimate society. This disrespect increased the community's negativism, perpetuating the entire process of commitment to deviance. Lack of a commitment to deviance works the same way. In either case, the process will perpetuate itself unless some event (like a scholarship to college or a sudden failure) external to the established relationship intervenes. For two of the Roughnecks (Herb and Jack), receiving college athletic scholarships created new relations and culminated in a break with the established pattern of deviance. In the case of one of the Saints (Jerry), his parents' divorce and his failing to graduate from high school changed some of his other relations. Being held back in school for a year and losing his place among the Saints had sufficient impact on Jerry to alter his self-image and virtually to [ensure] that he would not go on to college as his peers did. Although the experiments of life can rarely be reversed, it seems likely in view of the behavior of the other boys who did not enjoy this special treatment by the school that Jerry, too, would have "become something" had he graduated as anticipated. For Herb and Jack outside intervention worked to their advantage; for Jerry it was his undoing.

Selective perception and labelling—finding, processing and punishing some kinds of criminality and not others [italics added]—means that visible, poor, nonmobile, outspoken, undiplomatic "tough" kids will be noticed, whether their actions are seriously delinquent or not. Other kids, who have established a reputation for being bright (even though underachieving), disciplined and involved in respectable activities, who are mobile and monied, will be invisible when they deviate from sanctioned activities. They'll sow their wild oats—perhaps even wider and thicker than their lower-class cohorts—but they won't be noticed. When it's time to leave adolescence most will follow the expected path, settling into the ways of the middle class, remembering fondly the delinquent but unnoticed fling of their youth. The Roughnecks and others like them may turn around, too. It is more likely that their noticeable deviance will have been so reinforced by police and community that their lives will be effectively channeled into careers consistent with their adolescent background.

Legal Stigma

RICHARD D. SCHWARTZ and JEROME H. SKOLNICK

A maxim to which some criminal court personnel subscribe holds that "no one comes into court with clean hands." And this belief about defendants' past actions also contains inferences about their future actions. The popular saying "where there's smoke there's fire" similarly derives from the belief that if you are suspected of deviance you must be a "bad person." Just the fact that a person is alleged to be deviant can establish the conditions for that person to embark upon a social career as a deviant. Just by having had contact with an agency of social control, a person carries a stigma that can constrict his or her legitimate opportunities while expanding subsequent illegitimate opportunities.

The study by Richard D. Schwartz and Jerome H. Skolnick demonstrates that contact with social control agencies, regardless of the outcome, can seriously influence a person's postagency life chances. In sum, their research offers strong empirical support for the powerful effect that folk beliefs can have. In the conventional wisdom of everyday life, contact with an agency of social control suffices to assign deviant status and moral stigma.

Legal thinking has moved increasingly toward a sociologically meaningful view of the legal system. Sanctions, in particular, have come to be regarded in functional terms.[1] In criminal law, for instance, sanctions are said to be designed to prevent recidivism by rehabilitating, restraining, or executing the offender. They are also said to deter others from the performance of similar acts and, sometimes, to provide a channel for the expression of retaliatory motives. In such civil actions as tort or contract, monetary awards may be intended as retributive and deterrent, as in the use of punitive damages, or may be regarded as a *quid pro quo* to compensate the plaintiff for his wrongful loss.

While these goals comprise an integral part of the rationale of law, little is known about the extent to which they are fulfilled in practice. Lawmen do not as a rule make such studies, because their traditions and techniques are not designed for a systematic examination of the operation of the legal system in action, especially outside the courtroom. Thus, when extra-legal consequences—e.g., the social stigma of a prison sentence—are taken into account at all, it is through the discretionary actions of police, prosecutor, judge, and jury. Systematic information on a variety of unanticipated outcomes, those which benefit the accused as well as those which hurt him, might help to inform these decision makers and perhaps lead to changes in substantive law as well. The present paper is an attempt to study the consequences of stigma associated with legal accusation....

THE EFFECTS OF A CRIMINAL COURT RECORD ON THE EMPLOYMENT OPPORTUNITIES OF UNSKILLED WORKERS

In [a] field experiment, four employment folders were prepared, the same in all respects except for

Reprinted from "Two Studies of Legal Stigma," *Social Problems*, Vol. 10, No. 2 (Fall 1962), pp. 133–38, by permission of the Society for the Study of Social Problems and the authors. Copyright © 1962 by the Society for the Study of Social Problems.

the criminal court record of the applicant. In all of the folders he was described as a thirty-two-year-old single male of unspecified race, with a high school training in mechanical trades, and a record of successive short term jobs as a kitchen helper, maintenance worker, and handyman. These characteristics are roughly typical of applicants for unskilled hotel jobs in the Catskill resort area of New York State where employment opportunities were tested.[2]

The four folders differed only in the applicant's reported record of criminal court involvement. The first folder indicated that the applicant had been convicted and sentenced for assault; the second, that he had been tried for assault and acquitted; the third, also tried for assault and acquitted, but with a letter from the judge certifying the finding of not guilty and reaffirming the legal presumption of innocence. The fourth folder made no mention of any criminal record.

A sample of one hundred employers was utilized. Each employer was assigned to one of four "treatment" groups.[3] To each employer only one folder was shown; this folder was one of the four kinds mentioned above, the selection of the folder being determined by the treatment group to which the potential employer was assigned. The employer was asked whether he could "use" the man described in the folder. To preserve the reality of the situation and make it a true field experiment, employers were never given any indication that they were participating in an experiment. So far as they knew, a legitimate offer to work was being made in each showing of the folder by the "employment agent."

The experiment was designed to determine what employers would do in fact if confronted with an employment applicant with a criminal record....

Of the twenty-five employers shown the "no record" folder, nine gave positive responses. Subject to reservations arising from chance variations in sampling, we take this as indicative of the "ceiling" of jobs available for this kind of applicant under the given field conditions. Positive responses by these employers may be compared with those in the other treatment groups to obtain an indication of job opportunities lost because of the various legal records.

Of the twenty-five employers approached with the "convict" folder, only one expressed interest in the applicant. This is a rather graphic indication of the effect which a criminal record may have on job opportunities. Care must be exercised, of course, in generalizing the conclusions to other settings. In this context, however, the criminal record made a major difference.

From a theoretical point of view, the finding leads toward the conclusion that conviction constitutes a powerful form of "status degradation"[4] which continues to operate after the time when, according to the generalized theory of justice underlying punishment in our society, the individual's "debt" has been paid. A record of conviction produces a durable if not permanent loss of status. For purposes of effective social control, this state of affairs may heighten the deterrent effect of conviction—though that remains to be established. Any such contribution to social control, however, must be balanced against the barriers imposed upon rehabilitation of the convict. If the exprisoner finds difficulty in securing menial kinds of legitimate work, further crime may become an increasingly attractive alternative.[5]

Another important finding of this study concerns the small number of positive responses elicited by the "accused but acquitted" applicant. Of the twenty-five employers approached with this folder, three offered jobs. Thus, the individual accused but acquitted of assault has almost as much trouble finding even an unskilled job as the one who was not only accused of the same offense, but also convicted.

From a theoretical point of view, this result indicates that permanent lowering of status is not limited to those explicitly singled out by being convicted of a crime. As an ideal outcome of American justice, criminal procedure is supposed to distinguish between the "guilty" and those who have been acquitted. Legally controlled conse-

quences which follow the judgment are consistent with this purpose. Thus, the "guilty" are subject to fine and imprisonment, while those who are acquitted are immune from these sanctions. But deprivations may be imposed on the acquitted, both before and after victory in court. Before trial, legal rules either permit or require arrest and detention. The suspect may be faced with the expense of an attorney and a bail bond if he is to mitigate these limitations on his privacy and freedom. In addition, some pre-trial deprivations are imposed without formal legal permission. These may include coercive questioning, use of violence, and stigmatization. And, as this study indicates, some deprivations not under the direct control of the legal process may develop or persist after an official decision of acquittal has been made.

Thus two legal principles conflict in practice. On the one hand, "a man is innocent until proven guilty." On the other, the accused is systematically treated as guilty under the administration of criminal law until a functionary or official body—police, magistrate, prosecuting attorney or trial judge—decides that he is entitled to be free. Even then, the results of treating him as guilty persist and may lead to serious consequences.

The conflict could be eased by measures aimed at reducing the deprivations imposed on the accused, before and after acquittal. Some legal attention has been focused on pre-trial deprivations. The provision of bail and counsel, the availability of habeas corpus, limitations on the admissibility of coerced confessions, and civil actions for false arrest are examples of measures aimed at protecting the rights of the accused before trial. Although these are often limited in effectiveness, especially for individuals of lower socioeconomic status, they at least represent some concern with implementing the presumption of innocence at the pre-trial stage.

By contrast, the courts have done little toward alleviating the post-acquittal consequences of legal accusation. One effort along these lines has been employed in the federal courts, however. Where an individual has been accused and exonerated of a

TABLE 7.1   Effect of Four Types of Legal Folder on Job Opportunities (in per cent)

	NO RECORD	ACQUITTED WITH LETTER	ACQUITTED WITHOUT LETTER	CONVICTED	TOTAL
	(N = 25)	(N = 25)	(N = 25)	(N = 25)	(N = 100)
Positive response	36	24	12	4	19
Negative response	64	76	88	96	81
Total	100	100	100	100	100

crime, he may petition the federal courts for a "Certificate of Innocence" certifying this fact.[6] Possession of such a document might be expected to alleviate post-acquittal deprivations.

Some indication of the effectiveness of such a measure is found in the responses of the final treatment group. Their folder, it will be recalled, contained information on the accusation and acquittal of the applicant, but also included a letter from the judge addressed "To whom it may concern" certifying the applicant's acquittal and reminding the reader of the presumption of innocence. Such a letter might have had a boomerang effect, by reemphasizing the legal involvement of the applicant. It was important, therefore, to determine empirically whether such a communication would improve or harm the chances of employment. Our findings indicate that it increased employment opportunities, since the letter folder elicited six positive responses. Even though this fell short of the nine responses to the "no record" folder, it doubled the number for the "accused but acquitted" and created a significantly greater number of job offers than those elicited by the convicted record. This suggests that the procedure merits consideration as a means of offsetting the occupational loss resulting from accusation. It should be noted, however, that repeated use of this device might reduce its effectiveness.

The results of the experiment are summarized in Table 7.1. The differences in outcome found there indicate that various types of legal records are systematically related to job opportunities. It seems fair to infer also that the trend of job losses corresponds with the apparent punitive intent of the authorities. Where the man is convicted, that intent is presumably greatest. It is less where he is accused but acquitted and still less where the court makes an effort to emphasize the absence of a finding of guilt. Nevertheless, where the difference in punitive intent is ideally greatest, between conviction and acquittal, the difference in occupational harm is very slight....

NOTES

1. Legal sanctions are defined as changes in life conditions imposed through court action.
2. The generality of these results remains to be determined. The effects of criminal involvement in the Catskill area are probably diminished, however, by the temporary nature of employment, the generally poor qualifications of the work force, and the excess of demand over supply of unskilled labor there. Accordingly, the employment differences among the four treatment groups found in this study are likely, if anything, to be *smaller* than would be expected in industries and areas where workers are more carefully selected.
3. Employers were not approached in pre-selected random order, due to a misunderstanding of instructions on the part of the law student who carried out the experiment during a three and one-half week period. Because of this flaw in the experimental procedure, the results should be treated with appropriate caution. Thus, chi-squared analysis may not properly be utilized. (For those used to this measure, $P < .05$ for Table 7.1.)
4. Harold Garfinkel, "Conditions of Successful Degradation Ceremonies," *American Journal of Sociology,* 61 (March, 1956), pp. 420–24.
5. Severe negative effects of conviction on employment opportunities have been noted by Sol Rubin, *Crime and Juvenile Delinquency,* New York: Oceana, 1958. A fur-

ther source of employment difficulty is inherent in licensing statutes and security regulations which sometimes preclude convicts from being employed in their pre-conviction occupation or even in the trades which they may have acquired during imprisonment. These effects, may, however, be counteracted by bonding arrangement, prison associations, and publicity programs aimed at increasing confidence in, and sympathy for, exconvicts. See also, B. F. McSally, "Finding Jobs for Released Offenders," *Federal Probation,* 24 (June, 1960), pp. 12–17; Harold D. Lasswell and Richard C. Donnelly, "The Continuing Debate over Responsibility: An Introduction to Isolating the Condemnation Sanction," *Yale Law Journal,* 68 (April, 1959), pp. 869–99; Johs Andenaes, "General Prevention—Illusion or Reality?" *J. Criminal Law, Criminology and Police Science,* 43 (July–August, 1952), pp. 176–98.

6. 28 United States Code, Secs. 1495, 2513.

The Positive Consequences of Stigma

NANCY J. HERMAN and CHARLENE E. MIALL

Early interpreters of labeling theory stressed the negative consequences of official labeling. Some interpreters actually conceived of it as a theory of stigma determinism. Once people had been processed by some agency of social control, they had no choice but to become the kind of people the agency said they now were. It was as if they were being cast in a play. Thus, they took on the role, status, and self-conception implicit in the part the control agency had cast them. In effect, the people processed by these agencies and their agents now saw themselves through agency eyes and became the kinds of people that they were said to be.

Nancy J. Herman and Charlene E. Miall's case study explores how ex–psychiatric patients and involuntarily childless women responded to being processed in treatment agencies and how they responded to the stigmatizing label of "mental patient" or "infertile." If stigma determinism held for all such labeled persons, then all mental patients and infertile women, once labeled, would experience a lowering of their self-esteem and an increase in their deviant behavior directly proportional to their lowered self-esteem. In contrast, Herman and Miall found a number of outcomes that they define as the "positive consequences of stigma." The label provided an explanation of their conduct to others. By lowering what others expected from them, it also was able to increase their sense of competence. It often engendered a number of opportunities and exempted them from what are defined as "normal" social roles. Finally, in many cases, it not only drew their families closer to them but also enabled them to gain a better understanding of themselves.

INTRODUCTION

The labeling theory perspective stresses the importance of studying social definitions and the so-

Reprinted from "The Positive Consequences of Stigma: Two Case Studies in Mental and Physical Disability," *Qualitative Sociology,* Vol. 13, No. 3 (1990), pp. 251–269, by permission of Plenum Publishers and the authors. Copyright © 1990 by Plenum Publishers.

cial processes by which actions and individuals are labeled or defined as deviant. The significance of labeling resides in the stigma that accompanies the label. Stigmatizing labels may produce the deviant behavior that is being condemned, and individuals may become the very thing that they are labeled (Becker, 1973; Lemert, 1972; Manning, 1975; Tannenbaum, 1938). This may occur as a consequence of social rejection which encourages maladaptive withdrawal into deviant subcultures.

Theorists, however, have argued that labeling may have both adaptive and maladaptive consequences (Plummer, 1979:118). Prior to the emergence of the labeling perspective, Parsons (1951:239–294) noted that the development of a strong defensive morale within deviant subcultures was a secondary gain for individuals involved in deviant behavior. More recently, others have argued that stigmas or identity marks themselves may be exploitable and used for secondary gains (cf. Gramling and Forsyth, 1987; Lorber, 1967; and Schur, 1979). Notably, systematic examination of the positive social and social psychological effects of possessing a stigma or identity mark is lacking.

Most sociological research on mental and physical disability using a labeling theory approach has focused on the negative consequences of possessing a stigmatizing attribute (cf. Davis, 1961; Gove, 1976:68; and Hanks and Poplin, 1981:322).[1] However, labeling behavior as disability may legitimate incapacity, reduce role strain, and provide the disabled with adaptive opportunities (cf. Haber and Smith 1971:95). We consider two substantively different deviant and stigmatized populations—ex-psychiatric patients and involuntarily childless women—and explore whether stigma has positive consequences for these individuals.[2] Using their meanings, we document the experiences defined as positive and construct three generic categories of positive consequences of stigma....

METHODOLOGY, SETTING, AND SAMPLES

Descriptive data were gathered on the nature of deinstitutionalized patient life over a period of four years by means of participant observation, informal, and semi-formal interviewing techniques with 285 chronic and non-chronic ex-psychiatric patients in Southern Ontario, Canada.[3] Qualitative data were collected at drop-in facilities for ex-patients, self-help group meetings such as "Re-

covery Inc.," at activist group headquarters, at sheltered workshops for the emotionally disturbed, at non-sheltered places of employment, at a psychiatric hospital canteen, in coffee shops, at boarding and nursing homes, and, in general, where subjects "hung out."

A disproportionate, stratified random sample of 285 former mental patients was drawn from a listing which included all psychiatric clients discharged from a government psychiatric facility in Southern Ontario between 1975 and 1981; all patients discharged from psychiatric wards in several general hospital facilities; those treated as outpatients between 1978 and 1981 in community psychiatric clinics; and all clients treated privately by a psychiatric team associated with a university hospital.[4]

The sample of 285 was disproportionately stratified to include six subgroups divided according to age, chronicity, and type of hospitalization. Comparisons were made among elderly, middle-aged, and young long-term male and female ex-patients; and elderly, middle-aged, and young short-term male and female ex-patients.[5] Initial interviews were done at home or after group meetings, were unstructured and open-ended, and lasted approximately one and a half hours. Subjects were subsequently asked if the researcher could accompany them to the various functions and activities in which they were involved. Many subjects sponsored the researcher into various ex-patient groups, which facilitated participant observation with ex-psychiatric patients interacting with other ex-patients and "normal" societal members.

Qualitative data were gathered on involuntarily childless women in Southern Ontario over a period of two years.[6] In order to obtain participants, a snowball sampling technique was used. Volunteers were recruited through social work agencies, adoptive parent groups, and through other research participants. The very secretive processes surrounding infertility (Miall, 1986) and the institutional confidentiality surrounding adoption (Miall, 1987) made it very difficult to obtain a sample of participants. Respondents were included if they had a desire for children and experienced infertility in past and present relationships.[7]

A pre-tested, standardized open-ended interview was conducted with 30 involuntarily childless women. Given recruitment problems, a questionnaire identical to the interview schedule was completed by 41 other subjects who would not agree to be interviewed but who were willing to complete the questionnaire. Questions were based on previous academic work on adoption, more than one and a half years of participant observation in an infertility self-help group, discussions with infertile adoptive parents, and anecdotal literature on infertility and adoption. Interviews lasted from two and a half to four hours.

The women ranged in age from 25 to 45, were well educated, from middle to upper class backgrounds, white, and Protestant, although 16 respondents were Jewish. In this sample, 58 (82%) had adopted children and 13 (18%) were in the process of adopting for the first time. In sociodemographic terms, the respondents were similar to those surveyed by Bachrach (1983) in the United States.

EX–PSYCHIATRIC PATIENTS:
THE EXPERIENCE OF STIGMA

Using the same sample, Herman has examined perceptions of mental illness as stigma, deviant identities, information/stigma management techniques, and identity transformation (cf. Herman, 1986, 1988, 1989, 1990). The data indicate that 98% of the sample categorize mental illness in negative terms and have learned the social meaning of their "failing" through formal societal reaction, official labeling, and institutional processing; direct, negative, disvaluing post-treatment experiences with others; a combination of societal reaction, institutional processing and negative experiences with "normals"; or through self-labeling (cf. Link, 1987; Link et al., 1987; Link et al., 1989).

To avoid potential or further stigma, chronic and non-chronic ex-psychiatric patients develop

and use "defensive" and "offensive" strategies of stigma management (cf. Link and Cullen, 1986). Defensive strategies include institutional retreatism, societal retreatism, capitulation, passing, and subcultural participation—strategies having negative implications for identity transformation. Offensive strategies include selective concealment, therapeutic disclosure, preventive disclosure, and political activism, strategies having positive implications for identity transformation and the resumption of normal roles, identities, and statuses.

INVOLUNTARILY CHILDLESS WOMEN: THE EXPERIENCE OF STIGMA

Estimates of involuntary childlessness range from 1 in 5 (Burgwyn, 1981; Kraft et al., 1980) to 1 in 10 couples (Mosher, 1982).[8] Within western nations, 10% to 15% of the population may be infertile (National Center for Health Statistics, 1985). Western cultural norms and values encourage reproduction and celebrate parenthood, particularly for women. Sociologists characterize childlessness, whether voluntary or involuntary, as a form of deviant behavior because it violates rules of acceptable conduct (Miall, 1985, 1986; Veevers, 1972).

Using the same sample, Miall (1986) examined involuntary childlessness as a stigmatizing attribute and discovered that the women studied feel stigmatized by their inability to reproduce. Nearly all categorize infertility as representing failure or an inability to "work" normally. These women have also provided detailed descriptions of real sanctions related to their childlessness (Miall, 1985). Their sexuality, femininity, and psychological health [have] been subject to question. In addition, infertile women are often divorced by their husbands, may not receive an equal share in the wills of relatives, are excluded from groups of mothers and children, and subjected to negative comments on an on-going basis, all because of their inability to reproduce.

Infertile couples who wish to rear children often resort to adoption. In western society, biological kinship ties are valued such that the lack of a blood tie between an adoptive mother and her children might also be discrediting. To explore the stigma potential of adoptive parent status, respondents were asked to detail their perceptions of societal beliefs about adoption. The beliefs generated contained strong elements of stigmatization based on the absence of a blood tie.[9] These women also experienced formal and informal social sanctions related to their adoptive parent status (Miall, 1987).

When compared with ex–psychiatric patients, similarities emerge in how involuntarily childless women learn the social meaning of their "failing."

Childless women experienced direct, negative, disvaluing experiences with "normals" during and after treatment for infertility, and during and after the adoption of their children. They also engaged in self-labeling apart from formal or informal processing.

To avoid potential or further stigma from others, infertile women who adopt also employ selective concealment, therapeutic disclosure, and preventive disclosure—strategies having positive implications for identity transformation (Miall, 1986, 1989).

POSITIVE RESPONSES TO STIGMA

Versions of labeling theory that focus on social reactions to deviance have been criticized for their neglect of the perceptions, interpretations, and behavior of the deviant actor (cf. Rogers and Buffalo, 1974); and their tendency to conceptualize the labeled individual as overly passive (cf. Davis, 1975). Warren and Johnson (1972:76) argue that labeling theorists have thrown out all concern with "the deviant being of the deviant" and what such a being means to the individual concerned. To correct this omission, they suggest a focus on "the everyday social reality of the individual social actor and his interpretations of that reality" (Warren and Johnson, 1972:82). As authors, we have extensively documented the negative social psychological and "real" consequences, such as

restriction on rights and limitation on life chances, that occur to individuals who have been labeled mentally ill or infertile. We do not, however, only presuppose negative experiences with stigma. Rather we focus on the meanings and interpretations, both positive and negative, that our respondents bring to their life experiences. Using these meanings, we document, in this paper, those experiences defined as positive and construct three generic categories of positive consequences of stigma.

CHRONIC AND NON-CHRONIC EX–PSYCHIATRIC PATIENTS

Several authors have established the profound negative effects of the stigma of mental illness—for example, limits on future participation in society; problems re-establishing normal social roles and identities; and employment difficulties (Herman, 1987, 1988, 1989, 1990; Link, 1987; Link et al., 1987, 1989). Herman's data indicate, however, that certain positive consequences result from labeling, institutional processing and treatment, and subsequent stigmatization. These positive consequences are that: (1) labeling provides ex-patients with legitimation for their post- and some pre-treatment behavior; (2) it exempts them from usual role obligations and relieves ex-patients from taxing, onerous duties; (3) it provides ex-patients, in their own terms, with certain adaptive opportunities; (4) in some cases, it leads to stronger familial ties (cf. Link et al., 1989); and (5) for some, it serves as a personal growth experience.

Approximately one half of the chronic ex-patients felt being diagnosed and treated for mental illness provided them with an identity that legitimated most or all of their post-hospital deviant behavior. As one young chronic male stated:

> This is how it is. You're an ex-nut. Society has this image of you, that you're at any moment going to do something "crazy." They almost expect it of you. And this is really great. Because if you want to go up to a woman and grab her tits or touch her ass, or even if I rip off a TV and get caught, all's I have

to explain is that I'm a nut that's been let out. It tells them that I'm not in my right mind, so they don't go too hard on me. Being mental gives you just the excuse you need!

Another ex-patient explained how she "got away" with committing deviant acts following release from the hospital:

I know that having mental illness is a bitch. I've gone through hell at times, but it does have its certain benefits. Like, if you hate someone's guts or if they've treated you meanly, you can get back at them without fear of retaliation. I had this neighbor who used to constantly pick on me and be sarcastic. He always used to be on his porch staring. One day, when I was sure he was watching, I undid my jeans and "mooned" him with my big ass. Ordinarily, I wouldn't have been able to get away with this act, but my mother explained to the man later that I was "mentally ill and we have to expect that she may do strange things from time to time."

Twelve percent of the sample also indicated that being defined as mentally ill provided justification for previous bizarre acts:

When I was finally hospitalized and they diagnosed my condition, my family absolved me from a lot of the things I had done in the past. They didn't realize that I smashed things and hit people because I was "sick"...that I was psychotic, and neither did I.

One third of the ex-patients remarked that awareness of their stigmatizing attribute exempted them from many social role obligations (cf. Haber and Smith, 1971) and excused them from taxing, onerous duties (cf. Sagarin, 1975; Scheff, 1981). One female ex-patient observed:

Being crazy does have its benefits. Like people don't expect the same things from you. You don't have to perform up to certain standards like you would if you hadn't had the breakdown. You don't have to be as responsible, to meet certain obligations, to be the ideal mother, et cetera.

Ex–psychiatric patients also feel that the stigma of mental illness provides them with certain adaptive

opportunities. Through participation in deviant subcultures, 42% of the chronic ex-patients learned how to capitalize on their stigmatizing attribute and "make it on the outside." Ex-patients learned where, how, and when they could pick up "quick cash," "free eats," and where to get a "free place to crash."[10] One young male ex–psychiatric patient stated:

There are certain advantages. Being a mental means that there are people and places out there that are dying to "help you." You know, like social agencies, churches, and so-called "do-gooders" in society. Some will give you a few bucks; others will give you a hot meal. You quickly find out where they are, hand them a line, and they fork over. It's better than working for a living.

A second female ex-patient, who called herself a "professional crazy," explained how she used the system to her advantage and capitalized on her stigmatized identity:

I'm actually better off now than before I was hospitalized. Such mental illness is the shits, but you can benefit from the status too. I learned from the others that I can sell my "meds" to Dirk on Jackson Street. He usually gives me about ten bucks. I also learned which fast food joints hand out free food, so I'm eating better than ever; and if I want to make some real money, I just have to act sorrowful on some street in "Streetsville" and hold out my hand and tell 'em that I need money to help with my treatment....One week, I made a hundred bucks.

The data indicate that, in the actors' terms, being labeled with a stigmatizing attribute generates certain opportunities that might otherwise not be available.

In terms of other gratifications, stronger familial relationships arose. Thirty-eight percent of the chronic and non-chronic ex-patients felt that having been labeled and treated for mental illness solidified and strengthened social relationships with family members.[11] Link *et al.* (1989) noted a similar phenomenon with relatives who were members of the patient's household. As one middle-aged male stated:

Things never used to be good between my family and me. There was no true genuine affection and caring. We used to fight a lot...big blow ups. No one pulled together. But since my sickness, things have really changed. Pop and my sisters and me are now on better terms. Tragedy can really bring people together.

Similarly, another ex-patient noted the strengthening of family ties:

I'm now sixty-two years old. Having mental illness is no picnic, don't get me wrong, but it did something so wonderful for me. It brought my family together as a unit. They rallied around me. We all banded together the way it's supposed to be.

For others, being labeled and treated for mental illness functioned as a growth experience. Although experiencing great frustration, anxiety, and pain, approximately 33% of chronic and non-chronic ex-patients felt they had grown from their social experiences within and outside of the hospital. Similarly, Warren (1987:227) has noted that her respondents attributed positive changes to themselves and to their marriages following hospitalization for mental illness. One ex-patient spoke of the acquired ability to engage in self-reflective activities, a consequence of hospitalization but not necessarily stigma:

Through the psychotherapy and shrink sessions, I must say that I did learn a lot—in particular about who I am, and why I do the things I do. Before my treatment, I was never the kind of guy to stop and think about things—what the hell is it that I'm doing and why? But now I do this on a regular basis. Sometimes, it's extremely painful, but ultimately, it's very enlightening.

Another ex-patient commented on how she "grew" from direct negative post-hospital experiences with "normals" who stigmatized her:

Once I was let out, friends, people just shunned me, or they acted as if I couldn't be trusted with their kids, or with a knife or something. Before my hospitalization, how people treated me or what they thought of me, was absolutely important to me. I was very insecure and had a low opinion of

myself. Through this fucking ordeal, I came to the realization that what others think is not important, it's how I think about myself that counts. I realized through all of this that I call stand on my own two feet.

To conclude, the possession of the discreditable label of mental illness has positive consequences such as legitimating subsequent deviant acts, exempting individuals from social role obligations and taxing duties, providing opportunities and gratifications, strengthening family relationships, and providing positive growth experiences.

INVOLUNTARILY CHILDLESS WOMEN

As already noted, involuntarily childless couples experience profound negative social psychological consequences and "real" sanctioning from others when they fail to reproduce. However, the infertile women studied by Miall also experienced certain positive consequences as a result of labeling and stigmatization, The positive consequences of being labeled infertile included: (1) legitimation of the childless role particularly as it pertained to interaction with family and friends; and (2) legalization of the disabled role within adoption agencies. The experience of stigma associated with being infertile and an adoptive parent also resulted in (3) personal growth as subjectively defined by the respondents; (4) the strengthening of dyadic ties; (5) opportunities for heightened interpersonal interaction with others; and (6) opportunities for career growth and change.

In terms of role legitimation, respondents diagnosed as infertile spoke of the relief they felt when others learned that their childlessness was involuntary and not by choice. Veevers (1979:4–5) has already concluded that childlessness in general is subject to stigmatization and voluntary childlessness most of all. Whereas the involuntarily childless are stigmatized by their "physical blemish," the childless by choice are stigmatized by their "moral blemish." Respondents reluctant to reveal their infertility shared this sentiment, noting feelings of frustration and hurt when others assumed they didn't *want* children. As one woman observed:

> I know at one point I overheard someone saying, "Oh, they're too selfish, they're too interested in going on fancy holidays. Material things, that's why they're not having children." It was so untrue and it hurt.

These women subsequently used the infertile label to avoid being labeled voluntarily childless—something the childless by choice have been known to do (cf. Veevers, 1980). As one respondent put it:

> We had been married five years when we decided to start our family. Up to that point, we'd been getting hints but we always ignored them. We'd have our family when we were ready, right? Well, we didn't because we found out we couldn't and it was terrible....His mother was always commenting on how many trips we were taking, the money we were spending on ourselves. Finally I had enough and told her that there was nothing we could do about it. The experience was negative, there's no getting around that but at least she didn't bug me anymore.

The use of the infertile label to deflect criticism about childlessness served as a "medical disclaimer"; that is, respondents presented a "...blameless, beyond-my-control medical interpretation" as a way "...to reduce the risk that more morally disreputable interpretations might be applied by naive others" (Schneider and Conrad, 1980:41). As another woman observed:

> If the reason [for childlessness] is not an anatomical reason or a reason for which they can't find a reason, I think people will chime in with, "Well, maybe you're not doing it right" and you don't want to leave yourself open to that [sic].

Thus, assuming the stigmatizing infertile label relieved respondents of the burden of being perceived as childless by choice, sexually incompetent, or both.

Similarly, a medical diagnosis of infertility legitimated respondents in the eyes of adoption agencies. In the United States and Canada, many adoption agencies require documented medical proof of infertility in order for couples to be considered for infants. Given that legal definitions of disability made with reference to medical, psychological, and social criteria can have the force of law, the infertile label facilitated access to help-giving agencies.

Being diagnosed as infertile and experiencing the stigma accompanying the label also generated other opportunities and gratifications. Several respondents spoke of the personal growth they experienced as a consequence of surviving this major life crisis. As one woman noted:

> Well, I'm more confident.... I'm more able to help others now I think because I've taken courses on group leadership, sensitivity training and so on, things I would probably not have become involved in otherwise. My outlook has broadened. I'm more sympathetic to others now.

Other respondents referred to stronger relationships as benefits arising from infertility and stigmatization and subsequent adoption. As another woman observed:

> I think the biggest thing that we've got out of [it] is that it has made our marriage stronger. We feel we went through a hell of a lot to get to that point and I've said it to my husband, I wouldn't change a thing.

The desire to avoid or lessen stigma arising from infertility prompted these respondents to seek out adoption as a means to obtain children to raise. Although not a positive consequence of stigma per se, official agency processing mitigated feelings of inadequacy engendered by infertility by providing respondents with legitimation as potential parents.[12] As one adoptive mother observed:

> I'm not as much of a failure as I thought I was. I can't have my own children but at least they think I'm good enough to adopt....Adoption has helped. It's not been the whole answer but it certainly has helped by being accepted, by being deemed a good parent in their eyes.

Miall (1987) has already documented the stigma and social sanctioning that can accompany adoptive parent status. Among the benefits perceived by respondents to be linked to adoption were opportunities for heightened interpersonal experiences with others "sharing the fate"; and initiatives for career growth and change. As one adoptive mother noted:

> I behave quite differently with other adoptive parents. We share the situation, we can discuss how other people react and achieve that understanding and rapport we can't get elsewhere. We know the secrets of adoption, we know about the love, the feelings that those other people can't understand. It's liberating.

As another adoptive mother observed, the experience of infertility and the pain which accompanies it resulted in a career change:

> I've had a real career change as a result of my infertility and adoption. I'm doing a degree in counselling and hope to continue to work in this area. I'm a helper now and a role model. I'm more sensitive to others regardless of what kind of life crisis they're going through.

Although not an obvious consequence of the experience of stigma itself, another respondent observed:

> It's interesting you know because one area of the law that sort of perked my interest was juvenile and adoption legal work. I tend to spend more time studying it where I might otherwise not have done.

To conclude, involuntarily childless women, when given the opportunity, were able to provide detailed information on the positive gratifications and opportunities arising from possessing a stigmatizing attribute. The relevance of these findings with ex–psychiatric patients and involuntarily childless women for labeling theory will now be considered.

DISCUSSION AND CONCLUSIONS

Previous research on labeling theory has tended to focus on the negative consequences of labeling an individual as deviant. These studies have suggested that deviants are more acted upon than acting and even when consideration has been given to strategies for managing stigma, these have focused also on managing negative consequences.[13] It is apparent from the data presented in this paper, however, that in the areas of mental and physical disability, deviants are active in refuting labels, in transforming stigma into something positive, and in utilizing stigmatizing identify marks for secondary gains—in other words, exploiting stigma for positive gains.

In the case of ex–psychiatric patients, the possession of a stigmatizing attribute legitimated pre- and post-treatment deviant behavior; exempted these individuals from normal social roles and obligations; provided opportunities and rewards (as they defined them); strengthened familial ties; and facilitated personal growth experiences.

Similarly, involuntarily childless women labeled infertile were able to legitimate their childless role; legalize a disabled role within adoption agencies with resultant access to services; experience personal growth through the management of stigma; strengthen dyadic ties; enjoy heightened interpersonal social interaction with others like-situated; and explore new opportunities for career growth not previously considered.

Using these two substantive cases, we have clearly demonstrated the positive consequences actors derive from being labeled discreditable through mental illness or infertility. We wish now to propose an addition to the literature on stigma by establishing a three-fold generic categorization of positive consequences of stigma. These generic categories are: (1) therapeutic opportunities; (2) personal growth experiences; and (3) interpersonal opportunities.

In recent years, scholars have argued for a renewed focus on generic concepts in ethnographic research (cf. Couch, 1984; Lofland, 1970; Miyomato, 1959; Prus, 1985). An emphasis on examining parallel processes and concepts across different social contexts and types of social actors can maximize conceptual development. Future research on other deviant populations might fruitfully benefit from an examination of the three-fold generic categorization of positive consequences of stigma advanced here.

In more general terms we also wish to extend the analysis of responses to labeling by considering not only positive and negative responses to negative labeling, but also positive and negative responses to positive labeling. By combining the dimensions of positive and negative labeling with the dimensions of positive and negative consequences of stigma, we may establish a four-fold classificatory system or typology of stigma and responses to it. (See Table 7.2.)

Labeling an individual in a negative fashion, whether it be homosexual, thief, or child molester, may have negative consequences in that the label may act as a "master status" (Becker, 1973), limiting the person's future participation in society. Although the deviant may seek moral reinstatement into society, others see and treat the person only in terms of the deviant status. Resumption of normal roles and statuses is inhibited. Symbolic reorganization of self occurs wherein the reactions of others create for the individual the experience of viewing the self as disvalued and deviant. The individual may be unable to act except in relation to the imputed self and its concomitant disvalued, degrading status. Normal channels being blocked off, prevented from resuming normal social roles and status, the individual may ultimately become confirmed in a deviant role.

Second, labeling an individual in a negative manner may have positive consequences for the individual and, paradoxically, for society at large. As we have demonstrated in this paper, the possession of a discrediting attribute can be a positive experience dependent on actor definitions and actions. Positive consequences can include therapeutic opportunities, personal growth experiences, and interpersonal opportunities for the individual. On the other hand, Warren (1974) has noted that labeling an individual deviant may in fact conventionalize deviant behavior and return the individual to a more acceptable way of acting, a positive consequence from a societal viewpoint.

Third, labeling an individual in a positive fashion may also have certain negative social psychological implications. For example, labeling a child as a star baseball player, a future Wayne Gretzky, or a person as exceptionally bright may place a great deal of stress and strain on the individual. Others may establish standards and expectations which may or may not be realistic for the positively labeled individual to live up to. Failing to meet expectations set and experiencing the disappointment of others may also result in self-devaluation and withdrawal from normal social roles and statuses.

Fourth, labeling individuals in a positive manner may generate positive consequences or benefits. Indeed, self-fulfilling prophecy is a well established principle in the social psychological literature. The deviance literature has limited this

TABLE 7.2   A Typology of Consequences of Stigma

CONSEQUENCES OF STIGMA	TYPE OF LABELING	
	Negative	*Positive*
Negative	Adversely affects self-images and identities; acts as a "master status," limiting future participation in society	Emotional stress, strain, and pressures
Positive	Personal growth experiences, therapeutic opportunities, interpersonal opportunities	Elevated self-images, self-esteems

principle, however, to the examination of negative labels. Positive labeling can result in elevated self-image and self-esteem and facilitate
access to valued statuses in society. We strongly
suggest that future research on labeling should
consider the dimensions outlined in this typology, considering both the positive and negative
consequences which can follow from positive
and negative labeling.

Finally, we contend that sociologists, as
members of the larger society, have focused almost exclusively on the disadvantaged status of
deviants. There is no doubt that the "normal"
world is powerful and individuals (deviants) who
are denied full participation in it actively suffer as
a result. Our attempts as sociologists to act as advocates for deviants, however, to take on an "un-
derdog" ideological stance, may in fact be
conceptually and methodologically flawed. Specifically, unstated assumptions about the relative
merits or benefits of social worlds introduce biases in data collection that are reflected in the negative, suffering, disadvantaged slant of much of our
research on deviant groups.

We have clearly demonstrated with our research groups that, given the opportunity, the so-
called disadvantaged are able to establish positive effects or benefits of being labeled—effects
or benefits that are real for them regardless of the
observer's interpretations of their status or situation. Indeed, being labeled, prevented from reas-
suming normal roles and statuses, and forced
into subcultures may provide individuals with alternate roles and statuses that are equally or even
more satisfying to them and may provide them
with the most intense, intimate social exchanges
that they will ever know. We so-called normals,
by contrast, may in fact be disadvantaged in that
in our significant relationships we will never experience the intensity and understanding of
those of the deviant, nor the opportunities for
change. From a humanistic point of view, we, as
sociologists, should not close the door to that
possibility.

NOTES

1. Theoretical arguments about the stigmatized status
of the disabled have been advanced by Freidson (1966);
Safilios-Rothschild (1970); and Scheff (1966, 1967,
1975).
2. The severe negative consequences arising from the
possession of these stigmatizing attributes are discussed
in Herman (1986, 1987, 1988, and 1990) and Miall
(1984, 1985, and 1986).
3. The term "chronic" is not defined in diagnostic terms
(e.g., manic-depressive); but in terms of duration, continuity, frequency, and type of hospitalization. It refers to
individuals institutionalized in a psychiatric facility for
two years or more, on a continual basis, or on five or
more occasions. Non-chronic refers to those individuals
hospitalized in general hospital facilities or psychiatric
institutions for less than two years, on a discontinuous
basis, or on less than five occasions.
4. Initially, 300 persons were selected for study. However 15 subjects were not included because of refusal,
death, inability to locate, or bureaucratic mixups.
5. Age was trichotomized so that elderly included 60
years or over, middle-aged was 30 to 59 years, and young
was 16 to 29 years. Hospitalization included individuals
treated primarily in a general hospital psychiatric ward,
and institutionalization included individuals treated primarily within government psychiatric facilities.
6. Despite two years of concerted effort, the researcher
was unable to recruit sufficient men to compare responses to infertility and adoption. Men may regard infertility as more stigmatizing than women (Miall, 1986)
or may regard infertility and adoption as "women's" issues.
7. Sub-classifications controlling for age, education,
occupation, religion, ethnicity, duration of marriage, and
presence of adopted children did not yield significant differences in responses on infertility and adoption.
8. From a social psychological viewpoint, the essential
component in defining individuals as involuntarily childless is not their biological status as fertile or infertile, but
their psychological preference to procreate and their inability in present circumstances to do so.
9. These beliefs were that the biological tie is important
in bonding and love, and therefore, bonding and love in
adoption are second-best; adopted children are second
rate because of their unknown genetic past; and adoptive
parents are not "real" parents (cf. Miall, 1987).

10. Membership in a sub-culture was, of course, partially dependent on the stigma drawing ex-patients together. Through this subcultural participation, ex-patients learned to pick up quick cash by selling their bodies and their medication, where to sell, and how much to ask. The dichotomy between an actor's and an observer's interpretation of lived reality is clearly illustrated here. Whereas respondents saw this as a positive aid to survival possible only because of access to the ex-patient subculture, others might regard this as a negative consequence of stigmatization. Indeed despite the possibility of benefiting from stigma, in real terms these ex-patients remained in a devalued position. Dear (1987), for example, has linked deinstitutionalization to homelessness.

11. It may be that stronger family ties also result from the "courtesy stigma" experienced by family members when a relative is diagnosed as mentally ill. A "courtesy stigma" is a "situationally induced social construct rather than a constant attribute of the person" (Birenbaum, 1975:348; Goffman, 1963), and this shared sense of stigma may bring the family closer together.

12. Adoption agency processing can also induce deep feelings of stigma in infertile couples (cf. Miall, 1987, 1989).

13. While this paper provides ethnographic information on substantive gratifications and opportunities associated with being labeled mentally ill or infertile, such positive consequences have been documented by a few notable others with respect to other deviant populations (Gramling and Forsyth, 1987; Hanks and Poplin, 1981). Stigma management techniques identified in the literature include selective concealment, passing, capitulation, preventive disclosure, political activism, and conventionalization. See, for example, Edgerton (1967); Goffman (1963); Herman (1986, 1987); Scott and Lyman (1968); Schneider and Conrad (1980).

REFERENCES

Bachrach, Christine, 1983. Children in families: Characteristics of biological, step-, and adopted children. *Journal of Marriage and the Family* 45:171–179.

Becker, Howard, 1973. *Outsiders: Studies in the sociology of deviance.* Rev. ed. New York: Free Press.

Birenbaum, Arnold, 1975. On managing a courtesy stigma. pp. 347–357. In *Deviance: Action, reaction, interaction.* Frank Scarpitti & Paul McFarlane (eds.). Reading, Massachusetts: Addison-Wesley.

Burgwyn, Diana, 1981. *Marriage without children.* New York: Harper & Row.

Couch, Carl, 1984. Symbolic interaction and generic sociological principles. *Symbolic Interaction* 7:1–14.

Davis, Fred, 1961. Deviance disavowal: The management of strained interaction by the visibly handicapped. *Social Problems* 9:120–132.

Davis, Nanette, 1975. *Sociological constructions of deviance.* Iowa: W. C. Brown Company.

Dear, Michael, 1987. *Landscapes of despair: From deinstitutionalization to homelessness.* Princeton, New Jersey: Princeton University Press.

Edgerton, Robert, 1967. *The cloak of competence: Stigma in the lives of the mentally retarded.* Berkeley: University of California Press.

Freidson, Elliot, 1966. Disability as social deviance. pp. 71–99. In *Sociology and rehabilitation.* Marvin Sussman (ed.). Washington, D.C.: American Sociological Association.

Goffman, Erving, 1963. *Stigma.* Englewood Cliffs, New Jersey: Prentice-Hall.

Gove, Walter, 1976. Social reaction theory and disability. pp. 51–71. In *The sociology of physical disability and rehabilitation.* Gary Albrecht (ed.). Pittsburgh, Pennsylvania: University of Pittsburgh Press.

Gramling, Robert & Craig Forsyth, 1987. Exploiting stigma. *Sociological Forum* 2:401–415.

Haber, Lawrence & Richard Smith, 1971. Disability and deviance: Normative adaptations of role behavior. *American Sociological Review* 36:87–97.

Hanks, Michael & Dennis Poplin, 1981. The sociology of physical disability: A review of literature and some conceptual perspectives. *Deviant Behavior* 2:309–328.

Herman, Nancy, 1986. Crazies in the community: An ethnographic study of ex-psychiatric clients in Canadian society—Stigma, management strategies, and identity transformation. Ph.D. dissertation, McMaster University, Hamilton, Ontario, Canada.

Herman, Nancy, 1987. The "mixed nutters" and "looney tuners": The emergence, development, nature and functions of two informal deviant subcultures of chronic ex-psychiatric patients. *Deviant Behavior* 8:235–258.

Herman, Nancy, 1988. The chronic elderly mentally ill in Canada. pp. 111–121. In *The North American elders: A comparison of U.S. and Canadian issues.*

Betty Havens & Edward Rathbone-McCuan (eds.). New Haven: Greenwood Press.

Herman, Nancy, 1989. Mental hospital depopulation in Canada: Patient perspectives. *Canadian Journal of Psychiatry* 34:386–391.

Herman, Nancy, 1990. *Crazies in the community: An ethnographic study of the post-hospital worlds of chronic and non-chronic ex-patients.* Dix Hills, New York: General Hall. Forthcoming.

Kraft, Adrienne, Joseph Palombo, Dorena Mitchell, Catherine Dean, Steven Meyers, & Anne Wright-Schmidt, 1980. The psychological dimensions of infertility. *American Journal of Orthopsychiatry* 50:618–628.

Lemert, Edwin, 1972. *Human deviance, social problems, and social control.* 2nd ed. Englewood Cliffs, New Jersey: Prentice-Hall.

Link, Bruce, 1987. Understanding labeling effects in the area of mental disorders: An assessment of the effects of expectations of rejection. *American Sociological Review* 52:96–112.

Link, Bruce & Francis Cullen, 1986. Contact with the mentally ill and perceptions of how dangerous they are. *Journal of Health and Social Behavior* 27:289–302.

Link, Bruce, Francis Cullen, James Frank, & John Wozniak, 1987. The social rejection of former mental patients: Understanding why labels matter. *American Journal of Sociology* 92:1461–1500.

Link, Bruce, Francis Cullen, Elmer Struening, Patrick Shrout, & Bruce Dohrenwend, 1989. A modified labeling theory approach to mental disorders. *American Sociological Review* 54:400–423.

Lofland, John, 1970. Interactionist imagery and analytic interruptus. pp. 35–45. In *Human nature and collective behavior: Papers in honor of Herbert Blumer.* Tamotsu Shibutani (ed.). Englewood Cliffs, New Jersey: Prentice-Hall.

Lorber, Judith, 1967. Deviance as performance: The case of illness. *Social Problems* 14:302–310.

Manning, Peter, 1975. Deviance and dogma. *The British Journal of Criminology* 15:1–20.

Miall, Charlene, l984. Women and involuntary childlessness: Perceptions of stigma associated with infertility and adoption. Ph.D. dissertation, York University, Toronto, Ontario, Canada.

Miall, Charlene, 1985. Perceptions of informal sanctioning and the stigma of involuntary childlessness. *Deviant Behavior* 6:383–403.

Miall, Charlene, 1986. The stigma of involuntary childlessness. *Social Problems* 33:268–282.

Miall, Charlene, 1987. The stigma of adoptive parent status: Perceptions of community attitudes toward adoption and the experience of informal social sanctioning. *Family Relations* 36:34–39.

Miall, Charlene, 1989. Authenticity and the disclosure of the information preserve: The case of adoptive parenthood. *Qualitative Sociology* 12:279–302.

Miyamato, S. Frank, 1959. The social act: Re-examination of a concept. *Pacific Sociological Review* 2:51–55.

Mosher, William, 1982. Infertility trends among U.S. couples: 1965–1976. *Family Planning Perspectives* 14:22–27.

Nagi, Saad, 1966. Some conceptual issues in disability and rehabilitation. pp. 100–113. In *Sociology and rehabilitation.* Marvin Sussman (ed.). Washington, D.C.: American Sociological Association.

National Center for Health Statistics, 1985. Fecundity and infertility in the United States, 1965–82. *Advance data from vital and health statistics,* No. 104, DHHS Pub. No. (PHS) 85–1250. Public Health Service. Hyattsville, Maryland. February.

Parsons, Talcott, 1951. *The social system.* New York: Free Press.

Plummer, Kenneth, 1979. Misunderstanding labeling perspectives. pp. 85–121. In *Deviant interpretations.* David Downes & Paul Rock (eds.). Oxford: Martin Robertson & Company.

Prus, Robert, 1985. Generic sociology: Maximizing conceptual development in ethnographic research. Paper presented at the Qualitative research conference: An ethnographic-interactionist perspective. University of Waterloo, Waterloo, Ontario, Canada. May.

Rogers, Joseph & M. D. Buffalo, 1974. Fighting back: Nine modes of adaptation to a deviant label. *Social Problems:* 22:101–118.

Safilios-Rothschild, Constatina, 1970. *The sociology and social psychology of disability and rehabilitation.* New York: Random House.

Sagarin, Edward, 1975. *Deviants and deviance.* New York: Praeger.

Scheff, Thomas, 1966. *Being mentally ill: A sociological theory.* Chicago, Illinois: Aldine.

Scheff, Thomas, 1967. *Mental illness and social processes.* New York: Harper & Row.

Scheff, Thomas, 1975. *Labeling madness.* Englewood Cliffs, New Jersey: Prentice-Hall.

Scheff, Thomas, 1981. Cultural stereotypes and mental illness. pp. 84–88. In *Deviance: The interactionist perspective.* Earl Rubington & Martin Weinberg (eds.). New York: Macmillan.

Schneider, Joseph & Peter Conrad, 1980. In the closet with illness: Epilepsy, stigma potential and information control. *Social Problems* 28:32–44.

Schur, Edwin, 1979. *Interpreting deviance.* New York: Harper & Row.

Scott, Martin & Stanford Lyman, 1968. Accounts. *American Sociological Review* 33:46–62.

Tannenbaum, Frank, 1938. *Crime and the community.* Boston: Ginn.

Veevers, Jean, 1972. The violation of fertility mores: Voluntary childlessness as deviant behavior. pp. 571–592. In *Deviant behavior and societal reaction.* Craig Boydell, Carl Grindstaff & Paul Whitehead (eds.). Toronto: Holt, Rinehart & Winston.

Veevers, Jean, 1979. Voluntary childlessness: A review of issues and evidence. *Marriage and Family Review* 2:1–26.

Veevers, Jean, 1980. *Childless by choice.* Toronto: Butterworth.

Warren, Carol, 1974. The use of stigmatizing social labels in conventionalizing deviant behavior. *Sociology and Social Research* 58:303–311.

Warren, Carol, 1987. *Madwives: Schizophrenic women in the 1950's.* London: Rutgers University Press.

Warren, Carol & John Johnson, 1972. A critique of labeling theory from the phenomenological perspective. pp. 69–92. In *Theoretical perspectives on deviance.* Robert Scott & Jack Douglas (eds.). New York: Basic Books.

PART THREE

RELATIONS AMONG DEVIANTS

Despite popular stereotype, deviant careers are not unilinear; nor do they have fixed and inevitable stages. Some people who commit deviant acts may never be typed as deviant or may discontinue those acts, while others may become "hard-core" career deviants. And even those who do become career deviants may do so through widely different routes. Thus there is no single natural history of deviant careers; there are many career histories. One hypothetical deviant career might proceed as follows. A person lives in a culture where certain acts are viewed as deviant. This person is believed, rightly or wrongly, to have committed such deviance. Someone (e.g., teacher, neighbor) types the person as a certain type of deviant. The person comes to the attention of an official agency (e.g., juvenile authorities) and becomes an official case. This social processing propels the person into organized deviant life (e.g., the person is now a "hoodlum"—ostracized by "good kids" and accepted only in disreputable circles). Finally, in self-redefinition, the person assumes the deviant role (i.e., actually becomes a "hood"), thus confirming the initial typing.

This, however, is only one developmental model. Another hypothetical deviant career (which is probably more characteristic of certain kinds of deviance such as professional crime) might proceed along opposite lines. First, the person defines himself or herself as a certain kind of deviant, then enters a deviant world to confirm that identity, comes to official notice, becomes an official case, and engages in more persistent and patterned deviations, thus reinforcing the system of social types. Still other types of deviant careers may require different models. In fact, deviant careers vary so widely that a person might enter the deviance process at any one of the various stages and move forward, backward, or out of the process completely.

Perhaps a visual image will help. Suppose we visualize deviant careers as a long corridor. Each segment of the corridor represents one stage in a deviant career, with doors that allow people to directly enter into or exit from that stage. Some people can enter the deviance corridor from a side door, without previous experience in a deviant career. Others can leave by a side door, thus terminating their deviant careers. Finally, there are some who will enter at one end of the corridor and proceed through all the stages to the other end. The diagram on page 222 shows how the traffic of deviance may flow.

The dotted lines represent the invisible boundaries marking stages of a person's deviant career. At each of these symbolic boundaries there are defining agents who speed certain people farther along the corridor and usher others out the side doors or back to where they started.

The Deviance Corridor

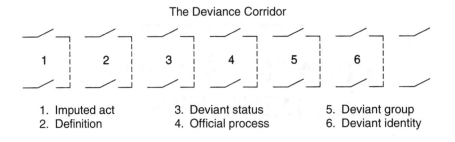

1. Imputed act   3. Deviant status   5. Deviant group
2. Definition   4. Official process   6. Deviant identity

The rate and direction of a person's progress through the corridor are based largely on the person's responses to others' symbolic definitions of him or her. In addition to conventional people, those who type and respond to the deviant often include members of the deviant group; thus these people can be an important influence in solidifying a person's deviant career.

The fact that a person has been assigned a deviant label does not mean that she or he will automatically be drawn into a deviant group. Nonetheless, dilettantes in deviance and career deviants alike are likely to become involved with a deviant group at some time. Thus Part Three of this book examines the social organization of deviants. It then goes on to examine how people enter deviant worlds and how they learn their traditions. Finally, it considers social diversity within deviant worlds.

THE SOCIAL ORGANIZATION OF DEVIANTS

A deviant group is apt to come into being when people are in contact with one another, suffer a common fate, and have common interests. These common interests generally arise from their social situation and are shared because these people face more or less the same dilemma.

The general dilemma for the persons who ultimately become involved in deviant groups is that they want to carry out activities that the society labels deviant but at the same time they want to avoid punishment. When people become aware that they share such a problem, a deviant group can arise to provide a solution.

When these people are especially concerned with pursuing their activities, the deviant group forms on the basis of a common attraction; an example would be the gay subculture. In contrast, when people are thrust together because of official typing, the deviant group forms on the basis of shared punishment; the prison subculture is one example. Finally, if it is merely by chance that the persons engage together in deviant activities, they do not actually form a structured group. Spontaneous riots provide an example.

ENTRY AND ACCULTURATION

Entry refers to the ways in which a person comes to participate in and gain admittance to a deviant group. *Acculturation* refers to the new ways and meanings a person acquires from it. Entry can be clearly defined (where a person clearly is or is not a member), or it can be rather loose in character. Likewise, acculturation can be highly specialized or casual and offhand. Like colleges, groups vary in how hard they are to get into and how hard they are to stay in. Much depends on the complexity of the activities involved, on how much commitment others in the group expect from newcomers, and on how much they must rely on them for their own safety and welfare. With a team of pickpockets, for example, entry and socialization are rigorous. On the other hand, admission and socialization to a skid row bottle gang are relatively simple. Here all a person needs is a few coins to "go in on a bottle," and there is relatively little to learn.

DIVERSITY IN SUBCULTURES

Some deviants become highly involved in deviant groups, but this is not true for all deviants. Within a particular group some people may be highly immersed while others (e.g., weekend visitors) may participate only occasionally. Also, some forms of deviance lend themselves to more involvement than do others. Because they have to be highly mobile, check forgers, for example, may be marginal to any kind of social group, conventional or deviant. Skid row drunks, on the other hand, are freer to immerse themselves in a deviant group. In addition, covert deviants (e.g., people in the "closet") are generally less engulfed in an unconventional way of life and engage in the unconventional world sporadically and secretly. Overt deviants (e.g., gay activists) ordinarily find themselves more involved in an unconventional way of life that stipulates a regular schedule of activities and a circle of intimate acquaintances.

Sanctions that deviants bring against one another are also important. Social control operates in deviant ways of life just as it does in the conventional world. How well do deviant groups control members? In general, it seems that members are subject to more social control in some groups (e.g., organized crime) than in others (e.g., the gay subculture). Also, it seems that within a group more social control is exerted over some members (e.g., a novice) than over others (e.g., a leader in the group).

Groups have beliefs, values, and norms that are supposed to regulate conduct. These prescriptions contribute to a form of social order. Deviant groups vary in the extent to which they organize their activities and define them by rules: some have elaborate rules that specify beliefs and actions; others have simpler codes. A simple, tightly organized code leads to one set of consequences, a complex, loosely organized code to another. In addition, some deviant groups have rules and beliefs that protect and dignify their members while others spawn normlessness, induce exploitation, and set members against one another.

Within a group some members show more commitment to the deviant way of life than do others. How dependent the person is on the group, the person's identity, how much the person shares the viewpoints of others in the group—all these seem to be factors influencing a person's commitment to the group.

CHAPTER 8

THE SOCIAL ORGANIZATION OF DEVIANTS

Types of Relationships

JOEL BEST and DAVID F. LUCKENBILL

Deviants are often persons who frequently break rules, are assigned a deviant status, perform the related role, and see themselves as deviants. And there are various networks of social relationships in which deviant persons can be involved. It is important to pay attention to these networks, the frequency of deviations, and the types of deviations (instrumental or expressive). The number of deviant persons involved, their relations with nondeviant people, and the stability of their deviant careers all vary with the networks in which the deviant transactions are implicated.

Joel Best and David F. Luckenbill note that deviations are both the process and product of social organization. They point out that deviant transactions involving force, fraud, or consent vary in the ways they are socially organized. In turn, the regularity, rewards, and costs of these transactions also vary in the ways they have been organized socially. The authors present a number of generalizations from their conceptual scheme concerning the effects of sophistication in forms of deviant organization.

Ethnographic research on particular social scenes provides data for general, grounded theories (Glaser and Strauss, 1967). For the study of deviance, field studies have supplied the basis for the development of general theories of the social psychology of deviance (Goffman, 1963; Lofland, 1969; Matza, 1969). However, while several reports about specific forms of deviance focus on social organization (Einstader, 1969; McIntosh, 1971; Mileski and Black, 1972; Shover, 1977; Zimmerman and

Reprinted from "The Social Organization of Deviants," *Social Problems,* Vol. 28, No. 1 (October 1980), pp. 14–31, by permission of the Society for the Study of Social Problems and the authors. Copyright © 1980 by the Society for the Study of Social Problems.

Wieder, 1977), there is no satisfactory general theory of the social organization of deviance.

Sociologists of varying perspectives have debated the nature of social organization among juvenile delinquents, professional criminals, organized criminals, and white-collar criminals. Others have developed typologies of deviants that include social organizational features (Clinard and Quinney, 1973; Gibbons, 1965, 1977; Miller, 1978). However, these treatments of social organization suffer from several flaws. First, they are often too narrow, focusing on a single type of deviance, such as burglary or more broadly, crime. Second, they usually are content with describing the organizational forms of different types of deviance. They fail to locate such forms along a dimension of organization or examine the consequences of organizational differences for deviants and social control agents. Third, they typically confuse two different bases for analyzing social organization: a general theory must distinguish between the social organization of *deviants* (the patterns of relationships between deviant actors) and the social organization of *deviance* (the patterns of relationships between the various roles performed in deviant transactions).

In this paper, we present a framework for understanding the social organization of deviants.[1] By examining reports of field research, several forms of social organization are identified and located along a dimension of organizational sophistication. Then some propositions are developed regarding the consequences of organizational variation for deviants and social control agents. Finally, some implications for the study of social organization are considered.

FORMS OF DEVIANT ORGANIZATION

The social organization of deviants refers to the structure or patterns of relationships among deviant actors in the context of deviant pursuits. The social organization of deviants varies along a dimension of sophistication. Organizational sophistication involves the elements of complexity, coordination and purposiveness (cf. Cressey, 1972). Organizations vary in the complexity of their division of labor including the size of membership, degree of stratification, and degree of specialization of organizational roles. Organizations also vary in their coordination among roles including the degree to which rules, agreements, and codes regulating relationships are formalized and enforced. Finally, organizations vary in the purposiveness with which they specify, strive toward, and achieve their objectives. Forms of organization which display high levels of complexity, coordination, and purposiveness are more sophisticated than those forms with lower levels.

Research reports suggest that deviants organize in several identifiable ways along the dimension of sophistication. Beginning with the least sophisticated, we will discuss five forms: loners, colleagues, peers, mobs, and formal organizations. These organizational forms can be defined in terms of four variables: (1) whether the deviants associate with one another; (2) whether they participate in deviance together; (3) whether their deviance requires an elaborate division of labor; and (4) whether their organization's activities extend over time and space (see Table 8.1). *Loners* do not associate with other deviants, participate in shared deviance, have a division of labor, or maintain their deviance over extended time and space. *Colleagues* differ from loners because they associate with fellow deviants. *Peers* not only associate with one another, but also participate in deviance together. In *mobs,* the shared participation requires an elaborate division of labor. Finally, *formal organizations* involve mutual association and participation, an elaborate division of labor,

TABLE 8.1   Characteristics of Different Forms of the Social Organization of Deviants

VARIABLE	TYPE OF ORGANIZATION				
	Loners	*Colleagues*	*Peers*	*Mobs*	*Formal Organizations*
Mutual association	−	+	+	+	+
Mutual participation	−	−	+	+	+
Division of labor	−	−	−	+	+
Extended organization	−	−	−	−	+

and deviant undertakings extended over time and space.

The descriptions of these forms of organization must be qualified in two ways. First, the forms are presented as ideal types. There is variation among the types of deviants within each form, as well as between one form and another. The intent is to sketch out the typical features of each form, recognizing that particular types of deviants may not share all of the features of their form to the same degree. Organizational sophistication can be viewed as a continuum, with deviants located between, as well as on, the five points. Describing a number of forms along this continuum inevitably understates the complexities of social life. Second, the descriptions of these forms draw largely from field studies of deviance in the contemporary United States, and attempt to locate the deviants studied along the dimension of organizational sophistication. A particular type of deviant can be organized in various ways in different societies and at different times. The references to specific field studies are intended to place familiar pieces of research within this framework; they are not claims that particular types of deviants invariably organize in a given way.

LONERS

Some deviants operate as individuals. These loners do not associate with other deviants for purposes of sociability, the performance of deviant activities, or the exchange of supplies and information. Rather, they must supply themselves with whatever knowledge, skill, equipment, and ideology their deviance requires. Loners lack deviant associations, so they cannot receive such crucial forms of feedback as moral support or information about their performance, new opportunities, or changes in social control strategies. They often enter deviance as a defensive response to private troubles (Lofland, 1969). Because their entry does not require contact with other deviants, as long as they can socialize themselves, loners frequently come from segments of the population which are less likely to be involved in the more sophisticated forms of deviance; it is not uncommon for loners to be middle-aged, middle-class, or female. Because their deviance often is defensive, and because they lack the support of other deviants, loners' careers typically are short-lived. Examples of loners include murderers (Luckenbill, 1977), rapists (Amir, 1971), embezzlers (Cressey, 1953), check forgers (Lemert, 1967:99–134; Klein and Montague, 1977), physician narcotic addicts (Winick, 1961), compulsive criminals (Cressey, 1962), heterosexual transvestites (Buckner, 1970), amateur shoplifters (Cameron, 1964), some gamblers (Lesieur, 1977), and many computer criminals (Parker, 1976).[2]

COLLEAGUES

Like loners, colleagues perform as individuals. Unlike loners, however, colleagues associate with others involved in the same kind of deviance. Colleagues thus form a simple group which provides important services for members. First, colleagues often socialize newcomers, providing training in deviant skills as well as an ideology which accounts for and justifies their deviance. Association also offers sociability among members with whom one's deviant identity need not be concealed: an actor can take down his or her guard without fear of discovery by agents of social control (Goffman, 1959, 1963). Also, association provides a source of information about ways to obtain deviant equipment, new techniques, new opportunities for engaging in deviance, and strategies for avoiding sanctioning. Colleagues learn and are held to a loose set of norms which direct conduct in both deviant and respectable activities. "Don't inform on a colleague" and "Never cut in on a colleague's score" exemplify such norms. The moral climate established by these expectations increases the stability of colleagues' social scene. At the same time, only some deviant activities and some people are suited for such a loose form of organization. A successful career as a colleague depends ultimately on the individual's performance when operating alone. As a result, newcomers often sample the scene and, when they encounter difficulties, drift away. Only the more successful colleagues maintain extended deviant careers. Some examples of colleagues include most prostitutes (Hirschi, 1962; Bryan, 1965, 1966), pimps (Milner and Milner, 1972), and pool hustlers (Polsky, 1967).

PEERS

Like colleagues, peers associate with one another and benefit from services provided by their fellows. Peers are involved in the socialization of novices, considerable sociable interaction, and the maintenance of a loose, unwritten code of conduct to be followed by individuals who wish to remain in the peer group. Unlike colleagues, peers participate in deviant acts together; they are involved in deviant transactions at the same time and in the same place. In some cases, such mutual participation is required by the nature of the deviant activity. This is exemplified in the performance of homosexual acts, or in the "task force raids" where a collection of young men engages in simple acts of violence such as gang fighting or rolling drunks (Cressey, 1972). In other cases, mutual participation is required because peers form a network for supplying one another with essential goods and services, as found in the distribution of illicit drugs. In either event, peers interact basically as equals; there is a minimal division of labor and specialized roles are uncommon. Although individuals pass through these social scenes, peer groups often are quite stable, perhaps because peer groups solve structural problems within society for their members. Two common varieties of deviant peers are young people who have not yet entered integrated adult work roles, and those who frequent a deviant marketplace and depend on their contacts with one another for the satisfaction of illicit needs. Examples of peers include hobos (Anderson, 1923), homosexuals (Humphreys, 1970; Mileski and Black, 1972; Warren, 1974), group-oriented gamblers (Lesieur,

1977), swingers (Bartell, 1971), gang delinquents (Shaw, 1930; Matza, 1964; Rosenberg and Silverstein, 1969), motorcycle outlaws (Thompson, 1966), skid row tramps (Wiseman, 1970; Rubington, 1978), and illicit drug users (Blumer, 1967; Carey, 1968; Feldman, 1968; Stoddart, 1974).

MOBS

Mobs are small groups of professional or career deviants organized to pursue specific, profitable goals.[3] Their deviance requires the coordinated actions of members performing specialized roles—a more sophisticated division of labor than that found among peers. Thus, work is divided among confidence artists (the inside man and the outside man), pickpockets (the tool and the stall), or card and dice hustlers (the mechanic and the shootup man; Maurer, 1962, 1964; Prus and Sharper, 1977). Ordinarily, at least one of the roles in the mob is highly skilled, requiring considerable practice and training to perfect. This training (normally via apprenticeship), the need for on-the-job coordination, and the common practice of traveling from city to city as a mob lead to intensive interaction between mobsters. Elaborate technical argots develop, as well as elaborate codes specifying mobsters' obligations to each other.

Mobs have complex links to outsiders. They are organized to accomplish profitable yet safe crimes. McIntosh (1971) describes the historical shift from craft thieving, where mobs develop routine procedures for stealing relatively small sums from individuals, to project thieving, where larger amounts are taken from corporate targets using procedures specifically tailored to the particular crime. In either case, mob operations are planned and staged with an eye toward avoiding arrest. Also, mobs may attempt to neutralize the criminal justice system by bribing social control agents not to make arrests, "fixing" those cases where arrests take place, or making restitution to victims in return for dropped charges. Mobs also have ties to others who purchase stolen goods, provide legal services, and supply information and deviant equipment. Finally, a network of sociable and business contacts ties mobs to one another, enabling strategic information to spread quickly. These arrangements ensure that mobs can operate at a consistently profitable level with minimal interference. Consequently, the careers of individual mobsters, as well as those of specific mobs, seem to be more stable than those of deviants organized in less sophisticated ways.[4] Examples of mobs are the groups of professional criminals specializing in confidence games (Sutherland, 1937; Maurer, 1962), picking pockets (Maurer, 1964), shoplifting (Cameron, 1964), armed robbery (Einstader, 1969; Letkemann, 1973), burglary (Shover, 1977), and card and dice hustling (Prus and Sharper, 1977).

FORMAL ORGANIZATIONS

Formal organizations of deviants differ from mobs in the scope of their actions.[5] Normally they involve more people, but, more importantly, their actions are coordinated to efficiently handle deviant tasks on a routine basis over considerable time and space. While mobsters work as a group in a series of episodic attacks, formal organizations are characterized by delegated responsibility and by routine and steady levels of productivity. In many ways, formal organizations of deviants share the features which characterize such respectable bureaucracies as military organizations, churches, and business firms. They have a hierarchical division of labor, including both vertical and horizontal differentiation of positions and roles and established channels for vertical and horizontal communication. A deviant formal organization may contain departments for planning, processing goods, public relations and rule enforcement, with positions for strategists, coordinators, accountants, lawyers, enforcers, and dealers in illicit goods. There may be recruitment policies for filling these diversified positions, and entry into the organization may be marked by a ritual ceremony of passage. Formal organizations usually have binding, but normally unwritten, rules

and codes for guiding members in organizational action, and these rules are actively enforced.

Formal organizations of deviants can make large profits by operating efficiently. At the same time, they must protect themselves from harm or destruction. As in less sophisticated forms of organization, loyal members are expected to maintain the group's secrets. In addition, deviant formal organizations attempt to locate power in the office, rather than in an individual charismatic leader. Although charismatic leadership obviously plays a part in some deviant formal organizations, the successful organization is able to continue operations when a leader dies or is arrested. Finally, deviant formal organizations typically invest considerable energy in neutralizing the criminal justice system by corrupting both high- and low-level officials. The scope and efficiency of their operations, their organizational flexibility, and their ties to agencies of social control make formal organizations of deviants extremely stable. Examples of such deviant formal organizations include very large urban street gangs (Keiser, 1969; Dawley, 1973), smuggling rings (Green, 1969), and organized crime "families" (Cressey, 1969; Ianni, 1972).

THE SIGNIFICANCE OF THE SOCIAL ORGANIZATION OF DEVIANTS

The identification and description of these different organizational forms permit a comparative analysis. What are the consequences of organizing as loners, colleagues, peers, mobs, or formal organizations? A comparison suggests that the sophistication of a form of deviant social organization has several consequences for both deviants and social control agents. Five propositions can be advanced.

I. *The more sophisticated the form of deviant organization, the greater its members' capability for complex deviant operations.* Deviant activities, like conventional activities, vary in their complexity. The complexity of a deviant operation refers to the number of elements required to carry it through; the more component parts to an activity, the more complex it is.[6] Compared to simple activities, complex lines of action demand more careful preparation and execution and take longer to complete. The complexity of a deviant activity depends upon two identifiable types of elements. First, there are the *resources* which the actors must be able to draw upon. Some activities require that the deviant utilize special knowledge, skill, equipment, or social status in order to complete the operation successfully, while simple acts can be carried out without such resources. Second, the *organization of the deviant transaction* affects an activity's complexity.[7] Some deviant acts can be accomplished with a single actor, while others require two or more people. The actors in a transaction can share a common role, as in a skid row bottle gang, or the transaction may demand different roles, such as offender and victim or buyer and seller. Furthermore, the degree to which these roles must be coordinated, ranging from the minimal coordination of juvenile vandals to the precision routines performed by mobs of pickpockets, varies among situations. The more people involved, the more roles they perform; and the more coordination between those roles, the more complex the deviant transaction's organization. The more resources and organization involved in a deviant operation, the more complex the operation is.

In general, deviants in more sophisticated forms of organization commit more complex acts.[8] The deviant acts of loners tend to be simple, requiring little in the way of resources or organization. Although colleagues work apart from one another, they generally share certain resources, such as shared areas. The hustlers' pool hall and the prostitutes' red light district contain the elements needed to carry out deviant operations, including victims and clients. Peers may interact in situations where they are the only ones present, performing complementary or comparable roles, as when two people engage in homosexual intercourse or a group of motorcycle outlaws makes a "run." Peers also may undertake activities which

involve nonmembers, as when members of a delinquent gang rob a passerby. The activities carried out by mobs involve substantially more coordination among the members' roles. In an armed robbery, for instance, one member may be assigned to take the money, while a second provides "cover" and a third waits for the others in the car, ready to drive away on their return. Finally, the activities of formal organizations tend to be particularly complex, requiring substantial resources and elaborate organization. Major off-track betting operations, with staff members at local, district, and regional offices who carry out a variety of clerical and supervisory tasks on a daily basis, represent an exceedingly complex form of deviance.

The relationship between the sophistication of organization and the complexity of deviant activities is not perfect. Loners can engage in acts of considerable complexity, for example. The computer criminal who single-handedly devises a complicated method of breaking into and stealing from computerized records, the embezzler who carries through an elaborate series of illicit financial manipulations, and the physician who juggles drug records in order to maintain his or her addiction to narcotics are engaged in complex offenses requiring substantial resources. However, these offenses cannot be committed by everyone. These loners draw upon resources which they command through their conventional positions, turning them to deviant uses. The computer criminal typically is an experienced programmer, the embezzler must occupy a position of financial trust, and the physician has been trained in the use of drugs. Possessing these resources makes the loner's deviance possible. Thus, the more concentrated the resources necessary for a deviant operation, the less sophisticated the form of organization required. However, when resources are not concentrated, then more sophisticated forms of organization are necessary to undertake more complex deviant operations.

Sophisticated forms of deviant organization have advantages beyond being able to undertake complex operations by pooling resources distributed among their members. Some deviant activities require a minimal level of organization; for example, homosexual intercourse demands the participation of two parties. In many other cases, it may be possible to carry out a deviant line of action using a relatively unsophisticated form of organization, but the task is considerably easier if a sophisticated form of organization can be employed. This is so because more sophisticated forms of deviant organization enjoy several advantages: they are capable of conducting a larger number of deviant operations; the operations can occur with greater frequency and over a broader range of territory; and, as discussed below, the members are better protected from the actions of social control agents. Of course, sophisticated organizations may engage in relatively simple forms of deviance, but the deviant act is often only one component in a larger organizational context. Taking a particular bet in the policy racket is a simple act, but the racket itself, handling thousands of bets, is complex indeed. Similarly, a murder which terminates a barroom dispute between two casual acquaintances is very different from an execution which is ordered and carried out by members of a formal organization, even though the two acts may appear equally simple. In the latter case, the killing may be intended as a means of maintaining discipline by demonstrating the organization's ability to levy sanctions against wayward members.

II. *The more sophisticated the form of deviant organization, the more elaborate the socialization of its members.* Neophyte deviants need to acquire two types of knowledge: (1) they must learn how to perform deviant acts, and how to gain appropriate *skills and techniques;* (2) they must develop a *cognitive perspective,* a distinctive way of making sense of their new, deviant world (cf. Shibutani, 1961:118–127). Such a perspective includes an ideology which accounts for the deviance, the individual's participation in deviance, and the organizational form, as well as a distinctive language for speaking about these and other matters.

As forms of deviant organization increase in sophistication, socialization becomes more elaborate. Loners do not depend upon other deviants for instruction in deviant skills or for a special cognitive perspective; they learn through their participation in conventional social scenes. Murderers, for instance, learn from their involvement in conventional life how to respond in situations of interpersonal conflict, and they employ culturally widespread justifications for killing people (Bohannon, 1960; Wolfgang and Ferracuti, 1967). Embezzlers learn the technique for converting a financial trust in the course of respectable vocational training, adapting justifications such as "borrowing" from conventional business ideology (Cressey, 1953). In contrast, colleagues teach one another a great deal. Although pool hustlers usually know how to shoot pool before they enter hustling, their colleagues provide a rich cognitive perspective, including a sense of "we-ness," some norms of behavior, a system for stratifying the hustling world, and an extensive argot (Polsky, 1967).[9] Peers receive similar training or, in some cases, teach one another through a process of emerging norms (Turner, 1964). Juvenile vandals, for example, can devise new offenses through their mutually constructed interpretation of what is appropriate to a particular situation (Wade, 1967). Sometimes, the knowledge peers acquire has largely symbolic functions that affirm the group's solidarity, as when a club of motorcycle outlaws devises a written constitution governing its members (Reynolds, 1967:134–136). In mobs and formal organizations, the cognitive perspective focuses on more practical matters; their codes of conduct specify the responsibilities members have in their dealings with one another, social control agents and others. Greater emphasis is also placed on the acquisition of specialized skills, with an experienced deviant coaching an apprentice, frequently over an extended period of time.

Two circumstances affect the socialization process in different forms of deviant organization. First, the sophistication of the organization affects the scope and style of the training process. The amount of training tends to increase with the sophistication of the organization. The skills required to perform deviant roles vary, but there is a tendency for more sophisticated forms of organization to incorporate highly skilled roles. Further, the more sophisticated forms of organization often embody cognitive perspectives of such breadth that the deviant must acquire a large body of specialized knowledge. In addition, the socialization process tends to be organized differently in different forms of deviant organization. While loners serve as their own agents of socialization, and colleagues and peers may socialize one another, mobs and formal organizations almost always teach newcomers through apprenticeship to an experienced deviant. Second, the socialization process is affected by the newcomer's motivation for entering deviance. Loners, of course, choose deviance on their own. In the more sophisticated forms, newcomers may ask for admission, but they often are recruited by experienced deviants. While peers may recruit widely, as when a delinquent gang tries to enlist all of the neighborhood boys of a given age, mobs and formal organizations recruit selectively, judging the character and commitment of prospective members and sometimes demanding evidence of skill or prior experience. For loners, entry into deviance frequently is a defensive act, intended to ward off some immediate threat. Peers, on the other hand, often are using deviance to experience stimulation; their deviance has an adventurous quality (Lofland, 1969). In contrast, mobs and formal organizations adopt a more professional approach: deviance is instrumental, a calculated means of acquiring economic profits.[10] These differences in the scope of socialization, the way the process is organized, and the neophyte's motivation account for the relationship between sophistication of organization and the elaborateness of the socialization.

III. *The more sophisticated the form of deviant organization, the more elaborate the services provided its members.* Every social role poses practical problems for its performers. In some cases these problems can be solved by providing the actors with supplies of various sorts. Actors may require certain *equipment* to perform a role. They

may also need *information* about their situation in order to coordinate their behavior with the ongoing action and successfully accomplish their part in an operation. One function of deviant social organization is to solve such practical problems by supplying members with needed equipment and information. More sophisticated forms of social organization are capable of providing more of these services.

Deviants differ in their requirements for equipment. Some need little in the way of equipment; a mugger may be able to get by with a piece of pipe. In other cases, deviants make use of specialized items which have few, if any, respectable uses (e.g., heroin or the booster boxes used in shoplifting).[11] Most loners require little equipment. When specialized needs exist, they are met through conventional channels accessible to the deviants, as when a physician narcotic addict obtains illicit drugs from hospital or clinic supplies. Colleagues also supply their own equipment, for the most part, although they may receive some assistance; pool hustlers, for example, provide their own cues, but they may rely on financial backers for funding. Peers adopt various patterns toward equipment. In some cases, peer groups develop to facilitate the distribution and consumption of deviant goods, such as illicit drugs. In other instances, peers use equipment as a symbol of their deviant status, as when gang members wear special costumes. The equipment used by mobsters is more utilitarian; many of their trades demand specialized tools, for safecracking, shoplifting, and so forth. In addition to a craftsman's personal equipment, the mob may require special materials for a specific project. Norms often exist that specify the manner in which these equipment purchases will be financed. In still other instances, some mobsters with expensive pieces of equipment may cooperate with several different mobs who wish to make use of them (such as the "big store" which is centrally located for the use of several confidence mobs). Formal organizations also have extensive equipment requirements. Because their operations extend over considerable time, formal organizations may find it expedient to invest in an elaborate array of fixed equipment. Off-track bookmaking, for example, may involve the purchase or rental of offices, desks, calculators, computer lines, special telephone lines, office supplies, and automobiles. Special staff members may have the responsibility for maintaining this equipment (Bell, 1962:134). In addition, some formal organizations are involved in producing or distributing deviant equipment for the consumption of other deviants; drug smuggling offers the best example.

Deviants need information in order to determine their courses of action. To operate efficiently, they need to know about new opportunities for deviant action; to operate safely, they need to know about the movements of social control agents. The more sophisticated forms of organization have definite advantages in acquiring and processing information. Loners, of course, depend upon themselves for information; opportunities or threats outside their notice cannot be taken into account. Colleagues and peers can learn more by virtue of their contacts with the deviant "grapevine," and they may have norms regarding a member's responsibility to share relevant information. In mobs, information is sought in more systematic ways. In the course of their careers, mobsters develop perceptual skills, enabling them to "case" possible targets (Letkemann, 1973). In addition, some mobs rely on outsiders for information; spotters may be paid a commission for pointing out opportunities for theft. A formal organization can rely upon its widely distributed membership for information and its contacts with corrupted social control agents.

The degree to which deviants need special supplies varies with the requirements of their operations, the frequency with which they interact with victims or other nondeviants, and their visibility to social control agents. Supplies other than equipment and information may be required in some instances. However, for most supply problems, sophisticated forms of social organization enjoy a comparative advantage.

IV. *The more sophisticated the form of deviant organization, the greater its members' involve-* *ment in deviance.* Complex deviant operations require planning and coordinated action during the deviant act. Socialization and supply also involve interaction among an organization's members. More sophisticated forms of deviant organization, featuring complex operations and elaborate socialization and supply, are therefore more likely to involve intensive social contact with one's fellow deviants. Furthermore, because deviants face sanctions from social control agents and respectable people, their contacts with other deviants are an important source of social support. The differences in the ability of forms…[of] social organization to provide support for their members have important social psychological consequences for deviants' careers and identities.

The dimensions of deviant careers vary from the form of deviant organization. Longer deviant careers tend to occur in more sophisticated forms of organization. For naive loners, deviance can comprise a single episode, a defensive act to ward off an immediate threat. For systematic loners, and many colleagues and peers, involvement in deviance is limited to one period in their life. Prostitutes grow too old to compete in the sexual marketplace, delinquents move into respectable adult work roles, and so forth. Members of mobs and formal organizations are more likely to have extended careers. Where the roles are not too physically demanding, deviance can continue until the individual is ready to retire from the work force (Inciardi, 1977). Deviant careers also vary in the amount of time they demand while the individual is active; some kinds of deviance take up only a small portion of the person's hours, but other deviant roles are equivalent to full-time, conventional jobs. Although the relationship is not perfect, part-time deviance is associated with less sophisticated forms of deviant organization.[12]

Social organization is also related to the relative prominence of the deviant identity in the individual's self-concept. Individuals may view their deviance as tangential to the major themes in their lives, or as a central focus, an identity around which much of one's life is arranged. The latter pattern is more likely to develop in sophisticated forms of deviant organization, for, as Lofland (1969) points out, several factors associated with deviant social organization facilitate the assumption of deviant identity, including frequenting places populated by deviants, obtaining deviant equipment, and receiving instruction in deviant skills and ideology. These factors also would appear to be associated with the maintenance of deviance as a central identity. Loners seem especially adept at isolating their deviance, viewing it as an exception to the generally conventional pattern their lives take. This is particularly true when the deviance was initially undertaken to defend that conventional life style from some threat. Even when an individual is relatively committed to deviance, normal identities can serve as an important resource. In his discussion of the World War II underground, Aubert (1965) notes that normal identities served to protect its members. In the same way, an established normal status shields the deviant from the suspicion of social control agents and, if the members refrain from revealing their conventional identities to one another, against discovery brought about by deviant associates who invade their respectable lives. Such considerations seem to be most important in middle-class peer groups organized around occasional leisure-time participation in a deviant marketplace, such as homosexuality and swinging.[13] Other deviants, particularly members of mobs and formal organizations, may associate with their fellows away from deviant operations, so that both their work and their sociable interaction take place among deviants. This is also true for peer groups that expand into "communities" and offer a wide range of services to members. Active members of urban gay communities can largely restrict their contacts to other homosexuals (Harry and Devall, 1978; Wolf, 1979). In these cases there is little need to perform conventional roles, aside from their obvious uses as concealment, and the deviant identity is likely to be central for the individual.

The degree to which an individual finds a deviant career and a deviant identity satisfying depends, in part, on the form of deviant organization of which he or she is a part. As in any activity, persons continue to engage in deviance only as long as the rewards it offers are greater than the rewards which could be obtained through alternative activities. The relevant rewards vary from one person to the next and from one type of deviance to another; a partial list includes money, physical and emotional satisfaction, valued social contacts, and prestige. Because the relative importance of these rewards varies with the individual, it is impossible to measure the differences in rewards between forms of deviant organization. There is some evidence that monetary profits are generally higher in more sophisticated forms of deviant organization. While an occasional loner can steal a very large sum through an embezzlement or a computer crime, most mobs can earn a reasonably steady income, and rackets run by formal organizations consistently bring in high profits. A more revealing measure of satisfaction is career stability; members of more sophisticated forms of deviant organization are more likely to remain in deviance. Loners' careers are short-lived, even when they are involved in systematic deviance. Lemert's (1967) account of the failure of professional forgers to remain at large suggests that the lack of social support is critical. As noted above, persons frequently drift out of their roles as colleagues and peers when other options become more attractive. The long-term careers of members of mobs and formal organizations suggest that these forms are more likely to satisfy the deviant.[14]

V. *The more sophisticated the form of deviant organization, the more secure its members' deviant operations.* The social organization of deviants affects the interaction between deviants and social control agents. This relationship is complicated because increased sophistication has consequences which would seem to make social control effects both easier and more difficult. On the one hand, the more sophisticated the deviant organization, the greater its public visibility and its chances of being subject to social control actions.

Because more sophisticated forms of organization have more complex deviant operations, there are more people involved with the organization as members, victims, customers, and bystanders. Therefore, there are more people capable of supplying the authorities with information about the identities, operations, and locations of organizational members. On the other hand, more sophisticated forms of organization are more likely to have codes of conduct requiring their members to be loyal to the organization and to maintain its secrets. Further, more sophisticated forms of organization command resources which can be used to protect the organization and its members from social control agents. While highly sophisticated organizations find it more difficult to conceal the fact that deviance is taking place, they often are more successful at shielding their members from severe sanctions.

NOTES

1. A second paper, in preparation, will discuss the social organization of deviance.

2. Following Lemert (1967), loners can be subdivided into naive loners, for whom deviance is an exceptional, one-time experience, and systematic loners, whose deviance forms a repeated pattern. Lemert's analysis of the problems confronting systematic check forgers, who have trouble maintaining a deviant identity with little social support, suggests that systematic loners may have particularly unstable careers.

3. The term "mob," as it is used here, is drawn from the glossary in Sutherland: "A group of thieves who work together; same as 'troupe' and 'outfit'" (1937:239; cf. Maurer, 1962, 1964). A more recent study uses the term "crew" (Prus and Sharper, 1977).

4. Although the mob is able to accomplish its ends more efficiently, the same tasks are sometimes handled by loners. For example, see Maurer (1964:166–168) and Prus and Sharper (1977:22).

5. Our use of the term "formal organization" is not meant to imply that these organizations have all of the characteristics of an established bureaucracy. Rather, "formal" points to the deliberately designed structure of the organization—a usage consistent with Blau and Scott (1962:5).

6. The complexity of a deviant activity must be distinguished from two other types of complexity. First, the definition of organizational sophistication, given above, included the complexity of the division of labor among the deviants in a given organizational form as one criterion of sophistication. Second, the complexity of an activity should not be confused with the complexity of its explanation. A suicide, for example, can be easily accomplished, even though a complex social-psychological analysis may be required to explain the act.

7. This point illustrates the distinction, made earlier, between the social organization of deviance (the pattern of relationships between the roles performed in a deviant transaction) and the social organization of deviants (the pattern of relationships between deviant actors). The former, not the latter, affects an activity's complexity.

8. In most cases, loners do not possess the resources required for more than one type of complex deviance; physicians, for instance, are unable to commit computer thefts. In contrast, members of more sophisticated forms of organization may be able to manage several types of operations, as when a mob's members shift from picking pockets to shoplifting in order to avoid the police, or when an organized crime family is involved in several different rackets simultaneously (Maurer, 1964; Ianni, 1972:87–106).

9. Within a given form of organization, some cognitive perspectives may be more elaborate than others. While pool hustlers have a strong oral tradition, founded on the many hours they share together in pool halls, prostitutes have a relatively limited argot. Maurer (1939) argues that this is due to the restricted contact they have with one another during their work.

10. Here and elsewhere, colleagues represent a partial exception to the pattern. Colleagues resemble members of mobs and formal organizations in that they adopt an instrumental perspective, view deviance as a career, are socialized through apprenticeship to an experienced deviant, and accept deviance as a central identity. While peers have a more sophisticated form of organization, their mutual participation in deviance is based on their shared involvement in an illicit marketplace or leisure-time activity. In contrast, colleagues usually are committed to deviance as means of earning a living.

Yet, because colleagues share a relatively unsophisticated form of organization, they labor under restrictions greater than those faced by mobs and formal organizations. Socialization is of limited scope; call girls learn about handling money and difficult clients, but little about sexual skills (Bryan, 1965). The code of conduct governing colleagues is less encompassing and less binding than those for more sophisticated forms, and the deviance of colleagues is usually less profitable. The absence of the advantages associated with organizational sophistication leads colleagues, despite their similarities to mobs and formal organizations, into an unstable situation where many individuals drift away from deviance.

11. Sometimes such equipment is defined as illicit, and its possession constitutes a crime.

12. Two reasons can be offered to explain this relationship. If a type of deviance is not profitable enough to support the individual, it may be necessary to take other work, as when a pool hustler moonlights (Polsky, 1967). Also, many loners have only a marginal commitment to deviance and choose to allocate most of their time to their respectable roles. This is particularly easy if the form of deviance requires little time for preparation and commission.

13. Swingers meeting new couples avoid giving names or information which could be used to identify them (Bartell, 1971:92–95); and Humphreys (1970) emphasizes that many tearoom participants are attracted by the setting's assurance of anonymity.

14. During their careers, deviants may shift from one organizational form or one type of offense to another. The habitual felons interviewed by Petersilia et al. (1978) reported that, while many of their offenses as juveniles involved more than one partner (presumably members of a peer group), they preferred to work alone or with a single partner on the crimes they committed as adults. The most common pattern was for juveniles who specialized in burglaries to turn to robbery when they became adults.

REFERENCES

Amir, Menachem. 1971. *Patterns in Forcible Rape.* Chicago: University of Chicago Press.

Anderson, Nels. 1923. *The Hobo.* Chicago: University of Chicago Press.

Aubert, Vilhelm. 1965. *The Hidden Society.* Totowa, N.J.: Bedminster.

Bartell, Gilbert. 1971. *Group Sex.* New York: New American.

Bell, Daniel. 1962. *The End of Ideology.* Revised edition. New York: Collier.

Blau, Peter M. and W. Richard Scott. 1962. *Formal Organizations.* San Francisco: Chandler.

Blumer, Herbert. 1967. *The World of Youthful Drug Use.* Berkeley: University of California Press.

Bohannon, Paul. 1960. *African Homicide and Suicide.* Princeton: Princeton University Press.

Bryan, James H. 1965. "Apprenticeships in prostitution." *Social Problems* 12:287–297.

———. 1966. "Occupational ideologies and individual attitudes of call girls." *Social Problems* 13:441–450.

Buckner, H. Taylor. 1970. "The transvestic career path." *Psychiatry* 33:381–389.

Cameron, Mary Owen. 1964. *The Booster and the Snitch.* New York: Free Press.

Carey, James T. 1968. *The College Drug Scene.* Englewood Cliffs, N.J.: Prentice-Hall.

Clinard, Marshall B. and Richard Quinney. 1973. *Criminal Behavior Systems: A Typology.* Second edition. New York: Holt, Rinehart and Winston.

Cressey, Donald R. 1953. *Other People's Money.* New York: Free Press.

———. 1962. "Role theory, differential association, and compulsive crimes." Pp. 443–467 in Arnold M. Rose (ed.), *Human Behavior and Social Processes.* Boston: Houghton Mifflin.

———. 1969. *Theft of the Nation.* New York: Harper & Row.

———. 1972. *Criminal Organization.* New York: Harper & Row.

Dawley, David. 1973. *A Nation of Lords.* Garden City, N.Y.: Anchor.

Einstader, Werner J. 1969. "The social organization of armed robbery." *Social Problems* 17:64–83.

Feldman, Harvey W. 1968. "Ideological supports to becoming and remaining a heroin addict." *Journal of Health and Social Behavior* 9:131–139.

Gibbons, Don C. 1965. *Changing the Lawbreaker.* Englewood Cliffs, N.J.: Prentice-Hall.

———. 1977. *Society, Crime, and Criminal Careers.* Third edition. Englewood Cliffs, N.J.: Prentice-Hall.

Glaser, Barney G. and Anselm L. Strauss. 1967. *The Discovery of Grounded Theory.* Chicago: Aldine.

Goffman, Erving. 1959. *The Presentation of Self in Everyday Life.* Garden City, N.Y.: Anchor.

———. 1963. *Stigma.* Englewood Cliffs, N.J.: Prentice-Hall.

Green, Timothy. 1969. *The Smugglers.* New York: Walker.

Harry, Joseph and William B. Devall. 1978. *The Social Organization of Gay Males.* New York: Praeger.

Hirschi, Travis. 1962. "The professional prostitute." *Berkeley Journal of Sociology* 7:33–49.

Humphreys, Laud. 1970. *Tearoom Trade.* Chicago: Aldine.

Ianni, Francis A. J. 1972. *A Family Business.* New York: Sage.

Inciardi, James A. 1977. "In search of the class cannon." Pp. 55–77 in Robert S. Weppner (ed.), *Street Ethnography.* Beverly Hills, Calif.: Sage.

Keiser, R. Lincoln. 1969. *The Vice Lords.* New York: Holt, Rinehart and Winston.

Klein, John F. and Arthur Montague. 1977. *Check Forgers.* Lexington, Mass.: Lexington.

Lemert, Edwin M. 1967. Human Deviance, *Social Problems, and Social Control.* Englewood Cliffs, N.J.: Prentice-Hall.

Lesieur, Henry R. 1977. *The Chase.* Garden City, N.Y.: Anchor.

Letkemann, Peter. 1973. *Crime as Work.* Englewood Cliffs, N.J.: Prentice-Hall.

Lofland, John. 1969. *Deviance and Identity.* Englewood Cliffs, N.J.: Prentice-Hall.

Luckenbill, David F. 1977. "Criminal homicide as a situated transaction." *Social Problems* 25:176–186.

Matza, David. 1964. *Delinquency and Drift.* New York: Wiley.

———. 1969. *Becoming Deviant.* Englewood Cliffs, N.J.: Prentice-Hall.

Maurer, David W. 1939. "Prostitutes and criminal argots." *American Journal of Sociology* 44:346–350.

———. 1962. *The Big Con.* New York: New American.

———. 1964. *Whiz Mob.* New Haven, Conn.: College and University Press.

McIntosh, Mary. 1971. "Changes in the organization of thieving." Pp. 98–133 in Stanley Cohen (ed.), *Images of Deviance.* Baltimore, Md.: Penguin.

Mileski, Maureen and Donald J. Black. 1972. "The social organization of homosexuality." *Urban Life and Culture* 1:131–166.

Miller, Gale. 1978. *Odd Jobs: The World of Deviant Work.* Englewood Cliffs, N.J.: Prentice-Hall.

Milner, Christina and Richard Milner. 1972. *Black Players.* Boston: Little, Brown.

Parker, Donn B. 1976. *Crime by Computer.* New York: Scribner's.

Petersilia, Joan, Peter W. Greenwood and Marvin Lavin. 1978. *Criminal Careers of Habitual Felons.* Santa Monica, Calif.: Rand.

Polsky, Ned. 1967. *Hustlers, Beats, and Others.* Chicago: Aldine.

Prus, Robert C. and C. R. D. Sharper. 1977. *Road Hustler.* Lexington, Mass.: Lexington.

Reynolds, Frank. 1967. *Freewheelin' Frank.* New York: Grove.

Rosenberg, Bernard and Harry Silverstein. 1969. *Varieties of Delinquent Experience.* Waltham, Mass.: Blaisdell.

Rubington, Earl. 1978. "Variations in bottle-gang controls." Pp. 383–391 in Earl Rubington and Martin S. Weinberg (eds.), *Deviance: The Interactionist Perspective.* Third edition. New York: Macmillan.

Shaw, Clifford R. 1930. *The Jack-Roller.* Chicago: University of Chicago Press.

Shibutani, Tamotsu. 1961. *Society and Personality.* Englewood Cliffs, N.J.: Prentice-Hall.

Shover, Neal. 1977. "The social organization of burglary." *Social Problems* 20:499–514.

Stoddart, Kenneth. 1974. "The facts of life about dope." *Urban Life and Culture* 3:179–204.

Sutherland, Edwin H. 1937. *The Professional Thief.* Chicago: University of Chicago Press.

Thompson, Hunter S. 1966. *Hell's Angels.* New York: Ballantine.

Turner, Ralph H. 1964. "Collective behavior." Pp. 382–425 in Robert E. L. Faris (ed.), *Handbook of Modern Sociology.* Chicago: Rand McNally.

Wade, Andrew L. 1967. "Social processes in the act of juvenile vandalism." Pp. 94–109 in Marshall B. Clinard and Richard Quinney (eds.), *Criminal Behavior Systems: A Typology.* New York: Holt, Rinehart and Winston.

Warren, Carol A. B. 1974. *Identity and Community in the Gay World.* New York: Wiley.

Winick, Charles. 1961. "Physician narcotic addicts." *Social Problems* 9:174–186.

Wiseman, Jacqueline P. 1970. *Stations of the Lost.* Englewood Cliffs, N.J.: Prentice-Hall.

Wolf, Deborah G. 1979. *The Lesbian Community.* Berkeley: University of California Press.

Wolfgang, Marvin E. and Franco Ferracuti. 1967. *The Subculture of Violence.* London: Tavistock.

Zimmerman, Don H. and D. Lawrence Wieder. 1977. "You can't help but get stoned." *Social Problems* 25:198–207.

Capitalism and the Gay Subculture

JOHN D'EMILIO

In 1955, Albert K. Cohen specified a number of conditions that must be present if a deviant subculture is to emerge.* In sequence, there is the experience of a problem of adjustment; next, communication exists (sharing of the problem with others); subsequent interaction then evolves a collective solution to the problem; and finally joint action in time creates a tradition. Since Cohen's formulation, numerous field studies have depicted the subculture of drug addicts, bikers, skid row alcoholics, prostitutes, thieves, and gays and lesbians.

John D'Emilio argues that capitalism established the conditions for the formation of both gay identity and subsequent gay subcultures. Identity depends upon the fusion of acts, roles, and selves. People have always engaged in occasional homosexual acts without necessarily adopting a homosexual identity and social role. D'Emilio points out that capitalism has slowly weakened the affectional bonds of the family at the same time that it has increased the chances of contact, particularly in urban places, of people who are aware of their desires for expressing themselves sexually with persons of the same sex. It was only in the urban enclaves where large numbers of gay people could interact regularly that the fusion of their acts, roles, and selves took place. After the development of capitalism, subcultures formed and gay identity became a social fact.

...There is [a] historical myth that enjoys nearly universal acceptance in the gay movement, the myth of the "eternal homosexual." The argument runs something like this: Gay men and lesbians always were and always will be. We are everywhere; not just now, but throughout history, in all societies and all periods. This myth served a positive political function in the first years of gay liberation. In the early 1970s, when we battled an ideology that either denied our existence or defined us as psychopathic individuals or freaks of nature, it was empowering to assert that "we are everywhere." But in recent years it has confined us as surely as the most homophobic medical theories, and locked our movement in place.

Here I wish to challenge this myth. I want to argue that gay men and lesbians have not always existed. Instead, they are a product of history, and have come into existence in a specific historical era. Their emergence is associated with the relations of capitalism; it has been the historical development of capitalism—more specifically, its free-labor system—that has allowed large numbers of men and women in the late twentieth century to call themselves gay, to see themselves as part of a community of similar men and women, and to organize politically on the basis of that identity.[1] Finally, I want to suggest some political lessons we can draw from this view of history.

What, then, are the relationships between the free-labor system of capitalism and homosexuality? First, let me review some features of capitalism. Under capitalism workers are "free" laborers

*Albert K. Cohen, *Delinquent Boys* (Glencoe, IL: Free Press, 1955).

in two ways. We have the freedom to look for a job. We own our ability to work and have the freedom to sell our labor power for wages to anyone willing to buy it. We are also freed from the ownership of anything except our labor power. Most of us do not own the land or the tools that produce what we need, but rather have to work for a living in order to survive. So, if we are free to sell our labor power in the positive sense, we are also freed, in the negative sense, from any other alternative. This dialectic—the constant interplay between exploitation and some measure of autonomy—informs all of the history of those who have lived under capitalism.

As capital—money used to make more money—expands so does this system of free labor. Capital expands in several ways. Usually it expands in the same place, transforming small firms into larger ones, but it also expands by taking over new areas of production: the weaving of cloth, for instance, or the baking of bread. Finally, capital expands geographically. In the United States, capitalism initially took root in the Northeast, at a time when slavery was the dominant system in the South and when noncapitalist Native American societies occupied the western half of the continent. During the nineteenth century, capital spread from the Atlantic to the Pacific, and in the twentieth, U.S. capital has penetrated almost every part of the world.

The expansion of capital and the spread of wage labor have [effected] a profound transformation in the structure and functions of the nuclear family, the ideology of family life, and the meaning of heterosexual relations. It is these changes in the family that are most directly linked to the appearance of a collective gay life.

The white colonists in seventeenth-century New England established villages structured around a household economy, composed of family units that were basically self-sufficient, independent, and patriarchal. Men, women, and children farmed land owned by the male head of the household. Although there was a division of labor between men and women, the family was truly an interde-

pendent unit of production: the survival of each member depended on the cooperation of all. The home was a workplace where women processed raw farm products into food for daily consumption, where they made clothing, soap, and candles, and where husbands, wives, and children worked together to produce the goods they consumed.

By the nineteenth century, this system of household production was in decline. In the Northeast, as merchant capitalists invested the money accumulated through trade in the production of goods, wage labor became more common. Men and women were drawn out of the largely self-sufficient household economy of the colonial era into a capitalist system of free labor. For women in the nineteenth century, working for wages rarely lasted beyond marriage; for men, it became a permanent condition.

The family was thus no longer an independent unit of production. But although no longer independent, the family was still interdependent. Because capitalism had not expanded very far, because it had not yet taken over—or socialized—the production of consumer goods, women still performed necessary productive labor in the home. Many families no longer produced grain, but wives still baked into bread the flour they bought with their husbands' wages; or, when they purchased yarn or cloth, they still made clothing for their families. By the mid-nineteenth century, capitalism had destroyed the economic self-sufficiency of many families, but not the mutual dependence of the members.

This transition away from the household family-based economy to a fully developed capitalist free-labor economy occurred very slowly, over almost two centuries. As late as 1920, fifty percent of the U.S. population lived in communities of fewer than 2,500 people. The vast majority of blacks in the early twentieth century lived outside the free-labor economy, in a system of sharecropping and tenancy that rested on the family. Not only did independent farming as a way of life still exist for millions of Americans, but even in towns and small cities women continued to grow and process food, make clothing, and engage in other kinds of domestic production.

But for those people who felt the brunt of these changes, the family took on new significance as an affective unit, an institution that provided not goods but emotional satisfaction and happiness. By the 1920s among the white middle class, the ideology surrounding the family described it as the means through which men and women formed satisfying, mutually enhancing relationships and created an environment that nurtured children. The family became the setting for a "personal life," sharply distinguished and disconnected from the public world of work and production.[2]

The meaning of heterosexual relations also changed. In colonial New England the birth rate averaged over seven children per woman of childbearing age. Men and women needed the labor of children. Producing offspring was as necessary for survival as producing grain. Sex was harnessed to procreation. The Puritans did not celebrate heterosexuality but rather marriage; they condemned all sexual expression outside the marriage bond and did not differentiate sharply between sodomy and heterosexual fornication.

By the 1970s, however, the birth rate had dropped to under two. With the exception of the post–World War II baby boom, the decline has been continuous for two centuries, paralleling the spread of capitalist relations of production. It occurred even when access to contraceptive devices and abortion was systematically curtailed. The decline has included every segment of the population—urban and rural families, blacks and whites, ethnics and WASPs, the middle class and the working class.

As wage labor spread and production became socialized, then, it became possible to release sexuality from the "imperative" to procreate. Ideologically, heterosexual expression came to be a means of establishing intimacy, promoting happiness, and experiencing pleasure. In divesting the household of its economic independence and fostering the separation of sexuality from procreation, capitalism has created conditions that allow some men and women to organize a personal life around their erotic/emotional attraction to their own sex. It has made possible the formation of urban communities of lesbians and gay men and, more recently, of a politics based on sexual identity.

Evidence from colonial New England court records and church sermons indicates that male and female homosexual behavior existed in the seventeenth century. Homosexual behavior, however, is different from homosexual identity. There was, quite simply, no "social space" in the colonial system of production that allowed men and women to be gay. Survival was structured around participation in a nuclear family. There were certain homosexual acts—sodomy among men, "lewdness" among women—in which individuals engaged, but family was so pervasive that colonial society lacked even the category of homosexual or lesbian to describe a person. It is quite possible that some men and women experienced a stronger attraction to their own sex than to the opposite sex—in fact, some colonial court cases refer to men who persisted in their "unnatural" attractions—but one could not fashion out of that preference a way of life. Colonial Massachusetts even had laws prohibiting unmarried adults from living outside family units.[3]

By the second half of the nineteenth century, this situation was noticeably changing as the capitalist system of free labor took hold. Only when individuals began to make their living through wage labor, instead of as parts of an interdependent family unit, was it possible for homosexual desire to coalesce into a personal identity—an identity based on the ability to remain outside the heterosexual family and to construct a personal life based on attraction to one's own sex. By the end of the century, a class of men and women existed who recognized their erotic interest in their own sex, saw it as a trait that set them apart from the majority, and sought others like themselves. These early gay lives came from a wide social spectrum: civil servants and business executives, department store clerks and college professors, factory operatives, ministers, lawyers, cooks, domestics, hoboes, and the idle rich; men and women, black and white, immigrant and native-born.

In this period, gay men and lesbians began to invent ways of meeting each other and sustaining a group life. Already, in the early twentieth century, large cities contained male homosexual bars. Gay men stalked out cruising areas, such as Riverside Drive in New York City and Lafayette Park in Washington. In St. Louis and the nation's capital, annual drag balls brought together large numbers of black gay men. Public bathhouses and YMCAs became gathering spots for male homosexuals. Lesbians formed literary societies and private social clubs. Some working-class women "passed" as men to obtain better-paying jobs and lived with other women—forming lesbian couples who appeared to the world as husband and wife. Among the faculties of women's colleges, in the settlement houses, and in the professional associations and clubs that women formed, one could find lifelong intimate relationships supported by a web of lesbian friends. By the 1920s and 1930s, large cities such as New York and Chicago contained lesbian bars. These patterns of living could evolve because capitalism allowed individuals to survive beyond the confines of the family.[4]

Simultaneously, ideological definitions of homosexual behavior changed. Doctors developed theories about homosexuality, describing it as a condition, something that was inherent in a person, a part of his or her "nature." These theories did not represent scientific breakthroughs, elucidations of previously undiscovered areas of knowledge; rather, they were an ideological response to a new way of organizing one's personal life. The popularization of the medical model, in turn, affected the consciousness of the women and men who experienced homosexual desire, so that they came to define themselves through their erotic life.[5]

These new forms of gay identity and patterns of group life also reflected the differentiation of people according to gender, race, and class that is so pervasive in capitalist societies. Among whites,

for instance, gay men have traditionally been more visible than lesbians. This partly stems from the division between the public male sphere and the private female sphere. Streets, parks, and bars, especially at night, were "male space." Yet the greater visibility of white men also reflected their larger numbers. The Kinsey studies of the 1940s and 1950s found significantly more men than women with predominantly homosexual histories, a situation caused, I would argue, by the fact that capitalism had drawn far more men than women into the labor force, and at higher wages. Men could more easily construct a personal life independent of attachments to the opposite sex, whereas women were more likely to remain economically dependent on men. Kinsey also found a strong positive correlation between years of schooling and lesbian activity. College-educated white women, far more able than their working-class sisters to support themselves, could survive more easily without intimate relationships with men.[6]

Among working-class immigrants in the early twentieth century, closely knit kin networks and an ethic of family solidarity placed constraints on individual autonomy that made gayness a difficult option to pursue. In contrast, for reasons not altogether clear, urban black communities appeared relatively tolerant of homosexuality. The popularity in the 1920s and 1930s of songs with lesbian and gay male themes—"B. D. Woman," "Prove It on Me," "Sissy Man," "Fairy Blues"—suggests an openness about homosexual expression at odds with the mores of whites. Among men in the rural West in the 1940s, Kinsey found extensive incidence of homosexual behavior, but, in contrast with the men in large cities, little consciousness of gay identity. Thus even as capitalism exerted a homogenizing influence by gradually transforming more individuals into wage laborers and separating them from traditional communities, different groups of people were affected in different ways.[7]

The decisions of particular men and women to act on their erotic/emotional preference for the same sex, along with the new consciousness that this preference made them different, led to the formation of an urban subculture of gay men and lesbians. Yet at least through the 1930s this subculture remained rudimentary, unstable, and difficult to find. How, then, did the complex, well-developed gay community emerge that existed by the time the gay liberation movement exploded? The answer is to be found in the dislocations of World War II, a time when the cumulative changes of several decades coalesced into a qualitatively new shape.

The war severely disrupted traditional patterns of gender relations and sexuality, and temporarily created a new erotic situation conducive to homosexual expression. It plucked millions of young men and women, whose sexual identities were just forming, out of their homes, out of towns and small cities, out of the heterosexual environment of the family, and dropped them into sex-segregated situations—as GIs, as WACs and WAVEs, in same-sex rooming houses for women workers who relocated to seek employment. The war freed millions of men and women from the settings where heterosexuality was normally imposed. For men and women already gay, it provided an opportunity to meet people like themselves. Others could become gay because of the temporary freedom to explore sexuality that the war provided.[8]

The gay men and women of the 1940s were pioneers. Their decisions to act on their desires formed the underpinnings of an urban subculture of gay men and lesbians. Throughout the 1950s and 1960s the gay subculture grew and stabilized, so that people coming out then could more easily find other gay women and men than in the past. Newspapers and magazines published articles describing gay male life. Literally hundreds of novels with lesbian themes were published.[9] Psychoanalysts complained about the new ease with which their gay male patients found sexual partners. And the gay subculture was not to be found just in the largest cities. Lesbian and gay male bars existed in places like Worcester, Massachusetts, and Buffalo, New York; in Columbia, South Carolina, and Des Moines, Iowa. Gay life in the 1950s and 1960s became a nationwide phenomenon. By the

time of the Stonewall Riot in New York City in 1969—the event that ignited the gay liberation movement—our situation was hardly one of silence, invisibility, and isolation. A massive, grass-roots liberation movement could form almost overnight precisely because communities of lesbians and gay men existed.

Although gay community was a precondition for a mass movement, the oppression of lesbians and gay men was the force that propelled the movement into existence. As the subculture expanded and grew more visible in the post–World War II era, oppression by the state intensified, becoming more systematic and inclusive. The Right scapegoated "sexual perverts" during the McCarthy era. Eisenhower imposed a total ban on the employment of gay women and men by the federal government and government contractors. Purges of lesbians and homosexuals from the military rose sharply. The FBI instituted widespread surveillance of gay meeting places and of lesbian and gay organizations, such as the Daughters of Bilitis and the Mattachine Society. The Post Office placed tracers on the correspondence of gay men and passed evidence of homosexual activity on to employers. Urban vice squads invaded private homes, made sweeps of lesbian and gay male bars, entrapped gay men in public places, and fomented local witch-hunts. The danger involved in being gay rose even as the possibilities of being gay were enhanced. Gay liberation was a response to this contradiction....

NOTES

1. I do not mean to suggest that no one has ever proposed that gay identity is a product of historical change. See, for instance, Mary McIntosh, "The Homosexual Role," *Social Problems* 16 (1968): 182–92; Jeffrey Weeks, *Coming Out: Homosexual Politics in Britain* (New York: Quartet Books, 1977). It is also implied in Michel Foucault, *The History of Sexuality, vol. 1: An Introduction.* tr. Robert Hurley (New York: Pantheon, 1978). However, this does represent a minority viewpoint and the works cited above have not specified how it is that capitalism as a system of production has allowed for

the emergence of a gay male and lesbian identity. As an example of the "eternal homosexual" thesis, see John Boswell, *Christianity, Social Tolerance, and Homosexuality* (Chicago: University of Chicago Press, 1980), where "gay people" remains an unchanging social category through fifteen centuries of Mediterranean and Western European history.

2. See Eli Zaretsky, *Capitalism, the Family, and Personal Life* (New York: Harper & Row, 1976); and Paul Fass, *The Damned and the Beautiful: American Youth in the 1920s* (New York: Oxford University Press, 1977).

3. Robert F. Oaks, "'Things Fearful to Name': Sodomy and Buggery in Seventeenth-Century New England," *Journal of Social History* 12 (1978): 268–81; J. R. Roberts, "The Case of Sarah Norman and Mary Hammond," *Sinister Wisdom* 24 (1980): 57–62; and Jonathan Katz, *Gay American History* (New York: Crowell, 1976), pp. 16–24, 568–71.

4. For the period from 1870 to 1940 see the documents in Katz, *Gay American History,* and idem, *Gay/Lesbian Almanac* (New York: Crowell, 1983). Other sources include Allan Bérubé, "Lesbians and Gay Men in Early San Francisco: Notes Toward a Social History of Lesbians and Gay Men in America," unpublished paper, 1979; Vern Bullough and Bonnie Bullough, "Lesbianism in the 1920s and 1930s: A Newfound Study," *Signs* 2 (Summer 1977): 895–904.

5. On the medical model see Weeks, *Coming Out,* pp. 22–32. The impact of the medical model on the consciousness of men and women can be seen in Louis Hyde, ed., *Rat and the Devil: The Journal Letters of F. O. Matthiessen and Russell Cheney* (Hamden, CT.: Archon, 1978), p. 47, and in the story of Lucille Hart in Katz, *Gay American History,* pp. 258–79. Radclyffe Hall's classic novel about lesbianism, *The Well of Loneliness,* published 1928, was perhaps one of the most important vehicles for the popularization of the medical model.

6. See Alfred Kinsey et al., *Sexual Behavior in the Human Male* (Philadelphia: W. B. Saunders, 1948) and *Sexual Behavior in the Human Female* (Philadelphia: W. B. Saunders, 1953).

7. On black music, see "AC/DC Blues: Gay Jazz Reissues," Stash Records, ST-106 (1977), and Chris Albertson, *Bessie* (New York: Stein & Day, 1974); on the persistence of kin networks in white ethnic communities see Judith Smith, "Our Own Kind: Family and Community Networks in Providence," in *A Heritage of Her Own,* ed. Nancy F. Cott and Elizabeth H. Pleck (New York: Simon & Schuster, 1979), pp. 393–411; on differences between rural and urban male homoeroticism see Kinsey et al., *Sexual Behavior in the Human Male,* pp. 455–57, 630–31.

8. The argument and the information in this and the following paragraphs come from my book *Sexual Politics, Sexual Communities: The Making of a Homosexual Minority in the United States, 1940–1970* (Chicago: University of Chicago Press, 1983). I have also developed it with reference to San Francisco in "Gay Politics, Gay Community: San Francisco's Experience," *Socialist Review* 55 (January–February 1981): 77–104.

9. Donald Vining, *A Gay Diary, 1933–1946* (New York: Pepys Press, 1979); "Pat Bond," in Nancy Adair and Casey Adair, *Word Is Out* (New York: New Glide Publications, 1978), pp. 55–65; and Allan Bérubé, "Marching to a Different Drummer: Coming Out During World War II," a slide/talk presented at the annual meeting of the American Historical Association, December 1981, Los Angeles. A shorter version of Bérubé's presentation can be found in *The Advocate,* October 15, 1981, pp. 20–24.

"Mixed Nutters," "Looney Tuners," and "Daffy Ducks"

NANCY J. HERMAN

Ever since Edwin H. Sutherland developed his concept of the "behavior system," sociologists have theorized about the subject of deviant subcultures. They have also studied the varieties of subcultures among such deviant groups as addicts, bikers, crooks, drunks, gays, juvenile gangs, lesbians, pickpockets, and prisoners. Unstudied, however, until very recently were ex–psychiatric patients.

Nancy J. Herman, in her study of three distinct ex–psychiatric patient subcultures, specifies the social conditions for their emergence, and then goes on to describe the characteristics of these subcultures in some detail. The shift from hospital to community treatment concentrated a large number of chronic ex–mental patients in certain sections of large cities. "Mentals" began talking with one another only to find out that they all faced common problems of living, that they "were all in the same boat." In a very short period of time, they devised collective solutions to their common problems of loneliness, poverty, alienation, stigma, and just "getting by."

In response to society's disapproval and harassment, deviants usually band together with others in the same plight. Beyond the ties of similar interests and views…deviants find that establishing fairly stable relationships with other deviants does much to ease procurement and coping problems and to provide a more stable and reliable source of direct support and interaction. In these indirect ways, society's condemnation "creates" the deviant subculture. (Simmons, 1969:88)

INTRODUCTION

This sociological study on subcultures of chronic ex–mental patients was stimulated by the observation that a wealth of sociological research has been conducted on such various deviant subcultures as: delinquent gangs (Cohen, 1979; Demotte, 1984; Yablonsky, 1959), the drug subculture (Burr, 1984;

Johnson, 1980; Lipton and Johnson, 1980; Ray, 1961), the prison subculture (Webb, 1984), religious subcultures (Lofland, 1966; Melville, 1972; Shupe and Bromley, 1980), the skid row subculture (Rubington, 1968; Wallace, 1965), the motorcycle gang subculture (Hopper and Moore, 1993), and even the subculture of female impersonators (Tewksbury, 1995).

Despite the preponderance of sociological research on such diverse, deviant groups, and the concomitant theoretical approaches[1] used to explain such phenomena, no systematic research has centered on subcultures of ex–psychiatric patients.[2]

Since the advent of the movement toward deinstitutionalization and development of community psychiatry, some thirty years ago, there has been a marked shift *away* from the hospital *to* the community.[3] As a result of the movement toward deinstitutionalization, hundreds of thousands of persons once institutionalized for long periods of time in mental hospitals in the United States, Canada, and Great Britain, have been released into the community. Moreover, with this shift in policy and treatment of the mentally ill, newly diagnosed or defined psychiatric patients

This is an expanded and updated version of Nancy J. Herman, "'Mixed Nutters' and 'Looney Tuners': The Emergence, Development, Nature and Functions of Two Informal, Deviant Subcultures of Chronic, Ex-Psychiatric Patients," *Deviant Behavior,* 8, 235–258, 1987. Reprinted with permission of the author.

are no longer being sent directly to the government or state institutions, but rather, are being treated primarily on an out-patient basis in community mental health centers or are admitted on a short-term basis to psychiatric wards in general hospital facilities, and are only admitted to mental institutions or "tertiary care facilities" as a last resort.

Further, what research has been conducted on discharged or deinstitutionalized psychiatric patients has been done largely from a psychiatric, social work, or psychological perspective.[4] With the exception of a few studies (Cheadle et al., 1978; Dear et al., 1980; Estroff, 1981; Reynolds and Farberow, 1977), little sociological research has focused on the effects of deinstitutionalization from the perspectives of the ex-patients themselves. No published work has documented the origins, development, and functions of informal deviant subcultures of chronic[5] ex–psychiatric patients.

It is the purpose of this paper, then, to fill such a void. Specifically, it seeks to examine the effects of deinstitutionalization from the perspectives of chronic discharged psychiatric patients, individuals who are directly affected by this shift in treatment, housing, and policies. Adopting a symbolic interactionist perspective, this study seeks to discover the social meanings that the ex-patients define and determine to be important and real. Specifically, this paper examines the ex-patient subculture[6]—one major organizational adaptive response former chronic ex-patients develop and utilize to deal with their "deviantness"—the structural and interactional factors giving rise to this formation, its characteristic traits, and the various functions it serves for its members.

METHODOLOGY, SAMPLE AND SETTINGS

For the purposes of this study, data were collected from December 1981 to June 1984, and from November 1987 to April 1990 largely by means of participant observation and informal interviewing with one hundred and thirty-nine chronic ex–psychiatric patients living in three large cities in southern Ontario, Canada, and in central Michigan....

In the case of the Canadian cohort, as part of a larger, ongoing study, the researcher initially obtained a disproportionate, stratified random sample[7] of two hundred and eighty-five chronic and non-chronic ex–psychiatric patients living in eight communities in southern Ontario. Through semiformal and informal interviewing with the respondents, this researcher came upon, quite by accident,...of two informal ex-psychiatric patient subcultures, referred to here as the "Mixed Nutters" and "Looney Tuners."[8]

In terms of the Mixed Nutters, this cultural formation is comprised of forty-nine members (thirty-six males and thirteen females) living in rooming houses, boarding homes, and cheap hotels in the southwest section of a large metropolitan city of 2.5 million. Subjects ranged in age from twenty-one to forty-two, were predominantly from working-class backgrounds and were poorly educated, with a mean level of educational attainment being grade seven.

In terms of the Looney Tuners, this subculture is comprised of forty-eight members (twenty-six males and twenty-two females) living in boarding homes, rooming houses, in missions, or simply on the streets in the northern section of a smaller city of 300,000 in southern Ontario. Similar to the Mixed Nutters, the Looney Tuners were also poorly educated with a mean level of educational attainment being grade eight, were from working- and middle-class backgrounds, and ranged in age from twenty-two to forty-five. In terms of their "moral careers" as mental patients, the mean number of years that the Mixed Nutters and Looney Tuners were institutionalized was nine years. The mean number of occasions upon which such persons were institutionalized was seven.

The Daffy Duck subculture is an all-male group comprised of forty-two members. These individuals were living in downtown missions, rooming houses, flop hotels, on their own in one-room apartments, or simply on the streets of a large city of 250,000 in central Michigan. In terms of their psychiatric history, the mean number of years the Daffy Ducks were institutionalized was ten years and the mean number of occasions upon which they were hospitalized throughout their life was twelve. Unlike the Mixed Nutter and Looney Tuner groups, which were comprised almost exclusively by Caucasian members, the Daffy Ducks was made up of 75 percent African Americans, 15 percent Hispanics, and only 10 percent Caucasians.

THE EMERGENCE OF THREE INFORMAL EX–PSYCHIATRIC PATIENT SUBCULTURES

Early subcultural theorists (Gans, 1962; Gillin, 1955; Lewis, 1961) contended that deviant subcultures emerge largely in response to particular problems or social situations. Speaking on the subculture of poverty, Lewis (1961:27) argues that:

> Many of the traits of the subculture of poverty can be viewed as attempts at local solutions for problems not met by existing institutions and agencies because the people are not eligible for them, cannot afford them, or are suspicious of them.

In a similar vein, Gans (1962:248) argues:

> Each subculture is an organized set of related responses that has developed out of people's efforts to cope with the opportunities, incentives, and rewards, as well as the deprivations, prohibitions, and pressures which the natural environment and society—that complex of coexisting and competing subcultures—offer to them.

Reacting against this primary emphasis on *response* to the neglect of [the] secondary role of *interaction* as having importance for the development of subcultures, other theorists (Becker, 1963; Cohen, 1955; Hughes, 1961; Shibutani, 1955; and Wallace, 1965) proposed an alternative explanation that places equal importance on *both* factors for subcultural development. Wallace (1965:149), speaking on the emergence of the skid row subculture, for example, states:

> One effect of the self and community imposed isolation [of skid row persons] has been the emergence of skid row subculture. Skid rowers share similar problems of adjustment to their deviance and are in effective interaction with one another.

Cohen (1955), in his systematic attempt to develop a theory of subcultures, states that the following conditions are important in the development of this cultural form: (1) experiencing a problem or set of problems; (2) communicating such problems; (3) effectively interacting over an extended period of time with like others on the basis of such problems; and (4) developing solutions to these common problems.

In the case of the Mixed Nutters, Looney Tuners, and Daffy Ducks, the data suggest that these ex–psychiatric patient subcultures emerged in 1978, 1980, and 1987, respectively.[9] Prior to their formation, chronic ex–psychiatric patients were experiencing a number of post-hospital problems. These problems included: abandonment; the stigma of mental illness; physical, mental, and sexual exploitation; social isolation; poverty; and coping. Speaking on the problems of isolation and poverty, a Mixed Nutter states:

> You think it's bad in the hospital but on the outside it's a lot worse. You're all alone in the world, no one gives a fucking damn; you're trying to survive on a few measly bucks a month and most goes to the landlord.... People in this society care more about their pets, what's going on in South Africa or the Middle East.... America has really let us mentals down!

A Daffy Duck, addressing the problems of the stigma of mental illness and sexual exploitation, remarks:

> Mary [another patient] and I have a lot of problems on the outside.... The biggest ones center on people taking advantage of us sexually—I mean, the bosses of the boarding homes expect you to screw 'em. If you say no, they rough you up real bad and threaten to throw you out on the street— they also threaten to give you an OD of your meds. They have all the power—you have to do what they

want. But where can we go; no one wants to take in a mental—your friends and so-called family all treat you like you've got AIDS!

The three ex–psychiatric patient subcultures studied originated when the individuals began communicating with one another and realizing that they had a number of problems in common, they shared a common fate of being "in the same boat." Commenting on her discovery of others experiencing the same problems in the community, Sally says:

Nobody organized us or anything. We all just got together on a fluke. Each one of us, for a long time, thought we were the only ones going through the shit of being an ex-mental. But gradually we found out, by talking and bitching to a couple of others, that we were all in the "same leaky lifeboat" trying not to drown in the choppy sea of society.

Analysis of the data indicates that, subsequent to this initial communication of their problem(s) with others, individuals began interacting with one another over an extended period of time on the basis of their newly discovered shared fate:

It wasn't like we started a formal club but we would first get together 'cause we realized that we had this common bond—we all shared the same blight of humanity. We'd just get together once in a while and listen to other's problems and tribulations.... We gradually realized that we were benefiting and then decided to make it a twice a week thing at the Mall over in the Food Court Area.

Out of this semi-regular interaction with others of their own kind, chronic ex–psychiatric patients attempt to develop solutions to the various problems they are collectively experiencing. Three young male members of the Daffy Ducks, discussing their attempts to develop solutions to the problem of poverty, comment:

We first thought about pooling our money together and buying lotto tickets, but we realized that that would be a waste.... We moved to some thoughts about illegal activities.... B and E and even

thought about carjacking.... In the end, we decided that these ventures were too dangerous, that we didn't have any experience, so we decided on collecting cans to add to our income and doing odd jobs for people and sometimes even playing our guitar in the park.

In short then, the data reveal that certain interactional and structural factors contribute to the rise of the ex–mental patient subculture. This subcultural formation arises essentially in response to the various problems and negative post-hospital situations collectively faced by a number of chronic ex-patients, insofar as they are able to effectively communicate and interact with one another over an extended period of time. Given that, upon discharge, these ex–psychiatric patients are "placed" in rooming houses, boarding homes, and "approved homes" in specific geographical sections of the city, such concentrated placement in specific neighborhoods increases the probability of social interaction among ex-patients. When ex–psychiatric patients have the opportunity to interact with one another, they are likely to develop a subculture to deal with such specific problems as abandonment, poverty, sexual, physical and emotional exploitation, stigma, social isolation, and in general, with problems developing out of the discrepancies between their personal perceptions of mental illness and mental patients and the stereotypical perceptions held by society.

THE SOCIAL CHARACTERISTICS OF THE MIXED NUTTERS, LOONEY TUNERS, AND DAFFY DUCKS

As mentioned previously, chronic ex–psychiatric patients have one thing in common: their deviant attribute (and the problems associated with it). Such things give chronic ex-patients a sense of a common fate. It is from this feeling of a shared fate that the Mixed Nutters, Looney Tuners, and Daffy Ducks have developed subcultures consisting of: a set of perspectives or world-view about the nature of society, its members, and how to deal with each other, and a set of activities based on this world-view, some of which are specifically centered on providing solutions to the problems associated with the attribute of mental illness. These deviant subcultures possess four major characteristics to which attention will now turn.

BEHAVIORAL PATTERNS

The ex–mental patient subculture generally focuses its attention, interests, and activities around their deviant attribute and the problems associated with it. Specifically, the Mixed Nutters and Looney Tuners participate in three major activities referred to by the subjects as: (1) "hanging around"; (2) "shrink sessions"; and (3) "schooling." The data indicate that a major portion of the chronic ex-patients' day is usually spent at a specified location such as a park, parking lot, at the riverfront, shopping mall, street corner, donut shop, or hospital canteen:

> Most of us live at the mission, in a boarding home and a couple of us live in the streets. If you live in one of those places, they got strict rules and we're kicked out early in the day...which leaves a lot of time to "kill" before we can go back to eat or sleep.... So the guys and me meet up in the park and then we go to "our table" at the mall and we kill five or six hours.

In a similar vein, a member of the Mixed Nutters, discussing the activity of "hanging around," remarks:

> There's three, four, or sometimes even six of us that meet every day. It's not always the same crowd though. Each day, different faces show up at the Delicious Donut Shop.... It's our second home and that's why we do our hanging around there. We scrape up our money and drink coffee until we got no more left and Gus, the owner, "invites" us to leave.

In order to be allowed to "hang around" in such locations as donut shops or hospital canteens, it is a prerequisite that ex-patients purchase (and continue to purchase) food and/or drink. For those ex-patients unable to purchase items on their own, other group members make contributions, thus enabling them to remain with the others:

> "Chipping in" is the name of the game.... Everyone in the group knows [that]...you give what you got, you ante up. If you don't got nothin' this time, maybe you will put in double next time. The group will let you ride and pull up the slack 'cause they know that you will come through for them when they are short of cash.

The activity of "hanging around" or being in the company of other ex–psychiatric patients serves to combat feelings of alienation, social isolation, and fear experienced by such persons. As one middle-aged Looney Tuner put it:

> It makes me feel a million times better when I meet up with the guys; it really lifts me up mentally.... I don't feel so alone.... They're my brothers and they'd do anything for me. I don't have to be scared when I'm with them.

Similarly, a second chronic ex-patient adds:

> We're a tight network of buddies, more like family than friends, out to help each other any way we can. We can count on them any time.... We can also learn from each other—how to combat people being shitty to us, our anxiety about being alone and things like that.

Another activity (somewhat related to the first) in which chronic ex–psychiatric patients frequently engage are "shrink sessions." Shrink sessions, or informal self-help meetings, usually occur (in the case of the Mixed Nutters) at the hospital canteen where ex-patients frequent, at a drop-in center for discharged patients (in the case of the Looney Tuners), or at the mall (in the case of the Daffy Ducks). Such meetings vary in duration from half an hour up to four hours with members coming and going throughout. The data indicate that the sessions begin when an individual initiates the topic of conversation and petitions others for advice. During these sessions, members of the subculture complain about such problems as fear, anxiety, stress, the stigma of mental illness, depression, deteriorating psychiatric conditions, poor follow-up care by psychiatric professionals, and the negative side-effects of their maintenance medications. During these sessions, some air such problems while other ex-patient "experts" supportively respond. Speaking of post-hospital anxiety and stress in his life and the helpful suggestions proposed by the group, one chronic male remarks:

> When we sit down and start "shrinking" each other, I sometimes talk about how tense and nervous I get being out [discharged]. Everything is moving at such a fast pace that it freaks me out. There's too much stress for me.... When I talked about it to the other guys, it felt so good to let it all out, and the guys really helped me get a handle on it.... They really know about these things, because, after all, they've been through it themselves a hundred times before.

Another ex-patient speaking of airing, to the group, the problems he was experiencing with respect to his deteriorating mental condition, drug side-effects, and his condemnation of the type of psychiatric aftercare (or lack thereof), states:

> It's real shitty.... I feel that I'm getting sicker each day...but where is my social worker? She's supposed to be assigned to me but I haven't seen her in months. The drugs they got me are dozing me up— they make me so confused that I can't function— I'm like I'm moving in slow motion. The times that I've gone over the _____ Clinic [out-patient psychiatric facility], they tell me to get lost. Telling the group about these problems made me feel better, and they gave me some good advice on how to handle things.

These "shrink sessions," then, serve a threefold function for the ex–psychiatric patients: (1) disclosure of concerns and complaints in a cathartic fashion serves to alleviate a portion of the burden of their loads; (2) ex-patients are given social support and helpful suggestions to deal with various problems; and (3) they are presented with an ideology and positive self-image of ex–psychiatric patients that refute stereotypical

beliefs about mental patients held by conventional society, thereby elevating their self-esteem.

Just as chronic ex–psychiatric patients frequently engage in the activities of "hanging around" and "shrink sessions," so too do they participate in one other activity referred to by the subjects as "schooling." Schooling involves ex-patients teaching each other various methods for "making it on the outside" or how to capitalize[10] on their deviant identities. By making it on the outside, ex-patients, through informal interaction with other subcultural members, learn how to make the most of their deviant identities. They are taught such things as: where, how, and when they can pick up "quick cash," or "free eats," the art of begging, and where to get a "free place to crash." So, for example, neophytes entering the ex-patient subculture are taught that they can pick up "quick cash" by selling their "meds" and their bodies for money (not only where to sell these commodities, but for how much), and they are given a set of rationalizations justifying such actions:

> When I first started hanging around with those guys, they showed me the ropes. I was pretty green about things, and I never had any money. But they told me that if I ran short of bucks, I could pick up an extra twenty or fifty by selling my meds. They even pointed out this group of young boys who would be willing to buy the stuff.

Margo, a Mixed Nutter, adds:

> We're not prosties, we only sell ourselves when it's absolutely necessary. We don't turn tricks. It's only done when it's a matter of life and death, like getting some cash for food or to pay rent or for a place to sleep. Mavis and Flo was the ones who turned me on to the idea. They'd been doing it for five years. It's a way to survive out here.

Moreover, in the context of the ex-patient subculture, members learn which religious and social agencies give "hand-outs"—where such agencies are located, how much they may give, and how to approach them:

You learn from your friends how to go about getting what you want and which agencies is good for it, which want you to sign your life away, which want to "religicize" you or sign away your soul. These guys sure pointed me in the right direction to help me get what I need with no hassle.

Another chronic ex-patient, discussing the skills and knowledge about various agencies she acquired through interaction with others in the subculture, remarks:

If it wasn't for my friends, I would be out in the cold. I wouldn't know nothing about where to get a hand-out when I really needed it. They took me by the hand when I met them and pointed out each and every one of them in the area, and not only that, they teached me to dress poorly, muss up my hair and cry a lot when I went to them.

Further, ex-patients learn through participation in their subculture which agencies, missions, and restaurants provide such things as free food, clothing, and shelter:

At first, I didn't know nothing. But my friends taught me where I could get free food whenever I wanted it, like down at the Lakeside Mission. You gotta put up with their praying and singing, but that's O.K. They also showed me where to go to this church if I needed new threads and some lady will give you whatever you want.

Speaking on his major source of free food from one fast-food restaurant, a middle-aged male says:

Moe was the one who wised me up about the free eats from Burger Town. A couple of times the manager caught us snatching leftovers from the garbage and we told him how hungry we were and really laid it on thick to him. He felt sorry for us, I guess, so he told me to come back near closing and we get a lot of the hamburgers and fries that they don't sell.

Through participation in such groups as the Mixed Nutters, Looney Tuners, and Daffy Ducks, individuals not only learn the "ins and outs" of the system and how to use it to their advantage but also learn how to capitalize on their deviant identities by becoming "professional crazies":

Look, if you've got the curse of psychosis or manic depression, or even schizophrenia, I've learned that you might as well make the most of it.... I mean, you take advantage of what you've got.... So we often go right into the downtown area and beg for money. We tell 'em a sad tale—that we're mentally ill and need money for our treatment. Sometimes we hit the jackpot—like from decked-out businessmen or old ladies, especially if the cops don't chase us away.

A second ex-patient, speaking on the capitalization of his deviant identity, says:

There are places where a mental can make a killing.... Like standing outside of St. Mark's right after Sunday services. People are usually in a charitable mood and if you approach them with the proper spiel about being a sick mental person, they will usually fork over a few bucks.

In short then, these three behavioral patterns serve to combat the social isolation ex-patients are experiencing, provide a therapeutic function, enhance their self-esteem, provide pragmatic solutions to various problems, and equip ex-patients with important knowledge and skills for "making it on the outside."

ARGOT

The Mixed Nutters, Looney Tuners, and Daffy Ducks communicate with their respective members by means of an argot, a distinctive vocabulary that demarcates not only outsiders from insiders but also neophytes from veterans. Speaking on the role of argot, one Mixed Nutter remarks:

Our way of rapping with each other is real cool. You can be in any public place and talking about whatever and nobody eavesdropping has a clue about what the hell you're saying.

In a similar vein, a member of the Daffy Ducks adds:

It's them against us. Having a special language all our own protects us.... You can clearly tell who is one of us and who isn't. You can test them by using a few code words. If they don't understand you, they ain't part of the group and are not to be trusted.

Moreover, their argot prescribes symbols for cognition and communication regarding matters of interest to chronic ex–psychiatric patients. So, for example, "shaking it" refers to the act of sexual solicitation; "plucking the rooster" refers to receiving hand-outs from clergy or social agency members; "going to a banquet" refers to individuals discovering a place giving out large amounts of free food; and "doing the groceries" refers to shoplifting various foodstuffs.

In an effort to maintain some sense of order and stability, all social groups make evaluations of its members. So, for example, in the case of the Looney Tuners, at certain times, usually when "hanging around," members will talk about "cheapers," those ex-patients who violated the norm of reciprocity. So, too, do they speak about "dozers," those individuals who were caught committing a deviant act. The Mixed Nutters also refer to members being "turncoats" or "fruitcakes." The former term refers to those ex-patients who have violated norms of trust and confidentiality. The latter term refers to individuals with little common sense. Moreover, they use the terms "oldies" and "shit-kid" to make [a] distinction between veterans and novices.

In their demarcation between themselves and outsiders, the Daffy Ducks use such terms as the "pigs" or "terminators," while the Mixed Nutters refer to outsiders as "Nazis"—individuals who reject or stigmatize them; the term "moron" refers to unacceptable ex-patients who do not meet the standards for acceptance into the group. Similarly, the Looney Tuners use such terms as "head shrinkers" and "cop patrols" to refer to psychiatric professionals and social workers, respectively.

BOUNDARIES

Similar to other subcultural groups such as the nudist (Weinberg, 1966) and motorcycle gang (Hopper and Moore, 1993) subcultures, which have territorial boundaries, the data indicate that the ex–psychiatric patient subcultures also have sharply defined territorial boundaries, within which they carry out their daily rounds. In the case of the Looney Tuners, members live and carry out their daily activities in a territorial area of approximately 2.5 to 3.0 square miles. This territory contains a mixture of residential housing and commercial and service-oriented properties. The Mixed Nutters live and carry out their activities in a somewhat larger territorial area of approximately 3.0 to 4.0 square miles. This territory contains a mixture of commercial and service-oriented properties, residential housing, and some light industries. The Daffy Ducks, by contrast, have a still larger territorial area of approximately 5.5 square miles, consisting of commercial and service-oriented industries/businesses, low-rent housing, and many abandoned buildings.

During the five years this researcher studied these three groups, individuals rarely stepped outside their respective territories. The territories of these three subcultures essentially provide expatients with everything they need to "get by on." Remaining inside imaginary boundaries brings the world down to size and makes life more manageable for the ex-patients. The individuals come to know every inch of their territory—a knowledge that gives them a sense of security:

This is my world cut down to size. The guys and me know everything about it and everybody living there. There are no real surprises for me. You get to know it like the back of you hand, inside out.

IDEOLOGY

Similar to other deviant subcultures, the ex-psychiatric subcultures develop an ideology: a perspective on themselves and on their relations with other societal members, a set of ideas repudiating conventional, stereotypical attitudes about their deviant attribute, and a set of justifications for engaging in deviant/illegal activities.

The ideology of the Mixed Nutters, Looney Tuners, and Daffy Ducks provides their members with a set of ideas about the mentally ill, about "normals" in society, and about the relations between the two groups. Normals are generally perceived as evil, cruel, untrustworthy, uncaring, dangerous, and unknowledgeable about mental illness, an ideology prescribing avoidance on the part of ex-patients. As one member of the Daffy Ducks puts it:

> It's terrible to be mentally ill. The world doesn't care one iota about us. We're lumped in with the homeless, serial killers, and druggies. Society is so mean to us—they're not kind and caring; they won't give us a break. They just want us to fall down and slip between one of those cracks and disappear from sight.

Moreover, the ideology of these ex–psychiatric patient subcultures refutes stereotypical perceptions about mental patients and mental illness generally held by conventional society. Members are provided with a set of excuses for their illnesses mitigating their blameworthiness,[11] thereby enabling ex-patients to redefine themselves in a more positive, although still deviant, light. According to one male Looney Tuner:

> The group taught me that I'm not to blame for my illness. It was something genetic and I couldn't stop it. I am not responsible, therefore, I should not be ashamed or feel bad.

Similarly, a Mixed Nutter remarks:

> My friend told me that I wasn't responsible for my situation. How could I be? It's not my own fault.... They helped me to see that my sickness was caused by others, and that's what I try to convince other [ex-patients] of. It makes them feel less guilt and really picks them up mentally.

Just as the ideology of the subculture provides ex-patients with ideas about normal others and a set of excuses holding others accountable for their deviant attribute, so, too, does it function in one final respect: specifically, it provides members with a set of justifications for carrying out deviant/illegal acts. This self-justifying rationale then, furnishes ex-patients with "sound" reasons for engaging in such activities as prostitution, selling their medication, and shoplifting:

> We're not doing anything that's really wrong. We don't murder or rob or things like that. We only take a few groceries once in a while from the A & P store. And we only do that when it's absolutely necessary. Other people who have lots of money do it all the time, and they take things much bigger than we do. We do it for medical reasons—our health, but they just do it for greed.

In a similar vein, another ex-patient discussing her rationale for engaging in prostitution, says:

> The world is against us patients and we got to get by somehow. And we can't make ends meet on a disability pension. The boarding home takes most of the monthly cheque and we're only left with a few bucks for the whole month. There is nothing wrong with what we do. Most patients do it to survive. So, what the hell, we "work under the covers" once in a while. It's not that we do it for pleasure, it's necessary. No one will give me a "normal" job because of my sickness, so this is my only option. You look down the big streets and avenues and see lots of girls doing it anyway. It's just another way to make a buck!

In short then, the chronic ex-patients in this study develop and utilize an ideology: a set of ideas that suit their own interests, justify their post-hospital actions, and hold others accountable for their mental illness. Moreover, this ideology contains a set of ideas and judgments about others in society and provides ex-patients with specific prescriptions for action.

SUMMARY AND DISCUSSION

The results of this study have indicated that this subcultural formation emerged when ex-patients began experiencing a number of problems (created by the deinstitutionalization of mental health services and societal attitudes toward the mentally ill), communicating such problems to other discharged chronic ex-patients, subsequently interacting with like others on the basis of their problems, and attempting to provide solutions to their difficulties. Ex–psychiatric patient subcultures were characterized by crystallized patterns of behavior centered around their social plights, a set of clearly defined norms and values, and an ideology: a set of ideas developed to suit their own interests and justify their actions.

Analysis of the data revealed that the ex–psychiatric patient subcultures provided a number of functions for their members. First, through subcultural participation, ex-patients established social relationships with understanding others—a relationship that was supportive in nature and served to combat feelings of fear and social isolation. Second, group activities, in particular "shrink sessions," allowed members to discuss problems of anxiety, stress, depression, stigma, and the like, and ask fellow group members for advice on how to deal with such problems. Through such "shrink sessions" ex-patients were able to disclose various concerns and dilemmas in a cathartic fashion; by so doing, they were able to alleviate a portion of the burden of their loads, thereby elevating their self-esteem. Moreover, in the context of their daily interactions, in general, and during "shrink sessions" specifically, fellow members provided "expert advice" and practical strategies for mitigating the stigma potential of mental illness on their daily rounds. Given that others in the subculture had experienced the stigma of mental illness on numerous occasions during the post-patient phase of their careers, such persons had indeed become "expert managers"— they had a great deal of advice on the "do's and don'ts" of avoiding stigma associated with their discreditable attribute. In the context of this subcultural formation, various stigma management strategies were imparted upon new charges. Third, in the context of participating in the ex–mental patient subcultures, members were provided with an ideology, a set of justifications or "sound" rationales about their deviant attribute. The ideology of the Mixed Nutters, Looney Tuners, and Daffy Ducks provided ex-patients with a set of rationalizations which mitigated their blameworthiness; instead, blame was placed upon various others, ranging

from spouses, children, teachers, parents, to society, in general. By placing blame on others for their discreditable attribute, this enables ex-patients to redefine themselves in a more positive, although still deviant, light. Further, the ideology that normals were untrustworthy, callous, and uneducated about mental illness...prescribed "avoidance of normals" to members of the subculture. Also, the ideology of the ex-patient subcultures furnished members with a self-justifying rationale for engaging in various deviant/illegal activities. Ex-patients, through subcultural participation, were provided with a set of "sound" reasons for engaging in such activities as selling drugs, shoplifting, and prostitution, enabling them to maintain positive self-images. A final function of the ex–psychiatric patient subcultures was that they provided members with various practical stratagems for "making formal sense," how to capitalize on their deviant identities, specifically, by selling their bodies, selling their medication, locations where to get "free eats" or a "free place to crash." In short, in the context of this subcultural form, individuals were taught how to make the most of their attributes by becoming "professional crazies."

This is not to say, however, that ex–psychiatric patients experienced only positive consequences from participation in the subcultures. In fact, on a number of occasions the author observed situations of conflict surrounding authority, verbal abuse among members, stolen wallets, tobacco, cigarettes, and various articles of clothing. However, the positive consequences of subcultural participation far outweighed the negative effects:

> Overall, I think that this group has help[ed] me tremendously, but society is also threatened by people that group themselves together. This is what happened in our area. The neighborhood got up in arms, spit on us as we walked by, the kids threw garbage at us, and one of our guys, Frank, was found beaten to death in the alley.... That was a grim message that we weren't wanted.

According to the ideology behind the movement toward deinstitutionalization of mental health services, individuals would be released or discharged from the institution. However, "stone walls do not a prison make, nor iron bars a cage." Many chronic ex–psychiatric patients, even though discharged, remain imprisoned in a metaphorical sense with their guards and wardens being the family, friends, potential employers, and society in general who are unable to tolerate mental illness. The term, "deinstitutionalization" is defined by chronic ex-patients as a form of "social segregation and reinstitutionalization in *certain* areas in the community." Such persons are *in* but not *of* the community. Ex-patients, for the most part, are confined in "institutions without walls, bars or locks," living lives of frustration, disappointment, fear, exploitation, and poverty. In response to their undesirable social situations, these persons (similar to other stigmatized deviants in society) have developed and entered into deviant subcultures or "informal self-help groups"—an "expressive group exist[ing] primarily to furnish activities for members" (Gordon and Babchuk, 1959:25), including evading stigma.

NOTES

1. See Cloward and Ohlin (1964); Cohen (1955); Gordon (1964); Kitsuse and Dietrick (1959); Matza (1964); Sykes and Matza (1957); Wallace (1965); and Wolfgang and Ferracuti (1967).
2. See Anspach (1979) and Landy and Singer (1961) for discussions of *formal* social organizations for ex–mental patients.
3. For detailed discussions concerning the origins and development of the movement toward deinstitutionalization of psychiatric services, consult: Bassuk and Gerson (1978); Bellak (1964); Brown (1979); Chu and Trotter (1974); Herman (1986); Leifer (1967); Ralph (1980); and Scull (1977).
4. For an extensive review of the body of literature which examines the ideological foundations, background philosophies, treatment programs, the medical and psychological consequences of such treatments, and the aftercare programs for discharged patients, the reader may consult Herman (1986).

5. For the purposes of this study, the term "chronic" is defined *not* in diagnostic terms, i.e., "chronic schizophrenic"; rather it is defined in terms of duration, continuity, and frequency of hospitalizations. Specifically, chronicity refers to those individuals institutionalized on a continual basis, or those institutionalized on five or more occasions.
6. Following Rubington (1982), the concept of deviant subculture is defined in this paper as: "the shared ways of thinking, feeling, and acting that members of a deviant group have developed for engaging in deviant behavior, organizing relations among themselves, and defending themselves against social punishment."
7. For specific details concerning the sample, consult Herman (1986).
8. The names used here to refer to the three subcultures are pseudonyms that closely approximate the actual names that the groups call themselves.
9. In contrast to the Mixed Nutters, who had been in existence for three years prior to the beginning of this research project, the researcher was able to directly follow the development of the Looney Tuners and Daffy Ducks shortly following their inception.
10. See Goffman (1963) and Scott (1969) for related discussions on the capitalization of the visually impaired.
11. See Sykes and Matza (1957) for a discussion of similar neutralizing techniques employed by juvenile delinquents.

REFERENCES

Anspach, Renee. 1979. "From Stigma to Identity Politics: Political Activism among the Physically Disabled and Former Mental Patients." *Social Science and Medicine* 13A: 765–773.

Bassuk, Ellen L., and Samuel Gerson. 1978. "Deinstitutionalization and Mental Health Services." *Scientific American* 238: 46–53.

Becker, Howard S. 1963. *Outsiders: Studies in the Sociology of Deviance.* New York: Free Press.

Bellak, Leopold. 1964. "Community Psychiatry: The Third Psychiatric Revolution." In L. Bellak (ed.), *Handbook of Community Psychiatry and Community Mental Health.* New York: Grune and Stratton.

Brown, Philip. 1979. "The Transfer to Care: U.S. Mental Health Policy since World War II." *International Journal of Health Services* 9: 645–662.

Burr, Angela. 1984. "The Illicit Non-Pharmaceutical Heroin Market and Drug Scene in Kensington Market." *British Journal of Addiction* 79 (3): 337–343.

Cheadle, A. J., H. Freeman, and J. Korer. 1978. "Chronic Schizophrenics in the Community." *British Journal of Psychiatry* 132: 221–227.

Chu, F. D., and S. Trotter. 1974. *The Madness Establishment: Ralph Nader's Study Group Report on the National Institute of Mental Health.* New York: Grossman.

Cloward, R. A., and L. E. Ohlin. 1964. *Delinquency and Opportunity.* New York: Free Press.

Cohen, Albert. 1955. *Delinquent Boys.* Glencoe, Illinois: Free Press.

Cohen, Jere. 1979. "High-School Subcultures and the Adult World." *Adolescence* 14 (55): 491–502.

Dear, Michael, L. Bayne, G. Boyd, E. Callaghan, and E. Goldstein. 1980. *Coping in the Community: The Needs of Ex-Psychiatric Patients.* Mental Health Hamilton Project.

Demotte, Charles. 1984. "Conflicting Worlds of Meaning: Juvenile Delinquency in 19th Century Manchester." *Deviant Behavior* 5: 193–215.

Estroff, Sue E. 1981. *Making It Crazy: An Ethnography of Psychiatric Clients in an American Community."* Berkeley: University of California Press.

Gans, Herbert. 1962. *The Urban Villagers.* New York: Free Press.

Gillin, John. 1955. "National and Regional Cultural Values in the United States." *Social Forces* (Dec.): 110–115.

Goffman, Erving. 1963. *Stigma.* Englewood Cliffs, New Jersey: Prentice-Hall.

Gordon, C. Wayne, and Nicholas Babchuk. 1959. "A Typology of Voluntary Associations." *American Sociological Review* 24 (February): 22–29.

Gordon, Milton M. 1964. *Assimilation in American Life.* London: Oxford University Press.

Herman, Nancy J. 1986. "Crazies in the Community: An Ethnographic Study of Ex–Psychiatric Clients in Canadian Society." Unpublished Ph.D. dissertation, McMaster University, Hamilton, Ontario, Canada.

Hopper, Columbus, and J. Moore. 1993. "Women in Outlaw Motorcycle Gangs." Pp. 389–400 in Patricia A. Adler and Peter Adler, *Constructions of Deviance.* Belmont, California: Wadsworth.

Hughes, Everett Cherington. 1961. *Students' Culture and Perspectives: Lectures on Medical and General Ed-*

ucation. Lawrence, Kansas: University of Kansas Law School.

Johnson, Bruce. 1980. "Towards a Theory of Drug Subculture." Paper presented at the annual meetings of the Society for the Study of Social Problems.

Kitsuse, J. I., and D. C. Dietrick. 1959. "Delinquent Boys: A Critique." *American Sociological Review* 24: 213–215.

Landy, David, and Sara Singer. 1961. "The Social Organization and Culture of a Club for Former Mental Patients." *Human Relations* 14: 31–40.

Leifer, Rod. 1967. "Community Psychiatry and Social Power." *Social Problems* 14: 16–22.

Lewis, Oscar. 1961. *The Children of Sanchez.* New York: Vintage Books.

Lipton, D. S., and B. D. Johnson. 1980. "Control at the Subcultural Interface: Heroin vs. Methadone." Paper presented at the annual meetings of the Society for the Study of Social Problems.

Lofland, John. 1966. *Doomsday Cult.* Englewood Cliffs, New Jersey: Prentice-Hall.

Matza, David. 1964. *Delinquency and Drift.* New York: Wiley.

Melville, K. 1972. *Communes in the Counter Culture.* New York: Morrow.

Ralph, Diana. 1980. "Where Did Community Psychiatry Come From? The Labour Theory of Community Psychiatry." Mimeo. University of Regina, Saskatchewan, Canada.

Ray, Marsh B. 1961. "Abstinence Cycles and Heroin Addicts." *Social Problems* 9: 132–140.

Reynolds, David K., and Norman Farberow. 1977. *Endangered Hope: Experiences in Psychiatric Aftercare Facilities.* Berkeley: University of California Press.

Rubington, Earl. 1968. "The Bottle Gang." *Quarterly Journal of Studies on Alcohol* 29: 943–955.

———. 1982. "Deviant Subcultures." In M. Michael Rosenberg, R. Stebbins, and A. Turowetz (eds.), *The Sociology of Deviance.* New York: St. Martin's, pp. 42–70.

Scott, Robert. 1969. *The Making of Blind Men: A Study of Adult Socialization.* New York: Russell Sage Foundation.

Scull, Andrew. 1977. *Decarceration: Community Treatment and the Deviant: A Radical View.* Englewood Cliffs, New Jersey: Prentice-Hall.

Shibutani, Tamotsu. 1955. "Reference Groups as Perspectives." *American Journal of Sociology* (May): 565–566.

Shupe, Anson, and David Bromley. 1980. "Some Continuities in American Religion: Witches, Moonies, and Accusations of Evil." In Thomas Robbins and Dick Anthony (eds.), *God We Trust: New Patterns of American Religious Pluralism.* New Brunswick, New Jersey: Transaction.

Simmons, J. L. 1969. *Deviants.* Berkeley: The Glendessary Press.

Sykes, G. M., and D. Matza. 1957. "Techniques of Neutralization: A Theory of Delinquency." *American Sociological Review* 22: 124–136.

Tewksbury, Richard. 1995. "Constructing Women and Their World: The Subculture of Female Impersonation." In Nancy J. Herman (ed.), *Creating Deviance.* Dix Hills, New York: General Hall.

Wallace, Samuel E. 1965. *Skid Row as a Way of Life.* New York: Harper Torchbook.

Webb, Gary. 1984. "The Inmate Subculture: A Case Study." Paper presented at the Western Social Science Association Meetings.

Weinberg, Martin S. 1966. "Becoming a Nudist." *Psychiatry: Journal for the Study of Interpersonal Processes* 29 (1): 15–24.

Wolfgang, Marvin, and Franco Ferracuti. 1967. *The Subculture of Violence.* London: Tavistock.

Yablonsky, Lewis. 1959. "The Delinquent Gang as a Near Group." *Social Problems* 7 (2): 108–117.

CHAPTER 9

GETTING INTO DEVIANT GROUPS

Becoming a Nudist

MARTIN S. WEINBERG

Sociologists focus considerable attention on experiences people have in groups. One of their major concerns is establishing the influence of group membership on conduct. But people must first become members of a particular group. Since the costs of membership in deviant groups may seem to outweigh the benefits, questions arise as to what might attract people to deviant groups, what the circumstances are under which they have their initial experiences in such groups, and under what conditions and at what costs they continue their involvement.

 Martin S. Weinberg asks, Why do people go to a nudist camp for the very first time? How do they decide to continue their association with people who are nude in the company of others? His work suggests a set of generalizations that help to account for both initial entry into other deviant groups and continued affiliation after the initial experience. Initial association with a deviant group quickly dissipates anxiety and replaces it with the rewards of fellowship. Fellowship strengthens the bonds to unconventionality. At the same time, it weakens social ties to certain members of the conventional world, in turn reinforcing the ties to the unconventional group.

In order to better understand deviant lifestyles and the meanings they have for those engaged in them, it is often useful to conceptualize a lifestyle as a career, consisting of various stages. We can then study the interpersonal processes that draw and sustain people at each of these various stages. In this way, we can appreciate the motivations, perceptions, and experiences that characterize involvement in that way of life at various points in

time—e.g., these may differ for novices, "veterans," etc.

 Using such a career model, this paper deals with the interpersonal processes and phases involved in nudist camp membership. Specifically, it deals with the processes by which people come to contemplate a visit to a nudist camp, attend for the first time, and then continue attending over a period of time. The data come from three sources— 101 interviews with nudists in the Chicago area; two successive summers of participant observation in nudist camps; and 617 mailed questionnaires completed by nudists located throughout the United States and Canada.[1]

Reprinted by special permission of The William Alanson White Psychiatric Foundation, Inc., from *Psychiatry: Journal for the Study of Interpersonal Processes,* Vol. 29, No. 1 (February 1966), pp. 15–24. Copyright 1966 by The William Alanson White Psychiatric Foundation, Inc.

PRENUDIST ATTITUDES TOWARD NUDISM

Most people seldom give much thought to the subject of nudism.[2] Responses in the interviews indicated that nudism is not a prominent object of thought even for many persons who will later become nudists. Thus when nudist members were asked what they had thought of nudism before visiting a camp, many stated that they had never really given it any thought. Until their initial experience, the interviewees' conceptions of nudism had been vague stereotypes, much like those held by the general public. In the words of a now active nudist:

> I never gave it too much thought. I thought it was a cult—a nut-eating, berry-chewing bunch of vegetarians, doing calisthenics all day, a gymno-physical society. I thought they were carrying health to an extreme, being egomaniacs about their body.

Many of those who had thought about the subject conceived of nudists' camps as more exclusive, luxurious, and expensive than they actually are. Others had different conceptions:

> I'm afraid I had the prevailing notion that they were undignified, untidy places populated (a) by the very poor, and (b) by languishing bleached blonds, and (c) by greasy, leering bachelors.

Table 9.1 sums up the attitudes that nudists reported themselves to have taken before their affiliation.

THE INITIAL INTEREST IN NUDISM

If prenudist attitudes are of the nature indicated by Table 9.1, how does one become interested enough to make a first visit to a nudist camp? As shown in Table 9.2, the highest percentage of men mentioned magazines as the source of their interest, and the next largest source was other persons (exclusive of parents or parents-in-law). For women, the pattern was different; the highest percentage were first informed about nudism by their husbands. In 78 percent of the families, the husband had been more interested in visiting a camp.

TABLE 9.1 Prenudist Attitudes Toward Nudism*

ATTITUDE	PERCENTAGE OF INTERVIEWEES
Positive	35
Live and let live	16
Negative	19
Very negative	1
Does not know	29

*For coding purposes, "positive" was defined as a desire to participate in nudism or to become a nudist. "Live and let live" included those who did not desire participation in nudism, but did not think ill of those who did participate; however, some of these respondents would have imposed social distance from nudists, and some would not.

In all other cases both spouses had equally wanted to go. There were no cases in which the wife had wanted to go more than the husband.

The fact that the overwhelming majority of women became interested in nudism through their relationships with other people, rather than through the mass media which played such an important part with men, was reflected in the finding that interpersonal trust had to be sustained in order to evoke the women's interest.[3] This was indicated in the content of many interviews. The interviews also indicated that commonsense justifications and "derivations"[4] were important in overcoming the women's anxieties.

TABLE 9.2 Source of Initial Interest in Nudism

SOURCE	MALE	FEMALE
Magazines	47%	14%
Movies	6	6
Newspapers	6	0
Spouse	0	47
Parents or parents-in-law	2	8
Other person	31	23
Medical advice from physician	0	2
Other source	8	0

The following quotation is from an interview with a woman who became interested in nudism after being informed about it by a male friend. Here she was describing what her feelings would have been prior to that time. (In this quotation, as in others in this paper, Q is used to signify a neutral probe by the interviewer that follows the course of the last reply—such as "Could you tell me some more about that?" or "How's that?" or "What do you mean?" Other questions by the interviewer are given in full.)

> *…[Whether or not I would go to a nudist camp would] depend on who asked me. If a friend, I probably would have gone along with it…. [Q] If an acquaintance, I wouldn't have been interested. [Q] I don't know, I think it would depend on who was asking me to go. [Q] If it was someone you liked or had confidence in, you'd go along with it. If you didn't think they were morally upright you probably wouldn't have anything to do with it.*

A man described how he had persuaded his wife to become interested in nudism:

> *I expected difficulty with my wife. I presented it to her in a wholesome manner. [Q] I had to convince her it was a wholesome thing, and that the people there were sincere…. [Q] That they were sincere in efforts to sunbathe together and had only good purposes in mind when they did that. [Q] All the things that nudism stands for: a healthy body and a cleansed mind by killing sex curiosities.*

The anxieties that enter into the anticipation of public nudity were described in the following interview excerpts:

> *I was nervous…. [Q] It's different. It's not a daily practice…. I'm heavy, that added to the nervousness.*

> *They said they were ashamed of their builds. They think everyone there is perfection. [Q] They think everyone will look at them.*

> *He [a friend] said he'd never go, but that he could understand it. He saw nothing wrong in it. [Q] He said he wouldn't want other men looking at his wife.*

Even though they had enough confidence to make the decision to visit a camp, the respondents did not necessarily anticipate becoming nudists themselves. For many the first trip was merely a joke, a lark, or a new experience, and the main motivation was curiosity. They visited the camp as one might make a trip to the zoo, to see what it was like and what kind of characters would belong to such a group. There was also curiosity, on the part of many of the respondents, about seeing nude members of the opposite sex.

> *The original thought was that we were going to see a bunch of nuts. It was a joke going out there.*

> *I thought they must be a little nutty. Eccentric. I didn't think there'd be so many normal people…. [Q] I felt that people that are nudists are a little bohemian or strange. [Q] I don't feel that way now. I thought we'd be the only sane people there. I thought it was kind of an adventure…. [Q] I like feeling I'm doing something unusual that no one knows about. It's a big secret…. [Q] The novelty, the excitement of driving up in the car; no one knew we were going….*

Table 9.3 presents the motivations given by interviewees for their first trip to a nudist camp.

TABLE 9.3 Motivations for the First Visit to a Nudist Camp

MOTIVATION	MALE	FEMALE
Curiosity over what it was like	33%	25%
Sexual curiosity	16	2
To satisfy spouse or relative	2	38
Combination of curiosity and to satisfy spouse	0	13
For relaxation	2	4
For health	12	6
To sunbathe	8	2
To make friends	6	0
Other	21	10

THE FIRST VISIT

The first trip to camp was frequently accompanied by extreme nervousness. Part of this might be attributed simply to the experience of entering a new group. The visitors did not know the patterns common to the group, and they were uncertain about their acceptance by group members. For example, a nudist said, referring to his participation in a nudist camp in which he was not well known:

> I guess I'm a little nervous when I get there, 'cause I'm not recognized as a member of the group.[5]

But, in the instance of a first visit to a nudist camp, this anxiety on entering a new group was considerably heightened by the unknown nature of the experience that lay ahead. Mead, in his discussion of the "social psychology of the act," has described how people, in planning an action, imaginatively rehearse it and its anticipated consequences.[6] The nudist camp, however, presents a totally unfamiliar situation; the person planning a visit has no past of similar situations, and usually no one has effectively described the situation to him in advance. This gap in effective imagination produces apprehension, anxiety, and nervousness.

> [On the trip up] I was very nervous. [Q] Because the idea was foreign. [Q]...The unknown factor. Just seeing a lot of people without clothes on is an unusual situation. Different or new experiences make one nervous.

> You're nervous and apprehensive. You don't know what to expect.... I was very nervous.... I thought of everything under the sun.... I didn't know what to expect.

> I felt a little inferior at first, because I had no knowledge of nudist camps.... I started to enjoy myself, but I couldn't quite feel comfortable. [Q] In the nude. In front of a lot of people. A lack of confidence, self-confidence. [Q] By not having a complete knowledge. I really didn't know what to expect.

> I was afraid of the unknown. I didn't know what to expect. If we had known nudists, I wouldn't have had those fears.

In most instances, the initial nervousness dissipated soon after the newcomer's arrival. Forty-six percent of the interviewees said that they were not nervous at all after arriving at camp. An additional 31 percent felt at ease in less than three hours. Thus most visitors adjusted rapidly to the nudist way of life. Seventy-one percent of those interviewed reported that *no* major adjustment was necessary. Sixteen percent of the residual group reported that undressing for the first time, or becoming used to being nude, was the only adjustment. Of these people who had to adjust, only 15 percent found the adjustment to be difficult.

> I really was afraid and shy and I didn't feel too well. We had discussed going, but when the time came to go I couldn't sleep that night.... Once we got nude then everything just seemed to come natural. I was surprised at how at ease I felt.

A variety of other response patterns, which I shall not discuss in detail, were characteristic of the initial visit. For example, one pattern related to the visitor's socioeconomic position.[7] Because facilities in many camps are relatively primitive, those used to more comfortable circumstances were likely to be disappointed. One professional man said:

> I was disappointed to see it was as rustic and unkempt as it was.... If people wore clothes and nothing else changed it would be a fourth-class resort. [Q] Everything there is shabby and not well cared for.

THE ADOPTION OF NUDISM AS A WAY OF LIFE

COACHING AND SOCIAL VALIDATION

The newcomers to camps received no formal indoctrination in the nudist perspective, but acquired it almost imperceptibly as the result of a subtle social process. Informal coaching, either prior to or after arrival, appears to have eased adjustment problems.[8]

My husband said the men are gentlemen. He told me I'd have fun, like play in the sun, play games, and swim.

She didn't want to undress.... [Q] I tried to talk to her and her husband did; she finally got convinced. [Q] I told her you feel better with them off, and that no one will pay any attention.

The consensus of 95 percent of the interviewees was that, as one of them put it, "Things run along very smoothly when you first become a nudist." Asked if they ever had any doubts that becoming a nudist was the right decision, once they had made up their minds, 77 percent reported that they had never had any doubts. Fourteen percent had doubts at the time of the interview. The following quotations illustrate the process of social validation that tends to quell doubts:[9]

I do and I don't [have doubts], because of my religion. [Q] Nobody knows about it, and I wonder about that. [Q] Whether it's the right thing. But as I read the pamphlets [nudist literature] I realize it's up to the individual. God made Adam and Eve and they had no clothes. You don't have to be ashamed of your body. Some are fat and some are thin, but it doesn't matter; it's your personality that matters. I don't know, if my minister found out, I'd defend it. We don't use bad language. Sometimes I wonder, but down underneath I think it's all right. We've just been taught to hide our bodies. Sometimes I wonder, but then I think what the pamphlets say. [Q: At what time do you have these doubts?] When I'm in church. [Q] Yes, when I get to thinking about religion. Not very often. Sometimes I just wonder. [Q: Do you ever have these doubts while at camp?] No, I forget about everything. I'm having too much fun. I remind myself that this is something good for the children. My children won't become Peeping Toms or sex maniacs.

[At first] I felt ridiculous. I thought all those people looked so funny. [Q: Why's that?] All your life you've seen people with their clothes on; now they all have them off. After a while, you feel ridiculous with your clothes on. [Q] I liked the people. They were all very nice. They came from nice families. It

couldn't just be something anyone would do, or just people from a lower class.

The nudist way of life becomes a different reality, a new world:

It seems like a different world from the world we live in every day. No washing, ironing, worries. You feel so free there. The people are friendly there, interested in each other. But not nosy. You can relax among them more easily than in the city.

And this new reality imposes a different meaning on the everyday life of the outside world:

My daughter told us today the boys and girls don't sit together at school, but it makes no difference to her. Several times they're out playing and the boys get excited when they see their panties. My children don't understand that. They have a different state of mind toward different sexes.

MOTIVES FOR BECOMING A NUDIST

Persons who became nudists—that is, became members of a camp and conceived of themselves as nudists—usually demonstrated an autonomy of motives,[10] in the sense that their motives for doing so differed from their motives for first visiting a camp. That is to say, participation in different stages of the "nudist career" were usually characterized by different sets of motives. Hence the curiosity that had often been the overriding motive for initial visits was satisfied, and the incentive for affiliating with a nudist camp was based on the person's experiences at the camp, experiences which may not have been anticipated before visiting the camp.[11] It should be noted, however, that the decision was sometimes prompted by the owner's insistence that visitors join if they wished to return. As Table 9.4 shows, there was a considerable change, after the first visit, in the pattern of male versus female desire to attend the camp.

The following quotations are illustrative of the autonomous motives of respondents for the first and subsequent visits:

[Q: What was your main reason for wanting to attend camp the first time?] Curiosity. [Q] To see

TABLE 9.4 Comparative Desires of Male and Female Members of Couples to Visit a Nudist Camp*

	MALE WANTED TO GO MORE	MALE AND FEMALE WANTED TO GO EQUALLY	FEMALE WANTED TO GO MORE
First visit	79%	21%	0%
Return visits	40	51	9

*Two unmarried couples are included in these data.

how people behave under such circumstances, and maybe also looking at the girls. [Q] Just that it's interesting to see girls in the nude. [Q: What is the main reason you continue to attend?] I found it very relaxing. [Q] It's more comfortable to swim without a wet suit, and not wearing clothes when it's real warm is more comfortable and relaxing.

[I went up the first time] to satisfy my husband. He wanted me to go and I fought it. But he does a lot for me, so why not do him a favor. [She had told him that people went to nudist camps only for thrills and that she would divorce him before she would go. Although he talked her into it, she cried all the way to camp. Asked why she continued to attend, she looked surprised and replied:] Why, because I thoroughly enjoy it!

This last quotation describes a common pattern for women, which appears also in the following recollection:

[I went the first time] because my husband wanted me to go. [Q: What is the main reason that you continue to attend?] Because we had fun...and we met a lot of nice people.

The interviewees were asked what they liked most about nudism, with the results shown in Table 9.5. Three of the benefits cited are of special sociological interest—the concept of nudist freedom, the family-centered nature of the recreation, and the emphasis on friendliness and sociability.

"Freedom"

Echoing the nudist ideology, many respondents mentioned "freedom"—using the term in various contexts—as a major benefit. There were varied definitions of this freedom and its meaning for the participant. Some defined it in terms of free body action, of being unhindered by clothing.

Nudism...gives me an opportunity to be in the sunshine and fresh air. Also to take a swim nude gives me free expression of body. [Q] I'm not hindered by clothes, a freedom of body movement and I can feel the water all over my body.

Nothing was binding; no socks, no tight belt, nothing clothing-wise touching me.

You don't have garter belts or bras. Your body can breathe.

With perspiration your clothes start to bind and you develop rashes. [Q] You just feel more relaxed

TABLE 9.5 What Interviewees Liked Most About Nudism

	PERCENT OF SAMPLE MENTIONING THE ITEM
Friendliness, sociability	60%
Relaxation, getting away from the city	47
Enjoyment of outdoors and sports	36
Freedom	31
Sunbathing	26
Physical health	26
Children becoming informed about the human body	11
Mental health	8
Economical vacations	4
Family recreation, keeping family together	4
Seeing people nude	1
Other aspects	15

when you're nude, and more comfortable from hot, sticky clothing.

Others interpreted freedom from clothing in a different way:

Freedom from a convention of society. It's a relief to get away from it. [Q] A physical relief in that wearing clothes is something you must do. I hate wearing a choking tie at a dinner party, but I have to because it is a society convention.

You don't have to dress appropriate for the occasion. You aren't looking for the smartest slacks and sports clothes.

The freedom.... You don't have to worry about the way you're dressed. You don't try to outdo someone with a thirty-dollar bathing suit.

For others, freedom meant the absence of routine and restraint:

A nudist camp has a lot more freedom [than a summer resort]. You do just as you want.... [Q] Just to do what you want to do, there is nothing you have to do. At a resort you have to participate in activities.

The freedom. [Q] You can do as you please. [Q] I can read or just lay in the sun.

The freedom. [Q] You can go any place you want in the camp. You can walk anywhere nude.

The range of conceptions of freedom is indicated by the following examples:

I felt free in the water. No one staring at you.

I like the complete freedom of...expression. With nudist people, I find them more frank and outspoken, not two-faced. You don't have to be cagey and worry about saying the wrong thing.

Feeling free with your body. [Q] I can't really explain it. Feeling more confident, I guess.

The varying constructions of nudist freedom support Schutz's model of man as a commonsense actor.[12] According to Schutz, man lives very naively in his world; clear and distinct experiences are mixed with vague conjectures, and "cook-

book" descriptions of experiences are uncritically adopted from others. When these standard descriptions are vague, and are called into question—for example, by an interviewer who asks what is meant by "freedom"—a wide variety of constructions is elicited from respondents. Nudists, as devotees to a "cause," resemble other commonsense actors in their frequent inability to understand their stock answers critically.

Family Cohesion

As shown in Table 9.5, some respondents gave, as the feature of nudism they like most, its function in providing family recreation. One of the interview sample expressed this as follows:

Nudism tends to keep the family together. In the nonnudist society the family tends to split into different organizations; all have different interests. You can still do different things in camp, but you still have a common interest. And all your plans are made together.

One would expect that nudism would lead to family cohesiveness, as a result of this common interest, and also as a result of a tendency for the family members to conceal their nudist involvements in their dealings with the outside world. In regard to the element of secrecy, Simmel has pointed out how a group's intensified seclusion results in heightened cohesiveness.[13] Participation in nudism did not, however, always lead to increased family cohesiveness. For example, if one spouse did not appreciate the experience, the family's continued participation resulted in increased strain. And although nudist ideology claims that nudist participation brings the family closer together, 78 percent of the interviewees, and 82 percent of the questionnaire respondents, reported no change in their family relationships.

Relationships with Others

Friendliness and sociability were the characteristics of the nudist experience mentioned most often by interviewees. In addition, nudists extended the concept of "family" to include fellow nudists; they cited a "togetherness" that is rare in the clothed society. Some insight into this cohesiveness was displayed in the following remarks by an interviewee:

> Camaraderie and congeniality...come in any minority group that supports an unpopular position. [Q] Feelings develop by these in-groups because you are brought together by one idea which you share. On the street you may run into people you share no ideas with.

The interviewees were asked how the camp situation would change if everything remained constant except that clothes were required. Most of them anticipated that their bond would be dissolved.

> They would lose the common bond. They have a bond that automatically is a bond. They are in a minority. They are glad you're here. You are welcome there; they're glad you're one of us.

> I think the people would be less friendly. When you're all nude you feel the same as them. You all came here to be nude.... [Q] Everybody feels the other is the same; you have something in common to be doing this unusual thing.

A number of interviewees, supporting the nudist contention that social distinctions diminish in the nudist camp, believed that class distinctions would reappear if clothing were donned.[14] A 19-year-old respondent cited both class and age distinctions:

> You would have...your classes, and age. [Q] I wouldn't feel as close to B and G.

> There is a great age difference. Knowing them this way, though, gives us a common bond. You just don't think about their ages or anything else about them.

Several blue-collar workers remarked that one of the things they liked about nudism was that, without their uniforms or customary clothes, they and their families could associate with a better class of people. Status striving decreases with the removal of these important props of impression management.

> [If everyone in the camp wore clothes] everything I detest about country clubs I've seen would immediately become manifest. Namely: (1) social climbing with all its accompanying insincerity and ostentation; (2) wolves tracking down virgins; (3) highly formalized activities such as golf; (4) gambling and drinking; (5) embarrassment of having to swim under the appraising gaze of a gallery full of people sipping cocktails. This is the paradox, the curious thing; it doesn't embarrass me to swim at...[a nudist camp] whereas I can't be coaxed into the swimming pool at the country club in my hometown. [Q] I think that the reason is the fact that so much in that country club is so calculated to make tableaux or pictures, in which only the young and the handsome can really be a part. That's terribly true.

Another interviewee, when asked what he liked most about social nudism, replied:

> It is the best way to relax. [Q] Once you take your clothes off, people are on the same basis. [Q] Everyone is a person. There are no distinctions between a doctor or a mechanic because of clothing. [Q]...It's hard to describe. It's just that all have an equal basis, no distinctions because of clothing. That helps you to relax.

Although these statements may be somewhat idealized, the nudist camp does effectively break down patterns common to country clubs, resorts, and other settings in the outside society. Sex, class, and power lose much of their relevance in the nudist camp, and the suspension of the barriers they create effects a greater unity among the participants. This is not to say, however, that there is no social hierarchy—a point to which I shall return shortly.

The suspension of clothing modesty reinforces the atmosphere of "one big family" in another way. Clothing modesty is a *ceremony* of everyday life that sustains a nonintimate definition of relationships, and with its voluntary suspension relationships are usually defined as closer in character. However, for this to occur, trust must not be called into question, and each person must take for granted that he is differentiated from other social objects. Camp relationships usually meet these conditions. For example, they are differentiated from relationships elsewhere; being undressed in front of others is still out of the ordinary, since nudists do not appear nude among outsiders.

The social effect was significant enough to prompt members to describe the nudist way of life as a discovery that had brought new meaning to their lives. The experience provided many of them with "a sense of belonging." As one respondent put it:

> *...you feel like you're part of a whole family. You feel very close. That's how I feel.*

The feeling of being part of "one big family" was, of course, more common to the smaller camps. But even in the large camps, participants in camp activities felt themselves to be a part of a special group.

As I have suggested, however, the "togetherness" of nudists is exaggerated. Personality clashes, cliques, and intergroup disagreements exist, and social stratification remains in evidence. In the words of an unmarried neophyte:

> *Sometimes I think there is a hierarchy at...[a large nudist camp]. [Q] In any organization there are cliques. [Q] These cliques I believe are formed by seniority. [Q] Those who have been there the longest. [Q: What makes you think this?] Something that is in the air. [Q] Just an impression you get. It's hard to say; it's just a feeling. [Q] As a newcomer I felt not at ease. [Q] There is an air of suspicion; people are not really friendly. [Q] They are not really unfriendly, just suspicious, I suppose, of single men.... They suspect single men are coming for Peeping Tom purposes. [Q] Just to see the nude women.... Single men, I think, are the lowest class at camp.*

This attitude was borne out in the interviews with other single men; rarely did they describe nudism in *gemeinschaftlich* terms. The meaning of a person's experiences still depends on his social position.

Furthermore, it is doubtful that many people find a Utopia in nudism. The nudists interviewed were asked how seriously they felt that they would be affected if nudist camps were closed. As Table 9.6 shows, 30 percent of the interviewees consid-

TABLE 9.6 The Degree to Which the Closing of Nudist Camps Would Affect Interviewees*

CLOSING CAMPS WOULD AFFECT RESPONDENT	PERCENT OF RESPONDENTS
Very much	43
Somewhat	26
Not too much	17
Not at all	13

*Vague categories, such as those presented in this table, were occasionally used for their descriptive value in grossly delineating some point. In this case, respondents were asked to classify themselves (after completing their open-end response). In other cases, the coders used a large group of indicators in constructing such gross scales. Although these scales lacked intrinsic rigor, reliability between coders was high.

ered that they would be relatively unaffected. When they were asked to identify their three best friends, almost half of the interviewees did not name another nudist.[15] Table 9.7 details this information, as well as the degree of social involvement with other nudists, as rated by coders.

NUDISTS AND THE CLOTHED SOCIETY

Nudists envision themselves as being labeled deviant by members of the clothed society. In both the interviews and the questionnaires, the respondents were asked to conceptualize the view of nudists taken by the general public, and by their parents. No consistent difference was found between the views of the two groups, as described by the nudists.[16] Approximately one-third of the respondents conceptualized a live-and-let-live attitude on the part of parents and public. Two-thirds conceptualized a negative or very negative attitude.

> *They think we're fanatics. [Q] That we go overboard or something. That we're out of line.*

> *If I went by what the guys say at work, you'd have to be pretty crazy, off your head a little bit. [Q] They think you almost have to be...a sex fiend or*

TABLE 9.7   Social Involvement with Other Nudists*

	DEGREE OF SOCIAL INVOLVEMENT						
Best Friends Who Are Nudists	*Very Low*	*Moderately Low*	*Neither High nor Low*	*Moderately High*	*Very High*	*Totals*	
None	13	9	12	5	7	46	(47%)
One	3	2	6	9	5	25	(26%)
Two		1	3	3	10	17	(18%)
Three					9	9	(9%)
Total	16	12	21	17	31	97	(100%)
	(16%)	(12%)	(22%)	(18%)	(32%)		

*The data on the number of best friends who are nudists were drawn from the replies of interviewees. The degree of social involvement was rated by coders on the basis of the following instructions: Code the degree of social involvement with nudists throughout the year on the basis of answers to Question 40 (b and c). Think of this as a scale or continuum: (1) Very low involvement (no contact at all); (2) moderately low involvement (just write or phone occasionally); (3) neither low nor high involvement (get together every couple of months—or attend New Year's party or splash party together); (4) moderately high involvement (visit once a month); (5) very high involvement (visit every week or two).

something like that. They think there's sex orgies, or wife-swapping, or something.

They think we're a bunch of nuts. [Q] They just think that anyone who runs around without clothes is nuts. If they stopped to investigate, they'd find we weren't.

People think the body should be clothed and not exposed at any time. They associate that with vulgarity, indecency, and abnormality. [Q] Vulgarity is something that is unacceptable to the general public. [Q] Indecency in this respect would be exposing portions of the body which normally we hide. [Q] Abnormality? Well, the general public feels it's abnormal for the body to be undressed around other people, in a social group.

The fact that nudists were able to participate in a group which they viewed as stigmatized (and also the sense of belonging they claimed to have found in nudism) suggested that nudists might be isolated in the larger society. If they were isolated they could more easily participate in such a deviant group, being insulated from social controls.

A comparison of nudist interviewees with a sample of the general population[17] did show the nudists to fall substantially below the general population in frequency of informal association,[18] as shown in Table 9.8. Further, while members of the general population got together most often with relatives, nudists got together most often with friends,[19] as Table 9.9 indicates. The fact that 34 percent of the nudist sample got together with relatives less than once a month may reflect a considerable insulation from informal controls, since it is relatives who would probably provide the greatest pressure in inhibiting participation in such deviant groups.[20]

The degree to which nudists were isolated in the clothed society was found to be related to the

TABLE 9.8 Frequency of Informal Group Participation

	NUDISTS	GENERAL POPULATION
At least twice a week	17%	30%
Every 4 or 5 days	4	35
Once a week	12	16
Less often or never	67	19

TABLE 9.9 Frequency of Association with Several Types of Informal Groups

	RELATIVES		FRIENDS		NEIGHBORS		CO-WORKERS	
	Nudists	*General Population*	*Nudists*	*General Population*	*Nudists*	*General Population*	*Nudists*	*General Population*
At least once a week	38%	51%	49%	29%	26%	30%	17%	13%
A few times a month	16	13	21	20	11	9	10	8
About once a month	11	13	8	19	6	9	7	15
Less often	34	23	20	32	56	52	63	65

length of time they had been nudists. As shown in Table 9.10, the longer a person had been in nudism, the more likely he was to be isolated. This may be interpreted in different ways. For example, there may be a tendency to become more isolated with continued participation, perhaps to avoid sanctions. (Yet, in regard to formal organizations nudists did *not* drop out or become less active.) Or, in the past it is likely that nudism was considered even more deviant than it is today and therefore it may have appealed primarily to more isolated types of people.

TABLE 9.10 Social Isolation of Nudists According to Their Length of Time in Nudism

DEGREE OF SOCIAL ISOLATION*	YEARS IN NUDISM			
	1–2	*3–5*	*6–9*	*10 and Over*
Moderately or very isolated	22%	38%	44%	54%
Neither isolated nor active	39	31	25	35
Very or moderately active	39	31	32	12

*As rated by coders.

Regardless of which interpretation is correct, as previously discussed, many nudists found a sense of belonging in nudism.[21]

People are lonely. It gives them a sense of belonging.

Until I started going out…[to camp] I never felt like I was part of a crowd. But I do out there. I was surprised. [Q] Well, like I said, I was never part of a crowd…. I had friends, but never outstanding. My wife and I were [camp] King and Queen.

However, while the nudist experience helps solve this life problem for some, it creates this same problem for others. For the latter group, nudism may only ease the problem that it creates—that is, the isolation that results from concealing one's affiliation with a deviant group.[22]

NOTES

1. Interviews were the primary source of data, and all of the quotations and quantifications in this paper, unless otherwise specified, are drawn from interviews. All known nudists in the vicinity of Chicago were contacted for an interview; the mean interview time was three and one-half hours. Approximately one hundred camps were represented in the interviews and questionnaires. A detailed discussion of my methodology may be found in "Sex, Modesty, and Deviants," Ph.D. Dissertation, Northwestern University, June, 1965.

2. This statement is based on the results of a questionnaire study of social response to nudism.

3. My thanks are due to James L. Wilkins for initially pointing this pattern out in his analysis of the additional data on the response of college students to nudists.

4. For a discussion of Pareto's concept of derivation, see Talcott Parsons, *The Structure of Social Action* (second edition); Glencoe, Ill., Free Press, 1949; p. 198 *ff.*

5. It is this very fact of an established social system, however, that prevents a disruption of social order in nudist camps. Traditions and norms are stabilized, and even neophytes who think of themselves as leader-types are forced to fall into the pattern or be rejected. (For a small-group experiment that studies this phenomenon, see Ferenc Merei, "Group Leadership and Institutionalization," *Human Relations* [1949] 2:23–39.) In another paper I have shown how some of these traditions function to sustain a nonsexual definition of the nudist situation. See Martin S. Weinberg, "Sexual Modesty, Social Meanings, and the Nudist Camp," *Social Problems* (1965) 12:311–318.

6. Anselm Strauss, editor, *The Social Psychology of George Herbert Mead;* Chicago, Univ. of Chicago Press, 1956; p. xiii.

7. At the time of the interviews, the interviewers, making a commonsense judgment, placed 54 percent of the nudist respondents in the lower-middle class. This was the modal and median placement.

8. For a discussion of "coaching" relationships, see Anselm Strauss, *Mirrors and Masks: The Search for Identity;* New York, Free Press, 1959; pp. 109–118.

9. By "social validation," I mean the process by which the subjective comes to be considered objective—that is, true. The views of others (especially those considered to have more extensive knowledge) provide a social yardstick by which to measure truth. Pareto reaches a similar view of objectivity. Note the following statement: "…we apply the term 'logical actions' to actions that logically conjoin means to ends not only from the standpoint of the subject performing them, but from the standpoint of other persons who have more extensive knowledge—in other words, to actions that are logical both subjectively and objectively in the sense just explained." See Vilfredo Pareto, *The Mind and Society,* Vol. 1; New York, Harcourt, Brace, 1935; p. 77.

10. This concept was developed by Gordon Allport, "The Functional Autonomy of Motives," *Amer. J. Psychology* (1937) 50:141–156.

11. Attendance is usually confined to summer weekends, and sexual curiosity may arise again between seasons.

12. See Alfred Schutz, "The Dimensions of the Social World," in *Collected Papers, II: Studies in Social Theory,* edited by Arvid Broderson; The Hague, Martinus Nijhoff, 1964; p. 48 *ff.*

13. Kurt H. Wolff, *The Sociology of Georg Simmel;* New York, Free Press, 1950; see Part IV.

14. For discussions of clothes as "sign equipment," see Erving Goffman, "Symbols of Class Status," *British J. Sociology* (1951) 2:294–304; and *The Presentation of Self in Everyday Life;* Garden City, N.Y., Doubleday, 1959; p. 24 *ff.* Also see Gregory Stone, "Appearance and the Self," in *Human Behavior and Social Processes: An Interactionist Approach,* edited by Arnold Rose; Boston, Houghton Mifflin, 1962; pp. 86–118.

15. Although 59 percent of the interviewees had been nudists for over two years, and 27 percent of this group had been nudists for over ten years, involvement did not appear to be particularly high. Also, an estimated 17 percent of the membership drops out every year.

16. Although a positive versus negative differentiation of parents and general public was not found, there was a difference in the character of the typifications involved. In the case of parents, the typifications were derived from a history of experiences with an acting personality and were relatively concrete. In contrast, typifications of the general public were highly anonymous. Because such a collectivity could never be experienced directly, there was a much larger region of taken-for-granteds. This is due to the great number of substrata typifications underlying the general whole. This phenomenon is discussed by Alfred Schutz (see note 12).

17. In this comparison, Axelrod's data on a sample of the general population in the Detroit area were used. See Morris Axelrod, "Urban Structure and Social Participation," *Amer. Sociol. Review* (1956) 21:13–18.

18. A major limitation in this comparison, however, is that Axelrod has collapsed frequencies of association that are less than once a week into the category of "less often or never."

19. Axelrod finds this greater participation with friends only for members of his sample with high income or high educational or social status.

20. Also the absolute frequency of association with friends includes association with nudist friends. This reduces the apparent social-control function of their friendship associations.

Curiously, members of the nudist sample belonged to more formal organizations than did members of Axelrod's sample of the general population. The comparison was as follows: Membership in no group—general population, 37 percent; nudists, 18 percent. One group—general population, 31 percent; nudists, 27 percent. Two groups—general population, 16 percent; nudists, 19 percent.

21. Some nudists also viewed themselves as members of an elite, superior to clothed society because they had suspended the body taboo.

22. For a discussion of information control, see Erving Goffman, *Stigma: The Management of Spoiled Identity;* Englewood Cliffs, N.J., Prentice-Hall, 1963; pp. 41–104.

Getting into Gangs

MARTIN SANCHEZ JANKOWSKI

Traditional theories on why youth in low-income neighborhoods join gangs center on community, family, opportunities, and status. Youth join gangs because of (1) absence of community controls; (2) broken homes and the absence of primary group controls; (3) few opportunities to obtain money legitimately; and (4) chances to achieve status through gang membership.

Martin Sanchez Jankowski, after a field study of numerous gangs, argues that these theories ultimately fail as explanations of gang affiliation because of their tendency to stress one factor. He points out that there are a variety of reasons for joining, staying in, leaving, and rejoining groups.

Just as youth seek out gangs in the hope of becoming members, gangs, as social organizations, actively recruit and select candidates for membership from time to time. In addition, there are both variations in the times that youth seek membership and the times that gangs actively recruit.

Thus motives for joining and styles of recruitment vary in accordance with candidates' needs and gang needs. And so the nature of the interaction between the seekers and those sought changes as members of each category redefine their situation.

Earlier, I argued that one of the most important features of gang members was their defiant individualist character. I explained the development of defiant individualism by locating its origins in the material conditions—the competition and conflict over resource scarcity—of the low-income neighborhoods of most large American cities. These conditions exist for everyone who lives in such neighborhoods, yet not every young person

From Chapter Two, "Gang Involvement," in Martin Sanchez Jankowski, *Islands in the Street: Gangs and American Urban Society* (Berkeley: University of California Press, 1991). Copyright © 1991 The Regents of the University of California. Reprinted by permission of the publisher.

joins a gang. Although I have found that nearly all those who belong to gangs do exhibit defiant individualist traits to some degree, not all those who possess such traits join gangs. This…[section] explores who joins a gang and why in more detail.

Many studies offer an answer to why a person joins a gang, or why a group of individuals start a gang. These studies can be divided into four groupings. First, there are those that hold the "natural association" point of view. These studies argue that people join gangs as a result of the natural act of associating with each other.[1] Their contention is that a group of boys, interrelating with each other, decide to formalize their relationship in an attempt to reduce the fear and anxiety associated with their socially disorganized neighborhoods. The individual's impetus to join is the result of his desire to defend against conflict and create order out of the condition of social disorganization.

The second group of studies explains gang formation in terms of "the subculture of blocked opportunities": gangs begin because young males experience persistent problems in gaining employment and/or status. As a result, members of poor communities who experience the strain of these blocked opportunities attempt to compensate for socioeconomic deprivation by joining a gang and establishing a subculture that can be kept separate from the culture of the wider society.[2]

The third group of studies focuses on "problems in identity construction." Within this broad group, some suggest that individuals join gangs as part of the developmental process of building a personal identity or as the result of a breakdown in that process.[3] Others argue that some individuals from low-income families have been blocked from achieving social status through conventional means and join gangs to gain status and self-worth, to rebuild a wounded identity.[4]

A recent work by Jack Katz has both creatively extended the status model and advanced the premise that sensuality is the central element leading to the commission of illegal acts. In Katz's "expressive" model, joining a gang, and being what he labels a "badass," involves a process whereby an individual manages (through transcendence) the gulf that exists between a sense of self located within the local world (the here) and a reality associated with the world outside (the there). Katz argues that the central elements in various forms of deviance, including becoming involved in a gang and gang violence, are the moral emotions of humiliation, righteousness, arrogance, ridicule, cynicism, defilement, and vengeance. "In each," he says, "the attraction that proves to be most fundamentally compelling is that of overcoming a personal challenge to moral—not material—existence."[5]

Most of these theories suffer from three flaws. First, they link joining a gang to delinquency, there-

by combining two separate issues. Second, they use single-variable explanations. Third, and most important, they fail to treat joining a gang as the product of a rational decision to maximize self-interest, one in which both the individual and the organized gang play a role. This is especially true of Katz's approach, for two reasons. First, on the personal level, it underestimates the impact of material and status conditions in establishing the situations in which sensual needs/drives (emotions) present themselves, and overestimates/exaggerates the "seductive" impact of crime in satisfying these needs. Second, it does not consider the impact of organizational dynamics on the thought and action of gang members.

In contrast, the data presented here will indicate that gangs are composed of individuals who join for a variety of reasons. In addition, while the individual uses his own calculus to decide whether or not to join a gang, this is not the only deciding factor. The other deciding factor is whether the gang wants him in the organization. Like the individual's decision to join, the gang's decision to permit membership is based on a variety of factors. It is thus important to understand that who becomes a gang member depends on two decision-making processes: that of the individual and that of the gang.

THE INDIVIDUAL AND THE DECISION TO BECOME A MEMBER

Before proceeding, it is important to dismiss a number of the propositions that have often been advanced. The first is that young boys join gangs because they are from broken homes where the father is not present and they seek gang membership in order to identify with other males—that is, they have had no male authority figures with whom to identify. In the ten years of this study, I found that there were as many gang members from homes where the nuclear family was intact as there were from families where the father was absent.[6]

The second proposition given for why individuals join gangs is related to the first: it suggests that broken homes and/or bad home environments force them to look to the gang as a substitute family. Those who offer this explanation often quote gang members' statements such as "We are like a family" or "We are just like brothers" as indications of this motive. However, I found as many members who claimed close relationships with their families as those who denied them.

The third reason offered is that individuals who drop out of school have fewer skills for getting jobs, leaving them with nothing to do but join a gang. While I did find a larger number of members who had dropped out of school, the number was only slightly higher than those who had finished school.

The fourth reason suggested, disconfirmed by my data, is a modern version of the "Pied Piper" effect: the claim that young kids join gangs because they are socialized by older kids to aspire to gang membership and, being young and impressionable, are easily persuaded. I found on the contrary that individuals were as likely to join when they were older (mid to late teens) as when they were younger (nine to fifteen). I also found significantly more who joined when they were young who did so for reasons other than being socialized to think it was "cool" to belong to a gang. In brief, I found no evidence for this proposition.

What I did find was that individuals who live in low-income neighborhoods join gangs for a variety of reasons, basing their decisions on a rational calculation of what is best for them at that particular time. Furthermore, I found that they use the same calculus (not necessarily the same reasons) in deciding whether to stay in the gang, or, if they happen to leave it, whether to rejoin.

REASONS FOR DECIDING TO JOIN A GANG

Most people in the low-income inner cities of America face a situation in which a gang already exists in their area. Therefore the most salient question facing them is not whether to start a gang or not, but rather whether to join an existing one. Many of the reasons for starting a new gang are

related to issues having to do with organizational development and decline—that is, with the existing gang's ability to provide the expected services, which include those that individuals considered in deciding to join.... This section deals primarily, although not exclusively, with the question of what influences individuals to join an existing gang. However, many of these are the same influences that encourage individuals to start a new gang.

MATERIAL INCENTIVES

Those who had joined a gang most often gave as their reason the belief that it would provide them with an environment that would increase their chances of securing money. Defiant individualists constantly calculate the costs and benefits associated with their efforts to improve their financial well-being (which is usually not good). Therefore, on the one hand, they believe that if they engage in economic ventures on their own, they will, if successful, earn more per venture than if they acted as part of a gang. However, there is also the belief that if one participates in economic ventures with a gang, it is likely that the amount earned will be more regular, although perhaps less per venture. The comments of Slump, a sixteen-year-old member of a gang in the Los Angeles area, represent this belief:

> *Well, I really didn't want to join the gang when I was a little younger because I had this idea that I could make more money if I would do some gigs [various illegal economic ventures] on my own. Now I don't know, I mean, I wasn't wrong. I could make more money on my own, but there are more things happening with the gang, so it's a little more even in terms of when the money comes in.... Let's just say there is more possibilities for a more steady amount of income if you need it.*

It was also believed that less individual effort would be required in the various economic ventures in a gang because more people would be involved. In addition, some thought that being in a gang would reduce the risk (of personal injury) associated with their business ventures. They were aware that if larger numbers of people had knowledge of a crime, this would increase the risk that if someone were caught, others, including themselves, would be implicated. However, they countered this consideration with the belief that they faced less risk of being physically harmed when they were part of a group action. The comments of Corner, a seventeen-year-old resident of a poor Manhattan neighborhood, represent this consideration. During the interview, he was twice approached about joining the local gang. He said:

> I think I am going to join the club [gang] this time. I don't know, man, I got some things to decide, but I think I will.... Before I didn't want to join because when I did a job, I didn't want to share it with the whole group—hell, I was never able to make that much to share.... I would never have got enough money, and with all those dudes [other members of the gang] knowing who did the job, you can bet the police would find out.... Well, now my thinking is changed a bit 'cause I almost got hurt real bad trying something the other day and so I'm pretty sure I'll join the gang 'cause there's more people involved and that'll keep me safer. [He joined the gang two weeks later.]

Others decided to join the gang for financial security. They viewed the gang as an organization that could provide them or their families with money in times of emergency. It represented the combination of a bank and a social security system, the equivalent of what the political machine had been to many new immigrant groups in American cities.[7] To these individuals, it provided both psychological and financial security in an economic environment of scarcity and intense competition. This was particularly true of those who were fifteen and younger. Many in this age group often find themselves in a precarious position. They are in need of money, and although social services are available to help during times of economic hardship, they often lack legal means of access to these resources. For these individuals, the gang can provide an alternative source of aid. The comments of Street Dog and Tomahawk represent

these views. Street Dog was a fifteen-year-old Puerto Rican who had been in a New York gang for two years:

> Hey, the club [the gang] has been there when I needed help. There were times when there just wasn't enough food for me to get filled up with. My family was hard up and they couldn't manage all of their bills and such, so there was some lean meals! Well, I just needed some money to help for awhile, till I got some money or my family was better off. They [the gang] was there to help. I could see that [they would help] before I joined, that's why I joined. They are there when you need them and they'll continue to be.

Tomahawk was a fifteen-year-old Irishman who had been in a gang for one year:

> Before I joined the gang, I could see that you could count on your boys to help in times of need and that meant a lot to me. And when I needed money, sure enough they gave it to me. Nobody else would have given it to me; my parents didn't have it, and there was no other place to go. The gang was just like they said they would be, and they'll continue to be there when I need them.

Finally, many view the gang as providing an opportunity for future gratification. They expect that through belonging to a gang, they will be able to make contact with individuals who may eventually help them financially. Some look to meet people who have contacts in organized crime in the hope of entering that field in the future. Some hope to meet businessmen involved in the illegal market who will provide them with money to start their own illegal businesses. Still others think that gang membership will enable them to meet individuals who will later do them favors (with financial implications) of the kind fraternity brothers or Masons sometimes do for each other. Irish gang members in New York and Boston especially tend to believe this.

RECREATION

The gang provides individuals with entertainment, much as a fraternity does for college students or the Moose and Elk clubs do for their members. Many individuals said they joined the gang because it was the primary social institution of their neighborhood—that is, it was where most (not necessarily the biggest) social events occurred. Gangs usually, though not always, have some type of clubhouse. The exact nature of the clubhouse varies according to how much money the gang has to support it, but every clubhouse offers some form of entertainment. In the case of some gangs with a good deal of money, the clubhouse includes a bar, which sells its members drinks at cost. In addition, some clubhouses have pinball machines, soccer-game machines, pool tables, [Ping-Pong] tables, card tables, and in some cases a few slot machines. The clubhouse acts as an incentive, much like the lodge houses of other social clubs.[8]

The gang can also be a promoter of social events in the community, such as a big party or dance. Often the gang, like a fraternity, is thought of as the organization to join to maximize opportunities to have fun. Many who joined said they did so because the gang provided them with a good opportunity to meet women. Young women frequently form an auxiliary unit to the gang, which usually adopts a version of the male gang's name (e.g., "Lady Jets"). The women who join this auxiliary do so for similar reasons—that is, opportunities to meet men and participate in social events.[9]

The gang is also a source of drugs and alcohol. Here, most gangs walk a fine line. They provide some drugs for purposes of recreation, but because they also ban addicts from the organization, they also attempt to monitor members' use of some drugs.[10]

The comments of Fox and Happy highlight these views of the gang as a source of recreation.[11] Fox was a twenty-three-year-old from New York and had been in a gang for seven years:

Like I been telling you, I joined originally because all the action was happening with the Bats [gang's name]. I mean, all the foxy ladies were going to their parties and hanging with them. Plus their parties were great. They had good music and the

herb [marijuana] was so smooth.... Man, it was a great source of dope and women. Hell, they were the kings of the community so I wanted to get in on some of the action.

Happy was a twenty-eight-year-old from Los Angeles, who had been a gang member for eight years:

I joined because at the time, Jones Park [gang's name] had the best clubhouse. They had pool tables and pinball machines that you could use for free. Now they added a video game which you only have to pay like five cents for to play. You could do a lot in the club, so I thought it was a good thing to try it for awhile [join the gang], and it was a good thing.

A PLACE OF REFUGE AND CAMOUFLAGE

Some individuals join a gang because it provides them with a protective group identity. They see the gang as offering them anonymity, which may relieve the stresses associated with having to be personally accountable for all their actions in an intensely competitive environment. The statements of Junior J. and Black Top are representative of this belief. Junior J. was a seventeen-year-old who had been approached about becoming a gang member in one of New York's neighborhoods:

I been thinking about joining the gang because the gang gives you a cover, you know what I mean? Like when me or anybody does a business deal and we're members of the gang, it's difficult to track us down 'cause people will say, oh, it was just one of those guys in the gang. You get my point? The gang is going to provide me with some cover.

Black Top was a seventeen-year-old member of a Jamaican gang in New York:

Man, I been dealing me something awful. I been doing well, but I also attracted me some adversaries. And these adversaries have been getting close to me. So joining the brothers [the gang] lets me blend into the group. It lets me hide for awhile, it gives me refuge until the heat goes away.

PHYSICAL PROTECTION

Individuals also join gangs because they believe the gang can provide them with personal protection from the predatory elements active in low-income neighborhoods. Nearly all the young men who join for this reason know what dangers exist for them in their low-income neighborhoods. These individuals are not the weakest of those who join the gang, for all have developed the savvy and skills to handle most threats. However, all are either tired of being on the alert or want to reduce the probability of danger to a level that allows them to devote more time to their effort to secure more money. Here are two representative comments of individuals who joined for this reason. Chico was a seventeen-year-old member of an Irish gang in New York:

> When I first started up with the Steel Flowers, I really didn't know much about them. But, to be honest, in the beginning I just joined because there were some people who were taking my school [lunch] money, and after I joined the gang, these guys laid off.

Cory was a sixteen-year-old member of a Los Angeles gang:

> Man I joined the Fultons because there are a lot of people out there who are trying to get you and if you don't got protection you in trouble sometimes. My homeboys gave me protection, so hey, they were the thing to do.... Now that I got some business things going I can concentrate on them and not worry so much. I don't always have to be looking over my shoulder.

A TIME TO RESIST

Many older individuals (in their late teens or older) join gangs in an effort to resist living lives like their parents'. As Joan Moore, Ruth Horowitz, and others have pointed out, most gang members come from families whose parents are underemployed and/or employed in the secondary labor market in jobs that have little to recommend them.[12] These jobs are low-paying, have long hours, poor working conditions, and few opportunities for advancement; in brief, they are dead ends.[13] Most prospective gang members have lived through the pains of economic deprivation and the stresses that such an existence puts on a family. They desperately want to avoid following in their parents' path, which they believe is exactly what awaits them. For these individuals, the gang is a way to resist the jobs their parents held and, by extension, the life their parents led. Deciding to become a gang member is both a statement to society ("I will not take these jobs passively") and an attempt to do whatever can be done to avoid such an outcome. At the very least, some of these individuals view being in a gang as a temporary reprieve from having to take such jobs, a postponement of the inevitable. The comments of Joey and D. D. are representative of this group. Joey was a nineteen-year-old member of an Irish gang in Boston:

> Hell, I joined because I really didn't see anything in the near future I wanted to do. I sure the hell didn't want to take that job my father got me. It was a shit job just like his. I said to myself, "Fuck this!" I'm only nineteen, I'm too young to start this shit.... I figured that the Black Rose [the gang] was into a lot of things and that maybe I could hit it big at something we're doing and get the hell out of this place.

D. D. was a twenty-year-old member of a Chicano gang in Los Angeles:

> I just joined the T-Men to kick back [relax, be carefree] for awhile. My parents work real hard and they got little for it. I don't really want that kind of job, but that's what it looked like I would have to take. So I said, hey, I'll just kick back for a while and let that job wait for me. Hey, I just might make some money from our dealings and really be able to forget these jobs.... If I don't [make it, at least] I told the fuckers in Beverly Hills what I think of the jobs they left for us.

People who join as an act of resistance are often wrongly understood to have joined because they were having difficulty with their identity and the gang provided them with a new one. However, these individuals actually want a new identity less than they want better living conditions.

COMMITMENT TO COMMUNITY

Some individuals join the gang because they see participation as a form of commitment to their community. These usually come from neighborhoods where gangs have existed for generations. Although the character of such gangs may have changed over the years, the fact remains that they have continued to exist. Many of these individuals have known people who have been in gangs, including family members—often a brother, but even, in a considerable number of cases, a father and grandfather. The fact that their relatives have a history of gang involvement usually influences these individuals to see the gang as a part of the tradition of the community. They feel that their families and their community expect them to join, because community members see the gang as an aid to them and the individual who joins as meeting his neighborhood obligation. These attitudes are similar to attitudes in the larger society about one's obligation to serve in the armed forces. In a sense, this type of involvement represents a unique form of local patriotism. While this rationale for joining was present in a number of the gangs studied, it was most prevalent among Chicano and Irish gangs. The comments of Dolan and Pepe are representative of this line of thinking. Dolan was a sixteen-year-old member of an Irish gang in New York:

> *I joined because the gang has been here for a long time and even though the name is different a lot of the fellas from the community have been involved in it over the years, including my dad. The gang has helped the community by protecting it against outsiders so people here have kind of depended on it.... I feel it's my obligation to the community to put in some time helping them out. This will help me to get help in the community if I need it some time.*

Pepe was a seventeen-year-old member of a Chicano gang in the Los Angeles area:

> *The Royal Dons [gang's name] have been here for a real long time. A lot of people from the community have been in it. I had lots of family in it so I guess I'll just have to carry on the tradition. A lot of people from outside this community wouldn't understand, but we have helped the community whenever they've asked us. We've been around to help. I felt it's kind of my duty to join 'cause everybody expects it.... No, the community doesn't mind that we do things to make some money and raise a little hell because they don't expect you to put in your time for nothing. Just like nobody expects guys in the military to put in their time for nothing.*

In closing this section on why individuals join gangs, it is important to reemphasize that people choose to join for a variety of reasons, that these reasons are not exclusive of one another (some members have more than one), that gangs are composed of individuals whose reasons for joining include all those mentioned, that the decision to join is thought out, and that the individual believes this was best for his or her interests at the moment.

ORGANIZATIONAL RECRUITMENT

Deciding whether or not to join a gang is never an individual decision alone. Because gangs are well established in most of these neighborhoods, they are ultimately both the initiators of membership and the gatekeepers, deciding who will join and who will not.

Every gang that was studied had some type of recruitment strategy. A gang will frequently employ a number of strategies, depending on the circumstances in which recruitment is occurring. However, most gangs use one particular style of recruitment for what they consider a "normal" period and adopt other styles as specific situations present themselves. The three most prevalent styles of recruitment encountered were what I call the fraternity type, the obligation type, and the coercive type.

THE FRATERNITY TYPE OF RECRUITMENT

In the fraternity type of recruitment, the gang adopts the posture of an organization that is "cool," "hip," the social thing to be in. Here the gang makes an effort to recruit by advertising through word of mouth that it is looking for members. Then many of the gangs either give a party or circulate information throughout the neighborhood, indicating when their next meeting will be held and that those interested in becoming members are invited. At this initial meeting, prospective members hear a short speech about the gang and its rules. They are also told about the gang's exploits and/or its most positive perks, such as the dances and parties it gives, the availability of dope, the women who are available, the clubhouse, and the various recreational machinery (pool table, video games, bar, etc.). In addition, the gang sometimes discusses, in the most general terms, its plans for creating revenues that will be shared among the general membership. Once this pitch is made, the decision rests with the individual. When one decides to join the gang, there is a trial period before one is considered a solid member of the group. This trial period is similar, but not identical, to the pledge period for fraternities. There are a number of precautions taken during this period to check the individual's worthiness to be in the group. If the individual is not known by members of the gang, he will need to be evaluated to see if he is an informant for one of the various law enforcement agencies (police, firearms and alcohol, drug enforcement). In addition, the individual will need to be assessed in terms of his ability to fight, his courage, and his commitment to help others in the gang.

Having the *will* to fight and defend other gang members or the "interest" of the gang is considered important, but what is looked upon as being an even more important asset for a prospective gang member is the *ability* to fight and to carry out group decisions. Many researchers have often misinterpreted this preference by gangs for those who can fight as an indication that gang members, and thus gangs as collectives, are primarily interested in establishing reputations as fighters.[14] They interpret this preoccupation as being based on adolescent drives for identity and the release of a great deal of aggression. However, what is most often missed are the functional aspects of fighting and its significance to a gang. The prospective member's ability to fight well is not looked upon by the organization simply as an additional symbol of status. Members of gangs want to know if a potential member can fight because if any of them are caught in a situation where they are required to fight, they want to feel confident that everyone can carry his or her own responsibility. In addition, gang members want to know if the potential gang member is disciplined enough to avoid getting scared and running, leaving them vulnerable. Often everyone's safety in a fight depends on the ability of every individual to fight efficiently. For example, on many occasions I observed a small group of one gang being attacked by an opposing gang. Gang fights are not like fights in the movies: there is no limit to the force anybody is prepared to use—it is, as one often hears, "for all the marbles." When gang members were attacked, they were often outnumbered and surrounded. The only way to protect themselves was to place themselves back to back and ward off the attackers until some type of help came (ironically, most often from the police). If someone cannot fight well and is overcome quickly, everyone's back will be exposed and everyone becomes vulnerable. Likewise, if someone decides to make a run for it, everyone's position is compromised. So assessing the potential member's ability to fight is not done simply to strengthen the gang's reputation as "the meanest fighters," but rather to strengthen the confidence of other gang members that the new member adds to the organization's general ability to protect and defend the collective's interests. The comments of Vase, an eighteen-year-old leader of a gang in New York, highlight this point:

When I first started with the Silk Irons [gang's name], they checked me out to see if I could fight.

After I passed their test, they told me that they didn't need anybody who would leave their butts uncovered. Now that I'm a leader I do the same thing. You see that guy over there? He wants to be in the Irons, but we don't know nothing about whether he can fight or if he got no heart [courage]. So we going to check out how good he is and whether he going to stand and fight. 'Cause if he ain't got good heart or skills [ability to fight], he could leave some of the brothers [gang members] real vulnerable and in a big mess. And if [he] do that, they going to get their asses messed up!

As mentioned earlier, in those cases where the gang has seen a prospective member fight enough to know he will be a valuable member, they simply admit him. However, if information is needed in order to decide whether the prospective gang member can fight, the gang leadership sets up a number of situations to test the individual. One favorite is to have one of the gang members pick a fight with the prospective member and observe the response. It is always assumed that the prospective member will fight; the question is, how well will he fight? The person selected to start the fight is usually one of the better fighters. This provides the group with comparative information by which to decide just how good the individual is in fighting.[15] Such fights are often so intense that there are numerous lacerations on the faces of both fighters. This test usually doubles as an initiation rite, although there are gangs who follow up this test phase with a separate initiation ritual where the individual is given a beating by all those gang members present. This beating is more often than not symbolic, in that the blows delivered to the new members are not done using full force. However, they still leave bruises.

Assessing whether a prospective gang member is trustworthy or not is likewise done by setting up a number of small tests. The gang members are concerned with whether the prospective member is an undercover agent for law enforcement. To help them establish this, they set up a number of criminal activities (usually of medium-level illegality) involving the individual(s); then they observe whether law enforcement proceeds to make arrests of the specific members involved. One gang set up a scam whereby it was scheduled to commit an armed robbery. When a number of the gang members were ready to make the robbery, the police came and arrested them—the consequence of a new member being a police informer. The person responsible was identified and punished. Testing the trustworthiness of new recruits proved to be an effective policy because later the gang was able to pursue a much more lucrative illegal venture without the fear of having a police informer in the organization.

Recruiting a certain number of new members who have already established reputations as good fighters does help the gang. The gang's ability to build and maintain a reputation for fighting reduces the number of times it will have to fight. If a gang has a reputation as a particularly tough group, it will not have as much trouble with rival gangs trying to assume control over its areas of interest. Thus, a reputation acts as an initial deterrent to rival groups. However, for the most part, the gang's concern with recruiting good fighters for the purpose of enhancing its reputation is secondary to its concern that members be able to fight well so that they can help each other.

Gangs who are selective about who they allow in also scrutinize whether the individual has any special talents that could be useful to the collective. Sometimes these special talents involve military skills, such as the ability to build incendiary bombs. Some New York gangs attempted to recruit people with carpentry and masonry skills so that they could help them renovate abandoned buildings.

Gangs that adopt a "fraternity recruiting style" are usually quite secure within their communities. They have a relatively large membership and have integrated themselves into the community well enough to have both legitimacy and status. In other words, the gang is an organization that is viewed by members of the community as legitimate. The comments of Mary, a fifty-three-year-old garment worker who was a single parent in New York, indicate how some community residents feel about certain gangs:

> There are a lot of young people who want in the Bullets, but they don't let whoever wants to get in in. Those guys are really selective about who they want. Those who do get in are very helpful to the whole community. There are many times that they have helped the community…and the community appreciates that they have been here for us.

Gangs that use fraternity style recruitment have often become relatively prosperous. Having built up the economic resources of the group to a level that has benefited the general membership, they are reluctant to admit too many new members, fearing that increased numbers will not be accompanied by increases in revenues, resulting in less for the general membership. Hackman, a twenty-eight-year-old leader of a New York gang, represented this line of thought:

> Man, we don't let all the dudes who want to be let in in. We can't do that, or I can't, 'cause right now we're sitting good. We gots a good bank account and the whole gang is getting dividends. But if we let in a whole lot of other dudes, everybody will have to take a cut unless we come up with some more money, but that don't happen real fast. So you know the brothers ain't going to dig a cut, and if it happens, then they going to be on me and the rest of the leadership's ass and that ain't good for us.

THE OBLIGATION TYPE OF RECRUITMENT

The second recruiting technique used by gangs is what I call the "obligation type." In this form, the gang contacts as many young men from its community as it can and attempts to persuade them that it is their duty to join. These community pressures are real, and individuals need to calculate how to respond to them, because there are risks if one ignores them. In essence, the gang recruiter's pitch is that everyone who lives in this particular community has to give something back to it in order to indicate both appreciation of and solidarity with the community. In places where one particular gang has been in existence for a considerable

amount of time (as long as a couple of generations), "upholding the tradition of the neighborhood" (not that of the gang) is the pitch used as the hook. The comments of Paul and Lorenzo are good examples. Paul was a nineteen-year-old member of an Irish gang in New York:

> Yeah, I joined this group of guys [the gang] because they have helped the community and a lot of us have taken some serious lumps [injuries] in doing that.… I think if a man has any sense of himself, he will help his community no matter what. Right now I'm talking to some guys about joining our gang and I tell them that they can make some money being in the gang, but the most important thing is they can help the community too. If any of them say that they don't want to get hurt or something like that, I tell'm that nobody wants to get hurt, but sometimes it happens. Then I tell them the bottom line, if you don't join and help the community, then outsiders will come and attack the people here and this community won't exist in a couple of years.

Lorenzo was a twenty-two-year-old Chicano gang member from Los Angeles. Here he is talking to two prospective members:

> I don't need to talk to you dudes too much about this [joining a gang]. You know what the whole deal is, but I want you to know that your barrio [community] needs you just like they needed us and we delivered. We all get some battle scars [he shows them a scar from a bullet wound], but that's the price you pay to keep some honor for you and your barrio. We all have to give something back to our community.[16]

This recruiting pitch is primarily based on accountability to the community. It is most effective in communities where the residents have depended on the gang to help protect them from social predators. This is because gang recruiters can draw on the moral support that the gang receives from older residents.

Although the power of this recruiting pitch is accountability to the community, the recruiter can suggest other incentives as well. Three positive incentives generally are used. The first is that gang members are respected in the community. This means that the community will tolerate their illegal business dealings and help them whenever they are having difficulty with the police. As Cardboard, a sixteen-year-old member of a Dominican gang, commented:

> *Hey, the dudes come by and they be putting all this shit about that I should do my part to protect the community, but I told them I'm not ready to join up. I tell you the truth, I did sometimes feel a little guilty, but I still didn't think it was for me. But now I tell you I been changing my mind a little. I thinking more about joining.... You see the dudes been telling me the community be helping you do your business, you understand? Hey, I been thinking, I got me a little business and if they right, this may be the final straw to get me, 'cause a little help from the community could be real helpful to me. [He joined the gang three weeks later.]*

The second incentive is that some members of the community will help them find employment at a later time. (This happens more in Irish neighborhoods.) The comments of Andy, a seventeen-year-old Irish-American in Boston, illustrate this view:

> *The community has been getting squeezed by some developers and there's been a lot of people who aren't from the community moving in, so that's why some of the Tigers [gang's name] have come by while we've been talking. They want to talk to me about joining. Just like they been saying, the community needs their help now and they need me. I really was torn because I thought there might be some kind of violence used and I don't really want to get involved with that. But the other day when you weren't here, they talked to me and told me that I should remember that the community remembers when people help and they take care of their own. Well, they're right, the community does take care of its own. They help people get jobs all the time 'cause they got contacts at city hall and at the docks, so I been thinking I might join. [He joined three weeks later.]*

The third incentive is access to women. Here the recruiter simply says that because the gang is a part of the community and is respected, women look up to gang members and want to be associated with them. So, the pitch continues, if an individual wants access to a lot of women, it will be available through the gang. The comments of Topper, a fifteen-year-old Chicano, illustrate the effectiveness of this pitch:

> *Yeah, I was thinking of joining the Bangers [a gang]. These two homeboys [gang members] been coming to see me about joining for two months now. They've been telling me that my barrio really needs me and I should help my people. I really do want to help my barrio, but I never really made up my mind. But the other day they were telling me that the mujeres [women] really dig homeboys because they do help the community. So I was checking that out and you know what? They really do! So, I say, hey, I need to seriously check the Bangers out. [One week later he joined the gang.]*

In addition to the three positive incentives used, there is a negative one. The gang recruiter can take the tack that if a prospective member decides not to join, he will not be respected as much in the community, or possibly even within his own family. This line of persuasion can be successful if other members of the prospective recruit's family have been in a gang and/or if there has been a high level of involvement in gangs throughout the community. The suggestion that people (including family) will be disappointed in him, or look down on his family, is an effective manipulative tool in the recruiting process in such cases. The comments of Texto, a fifteen-year-old Chicano, provide a good example:

> *I didn't want to join the Pearls [gang's name] right now 'cause I didn't think it was best for me right now. Then a few of the Pearls came by to try to get me to join. They said all the stuff about helping your barrio, but I don't want to join now. I mean I do care about my barrio, but I just don't want to join now. But you heard them today ask me if my father wanted me to join. You know I got to think about this, I mean my dad was in this gang and I don't know. He says to me to do what you want, but I think he would be embarrassed with his*

friends if they heard I didn't want to join. I really don't want to embarrass my dad, I don't know what I'm going to do. [He joined the gang one month later.]

The "obligation method of recruitment" is similar to that employed by governments to secure recruits for their armed services, and it meets with only moderate results. Gangs using this method realized that while they would not be able to recruit all the individuals they made contact with, the obligation method (sometimes in combination with the coercive method) would enable them to recruit enough for the gang to continue operating.

This type of recruitment was found mostly, although not exclusively, in Irish and Chicano communities where the gang and community had been highly integrated. It is only effective in communities where a particular gang or a small number of gangs have been active for a considerable length of time.

THE COERCIVE TYPE OF RECRUITMENT

A third type of recruitment involves various forms of coercion. Coercion is used as a recruitment method when gangs are confronted with the need to increase their membership quickly. There are a number of situations in which this occurs. One is when a gang has made a policy decision to expand its operations into another geographic area and needs troops to secure the area and keep it under control. The desire to build up membership is based on the gang's anticipation that there will be a struggle with a rival gang and that, if it is to be successful, it will be necessary to be numerically superior to the expected adversary.

Another situation involving gang expansion also encourages an intense recruitment effort that includes coercion. When a gang decides to expand into a geographic area that has not hitherto been controlled by another gang, and is not at the moment being fought for, it goes into the targeted area and vigorously recruits members in an effort to establish control. If individuals from this area are not receptive to the gang's efforts, then coer-

cion is used to persuade some of them to join. The comment of Bolo, a seventeen-year-old leader of a New York gang, illustrates this position:

Let me explain what just happened. Now you might be thinking, what are these dudes doing beating up on somebody they want to be in their gang? The answer is that we need people now, we can't be waiting till they make up their mind. They don't have to stay for a long time, but we need them now.... We don't like to recruit this way 'cause it ain't good for the long run, but this is necessary now because in order for us to expand our business in this area we got to get control, and in order to do that we got to have members who live in the neighborhood. We can't be building no structure to defend ourselves against the Wings [the rival gang in the area], or set up some communications in the area, or set up a connection with the community. We can't do shit unless we got a base and we ain't going to get any base without people. It's that simple.

A third situation where a gang feels a need to use a coercive recruiting strategy involves gangs who are defending themselves against a hostile attempt to take over a portion of their territory. Under such conditions, the gang defending its interests will need to bolster its ranks in order to fend off the threat. This will require that the embattled gang recruit rapidly. Often, a gang that normally uses the fraternity type of recruitment will be forced to abandon it for the more coercive type. The actions of these gangs can be compared to those of nation-states when they invoke universal conscription (certainly a form of coercion) during times when they are threatened and then abrogate it when they believe they have recruited a sufficient number to neutralize the threat, or, more usually, when a threat no longer exists. The comments of M. R. and Rider represent those who are recruited using coercion. M. R. was a nineteen-year-old ex–gang member from Los Angeles:[17]

I really didn't want to be in any gang, but one day there was this big blowout [fight] a few blocks from here. A couple of O Streeters [gang's name] who were from another barrio came and shot up a number of the Dukes [local gang's name]. Then it was said that the O Streeters wanted to take over the area as theirs, so a group of the Dukes went around asking people to join for awhile till everything got secure. They asked me, but I still didn't want to get involved because I really didn't want to get killed over something that I had no interest in. But they said they wanted me and if I didn't join and help they were going to mess me up. Then the next day a couple of them pushed me around pretty bad, and they did it much harder the following day. So I thought about it and then decided I'd join. Then after some gun fights things got secure again and they told me thanks and I left.

Rider was a sixteen-year-old member of an Irish gang from New York:

Here one day I read in the paper there was fighting going on between a couple of gangs. I knew that one of the gangs was from a black section of the city. Then some of the Greenies [local Irish gang] came up to me and told me how some of the niggers from this gang were trying to start some drugs in the neighborhood. I didn't want the niggers coming in, but I had other business to tend to first. You know what I mean? So I said I thought they could handle it themselves, but then about three or four Greenies said that if I didn't go with them that I was going to be ground meat and so would members of my family. Well, I know they meant business because my sister said they followed her home from school and my brother said they threw stones at him on his way home. So they asked me again and I said OK...then after we beat the niggers' asses, I quit.... Well, the truth is that I wanted to stay, but after the nigger business was over, they didn't want me. They just said that I was too crazy and wouldn't work out in the group.

This last interview highlights the gang's movement back to their prior form of recruitment after the threat was over. Rider wanted to stay in the gang but was asked to leave. Many of the members of the gang felt Rider was too crazy, too prone to vicious and outlandish acts, simply too unpredictable to trust. The gang admired his fighting ability, but he was the kind of person who caused too much trouble for the gang. As T. R., an eighteen-year-old leader of the gang, said:

There's lots of things we liked about Rider. He sure could help us in any fight we'd get in, but he's just too crazy. You just couldn't tell what he'd do. If we kept him, he'd have the police on us all the time. He just had to go.

There is also a fourth situation in which coercion is used in recruiting. Sometimes a gang that has dominated a particular area has declined to such an extent that it can no longer control all its original area. In such situations, certain members of this gang often decide to start a new one. When this occurs, the newly constituted gang often uses coercive techniques to recruit members and establish authority over its defined territory. Take the comments of Rob and Loan Man, both of whom were leaders of two newly constituted gangs. Rob was a sixteen-year-old gang member from Los Angeles:

There was the Rippers [old gang's name], but so many of their members went to jail that there really wasn't enough leadership people around. So a number of people decided to start a new gang. So then we went around the area to check who wanted to be in the gang. We only checked out those we really wanted. It was like pro football scouts, we were interested in all those that could help us now. Our biggest worry was getting members, so when some of the dudes said they didn't want to join, we had to put some heavy physical pressure on them; because if you don't get members, you don't have anything that you can build into a gang.... Later after we got established we didn't need to pressure people to get them to join.

Loan Man was a twenty-five-year-old member of a gang in New York:

I got this idea to start a new gang because I thought the leaders we had were all fucked up. You know, they had shit for brains. They were ruining everything we built up and I wasn't going to go down with them and lose everything. So I talked to some others who didn't like what was going on and we decided to start a new club [gang] in the neighborhood we lived in. So we quit.... Well, we got new members from the community, one way or the other...you know we had to use a little persuasive muscle to build our membership and let the community know we were able to take control and hold it, but after we did get control, then we only took brothers who wanted us [they used the fraternity type of recruiting].

In sum, the coercive method of recruitment is used most by gangs that find their existence threatened by competitor gangs. During such periods, the gang considers that its own needs must override the choice of the individual and coercion is used to induce individuals to join their group temporarily.

NOTES

1. See Thrasher, *The Gang;* Suttles, *Social Order of the Slum;* Hagedorn, *People and Folks.*
2. Of course, some of the studies cited here overlap these categories, and I have therefore placed them according to the major emphasis of the study. See Cloward and Ohlin, *Delinquency and Opportunity;* Hagedorn, *People and Folks;* Moore, *Homeboys;* Short and Strodtbeck, *Group Process and Gang Delinquency.*
3. Here again it is important to restate that many of these studies overlap the categories I have created, but I have attempted to identify them by what seems to be their emphasis. See Bloch and Niederhoffer, *The Gang;* Yablonsky, *The Violent Gang.*
4. See the qualifying statement in nn. 2 and 3 above. See Horowitz, *Honor and the American Dream;* Cohen, *Delinquent Boys;* Miller, "Lower Class Culture as a Generating Milieu of Gang Delinquency"; Vigil, *Barrio Gangs.*
5. See Jack Katz, *The Seduction of Crime: Moral and Sensual Attractions in Doing Evil* (New York: Basic Books, 1988), p. 9.
6. Although the present study is not a quantitative study, the finding reported here and the ones to follow are based on observations of, and conversations and formal interviews with, hundreds of gang members.
7. For a discussion of the political machine's role in providing psychological and financial support for poor immigrant groups, see Robert K. Merton, *Social Theory and Social Structure* (New York: Free Press, 1968), pp. 126–36. Also see William L. Riordan, *Plunkitt of Tammany Hall* (New York: Dutton, 1963).
8. There are numerous examples throughout the society of social clubs using the lodge or clubhouse as one of the incentives for gaining members. There are athletic clubs for the wealthy (like the University Club and the Downtown Athletic Club in New York), social clubs in ethnic neighborhoods, the Elks and Moose clubs, the clubs of various veterans' associations, and tennis, yacht, and [racquetball] clubs.
9. See Anne Campbell, *Girls in the Gang* (New York: Basil Blackwell, 1987).
10. For the use of drugs as recreational, see Vigil, *Barrio Gangs;* and Fagan, "Social Organization of Drug Use and Drug Dealing among Urban Gangs," who reports varying degrees of drug use among various types of gangs. For studies that report the monitoring and/or prohibition of certain drugs by gangs, see Vigil, *Barrio Gangs,* on the prohibition of heroin use in Chicano gangs; and Thomas Mieczkowski, "Geeking Up and Throwing Down: Heroin Street Life in Detroit," *Criminology* 24 (November 1986): 645–66.
11. See Thrasher, *The Gang,* pp. 84–96. He also discusses the gang as a source of recreation.
12. See Moore, *Homeboys,* ch. 2.; Horowitz, *Honor and the American Dream,* ch. 8; Vigil, *Barrio Gangs;* and Hagedorn, *People and Folks.*
13. For a discussion of these types of jobs, see Michael J. Piore, *Notes for a Theory of Labor Market Stratification,* Working Paper no. 95 (Cambridge, Mass.: Massachusetts Institute of Technology, 1972).
14. See Horowitz, *Honor and the American Dream;* and Ruth Horowitz and Gary Schwartz, "Honor, Normative Ambiguity and Gang Violence," *American Sociological Review* 39 (April 1974): 238–51. There are many other studies that could have been cited here. These two are given merely as examples.
15. The testing of potential gang members as to their fighting ability was also observed by Vigil. See his *Barrio Gangs,* pp. 54–55.
16. This quotation was recorded longhand, not tape-recorded.
17. I first met M. R. when he was in one of the gangs that I was hanging around with. He subsequently left the gang, and I stayed in touch with him by talking to him when our paths crossed on the street. This quotation is from a long conversation that I had with him during one of our occasional encounters.

REFERENCES

Bloch, Herbert A., and Arthur Niederhoffer. *The Gang: A Study in Adolescent Behavior.* New York: Philosophical Library, 1958.

Campbell, Anne. *Girls in the Gang.* New York: Basil Blackwell, 1987.

Cloward, Richard A., and Lloyd B. Ohlin. *Delinquency and Opportunity: A Theory of Delinquent Gangs.* New York: Free Press, 1960.

Cohen, Albert K. *Delinquent Boys: The Culture of the Gang.* Glencoe, Ill.: Free Press, 1955.

Fagan, Jeffery. "The Social Organization of Drug Use and Drug Dealing among Urban Gangs." *Criminology* 27, no. 4 (November 1989): 633–70.

Hagedorn, John M. *People and Folks: Gangs, Crime and the Underclass in a Rustbelt City.* Chicago: Lakeview Press, 1988.

Horowitz, Ruth. *Honor and the American Dream: Culture and Identity in a Chicano Community.* New Brunswick: Rutgers University Press, 1983.

Horowitz, Ruth, and Gary Schwartz. "Honor, Normative Ambiguity and Gang Violence." *American Sociological Review* 39 (April 1974): 238–51.

Katz, Jack. *The Seduction of Crime: Moral and Sensual Attractions in Doing Evil.* New York: Basic Books, 1988.

Merton, Robert K. *Social Theory and Social Structure.* New York: Free Press, 1968.

Mieczkowski, Thomas. "Geeking Up and Throwing Down: Heroin Street Life in Detroit." *Criminology* 24 (November 1986): 645–66.

Miller, Walter B. "Lower Class Culture as a Generating Milieu of Gang Delinquency." *Journal of Social Issues* 14, no. 3 (Fall): 5–19.

Moore, Joan W. *Homeboys: Gangs, Drugs, and Prisons in the Barrios of Los Angeles.* Philadelphia: Temple University Press, 1978.

Piore, Michael J. *Notes for a Theory of Labor Market Stratification.* Working Paper no. 95. Cambridge, Mass.: Massachusetts Institute of Technology, 1972.

Riordan, William L. *Plunkitt of Tammany Hall.* New York: Dutton, 1963.

Short, James F., Jr., and Fred L. Strodtbeck. *Group Process and Gang Delinquency.* Chicago: University of Chicago Press, 1965.

Suttles, Gerald D. *The Social Order of the Slum: Ethnicity and Territory in the Inner City.* Chicago: University of Chicago Press, 1968.

Thrasher, Frederic. *The Gang: A Study of 1303 Gangs in Chicago.* Chicago: University of Chicago Press, 1928.

Vigil, James Diego. *Barrio Gangs: Street Life and Identity in Southern California.* Austin: University of Texas Press, 1988.

Yablonsky, Lewis. *The Violent Gang.* New York: Macmillan, 1966.

Getting into Porn

SHARON A. ABBOTT

Given the general processes by which people get into, hold onto, and move up in legitimate occupations, how do these processes compare with those used by people seeking to perform the kinds of work that are against the law, custom, or "morality"? Sharon A. Abbott offers some preliminary answers for men and women who act in "pornographic videos." Her answers, in turn, supply responses to the question, Why do some people get into a deviant subculture like the porn industry?

Unlike other deviant occupations such as prostitution, panhandling, or armed robbery, the porn video industry makes a product: a number of people collaborate in a specific place with special equipment, a division of labor, and a production schedule to make a video. Connections and opportunities are crucial to all three phases of entering, continuing in, and moving up in the industry.

People are more likely to get into this line of work if members of their family, friends, or acquaintances either work in or know others who work in the industry. Absence of opportunities for legitimate work increases the chances of entry. Holding onto work in the porn industry similarly involves a combination of connections and opportunities. Showing up for work, complying with schedules, and being able to perform the work on demand strengthen connections. A reputation for dependability increases the chances of being called back for additional work. Similarly, moving up involves the multiplication of connections along with the diversification of opportunities. Finally, regular participation in the porn industry increases involvement and immersion in a deviant subculture centering on erotic performances.

Many people choose a career based on what the job can provide for them. Benefits may include money, status and recognition, opportunities for career mobility, and social contacts. Some are drawn to jobs that provide a sense of freedom and independence, jobs in which workers can forge their own paths, set their own hours, and be free from rigid demands of authority. Others take jobs to meet new people and to have new experiences. Those who pursue careers in the pornography industry are often seeking these very things.

MOTIVATIONS

Women and men who choose to forge a career in the porn industry are motivated by several factors.

Prepared especially for this volume. Permission of the author.

The four most commonly cited motivations are (1) money, (2) fame and glamor, (3) a sense of freedom and independence, and (4) the desire to "be naughty" and have sex. Often there is a great deal of overlap in these motivations, and an individual's motivation to maintain a career in the industry can change over time. These motivations are also influenced by gender and the structure of the porn industry.

Heterosexual pornography production can be broadly divided into three categories: professional, pro-amateur, and amateur. Professional companies are the largest and most organized, typically employing between fifty and one hundred staff members for sales, marketing, distribution, promotion, and production scheduling. Each company releases more than twenty video tapes per month, which feature the most glamorous and popular talent in the industry. Budgets for professional features range from $50,000 to $150,000, averaging closer to the lower end. A second category, pro-amateur or "gonzo" companies, include small companies with large budgets, medium-size companies with small budgets, and subsidiaries of professional companies. Their budgets average between $15,000 and $25,000 per video. Unlike the specialized employees of professional companies, the staff at pro-amateur companies perform multiple functions within the organization. Pro-amateur productions create a bridge between professional and "homemade" productions by offering products with high production quality, relatively low cost, and known performers. The third type, amateur companies, are comprised of a few individuals who perform a variety of tasks, including acting, directing, sales, and marketing. Budgets range from a few hundred to a few thousand dollars. Most commonly, amateur companies do not produce but rather edit and market homemade materials that are sent in by the person or persons who videotaped the activities.

MONEY

Popular beliefs maintain that it is the lure of "easy money" that draws people, particularly the young, to the world of pornography. This belief is supported by trade and fan magazines that glamorize the industry by focusing on the lavish lifestyles of its members. While the industry cultivates the idea of porn as profitable, income varies greatly by individual. Furthermore, rather than "easy money," respondents reported that most of the work is boring and physically exhausting. Like prostitutes, only a few make a great deal of money, while most make a modest or meager living.

While money earned from appearing in pornography videos may seem high compared with that earned from many other jobs, annual incomes generated from porn alone typically approximate middle-class earnings. For example, in 1998, respondents reported that at the professional level, actresses receive between $300 and $1,000 for an individual scene. The fee is based on the actress's popularity, experience, and audience appeal, as well as what the scene entails. Masturbation and girl-girl (lesbian) scenes pay the least, while anal sex and double penetrations generate the most money. The most common scene combines oral sex and penile-vaginal intercourse, and pays, on average, $500. While the pay seems high per hour, income is limited by the amount of work offered. Furthermore, this money must often stretch between extended periods of no work.

Women earn more on average than men. Respondents in this study reported that male performers earn approximately 50 percent less than their female co-workers per scene. Pornography, therefore, is one of the few occupations in which men experience pay inequity. Furthermore, while actors often have more individual scenes per video than do actresses (with the exception of the star), they only rarely appear on box covers (which provide high fees). Therefore, actors' earnings are typically lower for the entire project. Since men in the industry make disproportionately less than women, money alone is an unlikely motivation for actors.

Earnings are also dependent on the category of porn. While money is a motivating factor at the professional and pro-amateur levels, participants in amateur productions are often paid little, if anything at all. When individuals sell amateur tapes to a distributer, they are paid, on average, $150 per tape. The fee is paid to the individual who sells the tape, not to the participants. It is unknown how much each participant receives. On the other hand, when videos are produced by amateur companies, each performer earns between $50 and $150 per scene. In addition to relatively low wages, amateur companies do not have the same connections to such money-making opportunities as erotic dancing and modeling, common at pro-amateur and professional levels. Therefore, actors and actresses at the amateur level were far less likely to cite money as a primary motivation than individuals at higher levels.

At the pro-amateur and professional levels, the effect of money may be a key factor in keeping members involved in the industry even after they decide to leave. Accustomed to periods in which money is plentiful (albeit sporadic), actors and actresses have a difficult time finding jobs that offer the perceived freedom and flexibility of porn work. This phenomenon is illustrated by the following exchange between a husband and wife acting team:

TIM: A friend of mine knew the contacts for porn and another friend of mine really pushed me into it, and once I tried it, I got hooked into it. I liked the lifestyle. And then I didn't like it. I went through a period where I didn't like it, and it was too late, because I was already in it, and I already changed my cost of living. And that's a mistake that porn actors and actresses make.

KERI: They start off making $5,000 a month in the beginning. And that is in the beginning.

TIM: They start off and bite off more than they can chew financially a month, and then you're stuck, because most of us can't turn around and go get a CEO job, because now we're in the $80,000 to $100,000 a year bracket. We are used to big houses and nice cars.

The inability to find jobs with similar benefits may keep participants involved in the industry. In addition, talent may begin to live beyond their means, which serves to keep them in their jobs in order to support their standard of living.

FAME AND GLAMOR

Many respondents report that "becoming known" is a greater motivating factor for entering the industry than money. This motivation is most common at the pro-amateur and professional levels, which have a large distribution of materials, and thus, more opportunities for recognition. Porn stars I interviewed reported being photographed, applauded, and having their autographs requested when appearing in public. In addition, fan clubs provide members of the public the opportunity to connect to their beloved stars while offering talent the chance to be admired.

Fan magazines often portray the world of porn as glamorous, and the industry attempts to promote this image. At the pro-amateur and professional levels, release of high-budget feature films and videos ("glamor pieces") are often accompanied by black-tie parties in highly visible settings (e.g., hotels or convention centers). A key component of these parties is the hordes of photographers from fan, trade, and entertainment magazines who serve as *paparazzi* for the industry. The mixing of glamorization and advertisement is best exemplified in a recent billboard erected over a busy street in Los Angeles featuring the "contract girls" of a large company. Other examples include the two domestic award shows each year hosted by the industry (a third is hosted abroad). While the focus of these ceremonies is often on high-budget features, amateur productions are also honored. The opportunity for fame is therefore available to participants at all levels. Only a limited number of seats for these black-tie affairs are available to the public, and typically cost $100 apiece. This glamorization serves to advertise specific companies while offering relatively low-cost perks to the talent.

Several actresses, actors, producers, and directors commented that the search for fame was a desirable trait in talent because enthusiasm for their work increases as popularity and recognition grow. In contrast, if talent are motivated only by money, they are often left frustrated, bored, or disinterested. As one actor argued, "If you are doing it for the money, you won't last long." Production companies similarly assume that interest in money is evident to viewers and disrupts the fantasy that the talent really enjoy their work.

In contrast to the "straight" (not-X-rated) entertainment industry, porn offers a relatively quick and easy means to earn public recognition. Acting in the straight industry is typically characterized by few opportunities, high competition, and waiting for "luck" or "big breaks" (Levy 1989). Straight actors and actresses often have to audition for hundreds of parts in order to obtain a scant few. In contrast, the porn industry is accom-

modating to people who are impulsive, spontaneous, and in need of immediate gratification.
According to a number of directors and talent, if
you are attractive enough, you can sign with an
agent and appear in a porn video within a matter
of days. Respondents reported that fame does not
take long to acquire in the world of pornography.

Unlike the motive of money, the motive of
fame and recognition is not gender-specific.
While actresses gets considerably more attention
in adult publications, there are fewer actors overall in the industry. Because the pool of actors is so
small, they become familiar and easily recognized. But while this motivation is not determined
by gender, the concept of fame varies between the
sexes. For females, being famous includes not
only being recognized and supported by the industry but also being desired by viewers.

A SENSE OF FREEDOM AND INDEPENDENCE

Research into the motivations of many other types
of sex workers suggests that individuals often become involved in the industry because of their low
socioeconomic status and restricted opportunities.
For example, in their study of table dancers, Ronai
and Ellis (1989) argue that women who work in
gentlemen's clubs have fewer resources and opportunities than other women. Other explanations
for why sex workers enter the trade include poor
schooling and/or job training, broken homes, poverty, sexual abuse, and limited opportunities to
make money legitimately (see, for example, Allen
1980).

By contrast, a number of my respondents reported that they turned to the adult industry because it offered them what they wanted in a job,
namely, flexible hours, good money, and fun. It is
thus not blocked opportunity but an understanding
of the often inflexible and demanding nature of
paid work that motivates entry into porn. Porn is
appealing because it offers more flexibility and independence to the workers. An experienced actress offered this explanation for choosing a career
in pornography:

> I just can't work in an office. I flip out—I get sick
> after two weeks. With this, I get to travel and have
> freedom. I got to come to the United States. I have
> enough money to take a vacation whenever I want.
> I just took two weeks off, although I am trying to
> save money. (Joanna)

Other respondents claimed that they were drawn
to the ease of the work. As one actor who has been
in the industry for six years explained:

> I might be on set from 8:00 A.M. to midnight, but I
> don't do a goddamn thing. They pay me to show
> up, read a book, flirt with girls, and fuck. As far as
> that goes, it's cake. (Ryan)

A sense of freedom and independence is supported by the structure of the industry itself.
While a few dozen female talent and two male talent hold exclusive contracts with professional
companies, most talent work as freelancers or under nonexclusive contracts in which a company is
guaranteed a set amount of available days each
month. Not being held to a contract allows talent
to select jobs and projects that best fit their schedules, interests, and preferences. As one actor explained, not being under an exclusive contract can
also increase overall earnings, because a person is
free to work on more projects and spends less
time on production sets:

> The reason I accepted a contract is because they
> are not keeping me exclusively. So, I can work
> around, and…I have a guarantee that's just about
> as big as a normal contract, but I can still work
> around and my hours are less. I don't stick around
> for dialogue and bullshit; I just show up and ba-
> da-bing, I'm done, like, in three hours. In a con-
> tract where I am doing a feature, I sit around for
> ten, twelve hours. If you spread $500 over twelve
> hours, it's not as much as if your spread $500 over
> three hours. Logically, it makes a lot of sense to be
> nonexclusive. (Dane)

Producers benefit from this freelancer system as
well by being able to select participants on a
project-by-project basis. Only a few well-publicized
stars are needed under exclusive contracts to promote the company.

While porn offers freedom and flexibility in comparison with most other jobs of equal pay, there are certain requirements for being regarded as professional and competent. In order to insure future projects, actresses and actors in all categories are expected to arrive on time, have all necessary paperwork available (identification and HIV test results), be sober and cooperative, and be willing to stay overtime. Being labeled as a "flake" is detrimental to a career, and includes everything from forgetting appointments to being uncooperative to having sexual problems (for males). Therefore, while the work is unconventional, aspects of the job are typical of many industries.

BEING NAUGHTY AND HAVING SEX

A number of my respondents reported that porn offered them a chance to snub the prevailing norms of acceptable sexuality. Few careers offer the same stigma attached to appearing on screen engaging in what many consider a private—and some a sacred—act. While porn undoubtedly attracts exhibitionists, it is also a vehicle for people who wish to violate, challenge, and refute social norms. This phenomenon is particularly relevant for women, as the double standard offers more stringent norms for female sexual expression, whose violations carry additional sanctions. In many ways, male stars embody sexual norms that equate masculine sex with prowess, adventure, and impersonality. The link between male sexuality and porn was humorously illustrated in the following comment.

> *[An actress] asked me if I had ever thought of being in the adult industry. I am an American male and I have seen porn—of course I have [thought of being in the industry]. (Chuck)*

One company in the study catered to and profited from this desire to be "naughty." The owner-director sought actresses and actors interested in being "bad." As he argued, talent interested in money were rarely interested in sex, while those who desired fame were "used-up" be-

fore they achieved it. Being "naughty" could easily be captured on film and would be appealing to viewers who want to see "real sex" (i.e., not acting). Interestingly, working for this producer offered actresses and actors an additional opportunity to be "naughty" since this particular company was marginal even within the industry (because of personnel, content matter, and geographical location).

In the course of violating social norms, porn offers the opportunity to have sex. Although it is widely assumed that the actresses are acting (at least to some degree), many respondents claimed that there was some sexual pleasure in their jobs. Being with "nice" and "gentle" guys was mentioned as increasing arousal. Several also reported that girl-girl scenes were more arousing or erotic because of the interpersonal dynamics between female participants. While female arousal is often exaggerated or faked, it is undeniable that males are obtaining erections and ejaculating as captured by the camera (typically constructed as "enjoying" sex). Even when filming soft-core versions (no penetration), sexual activities are rarely simulated. Furthermore, most scenes end with external ejaculation as a means to suggest that the sex was real. Not surprisingly, most actors cited "getting laid" as a primary motivation for entering a porn career. Once in the industry, sustaining an interest in sex is critical for a successful career. Experiencing sexual problems (inability to maintain an erection or control ejaculation) is the fastest way to end an acting career.

Being part of the porn world offers sexual opportunities for interested participants off the set as well. While many respondents said that they were in "monogamous" relationships outside of work, single participants and those involved in swinging reported many opportunities for sex as a result of being involved in the industry. It follows that individuals involved in norm-violating subcultures were likely to hold nontraditional attitudes toward sex and sexuality, and thus be drawn to an arena in which they can exercise these interests. For example, because girl-girl sex is a staple of mainstream productions, actresses have access to exploring such relationships, which may carry over into private behavior. About two-thirds of my female respondents (none of the males) self-identified as bisexual, although only half of them had engaged in sex with women prior to entering the industry.

OPPORTUNITIES

At the amateur and pro-amateur levels, individuals typically find their way into the industry via connections with friends, lovers, and co-workers. For example, amateur companies rely on actors and actresses to invite their friends to participate in a production. Agents are rarely involved with amateur productions because the fees are too low, but "talent scouts" are used to refer reliable performers (scouts are typically paid $25 to $50 per referral). The opportunity to enter pornography production therefore often comes from other participants. This avenue of entry applies to both women and men. Furthermore, once in the industry, it is easy to make connections that foster sustained contact with the business.

As in many other careers in deviance, once one is in a subculture, friends and social networks typically become limited to individuals who are also part of the subgroup. Being part of a stigmatized group fosters these relationships. In the porn business, industry parties and less-formalized social gatherings provide opportunities to socialize and network. Networking is as vital a function in porn production as it is in straight industries. These parties thus help in making contacts, forming alliances, and providing opportunities to be seen.

In addition to opportunities offered via friends, lovers, and acquaintances, other facets of the sex industry provide a means to enter the world of porn. For women, erotic dancing presents a primary opportunity. Dancers are often informed that they can make more money stripping if they appear in a few pornographic videos. If a dancer has established a name for herself, she may be recruited by the porn industry. Based on her physical attractiveness and name recognition, an actress may be offered both an exclusive contract and her pick of directors and co-talent. For example, at the time of data collection, the highest-paid actress under an exclusive contract, a former centerfold model, refused to participate in any boy–girl scenes on camera, and would engage only in masturbation and girl-girl scenes, typically the lowest paid in the industry. Her income, therefore, was tied to her appearance and status, rather than the acts she performed in the features.

The link between porn and stripping exists in the other direction as well. It is rare for a big-name actress not to "dance" (strip), at least periodically. Dancing provides an opportunity to increase recognition and fan appeal, and thus to make oneself more profitable to the industry. When an actress "headlines" (has a featured appearance) at a dance club, the owners advertise that they have a porn star performing, which in turn draws larger crowds. Bigger crowds and increased interest result in higher tips for dancers and more business (and thus more profit) for the clubs. Therefore, actresses, club owners, and porn companies all stand to benefit from this symbiotic relationship.

Porn companies, particularly those offering semiexclusive or exclusive contracts, will often encourage actresses to dance in order to advertise the company. Larger companies retain booking agents for their dancers so that arrangements and pay negotiations are handled in-house. In addition, videotapes in which the dancer has performed are often offered for sale. When state laws prohibit such sales, "one-sheets," or advertisements for videos with photographs taken on the set, are made available to the customers.

Increased recognition, however, can have negative effects on an actress's career. Porn companies are continuously searching for fresh faces in order to appeal to both new and old viewers. Actresses who are overexposed in regard to number of videos, magazine layouts, and dancing appearances are assumed to be unable to offer much appeal for viewers. Through popularity, their images become old and too familiar. Therefore, although publicity is mandatory for a profitable career, it is often of only limited interest to a company. In other words, the ingredients for having a successful career are the very things that can end one.

Because magazine spreads and dancing opportunities are far more available for women than for men, actors are not vulnerable to overexposure and, as a result, have careers commonly twice as long as females. As one actress explains:

Girls have a shelf life of nine months to two years, unless you are different. Like me, I am Asian, so it helps. Men stay forever. It is different for a man. If he can perform, he can stay in. There are guys that have been in the business ten or fifteen years. (Julie)

Furthermore, as Levy (1989) found in the straight industry, popular and successful actresses are younger on average than their male counterparts, suggesting the beauty norms held by both producers and audiences. In both the straight and adult industries, actors are able to age, while actresses are replaced by younger, newer talent.

CHANGES IN MOTIVATIONS

Actors and actresses who are searching for quick money and/or sexual adventure quickly leave the porn industry once those goals are met, as do those who take one-time opportunities to act in videos. Those who remain must build a career for themselves in an industry that centers on the temporary. Motivations change with experience and are replaced with other goals. Of the motivations that are associated with entry into the industry,

fame and recognition appear to be the most sustaining. In addition, although the construction of fame differs between actors and actresses, the desire for admiration and notoriety does not appear to be limited to women.

Initial motivations are often replaced by more substantial goals once performers are established in the industry. For example, although many respondents reported that "being naughty" was a primary motivation for entry, this goal is met in a relatively short time. It does not take many video appearances to establish one's rejection of traditional values. Over time, those interested in challenging mainstream societal values forge a career in which they receive approval for their actions and opportunities for recognition and exposure. Being "naughty" gives way to longer-term career goals. Those motivated by sex quickly learn that they must be able to preform on command in order to remain in the industry. Having sex becomes work, and actors and actresses are motivated to remain in the industry because they are among those who can "do the job." The motivation for sex is replaced by the desire to keep a satisfactory job.

REFERENCES

Allen, Donald M. 1980. "Young Male Prostitutes: A Psychosocial Study." *Archives of Sexual Behavior* 9(5): 399–426.

Levy, Emanuel. 1989. "The Democratic Elite: America's Movie Stars." *Qualitative Sociology* 12(1): 29–54.

Ronai, Carol Rambo, and Carolyn Ellis. 1989. "Turn-ons for Money: Interactional Strategies of the Table Dancer." *Journal of Contemporary Ethonography* 18: 271–298.

CHAPTER 10

LEARNING THE NORMS

The Nudist Management of Respectability

MARTIN S. WEINBERG

Through the continuous processes of socialization, people learn how they are expected to act in a variety of social situations. As a consequence, people usually perform as others expect them to act. The result, of course, is a body of routine practices that people come to see as natural. This attitude that people take toward the social facts of everyday life makes orderly social interaction possible. Violation of these expectations can constitute the basis upon which notions of unnatural behavior are formulated.

   Given all this, what are the conditions under which people cannot merely contemplate but actually carry out a set of actions that run directly counter to their basic assumptions about appropriate behavior? Martin S. Weinberg's study of nudist camp socialization offers some answers to the conditions under which people can, in concert, turn the conventionally unnatural into the natural—and vice versa!

   Nudist ideology says nudity is not shameful, that nakedness signifies health, not sexuality. In the nudist camp, nudity becomes taken-for-granted. A set of behavioral norms that nudists abide by when in the unclothed world sustains the definition of the new situation. These norms enjoin a variety of ways to deal with public nudity. Nudists all act as if being unclothed is what everybody does naturally.

Public nudity is taboo in our society. Yet there is a group who breach this moral rule. They call themselves "social nudists."

   A number of questions may be asked about these people. For example, how can they see their behavior as morally appropriate? Have they constructed their own morality? If so, what characterizes this morality and what are its consequences?[1]

   This article will attempt to answer these questions through a study of social interaction in nudist

Reprinted from *Sex Research: Studies from the Kinsey Institute* by Martin S. Weinberg, pp. 217–232. Copyright © 1976 by Martin S. Weinberg. Reprinted by permission of Oxford University Press, Inc. Updated version.

camps. The data come from three sources: two summers of participant observation in nudist camps; 101 interviews with nudists in the Chicago area; and 617 mailed questionnaires completed by nudists in the United States and Canada.[2]

THE CONSTRUCTION OF SITUATED MORAL MEANINGS: THE NUDIST MORALITY

The construction of morality in nudist camps is based on the official interpretations that camps provide regarding the moral meanings of public heterosexual nudity. These are (1) that nudity and sexuality are unrelated, (2) that there is nothing shameful about the human body, (3) that nudity promotes a feeling of freedom and natural pleasure, and (4) that nude exposure to the sun promotes physical, mental, and spiritual well-being.

This official perspective is sustained in nudist camps to an extraordinary degree, illustrating the extent to which adult socialization can affect traditional moral meanings. (This is especially true with regard to the first two points of the nudist perspective, which will be our primary concern since these are its "deviant" aspects.) The assumption in the larger society that nudity and sexuality are related, and the resulting emphasis on covering the sexual organs, make the nudist perspective a specifically situated morality. My field work, interview, and questionnaire research show that nudists routinely use a special system of rules to create, sustain, and enforce this situated morality.

STRATEGIES FOR SUSTAINING A SITUATED MORALITY

The first strategy used by the nudist camp to anesthetize any relationship between nudity and sexuality[3] involves a system of organizational precautions regarding who can come into the camp. Most camps, for example, regard single men as a threat to the nudist morality. They suspect that they may indeed see nudity as something sexual. Thus, most camps either exclude uncoupled men or allow only a small quota of them. Camps that do allow single men may charge them up to 35 percent more than they charge families. (This is intended to discourage single men, but since the cost is still relatively low compared with other resorts, this measure is not very effective. It seems to do little more than create resentment among the singles, and by giving formal organizational backing to the definition that singles are not especially desirable, it may contribute to the segregation of single and married members in nudist camps.)

Certification by the camp owner is another requirement for admission to camp grounds, and letters of recommendation regarding the applicant's character are sometimes required. These regula-

tions help preclude people whom members regard as a threat to the nudist morality.

> [The camp owner] invited us over to see if we were desirable people. Then after we did this, he invited us to camp on probation; then they voted us into camp. [Q: Could you tell me what you mean by desirable people?] Well, not people who are inclined to drink, or people who go there for a peep show. Then they don't want you there. They feel you out in conversation. They want people for mental and physical health reasons.

> Whom to admit [is the biggest problem of the camp]. [Q][4] Because the world is so full of people whose attitudes on nudity are hopelessly warped. [Q: Has this always been the biggest problem in camp?] Yes. Every time anybody comes, a decision has to be made. [Q]…The lady sitting at the gate decides about admittance. The director decides on membership.

A limit is sometimes set on the number of trial visits a non-member may make to camp. In addition, there is usually a limit on how long a person can remain clothed. This is a strategy to mark guests who may not sincerely accept the nudist perspective.

The second strategy for sustaining the nudist morality involves norms of interpersonal behavior. These norms are as follows:

No Staring. This rule controls overt signs of overinvolvement. As the publisher of one nudist magazine said, "They all look up to the heavens and never look below." Such studied inattention is most exaggerated among women, who usually show no recognition that the male is unclothed. Women also recount that they had expected men to look at their nude bodies, only to find, when they finally did get up the courage to undress, that no one seemed to notice. As one woman states: "I got so mad because my husband wanted me to undress in front of other men that I just pulled my clothes right off thinking everyone would look at me." She was amazed (and appeared somewhat disappointed) when no one did.

The following statements illustrate the constraints that result:

> [Q: Have you ever observed or heard about anyone staring at someone's body while at camp?] I've heard stories, particularly about men that stare. Since I heard these stories, I tried not to, and have even done away with my sunglasses after someone said, half-joking, that I hide behind sunglasses to stare. Toward the end of the summer I stopped wearing sunglasses. And you know what, it was a child who told me this.

> [Q: Would you stare…?] Probably not, 'cause you can get in trouble and get thrown out. If I thought I could stare unobserved I might. They might not throw you out, but it wouldn't do you any good. [Q] The girl might tell others and they might not want to talk to me…. [Q] They disapprove by not talking to you, ignoring you, etc.

> [Someone who stares] wouldn't belong there. [Q] If he does that he is just going to camp to see the opposite sex. [Q] He is just coming to stare. [Q] You go there to swim and relax.

> I try very hard to look at them from the jaw up— even more than you would normally.[5]

No Sex Talk. Sex talk, or telling "dirty jokes," is uncommon in camp. The owner of a large camp in the Midwest stated: "It is usually expected that members of a nudist camp will not talk about sex, politics, or religion." Or as one single male explained: "It is taboo to make sexual remarks here." During my field work, it was rare to hear "sexual" joking such as one hears at most other types of resort. Interview respondents who mentioned that they had talked about sex qualified this by explaining that such talk was restricted to close friends, was of a "scientific nature," or, if a joke, was a "cute sort."

Asked what they would think of someone who breached this rule, respondents indicated that such behavior would cast doubt on the situated morality of the nudist camp:

> One would expect to hear less of that at camp than at other places. [Q] Because you expect that the members are screened in their attitude for nudism— and this isn't one who prefers sexual jokes.

> I've never heard anyone swear or tell a dirty joke out there.

> No. Not at camp. You're not supposed to. You bend over backwards not to.

> They probably don't belong there. They're there to see what they can find to observe. [Q] Well, their mind isn't on being a nudist, but to see so and so nude.

No Body Contact. Although the extent to which this is enforced varies from camp to camp, there is at least some degree of informal enforcement in nearly every camp. Nudists mention that they are particularly careful not to brush against anyone or have any body contact for fear of how it might be interpreted:

> I stay clear of the opposite sex. They're so sensitive, they imagine things.

> People don't get too close to you. Even when they talk. They sit close to you, but they don't get close enough to touch you.

> We have a minimum of contact. There are more restrictions [at a nudist camp]. [Q] Just a feeling I had. I would openly show my affection more readily someplace else.

And when asked to conceptualize a breach of this rule, the following response is typical:

> They are in the wrong place. [Q] That's not part of nudism. [Q] I think they are there for some sort of sex thrill. They are certainly not there to enjoy the sun.

Also, in photographs taken for nudist magazines, the subjects usually have only limited body contact. One female nudist explained: "We don't want anyone to think we're immoral." Outsiders' interpretations, then, can also constitute a threat.

No Alcoholic Beverages in American Camps.
This rule guards against breakdowns in inhibition, and even respondents who admitted that they had "snuck a beer" before going to bed went on to say that they fully favor the rule.

> *Yes. We have [drunk at camp]. We keep a can of beer in the refrigerator since we're out of the main area. We're not young people or carousers.... I still most generally approve of it as a camp rule and would disapprove of anyone going to extremes. [Q] For commonsense reasons. People who overindulge lose their inhibitions, and there is no denying that the atmosphere of a nudist camp makes one bend over backwards to keep people who are so inclined from going beyond the bounds of propriety.*

> *Anyone who drinks in camp is jeopardizing their membership and they shouldn't. Anyone who drinks in camp could get reckless. [Q] Well, when guys and girls drink they're a lot bolder—they might get fresh with someone else's girl. That's why it isn't permitted, I guess.*

[Moderate use of alcohol has now become the rule.]

Rules Regarding Photography.   Photography in a nudist camp is controlled by the camp management. Unless the photographer works for a nudist magazine, his (or her) moral perspective is sometimes suspect. One photographer's remark to a woman that led to his being so typed was, "Do you think you could open your legs a little more?"

Aside from a general restriction on the use of cameras, when cameras are allowed, it is expected that no pictures will be taken without the subject's permission. Members blame the misuse of cameras especially on single men. As one nudist said: "You always see the singles poppin' around out of nowhere snappin' pictures." In general, control is maintained, and any infractions that take place are not blatant or obvious. Overindulgence in picture-taking communicates an overinvolvement in the subjects' nudity and casts doubt on the assumption that nudity and sexuality are unrelated.

> *Photographers dressed only in cameras and light exposure meters. I don't like them. I think they only go out for pictures. Their motives should be questioned.*

Photographers for nudist magazines recognize the signs that strain the situated morality that characterizes nudist camps.

Similarly, a nudist model showed the writer a pin-up magazine to point out how a model could make a nude picture "sexy"—through the use of various stagings, props, and expressions—and in contrast, how the nudist model eliminates these techniques to make her pictures "natural." Although it may be questionable that a nudist model completely eliminates a sexual perspective for the non-nudist, the model discussed how she attempts to do this.

> *It depends on the way you look. Your eyes and your smile can make you look sexy. The way they're looking at you. Here, she's on a bed. It wouldn't be sexy if she were on a beach with kids running around. They always have some clothes on too. See how she's "looking" sexy? Like an "oh dear!" look. A different look can change the whole picture.*

> *Now here's a decent pose.... Outdoors makes it "nature." Here she's giving you "the eye," or is undressing. It's cheesecake. It depends on the expression on her face. Having nature behind it makes it better. Don't smile like "come on honey!" It's that look and the lace thing she has on.... Like when you half-close your eyes, like "oh baby," a Marilyn Monroe look. Art is when you don't look like you're hiding it halfway.*

The element of trust plays a particularly strong role in socializing women to the nudist perspective. Consider this in the following statements made by another model for nudist magazines. She and her husband had been indoctrinated in the nudist ideology by friends. At the time of the interview, however, the couple had not yet been to camp, although they had posed indoors for nudist magazines.

> *[Three months ago, before I was married] I never knew a man had any pubic hairs. I was shocked when I was married.... I wouldn't think of getting*

undressed in front of my husband. I wouldn't make love with a light on, or in the daytime.

With regard to being a nudist model, this woman commented:

None of the pictures are sexually seductive. [Q] The pose, the look—you can have a pose that's completely nothing, till you get a look that's not too hard to do. [Q: How do you do that?] I've never tried. By putting on a certain air about a person; a picture that couldn't be submitted to a nudist magazine—using _____ [the nudist photographer's] language.... [Q: Will your parents see your pictures in the magazine?] Possibly. I don't really care.... My mother might take it all right. But they've been married twenty years and she's never seen my dad undressed.[6]

No Accentuation of the Body. Accentuating the body is regarded as incongruent with the nudist morality. Thus, a woman who had shaved her pubic area was labeled "disgusting" by other members. There was a similar reaction to women who sat in a blatantly "unladylike" manner.

I'd think she was inviting remarks. [Q] I don't know. It seems strange to think of it. It's strange you ask it. Out there, they're not unconscious about their posture. Most women there are very circumspect even though in the nude.

For a girl,...[sitting with your legs open] is just not feminine or ladylike. The hair doesn't always cover it. [Q] Men get away with so many things. But, it would look dirty for a girl, like she was waiting for something. When I'm in a secluded area I've spread my legs to sun, but I kept an eye open and if anyone came I'd close my legs and sit up a little. It's just not ladylike.

You can lay on your back or side, or with your knees under your chin. But not with your legs spread apart. It would look to other people like you're there for other reasons. [Q: What other reasons?]...To stare and get an eyeful...not to enjoy the sun and people.

[Currently you sometimes hear such remarks being made about people wearing nipple and genital jewelry.]

No Unnatural Attempts at Covering the Body. "Unnatural attempts" at covering the body are ridiculed since they call into question the assumption that there is no shame in exposing any area of the body. If such behavior occurs early in one's nudist career, however, members usually have more compassion, assuming that the person just has not yet fully assimilated the new morality.

It is how members interpret the behavior, however, rather than the behavior per se, that determines whether covering up is disapproved.

If they're cold or sunburned, it's understandable. If it's because they don't agree with the philosophy, they don't belong there.

I would feel their motives for becoming nudists were not well founded. That they were not true nudists, not idealistic enough.

A third strategy that is sometimes employed to sustain the nudist reality is the use of communal toilets. Not all the camps have communal toilets, but the large camp where I did most of my field work did have such a facility, which was marked, "Little Girls Room and Little Boys Too." Although the stalls had three-quarter-length doors, this combined facility still helped to provide an element of consistency; as the owner said, "If you are not ashamed of any part of your body or any of its natural functions, men and women do not need separate toilets." Thus, even the physical ecology of the nudist camp was designed to be consistent with the nudist morality. For some, however, communal toilets were going too far.

I think they should be separated. For myself it's all right. But there are varied opinions, and for the satisfaction of all, I think they should separate them. There are niceties of life we often like to maintain, and for some people this is embarrassing.... [Q] You know, in a bowel movement it always isn't silent.

THE ROUTINIZATION OF NUDITY

In the nudist camp, nudity becomes routinized; its attention-provoking quality recedes, and nudity becomes a taken-for-granted state of affairs. Thus, when asked questions about staring ("While at camp, have you ever stared at anyone's body? Do you think you would stare at anyone's body?") nudists indicate that nudity generally does not invoke their attention.

> Nudists don't care what bodies are like. They're out there for themselves. It's a matter-of-fact thing. After a while you feel like you're sitting with a full suit of clothes on.

> To nudists the body becomes so matter-of-fact, whether clothed or unclothed, when you make it an undue point of interest it becomes an abnormal thing. [Q: What would you think of someone staring?] I would feel bad and let down. [Q] I have it set up on a high standard. I have never seen it happen.... [Q] Because it's not done there. It's above that; you don't stare.... If I saw it happen, I'd be startled. There's no inclination to do that. Why would they?

> There are two types—male and female. I couldn't see why they were staring. I wouldn't understand it.

In fact, these questions about staring elicit from nudists a frame of possibilities in which what is relevant to staring is ordinarily not nudity itself. Rather, what evokes attention is something unusual, something the observer seldom sees and thus is not routinized to.[7]

> There was a red-haired man. He had red pubic hair. I had never seen this before.... He didn't see me. If anyone did, I would turn the other way.

> Well, once I was staring at a pregnant woman. It was the first time I ever saw this. I was curious, her stomach stretched, the shape.... I also have stared at extremely obese people, cripples. All this is due to curiosity, just a novel sight. [Q]...I was discreet. [Q] I didn't look at them when their eyes were fixed in a direction so they could tell I was.

> [Q: While at camp have you ever stared at someone's body?] Yes. [Q] A little girl. She had a birthmark on her back, at the base of her spine.

> [Q: Do you think you would ever stare at someone's body while at camp?] No. I don't like that. I think it's silly.... What people are is not their fault if they are deformed.

> I don't think it would be very nice, very polite. [Q] I can't see anything to stare at, whether it's a scar or anything else. [Q] It just isn't done.

> I've looked, but not stared. I'm careful about that, because you could get in bad about that. [Q] Get thrown out by the owner. I was curious when I once had a perfect view of a girl's sex organs, because her legs were spread when she was sitting on a chair. I sat in the chair across from her in perfect view of her organs. [Q] For about ten or fifteen minutes. [Q] Nobody noticed. [Q] It's not often you get that opportunity.[8]

> [Q: How would you feel if you were alone in a secluded area of camp sunning yourself, and then noticed that other nudists were staring at your body?] I would think I had some mud on me. [Q]...I would just ask them why they were staring at me. Probably I was getting sunburn and they wanted to tell me to turn over, or maybe I had a speck of mud on me. [Q] These are the only two reasons I can think of why they were staring.

In the nudist camp, the arousal of attention by nudity is usually regarded as *unnatural*. Thus, staring is unnatural, especially after a period of grace in which to adjust to the new meanings.

> If he did it when he was first there, I'd figure he's normal. If he kept it up I'd stay away from him, or suggest to the owner that he be thrown out. [Q] At first it's a new experience, so he might be staring. [Q] He wouldn't know how to react to it. [Q] The first time seeing nudes of the opposite sex. [Q] I'd think if he kept staring, that he's thinking of something, like grabbing someone, running to the bushes and raping them. [Q] Maybe he's mentally unbalanced.

> He just sat there watching the women. You can forgive it the first time, because of curiosity. But not every weekend. [Q] The owner asked him to leave.

> These women made comments on some men's shapes. They said, "He has a hairy body or ugly bones," or "Boy his wife must like him because

he's hung big." That was embarrassing.... I thought they were terrible. [Q] Because I realized they were walking around looking. I can't see that.

ORGANIZATIONS AND THE CONSTITUTION OF NORMALITY

The rules-in-use of an organization *and the reality they sustain* form the basis on which behaviors are interpreted as "unnatural."[9] Overinvolvement in nudity, for example, is interpreted by nudists as unnatural (and not simply immoral). Similarly, erotic stimuli or responses, which breach the nudist morality, are defined as unnatural.

> *They let one single in. He acted peculiar.... He got up and had a big erection. I didn't know what he'd do at night. He might molest a child or anybody.... My husband went and told the owner.*

> *I told you about this one on the sundeck with her legs spread. She made no bones about closing up. Maybe it was an error, but I doubt it. It wasn't a normal position. Normally you wouldn't lay like this. It's like standing on your head. She had sufficient time and there were people around.*

> *She sat there with her legs like they were straddling a horse. I don't know how else to describe it. [Q] She was just sitting on the ground. [Q] I think she's a dirty pig. [Q] If you sit that way, everyone don't want to know what she had for breakfast. [Q] It's just the wrong way to sit. You keep your legs together even with clothes on.*

> *[Q: Do you think it is possible for a person to be modest in a nudist camp?] I think so. [Q] If a person acts natural.... An immodest person would be an exhibitionist, and you find them in nudism too.... Most people's conduct is allright.*

When behaviors are constituted as *unnatural*, attempts to understand them are usually suspended, and reciprocity of perspectives is called into question. (The "reciprocity of perspectives" involves the assumption that if one changed places with the other, one would, for all practical purposes, see the world as the other sees it.[10])

> *[Q: What would you think of a man who had an erection at camp?] Maybe they can't control themselves. [Q] Better watch out for him. [Q] I would tell the camp director to keep an eye on him. And the children would question that. [Q: What would you tell them?] I'd tell them the man is sick or something.*

> *[Q: What would you think of a Peeping Tom—a nonnudist trespasser?] They should be reported and sent out. [Q] I think they shouldn't be there. They're sick. [Q] Mentally. [Q] Because anyone who wants to look at someone else's body, well, is a Peeping Tom, is sick in the first place. He looks at you differently than a normal person would. [Q] With ideas of sex. [A trespasser]...is sick. He probably uses this as a source of sexual stimulation.*

Such occurrences call into question the taken-for-granted character of nudity in the nudist camp and the situated morality that is officially set forth.

INHIBITING BREAKDOWNS IN THE NUDIST MORALITY

Organized nudism promulgates a nonsexual perspective toward nudity, and breakdowns in that perspective are inhibited by (1) controlling erotic actions and (2) controlling erotic reactions. Nudity is partitioned off from other forms of "immodesty" (e.g., verbal immodesty, erotic overtures). In this way, a person can learn more easily to attribute a new meaning to nudity.[11] When behaviors occur that reflect other forms of "immodesty," however, nudists often fear a voiding of the nonsexual meaning that they impose on nudity.

> *This woman with a sexy walk would shake her hips and try to arouse the men.... [Q] These men went to the camp director to complain that the woman had purposely tried to arouse them. The camp director told this woman to leave.*

Nudists are sensitive to the possibility of a breakdown in the nudist morality. Thus, they have a low threshold for interpreting acts as "sexual."

> *Playing badminton, this teenager was hitting the birdie up and down and she said, "What do you*

think of that?" I said, "Kind of sexy." _____ [the president of the camp] said I shouldn't talk like that, but I was only kidding.

Note the following description of "mauling":

I don't like to see a man and a girl mauling each other in the nude before others.... [Q: Did you ever see this at camp?] I saw it once.... [Q: What do you mean by mauling?] Just, well, I never saw him put his hands on her breasts, but he was running his hands along her arms.

This sensitivity to "sexual" signs also sensitizes nudists to the possibility that certain of their own acts, although not intended as "sexual," might nonetheless be interpreted that way.

Sometimes you're resting and you spread your legs unknowingly. [Q] My husband just told me not to sit that way. [Q] I put my legs together.

Since "immodesty" is defined as an unnatural manner of behavior, such behaviors are easily interpreted as being motivated by "dishonorable" intent. When the individual is thought to be in physical control of the "immodest" behavior and to know the behavior's meaning within the nudist scheme of interpretation, sexual intentions are assigned. Referring to a quotation that was presented earlier, one man said that a woman who was lying with her legs spread may have been doing so unintentionally, "but I doubt it. It wasn't a normal position. Normally you wouldn't lay like this. It's like standing on your head."

Erotic reactions, as well as erotic actions, are controlled in camp. Thus, even when erotic stimuli come into play, erotic responses may be inhibited.

When lying on the grass already hiding my penis, I got erotic thoughts. And then one realizes it can't happen here. With fear there isn't much erection.

Yes, once I started to have an erection. Once. [Q] A friend told me how he was invited by some young lady to go to bed. [Q] I started to picture the situation and I felt the erection coming on; so I immediately jumped in the pool. It went away.

I was once in the woods alone and ran into a woman. I felt myself getting excited. A secluded spot in the bushes which was an ideal place for procreation. [Q] Nothing happened, though.

When breaches of the nudist morality do occur, other nudists' sense of modesty may inhibit sanctioning. The immediate breach may go unsanctioned. The observers may feign inattention or withdraw from the scene. The occurrence is usually communicated, however, via the grapevine, and it may reach the camp director.

We were shooting a series of pictures and my wife was getting out of her clothes. _____ [the photographer] had an erection but went ahead like nothing was happening. [Q] It was over kind of fast.... [Q] Nothing. We tried to avoid the issue.... Later we went to see _____ [the camp director] and _____ [the photographer] denied it.

[If a man had an erection] people would probably pretend they didn't see it.

[Q: What do you think of someone this happens to?] They should try to get rid of it fast. It don't look nice. Nudists are prudists. They are more prudish. Because they take their clothes off they are more careful. [Q] They become more prudish than people with clothes. They won't let anything out of the way happen.

As indicated in the remark, "nudists are prudists," nudists may at times become aware of the fragility of their situated moral meanings.

At _____ [camp], this family had a small boy no more than ten years old who had an erection. Mrs. _____ [the owner's wife] saw him and told his parents that they should keep him in check, and tell him what had happened to him and to watch himself. This was silly, for such a little kid who didn't know what happened.

DEVIANCE AND MULTIPLE SCHEMAS

There are basic social processes that underlie responses to deviance. Collectivities control thresholds of response to various behaviors, determining the relevance, meaning, and importance of the behavior. In the nudist camp, as pointed out previously, erotic overtures and erotic responses are regarded as unnatural, and reciprocity of perspectives is called into question by such behaviors.

> We thought this single was all right, until others clued us in that he had brought girls up to camp. [Then we recalled that]…he was kind of weird. The way he'd look at you. He had glassy eyes, like he could see through you.[12]

Such a response to deviance in the nudist camp is a result of effective socialization to the new system of moral meanings. The deviant's behavior, on the other hand, can be construed as reflecting an ineffective socialization to the new system of meanings.

> I think it's impossible [to have an erection in a nudist camp]. [Q] In a nudist camp you must have some physical contact and a desire to have one.

> He isn't thinking like a nudist. [Q] The body is wholesome, not…a sex object. He'd have to do that—think of sex.

> Sex isn't supposed to be in your mind, as far as the body. He doesn't belong there. [Q] If you go in thinking about sex, naturally it's going to happen.… You're not supposed to think about going to bed with anyone, not even your wife.

As these quotes illustrate, the unnaturalness or deviance of a behavior is ordinarily determined by relating it to an institutionalized scheme of interpretation. Occurrences that are "not understandable" in the [schema] of one collectivity may, however, be quite understandable in the [schema] of another collectivity.[13] Thus, what are "deviant" occurrences in nudist camps probably would be regarded by members of the clothed society as natural and understandable rather than unnatural and difficult to understand.

Finally, a group of people may subscribe to different and conflicting interpretive schemes. Thus, the low threshold of nudists to anything "sexual" is a function of their marginality; the fact that they have not completely suspended the moral

meanings of the clothed society is what leads them to constitute many events as "sexual" in purpose.

NOTES

1. In my previous papers, I have dealt with other questions that are commonly asked about nudists. How persons become nudists is discussed in my "Becoming a Nudist," *Psychiatry,* XXIX (February, 1966), 15–24. A report on the nudist way of life and social structure can be found in my article in *Human Organization,* XXVI (Fall, 1967), 91–99.

2. Approximately one hundred camps were represented in the interviews and questionnaires. Interviews were conducted in the homes of nudists during the off season. Arrangements for the interviews were initially made with these nudists during the first summer of participant observation; selection of respondents was limited to those living within a one-hundred-mile radius of Chicago. The questionnaires were sent to all members of the National Nudist Council. The different techniques of data collection provided a test of convergent validation.

3. For a discussion of the essence of such relationships, see Alfred Schutz, *Collected Papers: The Problem of Social Reality,* Maurice Natanson, ed. (The Hague: Nijhoff, 1962), I, 287 ff.

4. [Q] is used to signify a neutral probe by the interviewer that follows the course of the last reply, such as "Could you tell me some more about that?" or "How is that?" or "What do you mean?" Other questions by the interviewer are given in full.

5. The King and Queen contest, which takes place at conventions, allows for a patterned evasion of the staring rule. Applicants stand before the crowd in front of the royal platform, and applause is used for selecting the winners. Photography is allowed during the contest, and no one is permitted to enter the contest unless willing to be photographed. The major reason for this is that this is a major camp event, and contest pictures are used in nudist magazines. At the same time, the large number of photographs sometimes taken by lay photographers (that is, not working for the magazines) makes many nudists uncomfortable by calling into question a nonsexual definition of the situation.

6. I was amazed at how many young female nudists described a similar pattern of extreme clothing modesty among their parents and in their own married life. Included in this group was another nudist model, one of

the most photographed of nudist models. Perhaps there are some fruitful data here for cognitive-dissonance psychologists.

7. Cf. Schutz, *op. cit.,* p. 74.

8. For some respondents, the female genitals, because of their hidden character, never become a routinized part of camp nudity; thus their visible exposure does not lose an attention-provoking quality.

9. Compare Harold Garfinkel, "A Conception of, and Experiments with, 'Trust' as a Condition of Stable Con-

certed Actions," in O. J. Harvey, ed., *Motivation and Social Interaction* (New York: Ronald, 1963).

10. See: Schutz, *op. cit.,* I, 11, for his definition of reciprocity of perspectives.

11. This corresponds with the findings of learning-theory psychologists.

12. For a study of the process of doublethink, see James L. Wilkins, "Doublethink: A Study of Erasure of the Social Past," unpublished doctoral dissertation, Northwestern University, 1964.

13. Cf. Schutz, *op. cit.,* p. 229 ff.

Cruising for Sex in Public Places

RICHARD TEWKSBURY

All people, deviants as well as conformists, must learn how to interact with other people. Taking instruction, watching others, and practicing their own actions, people, in time, master the roles that they customarily take when in the company of others. The main difference between conformists and deviants is that deviants have to learn how to engage in deviant acts and avoid social punishment (exposure, labeling, disapproval, criminal sanctions, etc.). Such punishment can come from intimates, associates, strangers, and agents of formal social control such as police or psychiatrists.

Richard Tewksbury points out that men seeking sex from other men in public parks have to learn cruising norms. A tacit code of etiquette regulates the conduct of men when cruising. In time, they learn (often from their own mistakes) to signal their intentions by gestures rather than by speech. Both parties negotiate by means of a series of nonverbal signals. The series of nonverbal acts tests in sequence whether both parties understand the signals and also the degree of risk that both may face when engaging in homosexual acts. Learning, then complying with, the silent code makes it possible for men to have sex in public places and to best evade social punishment.

To date, studies of interpersonal, especially sexual, attraction have focused almost entirely on heterosexual relationships. Although these relationships are important to understand, such studies are too narrow for practical use in contemporary society. Understanding how and why men may be attracted

From "Cruising for Sex in Public Places: The Structure and Language of Men's Hidden, Erotic Worlds," *Deviant Behavior, An Interdisciplinary Journal,* 17 (1996): 1–19. Taylor & Francis, Inc., Washington DC. Reproduced with permission. All rights reserved.

to other men, or women to other women, can lead to important conclusions regarding social structures, public health, marketing, legal implications, and daily work and/or leisure activities.[1]

The mere fact that some sexual settings are homosocial necessarily leads to expectations for varying sexual scripts based on differing values, desires, and expectations. Men are reputed, and shown in the research literature, to be more likely than women to have engaged in casual sex (Herold and Mewhinney 1993) and to be more willing to accept a sexual invitation from an un-known other (Clark and Hatfield 1989; Clark 1990). With this in mind, an examination of the ways and means by which men who have sex with men (MSMs) pursue and carry through with casu-al sexual encounters via cruising—seeking sexual partners, often in public places—becomes an im-portant and socially relevant topic of research....

RESEARCH METHOD

This research draws on in-depth interviews con-ducted by the author with 11 men who have cruised for male sexual partners in public parks.[2] All interviews were completed between March and November of 1992. Interviewees live in three Midwestern states, and report prolonged periods of cruising in a total of six states....

CRUISING FOR SEX PARTNERS

In order for an individual to participate in public cruising activities it is, of course, first necessary for him to know that such activities occur, and to know where, when, and how such activities occur. Within urban gay communities, the fact that cruis-ing and public sex occur is relatively common knowledge. Locations where cruising takes place are basic kernels of subcultural knowledge, often including specifics about particular "types" of men one may expect to find in particular settings (Lee 1979; Brodsky 1993). However, in the rare instance that a man does not know where or when he may find cruising activity, there are annually published guides to public sex locations for most American urban areas.[3] Therefore, the where is-sue is addressed, leaving a man to answer only when and how.

Both sexual scripting (Gagnon and Simon 1973; Simon and Gagnon 1986) and imaging (Ka-mel 1983) are important means by which individ-uals manage presentations of self, which in turn shape and direct interactional (especially sexual) possibilities and consequences. Depending on the imaging practices and scripts pursued by setting

participants, the encounters among men vary in form, degree, intensity, and success.

The playing out of sexual scripts and imaging practices occur everywhere in society, but are most common (and obvious) in subcultural loca-tions known for cruising and sexual activity. The process of cruising has a long history in gay male communities. The perpetuation of such behavior is so well known, and so commonly practiced, that one theorist has been led to critique cruising as a "ritual" (Pollack 1993).

Cruising can be a dangerous activity. Media and anecdotal accounts abound about violence and blackmail arising from public sex and the search for it. Consequently, many MSMs seek out protected environments for casual and recreational sex, places where access can be controlled and victimization potential limited. Such controlled environments—sex clubs, baths, and some gay bars—not only function to provide a sense of protection from invading cultural outsiders, but also allow for transformations of sexual and sex-seeking activities within the controlled boundaries. Lee (1979) outlines four specific issues/processes (for him unique to S&M encounters, but, as we can see, not necessarily so restricted) that are fa-cilitated by the control/bounding of a homosocial, sexual environment:

1. the function of protected territories in facili-tating the arrangement of (sexual) encounters between strangers;
2. the screening processes by which a potential partner is selected as an acceptable risk;
3. the negotiation of the "scenario" itself, so that the risks to be taken are clarified, and agree-able limits set;
4. control of interaction during the actual sce-nario (the sex act) so that the limits are not exceeded, real "consent" is maintained, and withdrawal possible at any point where one of the participants finds "the action too much to handle." (pp. 77–78)

These same issues may also be of concern in less restricted sexual environments, but are less subject to control by setting participants. As apparently universal concerns, these issues establish some similarities in activities across a diverse universe of cruising locales, lending support to the view of such activities as rituals. However, the virtual absence of access control and less authoritative means of enforcing situational norms means the structure and process of cruising public places [are] significantly different from the sex-seeking behaviors of other, more restricted, cruising locales. Understanding the men who cruise for sex with other men in public places, and how the ritual is performed, are the next topics of this discussion.

LEARNING THE ROPES

Once a man seeking to locate other men interested in anonymous sexual encounters identifies a location, all that he needs to do is go to the location and, as Steve succinctly explained, "just start walking, it'll be there. At least somebody there is waiting to service your every need." In other words, even the naive, inexperienced cruiser can expect to engage a willing sexual partner. Where the individual encounters challenges and has a need for subcultural knowledge is in the area of facilitating his likelihood for achieving a successful and safe encounter. As Lee (1979) has elaborated, concerns about finding structured and protected settings and establishing means to negotiate encounters are central to the experience of sexual encounters with anonymous or casual-acquaintance others. These are abilities and skills that must be learned.

Although public park cruising locales are widely known within the subculture of an urban area's MSMs, such locations cannot be approached as if everyone found there was interested in sex with everyone and anyone else. Obviously, not all individuals, or even all men, in public parks are in search of sexual encounters. Despite the apparent openness and unrestricted nature of the sexual activity, there are norms that regulate activities. Many of these norms may appear to be simple courtesies, maintaining a sense of civility within

the setting. Additionally, and more importantly, norms structure activities and foster avenues by which men may screen potential partners for safety and enter into familiar negotiation patterns. As Kirk, a well-practiced cruiser, explains,

You don't walk straight up to someone and put your hand in their crotch, that's for sure. That's a little forward. You don't assume that just because the other person's there to have sex, that they want to have sex with you.

It should be noted, however, that many men do report norm-violating experiences including things such as having another simply walk up and place a hand on their crotch. Such instances, where sexual receptiveness is assumed and contact is immediately initiated, do occur. However, typically men methodically seek out and negotiate sexual interactions, and only then perhaps enter into a sexual exchange. Regardless of whether an encounter is methodically negotiated or a surprise contact, both men are allowed to withdraw quickly, easily, and without negative consequence, at any time (Weinberg and Williams 1975; Brown 1976; Lee 1979; Tewksbury 1990; Brodsky 1993). Simply because sexual contact is initiated does not mean that it will necessarily result in both men's (or either individual's) ejaculation. When a man wishes to remove himself from a sexual interaction, he does just that. Replacing one's clothing and walking away are acceptable, although not always desirable, to one's anonymous sex partners.

How does one learn the norms of a public sex arena? Explicit instruction from a friend who is knowledgeable may be one way for some men to learn how to cruise. Or, simply being present and observing the actions and interactions of others may be the most fruitful method. Or, as has been the case for some, learning may occur as a result of violating the unknown norms and being subsequently sanctioned. To successfully learn via observation, and to successfully complete a sexual encounter, the trick is, as Vince puts it, to "look inconspicuous."

Meticulous scrutiny of co-present others is generally believed not only to be the key to locating desirable, willing sexual partners, but also to serve as a screening device to assess the situation for risk. Such a practice is by no means unique to public sex arenas. What may be unique here, though, is that the use of such an activity serves both to facilitate seeking and to assess the setting for possible threats to safety. If such a canvassing reveals the presence of men of dubious appearance, activities can be restricted, or the individual can safely retreat from the perceived threat.

CHARACTERISTICS OF MEN FOUND IN PUBLIC SEX ARENAS

The men found in public cruising areas are, according to Steve, "just your average build, average body, average hair, average, average. Very average-looking." In short, the men in public sex arenas run the full spectrum from highly unattractive to attractive, old to young, poor to wealthy, short to tall, and so forth. Stating this position more completely is Matt, who says cruising men are not stereotypical gay men, but rather:

> You're finding trolls, you're finding young adults, you're finding married men, you're finding truckers, you're finding the whole spectrum. I mean, that's who you would find in any cruising spots, I guess.... These are often people that don't want to admit their homosexuality yet.

Standing on the edge of social acceptability, and on the edge of being "out," the men who cruise in public parks (and in other public sex arenas) do not fit common stereotypes of gay men. Neither do men in public cruising areas adorn themselves in "costumes" common to other gay settings (Lee 1979; Kamel 1983; Brodsky 1993). Cruising men are not necessarily feminine, highly fashionable, flamboyant, or hypermasculine. If anything, it can be expected that cruising men fit more closely with stereotypes of "traditional masculine" presentations of self. This is clearly seen in Jack's definition of men in the park:

> They are not your average queen. They're not the little faggot down the street with the loose wrist and the lisp and the high heels that walks like they're stepping on eggshells. You will very seldom find that person in the park, because the park intones to them more masculinity.

For some, the more masculine nature of cruising for sex outdoors might suggest a parallel with ideals of heterosexuality. This may stand as one reason, together with the setting's norms of anonymity and quick sexual consumption, that all men interviewed believed a significant percentage of those who cruise in public are self-identified heterosexuals. Such "men who have sex with men" are more likely to venture into the more easily permeable setting of the public park than they are to cross the boundaries that maintain more recognizable gay settings (such as gay bars and baths).

This evidence suggests, then, that cruising public parks is something that is looked upon as, at best, marginal to the gay community. Although a sizable minority (or, perhaps a slight majority) of gay men may at one time or another seek out anonymous sex in a public sex arena, this is not an activity that is commonly discussed openly and honestly among gay men. Rather, to be known as a man who cruises in the park is to be, as Albert claims from personal experience, severely stigmatized. In his experiences, Albert says he has learned, "Oh God, everybody that goes to the park, if you are seen at the park you are automatically tagged a scuzz. You are a real slut."

All of the men interviewed for this project believe that most, if not nearly all, MSMs at one time or another cruise in public sex arenas. This universality accounts for the perception of participating men as both diverse and "average." Within the gay community, however, such activity remains stigmatized. Due in part to the increasing awareness of the health risks of having multiple anonymous partners, gay community norms have moved toward lower levels of acceptance of multiple anonymous sexual contacts. Rather than adhering to the very expressive sexual freedom perspective that characterized many urban gay communities in the

1970s and early 1980s, gay men in the 1990s are less apt to embrace sexual excesses. Consequently, those men who regularly engage in anonymous public sex are likely to be stigmatized.

WHEN IS CRUISING MOST PRODUCTIVE?

Knowing that cruising in public sex arenas is not a highly respected or respectable activity, men clearly guide the temporal aspects of cruising by a combination of utilitarian and self-protective interests. The utilitarian interests are seen in efforts to be present when other, similarly interested men will also be present. The self-protective interests are the efforts *not* to be present when "outsiders" are present; in this way, men seek to maximize the effects of screening procedures and to provide opportunities for sexual encounters that are not likely to be interrupted by the "unwise." In practice, most cruising activity in public parks occurs at night. Although men do visit the park during daylight hours, and may meet and leave with other men, actual consummation of relations most often is an after-dark activity. This is a practical practice, for, as Kirk says, "If you're intent on having sex in the park, yes, it is at night.... That's your cover; people don't see you." Darkness facilitates the anonymity of the setting and thus the sexual activity.

Minimizing the likelihood of intrusions (including arrest) means that cruising rarely takes place during hours when large numbers of "straight" people are using the park. Often referred to as "family time," these hours (afternoons, early evenings, weekend daylight hours) are perceived as both too dangerous for sexual activity and simply inappropriate. Marc explained this saying, "A bad time is when, well, family time.... It's our criteria. Family time is kind of an etiquette, you just don't do it. There is etiquette out there."

Even during the hours when supposedly "polite" men do not have sex where they may be detected, cruising does occur. Such hours host sex between men, but in more secluded areas, places

where "straight" people are unlikely to venture. Daytime sexual relations, when they occur, are most likely to be consummated deep in the woods, or in locations removed from the easily accessed regions of the park. In other words, especially when running increased risks of detection, active attempts are made to "hide" sexual activities. Delph (1978), discussing how men transform innocuous public settings into erotic oases, described prime locations as those having distinct boundaries and structural features that help acknowledge the approach of others. Out-of-sight, deep-in-the-woods locations offer these same attractions to men who transform public parks into erotic oases.

Therefore, both time of day and season (in most climates) influence the structure and amount of cruising that occurs in public parks. In the Midwest, late fall through early spring is a very slow time for cruising; weather turns cold, leaves fall from trees, and the setting loses its veils of secrecy. However, even on cold, sunlit days, at least a few men are likely to be cruising in the park. The setting, both physically and temporally, may facilitate or complicate cruising, but it does not strictly govern the who, when, where, or how.

CONTACTING AND CONTRACTING WITH ANONYMOUS SEXUAL PARTNERS

As outlined above, cruising for anonymous sexual partners in public sex arenas is a subcultural phenomenon that requires knowledge of locations, comprehension of norms, and often a period of time during which skills are acquired and refined. However, what remains to be discussed is the crux of the matter: the process by which men actually identify mutually interested others and the ways they communicate and negotiate sexual interactions. The "information game" (Goffman 1959) is a process by which individuals carefully seek to negotiate a mutual understanding of the situation: involved others and mutual needs, wants, and expectations. It is this process that cruising men re-create each and every time they return to the park and pursue a new sexual partner.

What is perhaps the most notable characteristic of interactions in pursuit of sexual relations in public sex arenas is the lack of verbal communications. As seen above, cover of darkness, bushes, and other obstacles to visibility are desirable elements of an erotic oasis, in part because they provide means to shield identities, as well as activities. Nonverbal communications are also, at least partially, a shield against identity disclosures. When one speaks, one conveys more information than the mere content of one's words. If the verbal aspects of communication are removed, so too may some of the additional identity elements be removed from an individual's interactions. Consequently, the great majority of cruising activities found in public sex arenas are conducted under the veil of silence.

Because verbal conversations are severely limited, and due to the subcultural stigmas associated with cruising public parks, men interested in other men they find in the park have restricted means to learn of others' sexual and social reputations. Whereas in other settings men may ask their associates about particular others, this is not generally possible in the arena of the public park. Additionally, because of both the very fluid nature of the park's patrons and their preference for after-dark cruising, identifying others can often be a very difficult task. Therefore, there may be only minimal assurances that a sexual partner is not prone to violence or to exposing others to social and physical dangers.

On those rare occasions when verbal conversation is used to establish contact, it is brief and presented in ambiguous fashion. One man may greet another, or make a simple request (ask for the time, a match, or directions to a landmark). Such opening comments allow for a quick appraisal of another man in a very low-risk form of contact. Once a man is deduced as willing to speak, the conversation starter will ask some type of leading, or double-meaning, question. This is the way that Adam makes initial contact with men

in the park. Adam says he likes to feel as if he knows *something* about the men with whom he has anonymous sexual encounters, so he always asks others a few questions.

> *I might say something about any subject that I knew would be of common interest...or, I'd ask if you were driving through enjoying the day, or looking? Everybody knows what that means! If you're driving through enjoying the day, or you're not interested, you'll tell me. That's a comfortable way out, and not being rude. If you are interested, you're going to tell me that you are—you are looking.*

As explained earlier, withdrawing from an unwanted interaction is acceptable, and provided for, in men's homosocial, sexual environments. Ambiguous questions not only facilitate the negotiation of sexual encounters but can also provide for easy withdrawal from undesirable potential encounters.

The way that men communicate their interest in other men, and contact and contract with others, is via five primary modes of nonverbal communication: eye contact, use of personal space, body language, subtle forms of touching (of both themselves and others), and movement through the park in pursuit or in tandem with other men. Nonverbal communication is the rule in erotic oases (Delph 1978; Donnelly 1981; Weatherford 1986; Tewksbury 1990). The "language" of such a subcultural location is well summarized by Ted, who explains the way men who cruise public parks communicate, saying,

> *It has its own language, and you don't—well, I'm sure I don't know all of it. But what I have come to learn and be able to recognize is that there is a subliminal language to it that is not words. It's certain actions, certain movement.... This is something I've never really put words to until now.*

To understand the language is to use it while not needing to think consciously about it. It is only when one develops a fluency in the "subliminal language" of the public sex arena that successful cruising is likely to occur. The way men communicate while cruising is indeed a language in its own right, just as is any patterned form of communication that requires study, skill, and practice.

The communication modes used are by no means unique to the public sex arena. Neither is the public sex arena the only setting in which such communication means are used to contact and contract with interactants. What is unique is the way that *men* use such means with *other men* in pursuit of sexual exchanges.

With verbal communication essentially absent, men need to have means of getting the attention of others, as well as a means of acknowledging the call for attention of another. This is the principal function of eye contact. As Goffman (1977) believed, "the male's assessing act—his ogling—constitutes the first move in the courtship process" (p. 309). Eye contact is the main means by which contact is made. Contact is not simply looking at a man, but looking consistently into his eyes and holding his gaze. The "prolonged" look, directly into the eyes of another, which might be considered deviant in ordinary, daily interactions, is the means by which men greet one another and quickly determine whether sufficient mutual interest exists to continue with increasingly intimate contact.[4]

Eye contact is relied upon to determine, first of all, whether another is knowledgeable about setting activities, and whether he understands and adheres to (at least in rudimentary fashion) the norms of the public sex arena. Duane, who knows that police regularly visit the parks undercover, says that when he is cruising in the park,

> Eye contact for me is ultimate. By being able to catch a person's eye and the way that—well, I can tell whether they're really comfortable or not. Even cops aren't comfortable enough to hold your gaze, you know—I mean 'cause they are just not to the point of doing it. That's one of the biggest clues for me.

Another way of looking at the functions of eye contact while cruising is offered by Matt, a self-described "long experienced" public sex arena cruiser: "Eye contact is the way you invite someone to participate with you.... It's not just looking at someone, but like *really* looking at someone, and them really looking at you."

Eye contact is the contact point, the initial way to investigate another man's subcultural experience, and perhaps motivations. Eye contact can open the door to continued, increasingly focused, sexually directed interactions. The eyes serve as the filter for determining which others in the setting may be appropriate, interested, and suitable partners, with whom one may wish to move into the initial contracting stage. As amount and intensity of eye contact increase, so too do interactants' personal investments in continued interactions (Iizuka 1992).

There are two general, and related, means by which increasingly focused interactions are pursued. Communicating an interest in contracting is put forth either through one man entering another man's "personal space" (see Hall 1959) or through body language signaling a sexual interest.

Body language—positioning oneself within the setting, posing in the line of another's vision, and contorting the body so as to present or emphasize certain parts of it—can communicate meaningful messages. Many men maintain that even though they don't speak with others, "body language says a lot." Or, more specifically, as Ted explains it:

> There are several forms of body language. If a person is standing facing toward you and they're moving about in place.... Fondling himself, making it apparent that they're interested in some kind of sexual contact. Maybe by fondling themselves directly at you, so that is something that they perceive is what you're looking for. Their intention is pretty clear and very tight. Then that followed with a smile.

Body language often involves motions and signals. As attention is maintained between men, these signals frequently involve touching oneself. Touching, stroking, and massaging parts of one's own body are taken to communicate interests (often specific sexual interests). Rubbing one's chest or lips, or stroking the inside of one's thighs, or, most obviously, stroking, massaging, or caressing one's genitals (usually, but not always, through one's clothing) communicates sexual interest, and for most men is taken as an invitation for sexual contact. Body rubbing is done in conjunction with eye contact. To create the most direct message possible, a man moves, rubs, or serially poses while maintaining what he hopes is a mutually held gaze.

Body language also means presenting one's body in what is self-perceived as an attractive manner. Often, especially during warm weather, careful attention is given to the apparel a man wears to the public sex arena. Clothing not only functions as costume, but ideally for the cruising man also provides easy access to critical sexual body parts. Ease and speed of removal and replacement are important. More important, though, is the way that clothing accentuates what a man perceives as his appearance strengths. On occasion men will be seen in cruising areas wearing very revealing clothing (e.g., bathing suits, leather accessories, workout clothing). The intention of men so attired is presumably obvious to others, both those cruising and not. Among many men in public sex arenas, "there's this whole mentality of putting yourself on display," says Duane. Being on display can be dangerous, though; this is why many gay men prefer cruising in controlled access environments (e.g., bars, baths, and clubs) where costuming can be beneficial to one's displays but only minimally dangerous (Brodsky 1993).

In addition to the presentation of oneself, communicating a sexual interest in another man involves personal space invasions and perhaps subtle, "accidental" forms of contact. When one man allows himself to be touched in any way by another man and does not indicate a dislike or unwillingness to have it continue or occur again, an agreement to progress in the form and intensity of touching is presumed. Vince explained that when he cruises for a sexual partner in the park, after making eye contact with a man he next moves to

invasion of personal space. Another thing after that is accidentally brushing up against him and neither one of you moves away. That's important, 'cause that dude not moving shows a willingness to be touched.

Touching, posing, placing oneself in another's line of vision, gazing at and receiving a return gaze: these are the tools of communication men in public sex arenas use to replace verbal exchanges when contacting and contracting for exchanges.

Intervening between the initial eye contact and an eventual sexual contact are a period of time and a series of interactions in which men pursue each other (both literally and figuratively). The pursuit involves men following each other through the park, whether on foot or in their automobiles, testing one another's resolve and commitment to an exchange. For many men, this phase takes on the quality of a game, or becomes a literal "hunt" and conquest series of interactions. Jack, who believes himself to be among the most skillful and experienced public park cruisers in his city, related the following description of "the chase":

It's more like playing a game. Basically, that's what it is with a lot of them, it's a big game. You see somebody, you walk by, they'll take off and you follow them from one end to the other, chasing each other. If you give up and turn around, then they'll start chasing after you. That will happen as much as seven or ten times; it's a two-way game, until the connection is made.

The rules of the "chase" game are fairly simple. If you make initial contact with someone that you are interested in, you either follow him or position yourself so that he can easily follow you. The chase is not supposed to be simply one man following another to a location where they have sex, however. Rather, the chase is a test of each man's dedication to the process and the possibility of a sexual encounter with his chosen other.

Many times the chase lasts for extended periods of time, perhaps 2 hours or more. During the course of this time, men report, they are consistently strategizing ways to read the intentions of the other and to seek ways to draw the other man into making a more assertive advance. Adam, a friend who often goes to the park with Jack, but who always cruises alone, describes how his mind is constantly at work strategizing while playing the "chase game." According to Adam, after making an initial move to follow a man with whom he has already made contact, his mind turns to:

> *The next move is his, what will he do? Will he go back the other way? Will he at that point take the initiative and come up to me, or will he pass me and go down the path 10 or 15 feet and stop? If he does that, it's quite obvious he knows how to play the game. He's interested. He knows that second stop on his part has told me something.... Then I know. He already knows, because I've already stopped. I was first following him, and I stopped to give him a chance to follow me. If he's not interested, he'll do something else. He'll go the other way or do something that will tell me that. It's all just a game!*

In the game, the role with the greater degree of both control and prestige is the role of the pursued. To be followed is to be complimented. Men who are sought after may, in fact, experience situations when more than one individual follows them. In such a situation the matter is complicated when only one of the others involved in the game is desirable to the sought-after man.

Throughout the chase game, communications remain on the nonverbal level, and they may often include heavy doses of eye contact. Whenever a man is being followed, he needs to be aware constantly of whether his pursuer is still in pursuit. This means both visually checking behind him and carefully listening for the other man.

Obviously, to be successful at the chase game requires skills, yet not every man in the park possesses these skills. They can be learned but frequently may require numerous futile (and therefore discouraging) forays. However, with time, dedication, and careful observation (if not direct instruction from a friend, such as Adam reports receiving from Jack), a man can become a skillful player of the game.

CONCLUSION

The processes employed by men who have anonymous sexual encounters with men in public places are culturally created and reinforced phenomena.

The idea that men seek out and consummate sexual relationships with anonymous others, while perhaps shocking or disturbing to some, actually carries many similarities to the processes by which men and women seek out both sexual and long-term relationship partners.

Regardless of the gender of those involved, partner-seeking activities require that an individual be aware of the locations where potential partners can be located, have a sense of when others are likely to be in these locations, understand the basic scripts for normative interactional patterns, and be at least somewhat fluent in the language and dialects of cruising. Where differences become apparent is in the fact that gender-based roles are altered, and only men are present. Rather than having attraction based on "natural" gender differences, these men must establish differences in roles, expectations, and desires among potential partners. Communication among and between those seeking partners must be clear and complete.

However, because men who cruise for male sexual partners in public settings must be ever attentive to the possibilities (and likely negative consequences) that other men present may not be seeking sex, common communication modes present obstacles. Therefore, the process of communication is tracked into a (typically) prolonged, carefully navigated cruise through double-entendres and ambiguous nonverbal statements. Communication modes include body language, movement throughout the setting, eye contact, and subtle forms of gestures and touch. In essence, men seeking male sex partners in anonymous public settings employ some of the traditionally feminine means of communication. The homosocial nature of the interactional environment necessitates reconfiguration of gendered interactions.

The language of cruising serves as a gatekeeping mechanism for the subcultural setting of the public sex arena. As an open, yet carefully guarded, subcultural setting, a closed set of discreditable (Goffman 1963) men are provided an environment that meets their needs and desires.

Although open, the setting does provide some degree of territorial bounding as well as a potential "cover" for men's presence.

NOTES

1. For an exception to the long-standing focus on heterosexual attraction, see Ross and Paul (1992) for an examination of the role of physical attractiveness in the sexual attractions of bisexual men and women.

2. Interviewees are all white men, with an average age of 31.3 years, and an age range from 21 to 50. Ten of the men in the sample self-identify as gay, and one identifies as bisexual. All but one of the men have some college education.

3. Some critics would argue, however, that such "guides" are often outdated and simply incorrect. For our purposes, however, the mere existence of such publications testifies to the wide knowledge of such locations among MSM community members.

4. Similarly, Walsh and Hewitt (1985) have shown that repeated instances of eye contact function as strong motivators for men to approach unknown women in a singles bar.

REFERENCES

Brodsky, Joel I. 1993. "The Mineshaft: A Retrospective Ethnography." *Journal of Homosexuality* 24: 233–251.

Brown, Rita Mae. 1976. "Strangers in Paradise." *Body Politic* (no volume):23.

Clark, Russell III. 1990. "The Impact of AIDS on Gender Differences in Willingness to Engage in Casual Sex." *Journal of Applied Social Psychology* 20:771–782.

Clark, Russell III, and Elaine Hatfield. 1989. "Gender Differences in Receptivity to Sexual Offers." *Journal of Psychology and Human Sexuality* 2:39–55.

Delph, Edward. 1978. *The Silent Community: Public Homosexual Encounters.* Beverly Hills, CA: Sage.

Donnelly, Peter. 1981. "Running the Gauntlet: The Moral Order of Pornographic Movie Theaters." *Urban Life* 10:239–264.

Gagnon, John, and William Simon. 1973. *Sexual Conduct: The Social Sources of Human Sexuality.* Chicago: Aldine.

Goffman, Erving. 1959. *The Presentation of Self in Everyday Life.* Garden City, NY: Doubleday.

Goffman, Erving. 1963. *Stigma: Notes on the Management of Spoiled Identity.* Englewood Cliffs, NJ: Prentice-Hall.

Goffman, Erving. 1977. "The Arrangement Between the Sexes." *Theory and Society* 4:301–331.

Hall, Edward. 1959. *The Silent Language.* Garden City, NY: Doubleday.

Herold, Edward, and Dawn-Marie Mewhinney. 1993. "Gender Differences in Casual Sex and AIDS Prevention: A Survey of Dating Bars." *The Journal of Sex Research* 30:36–42.

Iizuka, Yuichi. 1992. "Eye Contact in Dating Couples and Unacquainted Couples." *Perceptual and Motor Skills* 75:457–461.

Kamel, G. W. Levi. 1983. *Downtown Street Hustlers: The Role of Dramaturgical Imaging Practices in the Social Construction of Male Prostitution.* Unpublished Ph.D. dissertation, University of California, San Diego.

Lee, John Alan. 1979. "The Social Organization of Sexual Risk." *Alternative Lifestyles* 2:69–100.

Pollack, Michael. 1993. "Homosexual Rituals and Safer Sex." *Journal of Homosexuality* 25:307–317.

Ross, Michael, and Jay Paul. 1992. "Beyond Gender: The Basis of Sexual Attraction in Bisexual Men and Women." *Psychological Reports* 71:1283–1290.

Simon, William, and John Gagnon. 1986. "Sexual Scripts: Permanence and Change." *Archives of Sexual Behavior* 15:97–120.

Tewksbury, Richard. 1990. "Patrons of Porn: Research Notes on the Clientele of Adult Bookstores." *Deviant Behavior* 11:259–271.

Walsh, Debra, and Jay Hewitt. 1985. "Giving Men the Come-On: Effect of Eye Contact and Smiling in a Bar Environment." *Perceptual and Motor Skills* 61:873–874.

Weatherford, Jack McIver. 1986. *Porn Row.* New York: Arbor House.

Weinberg, Martin, and Colin Williams. 1975. "Gay Baths and the Social Organization of Impersonal Sex." *Social Problems* 23:124–136.

Lesbians' Resistance to
Culturally Defined Attractiveness

LIAHNA GORDON

The dominant culture of gender puts forth a set of expectations on how women are supposed to think, feel, and act about their bodies. In short, they are expected to be attractive. Conventional socialization presents a narrow view of attractiveness at the same time that it exerts high pressure to conform to this conception.

In studying lesbians, Liahna Gordon found that, after participation in a lesbian subculture, they learned a much broader conception of attractiveness, a wider set of beauty norms. In turn, they learned how to conform to and enact these norms with their intimate partners. Both they and their partners organized their actions on the basis of this broader conception of attractiveness. The women came to see themselves as their partners did—as attractive people—even though their bodies didn't represent the more rigid criteria of the dominant culture.

Popular stereotypes depict lesbians as looking butch and unfeminine with hairy legs, short hair, no makeup, and androgynous clothing. According to these stereotypes, all lesbians resist nearly all feminine forms of dress and appearance at all times. In 1998 I investigated the ways in which women in the lesbian community actually resist (and conform to) feminine appearance by conducting in-depth interviews with 24 women who belong to a lesbian community in Bloomington, Indiana. The women range in age from 21 to 61, are white, and are predominantly middle class. Consistent with these views, all the participants in the study discussed below *do* engage in some form of resistance to what they interpret as the mainstream heterosexual gender rules of appearance and attractiveness. Unlike the clichés, however, this resistance does not always take the most obvious or stereotypical forms. The resistant behavior of the participants is actually more complex than portrayed by the stereotypes, varying in degree, form, and motivation. Further, this resistance does not simply result from individuals acting out their true, gender-deviant natures, but consists of patterns of behavior, grounded in ideology, that are continually encouraged and reinforced by the lesbian community.

SUBCULTURAL RESOURCES

By engaging in resistant and nonconforming behaviors, the participants render themselves "deviant" in the larger cultures. I argue, however, that the members of the lesbian community are acting out not merely some true inner nature but a patterned set of behaviors based on ideology and values of the lesbian subcultures. Indeed, the community teaches, supports, and reinforces these behaviors. I use the term *subcultural resources* to signify all the sources of support the lesbian subcultures provide their members by way of encouragement for engaging in these resistant and nonconforming behaviors. In theory, these resources could include ideology, attitudes, norms, accounts, friendship networks, and formal organizational support. In the data presented here, the participants specifically cited the following as the subcultural resources from which they most com-

Prepared especially for this volume. Permission of the author.

monly gain their support: alternative constructions of beauty, norms encouraging the acceptance of these alternate constructions, lesbian media, lesbian festivals, and lesbian partners.

The beauty ideals in the lesbian subcultures seem more expansive than those in the hegemonic cultures. This comes across not only in what the participants themselves find attractive in women but also in what the subcultures have defined as its beauty ideals. In other words, the participants see the community as a whole, not just themselves as individuals, and have defined attractiveness in a way that differs from that of the mainstream cultures:

> It seems that lesbians, the ones I've been around, not the lesbians of fiction, that lesbians accept women and their bodies as they are, whatever shape or weight or endowment or whatever. This is the body you have. (Tiger)[1]

> I think that lesbians don't find [body] parts as attractive. We aren't like, "Oh, she has really nice breasts" or "She's got really pretty legs, too bad her shoulders are all wrong." I think lesbians are more physically attracted to the whole. Straight men will be like, "I'm a tit man" or "I'm a leg man." You don't see lesbians objectifying women; we don't tend to pick women apart and then be attracted to those parts. That may be why lesbians tend to be attracted to a broader range of body types. I think that what we find attractive to other women are what we would want others to be attracted to in us. (Harriet)

A few of the participants disagree in that they do not think that the community necessarily rejects the mainstream cultural definition of beauty, but neither do they believe that the community is confined to that definition; they believe that women who both fit and run counter to that cultural ideal are deemed attractive in the community:

> Well, I think a lot of lesbians like that Barbie-doll look [laughs]. I don't think they have to have that look to be attractive to someone. I think lesbians

have a more expansive view of what beauty is. Lesbians value strength. I think women value other strong women. I think women can look male and, in the lesbian community, be exactly right on. You can look like anything and be accepted in the lesbian community. (Julie)

Not everyone agrees that someone could "look like anything" and still be considered attractive to lesbians. But all of the participants do concur that the boundaries in the lesbian communities are more expansive than those of the heterosexual cultures:

> It's a different sort of standard, but is a standard of some sort. There are all sorts of standards for the female body. There's a generic male-defined one, and then another that women have for other women, and then another that straight women have for other women. They are different. The one in other lesbian women is more flexible, but is still a standard. It's not just how thin I am, but standards in terms of what a woman should be. A different standard, but still a standard. (Sarah)

Though participants hold slightly different opinions on this topic, this is perhaps attributable in part to the diversity of the lesbian community itself, in which these attractiveness norms may be stronger among certain parts of the community. Nonetheless, the participants agree overall: the lesbian subcultures generally promote broader, more accepting definitions of attractiveness than do the mainstream heterosexual cultures.

The lesbian media help to reinforce and reaffirm these alternate standards and constructions of beauty both by showing different images of women than those typically highlighted by mainstream media, and by confronting the issue head on, discussing the dangers done by the mainstream beauty ideals. As one participant explains:

> I think one of the things that lesbian women do is fight more vigorously against the expectations. I don't see very often in heterosexual women's magazines the notion that fat is beautiful. One of the Lesbian Connections has this huge woman on the cover. You never see that in heterosexual magazines.

---

[1] All names are pseudonyms chosen by the participants.

In Lesbian Connection, *there's at least debate about whether fat is beautiful or if it is healthy. Is it a reflection of self-esteem or a lack of it? These are not Christie Brinkley–type women, but they're beautiful. To lesbians, they're beautiful. (Anne)*

Additionally, musical performances aimed primarily at lesbians commonly include at least one song in their play list that critiques heterosexual beauty standards. Lesbian singer/songwriter Jamie Anderson sings several such songs, including *All of Me* and *Dark Chocolate*. Likewise, the Sapphire Uppity Blues Women sing the praises of large legs ("there's thunder in these thighs") in their song *Thunder Thighs*. Donna talks about such a song performed by the Bloomington Feminist Chorus:

Going to the Feminist Chorus concert a week ago, there was a song about being overweight, being fat. And one of the lines was, "Do I really want to be so thin that a man can count my ribs so that I will look beautiful for him while he's counting my ribs?" And I went, "That just sums up our whole life!"

The participants often cited the lesbian music festivals, especially the National Women's Music Festival and the Michigan Women's Music Festival, as spaces where these more expansive constructions of beauty are taught, reinforced, and reaffirmed. Women who have attended these festivals talked about how they offer opportunities for them to see women of all shapes and sizes together, and to feel accepted. For some, being in this crowd makes them feel "normal" at last:

Over half the womyn [sic] around are also shirtless. Wimmin [sic] of all sizes, shapes, ages, and breast sizes. I will fit in here fine, for I will not feel big or fat like [in] the outside world. Thank you, God!! (Donna, personal journal)

Alice explains that at these festivals one does more than just see all types of women, for the presence and prevalence of such a variety of bodies bring about an altered conception of beauty:

Women there on acres of forested ground where there are no men; it's totally safe. Women are in all kinds of stages of dress and undress. How wonderful that feels, to be walking around in a skirt and nothing else. To see every conceivable size, shape, ability, disability, scars, mastectomy scars. Every time I've been there, there's a moment of understanding how beautiful we all are. Miles and miles of women….I do think it is a common experience to go, "Wow! Aren't we beautiful!" The last time I was there, for two months preparing, there were eight or nine of us in a house, and the others were veterans, and were talking about the "festival moment." And then at one point I went, "Wow! Look at us! Aren't we incredible?! Look at all of us! We're beautiful!" Someone said, "Ha! You're having your festival moment!" So it must be pretty common.

Support for acceptance of these alternate constructions of beauty is found not only in the form of sudden realizations or informal opportunities for changes in one's consciousness. The festivals also offer formal organizational support. The feminist organizers often encourage women's acceptance of their bodies by scheduling workshops around issues of the body.

The expansive alternate constructions of beauty, and the norms encouraging women to adopt these alternate constructions, are strong enough that even the few participants who don't find a variety of body shapes (especially those of heavy women) attractive are apologetic about it. Their discourse around this issue resembles a confessional, and the women articulated that to not find large women attractive is somehow "against the rules":

I'm not attracted to girls who are real heavy for some reason. That's bad, I know, because society in general is like, "You're not attractive if you're fat," which is not true, because there are a lot of really pretty girls out there who are big girls. Which is cool. But I don't find myself attracted to those girls, although I can still say she's pretty. But I wouldn't necessarily want to hop in bed with her. (Gertrude)

PPAN: It's embarrassing to even say. I find that I tend not to look at very overweight people.

And that's very...I feel bad saying that, but it's true. I tend not to look twice at someone who's very overweight.

LIAHNA: Why do you feel bad?

PPAN: I think it's making a judgment on someone without getting to know them. I know a number of women who are overweight who are lovely women that I got to know through the National Women's Music Festival. But probably unless they approached me, I may not have approached them. Which doesn't feel good, you know? I am not proud of that fact.

Support for resistance to the heterosexual beauty rules is perhaps most often and most importantly manifested and reinforced at the individual level, where the participants receive continuing positive feedback from their partners about their attractiveness. Though based on the behaviors of individuals, this is a subcultural resource in that the community encourages a norm according to which partners are supposed to recognize and allay each others' insecurities regarding their bodies or attractiveness. Regardless of how far the participants lie from the heterosexual ideal in terms of appearance, nearly all the women say that their partners (or past partners) regularly compliment their appearance, and that they believe their partners find their bodies attractive, beautiful, and/or sexy:

She really seemed to like my body, and even the things I was self-conscious about. She really went out of her way, as I did with her, to make me think that was silly. There were things she was self-conscious about, but this is why I believe her. The things she was self-conscious about were things—I thought she had a beautiful body too. She always thought the normal girl things: "I have a big ass," or whatever. I wasn't just overlooking that. I really didn't think that. I thought she was beautiful. So I believe she really thought the same about me. (Sarah)

She likes my eyes, she likes my hair, she always says, "I think you're gorgeous!" She likes my body, she doesn't want me to be really thin. She definitely doesn't want me to be skinny. (Emily)

According to the participants, not only do their partners think the participants are sexy and beautiful, but they actively and continually let the participants know this through compliments and other regular verbalizations. This is a reciprocal endeavor, with the participants doing the same for their partners.

HARRIET: We both had pretty lousy feelings about our bodies. She was fairly heavy and really broad-shouldered, which I love! I thought they were really cool! But she hated it because she couldn't find clothes to fit. I like to think that I was a positive influence on her own body [image]. A fairly solidly built woman, not fat and soft, but more just solid. I thought she was very attractive. She would constantly give me compliments and I would say no way! But I finally started believing her.

LIAHNA: How did she tell you?

HARRIET: She used to say I was hot! It cracked me up because it was sooo different from my own image of myself. I don't know how much of that was just saying it to make me feel good. She would go on and on complimenting me. "Oooh, you need glasses!" [I'd say]. And finally I got tired of protesting, and I just dealt with it.

I feel sexy when she [my partner] compliments me. I feel sexy when I get dressed up and go out. She's always complimenting me and it makes me feel so good. (Julie)

Similarly, most of the participants described their partners' bodies positively. Only three made neutral or negative comments regarding their partners' bodies, and even those were more made as statements of fact than as value judgments. When asked to describe her last partner's body, for example, KT said, "I would say she's overweight, but it wasn't necessarily an issue [for me]." Yet, while this quote is one of the most negative ones made regarding a partner's body, KT indicated that she, too, complimented her partner regularly on her body, and appreciated her partner's attractiveness, despite her partner's insecurities:

LIAHNA: Were you aware of your partner feeling self-conscious [about her body during sex]?

KT: Yeah. Our opinions about ourselves are usually stronger than others' are about you. She felt like she was fat. So I felt as if I had to make her feel better about it. It wasn't an issue for me, but it was for her. I would tell her what I thought about her. Sometimes when you tell someone something, they don't believe it is the complete truth, even when it is.

Thus, the norms in the community are strong enough that even those making the most negative comments about their partners' appearance also try to allay their partners' fears and give them positive feedback on their attractiveness. Again, this evidences not only an individual expression of support but a patterned set of behaviors taught, expected, and reinforced by the lesbian subcultures.

SUMMARY AND CONCLUSION

In the lesbian subcultures, the rules regarding attractiveness are set up in opposition to the heterosexual norms. Thus, all the participants resist the mainstream heterosexual attractiveness norms (as they interpret them) to at least some extent. This resistance is more complex than popularly conceived, taking various forms and stemming from a variety of motivations. Further, resistance cannot be judged by appearance alone: the resistant behaviors engaged in by the women include redefining beauty ideals, holding certain beliefs and values about appearance and attractiveness, and, as members of the community, providing support for other women, especially partners, in terms of attractiveness.

A subcultural rule not discussed by many of the participants, but which I have observed in my time in the lesbian community, is that women simply do not talk about their bodies, especially in any sort of negative way. Unlike in heterosexual contexts where fat talk may be used either as a form of bonding or as a way to get positive feedback ("Don't say that! You're not fat!") (Nichter and Vuckovic 1994), in lesbian contexts negative self-body talk is met with silence. In the few instances in which I have witnessed lesbians mentioning their bodily attractiveness at all, I have literally seen those around them physically turn away, change the subject, or react with complete silence. While this may not seem as supportive as the heterosexual response of providing reassurance or joining in the self-critique, it does signal that those in the lesbian community are not willing to encourage such negative self-evaluations. Thus, unlike the dominant cultures in which discontent with one's body may be normative (Rodin, Silberstein, and Striegel-Moore 1984), the lesbian community promotes a norm in which women are satisfied with their bodies, whatever their shape or size.

Relatedly, unlike in the heterosexual cultures where weight control signals morality (Nichter and Vuckovic 1994), in the lesbian community a sense of morality is linked to not participating in the beauty game. The participants give a sense that to resist dominant attractiveness norms is to be more "real." In this formulation, wearing makeup or spending excessive amounts of time on clothing acts as a mask or costume, hiding the "real self." Thus, to discuss one's appearance at all, but especially in a judgmental way, is to exhibit shallowness and superficiality, a trait generally not considered acceptable within the lesbian community.

It is important to reiterate that, with the aid of subcultural resources, not only do all the participants resist the dominant heterosexual norms of attractiveness, but all the participants also engage in nonconforming behavior that they do not label resistant. Hence, we do not simply have a situation in which some women are more politically aware than others and call their behavior resistance, while others wish to minimize their "deviance" by accounting for it by claiming it falls outside their control. Rather, we see a complex system in which the participants account for appearance behavior they perceive as falling outside the mainstream attractiveness norms as both resistant *and* out of their control. Emphasizing this complexity, I witnessed the participants regularly giving these various and multiple accounts, highlighting the fact that the type of account given cannot be predicted according to the type of individual or type of appearance behavior. These multiple accounts likely stem from the different norms and resources provided the participants by both the lesbian and heterosexual communities. As members of the lesbian community, the women not only accept certain parts of the prevailing ideologies of the subcultures but are also expected, and given the opportunity, to follow at least some of the subcultural rules regarding appearance. Yet, the lesbian community does not exist apart from the heterosexual cultures, and it makes its own demands regarding attractiveness and appearance.

REFERENCES

Nichter, Mimi, and Nancy Vuckovic. 1994. "Fat Talk: Body Image Among Adolescent Girls," in *Many Mirrors: Body Image and Social Relations* (pp. 109–131), edited by Nicole Sault. New Brunswick: Rutgers University Press.

Rodin, Judith, Lisa Silberstein, and Ruth Striegel-Moore. 1984. "Women and Weight: A Normative Discontent," in *Nebraska Symposium on Motivation* (pp. 267–307), edited by T. B. Sonderegger. Lincoln: University of Nebraska Press.

CHAPTER 11

SOCIAL DIVERSITY

A Typology of Heroin Addicts

CHARLES E. FAUPEL

Street junkies, whose deviance is both frequent and visible, perform social functions. In addition to serving as negative role models, they supply ample evidence of the penalties for deviance. Perhaps more importantly, they help to sustain the popular negative stereotype about the relationship of deviance and downward social mobility. Thus, in the popular view of drug addiction, once people start, they cannot stop, and it is only a matter of time before they "hit bottom." In the popular view, deviant careers in substance use are irreversible. They move in only one direction—down. The relationship between use and deviant behavior is linear. As drug use increases, conformity with both conventional norms and norms of the addict subculture decreases.

Charles E. Faupel's study of drug addicts refutes this popular stereotype. Use and conformity to addict norms vary in accordance with two kinds of regularities in the addict's life: supply of drugs and work. Faupel categorizes four types of addicts according to changes in both routines. And he finds fluctuations in the deviant lifestyle rather than fixity in the downward direction. Thus, addicts can and do change in accordance with these other changes. The more regular the routines, the greater the conformity with addict norms.

A widely shared belief in American society holds that increased heroin addiction inevitably results in moral degeneracy. According to the "dope fiend mythology" (Lindesmith, 1940), as the addict becomes hopelessly enslaved to this deadliest of all drugs, all ethical restraints dissolve. In the words of a vice squad officer interviewed by Gould and his associates:

> These junkies become so degenerate it is sad. They live in such filth. You should see some of the apart-

Reprinted from *Urban Life and Culture,* Vol. 15 (October 1986–January 1987), pp. 395–419, by permission of Sage Publications, Inc. Copyright © 1989 by Sage Publications, Inc.

> ments I've been in. What's more, junkies have no consideration for their families and their friends.... I think the drug does something basic to a person. I don't know what it is. I'm not an expert on that sort of thing, but it seems as if drug users just don't have any morals left after a while. (Gould et al., 1974:71)

As this statement indicates, many believe that addicts will indiscriminately victimize anyone they know or encounter. One San Francisco journalist flatly asserts:

> He's after that money; he needs it to buy heroin. And he'll take it from you if you are his nearest

and dearest friend, even if he has to kill you to do it. (Quoted in Silver and Aldrich, 1979:42)

Similarly, the "dope peddler" is commonly depicted as an unscrupulous entrepreneur with a penchant for turning young children on to drugs (Anslinger and Tompkins, 1953; Ashley, 1972; Eldridge, 1967; Lindesmith, 1940; Rubington, 1967). "Every addict," say Anslinger and Tompkins (1953:272), "knowing himself to be a moral and social outcast, delights in bringing others into the outcast fold."

Recent research has openly questioned this assumption of the inevitable and totally morally destructive effects of heroin use. Studies by Ashley (1972), Bullington (1977), Coombs (1981), Hanson et al. (1985), Hughes (1977), Preble and Casey (1969), Reese (1975), Rosenbaum (1981a, 1981b), Waldorf (1973), and Zinberg (1984) suggest that most heroin addicts maintain a sense of ethical responsibility in the social world in which they function. Contrary to the popular imagery, this research has consistently reported that heroin addicts are not indiscriminate with regard to whom they will victimize. Rosenbaum (1981a:54) found, for example, not only that addicts espouse a distinct code of ethics, but also that the inclination and ability to adhere to this code [vary] with an addict's standing in the street world of heroin use:

A code of ethics is, in fact, a part of the stratification system in the addict world. Theft, for example, is graduated. The more impersonal the target of stealing, the better; the closer to home, the worse the addict feels about it. While it is seen as all right, even courageous and bold, to steal from a large store or a person unknown to the addict, stealing from friends, family, and to a lesser extent, other addicts is not sanctioned.

Ethnographic studies have also failed to support the image of the addict as promiscuously turning on the young and vulnerable. Most young users were first turned on by close friends who were themselves just beginning to experiment with drugs (Ashley, 1972; Blum, 1972; Blumer et

al., 1976; Crawford et al., 1983; Eldridge, 1967; Hughes, 1977; Sutter, 1969). Moreover, Sutter (1969:807) insists that "turning someone on"

is an expression of trust, friendship and acceptance. Most lower strata youth were introduced to drugs by a close friend or relative. After they learned to use drugs for pleasure, being turned on and turning others on became an established social practice, similar to the convention of buying a friend a drink or offering a drink to a guest when he comes to your house.

In spite of this body of research, however, we know that most addicts have at times engaged in behaviors that violated the standards and ideals of their own subculture. Despite ethical protestations to the contrary, young neophytes may be turned on to drugs by experienced addicts, and addicts may victimize those nearest and dearest to them. It is not sufficient simply to note that addicts engage in such norm-violating behaviors. Situational exceptions to idealized cultural standards can frequently be observed throughout various sectors of the population. Consequently, we should expect that there will also be times, places, and circumstances when normative standards in the heroin subculture will fail to invoke strict conformity. The more important consideration is the circumstances under which these standards are violated and the stance that addicts take toward these violations and the values they represent. For as Meier (1981:14) has argued:

The concept of norm…does not require a correspondence between what persons say and what they do; discrepancies are to be expected…. [B]ecause norms identify behavior that "ought" or "ought not" to occur, behavior may (and often does) depart from norms…. The more relevant consideration includes the conditions under which this potential for deviance is realized and the conditions under which norms guide specific conduct.

The subculture of heroin use provides an excellent opportunity to examine the situational contingencies affecting departure from or conformity to such subcultural normative standards. Heavily involved heroin addicts experience a daily demand for high-cost drugs, a harsh reality that may indeed come to overshadow all other concerns in the addict's life. This article seeks to identify and analyze those conditions that tend to undermine conformity to espoused subcultural ideals....

...All of the respondents had prior contact with the criminal justice system and most (24) were incarcerated at the time of interview....

DRUG AVAILABILITY AND LIFE STRUCTURE

The situational character of addict ethics must be understood in the context of addict careers. As Crawford et al. (1983) and Rubington (1967) point out, heroin-using careers are not an inevitable result of heroin use, but are shaped by external career contingencies. Two contingencies that have a profound influence both on the direction of addicts' careers and on their conformity to or departure from subcultural norms of behavior are *drug availability* and *life structure* (Faupel, 1981). *Availability* refers in the broadest sense to the extent to which heroin is accessible to any particular addict. At issue here is more than mere access to sellers of heroin who have quantities of the drug to sell, although this is certainly an important aspect of availability. Availability is also a function of the fluctuating cost of heroin, the resources and opportunities to obtain the drug in nonmonetary ways (for example, see Goldstein, 1981; Johnson et al., 1985), possession of the conventional and/or criminal skills necessary to provide money to purchase heroin, and the knowledge and techniques necessary to actually use heroin. In short, availability is a product of all of those opportunities and obstacles that may influence a heroin user's prospects for ultimately introducing a quantity of the drug into his or her bloodstream.

This feature of heroin-using careers has profound implications for the ethical behavior of addicts. Ready availability of drugs affords the addict the luxury of maintaining a comfortable level of consumption without engaging in many of the "low-down" or desperate tactics characteristic of less fortunate users. Rosenbaum (1981b:77) notes, for example, that

> *the addict who occupies the top of the stratification system—the successful dealer or hustler—does not have to resort to those activities more characteristic of poorer addicts. Such addicts do not have to become unscrupulous and without values or morals. However, those addicts who are sick from withdrawal and penniless find themselves in a situation that forces them to get money by* whatever *means possible.*

These moral dynamics are not, of course, limited to the experience of heroin addicts. Hughes (1971), for example, has observed a "moral division of labor" in the legal and medical professions where, because of their relative position in the professional hierarchy, some lawyers and physicians end up doing the "dirty work" enabling those of higher status to "stay clean."

Life structure refers to the regularly occurring patterns of domestic, recreational, work, and criminal activity that shape and constrain the daily life of heroin users. Recent ethnographic accounts of street heroin use in several major cities reveal that, like their "straight" counterparts, most addicts maintain reasonably predictable daily routines (Beschner and Brower, 1985; Walters, 1985). Throughout their lives all of the respondents in my study fulfilled conventional as well as criminal and other subcultural roles, both of which serve to structure the addict's daily routine. Indeed, although conventional roles are frequently overlooked in accounts of street addicts, the individuals I interviewed typically spent more time engaged in conventional activities than in criminal or deviant ones. Several worked conventional jobs. Women with children performed routine housekeeping and child-rearing duties. Many leisure-time activities did not differ from those of nonaddicts. These hard-core addicts spent time grocery shopping, tinkering with cars, visiting relatives, talking with friends, and watching television in totally unremarkable fashion.

Criminal activity, too, is an important source of life structure for the addicts I interviewed. Burglars spend time "casing" residential areas and business establishments. Shoplifters typically establish "runs," more or less stable sequences of targeted stores from which to "boost" during late morning, noon, and early afternoon hours, fencing their goods later in the afternoon. Most prostitutes keep a regular evening and nighttime schedule; mornings are usually spent sleeping and afternoons are typically occupied with conventional duties.

Although the source of these daily routines (conventional versus criminal) may have important implications for drug availability—as I shall point out momentarily—the degree of life structure exerts a significant force independently of its source. Durkheim's (1897) observation of the impact of economic disruption on suicide behavior is pertinent here; it is during such periods of instability that the usual structures of restraint lose their relevance, resulting in a state of "anomie." Lacking a routinized life structure, the heroin addict, too, finds himself or herself in an anomic condition. Under such conditions, when routine conventional and subcultural roles that serve to guide and constrain drug-using and criminal behavior are abandoned or suddenly altered, addicts typically find themselves in normative limbo. The problems of adjustment entailed in the shift from heroin to methadone maintenance, particularly as such a change disrupted the structuring of daily routine, provide a recurrent theme in the life histories. For example, "Belle," an older female addict who attempted to replace her heroin-using lifestyle with the use of "crank" (amphetamines), recalled:

> It was just like day and night between the person I had been when I was using heroin and the person I was when I got on this meth and crank...doing things in my home I had never done before; and taking things from my home that I had never done before. It was always a no-no touching my home in any way...and this last period—whew! it was really abominable.

This brief behavioral aberration, which lasted several weeks, captures the anomic reality encountered by addicts who experience an abandonment or sudden alteration of normal daily routine. In this respect, life structure exercises an important stabilizing force that helps regulate an otherwise insatiable appetite and provides the addict with a meaningful normative context.

Finally, drug availability and life structure are dynamically interrelated. Availability, for example, is often considerably enhanced when a beginning user abandons or curtails conventional routines for more lucrative criminal roles. Similarly, an addict may suffer reduced availability to drugs if he or she has a falling out with a connection (dealer), if his or her connection is arrested, or if a dealer decides to appreciably raise prices. Such eventualities may force the addict to abandon or alter normal routines in order to raise more money to obtain higher-priced drugs or to accommodate to lowered availability. Other factors, such as loss of a job, divorce, or problems from the police may result in an abandonment of normal routines, which in turn may have direct implications for an addict's ability to secure a stable supply of heroin. Consequently, the careers of addicts are characterized by periods of structured routine and relative ease of availability and by periods of disruption in routine and/or difficulty in obtaining drugs.

TYPES OF HEROIN USE AND THE CONTINGENCIES OF ETHICAL BEHAVIOR

Table 11.1 depicts four "heroin use types" that reflect the drug-use patterns produced by different combinations of drug availability and life structure. Since drug availability and life structure involve dynamic and fluctuating contingencies, these types do not represent static descriptions of particular addicts. Rather, any specific addict is likely to have experienced varying constellations of availability and structure at different times during his or her career. Furthermore, addicts do not necessarily move through these types in any sort of linear career path. Although some addicts did indeed seem to follow the sequence that will be discussed, others moved in different patterns or skipped types entirely. Moreover, it was not uncommon for there to be movement back and forth between types as the circumstances of an addict's life situation changed. Each heroin use type does represent, however, certain critical constraints and opportunities that profoundly affect addicts' inclinations and/or abilities to maintain the ethical ideals of the subculture.

THE OCCASIONAL USER

Initiates into the heroin-using subculture typically fall into this category, characterized by high life structure and low drug availability. A number of factors limit the availability of heroin to beginning users. They have not spent enough time in the subculture to have developed extensive connections for "copping dope." Moreover, their level of income is probably not capable of supporting substantial levels of heroin consumption inasmuch as successful hustling takes time to learn technique, to establish patterns, and to develop necessary connections within the subculture.

Corresponding to low levels of availability, this early period of drug use usually takes place within a structure of more conventional roles. In many cases, individuals experimenting with drugs are young and involved in school and related activities. Adolescents experimenting with drugs are

TABLE 11.1 A Typology of Heroin Use

Availability	Life Structure	
	High	Low
High	The Stabilized Junkie	The Free-Wheeling Junkie
Low	The Occasional User	The Street Junkie

also typically tied into a family structure. Conventional adult roles similarly serve to structure heroin consumption. Ron, an older black addict who had an unusually long period of occasional use, was shooting an average of only $10–$15 in street dope a day for eight years. During this eight-year period he was working a full-time job. At the same time he was living with his mother, who did not allow drug use in her home. At the end of this eight years he became a "tester" for a local dealer, a job that entailed injecting drug samples to test for quality. At that same time he lost his job and moved out of his mother's home. Hence, in addition to having more drugs available as a tester, Ron no longer maintained the rigorous daily routine that had been crucial in controlling his heroin use for eight years. His consumption escalated dramatically over a few short weeks as he quickly came to assume the "stabilized junkie" status.

All of the addicts I interviewed can be characterized as occasional users during the early period of their involvement in the subculture. Indeed, research by Zinberg (1984) suggests that there is a sizable number of users who never advance beyond such "controlled" use. Just beginning their careers as heroin users, many occasional users have not spent sufficient time in the subculture to internalize its normative expectations. Consequently, many of the respondents admitted to having violated commonly espoused subcultural standards during this phase of their careers. For example, a number of the addicts I interviewed turned friends on to heroin in a way analogous to that described by Sutter (1969). It was also during this period as young initiates that these individuals most frequently reported dipping into the family's petty cash box for some extra "spending" money. The following remarks by a veteran female addict, however, suggest that such behavior is not so much a violation of an internalized ethic, but rather a manifestation of inadequate socialization at this early point in one's career.

When you're real young…you don't have the same kind of ethics as when you get older…. All you think about in the beginning is just getting the money. But after a while as you go through the years...you begin to see that this is not the right way.

THE STABILIZED JUNKIE

Often, though not necessarily, the occasional user moves directly to the status of "stabilized junkie," characterized by a high level of availability and high, though usually modified, life structure. As occasional users, emerging addicts become socialized into the life of the subculture. Not only do they learn and internalize the normative expectations of the subculture, they also learn the essentials of copping (locating and purchasing), cooking (preparing), and spiking (injecting) themselves— all factors that, in effect, increase the availability of heroin. It was not uncommon for the addicts I interviewed, for example, to experience a sharp increase in their heroin consumption after they learned to inject themselves. They were no longer dependent on the presence of more experienced drug using friends to "get off."

In addition to enhancing these fundamental skills as a drug user, the stabilized junkie increases drug availability by upgrading copping skills and connections. The addict who must rely on the lower-quality, more expensive "street bag," who gets "ripped" by paying high prices for "bad dope," or who is totally dependent on the quality or quantity of heroin a single supplier happens to have available, does not have access to regularly available, high-quality heroin. As Belle explains, gaining such access usually requires extending and developing contacts in the drug subculture:

> *You got to start associating with different people. You got to be in touch with different people for the simple reason that not just one person has it all the time. You got to go from one person to the other, find out who's got the best bag and who hasn't.... You want to go where the best bag is for your money.... You got to mingle with so many different people.*

Not only must the aspiring stabilized junkie learn the essentials of shooting and copping, but the expensive nature of heroin usually requires that the addict become familiar with the art of hustling. Hustling provides an alternative basis for life structure capable of accommodating higher levels of drug use. Unlike the adolescent in school or some types of conventional jobs, the hustler role provides a daily structure capable of incorporating periodic visits to a copping connection to secure a "fix." At the same time, however, hustling does provide a routine structure that serves to limit one's habit and prevent it from "getting out of hand." Most hustles, for example, require regular commitments of time and patience, and must be practiced within certain unavoidable constraints. Just as important, however, the hustler role provides the addict with increased income that facilitates the ready availability of heroin without compromising the normative and ethical ideals of the subculture. "Little Italy," a young male addict in his early twenties, reports that his ready access to dependable supplies of heroin was crucial in maintaining ethical respectability:

> *I just kept right at it [using heroin] because...I had it in my possession every day.... I could go get it and that's just the way it was. With that in order, I didn't have to go out and burglarize. No one had to worry about me stealing from them.... I had money. I didn't have to beat anybody.*

For this reason, the stabilized junkie, which often represents a dominant phase in the career of the hard-core addict, is characterized by a high degree of *conformity* to subcultural norms and most closely reflects the recent ethnographic accounts of the normative structure of drug use.

THE FREE-WHEELING JUNKIE

In contrast to the stabilized junkie, the free-wheeling junkie lacks a daily structure to guide and constrain his or her consumption. A number of factors may undermine the stable life structure characteristic of the stabilized junkie. Addicts place particular importance on the inevitable vicissitudes of the hustler routine. Here it is not so much the hard times or difficulties in raising money that are critical. Addicts can often accommodate themselves to such lean periods by adjusting the level of their heroin use, substituting other drugs for heroin, or working longer and harder at hustling without undue disruption or abandonment of daily routine. "You can adjust yourself to a certain amount of drugs a day," explains Belle, "that you don't have to have but just that much." On the contrary, it is the unusual success, the "big sting," that distinctively undermines the stabilized junkie's high level of life structure. Often, in the course of hustling, addicts will confront an opportunity to make a score so big that they will not have to hustle so rigorously for a period of time. If successful, such a score brings a dramatic change in daily routine. Consider the experience of a burglar named Harry. Harry was working residential areas full time and supporting a modest habit. An associate stopped by one day with a roll of bills worth several thousand dollars and asked Harry if he would like to be partners in a new and more profitable hustle. Harry agreed and began holding up local grocery stores. His profits increased dramatically, and with his bigger earnings he started using drugs on a grand scale; not only did he increase his heroin use, but began using cocaine heavily as well.

However, the robberies brought a critical disjuncture to his normal daily routine. Harry no longer had to work eight hours a day for his copping money, but could secure a much more sizable income working only two or three hours per day three days a week. Harry now marvels that he was not even aware of the extensiveness of his habit until he voluntarily quit robberies because of the risk and returned once again to burglaries. All of these changes took place over a six-month period.

With drugs available, the free-wheeling junkie typically experiences a sharp escalation of his or her drug use. Moreover, because normal daily routine is suspended at least temporarily, the lifestyle of the addict tends to be erratic and often out of control. The free-wheeling junkie quite often resembles the sometimes stereotyped "flashy" junkie (often associated with pimps), engaged in

seemingly uncontrolled conspicuous consumption with a greatly expanded wardrobe, expensive cars, and extreme generosity; in short, the free-wheeling junkie typically finds himself or herself in a state of anomie, lacking the structures of restraint characteristic of the stabilized junkie.

The anomic condition peculiar to the free-wheeling junkie, however, relates specifically to patterns of personal consumption. The windfalls that catapult the addict to this type of heroin use usually allow him or her to maintain ethical integrity. As he mentally relives a particularly lucrative period of drug dealing, Little Italy recalls the following:

> So I'm a junkie now. But I'm not one of those scrub junkies, where I got to steal from my family.... I'm dealing. And I'm paying for my habit thataway. And man, listen here, don't you know that everybody that didn't know me, knew me now. Because I'm uptown on the Main Street Strip. You can drive by in your pretty car, blow at the girls. I had flashy clothes and the whole bit.

Provided that the free-wheeling junkie has not severed connections or alienated himself or herself in some way from the subculture, he or she may be able to rebuild the necessary daily routine and accommodate to new and lower levels of drug availability. Insofar as this can be managed the free-wheeling junkie may resume a stabilized junkie lifestyle. In many cases, however, the "big sting" has the effect of isolating the free-wheeling junkie from the subculture by decreasing the need to participate in the copping and hustling aspects of the subculture. Where this occurs the free-wheeling junkie is particularly susceptible to change toward the "street junkie" type.

THE STREET JUNKIE

The street junkie, characterized by low drug availability and minimal life structure, is the basis for the commonly held "junkie" stereotype. With drugs not freely available, the street junkie must typically cop his or her dope from the nearest street dealer who may be willing to provide credit on a bag or two. The cost is much higher on the street, and often the street junkie can afford only enough to take the edge off his or her "jones" (withdrawal) temporarily.

> *After I stopped going back and forth to New York, the street copping cost a lot more, too.... I might not have been shooting as much as I was [before] but I was spending a hell of a lot more money.*

Under these conditions, the street junkie lives from one "fix" to the next, often unable to maintain the most rudimentary routine. Personal hygiene and regular eating habits may be abandoned as the addict desperately seeks to scrape up enough money for his or her next shot. Not uncommonly, the street junkie will also abandon normal hustling routine, impulsively committing crimes that "happen" along, often in response to a felt need for dope due to withdrawal sickness. This happened to "Little Italy" who, after cutting himself off from his wholesale connection, turned to robberies to support his use. Lacking experience and technique, Little Italy staged these robberies largely on impulse:

> *I know today, I can say that if you don't have a plan you're gonna fuck up, man.... Now those robberies weren't no plan. They didn't fit in nowhere...just by the spur of the moment, you know what I mean? I had to find something to take that place so that income would stand off properly, 'cause I didn't have a plan or didn't know anything about robbery.*

The street junkie type might be precipitated by structural factors as well, particularly those that lead to the relinquishing of conventional roles. Some addicts, for example, report that "things started going downhill" after a divorce or the death of a loved one. Another common precipitator is the loss of conventional jobs. It is not uncommon for the stabilized junkie to be working a part-time job in addition to carrying out regular hustling activities. If an employer learns about drug use, the addict may well be fired. The emerging street junkie loses not only income, but also the high degree of daily routine provided by conventional employment. Desperately seeking to maintain even the most meager level of consumption to keep the edge off his or her "jones," the street junkie is forced to take chances that would ordinarily be quite unthinkable. Moreover, under those conditions, the street junkie becomes difficult to live with and family relationships become strained or perhaps even severed. Again, the addict faces a state of anomie, but this time without the luxury of easy access to drugs. This "down and out junkie," who has by now probably lost all semblance of respect and perhaps has been disenfranchised even by peers, has little stake in the moral order of the subculture. The addict in these desperate straits is likely to consider the possibility of "beating" friends or even family members for money to cop a street bag. Sylvia, a black woman in her twenties, explains:

> *After the money is coming in like that...and it gets to the point where their habit is worked up like that, then they might do anything [if they're cut off] and they have to find a new way of making their money. They might do anything.*

Rosenbaum (1981a:60) also reflects the dynamics of this situation for the female addict when she writes:

> *The woman addict's self-respect is at least temporarily damaged when, due to the fluidity of the money-stratification system, she finds herself down and out, with no way to earn money legally. It is at this point that she becomes temporarily unscrupulous and may rip off a personal friend, even family. It is important to note that this unscrupulousness is temporary and that in some way, most addicts become unscrupulous in some form, at some point in their careers.*

Similarly, the street junkie who has lost access to a stable network of copping connections is the most likely candidate to turn on a stranger (perhaps even a novice), introducing him or her to a dealer acquaintance in return for a bag of dope.

Such a situation almost always creates a dilemma for the street junkie. Rose had recently lost her copping connection and had to rely on a young neophyte to cop for her. Unfortunately for Rose, the young girl was not willing to make the purchase without compensation in drugs. Rose explained how she attempted to resolve her ethical dilemma:

> I gave her the least amount I figured she'd feel with a whole bunch of water so it would look like she had a lot.... It wasn't that I was trying to cheat her...it's just that I didn't want her to really get into it.

Lacking a daily routine and with drugs difficult to obtain, the street junkie must take more chances than would otherwise be the case. Under these circumstances addicts will engage in criminal hustles at which they are not adept. Unless their life circumstances change, arrest is virtually inevitable. Although not universally the case, it is the street junkie who typically encounters the criminal justice system. As Fiddle (1967:12–13) has observed,

> The police see junkies at their worst. They see them under the spur of need or pseudo-need...they see them violating even their own negative codes. The police rarely see the addict engaging in a purely voluntary humane act.

Moreover, that population of addicts most available to the media as well as to researchers are those who have been apprehended. For this reason, the image of the heroin addict generally available to the public is that of the stereotyped "street junkie." It is important to recognize, however, that the street junkie represents but one phase in the addict's career. For substantial portions of their careers, most addicts lead relatively stable, though fast-paced, lives. Far from being an inevitable result of the physiological dynamics of heroin use, the behavior of the street junkie, with all of its stereotyped ethical compromises, only emerges in response to the career contingencies

that limit accessibility and disrupt established patterns of behavior.

CONCLUSIONS

Drug using careers, like other careers, are subject to external constraints that affect the maintenance of ideal normative standards.[1] The testimony of the addicts I interviewed points to the importance of the career contingencies of drug availability and life structure in affecting their lifestyles. Most important, although most addicts generally proceed from a period of occasional use to more extensive stabilized use and often to the stereotyped down and out street junkie, these career contingencies are themselves affected by numerous factors in the addict's social environment so as to preclude a simple linear career model. Due to circumstances entirely beyond his or her control, for example, the stabilized junkie may lose access to a main connection, thereby reducing availability. If this unfortunate situation coincides with tighter law enforcement, forcing abandonment of usual hustling routine, the addict finds himself or herself in the situation of the street junkie without the benefit of "free wheeling." Similarly, it is not uncommon for free-wheeling junkies to reorganize their lives sufficiently by engaging in new or previous hustling role activities, thereby assuming once again the status of the stabilized junkie.

Regardless of the specific turns that an individual's drug using career may take, however, ethical conduct in the heroin subculture is dependent upon and sustained by the constraints and opportunities imposed by drug availability and life structure. That addict ethics are situated in this manner is hardly remarkable; the situational character of social behavior has long been documented in other contexts as well, particularly in the areas of racial attitudes and behavior (Deutscher, 1966; Kutner et al., 1952; LaPiere, 1934; Linn, 1965), classroom behavior (Freeman and Ataov, 1960; Henry 1959), and drinking behavior (Warriner, 1958), among others. Nevertheless, unlike individuals in these other contexts who fail to adhere to their stated principles, the failure of heroin addicts consistently to maintain ethical integrity is commonly understood to be evidence for a lack of any normative sensitivity whatsoever.

The testimony of the individuals reported here would suggest otherwise. These hard-core addicts readily articulated their ethical standards, often in a most forceful manner. Moreover, even as they failed to maintain their ethical standards behaviorally, addicts acknowledged and asserted the legitimacy of the very norms they violated. Many, like "Joy," expressed deep regret at their behavior during these desperate times:

> I felt bad…doing the things I was doing.… I didn't want to take nobody's check that I know [they] only get once a month and they probably got kids—and I know they did have kids or else they wouldn't be on welfare.

At other times these addicts used various sorts of excuses and rationalizations to mitigate or neutralize their culpability (see Sykes and Matza, 1957), as in Belle's emphasis on the deleterious effect of methamphetamines on her behavior. Then, too, some addicts attempted to lessen the impact of their indiscretion by pointing to the even more serious violations of actual or hypothetical peers. As one female addict put it, "There's things I've done that I've been ashamed of…but there's things that…I know I could have done that I didn't do."

In short, the credibility of the system of ethics embraced by street addicts cannot be measured by absolute behavioral conformity any more than the credibility of business ethics can be assessed in terms of the absolute absence of fraud. As Meier (1981:14) reminds us once again, "because norms identify behavior that ought or ought not to occur, behavior may (and often does) depart from norms." The legitimacy of these street ethics is rather established by the addict's reaction to their violation. The regrets expressed, and the very necessity of offering excuses, rationalizations, and moral comparisons, all acknowledge the legitimacy of those norms that have been breached.

Through these sorts of statements and reactions, then, addicts honor and reaffirm their own indigenous standards of conduct, even in pointing to and acknowledging their violation on particular occasions. In this way addict subculture is sustained and preserved in much the same way that interactional order, as Goffman (1967) reminds us, is sustained and preserved by displays of embarrassment at moments of incompetent performance.

NOTE

1. Such career contingencies are not, of course, limited to drug-using careers. Career contingencies have been discussed in relation to the fate of idealism in medical school (Becker and Geer, 1958); in nursing school (Psathas, 1968); and in dental school (Morris and Sherlock, 1971). Similarly, Cressey (1953) has discussed those external contingencies that are conducive to embezzlement among otherwise respectable businessmen. More generally, Lofland (1969) has specified a number of external conditions affecting the direction of deviant careers.

REFERENCES

Anslinger, H. J. and W. F. Tompkins (1953) *The Traffic in Narcotics*. New York: Funk and Wagnalls.

Ashley, R. (1972) *Heroin: The Myths and the Facts*. New York: St. Martin's.

Becker, H. S. and B. Geer (1958) "The fate of idealism in medical school." *Amer. Soc. Rev.* 23:50–56.

Beschner, G. M. and W. Brower (1985) "The scene," pp. 19–29 in B. Hanson et al. (eds.), *Life with Heroin: Voices from the Inner City*. Lexington, MA: D. C. Heath.

Blum, R. (1972) The Dream Sellers. San Francisco: Jossey-Bass.

Blumer, H., A. Sutter, R. Smith, and S. Ahmed (1976) "Recruitment into drug use," in R. Coombs et al. (eds.), *Socialization in Drug Use*. Cambridge, MA: Schenkman.

Bullington, B. (1977) *Heroin Use in the Barrio*. Lexington, MA: D. C. Heath.

Coombs, R. H. (1981) "Drug abuse as career." *J. of Drug Issues* 11:369–387.

Crawford, G. A., M. C. Washington, and E. C. Senay (1983) "Careers with heroin." *Intl. J. of the Addictions* 18:701–715.

Cressey, D. R. (1953) *Other People's Money.* Glencoe, IL: Free Press.

Deutscher, I. (1966) "Words and deeds: social science and social policy." *Social Problems* 13:235–254.

Durkheim, E. (1897) *Suicide* (trans., 1951). New York: Free Press.

Eldridge, W. B. (1967) *Narcotics and the Law: A Critique of the American Experiment in Narcotic Drug Control.* Chicago: Univ. of Chicago Press.

Faupel, C. E. (1981) "Understanding the relationship between heroin use and crime: contributions of the life history technique." Presented at the thirty-third Annual Meeting of the American Society of Criminology, Washington, DC.

Fiddle, S. (1967) *Portraits from a Shooting Gallery.* New York: Harper & Row.

Freeman, L. C. and T. Ataov (1960) "Invalidity of indirect and direct measures toward cheating." *J. of Personality* 28:443–447.

Goffman, E. (1967) "Embarrassment and social organization," pp. 97–112 in E. Goffman (ed.), *Interaction Ritual: Essays on Face to Face Behavior.* Chicago: Aldine.

Goldstein, P. J. (1981) "Getting over: economic alternatives to predatory crime among street drug users," pp. 67–84 in J. A. Inciardi (ed.), *The Drugs-Crime Connection.* Beverly Hills, CA: Sage.

Gould, L., A. L. Walker, L. E. Crane, and C. W. Lidz (1974) *Connections: Notes from the Heroin World.* New Haven, CT: Yale Univ. Press.

Hanson, B., G. Beschner, J. W. Walters, and E. Bovelle (1985) *Life with Heroin: Voices from the Inner City.* Lexington, MA: D. C. Heath.

Henry, J. (1959) "Spontaneity, initiative and creativity in suburban classrooms." *Amer. J. of Orthopsychiatry* 29:266–279.

Hughes, E. C. (1971) *The Sociological Eye: Selected Papers.* Chicago: Aldine-Atherton.

Hughes, P. H. (1977) *Behind the Wall of Respect.* Chicago: Univ. of Chicago Press.

Johnson, B. D., P. J. Goldstein, E. Preble, J. Schmeidler, D. S. Lipton, B. Spunt, and T. Miller (1985) *Taking Care of Business: The Economics of Crime by Heroin Abusers.* Lexington, MA: D. C. Heath.

Kutner, B., C. Wilkins, and P. R. Yarrow (1952) "Verbal attitudes and overt behavior involving racial prejudice." *J. of Abnormal and Social Psychology* 47:649–652.

LaPiere, R. T. (1934) "Attitudes vs. actions." *Social Forces* 13:230–237.

Lindesmith, A. (1940) "'Dope fiend' mythology." *J. of Criminal Law and Criminology* 31:199–208.

Linn, L. S. (1965) "Verbal attitude and overt behavior: a study of racial discrimination." *Social Forces* 43:353–364.

Lofland, J. (1969) *Deviance and Identity.* Englewood Cliffs, NJ: Prentice-Hall.

Meier, R. F. (1981) "Norms and the study of deviance: a proposed research strategy." *Deviant Behavior* 3:1–25.

Morris, R. and B. Sherlock (1971) "Decline of ethics and the rise of cynicism in dental school." *J. of Health and Social Behavior* 12:290–299.

Preble, E. and J. J. Casey (1969) "Taking care of business—the heroin user's life on the street." *Intl. J. of the Addictions* 4:1–24.

Psathas, G. (1968) "The fate of idealism in nursing school." *J. of Health and Social Behavior* 9:52–64.

Reese, A. (1975) "An addict's view of drug abuse," pp. 5–19 in R. H. Coombs (ed.), *Junkies and Straights.* Lexington, MA: D. C. Heath.

Rosenbaum, M. (1981a) *Women on Heroin.* New Brunswick, NJ: Rutgers Univ. Press.

Rosenbaum, M. (1981b) "Women addicts' experience of the heroin world: risk, chaos and inundation." *Urban Life* 10:65–91.

Rubington, E. (1967) "Drug addiction as a deviant career." *Intl. J. of the Addictions* 2:3–20.

Silver, G. and M. Aldrich (1979) *The Dope Chronicles: 1850–1950.* New York: Harper & Row.

Sutter, A. G. (1969) "Worlds of drug use on the street scene," pp. 802–829 in D. R. Cressey and D. A. Ward (eds.), *Delinquency, Crime and Social Process.* New York: Harper & Row.

Sykes, G. M. and D. Matza (1957) "Techniques of neutralization: a theory of delinquency." *Amer. Soc. Rev.* 22:664–670.

Waldorf, D. (1973) *Careers in Dope.* Englewood Cliffs, NJ: Prentice-Hall.

Walters, J. M. (1985) "'Taking care of business' updated: a fresh look at the daily routine of the heroin user," pp. 31–48 in B. Hanson et al. (eds.), *Life with Her-*

oin: Voices from the Inner City. Lexington, MA: D. C. Heath.

Warriner, C. K. (1958) "The nature and functions of official morality." *Amer. J. of Sociology* 64:165–168.

Zinberg, N. (1984) *Drug Set and Setting: The Basis for Controlled Intoxicant Use.* New Haven, CT: Yale Univ. Press.

Outsiders in a Hearing World

PAUL C. HIGGINS

Classification of people is a distinct pattern of culture. Social life without the sifting and sorting of people into their various categories seems most unlikely. And one of the more common classifications is typing people as being members of the "in-group" or the "out-group." Similar classification occurs when people make distinctions between those who conform and those who deviate. The former are marked for inclusion, the latter for exclusion. Relations between the majority group and the minority group follow from these social distinctions. And, to a large extent they border on stereotype.

Paul C. Higgins, in his study of the deaf community, calls attention to an important finding: Within a particular deviant social category, additional distinctions are made. This time, however, the people making the distinctions have themselves been excluded by the majority group. The deaf community consists of two categories based upon their modes of communicating with other people and the extent of their divergence from people with unimpaired hearing. This cleavage, at times, creates antagonisms in the deaf community. The distinctions that have real consequences for both categories turn on those who embrace deafness and those who still see themselves as participants in the hearing world.

Much of everyday life is based on the assumption that people can hear and speak. We communicate through telephones, radios, television, intercom systems and loudspeakers. Warning signals are often buzzers, sirens or alarms. Time is structured by bells and whistles. And, of course, people talk. Our world is an oral-aural one in which deaf people are typically left out (Higgins, 1978). They are *outsiders* in a hearing world (Becker, 1963). And like other outsiders, they are likely to create and maintain their own communities in order to survive and even thrive within an often hostile world.

Reprinted from *Urban Life and Culture,* Vol. 8, No. 1 (April 1979), pp. 3–22, by permission of Sage Publications, Inc. Copyright © 1979 by Sage Publications, Inc.

In this article I explore the deaf community. Unlike many other disabled populations—who often only establish self-help groups (Sagarin, 1969)—the deaf are not merely a statistical aggregate. For example, 85% of deaf people who lost their hearing before the age of 19 have hearing-impaired spouses (Schein and Delk, 1974:40).[1] Through marriage, friendships, casual acquaintances, clubs, religious groups, magazines published by and for themselves and sign language, the deaf create and maintain communities in the hearing world. Though scattered throughout a metropolitan area, members of the deaf community primarily confine their social relations to other members (Schein, 1968:74). Membership within those deaf communities and the organization of the relationships among members are the foci of this article. Each of these aspects of deaf communities revolves around the deaf being outsiders in a hearing world.

METHODS

This article is part of a larger study in Chicago which investigated the identity, interaction and community of the deaf in a hearing world (Higgins, 1977). I draw on materials from in-depth interviews with 75 hearing-impaired people and 15 counselors or friends of the deaf. My sample was developed through a snowballing technique.... National publications by and for the deaf, published writings of deaf individuals and articles or monographs about the deaf proved helpful. My research and analysis [were] primarily limited to the white deaf community. I soon learned that there was little interaction between white and black deaf. They form separate communities....

MEMBERSHIP

More than 13 million people in America have some form of hearing impairment. Almost 2 million are deaf. Of those 2 million approximately 410,000 are "prevocationally" deaf; they suffered their hearing losses before the end of adolescence (Schein and Delk, 1974).[2] It is from this latter group, the prevocationally deaf, that members of deaf communities are likely to come. I neither met nor heard of members of the Chicago-area deaf community who lost their hearing after adolescence. Surely some exist, but they are few. It will become evident later why that is so.

Deafness is not a sufficient condition for membership in deaf communities, though some degree of hearing impairment is a necessary condition as I will examine later. Deafness does not make "its members part of a natural community" (Furth, 1973:2). Membership in deaf communities must be *achieved*. It is not an ascribed status (Markowicz and Woodward, 1975). Membership in a deaf community is achieved through (1) *identification* with

the deaf world, (2) *shared experiences* of being hearing impaired, and (3) *participation* in the community's activities. Without all three characteristics one cannot be nor would one choose to be a member of a deaf community.

IDENTIFICATION

A deaf community is in part a "moral" phenomenon. It involves:

> a sense of identity and unity with one's group and a feeling of involvement and wholeness on the part of the individual. [Poplin, 1972:7]

A deaf woman, her hearing impaired since childhood, dramatically describes the realization in her late teens and early twenties that she was part of the deaf world:

> I didn't think I was very deaf myself. But when I saw these people [at a deaf organization] I knew I belonged to their world. I didn't belong to the hearing world. Once you are deaf, you are deaf, period. If you put something black in white paint, you can't get the black out. Same with the deaf. Once you are deaf, you're always deaf.

While it is problematic both physiologically and in terms of identification that "once you are deaf, you are always deaf," the woman's remarks express her commitment to the deaf world.[3] Whether members dramatically realize it or not, what is important is their commitment to and identification with the deaf. Other members, who attended schools and classes for the deaf since childhood and continued their interaction in the deaf world as adults, may, on looking back, find no dramatic moment when they realized that they had become part of a deaf community.

Members of the deaf community feel more comfortable with deaf people than they do with hearing people. They feel a sense of belonging. A young deaf woman explained:

> At a club for the deaf, if I see a deaf person whom I don't know, I will go up to that person and say, "Hi! What's your name?" I would never do that to a hearing person.

Not all deaf or hearing-impaired people, though, identify with the deaf world. Those who lost their hearing later in life through an accident, occupational hazard or presbycusis (i.e., aging process) do not seek to become members of deaf communities. Rather, as Goffman (1963) notes, they are likely to stigmatize members of deaf communities in the same way that those with normal hearing stigmatize them. Others, impaired from birth or from an early age, may never have developed such an identification. They probably had hearing parents and were educated in schools for the hearing. Some may participate in activities of deaf communities, but are not members. They are tolerated, though not accepted by the members. While audiologically they are deaf, socially they are not.

A hearing-impaired man, who participates in a deaf religious organization, but is not part of the deaf community, explained his self-identity in the following way:

In everyday life I consider myself a hearing person. [His hearing impaired wife interjected that she did too.] I usually forget it that I have a hearing problem. Sometimes I'm so lost [absorbed] in the hearing world; I mean I don't even realize I have a hearing problem. It seems automatic. I don't know what it is. I feel I'm hearing people to the deaf and hearing. I don't feel hearing impaired not even if I have a hard time to understand somebody. Still I don't feel I'm deaf because I couldn't hear you or understand you.

This man and his hearing-impaired wife are on the fringe of the deaf community. They participate in some community activities "just to show that we care" and "because they [the deaf] need help."

Hearing-impaired people like this man and his wife are often a source of both ill feelings and amusement for members of deaf communities. They are a source of ill feelings because their behavior does not respect the identity of the deaf community. Thus, this same hearing-impaired man was severely criticized for having someone at a board meeting of a religious group interpret his spoken remarks into sign language rather than

signing himself. As I will explain later, signing skill and communication preference are indications of one's commitment to the deaf community. Those who are opposed to signing or who do not sign are not members of the community.

They are a source of amusement for trying to be what members of deaf communities feel they are not—hearing. A deaf couple were both critical and amused at the attempt of the same hearing-impaired man's wife to hide her deafness. As they explained:

A hearing woman who signs well came up to her [the wife] at a religious gathering, and assuming that she was deaf, which she is, began to sign to her. The wife became flustered, put her own hands down and started talking.

Such hearing-impaired people serve as examples that members of deaf communities use in explaining to others what their community is like and in reaffirming to themselves who they are. These hearing-impaired people help to define for the members the boundary of their community and their identity as deaf people. The members reject the feelings of these "misguided" hearing-impaired people; feelings which deny their deafness. And in rejection, the members affirm who they are and what their community is.

SHARED EXPERIENCES

In developing an identification with the deaf world, members of deaf communities share many similar experiences. Those experiences relate particularly to the everyday problems of navigating in a hearing world (Higgins, 1978) and to being educated in special programs for the deaf.

Since childhood, members of deaf communities have experienced repeated frustration in making themselves understood, embarrassing misunderstandings and the loneliness of being left out by family, neighborhood acquaintances and others. Such past and present experiences help to strengthen a deaf person's identification with the deaf world. A *typical* instance of these experiences, remarkable only because it is so routine, was described by a deaf man:

> Most of my friends are deaf. I feel more comfortable with them. Well, we have the same feelings. We are more comfortable with each other. I can communicate good with hearing people, but in a group, no. For example, I go bowling. Have a league of hearing bowlers. Four of them will be talking, talking, talking and I will be left out. Maybe if there was one person I would catch some by lipreading, but the conversation passes back and forth so quickly. I can't keep up. I just let it go; pay attention to my bowling. Many things like that.

Yet, to be a member of a deaf community, one need not actually be deaf. Some members have lesser degrees of hearing impairment. As children, though, they were processed through educational programs for the deaf. These children were not necessarily mislabeled, though certainly some were. Rather, often no local programs for "hard of hearing" children were available. Children with various degrees of impairment were educated together. Through such processing, these children developed friendships with deaf children and an identification with the deaf world. As adults, they moved comfortably into deaf communities. With amplification these members of deaf communities are often able to use the telephone successfully, if also somewhat haltingly. Some converse with hearing people reasonably well. Yet, due to that childhood processing as deaf, these hearing-impaired people choose to live their lives within deaf communities. Audiologically they are not deaf; socially they are (Furfey and Harte, 1964, 1968; Schein, 1968).

Other members of a deaf community may have once been deaf, but through surgery or fortuitous circumstances they have regained some hearing. Though no longer severely hearing impaired, they remain active in the deaf community where their identity as a person developed. A dramatic case is that of a now slightly hearing-impaired man. He went to the state school for the deaf in Illinois. His childhood friends were deaf. During World War II, though, he regained much of his hearing while working in a munitions plant; the loud blasts from testing the bombs apparently improved his hearing. Consequently, his speech also improved. Only his modest hearing aid indicates that he has a slight impairment. Yet his wife is deaf, most of their friends are deaf, and he is active in a state organization for the deaf. As he explained:

> [As your speech got better, did you continue to associate with your deaf friends in _____ town?] Oh, yeh, I'm more involved with the deaf community now than I was back then [WW II]. To me they are still my family. I feel more at home when I walk into a room with 1,000 deaf people; more so than walking into a room with 1,000 hearing people, non-deaf. I feel at home. I can relate to them. We had something in common; our childhood, our education, our problems, and all that.

Since membership in a deaf community is based on shared experiences of being deaf and identification with the deaf world, it is difficult for hearing individuals to be members of such communities. A deaf woman put it simply: "Hearing people are lost in the deaf world just as deaf people are lost in the hearing world."

Outsiders are often wary and resentful of "normals": blacks of whites, gays of straights and so on. Likewise, deaf people are skeptical of hearing people's motives and intentions. A deaf man remarked:

> When a hearing person starts to associate with the deaf, the deaf begin to wonder why that hearing person is here. What does that hearing person want?

When a "hard of hearing" woman, who for years had associated exclusively with the hearing, started a north shore club for the deaf, her motives and behavior were questioned by some of the deaf members. I was warned myself by two deaf leaders to expect such skepticism and resistance by members of the deaf community. I encountered little in my research, but having deaf parents and clearly establishing my intentions probably allayed members' suspicions.

Outsider communities may grant courtesy membership to "wise" people who are not similarly stigmatized (Goffman, 1963). These individuals are "normal," yet they are familiar with and sympathetic to the conditions of outsiders. For example, gay communities grant courtesy membership to "wise" heterosexuals: heterosexual couples or single females known as "fag hags" (Warren, 1974:113). Researchers are often granted that status. Yet, that courtesy membership represents only a partial acceptance by the outsiders of the "normals."

Some hearing individuals are courtesy members of deaf communities. They may be educators, counselors, interpreters or friends of the deaf. Often they have deafness in their families: deaf parents, siblings, children or even spouses. Yet, their membership is just that, a courtesy, which recognizes the fundamental fact that no matter how empathetic they are, no matter that there is deafness in their families, they are not deaf and can never "really" know what it means to be deaf.[4]

Not surprisingly, hearing-impaired individuals who through their actions and attitudes would otherwise be part of a deaf community may be rejected by some members because they hear and speak too well. A hearing-impaired woman who speaks well and with amplification uses the telephone, who went to a state school for the deaf since childhood and to a college for the deaf and who is married to a deaf man is such an individual.

Yet, hearing-impaired people like that woman do receive some acceptance from those members who tend to reject them. They are called upon to act as go-betweens with the hearing world. This clearly differentiates these impaired people from the hearing. As the hearing-impaired woman mentioned above noted:

They [deaf people] can rely on me to do the talking for them [e.g., telephoning]. And in that sense they do accept me because I am somebody who can help them. Because they don't really want to turn around to a hearing person and ask them to do something.

The hearing and speech ability of this hearing-impaired woman creates a barrier between her and some members of the deaf community, but simultaneously allows her some acceptance by those who reject her. She is almost hearing; therefore, some members reject her. She is not quite hearing, though; therefore, members will rely on her for help in navigating through the hearing world. It is often only with greatest reluctance that members of deaf communities rely on hearing people for such assistance.[5]

PARTICIPATION

Active participation in the deaf community is the final criteria for being a member. Participation, though, is an outgrowth of identification with the deaf world and of sharing similar experiences in being hearing impaired. In that respect, then, it is the least important characteristic for being a member of the deaf community. Yet the deaf community is not merely a symbolic community of hearing-impaired people who share similar experiences. It is also created through marriages, friendships, acquaintances, parties, clubs, religious organizations and published materials. The activities provide the body of the community, whereas the identification and shared experiences provide the soul.

Thus, a deaf couple, who lived in the Chicago area for years, were not warmly received when they began to attend a deaf, Protestant congregation. The members of the congregation wondered where they had been all these years. Members interpreted that lack of participation as a lack of identification with themselves and a lack of commitment to the deaf community.

Participation, though, varies among the members of deaf communities. Involvement in community activities is tempered by outside commitments such as work, family and traveling time to and from activities as well as individual preference. More importantly, what activities one participates in and with whom one associates help to organize relationships among members of the deaf community.

SOCIAL ORGANIZATION

While normals may often treat outsiders as a homogeneous group, the outsiders themselves create distinctions among one another. Gays distinguish among "elite," "career" and "deviants" (Warren, 1972). Lower-class blacks may vilify middle-class blacks for being Uncle Toms (Pettigrew, 1964). The deaf community, too, is heterogeneous. Through differential participation with other members and in various activities of the deaf community, members organize their relationships with one another.

Members of the deaf community use several major characteristics in organizing relationships with one another. Some of these characteristics operate in much the same way as in the hearing world. Outsiders, whether they be deaf or not, live within a larger world. Some are not born as outsiders, but only later acquire that status. All are socialized to some degree within the dominant culture. Consequently, communities of outsiders and their subculture are continuous with the dominant culture of the larger society (Plummer, 1975:157). Therefore, it is not surprising that some characteristics which members of the dominant culture use to differentiate each other are also used by members of communities of outsiders. Sex, race, religion and sophistication (as often indicated by educational attainment) differentiate members in the deaf community as they do in the hearing world. Consequently, they will not receive special attention here.

Age, however, adds a special dimension to deaf communities. Unlike ethnic or racial outsiders, there are few deaf children in the deaf community. Less than 10% of deaf people have deaf parents (Schein and Delk, 1974:35). Consequently, deaf communities are actually adult deaf communities. As children, most members of the community were probably isolated in a hearing world except while attending educational programs for the deaf. The same holds true today, though deaf children may participate in such activities as religious worship where deaf adults are present. The intriguing question becomes: how are deaf children and adolescents socialized into the adult deaf community? I did not address this issue which clearly needs attention.

COMMUNICATION

Other characteristics which members of an outsider community use to organize their relationships with one another are related to their unique position within the dominant world. For example, within the black community skin color has played an important but diminishing role (Udry et al., 1971). Within the deaf community, communication preference and skill, the relative emphasis that members give to signing and speaking, is an important basis on which relationships are organized. I will examine this characteristic closely, because it is crucial for understanding the deaf community in a hearing world.

There are two general modes of communication used among the deaf. One is called the oral method; the other is the manual method. The oral method in its "purest" form is composed of speaking and lipreading. Manual communication is sign language and fingerspelling. Put very simply, sign language is a concept-based language of signs (i.e., various movements of the hands in relationship to one another and to the body in which the hands themselves take various shapes) that has a different structure from English, but one that is not yet fully understood (Stokoe et al., 1975). Within the deaf community there are oralists and manualists who I will refer to as *speakers* and *signers*.[6]

Speakers.   Speakers rely primarily on speaking and lipreading when communicating with fellow oralists. When communicating with signers, they may often accompany their speaking with signs, but they do not sign fluently. Those who are "pure" oralists in philosophy or communicative behavior are not part of the deaf community. A small number of these "pure" oralists are members of an oral association of the deaf; whereas, others go it alone in the hearing world (Oral Deaf Adults Section Handbook, 1975). Of course, the distinction between a "pure" oralist and a speaker is arbitrary. Speakers may accept as a member of the community an oralist who signers reject as too orally oriented to be a fellow member. Speakers are likely to have had hearing parents and attended day schools and classes for the deaf where signing was not permitted.

Signers. Signers sign and fingerspell when communicating to their deaf friends. For many signers their first language is sign language. They are native signers. Some have unintelligible speech and poor lipreading skills. Yet, others speak and lipread well, even better than speakers. Signers, though, prefer signing as compared to speech or lipreading when communicating with one another. Rarely will they use their voices or even move their mouths with other signers. Those who do may be teased. Signers reason that speaking and lipreading are for navigating in the hearing world, but they are not necessary among fellow signers.

Varieties of sign language exist. Many of those are due to the mixing of sign language and English. American Sign Language is least influenced by English. The use of varieties of sign language displays the social organization of the deaf community. The more educated the deaf individual is, the more likely that individual will be familiar with varieties which approximate English. Varieties of sign language which approximate English are more likely to be used at formal occasions (e.g., at a conference) than at informal ones. Social, educational, regional and ethnic (particularly black-white) variations in signing exist much as they do in English (Stokoe and Battison, 1975).

Becoming a signer follows no single path. Those who have deaf parents who sign most likely grew up as signers themselves. Others became signers in residential schools. Although signing often was not permitted in the classrooms of such schools, it was often allowed outside of the classrooms in the dorms and on the playgrounds. After leaving *oral* day school programs, many deaf individuals began to use signs which they learned from deaf adults. The hand rapping and monetary fines which were (and in some cases still are) administered to them when they were caught using their hands to communicate were not forgotten.

The frustration and bitterness from failing to understand and to learn through the oral approach is still felt.[7] Consequently, these converts are often the most adamantly opposed to oral education because they are the self-perceived victims of it.

Others who did not immediately seek out signers often found that their speech and lipreading skills did not gain them easy entrance into the hearing world. They were misunderstood and in turn misunderstood hearing people. Such experiences influenced these deaf individuals to become signers.

CLEAVAGE BETWEEN SIGNERS AND SPEAKERS

Signers and speakers are members of the same deaf community. They may attend the same religious organization, social club or community gala. They also marry one another. In such marriages the speaker typically becomes a signer. Yet, through their feelings toward each other and their differential involvement with each other, strong divisions and at times antagonisms are created. That cleavage within the deaf community relates historically to the deaf's position within a hearing world. Particularly, it is an outgrowth of how educators of the deaf have traditionally felt it best to teach deaf children.

Historically, throughout the United States and especially in Chicago, Boston, and a few other places, the oral method of instruction has been dominant in schools and classes for the deaf. Only since the early 1970s has the Chicago area begun to emphasize manual communication in the classroom. The combination of the two approaches along with writing and any other effective means of communication has been called total communication (O'Rourke, 1972).

The oral philosophy was stressed in the hope and desire that deaf children, trained in such a method, would be able to move easily into the hearing world as adults. Perhaps more importantly, it was also stressed due to the fear that [if] deaf children were allowed to sign and fingerspell with one another, especially in often isolated residential schools, then as adults they would marry one another and form deaf communities within, but apart from, the hearing world. Alexander Graham Bell, whose wife was deaf and who was an influential supporter of the oral philosophy, voiced such fears in an 1883 paper, "Upon the Formation of a Deaf Variety of the Human Race" (Boese, 1971). This emphasis of hearing educators on oralism and their suppression of signing among deaf children has not gone unnoticed by the deaf.

Through formal organizations as well as friendships and informal relations, signers and speakers organize the deaf community according to communication skill and preference. For example, a national fraternal organization for the deaf has several divisions in the Chicago area. One is attended by speakers; the other two by signers. Though the oral division has a dwindling membership, its members insist on being separate from the larger, manually oriented divisions. Further, respondents noted that most, if not all, of their friends had similar communication preferences as their own, be they manual or oral. Each group is not quite comfortable with the other's mode of communication. Speakers explain that it is difficult to follow fast signers, especially when the signers do not move their mouths. Signers complain that it is difficult to lipread the oralists or understand their modest or minimal signing.

The conflict between signing and speaking also disrupts family relationships. It is not unusual for deaf children who sign to communicate little with their parents who do not sign. As adults, their relationships with their parents may be bitter. Deaf siblings, too, can be divided by communication differences. For example, two deaf sisters in the Chicago area rarely see each other. Both grew up in the oral tradition but the older married a speaker while the younger married a signer. The younger sister has retained her oral skills, but has become more involved with signers. Rather than join the oral fraternal division at her sister's request, she remains in the larger, manual division where her friends are.

Although signing is not a basis for membership in deaf communities, it is clearly an out-

growth of becoming a member.[8] Signing is an indication of one's identity as a deaf person and one's commitment to the deaf world. It is perhaps the most obvious indication to hearing people that one is deaf. Because deafness is a relatively invisible impairment, deaf people would often go unnoticed in everyday, impersonal activities except for their signing to one another. Also, signing often attracts stares, unflattering imitations and ridicule from the hearing. Therefore, "pure" oralists are viewed by members of deaf communities, particularly by signers, as outsiders to the deaf world. Further, some signers wonder if speakers are ashamed of being deaf. Signers may interpret the speakers' not fully embracing signing as an indication that speakers are either trying to hide their deafness or are still hopelessly under the influence of misguided, hearing educators. Either way, the speakers' commitment to the deaf world becomes questioned. That commitment is partially based on the conviction that hearing people have too long dominated deaf people's lives; in education, in jobs, in even telling them how to communicate with each other.

CONCLUSION

Within the larger society, outsiders often create and maintain communities. Some of these communities are located within well-defined geographical areas of the city: ethnic neighborhoods, black ghettos or Mexican-American barrios. Other communities of outsiders may not be quite so geographically bounded. Through marriages (both legal and symbolic), friendships, clubs, formal organizations, publications and a special argot, outsiders who are scattered throughout a metropolitan area *create* their community. The deaf community is such a creation.

Membership in deaf communities, though, is neither granted to nor sought by all who are deaf. Rather, it is achieved through identification with the deaf world, shared experiences of being hearing impaired and involvement with other members. Most people who are audiologically deaf never become members. Some with lesser degrees of hearing impairment have been members for as long as they can remember.

Although the deaf community may appear to be homogeneous to the hearing, members of the community create distinctions among one another. These distinctions are used in organizing relationships within the community. Some of these distinguishing characteristics, such as sex, are used within the hearing world as well. Yet, due to the unique (historical and present) position of the deaf as outsiders in a hearing world, members of the community distinguish among one another based on communication preference. Signers and speakers find it easier to communicate with those who have preferences similar to their own. More importantly, speaking to fellow members is a vestige of the hearing's domination of and paternalism toward the deaf. Therefore, not fully embracing and using sign language may call into question one's identification with and commitment to the deaf community.

Within deaf communities the members seldom face the difficulties and frustrations which arise when they navigate through the hearing world. A sense of belonging and wholeness is achieved which is not found among the hearing. *Among* fellow members there is no shame in being deaf and being deaf does not mean being odd or different. Deafness is taken for granted. Within deaf communities those who cannot "turn a deaf ear" now become the outsiders.

NOTES

1. Ghettos for the blind have existed in the past in China and in many European cities. In 1935, a prominent worker in the field of blindness proposed establishing self-contained communities of the blind (Chevigny and Braverman, 1950). Few blind people, though, have blind spouses (Best, 1934).

A predominantly self-contained village of 400 physically disabled adults has been created by rehabilitation specialists in the Netherlands (Zola, unpublished). To what extent it is a community and to what extent it is

merely an extension of a long-term care facility is not clear.

2. Prevocationally deaf people were defined as those "who could not hear and understand speech and who had lost (or never had) that ability prior to 19 years of age" (Schein and Delk, 1974:2). A self-report hearing scale was used to determine the respondent's hearing ability. Schein (1968) discusses the factors (e.g., chronicity, age of onset and degree of loss) involved in defining deafness and examines previous definitions.

3. Most "coming out" among homosexuals, a process of defining oneself as gay, seems to occur in interaction with other homosexuals. Gays too feel that being gay is a permanent condition (Dank, 1971; Warren, 1974).

4. While members of deaf communities grant courtesy membership to "wise" hearing people, those members often subtly indicate that those hearing people are still not "one of them" (Markowicz and Woodward, 1975). When signing to a hearing person, the deaf may slow the speed of their signing or speak while signing. They would rarely do that when communicating with a fellow member.

5. This desire of the deaf to be independent from and their skeptical attitude toward help offered by the hearing [have] been documented in the more general situation of disabled-nondisabled relations (Ladieu et al., 1947).

6. It is difficult to estimate the relative proportion of oralists and manualists within deaf communities. Both the relative membership within the oral and manual divisions of a deaf fraternal organization (in Chicago) and the proportion of the prevocationally, adult deaf population who use signs (Schein, 1968; Schein and Delk, 1974) indicate that oralists are a numerical minority within deaf communities. Further, their numbers are likely to decline in the future as signing becomes more extensively employed in educational programs for the deaf.

7. On academic achievement tests, deaf children score several years behind their hearing counterparts (Trybus and Karchmer, 1977).

8. Some researchers have viewed deaf communities as language communities where American Sign Language use is necessary for membership (Markowicz and Woodward, 1975; Schlesinger and Meadow, 1972). This approach is too restrictive because it excludes speakers as well as many signers who are not ASL users from being members of deaf communities. Yet, speakers, nonnative signers and native signers associate with each other, marry one another and recognize each other as part of the

same community while also maintaining distinctions among one another.

REFERENCES

Becker, H. S. 1963. *Outsiders: Studies in the Sociology of Deviance.* New York: Free Press.

Best, H. 1934. *Blindness and the Blind in the United States.* New York: Macmillan.

Boese, R. J. 1971. "Native Sign Language and the Problem of Meaning." Ph.D. dissertation, University of California–Santa Barbara (unpublished).

Chevigny, H. and S. Braverman. 1950. *The Adjustment of the Blind.* New Haven, CT: Yale Univ. Press.

Dank, B. M. 1971. "Coming Out in the Gay World." *Psychiatry,* 34:180–197.

Furfey, P. H. and T. J. Harte. 1968. *Interaction of Deaf and Hearing in Baltimore City, Maryland.* Washington, DC: Catholic University Press.

———. 1964. *Interaction of Deaf and Hearing in Frederick County, Maryland.* Washington, DC: Catholic University of America Press.

Furth, H. G. 1973. *Deafness and Learning: A Psychosocial Approach.* Belmont, CA: Wadsworth.

Goffman, E. 1963. *Stigma: Notes on the Management of Spoiled Identity.* Englewood Cliffs, NJ: Prentice-Hall.

Higgins, P. C. 1978. "Encounters Between the Disabled and the Nondisabled: Bringing the Impairment Back In." American Sociological Association Meetings, San Francisco.

———. 1977. "The Deaf Community: Identity and Interaction in a Hearing World." Ph.D. dissertation, Northwestern University (unpublished).

Ladieu, G., E. Haufman, and T. Dembo. 1947. "Studies in Adjustment to Visible Injuries: Evaluation of Help by the Injured." *Journal of Abnormal and Social Psychology,* 42:169–192.

Markowicz, H. and J. Woodward. 1975. "Language and the Maintenance of Ethnic Boundaries in the Deaf Community." Conference on Culture and Communication, Temple University, March 13–15.

Oral Deaf Adults Section Handbook. 1975. Washington, DC: Alexander Graham Bell Association for the Deaf.

O'Rourke, T. J. (ed.). 1972. *Psycholinguistics and Total Communication: The State of the Art.* Washington, DC: American Annals of the Deaf.

Pettigrew, T. F. 1964. *A Profile of the Negro American.* Princeton, NJ: D. Van Nostrand.

Plummer, K. 1975. *Sexual Stigma: An Interactionist Account.* London: Routledge and Kegan Paul.

Poplin, D. E. 1972. *Communities: A Survey of Theories and Methods of Research.* New York: Macmillan.

Sagarin, E. 1969. *Odd Man In: Societies of Deviants in America.* Chicago: Quadrangle.

Schein, J. D. 1968. *The Deaf Community: Studies in the Social Psychology of Deafness.* Washington, DC: Gallaudet College Press.

Schein, J. D. and M. T. Delk, Jr. 1974. *The Deaf Population of the United States.* Silver Spring, MD: National Association of the Deaf.

Schlesinger, H. S. and K. P. Meadow. 1972. *Sound and Sign: Childhood Deafness and Mental Health.* Berkeley: Univ. of California Press.

Stokoe, W. C. and R. M. Battison. 1975. "Sign Language, Mental Health, and Satisfying Interaction." First National Symposium on the Mental Health Needs of Deaf Adults and Children. Chicago: David T. Siegel Institute for Communicative Disorders, Michael Reese Hospital and Medical Center, June 12–14.

Stokoe, W. C., C. G. Casterline, and C. G. Croneberg (eds.). 1975. *A Dictionary of American Sign Language on Linguistic Principles.* Washington, DC: Gallaudet College Press.

Trybus, R. J. and M. A. Karchmer. 1977. "School Achievement Scores of Hearing Impaired Children: National Data on Achievement Status and Growth Patterns." *American Annals of the Deaf,* 122(2): 62–69.

Udry, J. R., K. E. Bauman, and C. Chase. 1971. "Skin Color, Status, and Mate Selection." *American Journal of Sociology,* 76:722–733.

Warren, C. A. B. 1974. *Identity and Community in the Gay World.* New York: Wiley.

———. 1972. "Observing the Gay Community." In J. D. Douglas (ed.), *Research on Deviance.* New York: Random House, pp. 139–163.

Diversity in Panhandling

STEPHEN E. LANKENAU

With the resurgence of homelessness that began in the 1980s, there has been a marked increase in panhandling, a form of systematic deviance. As a result, there has been a community backlash, the passage of laws against "aggressive panhandling," and the spread of "compassion fatigue" in the general public. In short, as its nuisance value has increased, the tolerance for public displays of indigence has decreased. What underlies the negative reactions to panhandling, and how have panhandlers dealt with this situation?

The antipathy most people feel toward panhandlers is based on their breach of a number of expectations. One breach is of pedestrians' expectation about being able to go about their business without interruption. Another breach is the panhandlers' attempts to obtain money simply by asking for it rather than by earning it through some form of work. Consequently, the majority of pedestrians ignore panhandlers and act as though they are not even there.

Panhandlers want to gain the attention of people passing by, and get them to stop, look, and listen to their request for assistance with a minimum of disruption. Stephen E. Lankenau describes the diversity in roles that have developed as a way of requesting money while avoiding the creation of animosity. Thus, all of them are attention-getting devices, and all are designed to reduce social disruption as much as possible.

Some of the people just walk by and don't say nothin'. I call them zombies [laughs]. You ask them for change and they don't say "yes," "no," or "maybe I be back." They just walk by you like they don't even see you—it's like I'm not even sitting there. They could say "I ain't got none" or "no" or something. They just walk by.—Alice, a homeless panhandler

We use a variety of ploys to avoid the gaze or overtures extended by panhandlers—we avert our eyes, quicken our pace, increase the volume on our headphones. Some panhandlers manage to capture our attention, less frequently our money, using humor, offering services, telling stories, or by using other dramatic devices. A close examination of the exchanges between panhandler and passersby reveals that these interactions occur within a multi-layered, theatrical context; dramas are enacted at the face-to-face level yet display the larger social relations among the poor and nonpoor.

Goffman's (1959) dramaturgical perspective presents social life as a play in which persons or actors conduct themselves before various audiences according to scripted roles. Compared with the exchanges among everyday persons, however, interactions between panhandler and pedestrian more closely resemble the basic structural features of a play. The panhandler, who is the main actor, is like an improvisational performer who uses a repertoire of pieces or numbers to accomplish the act of panhandling. I refer to a panhandler's collection of these actions as his or her panhandling repertoire. Similarly, in reaction to the performer, pedestrians serve as the audience and respond to the panhandling routine by selecting from a menu of responses, like engaging or ignoring the panhandler. Being ignored by a passerby, which Goffman (1963) referred to as the

Reprinted from *Deviant Behavior: An Interdisciplinary Journal,* Vol. 20 (1999), pp. 183–206, by permission of Taylor and Francis, Inc. Copyright © 1999 by Taylor and Francis, Inc.

"nonperson treatment," is a primary problem confronted by panhandlers, but one that is directly addressed through a repertoire of panhandling routines.

On the basis of ethnographic observations and interviews of panhandlers on the streets of Washington, DC, I have conceptualized five primary panhandling routines: the entertainer, the greeter, the servicer, the storyteller, and the aggressor. These routines are premised on using various props, manipulating self-presentation, and engaging the sympathies and emotions of passersby. The fact that I am categorizing panhandlers according to various routines, however, does not necessarily imply that certain individuals are acting or feigning need and distress. Rather, panhandling repertoires are one way of describing the public dramas between panhandler and passersby.

A PRIMARY PROBLEM FACING PANHANDLERS—THE NONPERSON TREATMENT

The nonperson treatment of panhandlers, that is, passing by a panhandler as though he or she did not exist, originates in a disposition characterizing many city dwellers, which Simmel ([1903] 1971) called the "blasé attitude." The blasé attitude stems from the constant stimulation found in a city and causes inhabitants to react to new situations with minimal energy or to disregard differences between things....

A NEW APPROACH TO STUDYING PANHANDLERS

I propose that panhandlers devise a repertoire of panhandling routines to break out of the role of stranger or to awaken pedestrians from the blasé state; these dramaturgical actions then minimize the nonperson treatment and pave the way for encounters. Framing panhandling according to a repertoire of actions represents a different analytical approach to the study of panhandler practices and problems. Most prior research on the subject presents typologies that often lack analytical precision. Although these studies offer useful descriptive categories, such as white-collar beggars (Anderson [1923] 1961), child beggars (Freund 1925), store beggars (Gilmore 1940), professional beggars (Wallace 1965), executive beggars (Igbinova 1991), and character beggars (Williams 1995), I argue that they fail to provide a thorough understanding of the phenomenon of panhandling and of the problems faced by panhandlers.

First, past analyses often construct typologies that portray panhandlers not as actors but as types lacking agency and versatility. In contrast, panhandling repertoires highlight the drama and dynamism that often [underlie] the act of panhandling. I demonstrate how panhandlers confront ambivalent or negative reactions by using one or more routines in a single encounter. Ultimately, framing panhandling in terms of repertoires represents a departure from previous analyses as this strategy typifies action rather than essentializes or rigidifies persons.

Second, prior research typically fails to conceptualize panhandling in terms of interaction between two unequal sets of actors, the panhandler and the passerby. Framing panhandling as a theatrical exchange between two classes of actors with dissimilar material resources, different interactional objectives, and contrasting viewpoints, however, is a critical factor toward understanding the *repertoire of routines* enacted by panhandlers. Despite these inequalities, this analysis shows that panhandling repertoires lead to exchanges between the zombie and the stranger and thereby foster greater understanding among both classes of actors.

METHOD

I define a panhandler as a person who publicly and regularly requests money or goods for personal use in a face-to-face manner from unfamiliar others without offering a readily identifiable or valued consumer product or service in exchange for items received. Throughout the sampling process, I largely selected panhandlers who appeared mentally and physically fit for regular employment. Among both policymakers and the population at large, these able-bodied, often homeless individuals are generally regarded as the nondeserving poor (Wright 1989), that is, persons viewed as undeserving of sympathy or assistance as they violate basic norms surrounding work. I learned during interviews, however, that these seemingly fit fronts often belied health problems and circumstances that inhibited gainful employment, particularly work requiring physical stamina and strength. For instance, many panhandlers reported mild to serious illnesses and injuries occurring largely before their entry into panhandling, such as back and leg injuries, poorly healed broken bones, knife and gunshot wounds, burns, diabetes, and HIV exposure. Others admitted to past or current drug and alcohol problems, and a few appeared to have mental difficulties. However, no single health factor typically explained entry into panhandling and homelessness. Rather, a constellation of problems, including unemployment, homelessness, family conflicts, or health factors, often characterized each panhandler.

During the data collection period, which spanned from December 1994 to August 1996, I sampled mornings, afternoons, and evenings on both weekdays and weekends within five contiguous neighborhoods or sections of northwest Washington, DC. This area covered a three-mile corridor beginning in a largely White, well-educated, and affluent residential neighborhood at the northern point and terminating in a large downtown business section at the southern end. Both a major avenue and a common subway line connect four of these regions. I undertook about 80 official data collection efforts into this area, which were accomplished largely on foot since I lived in one of the five neighborhoods. Including interviews, each journey usually lasted between two and five hours. At the end of the data collection period in August 1996, I typically was able to identify two out of three panhandlers within this corridor as someone whom I had either interviewed or informally spoken to previously.

Interviews ($N = 37$) were tape recorded and followed a series of open-ended questions focusing on four aspects of the panhandler's experience: street work, relationships, self-issues, and demographics. Panhandlers received $10 for their tape-recorded interviews, which typically lasted between 45 minutes and an hour. On meeting a panhandler for the first time, I usually established basic rapport by giving $0.50, which was then followed by an explanation that I was a student studying panhandling. Other relevant information that may have influenced rapport with each panhandler is that I am White, male, and of a middle-class background. Only a handful of panhandlers, however, refused to be interviewed. In addition to these formal interviews, I informally spoke with dozens of other panhandlers and posed as a panhandler for two consecutive days in downtown Washington, DC.

On the basis of the formal interviews, the profile of the typical panhandler in this sample is as follows: a Black, single, unemployed homeless man in his early 40s who was born into a lower- or working-class family in the District of Columbia and who possessed a high school degree or higher. In addition, the typical panhandler began panhandling in his mid-30s or early 40s and had been panhandling consistently for the past five years after losing a job in the construction industry. A negative life event or events, such as an accident, an illness, a spell of homelessness, a layoff, or a drug or alcohol problem generally preceded job losses.

Largely owing to the disproportionate number of male panhandlers, only three female panhandlers were included in the sample of 37 persons. In addition, the city's demographic composition partially explains the high proportion of African American panhandlers in the sample: The District of Columbia is predominantly populated by African Americans (65.8 percent in 1990) and poverty and homelessness are most acute among African Americans (D.C. Government, 1993). When comparing my sample of panhandlers to a study of Washington, DC homeless individuals conducted by the National Institute on Drug Abuse (NIDA) in 1991, the NIDA sample captured a greater proportion of women, younger persons, White and Hispanic individuals, less educated persons, and employed individuals. Only a small proportion of the NIDA sample reported panhandling on a regular basis....

PANHANDLING REPERTOIRES

Panhandlers overcome the nonperson treatment by initiating encounters through the use of dramaturgical techniques, routines, acts, pieces, or numbers, which I collectively call panhandling repertoires. Often enacted in a performancelike manner, repertoires capture the attention and interest of passersby by appealing to a range of emotional qualities, such as amusement, sympathy, and fear.

I have conceptualized five primary panhandling routines: the entertainer, the greeter, the servicer, the storyteller, and the aggressor, along with strategies within certain routines. The entertainer offers music or humor, the greeter provides cordiality and deference, the servicer supplies a kind of service, the storyteller presents a sad or sympathetic tale, and the aggressor deals in fear and intimidation. Generally, the entertainer and greeter attempt to produce enjoyment or good feelings, whereas the storyteller and aggressor elicit more serious or hostile moods. The servicer, who occupies a more neutral position, is focused on providing some sort of utility. Fundamentally, the moods or impressions created by the routines are largely attempts to attenuate strangeness or awaken pedestrians from their blasé condition, which then paves the way for an encounter and possible contributions.

STORYTELLER

Of all the panhandling routines, the storyteller approach most clearly conveys the dramaturgical nature of panhandling. The storyteller routine is based on using stories to evoke understanding, pity, or guilt from pedestrians. The primary message is need in virtually all cases. Stories consist of various signs, appearances, lines, or narratives that focus on shaking pedestrians from their blasé state. The storyteller routine is then accomplished by means of one or more specific subroutines: the silent storyteller, the sign storyteller, the line storyteller, and the hard luck storyteller. Here, Duane, a long-time homeless panhandler, points to the tactics or arts of capturing the sympathy of passersby with a good story:

What makes my panhandlin' successful and any other panhandlin' successful is the emotions. Now if you were reared in a good moral background and I come up to you [he pulls his face close—about six inches away], "Excuse me sir, I'm really tired. I just moved in and I've got five kids. Me and my wife—we can't get jobs." Now when you say the word kids—*"Forget me—I've got babies I'm tryin' to feed." Or sickness—"I'm dyin'" or "my wife, my mother." More than just I'm givin' them money to get something to eat. These things are tactics. They'll be touched. [Duane gets up and demonstrates by calling out onto the sidewalk.] "Ma'am, my wife only has one hour to live! I'm tryin' to raise money. Please, someone help!" [He returns to the table.] Now, did you catch some of the arts? There's an appeal to your emotions. And you got those regulars who are sittin' down, "Hey, I'm homeless. Can you spare some change sir?" And you see the same jerk on the same corner everyday. And then you get into a habit, "Well here's a dollar." But the real money comes from the emotions.*

In addition to narratives, stories are conveyed symbolically through down-and-out facial expressions, as Ray indicates:

People look at me—the way I talk and you know—feel sorry for me. They know I'm homeless by the way I'm lookin'! And I give them a sad little look.

Clothing, appearances, and presentation of self may also be manipulated or used to tell the desired story. In fact, becoming a successful storyteller is contingent on developing a look that works, as Fox suggests:

When I first started panhandling I couldn't understand why people weren't giving me money—I looked too clean. So I grew this ratty beard and figured so that's the trick of the trade. As long as I was looking presentable like I was doing a 9-to-5 job—say working as a computer specialist—I wasn't getting a dime [laughs].

Hence, storytellers may have to consciously manage their appearance more than others to foster the impression of need. On buying or receiving new or secondhand clothes and shoes, for instance, storytellers find themselves in the difficult position of negotiating those symbols that do not suggest need, as compared with other routines that rely less on a sympathetic or pitiful appearance or story. I now discuss the four storyteller subroutines in greater detail.

The silent storyteller relies primarily on symbolic communication rather than verbal exchanges to gain the attention of passersby. The silent storyteller uses attire, expressions, movements, and other props to advertise his or her situation and needs. Movements might entail limping down the street or shivering unprotected in the rain and cold. Props may include crutches, a wheelchair, or other symbols of disability; bags of belongings; or children. Generally, silent storytellers, who often sit with their cup on the sidewalk and refrain from unnecessary interactions, are the most passive of all panhandlers. Harlan, a panhandler for the past six years, explains his silent approach:

Over the years I've looked at all the guys' styles and when I first started some of the guys used signs and some of the guys talked, some the guys sing, some of the guys danced, some of the guys do everything—I mean I can do all that too. I don't like to ask people for money so when I first started I used to say, "Excuse me sir, can you spare some change?" Then I started to develop my own thing—something told me not to say anything. In other words, I let my cup do the talking. People used to tell me a long time ago, if anyone wants you to have anything they'll give it to you. You know, you don't have to ask. I'm not gonna ask everybody that comes up and down the street to give me a nickel [laughs]. I've tried it, I've done it. You know, I just let my cup do the talking.

Like the silent storyteller, the sign storyteller typically waits passively for a pedestrian to initiate an encounter. A sign is a tool that effectively creates interest and concern within passersby with minimal effort exerted by the panhandler. A sign, as compared with a verbal exchange, reduces the likelihood of being subjected to a negative or humiliating interaction, as explained by Walt:

I let the sign do the talking. I don't speak unless I'm spoken to or unless to say "good morning" or something like that or "good afternoon." I just hold a sign and if people want to give me money they give me money and if they don't they walk by and nothing is ever said. There's no dirty looks, no nothin' because you can't look nasty to everyone that doesn't give you money because you'd [be] looking nasty to 90 percent of the world [chuckles].

Lou also uses a cardboard sign that reads, "Homeless and Hungry. Please Help. Thank you. God Bless All." He includes his name in the lower right corner of the sign. Lou sits on the sidewalk with his back against a building, his belongings on either side, and his sign and cup positioned in front of him. For Lou, the sign removes the uncomfortable process of verbally soliciting money and minimizes negative exchanges:

I don't like asking people for money straight out— that's why I use my sign. And incidentally, I don't feel as bad because I'm not asking people. A lot of people are afraid of me if I ask. With the sign they have the option of walking by or not walking by.

Thus, sign storytellers view the sign as an unobtrusive, nonthreatening device but one that still conveys a message of need. Generally, signs protect panhandlers from degrading interactions by allowing agreeable donors to initiate an exchange without compulsion or intimidation.

The line storyteller is the most common among all storytellers and possibly the most ubiquitous routine in the panhandling repertoire. The line storyteller typically remains stationary and simply presents a line to pedestrians as they pass. Almost all lines focus on money in one form or another. The most basic, unadorned money line is

"Can you spare some change?" but specific higher amounts, such as a quarter or a dollar are often inserted in place of *change*. Another variation on the money line is to ask for very little money, such as "Can you help me out? Pennies will do" or an odd amount of money, such as "Can you spare 27 cents?"

Other lines may refer to "help" rather than money while specifying how the help would be put to good use. In these instances, food is a typical theme, such as "Can you help me get something to eat?" or "Can you spare some change to get a burrito?" In addition to food, transportation needs are another common theme used by line storytellers, such as "Can you spare two or three dollars for bus fare?" Lines invoking transportation may also include a destination and purpose, like returning to the shelter for the evening, buying medication at a hospital, or going to a job interview. Lines also focus on the return from unintended destinations, such as a hospital or jail, which may involve displaying evidence of a stay, like an institutionally marked identification wristband. Beyond money, food, transportation, and destinations, line storytellers focus on innumerable topics, but lines typically center on subjects that a homeless or poor person might realistically need.

The hard luck storyteller uses a more direct approach than the teller of a line story and offers an in-depth narrative focusing on difficult or unusual circumstances. On gaining the person's attention, the hard luck storyteller then presents an extended narrative to elicit sympathy and a contribution. Often, hard luck storytellers elaborate and combine themes used by line and sign storytellers. Here is an example of a hard luck story told to me one afternoon:

> I know this is a little unusual but I need you to save me. God told me to approach the man with the pink shirt. [I was wearing a pink shirt.] I almost just committed suicide by jumping off the bridge. You need to help me and my two daughters. We're trying to get a bus ticket to Philadelphia. I've been in prison for the past five years and I've been out a

> month and I'm broke. When I was in prison my wife was raped and murdered. I need $15—Travelers Aid is going to pay the rest of the ticket. [I gave him a dollar from my wallet.] Can you help me get something to eat from Roy Rogers then? I'll put that dollar towards the bus but I need some money for food as well.

In sum, storytellers attempt to negate the blasé state by emphasizing the apparent disparities between themselves and pedestrians. These differences then create feelings of sympathy or pity within passersby and often lead to encounters and contributions. The storyteller's dramatized tales or physical appearance, however, may actually exacerbate the level of strangeness between panhandler and pedestrians—a result that is in contrast to more positive routines that neutralize strangeness, such as the entertainer, greeter, and servicer numbers. Aggravating strangeness through stories or appearances, though, places storytellers in the "sick role" (Parsons 1951) or a position of alienated dependency, which then paves the way for sympathy and contributions.

AGGRESSOR

The aggressor technique is premised on evoking guilt and fear in pedestrians by using either real or feigned aggression. Compared with the storyteller, the aggressor captures the attention of a pedestrian in a more pointed and dramatic fashion. Like the storyteller routine, however, the aggressor increases feelings of strangeness by highlighting disparities and differences. Primarily, the aggressor obtains food, money, and other items through intimidation, persistence, and shame.

Intimidation is accomplished through sarcastic and abusive comments, or fearful movements, like walking alongside, grabbing hold of the pedestrian, or silently using intimidating looks or stares. For instance, I encountered an unidentified panhandler using a kind of physical intimidation by standing in front of an ATM machine and then darting and lunging at pedestrians as they passed. Finally, a woman who initially refused his overtures gave him some money after completing her transaction at the ATM machine.

Persistence entails doggedly pursuing a contribution after it has been refused or seeking more money after an initial donation. Rita, for example, displayed this kind of persistence, though politely, during our hour-long encounter. After meeting her in front of McDonald's and buying her lunch, she then requested the change from lunch, asked for additional money to help her pay rent, and then asked for any old articles of clothing. During our meeting, Rita clearly displayed need especially after describing how she had been partially disabled by a stroke. Her method of asking, however, conveyed this element of aggressiveness and persistence.

Shame is evoked by making the donor feel that his or her quarter or dollar donation is insufficient and cheap given the vast material discrepancies between donor and panhandler. For example, my first encounter with Mel incorporated a sad tale with a shameful admonishment. After meeting him on the street, he lifted his shirt with his left hand revealing a long scar extending from his sternum to his belly button. The scar was folded over like it had recently been sewn up. "See this," he said, pointing to the scar with his right hand, "I need to eat right now. It's also about time for me to take my insulin. I'm a diabetic." I responded by giving him a dollar. "Can you tell me what I can get with that?" he returned somewhat indignantly.

Any of these prior examples may have constituted a form of aggressive panhandling under the District of Columbia's Panhandling Control Act, enacted in 1993. This act prohibits panhandling in an aggressive manner, which includes "approaching, speaking to, or following a person in a manner as would cause a reasonable person to fear bodily harm" and "continuously asking, begging, or soliciting alms from a person after the person has made a negative response."

Most panhandlers are well aware of this law and the prohibitions surrounding aggressive panhandling. Consequently, panhandlers often distinguish themselves from other panhandlers who act in an aggressive fashion, as Lou suggests:

You have people out there with the cup going right up to people and saying, "Help me out." That's what they call aggressive panhandling. That makes a bad name for me because I use a sign. And I mean that says it all. I'm not in people's face. I'm just off on the side. That's how I do it.

Up until now, I have described the aggressor routine as one that is consciously initiated by the panhandler. However, it also is clear that due to the many negative comments and interactions panhandlers report receiving from passersby, at least some of the time behaving aggressively is a reaction rather than a role, as suggested by Vern:

I have no problem people askin' for change because you can always say no. Some people have attitudes but you got to keep a good mind because I've been through it with people: "You got some spare change?" "Get the hell out of my face." You can't lose your spot over that because as soon as you get aggressive [makes police siren noise]. Don't let one dollar mess you up from a hundred dollars. They [fellow panhandlers] tell me that four or five times a night.

Hence, panhandlers generally understand the economic and legal imperatives behind remaining silent when publicly humiliated. Although easier said than done, managing one's emotions in the face of rejection or abusive comments is part of the job, as suggested by Ray:

I don't do aggressive panhandling. I don't harass nobody. If you have a problem with me I have nothin' to say to you—I'm a panhandler. If people have something to say I just let it go—words are words.

Whereas the aggressor routine is often good at stirring pedestrians from their blasé condition, such action runs the risk of furthering strangeness and alienating potential donors. Particularly among panhandlers who are tempted to react aggressively to humiliating interactions with passersby or police, the job of panhandling is akin to service occupations that require emotional labor (Hochschild 1983) or publicly managing one's feelings.

SERVICER

In contrast to all other routines, the servicer provides specific services to stimulate social interaction and exchange. Using various dramaturgical techniques, the servicer transforms the exchange into something different than merely giving money to a panhandler. The servicer dispels the blasé attitude by ostensibly offering a service while lessening the sense of strangeness by converting the interaction into a kind of business transaction. In other words, giving money to a stranger in public is an unfamiliar practice, whereas being engaged by a salesperson offering a service is a familiar ritual. Regardless of whether a service is desired or not, however, providing a service dampens strangeness by establishing a sense of obligation and reciprocity between panhandler and pedestrian.... This rapport may be contrived in some cases and more akin to "counterfeit intimacy" (Enck and Preston 1988), that is, interaction supporting the illusion that a legitimate service is being performed when both parties know this to be false.

The servicer repertoire consists of a formal, proactive component and an informal, reactive aspect. The formal servicer consciously seeks out situations to provide a service in exchange for a tip, much like a bellhop or bathroom attendant. Roaming the streets in search of an opportunity is a particular characteristic of the formal servicer. In contrast, the informal servicer is more typically sought out by virtue of possessing something desirable, such as information. Additionally, the informal servicer can be viewed as a secondary type of routine that emerges owing to the failure of a primary one or arises when a panhandler is in the right place at the right time.

Car parking, that is, pointing out parking spaces to drivers in exchange for a tip, is the most prevalent type of formal service. This practice, however, is illegal under the Panhandling Control Act. The maximum penalties for violating the statute are a $300 fine and 90 days in jail. Despite its illegality and potential costs, parking

cars remains a booming business in certain neighborhoods.

I gained a sense of the car-parking routine one evening by observing Spike, who is one of among a half-dozen car parkers that work a certain neighborhood. As we spoke alongside a busy street, Spike motioned to an approaching luxury sedan that a spot would be vacant. As the vehicle backed diagonally into the space, Spike stood behind and yelled out directions: "Turn your wheel to the left. You're OK. Come on." The passenger—a tall, professionally dressed man—took several minutes to emerge. Spike noted the car's Georgia license plate and asked the man as he opened his door what part of Georgia he was from. "I'm from Atlanta," the car owner said. "Oh yeah, I'm from Statesboro," Spike responded. The man then gave Spike some change. During this exchange, Spike's friendly demeanor also demonstrates how car parkers often integrate the greeter rap into their parking routine.

In terms of earnings, car parking appears to be the most lucrative of all the panhandling routines. Although most car parkers panhandle in addition to parking cars, it is difficult to gain an accurate understanding of the payoffs of car parking alone. In any case, regular car parkers report a minimum of $40 of total earnings on a good evening compared with the median level of $35 among all panhandlers. However, earnings reportedly can exceed $100 if a car parker encounters extra-generous drivers who give $10 or $20 at a time.

The increased earnings netted by car parkers may stem from any one of numerous factors, including drivers giving out of fear, generosity, appreciation, a desire to impress friends or dates, or inebriation. However, Mel, a long-time car parker, offers his own explanation for why car parkers earn such high relative earnings:

> *It's free money out there. I don't ask for nothing. I just direct cars into parking spaces and people give me money—some change, one dollar, five dollars, ten dollars, twenty dollars. Sometimes they're so happy to give me money even though they could've paid for an actual space in a parking lot*

for less. If you ever get hard up for money, go over there and try it. It's almost like they're trained. They expect it when they come into the neighborhood.

In contrast to the formal servicer, such as the car parker, the informal servicer provides services to pedestrians, vendors, storeowners, and the police. These services, which result from a panhandler's propensity of being in the right place at the right time, include offering an umbrella to a soaked pedestrian, giving directions to specific street addresses, escorting unchaperoned, sometimes inebriated persons to their final destinations, or hailing a taxi for the less streetwise or infirm. These exchanges convert the panhandler into an informal service provider.

Beyond informally offering everyday information and help, panhandlers occasionally encounter more significant and valued news. Owing to their near omnipresence on the streets, panhandlers are frequently knowledgeable of many important happenings. Information absorbed by panhandlers, particularly facts and persons relating to crimes, are sought after by storeowners and police, as explained by Vance:

We provide services to some of the storeowners. If there's a break-in or vandalism, we usually know who did it within a 24–48 hour period, whereas it might take the police several days to a week to find out the same information.

However, not all panhandlers capitalize on the opportunity to provide information to the powers that seek it. Each panhandler may have personal reasons for not offering up important information, such as fear of retaliation, a code of silence among street people, not knowing the desired facts, or not trusting the police. Hence, a witness who fails to cooperate with the police when the stakes are high may feel the stick rather than being handed a carrot, as Mel explains:

I went to jail because I wouldn't open my mouth. So they said I was in contempt of court. I was the witness of a murder and they all pointed their fingers at me man—I'm telling you Joe—"He saw it. He was there." I was just walking past. I didn't see who

was blowing who away. I be everywhere. I see a whole lot of things—and that be my business. I hear the gunshot goin' off, but do you think I looked around to see what time it was? I keep with my straight steady walk—outta there—caught a cab.

In sum, the servicer captures a pedestrian's attention by creating the impression that he or she has some valuable utility to offer in exchange for payment, much like the relationship between salesclerk and patron. Although intimacy or familiarity may increase the likelihood of a pedestrian giving money to a servicer, the quality of strangeness is attenuated by the panhandler's ability to turn the interaction into a kind of neutral business exchange. Because of their presence on the streets, overcoming the nonperson treatment is occasionally a moot point as panhandlers are sometimes actively approached for information or assistance. As indicated, however, panhandlers must intermittently use other dramaturgical routines to avoid encounters (and thereby foster strangeness) with more powerful persons, such as the police, who seek to develop exchanges that may be disadvantageous or detrimental to their existence on the streets.

GREETER

The greeter offers friendliness, respect, flattery, and deference to passersby in exchange for contributions and cordial responses. This routine largely revolves around polite behavior, such as greeting pedestrians with a "hello" or "good morning," quite like department store employees who welcome customers at store entrances. Like these service occupations, the greeter number is firmly rooted in dramaturgically managing emotions. Additionally, the routine is enhanced when a panhandler becomes familiar with a panhandling locale and then remembers faces, names, and biographical facts about contributors. Hence, a command of these more intimate details about passersby allows the greeter to personalize each greeting and devise a more comprehensive panhandling repertoire.

Sanford personifies the greeter number. During numerous observations and encounters, Sanford always offered a pleasant greeting and a distinctive, friendly smile. Sanford typically stands at the top of the Metro (subway) or along a busy side street greeting passersby during their commute or afternoon stroll. As he explains,

I greet people in the morning—say "good morning" to them—say "hello." I try to make people happy and everything. I generally get a good response—a happy greeting in a happy way especially with a smile. They always like my smile. Everybody has their own different style. My style is my smile. That's how a lot of people remember me you know.

Whereas Sanford capitalizes on his friendly smile and good nature, Lonnie, a 40-year-old native of the West Indies, appeals to pedestrians through his pleasing Caribbean accent and interactional flair:

I just talk to people because I'm gifted. I know that I'm gifted, OK. It doesn't matter what you have on as long as you are a gentle person and your mind is proper. As long as you have a pleasant personality it doesn't matter [exclaimed] what you have on—how stinky you feel or whatever. If you are nice to people, people will give.

Although some panhandlers possess specific attributes that facilitate the greeter number, such as a friendly smile or a courteous manner, a certain amount of on-the-job learning is usually involved. Wally implicitly describes his evolution from the aggressor to the greeter, which required emotion management skills:

I always say "good morning" to the people. It makes them feel real good. And most of the time I'm good at it but I was a nasty motherfucker when I came here. But now I've learned my lesson—I've learned from my mistakes. Now that I'm so nice to the people I can get anything I want. When I was nasty and dirty I used the "f" word. Now I think things have changed. Now I just like being friendly with my cup in hand—"Hey, how are you doin'!"

Just as a panhandler's repertoire may undergo an evolution, city commuters often require a breaking-in period before moving from the non-person treatment toward being open to encounters with panhandlers new to their daily schedule. As Sanford explains, pedestrians were generally skeptical of him and his routine until he developed a presence in the neighborhood:

When I first came up here [to this neighborhood] people didn't really know me or nothin' and I didn't get no friendly greetin'. I got a couple right. But then they saw what kind of guy I was, right. There's a lot of stereotypes—guys who are homeless panhandlin'—cussin' people out, bein' disrespectful to people and everything. Or they feel a lot of them are alcoholics or crack addicts or whatever. So you know, they saw that it wasn't like that with me so as soon as they got to know me I got a better greetin'. Cause I couldn't even get a dollar when I first got here [laughs].

Once a panhandler is known in a certain area and rapport is established with a group of regular contributors, the greeter may be emboldened to mix compliments, such as "You're looking good today," with more conservative salutations, like "good morning." Alternatively, a more confidant, forward greeter may deal largely in compliments.

In sum, the greeter deploys pleasantries to maintain friendships with regular contributors or displays politeness and deference to newcomers. Given its versatility, it is a routine used by nearly all panhandlers. Although some use it as a primary part of their repertoire when dealing with large processions of anonymous crowds, storytellers and others typically use it as a secondary routine on encountering persons who give regularly.

ENTERTAINER

The entertainer provides humor and enjoyment and encompasses two more specific numbers: the joker and the musician. Both typically awaken pedestrians from their blasé state through a benign or positive offering, such as a joke or a song. Strangeness is then reduced by creating rapport or intimacy by performing a familiar tune or by developing an ongoing presence in a particular neighborhood. Generally, the entertainer routine most clearly resembles an actor staging a performance before an audience.

The joker entertains by telling funny stories, making irreverent comments, or offering bizarre appearances. Minimally, the joker's goal is to make an unsuspecting pedestrian smile or laugh. Once the pedestrian is loosened up, it is hoped that a contribution will follow.

For instance, Yancy demonstrates the joker by presenting a strange appearance in conjunction with humorous lines. One evening, I observed Yancy walking along a crowded sidewalk with the collar of his blue shirt pulled over his forehead, exposing only his face and a green leaf drooping over his left eye and cheek. Donning this clownish look and occasionally saying, "Can you help me out? I'm trying to get on the Internet," he moved about holding out an upturned baseball cap. During an interview, Yancy explained how confronting a weary afternoon commuter with a humorous scenario, like the incongruity between a homeless panhandler and the Internet, is a good antidote for the nonperson treatment:

> A certain line can make their day or a little bit of laughter. If a person may have his briefcase or purse and whatnot and they may have two bags of groceries from Sutton Place Gourmet and a bottle of beaujolais nouveau. They want to go home and smoke a cigarette and watch cable and you're telling them that you're panhandling and trying to get on the Internet. And they're falling out—you know what I'm saying?

Humor sometimes emerges spontaneously, seemingly without any instrumental intentions. For instance, while standing outside the Metro late one quiet evening, Ralph called out to a Metro system repairman riding up the escalator: "Hey, I caught my foot in the escalator last week." While walking away, the repairman sarcastically replied, "Sue Metro." Ralph then excitedly responded, "But you're the Metro man!" And then to the ca-

dence of the Village People's song "Macho Man," Ralph sang "Metro, Metro man, I'd like to be a Metro man." No money was exchanged, but all parties within earshot appeared amused.

The musician is another variation on the entertainer routine and covers a range of musical acts from polished saxophonist to struggling crooner. Often, musicians play familiar and fun tunes to maximize appeal. Likewise, singers frequently enhance their act by interspersing humorous lines or jokes into songs.

For instance, a companion and I were abruptly accosted one evening by a man standing five-and-a-half feet tall with long sideburns and cowboy boots who introduced himself as "Blelvis"—Black Elvis. Blelvis announced that he could sing over 1,000 Elvis songs and could relate any word to an Elvis song. As we continued walking toward our destination, I mentioned the word *cat* and Blelvis began singing a tuneful Elvis melody containing the word *cat*. Eventually, Blelvis asked for $1.50 for his performance.

This encounter with Blelvis, though largely promoted as a musical/comedy act, also contained elements of the aggressor technique. After initiating the encounter, Blelvis followed close behind and offered us little choice but to engage him. When my companion produced only $0.50 in response to his solicitation, Blelvis deftly grabbed a bottle of beer from the bag I was carrying.

Because many street performers are less aggressive than Blelvis or lack genuine musical talent, contributions may be more linked to sympathy and respect than to performing abilities. For example, late one afternoon, Alvin sat on a milk crate and played a Miles Davis tune, "Solar," on his worn clarinet. Several moments after Alvin ceased his playing, which was inspired but not exceptional, a group of young men walked past, and one dropped a handful of coins into Alvin's green canvas bag. Alvin responded to the contributions by pulling the bag next to his side and reasserting his identity as a musician: "Sometimes people hear me when I'm playing good but give me money when I'm playing bad or just warming up.

They might give me money now or later. But I don't want anyone to think I'm a panhandler."

Hence, some ambiguous performers, like Alvin, occasionally struggle to prevent one routine, such as the musician, from being misinterpreted for another act that may be more degrading to the self, like the storyteller.

In sum, entertainers awaken pedestrians from their blasé state through benign or positive offerings, such as a song or a joke. Strangeness is reduced by performing familiar tunes or developing a welcoming presence in a particular neighborhood. Many panhandlers devise a coherent repertoire based largely on the entertainer and greeter routines, given the affinity between these two numbers....

REFERENCES

Anderson, Nels. [1923] 1961. *The Hobo: The Sociology of the Homeless Man.* Chicago: University of Chicago Press.

Council of the District of Columbia. 1993. "The Panhandling Control Act." Law No.10-54. D. C. Register, Washington, DC.

District of Columbia Government. 1993. *Indices: A Statistical Index to District of Columbia Services.* Vol. X. Washington, DC.

Enck, Graves E. and James D. Preston. 1988. "Counterfeit Intimacy: A Dramaturgical Analysis of an Erotic Performance." *Deviant Behavior* 9:369–81.

Freund, Roger Henry. 1925. "Begging in Chicago." Master's thesis, University of Chicago, Chicago, IL.

Gilmore, Harlan W. 1940. *The Beggar.* Chapel Hill: University of North Carolina Press.

Goffman, Erving. 1959. *The Presentation of Self in Everyday Life.* New York: Anchor/Doubleday.

———. 1963. *Behavior in Public Place.* New York: Free Press.

Hochschild, Arlie. 1983. *The Managed Heart: Commercialization of Human Feelings.* Berkeley: University of California Press.

Igbinova, Patrick. 1991. "Begging in Nigeria." *International Journal of Offender Therapy and Comparative Criminology* 35(1):21–33.

Parsons, Talcott. 1951. *The Social System.* New York: Free Press.

Simmel, Georg. [1903] 1971. "Mental Life and the Metropolis." Pp. 324–339, in *On Individuality and Social Forms,* edited by Donald N. Levine. Chicago: University of Chicago Press.

Wallace, Samuel. 1965. *Skid Row as a Way of Life.* Totowa, NJ: Bedminister Press.

Williams, Brackette. 1995. "The Public I/Eye: Conducting Fieldwork to Do Homework on Homeless and Begging in Two U.S. Cities." *Current Anthropology* 36(1)25–39.

Wright, James D. 1989. *Address Unknown: The Homeless in America.* New York: Aldine de Gruyter.

PART FOUR

DEVIANT IDENTITY

When a person asks "Who am I?" there are private answers as well as public ones. The private answers—how a person views himself or herself—form one's *personal* identity. The public answers—the image others have of the person—provide one's *social* identity. There is sometimes little consistency between the two. Con men, for example, may studiously present social identities that diverge widely from their true, personal identities. Thus they assume social identities that their personal identities, if known, would discredit. This is true for covert deviants generally. When in the company of heterosexuals, for example, the secret homosexual may ridicule or condemn homosexuality, or pretend to be interested in the other sex, in order to achieve a heterosexual social identity. The task of harmonizing one's personal and social identities is hard enough for conventional people. For certain kinds of deviants, particularly secret deviants, it is even more complex.

A deviant social identity may lead to a deviant personal identity when a person finds it prudent to accept a publicly attributed deviant status. This passive style of bringing personal and social identities together probably produces relatively little identity conflict. When a person identified as a deviant refuses to take on a deviant personal identity, however, greater identity problems are likely to result.

Social identities may be devised by the person or by others. Spies, for example, consciously devise and enact their own deceptive social identities. Public relations people, gossips, and agents of social control, on the other hand, often cast other people into social identities that may or may not conform to their personal identities.

In a complex, urban society where many people relate to a wide assortment of new, previously unknown people, the opportunity for taking on a new social identity comes up all the time. Similarly, the chance of being cast by someone else into a new social identity is also more likely. In addition, the possibility of having multiple social identities, with different identities for different audiences, also arises. In such a society, then, people often find it difficult to develop a single, coherent social identity; they may also find it difficult to harmonize their personal and social identities. In fact, attempts to manage this problem may produce the very deceitfulness that is presumed to be characteristic of so many deviants.

Because a social identity as a conforming person is usually preferred to a deviant social identity, most deviants need to practice some duplicity. The steady practice of duplicity may enable the deviant to avert conflict between his or her various positions and roles. On the other hand, duplicity may cause such a strain that the deviant gives it up. For example, Edwin Lemert found that with regard to the systematic check forger the need to assume many legitimate social roles and social identities produces a heavy strain;[1] constant impersonations are not easy to maintain. Hence, paradoxically, discovery and arrest actually solve an identity problem for the forger. In prison the forger at least has an authentic social identity. The strains confronting the systematic check forger typify the kinds of identity problems that many deviants must come to terms with in one way or another.

In this part of the book we examine the issue of deviant identity more specifically. First we consider the process of acquiring a deviant identity. Then we look at the ways a person sustains a particular identity. Finally, we consider the conditions under which a person is most likely to change a deviant identity.

ACQUIRING A DEVIANT IDENTITY

People acquire deviant identities in what is often a long-drawn-out interactive process. For example, a person performs a deviant act for the very first time, and then others respond to the act, usually with some form of social punishment. If the deviant act is repeated, the chances are that the social penalties will be repeated and may even increase. These social penalties, in turn, can alienate the alleged deviant; if the deviant act is repeated again, it may now be done with a degree of defiance. In time, then, a vicious circle tends to evolve. This cycle continues until others have come to expect a pattern of systematic deviant behavior from the "deviant"; in effect they have assigned that person to a deviant role. Reciprocally, the person who is now expected to perform a deviant role comes to see himself or herself in the same terms and may begin to devise ways of continuing the deviant line of action without getting caught. Thus, we see how the interactive process works: the alleged deviant *act* produces the negative *social response*, which in time elicits the deviant *social role*, which in turn after a while culminates in the person's adopting a deviant *identity.* The initial deviance, as proposed by Edwin Lemert, is referred to as *primary deviance,* and the deviant role and identity that develop as a result of people's reactions to the initial deviance, *secondary deviance.*[2]

Acquiring a deviant identity follows no consistent pattern, since a reduction in either the frequency of the deviant acts or the severity of the responses of others can diminish the chances of adopting a deviant identity. Reductions in either or both may prevent assignment to a deviant role and the reciprocal deviant self-definition. Increases in either or both, on the other hand, can increase the chances of the social acquisition of a deviant identity.

Several social and cultural conditions affect the process by which people assume deviant identities. These include factors that influence the performance of deviant acts, responses of others, and the definitions of various deviant roles. For example, social responses to initial deviant acts can be extremely effective in discouraging a future career in deviance. Social responses have this effect when they call attention to the marked discrepancy between the deviant act and the kind of person most likely to perform the role, on the one hand, and the identity of the person on the other hand. Thus, middle-class housewives caught in the act of shoplifting see themselves as being treated as if they were thieves. Being caught awakens them for the first time to the way their families and friends would regard their actions if they knew of them. This awakening usually is sufficient to discourage them from future thievery because they do not see themselves as "thieves."

Usually, when a person embarks on a deviant activity such as shoplifting for the very first time, he or she does not think too much about getting caught. At the same time, the person may justify the act in one way or another. Some justifications before the fact hamper a self-definition as deviant. People who embezzle money, for example, may not define their actions as stealing. Instead, they often tell themselves that they are only borrowing the money and will repay it at the earliest opportunity. Seeing themselves as borrowers, not thieves, embezzlers can justify taking the money.

On the other hand, occasionally a person acquires a deviant identity *before* taking on a deviant role. For example, male adolescents who are aware of a sexual interest in men and who grow up in an environment that defines homosexuality negatively may come to regard themselves as "sick." In their case, though they have a personal and secret deviant identity, they may refrain from engaging in any form of homosexual behavior. Hence, they cannot be said to have assumed a homosexual role, though they do have a personal identity as homosexual. We might speculate that the greater the stigma, the more likely it is that a deviant identity can exist without either deviant acts or a deviant role to support it.

People may also engage in a deviant act and expect a severely negative social reaction, only to find that this reaction does not occur. Without a negative social reaction, there is much less chance of being officially labeled as deviant. As a result, although the act has occurred, there is no significant social response to thrust the person into the role of deviant and thereby evoke the reciprocal deviant identity that goes with such a role assignment.

Thus, the responses of others are crucial when it comes to acquiring a deviant identity. Frequently these others are family or friends. Or they can be agents of social control, such as police officers, teachers, social workers, doctors, or priests. Sometimes, they can be fellow deviants. For instance, a person might experiment with heroin. In an initial act of experimenting with drugs in the company of others, the novice may see himself or herself as merely satisfying a curiosity about the effects of the drug. But later on, drug-using friends may tell the novice that the way to cure withdrawal distress is to take more heroin. The novice may now be on his way or her way to becoming a drug addict, along with its correlative deviant identity, acts, and roles. In this last instance, the responses of deviant others redefine the novice's situation for him or her.

MANAGING A DEVIANT IDENTITY

In order to sustain a deviant social identity and membership in a deviant group, new members have to incorporate the group's signs and symbols into their own personal styles and to behave according to deviant norms even when they may not especially want to. The novice's deviant identity may then be confirmed by the group. A deviant who fails to learn the appropriate ways probably will not be truly accepted as a member of the group.

Attempts at being a deviant can fail if the audience refuses to confirm the person's deviant social identity. Then there is no effective audience to reward the person's deviant actions or to confirm his or her self-typing. A jack-of-all-trades offender, for instance, may be considered too inept or "unprofessional" to be accepted into more skillful criminal circles. An audience—conformist or deviant—will not confirm the social identity desired by a person who has obviously miscast himself or herself, who does not look the part.

Some deviant statuses imply more than one audience, and the various audiences may demand different, sometimes contradictory, roles on the part of the deviant. Deviants with multiple audiences will have problems of identity unless they can clearly understand which audience they are confronting and which role is required at a particular time. It is often the case, for example, that "front ward" patients in mental hospitals are expected by fellow inmates to act "normal," while they are expected by outsiders to act "sick" and in need of treatment.

It should be noted that deviants can often choose among deviant identities, and this ability is often one facet of managing a deviant identity. As a result, there can be "imposters" who sustain deviant identities as well as "imposters" who sustain conventional identities. Some epileptics, for example, try to pass as alcoholics because they see alcoholism as less stigmatized than epilepsy. As long as these pseudoalcoholics have only limited contact with genuine alcoholics, their secret is probably safe.

To sustain a deviant identity and membership in a deviant group, then, it is necessary to act like other members of the group. Some social conditions are more conducive to this than others. For example, becoming more involved with other deviants and avoiding contact with nondeviants facilitates developing the deviant identity and maintaining the deviant role. It also makes it easier to cast off conventional traits and loyalties. Thus a deviant identity is easier to sustain under these optimum conditions.

Persons who wish to conceal their deviant identity also confront both role and self problems. As Erving Goffman has pointed out, they can seek to control information about their identity or, if already known about, try to control the tension possible in their face-to-face contacts with others.[3] Stutterers, for instance, may solve these role problems by hiding the fact that they stutter, revealing it on their own terms, or refusing to acknowledge the fact that they are stuttering. And, similarly, when control agents seek to assign a deviant identity, the person at risk of being so designated may try to neutralize the deviant identity. As Gresham Sykes and David Matza have pointed out with regard to delinquency, juveniles may deny responsibility for the behavior, any injury or harm to anyone, or the existence of any victim who really matters. In addition, the delinquent may cite an appeal to higher loyalties (e.g., that his behavior showed loyalty to his friends), or he may condemn the persons condemning him (e.g., as being hypocrites).[4]

TRANSFORMING DEVIANT IDENTITY

As we have suggested, some deviants have trouble managing a deviant identity. Fitting social positions, roles, and self-concepts together is too hard or undesirable. Thus the deviant may face an identity crisis that can become the turning point in his or her deviant career. Nonetheless, it is not necessarily true that most deviants are unhappy and wish to renounce their deviance. Conventional stereotypes of deviants suggest as much, but the facts are otherwise. If people can successfully conceal their deviance, for example, they can continue to enjoy their deviance without "paying the price."

A profound identity crisis can be one of the conditions for transforming a deviant identity back to a more conventional one. Discovery, or recurrent feelings of remorse, can produce the crisis, impelling the person to contemplate making some radical changes in his or her life. In such a crisis the mechanisms that successfully sustain a deviant identity usually show signs of breaking down, and these breakdowns in turn intensify the crisis.

As already noted, assuming and maintaining a deviant identity is not an easy matter. Renouncing one is even more difficult. Even if a deviant experiences an extreme identity crisis, that person may not succeed in transforming his or her deviant identity to a more conventional one. Three factors imperil successful transformation: lack of practice in conventional roles, continued distrust by conventional people, and pressure from fellow deviants to return to their group. Time spent in deviance is time spent away from the conventional world. Legitimate skills may fall into disuse; for example, alcoholic toolmakers who return to their craft after years of heavy drinking and unemployment may find that they cannot pick up where they left off. The ex-convicts' difficulty in finding work may exemplify the continued suspicion and disapproval that deviants arouse in the larger society. Finally, fellow deviants may press one to continue former deviations; thus the drug addict, on release from a hospital, may be quickly surrounded by former friends who are eager to supply a free fix.

Deviants who want to return to a more conventional way of life ordinarily have the best chance of success if they join a primary group with similar intentions. The best-known example of such a primary group is Alcoholics Anonymous. The group members reward the ex-drinker for making changes toward conventionality, and they confirm his or her new social identity as a nondrinker. These conditions encourage the deviant to return to conventional life. Such social and cultural supports are not available, however, to many deviants who might want to return to conformity.

Finally, in order to change deviant identities, deviants may enter into a "politics of protest" with political activism being directed at society. This method of transformation seeks to alter the labelers' attitudes and responses to them rather than the deviants' own attributes or behaviors. Thus, people who are unconventional—in their physical characteristics, sexual patterns, choice of intoxicating substances, and so forth—will only be defined as deviants if people continue to view them in a deviance framework. However, to the degree that labelers' change in these conceptions, the people who are subjects of their reaction will decrease in the extent to which they are sociologically deviant.

NOTES

1. Edwin M. Lemert, *Human Deviance, Social Problems, and Social Control,* 2nd ed. (Englewood Cliffs, NJ: Prentice-Hall, 1972), pp. 162–182.

2. Edwin M. Lemert, *Social Pathology: A Systematic Approach to the Theory of Sociopathic Behavior* (New York: McGraw-Hill, 1951), p. 76.

3. Erving Goffman, *Stigma: Notes on the Management of Spoiled Identity* (Englewood Cliffs, NJ: Prentice-Hall, 1963).

4. Gresham M. Sykes and David Matza, "Techniques of Neutralization: A Theory of Delinquency," *American Sociological Review,* 22 (December, 1957), pp. 667–670.

CHAPTER 12

ACQUIRING A DEVIANT IDENTITY

Becoming Bisexual

MARTIN S. WEINBERG, COLIN J. WILLIAMS, and DOUGLAS W. PRYOR

Whenever there is a discrepancy between personal and social identity, people facing this conflict have difficulty answering the question of what kind of people they are. Those facing questions about their "sexual identity" often have this problem. Studies of gays and lesbians, for example, report that the kind of identity problems they face may well last a lifetime. If so, then persons who find themselves attracted to both sexes could face even more in the way of such problems.

Martin S. Weinberg, Colin J. Williams, and Douglas W. Pryor examine how bisexuals become aware of these problems and how they try to come to terms with their "sexual identity." In part, their sexuality is always at issue because the homosexual community demands that they be homosexual whereas the heterosexual world continues to assume their heterosexuality. Given these persistent cross-pressures, they experience continual uncertainty with regard to labeling their sexual identity. The authors posit a stages model of bisexual identity and characterize each of these stages.

Becoming bisexual involves the rejection of not one but two recognized categories of sexual identity: heterosexual and homosexual. Most people settle into the status of heterosexual without any struggle over the identity. There is not much concern with explaining how this occurs; that people are heterosexual is simply taken for granted. For those who find heterosexuality unfulfilling, however, developing a sexual identity is more difficult.

How is it then that some people come to identify themselves as "bisexual"? As a point of departure we take the process through which people come to identify themselves as "homosexual." A number of models have been formulated that chart the development of a homosexual identity through a series of stages.[1] While each model involves a different number of stages, the models all share three elements. The process begins with the person in a state of identity confusion—feeling different from others, struggling with the acknowledgment of same-sex attractions. Then there is a period of thinking about possibly being homosexual—involving associating with self-identified homosexuals, sexual experimentation, forays into the homosexual subculture. Last is the attempt to integrate one's self-concept and social identity as homosexual—acceptance of the label, disclosure about being homosexual, acculturation to a homosexual way of life, and the development of love relationships. Not every person follows through each stage. Some remain locked in at a certain point. Others move back and forth between stages.

To our knowledge, no previous model of *bisexual* identity formation exists.... [W]e present such a model based on the following questions: To what extent is there overlap with the process involved in becoming homosexual? How far is the label "bisexual" clearly recognized, understood, and available to people as an identity? Does the absence of a bisexual subculture in most locales affect the information and support needed for sustaining a commitment to the identity? For our subjects, then, what are the problems in finding the "bisexual" label, understanding what the label means, dealing with social disapproval from two directions, and continuing to use the label once it is adopted? From our fieldwork and interviews, we found that four stages captured our respondents' most common experiences when dealing with questions of identity: initial confusion, finding and applying the label, settling into the identity, and continued uncertainty.

THE STAGES

INITIAL CONFUSION

Many of the people interviewed said that they had experienced a period of considerable confusion, doubt, and struggle regarding their sexual identity before defining themselves as bisexual. This was ordinarily the first step in the process of becoming bisexual.

They described a number of major sources of early confusion about their sexual identity. For some, it was the experience of having strong sexual feelings for both sexes that was unsettling, disorienting, and sometimes frightening. Often these were sexual feelings that they said they did not know how to easily handle or resolve.

> In the past, I couldn't reconcile different desires I had. I didn't understand them. I didn't know what I was. And I ended up feeling really mixed up, unsure, and kind of frightened. (F)

> I thought I was gay, and yet I was having these intense fantasies and feelings about fucking women. I went through a long period of confusion. (M)

Others were confused because they thought strong sexual feelings for, or sexual behavior with, the same sex meant an end to their long-standing heterosexuality.

> I was afraid of my sexual feelings for men and...that if I acted on them, that would negate my sexual feelings for women. I knew absolutely no one else who had...sexual feelings for both men and women, and didn't realize that was an option. (M)

> When I first had sexual feelings for females, I had the sense I should give up my feelings for men. I think it would have been easier to give up men. (F)

A third source of confusion in this initial stage stemmed from attempts by respondents trying to categorize their feelings for, and/or behaviors with, both sexes, yet not being able to do so. Unaware of the term "bisexual," some tried to organize their sexuality by using the readily available labels of "heterosexual" or "homosexual"— but these did not seem to fit. No sense of sexual identity jelled; an aspect of themselves remained unclassifiable.

> When I was young, I didn't know what I was. I knew there were people like Mom and Dad— heterosexual and married—and that there were "queens." I knew I wasn't like either one. (M)

> I thought I had to be either gay or straight. That was the big lie. It was confusing.... That all began to change in the late 60s. It was a long and slow process.... (F)

Finally, others suggested they experienced a great deal of confusion because of their "homophobia"—their difficulty in facing up to the same-sex component of their sexuality. The consequence was often long-term denial. This was more common among the men than the women, but not exclusively so.

> *At age seventeen, I became close to a woman who was gay. She had sexual feelings for me. I had some…for her but I didn't respond. Between the ages of seventeen and twenty-six I met another gay woman. She also had sexual feelings towards me. I had the same for her but I didn't act on…or acknowledge them.… I was scared.… I was also attracted to men at the same time.… I denied that I was sexually attracted to women. I was afraid that if they knew the feelings were mutual they would act on them…and put pressure on me. (F)*

> *I thought I might be able to get rid of my homosexual tendencies through religious means—prayer, belief, counseling—before I came to accept it as part of me. (M)*

The intensity of the confusion and the extent to which it existed in the lives of the people we met at the Bisexual Center, whatever its particular source, was summed up by two men who spoke with us informally. As paraphrased in our field notes:

> *The identity issue for him was a very confusing one. At one point, he almost had a nervous breakdown, and when he finally entered college, he sought psychiatric help.*

> *Bill said he thinks this sort of thing happens a lot at the Bi Center. People come in "very confused" and experience some really painful stress.*

FINDING AND APPLYING THE LABEL

Following this initial period of confusion, which often spanned years, was the experience of finding and applying the label. We asked the people we interviewed for specific factors or events in their lives that led them to define themselves as bisexual. There were a number of common experiences.

For many who were unfamiliar with the term bisexual, the discovery that the category in fact existed was a turning point. This happened by simply hearing the word, reading about it some-

where, or learning of a place called the Bisexual Center. The discovery provided a means of making sense of long-standing feelings for both sexes.

> *Early on I thought I was just gay, because I was not aware there was another category, bisexual. I always knew I was interested in men and women. But I did not realize there was a name for these feelings and behaviors until I took Psychology 101 and read about it, heard about it there. That was in college. (F)*

> *The first time I heard the word, which was not until I was twenty-six, I realized that was what fit for me. What it fit was that I had sexual feelings for both men and women. Up until that point, the only way that I could define my sexual feelings was that I was either a latent homosexual or a confused heterosexual. (M)*

> *Going to a party at someone's house, and finding out there that the party was to benefit the Bisexual Center. I guess at that point I began to define myself as bisexual. I never knew there was such a word. If I had heard the word earlier on, for example as a kid, I might have been bisexual then. My feelings had always been bisexual. I just did not know how to define them. (F)*

> *Reading* The Bisexual Option…*I realized then that bisexuality really existed and that's what I was. (M)*

In the case of others the turning point was their first homosexual or heterosexual experience coupled with the recognition that sex was pleasurable with both sexes. These were people who already seemed to have knowledge of the label "bisexual," yet without experiences with both men and women, could not label themselves accordingly.

> *The first time I had actual intercourse, an orgasm with a woman, it led me to realize I was bisexual, because I enjoyed it as much as I did with a man, although the former occurred much later on in my sexual experiences.… I didn't have an orgasm with a woman until twenty-two, while with males, that had been going on since the age of thirteen. (M)*

Having homosexual fantasies and acting those out.... I would not identify as bi if I only had fantasies and they were mild. But since my fantasies were intensely erotic, and I acted them out, these two things led me to believe I was really bisexual.... (M)

After my first involved sexual affair with a woman, I also had feelings for a man, and I knew I did not fit the category dyke. I was also dating gay-identified males. So I began looking at gay/lesbian and heterosexual labels as not fitting my situation. (F)

Still others reported not so much a specific experience as a turning point, but emphasized the recognition that their sexual feelings for both sexes were simply too strong to deny. They eventually came to the conclusion that it was unnecessary to choose between them.

I found myself with men but couldn't completely ignore my feelings for women. When involved with a man I always had a close female relationship. When one or the other didn't exist at any given time, I felt I was really lacking something. I seem to like both. (F)

The last factor that was instrumental in leading people to initially adopt the label bisexual was the encouragement and support of others. Encouragement sometimes came from a partner who already defined himself or herself as bisexual.

Encouragement from a man I was in a relationship with. We had been together two or three years at the time—he began to define as bisexual.... [He] encouraged me to do so as well. He engineered a couple of threesomes with another woman. Seeing one other person who had bisexuality as an identity that fit them seemed to be a real encouragement. (F)

Encouragement from a partner seemed to matter more for women. Occasionally the "encouragement" bordered on coercion as the men in their lives wanted to engage in a *ménage à trois* or group sex.

I had a male lover for a year and a half who was familiar with bisexuality and pushed me towards it. My relationship with him brought it up in me.

He wanted me to be bisexual because he wanted to be in a threesome. He was also insanely jealous of my attractions to men, and did everything in his power to suppress my opposite-sex attractions. He showed me a lot of pictures of naked women and played on my reactions. He could tell that I was aroused by pictures of women and would talk about my attractions while we were having sex.... He was twenty years older than me. He was very manipulative in a way. My feelings for females were there and [he was] almost forcing me to act on my attractions.... (F)

Encouragement also came from sex-positive organizations, primarily the Bisexual Center, but also places like San Francisco Sex Information (SFSI),[2] the Pacific Center, and the Institute for Advanced Study of Human Sexuality....

At the gay pride parade I had seen the brochures for the Bisexual Center. Two years later I went to a Tuesday night meeting. I immediately felt that I belonged and that if I had to define myself that this was what I would use. (M)

Through SFSI and the Bi Center, I found a community of people...[who] were more comfortable for me than were the exclusive gay or heterosexual communities.... [It was] beneficial for myself to be...in a sex-positive community. I got more strokes and came to understand myself better.... I felt it was necessary to express my feelings for males and females without having to censor them, which is what the gay and straight communities pressured me to do. (F)

Thus our respondents became familiar with and came to the point of adopting the label bisexual in a variety of ways: through reading about it on their own, being in therapy, talking to friends, having experiences with sex partners, learning about the Bi Center, visiting SFSI or the Pacific Center, and coming to accept their sexual feelings.

SETTLING INTO THE IDENTITY

Usually it took years from the time of first sexual attractions to, or behaviors with, both sexes before people came to think of themselves as bisexual.

The next stage then was one of settling into the identity, which was characterized by a more complete transition in self-labeling.

Most reported that this settling-in stage was the consequence of becoming more self-accepting. They became less concerned with the negative attitudes of others about their sexual preference.

I realized that the problem of bisexuality isn't mine. It's society's. They are having problems dealing with my bisexuality. So I was then thinking if they had a problem dealing with it, so should I. But I don't. (F)

I learned to accept the fact that there are a lot of people out there who aren't accepting. They can be intolerant, selfish, shortsighted and so on. Finally, in growing up, I learned to say, "So what, I don't care what others think." (M)

I just decided I was bi. I trusted my own sense of self. I stopped listening to others tell me what I could or couldn't be. (F)

The increase in self-acceptance was often attributed to the continuing support from friends, counselors, and the Bi Center, through reading, and just being in San Francisco.

Fred Klein's The Bisexual Option *book and meeting more and more bisexual people...helped me feel more normal.... There were other human beings who felt like I did on a consistent basis. (M)*

I think going to the Bi Center really helped a lot. I think going to the gay baths and realizing there were a lot of men who sought the same outlet I did really helped. Talking about it with friends has been helpful and being validated by female lovers that approve of my bisexuality. Also the reaction of people who I've told, many of whom weren't even surprised. (M)

The most important thing was counseling. Having the support of a bisexual counselor. Someone who acted as somewhat of a mentor. [He] validated my frustration..., helped me do problem solving, and guide[d] me to other supportive experiences like SFSI. Just engaging myself in a supportive social community. (M)

The majority of the people we came to know through the interviews seemed settled in their sexual identity. We tapped this through a variety of questions.... Ninety percent said that they did not think they were currently in transition from being homosexual to being heterosexual or from being heterosexual to being homosexual. However, when we probed further by asking this group, "Is it possible, though, that someday you could define yourself as either lesbian/gay or heterosexual?" about 40 percent answered yes. About two-thirds of these indicated that the change could be in either direction, though almost 70 percent said that such a change was not probable.

We asked those who thought a change was possible what it might take to bring it about. The most common response referred to becoming involved in a meaningful relationship that was monogamous or very intense. Often the sex of the hypothetical partner was not specified, underscoring that the overall quality of the relationship was what really mattered.

Love. I think if I feel insanely in love with some person, it could possibly happen. (M)

If I should meet a woman and want to get married, and if she was not open to my relating to men, I might become heterosexual again. (M)

Getting involved in a long-term relationship like marriage where I wouldn't need a sexual involvement with anyone else. The sex of the...partner wouldn't matter. It would have to be someone who I could commit my whole life to exclusively, a lifelong relationship. (F)

A few mentioned the breaking up of a relationship and how this would incline them to look toward the other sex.

Steve is one of the few men I feel completely comfortable with. If anything happened to him, I don't know if I'd want to try and build up a similar relationship with another man. I'd be more inclined to look towards women for support. (F)

Changes in sexual behavior seemed more likely for the people we interviewed...than changes in how they defined themselves. We asked, "Is it possible that someday you could behave either exclusively homosexual or exclusively heterosexual?" Over 80 percent answered yes. This is over twice as many as those who saw a possible change in how they defined themselves, again showing that a wide range of behaviors can be subsumed under the same label. Of this particular group, the majority (almost 60 percent) felt that there was nothing inevitable about how they might change, indicating that it could be in either a homosexual or a heterosexual direction. Around a quarter, though, said the change would be to exclusive heterosexual behavior and 15 percent to exclusive homosexual behavior. (Twice as many women noted the homosexual direction, while many more men than women said the heterosexual direction.) Just over 40 percent responded that a change to exclusive heterosexuality or homosexuality was not very probable, about a third somewhat probable, and about a quarter very probable.

Again, we asked what it would take to bring about such a change in behavior. Once more the answers centered on achieving a long-term monogamous and involved relationship, often with no reference to a specific sex.

> For me to behave exclusively heterosexual or homosexual would require that I find a lifetime commitment from another person with a damn good argument of why I should not go to bed with somebody else. (F)

> I am a romantic. If I fell in love with a man, and our relationship was developing that way, I might become strictly homosexual. The same possibility exists with a woman. (M)

Thus "settling into the identity" must be seen in relative terms. Some of the people we interviewed did seem to accept the identity completely. When we compared our subjects' experiences with those characteristic of homosexuals, however, we were struck by the absence of closure that characterized our bisexual respondents—even those who appeared most committed to the identity. This led us to posit a final stage in the forma-tion of sexual identity, one that seems unique to bisexuals.

CONTINUED UNCERTAINTY

The belief that bisexuals are confused about their sexual identity is quite common. This conception has been promoted especially by those lesbians and gays who see bisexuality as being in and of itself a pathological state. From their point of view, "confusion" is literally a built-in feature of "being" bisexual. As expressed in one study:

> While appearing to encompass a wider choice of love objects...[the bisexual] actually becomes a product of abject confusion; his self-image is that of an overgrown young adolescent whose ability to differentiate one form of sexuality from another has never developed. He lacks above all a sense of identity.... [He] cannot answer the question: What am I?[3]

One evening a facilitator at a Bisexual Center rap group put this belief in a slightly different and more contemporary form:

> One of the myths about bisexuality is that you can't be bisexual without somehow being "schizoid." The lesbian and gay communities do not see being bisexual as a crystallized or complete sexual identity. The homosexual community believes there is no such thing as bisexuality. They think that bisexuals are people who are in transition [to becoming homosexual] or that they are people afraid of being stigmatized [as homosexual] by the heterosexual majority.

We addressed the issue directly in the interviews with two questions: "Do you *presently* feel confused about your bisexuality?" and "Have you *ever* felt confused...?"...For the men, a quarter and 84 percent answered "yes," respectively. For the women, it was about a quarter and 56 percent.

When asked to provide details about this uncertainty, the primary response was that *even after having discovered and applied the label "bisexual" to themselves, and having come to the point of apparent self-acceptance, they still experienced continued intermittent periods of doubt and uncertainty regarding their sexual identity.* One reason was the lack of social validation and support that came with being a self-identified bisexual. The social reaction people received made it difficult to sustain the identity over the long haul.

While the heterosexual world was said to be completely intolerant of any degree of homosexuality, the reaction of the homosexual world mattered more. Many bisexuals referred to the persistent pressures they experienced to relabel themselves as "gay" or "lesbian" and to engage in sexual activity exclusively with the same sex. It was asserted that no one was *really* bisexual, and that calling oneself "bisexual" was a politically incorrect and inauthentic identity. Given that our respondents were living in San Francisco (which has such a large homosexual population) and that they frequently moved in and out of the homosexual world (to whom they often looked for support) this could be particularly distressing.

Sometimes the repeated denial the gay community directs at us. Their negation of the concept and the term bisexual has sometimes made me wonder whether I was just imagining the whole thing. (M)

My involvement with the gay community. There was extreme political pressure. The lesbians said bisexuals didn't exist. To them, I had to make up my mind and identify as lesbian.... I was really questioning my identity, that is, about defining myself as bisexual.... (F)

For the women, the invalidation carried over to their feminist identity (which most had). They sometimes felt that being with men meant they were selling out the world of women.

I was involved with a woman for several years. She was straight when I met her but became a lesbian. She tried to "win me back" to lesbianism. She tried to tell me that if I really loved her, I would leave Bill. I did love her, but I could not deny how I felt about him either. So she left me and that hurt. I wondered if I was selling out my woman identity and if it [being bisexual] was worth it. (F)

A few wondered whether they were lying to themselves about their heterosexual side. One woman questioned whether her heterosexual desires were a result of "acculturation" rather than being her own choice. Another woman suggested a similar social dimension to her homosexual component:

There was one period when I was trying to be gay because of the political thing of being totally woman-identified rather than being with men. The Women's Culture Center in college had a women's studies minor, so I was totally immersed in women's culture.... (F)

Lack of support also came from the absence of bisexual role models, no real bisexual community aside from the Bisexual Center, and nothing in the way of public recognition of bisexuality, which bred uncertainty and confusion.

I went through a period of dissociation, of being very alone and isolated. That was due to my bisexuality. People would ask, well, what was I? I wasn't gay and I wasn't straight. So I didn't fit. (F)

I don't feel like I belong in a lot of situations because society is so polarized as heterosexual or homosexual. There are not enough bi organizations or public places to go to like bars, restaurants, clubs.... (F)

For some, continuing uncertainty about their sexual identity was related to their inability to translate their sexual feelings into sexual behaviors. (Some of the women had *never* engaged in homosexual sex.)

Should I try to have a sexual relationship with a woman?...Should I just back off and keep my distance, just try to maintain a friendship? I question whether I am really bisexual because I don't know if I will ever act on my physical attractions for females. (F)

I know I have strong sexual feelings towards men, but then I don't know how to get close to or be sexual with a man. I guess that what happens is I start wondering how genuine my feelings are.... (M)

For the men, confusion stemmed more from the practical concerns of implementing and managing multiple partners or from questions about how to find an involved homosexual relationship and what that might mean on a social and personal level.

I felt very confused about how I was going to manage my life in terms of developing relationships with both men and women. I still see it as a difficult lifestyle to create for myself because it involves a lot of hard work and understanding on my part and that of the men and women I'm involved with. (M)

I've thought about trying to have an actual relationship with a man. Some of my confusion revolves around how to find a satisfactory sexual relationship. I do not particularly like gay bars. I have stopped having anonymous sex.... (M)

Many men and women felt doubts about their bisexual identity because of being in an exclusive sexual relationship. After being exclusively involved with an opposite-sex partner for a period of time, some of the respondents questioned the homosexual side of their sexuality. Conversely, after being exclusively involved with a partner of the same sex, other respondents called into question the heterosexual component of their sexuality.

When I'm with a man or a woman sexually for a period of time, then I begin to wonder how attracted I really am to the other sex. (M)

In the last relationship I had with a woman, my heterosexual feelings were very diminished. Being involved in a lesbian lifestyle put stress on my self-identification as a bisexual. It seems confusing to me because I am monogamous for the most part, monogamy determines my lifestyle to the extremes of being heterosexual or homosexual. (F)

Others made reference to a lack of sexual activity with weaker sexual feelings and affections for one sex. Such learning did not fit with the perception that bisexuals should have "balanced" desires and behaviors. The consequence was doubt about "really" being bisexual.

On the level of sexual arousal and deep romantic feelings, I feel them much more strongly for women than for men. I've gone so far as questioning myself when this is involved. (M)

I definitely am attracted to and it is much easier to deal with males. Also, guilt for my attraction to females has led me to wonder if I am just really toying with the idea. Is the sexual attraction I have for females something I constructed to pass time or what? (F)

Just as "settling into the identity" is a relative phenomenon, so too is "continued uncertainty," which can involve a lack of closure as part and parcel of what it means to be bisexual.

We do not wish to claim too much for our model of bisexual identity formation. There are limits to its general application. The people we interviewed were unique in that not only did *all* the respondents define themselves as bisexual (a consequence of our selection criteria), but they were also all members of a bisexual social organization in a city that perhaps more than any other in the United States could be said to provide a bisexual subculture of some sort. Bisexuals in places other than San Francisco surely must move through the early phases of the identity process with a great deal more difficulty. Many probably never reach the later stages.

Finally, the phases of the model we present are very broad and somewhat simplified. While the particular problems we detail within different phases may be restricted to the type of bisexuals in this study, the broader phases can form the basis for the development of more sophisticated models of bisexual identity formation.

Still, not all bisexuals will follow these patterns. Indeed, given the relative weakness of the bisexual subculture compared with the social pressures toward conformity exhibited in the gay subculture, there may be more varied ways of acquiring a bisexual identity. Also, the involvement of bisexuals in the heterosexual world means that various changes in heterosexual lifestyles (e.g., a decrease in open marriages or swinging) will be a continuing, and as yet unexplored, influence on bisexual identity. Finally, wider societal changes, notably the existence of AIDS, may make for changes in the overall identity process. Being used to choice and being open to both sexes can give bisexuals a range of adaptations in their sexual life that are not available to others.

NOTES

1. Vivien C. Cass, "Homosexual Identity Formation: Testing a Theoretical Model." *Journal of Sex Research*

20 (1984), pp. 143–167; Eli Coleman, "Developmental Stages of the Coming Out Process." *Journal of Homosexuality* 7 (1981/2), pp. 31–43; Barbara Ponse, *Identities in the Lesbian World: The Social Construction of Self* (Westport, CT: Greenwood Press, 1978).
2. Martin S. Weinberg, Colin J. Williams, and Douglas W. Pryor, "Telling the Facts of Life: A Study of a Sex Information Switchboard." *Journal of Contemporary Ethnography* 17 (1988), pp. 131–163.
3. Donald Webster Cory and John P. Leroy, *The Homosexual and His Society* (New York: The Citadel Press, 1963), p. 61.

Getting a Tattoo

CLINTON R. SANDERS

Marks on the human body are significant symbols. Their significance derives from who made the marks and the meaning people attach to the marks. Governments in earlier times branded people who had committed crimes, thereby labeling them permanently as criminals. Marks that people have acquired through injury or illness often increase their chances of being assigned the master status of a disabled person. If some self-induced marks can engender a positive societal reaction, other varieties, such as tattooing, can engender negative societal reactions. Given the ambivalent status of tattoos, people who decide to get a tattoo may experience the kinds of problems other social deviants face.

Clinton R. Sanders finds that people acquire a tattoo because it literally marks a change in their lives. And so they intend for the tattoo to set them off from others. The bodily display indicates their obvious difference from most conventional others. Because the conventional world, in general, tends to regard people with tattoos as social deviants, tattooed people have to develop some resistance to social stigma. Thus, membership in groups favorable to tattooing increases their chances of getting a tattoo. In turn, because of the awareness of negative societal reactions, tattooed people become quite selective about the audience to whom they display their tattoos.

Becoming tattooed is a highly social act. The decision to acquire a tattoo…is motivated by how

Excerpted and reprinted from the chapter entitled "Becoming and Being a Tattooed Person," included in *Customizing the Body: The Art and Culture of Tattooing* by Clinton R. Sanders, by permission of Temple University Press. © 1989 by Temple University. All rights reserved.

the recipient defines him- or herself. The tattoo becomes an item in the tattooee's personal identity-kit (Goffman, 1961:14–21) and, in turn, it is used by those with whom the individual interacts to place him or her into a particular, interaction-shaping social category (cf. Solomon, 1983; Csikszentmihalyi and Rochberg-Halton, 1981).

When asked to describe how they decided to get a tattoo, the vast majority of respondents made reference to another person or group. Family members, friends, business associates, and other people with whom they regularly interacted were described as being tattooed. Statements such as, "Everyone I knew was really into tattoos," "It was a peer decision," "Everyone had one so I wanted one," and "My father got one when he was in the war and I always wanted one, too," were typical. Entrance into the actual tattooing "event," however, has all of the characteristics of an impulse purchase. It typically is based on very little information or previous experience (58 percent of the questionnaire respondents reported never having been in a studio prior to the time they received their first tattoo). While tattooees commonly reported having "thought about getting [a tattoo] for a long time," they usually drifted into the actual experience when they "didn't have anything better to do," had sufficient money to devote to a nonessential purchase, and were, most importantly, in the general vicinity of a tattoo establishment. The following accounts were fairly typical.

> We were up in Maine and a bunch of us were just talking about getting tattoos—me and my friends and my cousins. One time my cousin came back from the service with one and I liked it.... The only place I knew about was S——'s down in Providence. We were going right by there on our way back home so we stopped and all got them.

> My friends were goin' down there to get some work, you know. That was the only place I knew about anyway. My friends said there was a tattoo parlor down by the beach. Let's go! I checked it out and seen something I liked. I had some money on me so I said, "I'll get this little thing and check it out and see how it sticks." I thought if I got a tatty it might fade, you know. You never know what's goin' to happen. I don't want anything on my body that is goin' to look fucked up.

The act of getting the tattoo itself is usually, as seen in these quotes, a social event experienced with close associates. Sixty-nine percent of the interviewees (11 of 16) and 64 percent of the ques-

tionnaire sample reported having received their first tattoo in the company of family members or friends. These close associates act as "purchase pals" (Bell, 1967). They provide social support for the decision, help to pass anxiety-filled waiting time, offer opinions regarding the design and body location, and commiserate with or humorously ridicule the recipient during the tattoo experience (see Becker and Clark, 1979).

The tattoo event frequently involves a ritual commemoration of a significant transition in the life of the recipient (cf. Van Gennep, 1960; Ebin, 1979:39–56; Brain, 1979:174–184). The tattooee conceives of the mark as symbolizing change—especially, achieving maturity and symbolically separating the self from individuals or groups (parents, husbands, wives, employers, and so on) who have been exercising control over the individual's personal choices. A tattoo artist related his understanding of his clients' motivations in this way:

> I do see that many people get tattooed to find out again...to say, "Who was I before I got into this lost position?" It's almost like a tattoo pulls you back to a certain kind of reality about who you are as an individual. Either that or it transfers you to the next step in your life, the next plateau. A woman will come in and say, "Well, I just went through a really ugly divorce. My husband had control of my fucking body and now I have it again. I want a tattoo. I want a tattoo that says that I have the courage to get this, that I have the courage to take on the rest of my life. I'm going to do what I want to do and do what I have to do to survive as a person." That's a motivation that comes through the door a lot.

One interviewee expressed her initial reason for acquiring her first tattoo in almost exactly these terms:

> [My friend and I] both talked semi-seriously about getting [a tattoo]. I mentioned it to my husband and he was adamantly opposed—only certain seedy types get tattoos. He didn't want someone else touching my body intimately, which is what a tattoo would involve...even if it was just my arm.

He was against it, which made me even more for it.... I finally really decided sometime last year when my marriage was coming apart. It started to be a symbol of taking my body back. I was thinking that about the time I got divorced would be a good time to do it.

LOCATING A TATTOOIST

Like the initial decision to get a tattoo, the tattooist one decides to patronize commonly is chosen through information provided by members of the individual's personal network. Fifty-eight percent of the questionnaire respondents located the shop in which they received their first tattoo through a recommendation provided by a friend or family member. Since, in most areas, establishments that dispense tattoos are not especially numerous, many first-time tattooees choose a studio on a very practical basis—it is the only one they know about or it is the studio that is closest to where they live (20 percent of the questionnaire sample chose the shop on the basis of location, 28 percent because it was the only one they knew about).[1]

Most first-time tattooees enter the tattoo setting with little information about the process or even about the relative skill of the artist. Rarely do recipients spend as much time and effort acquiring information about a process which is going to indelibly mark their bodies as they would were they preparing to purchase a TV set or other far less significant consumer item.

Consequently, tattooees usually enter the tattoo setting ill-informed and experiencing a considerable degree of anxiety. Their fears center around the anticipated pain of the process and the permanence of the tattoo. Here, for example, is an interaction (quoted from fieldnotes) that took place while a young man received his first tattoo.

RECIPIENT: Is this going to fade out much? There's this guy at work that has these tattoos all up and down his arms and he goes back to the guy that did them every couple of months and gets them recolored because they fade out. [General laughter.]

SANDERS: Does this guy work in a shop or out of his house?

R: He just does it on the side.

TATTOOIST: He doesn't know what the fuck he's doing.

R: This friend of mine told me that getting a tattoo really hurts. He said there would be guys in here hollering and bleeding all over the place.

S: Does he have any tattoos?

R: No, but he says he wants to get some.... Hey, this really doesn't hurt that much. It doesn't go in very deep, does it? It's like picking a splinter out of your skin. I was going to get either a unicorn or a Pegasus. I had my sister draw one up because I thought they just drew the picture on you or something. I didn't know they did it this way [with an acetate stencil]. I guess this makes a lot more sense.

S: You ever been in a tattoo shop before this?

R: No, this is my first time. Another guy was going to come in with me, but he chickened out.

...[T]attooists, for the most part, are quite patient about answering the questions clients ask with numbing regularity (pain, price, and permanence). This helps to put the recipient more at ease, smooths the service delivery interaction, and increases the chances that a satisfied customer—[one] who will recommend the shop to his or her friends and perhaps return again for additional work—will leave the establishment (see Govenar, 1977; Becker and Clark, 1979; St. Clair and Govenar, 1981).

CHOOSING A DESIGN AND BODY LOCATION

Tattooees commonly described the basic reasons for deciding to become tattooed in very general terms. Wearing a tattoo connected the person to significant others who were similarly marked, made one unique by separating him or her from those who were too convention-bound to so alter their bodies, symbolized freedom or self-control, and satisfied an aesthetic desire to decorate the physical self.[2]

The image one chooses, on the other hand, is usually selected for a specific reason. Typically, design choice is related to the person's connection to other people, his or her definition of self, or, especially in the case of women, the desire to enhance and beautify the body.

One of the most common responses to my question, "How did you go about deciding on this particular tattoo?" was a reference to a personal associate with whom they had a close emotional relationship. Some chose a particular tattoo because it was like that worn by a close friend or a member of their family. Others chose a design that incorporated the name of their boy friend, girl friend, spouse, or child or a design associated with that person (for example, zodiac signs).

> I had this homemade cross and skull here and I needed a coverup. [The tattooist] couldn't just do anything so I thought to myself, "My daughter was born in May and that's the Bull." I'm leaving the rest of this arm clean because it is just for my daughter. If I ever get married I'll put something here [on the other arm]. I'll get a rose or something for my wife.

> This tattoo is a symbol of friendship. Me and my best friend—I've known him since I could walk—came in together and we both got bluebirds to have a symbol that when we do part we will remember each other by it.

The ongoing popularity of "vow tattoos" such as the traditional heart with "MOM" or flowers with a ribbon on which the loved one's name is written attests to the importance of tattooing as a way of symbolically expressing love and commitment (Hardy, 1982).

Similarly, tattoos are used to demonstrate connection and commitment to a group. For example, military personnel pick tattoos that relate to their particular service, motorcycle gang members choose club insignia, and members of sports teams enter a shop en masse and all receive the same design.

Tattoos are also employed as symbolic representations of how one conceives of the self, or interests and activities that are key features of self-definition. Tattooees commonly choose their birth sign or have their name or nickname inscribed on their bodies. Others choose more abstract symbols of the self.

> I put a lot of thought into this tattoo. I'm an English lit major and I thought that the medieval castle had a lot of significance. I'm an idealist and I thought that that was well expressed by a castle with clouds. Plus, I'm blond and I wanted something blue.

> [Quote from fieldnotes] Two guys in their twenties come in and look at the flash. After looking around for a while one of the guys come[s] over to me and asks if we have any bees. I tell him to look through the book [of small designs] because I have seen some bees in there. I ask, "Why do you want a bee? I don't think I have ever seen anyone come in here for one." He replies, "I'm allergic to bees. If I get stung by one again I'm going to die. So I thought I'd come in here and have a big, mean-looking bee put on. I want one that has this long stinger and these long teeth and is coming in to land. With that, any bee would think twice about messing with me."

Tattooees commonly represent the self by choosing designs that symbolize important personal involvements, hobbies, occupational activities, and so forth. In most street shops, the winged insignia of Harley-Davidson motorcycles and variants on that theme are the most frequently requested images. During one particularly busy week in the major shop in which I was observing, a rabbit breeder acquired a rabbit tattoo, a young man requested a cartoon frog because the Little League team he coached was named the "Frogs," a fireman received a fire fighter's cross insignia surrounded by flame, and an optician chose a flaming eye.

No matter what the associational or self-definitional meaning of the chosen tattoo, the recipient commonly is aware of the decorative/aesthetic function of the design. When I asked tattooees to explain how they went about choosing a particular design, they routinely made reference to aesthetic criteria—they "like the colors" or they "thought it was pretty."

[I didn't get this tattoo] because of being bad or cool or anything like that. It's like a picture. You see a picture you like and you put it in your room or your house or something like that. It's just a piece of work that you like. I like the art work they do here. I like the color [on my tattoo]. It really brings out—the orange and the green. I like that— the colors.[3]

A number of factors shape the tattooee's decision about where on the body the tattoo will be located. The vast majority of male tattooees choose to have their work placed on the arm. In his study of the tattoos carried by 2000 members of the Royal Navy, Scutt found that 98 percent had received their tattoo(s) on the arm (Scutt and Gotch, 1974:96). In my own research, 55 percent of the questionnaire respondents received their first tattoo on the arm or hand (71 percent of the males and 19 percent of the females). The sixteen interviewees had, all together, thirty-five tattoos, twenty-seven of which were carried by the ten males. Eighty-one percent (twenty-two) of the mens' tattoos were on their arms (of the remainder two were on hips, one was on the back, one on the face, and one on the recipient's chest). The six women interviewees possessed eight tattoos— three on the back or the shoulder area, three on the breast, one on an arm, and one on the lower back. Thirty-five percent of female questionnaire respondents received their first tattoo on the breast, 13 percent on the back or shoulder, and 10 percent on the hip….

Clearly, there is a definite convention affecting the decision to place the tattoo on a particular part of the body—men, for the most part, choose the arm while women choose the breast, hip, lower abdomen, back, or shoulder. To some degree the tendency for male tattooees to have the tattoo placed on the arm is determined by technical features of the tattoo process. Tattooing is a two-handed operation. The tattooist must stretch the skin with one hand while inscribing the design

with the other. This operation is most easily accomplished when the tattoo is being applied to an extremity. Tattooing the torso is more difficult and, commonly, tattooists have an assistant who stretches the client's skin when work is being done on that area of the body. Technical difficulty, in turn, affects price. Most tattooists charge 10 to 25 percent more for tattoos placed on body parts other than the arm or leg. The additional cost factor probably has some effect on the client's choice of body location.

Pain is another factor shaping the tattooee's decision. The tattoo machine contains needle groups that superficially pierce the skin at high speed, leaving small amounts of pigment in the tiny punctures. Obviously, this process will cause more or less pain depending on the sensitivity of the area being tattooed. In general, tattooing arms or legs generates less pain than marking body areas with a higher concentration of nerve endings or parts of the body where the bones are not cushioned with muscle tissue.[4]

The sex-based conventions regarding choice of body site are largely determined by the different symbolic functions of the tattoo for men and women. Women tend to regard the tattoo (commonly a small, delicate design) as a permanent body decoration primarily intended for personal pleasure and the enjoyment of those with whom they are most intimate. The chosen tattoos are, therefore, placed on parts of the body most commonly seen by those with whom women have primary relationships. Since tattoos on women are especially stigmatizing, placement on private parts of the body allows women to retain unsullied identities when in contact with casual associates or strangers (see Goffman, 1963a:53–55, 73–91). Here, for example, is a portion of a brief conversation with a young woman who carried an unconventional design (a snake coiled around a large rose) on what is, for women, an unconventional body location (her right bicep).

SANDERS: How did you decide on that particular design?

WOMAN: I wanted something really different and I'd never seen a tattoo like this on a woman before. I really like it, but sometimes I look at it and wish I didn't have it.

S: That's interesting. When do you wish you didn't have it?

W: When I'm getting real dressed up in a sleeveless dress and I want to look…uh, prissy and feminine. People look at a tattoo and think you're real bad…a loose person. But I'm not.

Another interviewee described the decision-making process she had gone through in choosing to acquire a small rose design on her shoulder, emphasizing aesthetic issues and stigma control.

> The only other place that I knew of that women got tattoos was on the breast. I didn't want it on the front of my chest because I figured if I was at work and had an open blouse or a scoop neck, then half would show and half wouldn't. I wanted to be able to control when I wanted it to show and when I didn't. If I go for a job interview I don't want a tattoo on my breast. I didn't want it, like, on my thigh or on the lower part of my stomach. I didn't like how they look there. I just thought it would look pretty on my shoulder.…The main reason is that I can cover it up if I want to.

Men, on the other hand, typically are less inclined than women to define the tattoo primarily as a decorative and intimate addition to the body. Instead, the male tattoo is an identity symbol—a more public display of interests, associations, separation from the normative constraints of conventional society, and, most generally, masculinity. The designs chosen by men are usually larger than those favored by women and, rather than employing the gentle imagery of nature and mythology (flowers, birds, butterflies, unicorns, and so forth), they frequently symbolize more violent impulses. Snakes, bloody daggers, skulls, dragons, grim reapers, black panthers, and birds of prey are dominant images in the conventional repertoire of tattoo designs chosen by men. Placement of the image on the arm allows both casual public display and, should the male tattooee anticipate a critical judgment from someone whose negative reaction could have untoward consequences (most commonly, an employer), easy concealment with clothing. One male interviewee spoke about the public meaning of tattoos and expressed his understanding of the difference between male and female tattoos as follows:

> You fit into a style. People recognize you by your hair-style or by your tattoo. People look at you in public and say, "Hey, they got a tattoo. They must be a particular kind of person," or, "He's got his hair cropped short [so] he must be a different kind of person." The person with a tattoo is telling people that he is free enough to do what he wants to do. He says, "I don't care who you think I am. I'm doing what I want to do." [The tattoo] symbolizes freedom. It says something about your personality. If a girl has a skull on her arm—it's not feminine at all—that would symbolize vengeance. If a woman gets a woman's tattoo, that's normal. If she gets a man's tattoo symbolizing vengeance or whatever, I feel that is too far over the boards. A woman should act like a woman and keep her tattoos feminine. Those vengeance designs say, "Look out." People see danger in them.

IMPACT ON SELF-DEFINITION

As indicated in the foregoing presentation of the initial motives that prompt the decision to acquire a tattoo, tattooees consistently conceive of the tattoo as having impact on their definition of self and demonstrating to others information about their unique interests and social connections. Interviewees commonly expressed liking their tattoos because they made him or her "different" or "special" (see Goffman, 1963a:56–62).

> Having a tattoo changes how you see yourself. It is a way of choosing to change your body. I enjoy that. I enjoy having a tattoo because it makes me different from other people. There is no one in the whole world who has a right arm that looks anything like mine. I've always valued being different from other people. Tattooing is a way of expressing that difference. It is a way of saying, "I am unique."

In describing his own understanding of his clients' motives, one tattoo artist employed the analogy of the customized car.

Tattooing is really just a form of personal adornment. Why does someone get a new car and get all of the paint stripped off of it and paint it candy-apple red? Why spend $10,000 on a car and then spend another $20,000 to make it look different from the car you bought? I associate it with ownership. Your body is one of the things you indisputably own. There is a tendency to adorn things that you own to make them especially yours.

Interviewees also spoke of the pleasure they got from the tattoo as related to having gone through the mysterious and moderately painful process of being tattooed. The tattoo demonstrated courage to the self ("for some people it means that they lived through it and weren't afraid"). One woman, when asked whether she intended to acquire other tattoos in the future, spoke of the excitement of the experience as the potential motivator of additional work.

[Do you think you will have more work done after you add something to the one you have now?] Oh, God! I don't know why, but my initial reaction is, "I hope I don't, but I think I'm going to." I think getting a tattoo is so exciting and I've always been kind of addicted to excitement. It's fun. While it hurt and stuff it was a new experience and it wasn't that horrible for me. It was new and different.

In a poignant statement, another woman spoke similarly of the tattoo as memorializing significant aspects of her past experience. "In the future when I'm sitting around and bored with my life and I wonder if I was ever young once and did exciting things, I can look at the tattoo and remember."

INTERACTIONAL CONSEQUENCES

In general, tattooees' observations concerning the effect on their self-definitions of having a tattoo and the process of being tattooed were rather basic and off-hand. In contrast, all interviewees spoke at some length about their social experi-

ences with others and how the tattoo affected their identities and interactions. *Some stressed the affiliational consequences of being tattooed—the mark identified them as belonging to a special group.* [Italics added.]

I got tattooed because I had an interest in it. My husband is a chef and our friends tend to be bikers, so it gets me accepted more into that community. They all think of me as "the college girl" and I'm really not. So this [tattoo] kind of brings the door open more.... The typical biker would tell you that you almost have to have tattoos to be part of the group. [Emphasis added.]

Most took pleasure in the way the tattoo enhanced their identities by demonstrating their affiliation with a somewhat more diverse group—tattooed people. [Italics added.]

Having a tattoo is like belonging to a club. I love seeing tattoos on other people. I go up and talk with other people with tattoos. It gives me an excuse because I'm not just going up to talk with them. I can say, "I have one, too." I think maybe subconsciously I got [the tattoo] to be part of that special club.

Having tattoos in some ways does affect me positively because people will stop me on the street and say, "Those are really nice tattoos," and show me theirs. We kind of...it is a way of having positive contact with strangers. We have something very much in common. We can talk about where we got them and the process of getting them and that sort of thing.

Given the symbolic meaning carried by tattoos in conventional social circles, all tattooees have the experience of being the focus of attention because of the mark they carry. The positive responses of others are, of course, the source of the most direct pleasure.

People seem to notice you more when you walk around with Technicolor arms. I don't think that everyone who gets tattooed is basically an exhibitionist, someone that walks down the street and says, "Hey, look at me," you know. But it does draw attention to yourself. [How do people respond when they see your tattoos?] Well, yesterday we were sitting in a bar and the lady brings a beer over and she says, "That's gorgeous," and she's looking at the wizard and she's touching them and picking up my shirt. Everyone in the bar was looking and it didn't bother me a bit.

Not all casual encounters are as positive as this one. Revelation of the tattoo is also the source of negative attention when defined by others as a stigmatizing mark.

Sometimes at these parties the conversation will turn to tattoos and I'll mention that I have some. A lot of people don't believe it, but if I'm feeling loose enough I'll roll up my sleeve and show my work. What really aggravates me is that there will almost always be someone who reacts with a show of disgust. "How could you do that to yourself?" No wonder I usually feel more relaxed and at home with bikers and other tattooed people.

I think tattoos look sharp. I walk down the beach and people look at my tattoos. Usually they don't say anything. [When they do] I wish they would say it to my face…like, "Tattoos are ugly." But, when they say something behind my back…. "Isn't that gross." Hey, keep your comments to yourself! If you don't like it, you don't like it. I went to the beach with my father and I said, "Hey, let's walk down the beach," and he said, "No, I don't feel like it." What are you, embarrassed to walk with me?

Given the negative responses that tattooees encounter with some frequency when casual associates or strangers become aware of their body decorations, most are selective about to whom they reveal their tattoos. This is particularly the case when the "other" is in a position to exercise control over the tattooee.

Usually I'm fairly careful about who I show my tattoos to. I don't show them to people at work unless they are really close friends of mine and I know I won't get any kind of hassle because of them. I routinely hide my tattoos…. I generally hide them from people who wouldn't understand or people who could potentially cause me trouble. I hide them from my boss and from a lot of the people I work with because there is no reason for them to know.

Tattooees commonly use the reactions of casual associates or relative strangers as a means of categorizing them. A positive reaction to the tattoo indicates social and cultural compatibility, while a negatively judgmental response is seen as signifying a narrow and convention-bound perspective.

I get more positive reactions than I do negative reactions. The negative reactions come from people who aren't like me—who have never done anything astray. It is the straight-laced, conservative person who really doesn't believe that this is acceptable in their set of norms. It seems as though I can actually tell how I'm going to get along with people, and vice-versa, by the way they react to my tattoo. It's more or less expressive of the unconventional side of my character right up front. Most of the people who seem to like me really dig the tattoo too. (Quoted in Hill, 1972:249)

While it is fairly easy to selectively reveal the tattoo in public settings when interacting with strangers or casual associates, hiding the fact that one is tattooed, thereby avoiding negative social response, is difficult when the "other" is a person with whom the tattooee is intimately associated. The majority of those interviewed recounted incidents in which parents, friends, and, especially for the women, lovers and spouses reacted badly when they initially became aware of the tattoo.

[What did your husband say when he saw your tattoo?] He said he almost threw up. It grossed him out. I had asked him years ago, "What would you think if…," and he didn't like the idea. So, I decided not to tell him. It seemed a smart thing to do. He just looked rather grossed out by the whole thing; didn't like it. Now it is accepted, but I don't think he would go for another one.

Another woman interviewee recounted a similar post-tattoo experience with her parents and boyfriend.

My family was devastated. I didn't tell them for a long time. My mother and I were on a train to New York City and I said to her, "Mom, I want to tell you something but I don't want you to get up-

set." She said, "You're pregnant!" I said, "No." She says, "You're getting married!" I said, "God, no!" It was downhill from there. When I said, "I got a tattoo," it was like, "Thank God! That's all it is." It wasn't that horrible. My father's reaction was just one of disgust because women who get tattoos to him are…I don't know…they just aren't nice girls. They aren't the type of girl he wants his daughter to be. He let me know that. He let me have it right between the eyes. He said, "Do you know what kind of girls get tattoos?" and just walked out of the room. That was enough. He thought tramps get tattoos or girls that ride on the back seats of motorcycles, you know. I got a strange reaction from my boyfriend. We had a family outing to go to and there was going to be swimming and tennis and all this stuff and I was real excited about going. He said, "Are you going to go swimming?" I said, "Yeah." I was psyched because I love to swim. He looked at me and said, "You know, your tattoo is going to show if you go swimming." Probably. He didn't want me to go swimming because he didn't want his parents to know that I had a tattoo. Lucky for him it was cloudy that day and nobody swam. I told him, "I'm sorry but I know your parents can handle this kind of news." To boot, he's got a shamrock on his butt! So he has a tattoo—a real double standard there. He didn't say anything for a while after I first got it. It was subtle. He let me know he didn't like it but that, because it was on me, he could excuse it. He's got adjusted to it though. He just let me know that he's never dated a girl who's got a tattoo before. He would prefer that I didn't have it, but there isn't much he can do about that now.

Given the negative social reaction often precipitated by tattoos, it would be reasonable to expect that tattooees who regretted their decision would have emphasized the unpleasant interactional consequences of the tattoo. Interviewees and questionnaire respondents rarely expressed any doubts about their decision to acquire a tattoo. Those that did indicate regret, however, usually did not focus on the stigmatizing effect of the tattoo. Instead, regretful tattooees most commonly were dissatisfied with the technical quality of the tattoo they purchased.[5]…

CONCLUSION: TATTOOING, STIGMA, SELF, AND IDENTITY

When potential tattooees begin to think about altering their bodies in this manner, they devise an understanding of what the tattoo will signify to themselves and others through contact with tattooed associates or by attending media presentations of tattooing and tattooed people (cf. Cohen, 1973; Matza, 1969). In general, they define that tattoo as a mark of affiliation—demonstrating connection to significant groups, primary associates, or those who share specific interests—or as an isolative symbol of unconventionality, or unique personal decoration. Having come to conceive of themselves as tattooed, potential recipients locate a tattoo establishment and acquire the mark.

When revealed to others, the newly acquired corporeal embellishment affects interactions and relationships. Positive responses from co-interactants tend to reinforce social connections, certify tattooees' positive evaluations of self and the tattoo acquisition decision, and increase the likelihood that tattooees will [expand] the universe of situations in which they choose to reveal their unconventional body decorations.

If being tattooed leads to negative social and self-definitional consequences, regretful tattooees are faced with various alternatives. When met with disapproval tattooees may negatively evaluate the disapproving other and subsequently become more selective in disclosing the fact that they bear a tattoo (see Goffman, 1963a:11). If regretful tattooees focus the responsibility for the negative consequences of having acquired the tattoo upon themselves, they can deny responsibility for the decision or take steps to obliterate the tattoo. Since negative evaluations of the tattoo decision are most commonly due to the perceived inferior quality of the work, regretful tattooees often have the offending mark covered or reworked by another, more skilled (one hopes), tattooist.…

The central factor shaping this process—from initial stages of interest through dealing with the consequences of being a tattooed person—is that the tattoo is conventionally regarded as a stigma symbol (Goffman, 1963a:43). The decision to acquire a tattoo is not only a decision to alter one's physical appearance; it is a choice to change how the person experiences his or her self and, in turn, how he or she will be defined and treated by others.

Definitions of tattoos and tattooees, held by both the general culture and the "scientific community," are predominantly negative. Tattoos are defined as being symptomatic of the psychological or social deviance of the bearer. Conventional repulsion imbues tattooing with significant power and appeal. For some tattooees the act of acquiring a tattoo marks them as being involved in an exotic social world centered around the pleasurable flaunting of authority and convention (cf. Lofland, 1969:106).

> *[Why do you think you initially wanted to put the tattoo someplace that is well hidden?] I guess I thought that someone would think it was creepy. It would have connotations of loose women or being foolish. Like kids don't think through the consequences of stuff. They do things impetuously. I thought that people might think I just ran down there in a fit of glee. [Actually] a tattoo is not serious. I think that is part of the pleasure of it. When I was first thinking about it it was, "Oh boy, let's do this!" It was sort of a gleeful thing. It is like being a little bit bad.*

> *I can't think of one nice compact reason [I got a tattoo]. They are pretty. But most of all they are a poke in the eye to people who don't have them— people who are straights or whatever.*

The tattoo acts as more than simply a "mark of disaffiliation" (Goffman, 1963a:143–147). It may also demonstrate connection to unconventional social groups. In some cases, it symbolizes membership in subcultures (for example, outlaw motorcyclists, youth gangs) centered around socially disvalued or law-violating interests and activities.[6]

The stigmatized social definition of tattooing and the negative response tattooees commonly ex-

perience when "normals" are aware of their stigma may also precipitate identification with a subculture in which the tattoo is of primary significance. Within the informal "tattoo community" consisting of those tattooees who positively define their unconventional mark, the tattoo acts as a source of "mutual openness" (Goffman, 1963b: 131–139), providing opportunities for spontaneous appreciative interaction with others who are also tattooed (Pfuhl, 1986:168–188; Goffman, 1963a:23–25).[7]

As is commonly the case with subcultural groups bound together by the problems associated with possession of a physical stigma, the tattoo world has developed an organized core. More-or-less formal groups such as the National Tattoo Association hold regular meetings and provide practitioners with technical information, legal assistance, access to the latest equipment and supplies, and other essential occupational resources. Serious tattoo "enthusiasts" and collectors are also active in this organized world. Tattoo conventions provide them with an opportunity to display their work, enlarge their collections, and associate with other tattooees in situations in which they are normal. Understandably, a major focus of organizational activity is the public redefinition of tattooing as a legitimate form of artistic production.

Contemporary commercial culture provides a variety of products (t-shirts, bumper stickers, buttons, and so forth) by which people may announce their perspectives, personal interests, and social attachments. Clothing, jewelry, hair style, and other aspects of personal decoration are used to demonstrate aesthetic taste. These modes of self-symbolization are, however, relatively safe and transitory expressions. For some, these conventional mechanisms are inadequate. Typically impelled by personal association with others who have chosen a more drastic and symbolically powerful approach, tattooees purchase what is, as yet, a "tarnished" cultural product (Shover, 1975). In so doing, tattooed people voluntarily shape their social identities and enhance their definitions of self. Drawn by both the affiliational and individuating consequences of their choice and despite the potential for disrupted interactions, tattooees choose to mark their bodies with indelible symbols of what they see themselves to be.

NOTES

1. The central importance of personal recommendation as the source of tattoo clients is well known to tattooists. All tattooists have business cards that they hand out quite freely (one maintained that he had dispensed over 50,000 cards in the past two years). Listing one's services in the Yellow Pages is the other major means employed to draw customers since it provides location information to those who, for a variety of reasons, do not have interpersonal sources....

2. Questionnaire respondents were given an open-ended question that asked them to speculate as to why people get tattooed. Of the 163 respondents, 135 provided some sort of reply to this item. Forty-four percent of those responding emphasized that becoming tattooed was motivated by a desire for self-expression (for example, "vanity," "it's a personal preference," "a statement of who you are"), 21 percent emphasized tattooing as a mechanism for asserting uniqueness and individuality (for example, "people like to be different," "personal originality," "it makes you special"), and 28 percent made some form of aesthetic statement (for example, "because it is beautiful," "a form of art that lasts forever," "body jewelry"). On their part, tattooists tend to recognize the aesthetic importance of their work as seen by their clients....

3. Of the thirty-five tattoos worn by the sixteen interviewees, 14 percent (five) represented a bird, 6 percent (two) represented a mammal, 14 percent (five) represented a mythical animal, 9 percent (three) represented an insect, 3 percent (one) represented a human female, 17 percent (six) represented a human male, 14 percent (five) were noncommercial symbols (hearts, crosses, military insignia, and so on), 14 percent (five) were floral, 3 percent (one) were names or vow tattoos, and 6 percent (two) were some other image.

Questionnaire respondents were asked to indicate the design of their first tattoo. They were: 14 percent (twenty-three) bird, 11 percent (eighteen) mammal, 12 percent (nineteen) mythical animal, 10 percent (seventeen) insect, 1 percent (two) human female, 6 percent (ten) human male, 4 percent (six) commercial symbols, 8

percent (thirteen) noncommercial symbols, 21 percent (thirty-four) floral/arboreal, 4 percent (seven) name/vow, and 9 percent (fourteen) other.

4. The painfulness of the tattoo process is the most unpleasant element of the tattoo event. Only 33 percent (fifty-four) of the questionnaire respondents maintained that there was something about the tattoo experience that they disliked. One-third of these (eighteen) said that the pain was what they found most unpleasant. Fourteen of the sixteen interviewees mentioned pain as a troublesome factor. Numerous observations of groups of young men discussing pain or expressing stoic disregard for the pain as they received tattoos demonstrated the importance of the tattoo event as a form of initiation ritual. In some cases the tattoo process provides a situation in which the male tattooee can demonstrate his manliness to his peers.... The cross-cultural literature on body alteration indicates that the pain of the process is an important factor. See Ebin, 1979:88–89; Brain, 1979:183–184; Ross and McKay, 1979:44–49, 67–69; Becker and Clark, 1979:10, 19; St. Clair and Govenar, 1981:100–135.

5. Other than simply accepting the regretted mark, there are few avenues of resolution open to dissatisfied tattooees. In the most extreme cases, the tattooee may try to obliterate the offending mark with acid or attempt to cut it off. A somewhat more reasoned (and considerably less painful) approach entails seeking the aid of a dermatologist or plastic surgeon who will medically remove the tattoo. The most common alternative, however, is to have the technically inferior piece redone or covered with another tattoo created by a more skilled practitioner. Tattooists estimate that 40 to 50 percent of their work entails reworking or applying cover-ups to poor quality tattoos. See Goldstein et al., 1979, and Hardy, 1983.

6. One traditional use of tattooing has been to mark indelibly social outcasts and defined deviants so that they can be easily identified and/or avoided by officials and "normals." In sixth-century Japan, for example, criminals and social outcasts were tattooed on the face or arms as a form of negative public identification and punishment (Richie and Buruma, 1980:12–13). Similarly, in the nineteenth century, inmates of the Massachusetts prison system had "Mass S. P." and the date of their release tattooed on their left arms (Ebensten, 1953:20). More recently, the Nazis tattooed identification numbers on the arms of concentration camp inmates. In April of 1986 conservative columnist William Buckley suggested that victims of AIDS (Acquired Immune Deficiency Syndrome) be tattooed on the buttocks in order to limit the

spread of the disease among homosexuals (*Hartford Courant,* April 19, 1986, p. C6).

7. The literature directed at the fan world surrounding tattooing consistently makes reference to the "tattoo community."...

REFERENCES

Becker, Nickie, and Robert E. Clark. 1979. "Born to Raise Hell: An Ethnography of Tattoo Parlors." Paper presented at the meetings of Southwestern Sociological Association, March 28–31, Fort Worth, Texas.

Bell, Gerald. 1967. "Self-Confidence, Persuasibility and Cognitive Dissonance Among Automobile Buyers." In *Risk-Taking and Information Handling in Consumer Behavior,* ed. Donald Cox, 442–468. Boston: Harvard University Graduate School of Business Administration.

Brain, Dennis. 1979. *The Decorated Body.* New York: Harper and Row.

Cohen, Sidney. 1973. "Mods and Rockers: The Inventory as Manufactured News." In *The Manufacture of News: A Reader,* ed. S. Cohen and J. Young, 226–241. Beverly Hills, CA: Sage.

Csikszentmihalyi, Mihaly, and Eugene Rochberg-Halton. 1981. *The Meaning of Things: Domestic Symbols and the Self.* Cambridge: Cambridge University Press.

Ebensten, Hans. 1953. *Pierced Hearts and True Love.* London: Derek Verschoyle.

Ebin, Victoria. 1979. *The Body Decorated.* London: Thames and Hudson.

Goffman, Erving. 1961. *Asylums.* Garden City, NY: Doubleday.

———. 1963a. *Stigma.* Englewood Cliffs, NJ: Prentice-Hall.

———. 1963b. *Behavior in Public Places.* New York: Free Press.

Goldstein, Norman, James Penoff, Norman Price, Roger Ceilley, Leon Goldman, Victor Hay-Roe, and Timothy Miller. 1979. "Techniques and Removal of Tattoos." *Journal of Dermatologic Surgery and Oncology* 5:901–910.

Govenar, Alan. 1977. "The Acquisition of Tattooing Competence: An Introduction." *Folklore Annual of the University Folklore Association* 7 & 8:43–53.

Hardy, D. E. 1982. "The Name Game." *Tattootime* 1 (Fall):50–54.

———. 1983. "Inventive Cover Work." *Tattootime* 2:12–17.

Hill, Amie. 1972. "Tattoo Renaissance." In *Side-Saddle on the Golden Calf,* ed. G. Lewis, 245–249. Pacific Palisades, CA: Goodyear.

Lofland, John. 1969. *Deviance and Identity.* Englewood Cliffs, NJ: Prentice-Hall.

Matza, David. 1969. *Becoming Deviant.* Englewood Cliffs, NJ: Prentice-Hall.

Pfuhl, Edward. 1986. *The Deviance Process,* 2d ed. Belmont, CA: Wadsworth.

Richie, Donald, and Ian Buruma. 1980. *The Japanese Tattoo.* New York: Weatherhill.

Ross, Robert, and Hugh McKay. 1979. *Self-Mutilation.* Lexington, MA: Heath.

Scutt, R. W. B., and C. Gotch. 1974. *Art, Sex, and the Symbol: The Mystery of Tattooing.* New York: A. S. Barnes.

Shover, Neal. 1975. "Tarnished Goods and Services in the Market Place." *Urban Life and Culture* 3:471–488.

Solomon, Michael. 1983. "The Role of Products as Social Stimuli: A Symbolic Interactionist Perspective." *Journal of Consumer Research* 10:319–329.

St. Clair, Leonard, and Alan Govenar. 1981. *Stoney Knows How: Life as a Tattoo Artist.* Lexington: University of Kentucky Press.

Van Gennep, Arnold. 1960. *The Rites of Passage.* Chicago: University of Chicago Press.

Anorexia, Bulimia, and Developing a Deviant Identity

PENELOPE A. McLORG and DIANE E. TAUB

One's self-identification as deviant ordinarily follows changes in social interaction. Some questions about the conditions of changed interaction due to typifying a person as deviant are: Which others are more apt to affix the label? Does the specific nature of the deviant activity speed assumption of deviant identity? Are there variations in time between application of the label and the self-acceptance of a deviant identity?

Penelope A. McLorg and Diane E. Taub offer some answers to these questions in their comparison of anorexics and bulimics. They say some young women take actions to change the way they think they look in the eyes of other people, in particular young men. Significant others, such as family or friends, see the patterned actions they take to become attractive as being deviant. However, while anorexics employ more accepted methods of weight control (dieting), bulimics use less accepted methods (such as binging and purging). These different methods lead to variations in both the application of the deviant labels by family and friends and the acceptance of those labels by the young women who experience these eating disorders. Given these different circumstances, bulimics are more apt to accept their deviant identity, and to conceal their binging and purging from others. Thus, they are more likely to look at themselves from the point of view of the others who have become aware of their behavior. Whereas bulimics show consistency between their self-image and their social role, anorexics take much longer to integrate a deviant self-conception with their social role.

Current appearance norms stipulate thinness for women and muscularity for men; these expectations, like any norms, entail rewards for compliance and negative sanctions for violations. Fear of being overweight—of being visually deviant—has led to a striving for thinness, especially among women. In the extreme, this avoidance of overweight engenders eating disorders, which themselves constitute deviance. Anorexia nervosa, or purposeful starvation, embodies visual as well as behavioral deviation; bulimia, binge-eating followed by vomiting and/or laxative abuse, is primarily behaviorally deviant.

Reprinted from "Anorexia Nervosa and Bulimia: The Development of Deviant Identities," *Deviant Behavior*, Vol. 8 (1987), pp. 177–189, by permission of Taylor and Francis, Inc. All rights reserved. Copyright 1987 by Taylor and Francis, Inc.

Besides a fear of fatness, anorexics and bulimics exhibit distorted body images. In anorexia nervosa, a 20–25 percent loss of initial body weight occurs, resulting from self-starvation alone or in combination with excessive exercising, occasional binge-eating, vomiting, and/or laxative abuse. Bulimia denotes cyclical (daily, weekly, for example) binge-eating followed by vomiting or laxative abuse; weight is normal or close to normal (Humphries et al., 1982). Common physical manifestations of these eating disorders include menstrual cessation or irregularities and electrolyte imbalances; among behavioral traits are depression, obsessions/compulsions, and anxiety (Russell, 1979; Thompson and Schwartz, 1982).

Increasingly prevalent in the past two decades, anorexia nervosa and bulimia have emerged as major health and social problems. Termed an epidemic on college campuses (Brody, as quoted in Schur, 1984: 76), bulimia affects 13% of college students (Halmi et al., 1981). Less prevalent, anorexia nervosa was diagnosed in 0.6% of students utilizing a university health center (Stangler and Printz, 1980). However, the overall mortality rate of anorexia nervosa is 6% (Schwartz and Thompson, 1981) to 20% (Humphries et al., 1982); bulimia appears to be less life-threatening (Russell, 1979).

Particularly affecting certain demographic groups, eating disorders are most prevalent among young, white, affluent (upper-middle to upper class) women in modern, industrialized countries (Crisp, 1977; Willi and Grossmann, 1983). Combining all of these risk factors (female sex, youth, high socioeconomic status, and residence in an industrialized country), prevalence of anorexia nervosa in upper class English girls' schools is reported at 1 in 100 (Crisp et al., 1976). The age of onset for anorexia nervosa is bimodal at 14.5 and 18 years (Humphries et al., 1982); the most frequent age of onset for bulimia is 18 (Russell, 1979).

Eating disorders have primarily been studied from psychological and medical perspectives.[1] Theories of etiology have generally fallen into three categories: the ego psychological (involving an impaired child-maternal environment); the family systems (implicating enmeshed rigid families); and the endocrinological (involving a precipitating hormonal defect). Although relatively ignored in previous studies, the sociocultural components of anorexia nervosa and bulimia (the slimness norm and its agents of reinforcement, such as role models) have been postulated as accounting for the recent, dramatic increases in these disorders (Schwartz et al., 1982; Boskind-White, 1985).[2]

Medical and psychological approaches to anorexia nervosa and bulimia obscure the social facets of the disorders and neglect the individuals' own definitions of their situations. Among the social processes involved in the development of an eating disorder is the sequence of conforming behavior, primary deviance, and secondary deviance. Societal reaction is the critical mediator affecting the movement through the deviant career (Becker, 1973). Within a framework of labeling theory, this study focuses on the emergence of anorexia and bulimia identities, as well as on the consequences of being career deviants.

METHOD...

Most research on eating disorders has utilized clinical subjects or non-clinical respondents completing questionnaires. Such studies can be criticized for simply counting and describing behaviors and/or neglecting the social construction of the disorders. Moreover, the work of clinicians is often limited by therapeutic orientation. Previous research may also have included individuals who were not in therapy on their own volition and who resisted admitting that they had an eating disorder.

Past studies thus disregard the intersubjective meanings respondents attach to their behavior and emphasize researchers' criteria for definition as anorexia or bulimia. In order to supplement these sampling and procedural designs, the present study utilizes participant observation of a group of self-defined anorexics and bulimics.[3] As the individuals had acknowledged their eating disorders, frank discussion and disclosure were facilitated.

Data are derived from a self-help group, BANISH, Bulimics/Anorexics In Self-Help, which met at a university in an urban center of the mid-South....

The group's weekly two-hour meetings were observed for two years. During the course of this study, thirty individuals attended at least one of the meetings....

In addition to field notes from group meetings, records of other encounters with all members were maintained. Participants visited the office of one of the researchers (D.E.T.), called both researchers by phone, and invited them to their homes or out for a cup of coffee. Such interaction facilitated genuine communication and mutual trust. Even among the fifteen individuals who did not attend the meetings regularly, contact was maintained with ten members on a monthly basis.

Supplementing field notes were informal interviews with fifteen group members, lasting from two to four hours. Because they appeared to represent more extensive experience with eating disorders, these interviewees were chosen to amplify their comments about the labeling process, made during group meetings. Conducted near the end of the two-year observation period, the interviews focused on what the respondents thought antedated and maintained their eating disorders. In addition, participants described others' reactions to their behaviors as well as their own interpretations of these reactions. To protect the confidentiality of individuals quoted in the study, pseudonyms are employed.

DESCRIPTION OF MEMBERS

The demographic composite of the sample typifies what has been found in other studies (Fox and James, 1976; Crisp, 1977; Herzog, 1982; Schlesier-Stropp, 1984). Group members' ages ranged from nineteen to thirty-six, with the modal age being twenty-one. The respondents were white, and all but one were female. The sole male and three of the females were anorexic; the remaining females were bulimic.[4]

Primarily composed of college students, the group included four non-students, three of whom had college degrees. Nearly all members derived from upper-middle or lower-upper class households. Eighteen students and two non-students were never-married and uninvolved in serious relationships; two non-students were married (one with two children); two students were divorced (one with two children); and six students were involved in serious relationships. The duration of eating disorders ranged from three to fifteen years.

CONFORMING BEHAVIOR

In the backgrounds of most anorexics and bulimics, dieting figures prominently, beginning in the teen years (Crisp, 1977; Johnson et al., 1982; Lacey et al., 1986). As dieters, these individuals are conformist in their adherence to the cultural norms emphasizing thinness (Garner et al., 1980; Schwartz et al., 1982). In our society, slim bodies are regarded as the most worthy and attractive; overweight is viewed as physically and morally unhealthy—"obscene," "lazy," "slothful," and "gluttonous" (Dejong, 1980; Ritenbaugh, 1982; Schwartz et al., 1982).

Among the agents of socialization promoting the slimness norm is advertising. Female models in newspaper, magazine, and television advertisements are uniformly slender. In addition, product names and slogans exploit the thin orientation; examples include "Ultra Slim Lipstick," "Miller Lite," and "Virginia Slims." While retaining pressures toward thinness, an Ayds commercial attempts a compromise for those wanting to savor food: "Ayds...so you can taste, chew, and enjoy, while you lose weight." Appealing particularly to women, a nationwide fast-food restaurant chain offers low-calorie selections, so individuals can have a "license to eat." In the latter two examples, the notion of enjoying food is combined with the message to be slim. Food and restaurant advertisements overall convey the pleasures of eating, whereas advertisements for other products, such as fashions and diet aids, reinforce the idea that fatness is undesirable.

Emphasis on being slim affects everyone in our culture, but it influences women especially because of society's traditional emphasis on women's appearance. The slimness norm and its concomitant narrow beauty standards exacerbate the objectification of women (Schur, 1984). Women view themselves as visual entities and recognize that conforming to appearance expectations and "becoming attractive object[s] [are] role obligation[s]" (Laws, as quoted in Schur, 1984: 66). Demonstrating the beauty motivation behind dieting, a recent Nielsen survey indicated that of the 56 percent of all women aged 24 to 54 who dieted during the previous year, 76 percent did so for cosmetic, rather than health, reasons (Schwartz et al., 1982). For most female group members, dieting was viewed as a means of gaining attractiveness and appeal to the opposite sex. The male respondent, as well, indicated that "when I was fat, girls didn't look at me, but when I got thinner, I was suddenly popular."

In addition to responding to the specter of obesity, individuals who develop anorexia nervosa and bulimia are conformist in their strong commitment to other conventional norms and goals. They consistently excel at school and work (Russell, 1979; Bruch, 1981; Humphries et al., 1982), maintaining high aspirations in both areas (Theander, 1970; Lacey et al., 1986). Group members generally completed college-preparatory courses in high school, aware from an early age that they would strive for a college degree. Also, in college as well as high school, respondents joined honor societies and academic clubs.

Moreover, pre-anorexics and -bulimics display notable conventionality as "model children" (Humphries et al., 1982: 199), "the pride and joy" of their parents (Bruch, 1981: 215), accommodating themselves to the wishes of others. Parents of these individuals emphasize conformity and value achievement (Bruch, 1981). Respondents felt that perfect or near-perfect grades were expected of them; however, good grades were not rewarded by parents, because "A's" were common for these children. In addition, their parents suppressed conflicts, to preserve the image of the "all-American family" (Humphries et al., 1982). Group members reported that they seldom, if ever, heard their parents argue or raise their voices.

Also conformist in their affective ties, individuals who develop anorexia nervosa and bulimia are strongly, even excessively, attached to their parents. Respondents' families appeared close-knit, demonstrating palpable emotional ties. Several group members, for example, reported habitually calling home at prescribed times, whether or not they had any news. Such families have been termed "enmeshed" and "overprotective," displaying intense interaction and concern for members' welfare (Minuchin et al., 1978; Selvini-Palazzoli, 1978). These qualities could be viewed as marked conformity to the norm of familial closeness.[5]

Another element of notable conformity in the family milieu of pre-anorexics and -bulimics concerns eating, body weight/shape, and exercising (Kalucy et al., 1977; Humphries et al., 1982). Respondents reported their fathers' preoccupation with exercising and their mothers' engrossment in food preparation. When group members dieted and lost weight, they received an extraordinary amount of approval. Among the family, body size became a matter of "friendly rival." One bulimic informant recalled that she, her mother, and her coed sister all strived to wear a size 5, regardless of their heights and body frames. Subsequent to this study, the researchers learned that both the mother and sister had become bulimic.

As pre-anorexics and -bulimics, group members thus exhibited marked conformity to cultural norms of thinness, achievement, compliance, and parental attachment. Their families reinforced their conformity by adherence to norms of family closeness and weight/body shape consciousness.

PRIMARY DEVIANCE

Even with familial encouragement, respondents, like nearly all dieters (Chernin, 1981), failed to maintain their lowered weights. Many cited their lack of willpower to eat only restricted foods. For the emerging anorexics and bulimics, extremes such as purposeful starvation or binging accompanied by vomiting and/or laxative abuse appeared as "obvious solutions" to the problem of retaining weight loss. Associated with these behaviors was a regained feeling of control in lives that had been disrupted by a major crisis. Group members' extreme weight-loss efforts operated as coping mechanisms for entering college, leaving home, or feeling rejected by the opposite sex.

The primary inducement for both eating adaptations was the drive for slimness: with slimness came more self-respect and a feeling of superiority over "unsuccessful dieters." Brian, for example, experienced a "power trip" upon consistent weight loss through starvation. Binges allowed the purging respondents to cope with stress through eating while maintaining a slim appearance. As former strict dieters, Teresa and Jennifer used binging/purging as an alternative to the constant self-denial of starvation. Acknowledging their parents' desires for them to be slim, most respondents still felt it was a conscious choice on their part to continue extreme weight-loss efforts. Being thin became the "most important thing" in their lives—their "greatest ambition."

In explaining the development of an anorexic or bulimic identity, Lemert's (1951; 1967) concept of primary deviance is salient. Primary deviance refers to a transitory period of norm violations which do not affect an individual's self-concept or performance of social roles. Although respondents were exhibiting anorexic or bulimic behavior, they did not consider themselves to be anorexic or bulimic.

At first, anorexics' significant others complimented their weight loss, expounding on their new "sleekness" and "good looks." Branch and Eurman (1980: 631) also found anorexics' families and friends describing them as well-groomed," "neat," "fashionable," and "victorious." Not until the respondents approached emaciation did some parents or friends become concerned and withdraw their praise. Significant others also became increasingly aware of the anorexics' compulsive exercising, preoccupation with food preparation (but not consumption), and ritualistic eating patterns (such as cutting food into minute pieces and eating only certain foods at prescribed times).

For bulimics, friends or family members began to question how the respondents could eat such large amounts of food (often in excess of 10,000 calories a day) and stay slim. Significant others also noticed calluses across the bulimics' hands, which were caused by repeated induce-

ment of vomiting. Several bulimics were "caught in the act," bent over commodes. Generally, friends and family required substantial evidence before believing that the respondents' binging or purging was no longer sporadic.

SECONDARY DEVIANCE

Heightened awareness of group members' eating behavior ultimately led others to label the respondents "anorexic" or "bulimic." Respondents differed in their histories of being labeled and accepting the labels. Generally first termed anorexic by friends, family, or medical personnel, the anorexics initially vigorously denied the label. They felt they were not "anorexic enough," not skinny enough; Robin did not regard herself as having the "skeletal" appearance she associated with anorexia nervosa. These group members found it difficult to differentiate between socially approved modes of weight loss—eating less and exercising more—and the extremes of those behaviors. In fact, many of their activities—cheerleading, modeling, gymnastics, aerobics—reinforced their pursuit of thinness. Like other anorexics, Chris felt she was being "ultra-healthy," with "total control" over her body.

For several respondents, admitting they were anorexic followed the realization that their lives were disrupted by their eating disorder. Anorexics' inflexible eating patterns unsettled family meals and holiday gatherings. Their regimented lifestyle of compulsively scheduled activities—exercising, school, and meals—precluded any spontaneous social interactions. Realization of their adverse behaviors preceded the anorexics' acknowledgment of their subnormal body weight and size.

Contrasting with anorexics, the binge/purgers, when confronted, more readily admitted that they were bulimic and that their means of weight loss was "abnormal." Teresa, for example, knew "very well" that her bulimic behavior was "wrong and unhealthy," although "worth the physical risks." While the bulimics initially maintained that their purging was only a temporary weight-loss method, they eventually realized that their disorder represented a "loss of control." Although these respondents regretted the self-indulgence, "shame," and "wasted time," they acknowledged their growing dependence on binging/purging for weight management and stress regulation.

The application of anorexic or bulimic labels precipitated secondary deviance, wherein group members internalized these identities. Secondary deviance refers to norm violations which are a response to society's labeling: "secondary deviation... becomes a means of social defense, attack or adaptation to the overt and covert problems created by the societal reaction to primary deviance" (Lemert, 1967: 17). In contrast to primary deviance, secondary deviance is generally prolonged, alters the individual's self-concept, and affects the performance of his/her social roles.

As secondary deviants, respondents felt that their disorders "gave a purpose" to their lives. Nicole resisted attaining a normal weight because it was not "her"—she accepted her anorexic weight as her "true" weight. For Teresa, bulimia became a "companion"; and Julie felt "every aspect of her life," including time management and social activities, was affected by her bulimia. Group members' eating disorders became the salient element of their self-concepts, so that they related to familiar people and new acquaintances as anorexics or bulimics. For example, respondents regularly compared their body shapes and sizes with those of others. They also became sensitized to comments about their appearance, whether or not the remarks were made by someone aware of their eating disorder.

With their behavior increasingly attuned to their eating disorders, group members exhibited role engulfment (Schur, 1971). Through accepting anorexic or bulimic identities, individuals centered activities around their deviant role, downgrading other social roles. Their obligations as students, family members, and friends became subordinate to their eating and exercising rituals.

Socializing, for example, was gradually curtailed because it interfered with compulsive exercising, binging, or purging.

Labeled anorexic or bulimic, respondents were ascribed a new status with a different set of role expectations. Regardless of other positions the individuals occupied, their deviant status, or master status (Hughes, 1958; Becker, 1973), was identified before all others. Among group members, Nicole, who was known as the "school's brain," became known as the "school's anorexic." No longer viewed as conforming model individuals, some respondents were termed "starving waifs" or "pigs."

Because of their identities as deviants, anorexics' and bulimics' interactions with others were altered. Group members' eating habits were scrutinized by friends and family and used as a "catch-all" for everything negative that happened to them. Respondents felt self-conscious around individuals who knew of their disorders; for example, Robin imagined people "watching and whispering" behind her. In addition, group members believed others expected them to "act" anorexic or bulimic. Friends of some anorexic group members never offered them food or drink, assuming continued disinterest on the respondents' part. While being hospitalized, Denise felt she had to prove to others she was not still vomiting, by keeping her bathroom door open. Other bulimics, who lived in dormitories, were hesitant to use the restroom for normal purposes lest several friends be huddling at the door, listening for vomiting. In general, individuals interacted with the respondents largely on the basis of their eating disorder; in doing so, they reinforced anorexic and bulimic behaviors.

Bulimic respondents, whose weight-loss behavior was not generally detectable from their appearance, tried earnestly to hide their bulimia by binging and purging in secret. Their main purpose in concealment was to avoid the negative consequences of being known as a bulimic. For these individuals, bulimia connoted a "cop-out": like "weak anorexics," bulimics pursued thinness but yielded to urges to eat. Respondents felt other people regarded bulimia as "gross" and had little sympathy for the sufferer. To avoid these stigmas or "spoiled identities," the bulimics shrouded their behaviors.

Distinguishing types of stigma, Goffman (1963) describes discredited (visible) stigmas and discreditable (invisible) stigmas. Bulimics, whose weight was approximately normal or even slightly elevated, harbored discreditable stigmas. Anorexics, on the other hand, suffered both discreditable and discredited stigmas—the latter due to their emaciated appearance. Certain anorexics were more reconciled than the bulimics to their stigmas: for Brian, the "stigma of anorexia was better than the stigma of being fat." Common to the stigmatized individuals was an inability to interact spontaneously with others. Respondents were constantly on guard against topics of eating and body size.

Both anorexics and bulimics were held responsible by others for their behavior and presumed able to "get out of it if they tried." Many anorexics reported being told to "just eat more," while bulimics were enjoined to simply "stop eating so much." Such appeals were made without regard for the complexities of the problem. Ostracized by certain friends and family members, anorexics and bulimics felt increasingly isolated. For respondents, the self-help group presented a non-threatening forum for discussing their disorders. Here, they found mutual understanding, empathy, and support. Many participants viewed BANISH as a haven from stigmatization by "others."

Group members, as secondary deviants, thus endured negative consequences, such as stigmatization, from being labeled. As they internalized the labels anorexic or bulimic, individuals' self-concepts were significantly influenced. When others interacted with the respondents on the basis of their eating disorders, anorexic or bulimic identities were encouraged. Moreover, group members' efforts to counteract the deviant labels were thwarted by their master statuses.

DISCUSSION

Previous research on eating disorders has dwelt almost exclusively on medical and psychological facets. Although necessary for a comprehensive understanding of anorexia nervosa and bulimia, these approaches neglect the social processes involved. The phenomena of eating disorders transcend concrete disease entities and clinical diagnoses. Multifaceted and complex, anorexia nervosa and bulimia require a holistic research design, in which sociological insights be included....

With only five to ten percent of reported cases appearing in males (Crisp, 1977; Stangler and Printz, 1980), eating disorders are primarily a women's aberrance. The deviance of anorexia nervosa and bulimia is rooted in the visual objectification of women and attendant slimness norm. Indeed, purposeful starvation and binging/purging reinforce the notion that "a society gets the deviance it deserves" (Schur, 1979: 71). As...noted (Schur, 1984), the sociology of deviance has generally bypassed systematic studies of women's norm violations. Like male deviants, females endure label applications, internalizations, and fulfillments.

The social processes involved in developing anorexic or bulimic identities comprise the sequence of conforming behavior, primary deviance, and secondary deviance. With a background of exceptional adherence to conventional norms, especially the striving for thinness, respondents subsequently exhibit the primary deviance of starving or binging/purging. Societal reaction to these behaviors leads to secondary deviance, wherein respondents' self-concepts and master statuses become anorexic or bulimic. Within this framework of labeling theory, the persistence of eating disorders, as well as the effects of stigmatization, is elucidated.

Although during the course of this research some respondents alleviated their symptoms through psychiatric help or hospital treatment programs, no one was labeled "cured." An anorexic is considered recovered when weight is normal for two years; a bulimic is termed recovered after being symptom-free for one and one-half years (American Anorexia/Bulimia Association Newsletter, 1985). Thus deviance disavowal (Schur, 1971), or efforts after normalization to counteract the deviant labels, remains a topic for future exploration.

NOTES

1. Although instructive, an integration of the medical, psychological, and sociocultural perspectives on eating disorders is beyond the scope of this paper.

2. Exceptions to the neglect of sociocultural factors are discussions of sex-role socialization in the development of eating disorders. Anorexics' girlish appearance has been interpreted as a rejection of femininity and womanhood (Orbach, 1979; Bruch, 1981; Orbach, 1985). In contrast, bulimics have been characterized as over-conforming to traditional female sex roles (Boskind-Lodahl, 1976).

3. Although a group experience for self-defined bulimics has been reported (Boskind-Lodahl, 1976), the researcher, from the outset, focused on Gestalt and behaviorist techniques within a feminist orientation.

4. One explanation for fewer anorexics than bulimics in the sample is that, in the general population, anorexics are outnumbered by bulimics at 8 or 10 to 1 (Lawson, as reprinted in American Anorexia/Bulimia Association Newsletter, 1985: 1). The proportion of bulimics to anorexics in the sample is 6.5 to 1. In addition, compared to bulimics, anorexics may be less likely to attend a self-help group as they have a greater tendency to deny the existence of an eating problem (Humphries et al., 1982). However, the four anorexics in the present study were among the members who attended the meetings most often.

5. Interactions in the families of anorexics and bulimics might seem deviant in being inordinately close. However, in the larger societal context, the family members epitomize the norms of family cohesiveness. Perhaps unusual in their occurrence, these families are still within the realm of conformity. Humphries and colleagues (1982: 202) refer to the "highly enmeshed and protective" family as part of the "idealized family myth."

REFERENCES

American Anorexia/Bulimia Association Newsletter. 1985. 8(3).

Becker, Howard S. 1973. *Outsiders.* New York: Free Press.

Boskind-Lodahl, Marlene. 1976. "Cinderella's stepsisters: A feminist perspective on anorexia nervosa and bulimia." *Signs, Journal of Women in Culture and Society* 2: 342–56.

Boskind-White, Marlene. 1985. "Bulimarexia: A sociocultural perspective." In S. W. Emmett (ed.), *Theory and Treatment of Anorexia Nervosa and Bulimia: Biomedical, Sociocultural, and Psychological Perspectives* (pp. 113–26). New York: Brunner/Mazel.

Branch, C. H. Hardin, and Linda J. Eurman. 1980. "Social attitudes toward patients with anorexia nervosa." *American Journal of Psychiatry* 137: 631–32.

Bruch, Hilde. 1981. "Developmental considerations of anorexia nervosa and obesity." *Canadian Journal of Psychiatry* 26: 212–16.

Chernin, Kim. 1981. *The Obsession: Reflections on the Tyranny of Slenderness.* New York: Harper and Row.

Crisp, A. H. 1977. "The prevalence of anorexia nervosa and some of its associations in the general population." *Advances in Psychosomatic Medicine* 9: 38–47.

Crisp, A. H., R. L. Palmer, and R. S. Kalucy. 1976. "How common is anorexia nervosa? A prevalence study." *British Journal of Psychiatry* 128: 549–54.

Dejong, William. 1980. "The stigma of obesity: The consequences of naive assumptions concerning the causes of physical deviance." *Journal of Health and Social Behavior* 21: 75–87.

Fox, K. C., and N. McI. James. 1976. "Anorexia nervosa: A study of 44 strictly defined cases." *New Zealand Medical Journal* 84: 309–12.

Garner, David M., Paul E. Garfinkel, Donald Schwartz, and Michael Thompson. 1980. "Cultural expectations of thinness in women." *Psychological Reports* 47: 483–91.

Goffman, Erving. 1963. *Stigma.* Englewood Cliffs, NJ: Prentice-Hall.

Halmi, Katherine A., James R. Falk, and Estelle Schwartz. 1981. "Binge-eating and vomiting: A survey of a college population." *Psychological Medicine* 11: 697–706.

Herzog, David B. 1982. "Bulimia: The secretive syndrome." *Psychosomatics* 23: 481–83.

Hughes, Everett C. 1958. *Men and Their Work.* New York: Free Press.

Humphries, Laurie L., Sylvia Wrobel, and H. Thomas Wiegert. 1982. "Anorexia nervosa." *American Family Physician* 26: 199–204.

Johnson, Craig L., Marilyn K. Stuckey, Linda D. Lewis, and Donald M. Schwartz. 1982. "Bulimia: A descriptive survey of 316 cases." *International Journal of Eating Disorders* 2(1): 3–16.

Kalucy, R. S., A. H. Crisp, and Britta Harding. 1977. "A study of 56 families with anorexia nervosa." *British Journal of Medical Psychology* 50: 381–95.

Lacey, Hubert J., Sian Coker, and S. A. Birtchnell. 1986. "Bulimia: Factors associated with its etiology and maintenance." *International Journal of Eating Disorders* 5: 475–87.

Lemert, Edwin M. 1951. *Social Pathology.* New York: McGraw-Hill.

———. 1967. *Human Deviance, Social Problems and Social Control.* Englewood Cliffs, NJ: Prentice-Hall.

Minuchin, Salvador, Bernice L. Rosman, and Lester Baker. 1978. *Psychosomatic Families: Anorexia Nervosa in Context.* Cambridge, MA: Harvard University Press.

Orbach, Susie. 1979. *Fat Is a Feminist Issue.* New York: Berkeley.

———. 1985. "Visibility/invisibility: Social considerations in anorexia nervosa—a feminist perspective." In S. W. Emmett (ed.), *Theory and Treatment of Anorexia Nervosa and Bulimia: Biomedical, Sociocultural, and Psychological Perspectives* (pp. 127–38). New York: Brunner/Mazel.

Ritenbaugh, Cheryl. 1982. "Obesity as a culture-bound syndrome." *Culture, Medicine and Psychiatry* 6: 347–61.

Russell, Gerald. 1979. "Bulimia nervosa: An ominous variant of anorexia nervosa." *Psychological Medicine* 9: 429–48.

Schlesier-Stropp, Barbara. 1984. "Bulimia: A review of the literature." *Psychological Bulletin* 95: 247–57.

Schur, Edwin M. 1971. *Labeling Deviant Behavior.* New York: Harper and Row.

———. 1979. *Interpreting Deviance: A Sociological Introduction.* New York: Harper and Row.

———. 1984. *Labeling Women Deviant: Gender, Stigma, and Social Control.* New York: Random House.

Schwartz, Donald M., and Michael G. Thompson. 1981. "Do anorectics get well? Current research and future needs." *American Journal of Psychiatry* 138: 319–23.

Schwartz, Donald M., Michael G. Thompson, and Craig L. Johnson. 1982. "Anorexia nervosa and bulimia: The socio-cultural context." *International Journal of Eating Disorders* 1(3): 20–36.

Selvini-Palazzoli, Mara. 1978. *Self-Starvation: From Individual to Family Therapy in the Treatment of Anorexia Nervosa.* New York: Jason Aronson.

Stangler, Ronnie S., and Adolph M. Printz. 1980. "DSM-III: Psychiatric diagnosis in a university population." *American Journal of Psychiatry* 137: 937–40.

Theander, Sten. 1970. "Anorexia nervosa." *Acta Psychiatrica Scandinavica Supplement* 214: 24–31.

Thompson, Michael G., and Donald M. Schwartz. 1982. "Life adjustment of women with anorexia nervosa and anorexic-like behavior." *International Journal of Eating Disorders* 1(2): 47–60.

Willi, Jurg, and Samuel Grossmann. 1983. "Epidemiology of anorexia nervosa in a defined region of Switzerland." *American Journal of Psychiatry* 140: 564–67.

CHAPTER 13

MANAGING A DEVIANT IDENTITY

Stutterers' Practices

MICHAEL PETRUNIK and CLIFFORD D. SHEARING

People who have been designated as social deviants may have difficulty in their interaction with other people. The frequency and severity of the reactions of others as well as their own reactions vary with how serious their deviant behavior is judged to be, the ratio of conformity to deviant behavior in their current situation, and the extent to which their "misconduct" is considered to be voluntary or involuntary. Most criminals have less trouble conforming with the rules of everyday life than do people who are considered mentally less able. However, if most people knew the seriousness of their crimes, conventional social reactions to them would be much more severe than to the less abled.

In general, the taken-for-granted assumption with regard to most actions is that people intended them. When people blame themselves for their inability to control their conduct, as stutterers often do, they have internalized the commonsense assumption that their stuttering is a failure in voluntary self-control. Stutterers' problems are compounded if in addition to social labeling they add their own self-labels as incompetent speakers. Michael Petrunik and Clifford D. Shearing show that their self-consciousness makes them give accounts for incompetent speech. Only in groups that accept them do they lose their excessive efforts at speech control, in the process becoming unaware that they have given up trying to control stuttering.

…Stuttering is a puzzling disorder of human communication which has defied explanation and cure for thousands of years (Van Riper, 1971:2). According to survey estimates in Europe and North America, stutterers constitute about 1 percent of the school-age population, regardless of language or dialect (Bloodstein, 1981:79; Van

Reprinted from "Fragile Facades: Stuttering and the Strategic Manipulation of Awareness," *Social Problems,* Vol. 31, No. 2 (December 1983), pp. 125–138, by permission of the Society for the Study of Social Problems and the authors. Copyright © 1983 by the Society for the Study of Social Problems.

Riper, 1971:39). Although systematic data are not available—there are only impressionistic accounts from anthropologists—stuttering appears to be less common in non-western, non-industrial societies.[1] Stuttering typically appears between two and nine years of age. There is some evidence that stuttering has a genetic basis; it tends to appear in successive generations of the same family and frequently in identical twins (Bloodstein, 1981:94). Stuttering is more common among males than females, by a ratio of three or four to one (Bloodstein, 1981:86). Only about one-fifth of those who stutter in early childhood continue to stutter into adulthood (Bloodstein, 1981:86; Van Riper, 1971:45).

Stuttering, as visible behavior, refers to interruptions in speech involving the prolongation or repetition of sounds or words, pauses between words or syllables, and "blocking" on words, sometimes accompanied by extraneous sounds such as grunts, facial grimaces, body movements, and postural freezing as the person struggles to "get the word out." These speech difficulties can range from a split second to, in the worst cases, about a minute (Bloodstein, 1981:3).

Like other perceived impairments, stuttering interferes with "the etiquette and mechanisms of communication" (Goffman, 1963:103) and disrupts the "feedback mechanics of spoken interaction" (1963:49). Depending on the social context, the culture, and the health and social status of the speakers (Petrunik, 1977:37), persons who unintentionally and chronically deviate from fluency standards are likely to be defined as stutterers and subjected to various penalizing social reactions, including pity, condescension, embarrassment, amusement, ridicule, and impatience (Johnson, 1959:239; Lemert, 1967:135).

The extent and frequency of stuttering varies. No one stutters all the time. Indeed, there are some situations in which virtually all stutterers are fluent, for example, when singing, speaking in unison with others (including other stutterers), and speaking to themselves, animals, and infants. In addition, stutterers are often more fluent when speaking with a drawl, accent, or different pitch (Petrunik, 1977:34, 71). Some individuals stutter on some words or sounds but not others. ("I can never say g's." "I always stutter on the word 'coffee.'") Setting is also important. Many stutter more during telephone conversations than they do in face-to-face conversation; others find speaking to strangers particularly difficult; still others are more fluent in formal than informal situations, or vice versa. Stutterers have good periods and bad periods. ("Some days I wake up and I'm fine, other days I'm in for hell all day.") There are even some

actors and entertainers who stutter but who are fluent when playing a role or facing an audience.

Studying the ways stutterers cope with their stuttering offers valuable insights into how people manage perceived disabilities (Freidson, 1965) and the potential stigma associated with them by highlighting processes that are usually taken for granted, and thus obscured (Davis, 1961). This strategy of using the specific to identify the general has recently been employed by Kitsuse (1980) who has used the "coming out of the closet" metaphor to examine the processes which establish new and legitimate identities. Schneider and Conrad (1980) have developed Kitsuse's analysis by using epilepsy to examine how persons manage discreditable information where there is "no clear identity to move to or from" (1980:32) and where "no 'new' readily available supportive...subculture exists" (1980:33).

Both Kitsuse, and Schneider and Conrad, focus on identity rather than interactional order, and on calculated and planned management rather than moment-to-moment strategies. We broaden this analysis by examining: (1) how people coordinate the requirements of creating acceptable identities *and* orderly interaction; (2) how they integrate management strategies thought out in advance with those selected on a moment-to-moment basis; and (3) how the subjective experience of disability, together with the reactions of others, shape the management process (Higgins, 1980; Petrunik, 1983). Stuttering has three features which facilitate an examination of these issues. First, stuttering is a potentially stigmatizing disability that disrupts interaction. Second, because stutterers experience speech as a function over which they exercise partial but precarious control, their management of speech is both spontaneous and premeditated. Third, the experience of stuttering is critical for how stutterers, and others, define and manage stuttering.... We examine the central importance of stuttering as a reality experienced by the stutterer. We then examine a variety of strategies which stutterers use to manipulate awareness of their stuttering and present the fragile facade of normal speech. Although we refer throughout to Goffman's (1963) analysis of stigma management as a benchmark in demonstrating how an understanding of stuttering contributes to a more general understanding of stigma, we go beyond Goffman and those who have extended his work, such as Conrad and Schneider, in emphasizing the importance of the experiential domain for sociological analysis....

THE EXPERIENCE OF STUTTERING

I suppose that the hope of every stutterer is to awaken some morning and find that his disability has vanished. There is just enough promise of this in his experience to make it seem possible. There are days when, for some reason, the entangled web of words trips him only occasionally. In such periods of relief, he may peer back into his other condition and puzzle over the nature of the oppressive "presence"...[hoping that it] is a transitory aberration which might fade and vanish.... One feels that only an added will-power, some accretion of psychic rather than physical strength, should be necessary for its conquest. Yet, try as I might, I could not take the final step. I had come up against some invisible power which no strength of will seemed to surmount. (Gustavson, 1944:466)

Like normal speakers, stutterers believe speech is something that should be intentionally controlled. Yet, somehow their words are mysteriously blocked or interrupted. Stutterers experience stuttering as the work of an alien inner force (often referred to in the third person as "it") which takes control of their speech mechanism. Stuttering is something which stutterers feel happens *to* them, not something they do: "somebody else is in charge of my mouth and I can't do anything about it" (Van Riper, 1971:158).

In coping with this subjective reality, stutterers use three general strategies: concealment, openness, and disavowal. Concealment strategies involve three principal tactics: avoidance, circumvention, and camouflage. These tactics allow most stutterers to avoid being seen as stutterers part of

the time and a few to become secret stutterers. Openness tactics include: treating stuttering as unproblematic struggle with the "it," and voluntary disclosure. Disavowal—which often calls for the tacit cooperation of others—involves the pretense that stuttering is not occurring when it is obvious that it is. We discuss in turn each of these strategies and their tactics.

CONCEALMENT

AVOIDANCE

The simplest way to conceal stuttering is to avoid speaking. Many stutterers select occupations they think will minimize speaking. Others avoid situations in which they fear stuttering will embarrass them.

I never went to the dances at school because I was afraid of stuttering and looking silly. Because I didn't go, I didn't learn to dance or mix socially. I always felt bad when people would ask me if I was going to a dance or party. I would make up some excuse or say that I didn't want to go. I felt that people thought I was some sort of creep because I didn't go. Each time I wouldn't go because of my fears, I felt even weirder.

Stutterers avoid specific types of encounters. Instead of using the telephone they will write a letter, "drop in on someone," or go to a store to see if it has the item they want. Stutterers avoid particular words, substituting "easy" words for "hard" ones. Word substitution sometimes results in convoluted phrasing in which nothing seems to be addressed directly.

If I didn't dodge and duck, I wouldn't be able to carry on a conversation. If I didn't circumlocute, I wouldn't be able to get certain words out at all. Unless I'm coming in through the back door and taking a run at it, I'd never get it out.

Where this tactic proves difficult or impossible, stutterers may structure conversations so others say the troublesome words for them. One way of doing this is by feigning forgetfulness:

You know what I mean, what was it we were talking about this morning, you know, John has one, it's ah, this is annoying, it's right on the tip of my tongue....

Another tactic is to structure the situation so that someone else will be called upon to do the talking. For example, most stutterers fear they will stutter on their name (Petrunik, 1982:306). To avoid introducing themselves when they meet strangers, stutterers sometimes arrange their entry so that someone who knows them will [precede] them into the situation. They then rely on the social conventions governing introductions to compel the other person to introduce them. Similarly, stutterers often fear placing orders in restaurants because here, too, word substitution is difficult. To cope with this situation, stutterers may encourage others to order before them; as soon as an item they would like—or at least find acceptable—is mentioned, they can use words they feel more confident with to duplicate the other person's order: "me too" or "same here." With close associates such cooperation may take on the character of finely tuned team work.

> *When we were visiting friends of ours and I was having blocks, my wife would sometimes get what seemed to be a slightly anxious look and would quietly supply the word. She did this in a way that seemed so natural to me that I wondered if the others noticed it.*

While the willing cooperation of others, especially intimates, has been well documented (Goffman, 1963:55, 97) a study of stuttering draws attention to how others may unknowingly be coopted to conceal a potential stigma.

CIRCUMVENTION AND CAMOUFLAGE

Stutterers sometimes use tactics based on timing and rhythm to outsmart the "it." Using these tactics requires a knowledge of both the etiquette of conversation and the patterns of one's own stuttering. Some speak quickly, for example, "building up" momentum to get "past" or "over" "difficult words." Others rhythmically pace their speech with the aid of coordinated hand and/or leg movements. Some arrange their sentences so that "easy" words precede "hard" ones, to establish a "flow" which carries them uneventfully over "trouble spots." Others arrange their speech so that "difficult" sounds are said on falling (or rising) pitches. Still others find that changing their tone of voice, or speaking in dialect or with an accent, is helpful.

A similar tactic involves delaying saying a troublesome word until the stutterer feels "it" no longer threatens to control speech and the word is ready to "come out." One way of doing this is to introduce starters and fillers (well, like, er, ah, um) into speech, to postpone troublesome words until the moment when they can be said. One stutterer, for example, was walking along a street when a stranger asked him for directions: "Where is the Borden Building?" A sudden panic gripped the stutterer. He knew exactly where the building was but, to permit him to wait for a moment when "it" could be caught off guard, he responded: "Well, let me see [pause with quizzical expression] oh, ah, near...let me see...near, I think Spadina and, ah, College." A variant of this tactic involves rearranging words. The late British humorist and stutterer, Patrick Campbell, gave an example of this in a television interview. While travelling on a London bus, he feared he would not be able to say, "May I have a ticket to Marble Arch?" without stuttering. So, when the conductor approached, he said instead, "May I have a ticket to that arch which is of marble made?"—which he executed fluently.

Where stutterers fail to outwit the "it" they may attempt to camouflage their problem by, for example, visually isolating others from evidence of their stuttering. A teacher who stutters accomplished this by writing on the blackboard just as he was about to stutter, thereby disguising a "block" as a pause to write.

SECRET STUTTERERS

Most stutterers avoid detection only part of the time. However, some stutterers manage to maintain the identity of a "normal speaker" virtually all the time. They define themselves as stutterers not because they stutter in secret, like Becker's (1963:11) "secret deviants," but because they confront and respond to an inner propensity to stutter. Some stutterers report going for years without overtly stuttering. This fact—that a deviant identity can exist in the absence of visible deviant behavior—adds weight to Jack Katz's (1972) critique of those conceptions of labeling which focus exclusively on deviance as behavior and ignore deviance as an inner essence imputed to individuals. Goffman's (1963:56) refusal to recognize that stigmatized people may define themselves in terms of an inner essence and "that what distinguishes an individual from others is the core of his being" has limited his ability to comprehend how both stigmatized and "normal" people perceive their differences and the consequences of this for defining their "real" or "natural" groupings (1963:112). Some speech pathologists, on the other hand, have long recognized that stigmatized people define themselves on the basis of their subjective experience. They refer to secret stutterers as interiorized, indicating that stuttering can be an internal experience as well as an external appearance (Douglass and Quarrington, 1952:378).

Interiorized stutterers place great importance on preserving a social identity and will go to extraordinary lengths to preserve it. For example, a self-employed businessman in his early forties concealed his stuttering from his first wife. He confided in his second wife, but continued to conceal his stuttering from his children. At work, he had his secretary handle potentially troublesome situations. He would, for example, have her make certain phone calls for him. He claimed he would lose business if his stuttering became known. At one time he fired a secretary who had been working with him for a number of years because he thought her facial expressions showed that she had noticed him stuttering. He took great care not to drink too much or become fatigued so that he would not lose control over his speech. He preferred to entertain at home rather than to go out

because he felt he could better regulate his drinking at home.

Successful interiorized stutterers develop a particular sensitivity to the intricacies of syntax. They "become 'situation conscious' [and display] special aliveness to the contingencies of acceptance and disclosure, contingencies to which normals will be less alive" (Goffman, 1963:111).

Avoiding stuttering has many costs. Some tactics exclude the stutterer from fully participating in social life as a "normal person," infringing on the very status the stutterer wishes to preserve. The interactional costs may be relatively trivial (not eating what one really wants in a restaurant, or saying something quite different from what one intended), or far more consequential (depriving oneself of a social life or not pursuing a desired occupation).

> *Because I wasn't normal I thought I couldn't do normal things like get married. I avoided going to parties, because I didn't want to feel bad, and then I felt bad because I didn't go and wasn't meeting people and having a good social life.*

Similarly, the consequences for social identity may be relatively benign (being defined as "quiet" or "shy") or even somewhat flattering (being a "good listener" or a "strong silent type"). On the other hand, avoiding interaction may result in derogatory characterizations ("nervous," "odd," "rude," "affected," "silly," "strange," or "retarded").[2] A border crossing incident illustrates how avoidance can be interpreted as evidence of impropriety:

> *The border guard asked me where I was born. Because I was afraid I would stutter on "Nova Scotia," I hesitated and started to "ah" and "um" to him. "Let me see now…it's the…uh, Maritimes…uh…" and so on. The outcome of all this evasion was that they made a thorough search of my car and even threatened to slit my seat covers.*

The importance which stutterers give to the costs of concealment determines the tactics they use. Some people will do almost anything to avoid stuttering; others prefer to stutter in some situations rather than face the consequences of concealment.

> *On the first day [of the Kerr course] we were gathering at the motel and going through the ritual of introductions. One man put his hand out to me and said, "My name is…uh…actually…my name is Jim." Afterwards one of the other men in the group who had a highly noticeable stutter shook his head and said, in an aside to me, "What a fool! I'd rather stammer my head off than avoid like that. It looks ridiculous. People must think he's crazy!"*

OPENNESS

UNPROBLEMATIC STUTTERING

Unlike interiorized stutterers, those with visible and audible speech disruptions find that some audiences become so familiar with their stuttering that they no longer have anything to conceal. ("All my friends know I stutter. I can't hide my stuttering long enough.") These stutterers simply go ahead and speak without thinking about the consequences. As a result, particularly when speaking with persons who know their problem, they can be barely conscious of their stuttering.

> *With Evelyn, if you asked me, I never stutter. If there was a tape recorder going it might show that I was stuttering. But I don't notice it and it doesn't bother me. I don't have any trouble talking to her on the phone unless others are there.*

At the same time those who know stutterers well seem less conscious of their stuttering. Spouses and friends remarked:

> *You know, since I've got to know you well, I hardly ever notice your stuttering.*

> *You know, sometimes I forget he stutters.*

> *I notice his stuttering only when others are present. I'm more conscious of it. At other times, I don't care.*

Goffman (1963:81) argues that friends are less aware of a stigmatized person's problem because they are more familiar with the stigma. In the case of stuttering, however, what is critical is its obtrusiveness—"how much it interferes with the flow of interaction" (Goffman, 1963:49)—rather than mere visibility. When stutterers are with friends they feel less constrained to meet the exacting requirements which talk requires in other circumstances, because both parties develop idiosyncratic rules which enable them to become less dependent on such things as precise timing. For example, in telephone conversations between stutterers and their friends silences can cease to be interpreted as cues indicating the end of a speaking turn or a break in the telephone connection.

Once such understandings are developed stutterers feel less pressure to account for their problems or to work at concealing and controlling the "it"; thus, the sense of stuttering as a subjective presence wanes. For stutterers who learn to speak fluently by meticulously learning a new set of speech behaviors (Webster, 1975), the experience of stuttering as an "it" may fade away because with their speech under control there is no longer any need to account for stuttering.[3]

STRUGGLING WITH THE "IT"

Stutterers who find it difficult to conceal their stuttering face the additional problem of how to converse with people who take interruptions in the speech of stutterers as a signal to resume talking themselves. Stutterers attempt to avoid this by making two claims: first, that they are competent persons who understand the conventions of talk; and second, that they have not relinquished their speaking turn—even though they are lapsing into unusually long silences—and should be permitted to continue speaking uninterrupted. These claims are important to the stutterer because together they provide the basis for participation in conversation and for maintaining an acceptable identity. One way stutterers make these claims is by confronting a block "head on" and trying to force out the word or sound: a typical pattern is a deep breath followed by muscle tension and visible strain as the stutterer attempts to "break through" the interruption and regain control of speech. The late Japanese novelist Yukio Mishima (1959:5) vividly described this phenomenon: "When a stutterer is struggling desperately to utter his first sound he is like a little bird that is trying to extricate itself from thick lime."

By making visible the "I/it" conflict through struggle, stutterers demonstrate to those they are conversing with that they have not given up their speaking turn and are doing their utmost to limit the interruption in their speech. This process of externalizing stuttering enables stutterers to share with others their experience of stuttering as a mysterious intrusive force. By demonstrating that their deviation from the conventions of speech is not intentional (Blum and McHugh, 1971; Goffman, 1963:128, 143; Mills, 1940) they hope to persuade others to bear with them and not to regard them as outsiders who reject, or do not understand, the norms others adhere to. The struggle that stutterers engage in is the "stigma symbol" (Goffman, 1963:46) that others recognize as stuttering. Struggle feeds into the troubles stutterers are trying to remedy in a classic vicious circle: stuttering is in part a product of attachment to the very social conventions that stutterers struggle to avoid breaking.

This analysis is supported by evidence that some members of the British upper classes view stuttering (or stammering as it is referred to in Britain) as a mark of distinction (Kazin, 1978: 124; Shenker, 1970:112). They openly cultivate stuttering as a display of their superior social status and expect others to wait at their convenience. These persons make no apology for their stuttering and accordingly do not struggle with it to demonstrate its involuntary character. Consequently, their stuttering typically takes the form of a "slight stammer" characterized by relaxed repetitions and hesitations without any of the facial distortions associated with struggle.

VOLUNTARY DISCLOSURE

Like concealment, struggle also involves costs. Stuttering presents the listener with the problem of knowing how to sustain an interaction punctuated with silences, prolongations, and facial contortions. As one observer noted:

What am I supposed to do when a stutterer is struggling to say something? Should I help him by saying the word—because I usually know what he is trying to say—or am I supposed to wait? Then if you wait, what do you do? Am I supposed to watch him struggling? It can be awful. And then there is just no knowing what to do with the time. It can be a long wait. It's embarrassing.

One way stutterers deal with this, and with the fear of exposure in the case of concealment, is by voluntarily disclosing their stuttering (Van Riper, 1971:211) in much the same manner as epileptics (Schneider and Conrad, 1980).

The person who has an unapparent, negatively valued attribute often finds it expedient to begin an encounter with an unobtrusive admission of his own failing, especially with persons who are uninformed about him. (Goffman, 1967:29)

Stutterers who make public speeches may begin by referring to their problem so their audiences won't be unduly shocked. One university professor started off each term by talking about his stuttering and inviting students to ask questions about it. Another began his courses by deliberately stuttering, so that he would not create expectations of fluency that he might later fail to meet.

Stutterers sometimes indicate the involuntary nature of their disability by apologizing or by noting that their present stuttering is worse than usual. Through such tactics they, in effect, argue that the stigmatized and normal categories represent poles of a continuum, and that they are much further toward the normal end of this continuum than their present behavior would suggest. In doing so, stutterers typically take advantage of the fact that while struggling with some sound or word they can often make fluent asides which display their relative normality.

We went to the shh—shh—(s's always give me trouble) shh—show last night.

I was talking to K—K—en (Wow! I had a hard time on that one) and he was saying....

Other stutterers put listeners at ease with retrospective accounts such as, "Boy, I'm having a hard time today. I must be really tired."

Sometimes humor is used to anticipate and defuse confusion or embarrassment. One stutterer told people at informal gatherings to "go ahead and talk amongst yourselves if I take too long about saying anything." A teacher attempted to put his students at ease by inviting them to "take advantage of my stuttering to catch up on your note-taking."

Other stutterers use humor to claim more desirable identities for themselves.

> *I use humor a lot now. If I'm having a problem, I'll make a comment like, "Boy, it's a problem having a big mouth like mine and not being able to use it." When I'm having a hard time getting out a word in a store I'll say something like, "Three tries for a quarter." Once a waitress started guessing when I blocked giving my order and kept on guessing and guessing wrong. Every so often, I would smile and say, "You just keep guessing." Everyone was laughing but they were laughing at her, not me.*

Stutterers may also take a more aggressive stance. By pitting themselves against the listener, they indicate that they refuse to allow others to use their stuttering to belittle them. One of our respondents referred to this as the "fuck you, Mac" approach.

> *I challenge the listener. I can make a game out of it. I look them straight in the eye and in my mind tell them to "fuck off." I might stutter like hell, but so what. It doesn't make them any better than me.*

In using this strategy stutterers attempt to disavow the implications that they suspect others will draw about their lack of control over speech by displaying "cool." This strategy draws its impetus from the fear that many stutterers have that they will be seen as nervous and easily ruffled persons when they perceive themselves as normal persons in every respect other than their inability to control speech.

Another non-apologetic, but less aggressive, strategy that is occasionally used is one in which the stutterer systematically attempts to redefine stuttering as a "new and proud identity" (Schneider and Conrad, 1980:32) and to use this new identity as a means of getting stuttering "out of the closet" (M. Katz, 1968; Lambidakis, 1972). Some of our respondents reported that talking about their problem to new acquaintances proved to be a good way of gaining rapport. Revealing one's weakness to another can be a way of appearing honest, frank, and "more human." Others claimed that their efforts to overcome their "handicap" had strengthened their character. A few (e.g., Van Riper, Sheehan, and Douglass) have even used their personal experience of stuttering professionally, in therapy and research, to gain knowledge and rapport with patients and/or subjects. Even in occupations such as sales or journalism, where stuttering might ordinarily be seen to be a great handicap, some stutterers have used stuttering to their advantage. A Canadian journalist was said to have "disarmed" those he interviewed with his stuttering so that they were sympathetic toward him and unusually frank. A salesman had his business cards printed: "B-B-Bob G-G-Goldman the stuttering Toyota salesman."

Public figures sometimes use their stuttering as a trademark and a means to success. Some examples are the comedian "Stuttering Joe" Frisco, the humorist Patrick Campbell, and the country and western singer Mel Tillis. In his autobiography, Campbell (1967:212) reports how his stuttering on British television made him famous:

> *While making the ginger ale commercials I looked upon my stammer as a nuisance that would have to be played down as much as possible if we weren't to have endless takes.... Although I didn't care to think about this aspect of it too much I did realize that my stammer fitted rather neatly into their campaign, the essence of which was never to mention the word "Schweppes," but merely to mention*

the first syllable 'sch—', and that was quite enough for me in every way. It wasn't until nearly a year later [when asked to advertise butter] that I realized my mistake. [Again Campbell tried to control his stuttering. The producer called him aside and said,] "I don't know quite how to put this—but could we have a little more of your trademark on the word 'butter'?"…I'd been trying to suppress the very thing it seemed that everyone wanted.

Reflecting on his "asset," Campbell claimed that while he tried to put the best possible light on it, he never really became proud of his identity as a stutterer. The frequent and fleeting gains did not offset the losses that recurred day after day.

If I was offered by some miraculous overnight cure the opportunity never to stammer again, I'd accept it without hesitation, even though it meant the end for me of television. (1967:213)

DISAVOWAL

While stutterers sometimes try to put listeners at their ease by drawing attention to themselves, there are often circumstances in which they prefer to define their stuttering out of existence. To do this successfully, they need the tacit cooperation of their listeners. Both parties must share the assumption that the embarrassment and awkwardness associated with stuttering and attempts to control it are best dealt with by acting as if the stuttering were not happening. This provides a "phantom normalcy" (Goffman, 1963:122). By overlooking stuttering, both parties act as if "nothing unusual is happening" (Emerson, 1970) rather than acknowledge something which would require a response for which no shared guidelines exist. This tactic leaves intact the stutterer's status as a normal and competent person and the other's as a decent and tactful person who avoids needlessly embarrassing others. Tactful overlooking, as Safilios-Rothschild (1970:129) has suggested, is normatively prescribed:

Regardless of any degree of aversion felt toward the disabled, the non-disabled are normatively not permitted to show these negative feelings in any way and their fear of making a verbal or a non-verbal "slip" indicating their emotions renders the interaction quite formal and rigid.

The importance of tacit disavowal of stuttering is indicated by the anxiety some stutterers feel when they enter a situation where they know it cannot, or will not, be ignored. Conversations with little children are one example.

Children give me the hardest time. They know something is wrong and they don't hide it. My little nephew embarrassed me terribly in front of the family. He said, "Your mouth moves funny." I tried to explain to him that I had something wrong with my mouth just like other people had something wrong with their ears or their eyes.

Another example is where stutterers are forced to watch and listen to themselves or others stuttering. Just as many fat people avoid scales and mirrors (Himelfarb and Evans, 1974:222), many stutterers shun mirrors and audio and video tape recorders. Similarly, stutterers are often uncomfortable watching others stutter. We witnessed stutterers in the speech clinic cover their faces with their hands or even walk out of the room rather than witness another person stutter. These attempts to distance themselves from stuttering appeared in some cases to be experienced as a disassociation of the body and the self through a loss or blurring of self-awareness. Stutterers talked of "slipping out of the situation" at the moment of stuttering and not being aware of what they or others were doing when they "returned." During these periods, stutterers experience a "time out" (Goffman, 1967:30; Scott and Lyman, 1968) from the situation. Time appears to stop so that when speech resumes it is as if the block did not occur. This sense of time having stopped, and of stuttering occurring outside the situation, is symbolized by the frozen poses stutterers sometimes adopt at the moment of stuttering: gestures are stopped, only to be resumed once speech continues. For example, one stutterer regularly "blocked" on a word just as he was about to tap the ash off his cigarette with his finger. During the few seconds he was "caught" in his block, his finger remained poised, frozen an inch or so above his cigarette. When he released the sound, the finger would simultaneously tap the ash into the ashtray.

Stutterers and their listeners manage time outs cooperatively by severing eye contact. Normally, people who are conversing indicate their attentiveness by facial expressions and eye contact, thereby reaffirming that they are listening and involved in the interaction. By breaking eye contact at the moment of stuttering, stutterers and their listeners jointly disengage from the conversation and exclude stuttering from the interaction. The moment fluent speech returns engagement is reestablished through a renewal of eye contact; the participants confirm their mutual subterfuge by acting as if nothing had happened. During time outs listeners may also confirm their disengagement by doing something unrelated, such as assuming an air of nonchalance, shuffling papers, glancing through a magazine or a book, fiddling with an object, or surveying the immediate surroundings. These signals indicate that the participants are not "in" the conversation.

While struggling to "get a word out" stutterers may avert their faces or hide their mouths with their hands. This phenomenon reveals an apparent difference in the social significance of sight and hearing. During this obscuring of the sight of stuttering, as with the time out, both parties are presumably aware that stuttering is taking place, and indeed that the stutterer is doing her or his best to "get past the block" and resume the conversation. Yet, at the same time, stuttering is denied. It is as if through the "thin disguises" (Goffman, 1963:81) which contradictory appearances provide it is possible to establish opposing social claims and thus "have one's cake and eat it too."

Time out, besides resolving the interactional problem of how to respond to stuttering, protects or hides one's vulnerability; it's much like the common response of averting your eyes when you

accidentally see someone naked. Stutterers are, in a sense, "naked" at the moment of stuttering; they are without a mask, their front is crumbling and their "raw self" exposed (Goffman, 1963:16). Averting their eyes is a cue to the other to look away from the stutterer's "nakedness," thus saving both from embarrassment. The stutterers we interviewed expressed this sense of "nakedness" or vulnerability with descriptions such as "weak," "helpless," "like a little kid," and "with my shell removed." Some even said that at the point of stuttering they felt transparent. This can be related to the saying that the eyes are the mirror of the soul, which stems from the belief that the eyes reflect one's true feelings even though the rest of one's face may camouflage them.

Loss of eye contact gives stutterers time to recover their composure, manage the "unsatisfactory" image that has emerged, and, if possible, project a new image. Listeners have their own self to consider. Because they too may be held partly responsible for the stutterer's embarrassment, they can use loss of eye contact to indicate that they did not intend the embarrassment to happen and, above all, that they are not amused or uncomfortable.

While the tactic of mutual disavowal is usually a situational one, the comment of one stutterer we interviewed indicates that in some cases it can be much more pervasive:

Ever since I was a young child I can't remember my parents ever directly mentioning stuttering. It seemed obvious that they saw me stuttering, and they knew I stuttered, but they never said anything. The only incident I can remember is my father singing "K-K-Katy" a couple of times. I felt badly about that. Nothing direct was ever said, even by my brothers. My younger brother always gave me a lot of trouble. But he never mentioned stuttering once. I wondered if my parents told them not to say anything. My parents did make lots of references to me as nervous, sensitive, or different, and were always saying they were going to take me to the doctor for my nerves. But except for brief references on very few occasions, they never mentioned anything about stuttering.

In such cases, the disavowal of stigma is extended across entire situations. This requires others to tacitly agree to ignore the stigma in all encounters with the stigmatized person.

DISCUSSION

Our study of stuttering provides a vehicle to elaborate upon and extend the work of Davis, Goffman, Schneider and Conrad, and others on the strategic manipulation of awareness to manage potential stigma. The implications of our analysis also extend beyond stigma management to a consideration of the importance of the experiential dimension for the construction of social order. Because the stutterer finds problematic what others take for granted, the stutterer's social world is the world of everyman writ large.

In our consideration of stuttering we have developed three major lines of argument. First, our analysis shows the importance of considering subjective experience as well as behavior when studying the management of identity and the construction of interactional order. Stutterers engage in the ongoing creation of a subjective reality which at once shapes, and is shaped by, the management strategies they employ to regulate awareness of their disability and claim or disown identities. This consideration of the subjective experience of stuttering supports Jack Katz's (1972) argument that deviance theory should recognize that people sometimes perceive deviance as an inner essence independent of behavior. In addition, our analysis extends rather than simply elaborates upon Goffman's work, for though he writes of "ego" or "felt" identity, which he defines as "the subjective sense of [the stigmatized person's] own situation" (1963:105), he does not develop this concept.

Second, we have shown that the management of potential stigma can involve strategies conceived of, and executed, on a moment-to-moment basis, in addition to the premeditated strategies that have attracted most sociologists' attention. Advance planning was usually necessary where

stutterers tried to conceal their problem through role avoidance. In speaking situations, management became more spontaneous: stutterers selected strategies in the light of opportunities and difficulties which arose in the course of interaction. In both cases, concealment strategies were marked by a high level of self-consciousness. When stutterers used openness or disavowal, however, only voluntary disclosure was consciously employed. Both struggling to overcome the "it" and time outs were non-calculated, though, especially in the latter case, stutterers were quick to recognize these tactics as coping and "restorative measures" (Goffman, 1963:128) once they were brought to their attention.

Finally, we have called attention to the fact that stutterers, like other stigmatized persons, seek to manage two interrelated, yet analytically distinguishable, problems. They are concerned both with preserving an acceptable identity and with preserving orderly interaction so that they can get on with the business of living. In exploring this issue we have shown how stutterers sometimes find themselves in situations in which it is not possible to simultaneously achieve both these objectives and thus are required to choose between them. The repertoire of tactics stutterers develop, and by implication the limits they place on their involvement in social life, depend on the importance they attach to these objectives.

NOTES

1. A good summary is provided in Bloodstein (1981:103). Some observers have reported an absence of stuttering among certain North American Midwest Indian tribes such as the Utes, the Shoshone, and the Bannock (Johnson, 1944a, 1944b; Snidecor, 1947). Other studies (Clifford, 1965; Lemert, 1967:135; Sapir, 1915; Stewart, 1959; Van Riper, 1946) have noted that this is by no means true for all North American Indian tribes. Both Lemert and Stewart found that tribes (particularly those on the Pacific Northwest coast of Canada) which encouraged competition and stricter child-rearing practices, and which placed more emphasis on self-control, reported

more instances of stuttering. Lemert (1967:146) also offered a similar explanation for a higher incidence of stuttering among Japanese than Polynesians.

2. See Goffman (1963:94) for a parallel between stutterers and the hard of hearing.

3. While fluency can be achieved and the sense of stuttering as an "it" can disappear, the continued maintenance of fluency is quite another matter. Time and again those who have achieved fluency—through whatever means—find themselves relapsing, even years later (Perkins, 1979; Sheehan, 1979, 1983).

REFERENCES

Becker, Howard S. 1963. *Outsiders: Studies in the Sociology of Deviance*. New York: The Free Press.

Bloodstein, Oliver. 1981. *A Handbook on Stuttering*. Chicago: National Easter Seal Society.

Blum, Alan and Peter McHugh. 1971. "The Social Ascription of Motives." *American Sociological Review*, 36 (February):98–109.

Campbell, Patrick. 1967. *My Life and Easy Times*. London: Anthony Blond.

Clifford, S. 1965. "Stuttering in South Dakota Indians." *Central States Speech Association Journal*, 26 (February):59–60.

Davis, Fred. 1961. "Deviance Disavowal: The Management of Strained Interaction by the Visibly Handicapped." *Social Problems*, 9 (Fall):120–132.

Douglass, Ernest and Bruce Quarrington. 1952. "Differentiation of Interiorized and Exteriorized Secondary Stuttering." *Journal of Speech and Hearing Disorders*, 17 (December):377–385.

Emerson, Joan. 1970. "Nothing Unusual Is Happening." In Thomas Shibutani (ed.), *Human Nature and Collective Behavior*. Englewood Cliffs, N.J.: Prentice-Hall, pp. 208–223.

Freidson, Eliot. 1965. "Disability as Social Deviance." In Marvin Sussman (ed.), *Sociology and Rehabilitation*. Washington, D.C.: American Sociological Association, pp. 71–99.

Goffman, Erving. 1963. *Stigma*. Englewood Cliffs, N.J.: Prentice-Hall.

———. 1967. *Interaction Ritual*. Garden City, N.Y.: Doubleday-Anchor.

Gustavson, Carl. 1944. "A Talisman and a Convalescence." *Quarterly Journal of Speech*, 30(1): 465–471.

Higgins, Paul C. 1980. "Social Reaction and the Physically Disabled: Bringing the Impairment Back In." *Symbolic Interaction*, 3 (Spring):139–156.

Himelfarb, Alex and John Evans. 1974. "Deviance Disavowal and Stigma Management: A Study of Obesity." In Jack Haas and Bill Shaffir (eds.), *Decency and Deviance*. Toronto: McClelland and Stewart, pp. 221–232.

Johnson, Wendell. 1944a. "The Indian Has No Word for It: Part 1, Stuttering in Children." *Quarterly Journal of Speech*, 30 (October):330–337.

———. 1944b. "The Indian Has No Word for It: Part 2, Stuttering in Adults." *Quarterly Journal of Speech*, 30 (December):456–465.

———. 1959. *The Onset of Stuttering*. Minneapolis: University of Minneapolis Press.

Katz, Jack. 1972. "Deviance, Charisma, and Rule-defined Behavior." *Social Problems*, 20(2):186–202.

Katz, Murray. 1968. "Stuttering Power." *Journal of the Council of Adult Stutterers* (January):5.

Kazin, Alfred. 1978. *New York Jew*. New York: Random House.

Kitsuse, John I. 1980. "Coming Out All Over: Deviants and the Politics of Social Problems." *Social Problems*, 28 (October):1–13.

Lambidakis, Elenore. 1972. "Stutterers' Lib." *Journal of the Council of Adult Stutterers* (Winter):4–6.

Lemert, Edwin. 1967. *Human Deviance, Social Problems and Social Control*. Englewood Cliffs, N.J.: Prentice-Hall.

Mills, C. Wright. 1940. "Situated Action and Vocabularies of Motives." *American Sociological Review*, 5 (December):904–913.

Mishima, Yukio. 1959. *The Temple of the Golden Pavilion*. New York: A. A. Knopf.

Perkins, William. 1979. "From Psychoanalysis to Discoordination." In Hugo Gregory (ed.), *Controversies About Stuttering Therapy*. Baltimore: University Park Press, pp. 97–129.

Petrunik, Michael. 1977. "The Quest for Fluency: A Study of the Identity Problems and Management Strategies of Adult Stutterers and Some Suggestions for an Approach to Deviance Management." Unpublished Ph.D. dissertation, University of Toronto.

———. 1982. "Telephone Troubles: Interactional Breakdown and Its Management by Stutterers and Their Listeners." *Symbolic Interaction*, 5 (Fall): 299–310.

————. 1983. "Being Deviant: A Critique of the Neglect of the Experiential Dimension in Sociological Constructions of Deviance." Paper presented at the annual meetings of the Society for the Study of Social Problems, Detroit, August.

Safilios-Rothschild, Constantina. 1970. *The Sociology and Social Psychology of Disability and Rehabilitation.* New York: Random House.

Sapir, Edward. 1915. *Abnormal Types of Speech in Nootka.* Canadian Geological Survey, Memoir 62, Anthropological Series No. 5. Ottawa: Government Printing Bureau.

Schneider, Joseph W. and Peter Conrad. 1980. "In the Closet with Illness: Epilepsy, Stigma Potential, and Information Control." *Social Problems,* 28 (October):32–44.

Scott, Marvin B. and Stanford Lyman. 1968. "Accounts." *American Sociological Review,* 33 (February): 44–62.

Sheehan, Joseph. 1979. "Current Issues on Stuttering Recovery." In Hugo Gregory (ed.), *Controversies About Stuttering Therapy.* Baltimore: University Park Press, pp. 175–209.

————. 1983. "Invitation to Relapse." *The Journal,* National Council on Stuttering (Summer):16–20.

Shenker, Israel. 1970. "Stammer Becomes Fashionable." *Globe and Mail* (Toronto), November 12:12.

Snidecor, John. 1947. "Why the Indian Does Not Stutter." *Quarterly Journal of Speech,* 33 (December):493–495.

Stewart, Joseph. 1959. "The Problem of Stuttering in Certain North American Societies." *Journal of Speech and Hearing Disorders* (Monograph Supplement 6):1–87.

Van Riper, Charles. 1946. "Speech Defects among the Kalabash." *Marquette County Historical Society,* 8 (December):308–322.

————. 1971. *The Nature of Stuttering.* Englewood Cliffs, N.J.: Prentice-Hall.

Webster, Ronald. 1975. *The Precision Fluency Shaping Program: Speech Reconstruction for Stutterers.* Roanoke, Virginia: Communication Development Corporation.

Stripteasers' Management of Their Deviant Identity

CAROL RAMBO RONAI and REBECCA CROSS

Striptease dancers, whether men or women, make their living in a deviant line of work. Since they perform frequently in public, they can expect questions to be raised about themselves and their deviant occupation.

Carol Rambo Ronai and Rebecca Cross interviewed 24 striptease dancers (10 men, 14 women) to see how they coped with the problem of a deviant identity. Since they could not deny that they did striptease dancing, their only line of defense was how they danced and how limited their involvement in the occupation was. They constructed a self-defense based upon a conception of fellow dancers. Dancing, like all lines of work, was found to have its own set of moral boundaries. The stripteasers pointed out that some dancers crossed such boundaries by, for example, flagrantly violating a code of public sexual expression or becoming totally immersed in their career as a dancer. They claimed some degree of self-respect by showing how much they differed from such "deviant" colleagues. Ronai and Cross also point out that although both men and women dancers distance themselves from these negative role models, the sexes construct their self-defenses with different social audiences in mind.

Alexis,[1] a 25-year-old striptease dancer who reported feelings of nonattractiveness during childhood and reported a rape during adolescence, is painfully aware that society considers her occupation to be "deviant" and that she is stigmatized accordingly:

> Society has the nerve to tell me to be a good girl, to shove their sexual ethics down my throat. What shit. What a crock. They hate me if I'm ugly and they blame me for what happens if I'm attractive. I'm a slut. Ugly and hated, a slut and hated. It looks to me as if they are going to think whatever they please, so I might as well not even listen to their rules. If they get their stories straight, they can give me a call. Otherwise, I'll do as I fucking please. I'll dance my ass off, rake in the money, and laugh all the way to the bank. Let them talk trash.

Alexis is aware that others are trying to constrain both her identity and her actions by supplying her with negative definitions of "self." She is also aware of the arbitrary, socially constructed character of the options being offered to her. The messages she receives about herself—ugly and hated versus attractive and hated—are contradictory terms and thus problematic as identity resources. No matter how Alexis presents herself, she perceives that she will be thought of negatively. As a consequence, both constructs lose credibility as legitimate concepts by which to define her "self."

However, even as she objects to being thought of as ugly or attractive, a good girl, or a slut, Alexis incorporates those concepts into her discourse as she practices identity. She defines her position in social space using these and other categories made available to her from the common

---

[1]All names and places have been changed to protect the identities of the respondents.

Reprinted from "Dancing with Identity: Narrative Resistance Strategies of Male and Female Stripteasers," *Deviant Behavior: An Interdisciplinary Journal*, Vol. 19 (1998), pp. 99–119, by permission of Taylor and Francis, Inc. Copyright © 1998 by Taylor and Francis, Inc.

stocks of knowledge (Berger & Luckmann 1966) about striptease dancers. Rather than passively accepting the negative identity labels, Alexis and other dancers become active participants in the construction of their personal and group identities by practicing narrative resistance and transforming negative labels into more positive terms.

In this article we use narrative materials from 24 life history interviews with striptease dancers as data to develop the concept of narrative resistance. We interview both men and women to avoid a possible gender bias, which we observed in some of the research on stripteasers. We do not focus on striptease dancing as a deviant activity. Instead, we explore how dancers themselves, both male and female, use the discourse of deviance to organize their identities through a process we call *narrative resistance.*

GENDER AND THE DEVIANCE ORIENTATION IN THE STRIPTEASE LITERATURE

The conventional literature on striptease dancing addresses the topic as a deviant activity. The research includes studies of lesbian behavior as an adaptation to the occupation (McCaghy & Skipper 1969), the career contingencies and anatomical measurements of strip-tease dancers (Skipper & McCaghy 1970, 1971), the emotional stability of stripteasers (Peretti & O'Connor 1989), and managing the stigma of a deviant occupation (Thompson & Harred 1992). Much of the literature has focused on the background factors that ostensibly cause striptease dancers' "deviant careers." Other works deal with dancers' deviant lifestyles and deviant self-conceptions (Boles & Garbin 1974; Carey, Petersen, & Sharpe 1974; Prus & Irini 1980; Salutin 1971). The literature's analytical orientations pathologize dancers' experiences.

Within this deviance orientation, the striptease research literature presents a possible gender bias—female dancers are often examined in the context of sexual deviance; male dancers in the context of work. For instance, male striptease articles have appeared in publications such as *Urban*

Life, Work and Occupations, Sociological Focus, and *Doing Women's Work: Men in Nontraditional Occupations* (Dressel & Petersen 1982a, 1982b; Petersen & Dressel 1982; Tewksbury 1994). Some female striptease articles have appeared in *Social Problems, Sociology of Sex, Sex Work,* and *Deviant Behavior* (Enck & Preston 1988; Mc-Caghy & Skipper 1969; Skipper & McCaghy 1970, 1971; Sundahl 1987; Thompson & Harred 1992). The tacit attitude informing where some researchers are submitting their work is that stripping is an unusual and curious occupation for men, and a deviant, sexualized, social problem for women.

By comparing the work of Skipper and Mc-Caghy to Petersen and Dressel, other possible biases emerge. We make this particular comparison because Petersen and Dressel acknowledge Charles McCaghy for commenting on earlier drafts of their work. Skipper and McCaghy, in their research, asked for and reported the anatomical measurements of their female striptease respondents, and they concluded that they tended to have large breasts. Dressel and Petersen did not report any similar anatomical information for the male respondents. Background variables such as ordinal position in the family, age at physical maturation, age at first coitus, age if and when their father left the home, and age when they left the home were reported for the female sample. Petersen and Dressel did not report similar information on the male sample. For female strippers, the tacit assumption was that stripping is a behavior *caused* by early life experiences; for male strippers, the orientation to the occupation was not pathologized, so there was no need to consider background variables.

These differences reflect a larger trend in deviance research that has been discussed by feminist scholars. According to Chaftez and Dworkin (1986, p. 3),

> *Male delinquents are overwhelmingly guilty of acts that are criminally illegal regardless of the perpetrator's age. Crimes against property and persons characterize their behavior. Girls, however, are most often adjudicated delinquent on the basis of status offenses specific to being minors. Such girls are defined as "ungovernable," which typically means they are sexually active.…In short, it means girls are rebelling against the feminine role requirements of docility, obedience, and chastity.…Boys are rarely penalized for sexual misconduct by itself.*

Marcia Millman (1975, p. 251) determined that "sociological stereotypes of deviance closely resemble those that appear in popular culture," and documented a consistent pattern within the deviance literature where male "deviants" were cast in positive terms whereas female "deviants" were cast negatively.

As an alternative, Gale Miller (1978, p. 243) posited that "research should not seek to distinguish deviant workers from others." Instead, their activities should be treated as an occupational category. By orienting to "deviance" as an accomplished status (rather than a preexisting one), Miller implied that deviance is a social construct rather than something inherent to an activity such as striptease dancing.

Another way to re-think Miller's thesis is to use a theoretical orientation atypical of deviance research. Here, we use biographical work (Gubrium, Holstein, & Buckholdt 1994), a perspective which originated in aging research. Cast in this light, striptease dancing is a context through which a subject is asked to narrate a biography. By focusing attention on what dancers have to say about themselves, we learn which issues are relevant to their lives and, in particular, their conceptions of their identities. Within this context, deviance, as a category of identity, emerges as a narrative resource for accomplishing biographical work. By treating deviance as a reality socially constructed through language instead of a status intrinsic to striptease dancers, and by interviewing both male and female striptease dancers within the context of the same study, we have attempted to reduce gender bias in our study of stripteasers.

SAMPLE AND PROCEDURE

In this work, we analyze the life narratives of 14 female and 10 male striptease dancers to develop a critical understanding of deviance as a component of biographical activity. Carol Rambo Ronai developed an interest in the biographical work of exotic dancers while reflecting on data gathered in an ongoing field study of striptease artists (1992a, 1992b, 1994, 1997; Ronai & Ellis, 1989). Rabecca Cross, as Carol's graduate assistant, helped to code the data Carol had gathered, and she developed a parallel interest in biographical work. Together, they analyzed the dancers' narratives noting the framing devices each used in their life history narratives.

In total, 10 men and 14 women, all stripteasers in the southeastern United States, participated in tape-recorded "life history" interviews. Eighteen of the dancers were White, three were African American, two were Hispanic, and one was Asian. Each of the 24 dancers in the sample had participated in one or more types of striptease: revues, strip-o-grams, topless/table dancing, and nude dancing.

A revue is a traveling striptease show, consisting of either all women, all men, or both women and men. The shows begin with each dancer performing an individual striptease routine, and they conclude with all the dancers participating in a choreographed dance performance. Some shows feature activities such as Jell-O® wrestling or boxing. Female traveling revue dancers usually strip down to a string bikini, occasionally appearing topless for extra money. In any form of striptease, the men strip down to a T-back strap that conceals the genitalia and exposes the buttocks. Dancers often find revues more exciting than other forms of striptease and enjoy receiving a flat rate-plus-tips as payment. However, revue dancers often complain of receiving lower tips than topless/table dancers or nude dancers.

Strip-o-grams are usually performed at a birthday party or other celebration. The person who "sends" the strip-o-gram selects a dancer from a photo album. The dancer appears at a designated time and place to perform a striptease dance for the recipient. Male strip-o-gram dancers often appear as a character such as a delivery person, a police officer, or a lost motorist. The female strip-o-gram dancer often arrives wearing a revealing outfit and strips down to a string bikini or lingerie. The stripteaser dances very close to the strip-o-gram recipient, and physical contact, such as caressing or kissing, may occur. The pros and cons of strip-o-grams are similar to those of traveling revues, with the added disadvantage of the danger inherent in entertaining in private homes. Dancers use a variety of methods to ensure their safety: they call management when they arrive at and leave a site, have a friend wait in the car outside while performing, or have a friend attend the performance with them.

Topless and nude dancing takes place in strip bars designed for the activity. In topless bars, where alcohol is served, dancers wear pasties and a T-back strap. Customers make physical contact with the dancer during a routine called a "table dance," although ordinances vary on how much contact is allowed. In settings where dancers are totally nude and no alcohol is served, customers are not permitted to touch dancers except to tip them on stage. If the customer is interested in more, dancers can conduct dances for them behind private Plexiglas® booths.

The advantages and disadvantages of topless and nude dancing vary considerably from those of revues and strip-o-grams. For example, most topless and nude dancers rely solely on tips. Strip clubs are thought to be more boring than other forms of striptease, because dancers have a set schedule. However, the club setting is the safest place to work because there are bouncers to look out for the dancers' safety. Nevertheless, it is easy for anyone who wants to harm a dancer to follow the dancer home.

Knowledge of the different occupational forms furthers our understanding of how deviance is constructed by exotic dancers. Dancers who engage in one form of striptease often regard group members who engage in other forms as deviant. The form of the occupation serves as an important way to organize the discourses that dancers use to narratively resist deviance attributions.

NARRATIVE RESISTANCE AS BIOGRAPHICAL WORK, DIALECTICS, AND MAPPING

When an interviewer asks a subject to narrate a biography, the subject and the interviewer jointly negotiate the subject's identity. The subject relies on at-hand categories and typifications to retrospectively construct the "life." Subjects seek to "frame and organize one's character and actions, selecting and highlighting the defining aspects of one's past" (Gubrium, Holstein, & Buckholdt 1994, p. 157). These verbal management techniques are "biographical work."

Jaber Gubrium, James Holstein, and David Buckholdt (1994, p. 156) define biographical work as the "ongoing effort to integrate accounts of a person's life," which the authors argue is "continually subject to reinterpretation because it is always the biography-at-hand." Narrated biography is a stationary process rather than a static product. The elements of biography change because of time passage and the context of the social situation in which the account is told. For Gubrium et al. (1994, p. 155), "Much of the work of assembling a life story is the management of consistency and continuity, assuring that the past reasonably leads up to the present to form a lifeline." Biographical work is an activity in which a subject attempts to "make sense" of his or her life experiences.

In this project, we use the discourse of exotic dancers to highlight one form of biographical work: narrative resistance. "Others have the ability to threaten our opinion of ourselves by suggesting negative categories to define ourselves by" (Ronai 1997, p. 125). This threat is experienced as "discursive constraint" (Ronai 1997, 1994) by the individual. For instance, a child who is being sexually abused may be told that she is a slut and if

she speaks about the abuse, others will know the "truth" about her. This form of discursive constraint simultaneously controls the child's behavior (stay silent so others won't know) and her narrated biography as she tells it to herself (I am a slut and that is why this is happening to me), thus setting her up for future abuses. If she does not have an alternative stock of knowledge which enables her to resist this definition of self, she may incorporate the negative label into her identity.

Narrative resistance is a response to discursive constraint which dialectically emerges from and constitutes an alternative stock of knowledge within a stigmatized group. Narrative resistance is an active speech behavior which serves to decenter the authority of specific individuals or society to dictate identity. The narrative resistance strategies presented here are forms of biographical work which cast self in frameworks which make use of the language of deviance, but reshape it in such a way as to resist taking on the negative identity for oneself. In reshaping the resources that the mainstream stocks of knowledge offer a stigmatized group, the group in question is remapping both their individual identities and their collective place in the terrain of social space.

Each time an individual narratively resists discursive constraint and another group member incorporates that particular strategy into their own stock of knowledge, that strategy eventually emerges as a part of the local or alternative stock of knowledge. These alternative stocks of knowledge, intersubjectively shared by the community, in turn, serve to positively alter the mainstream stocks of knowledge regarding the group in question. For instance, many of the dancers interviewed expressed that they were either supporting themselves through school or supporting a child. One has only to listen to television or radio talk shows on the topic of striptease to hear non-strippers reproducing these discourses.

"Well at least Allen is in school," [and] "Midnight does it to support her children" are remarks that represent a small shift in the public's perception of striptease. These discourses still make use of the language of deviance—"If someone strips for a living and she or he is not in school or supporting children, then she or he is doing something wrong." Now, however, instead of viewing striptease as always wrong in all contexts, there are occasionally fields in the common stocks of knowledge where stripping is understandable or even acceptable. This mainstream discourse, in turn, intersubjectively circulates back to striptease dancers as a resource for their use in future instances when they are called to narrate accounts of self.

NARRATIVE RESISTANCE STRATEGIES

This article focuses on a form of narrative resistance that uses images of deviance as negative exemplars—standards of comparison—to avoid negative identity assignations. The dancers in this study made use of a wide variety of narrative resources while constructing their biographies for our life history interviews, many more than we could discuss in a single article. Therefore, we limit our analysis of identity construction and narrative resistance to two particular strategies where images of deviance are used as exemplars: sleaze and immersion.

CONSTRUCTING DEVIANCE EXEMPLARS

Exemplars, as defined by Gubrium and Lynott (1985, p. 353), are "products of the collective work of representing experiences…recognizable means of sharing particular collective representations." For striptease dancers, the collective representations of their experiences are deviant images. Dancers construct deviance exemplars which delimit identity by serving as a narrative "straw man" or "straw woman" by which to compare oneself. A dancer practices biographical work to define herself or himself as an exception to the average striptease dancer. Her or his identity emerges narratively by resisting the deviant role that the exemplar represents. By engaging in this pattern of discourse, a dancer defines the deviance

frame as acceptable for some people, but not for herself or himself. Dancers, both male and female, triangulate their "selves" relative to the selves of other dancers, thus mapping identity claims in social space as they narrate their biographies. Through this process of comparison, they map their own position in the social world relative to other dancers.

Garcia, a 26-year-old strip-o-gram dancer, uses a deviance exemplar to describe another dancer whom he did not respect:

> I know a guy who is fool enough, he got accepted to medical school, because his father wanted him to be a doctor, but while he was doing his undergrad, he started stripping. He got accepted, and I think he did like three semesters of medicine school, and he went back to stripping and that is what he is doing now. So, like, to me, that is a pity. He could have done a lot of good to a lot of people, being a doctor. Now, he is a stripper, what good does he do? I don't see it as a job, but a way to get money. I think it should be the means to an end, not the ends to a mean.

Garcia constructs an exemplar, a model of someone who is treating the occupation of stripping as a permanent job. He defines himself conversely by stating that, for him, exotic dancing is only a "way to get money."

Nina, a 22-year-old revue and strip-o-gram dancer, gossips about a rival troupe, "In the Raw":

> Everyone knows about them. We know what's up. How do I say this? [giggles]. They's hos [euphemism for "They are whores"]. Say, "Hey ho" and those bitches'll turn around and answer you, "What?" [giggles]. Our group can't make the money they do because we don't **fuck** [her emphasis as she laughs out right] everyone we dance for. We may not make the money they do, but we aren't total sluts either.

Nina constructs "In the Raw" as the comparison group or exemplar by describing them, and then designates her troupe as superior because they do not engage in the same behavior. This time an entire group is set up as the triangulation coordinate by which to map and narratively resist a deviant identity.

Jessica, who is 25 years old, White, a senior in college and a revue dancer, displays a native awareness of how deviance exemplars are constructed and used:

> Other girls spend a lot of time talking about who they aren't by talking about someone else. I'm sure you got a lot of dancers to talk to you and I'm sure you got them talkin' trash. It's bad for the industry. You won't get trash from me. I'm one of the people that don't fall into the category of the misconception that dancers come from bad homes or are doing it out of some sort of sexual need or things like that. But that's the public talking. I don't see dancers as bad. And I don't need to bad-mouth to tell you who I am. Dancers are so catty, back stabbing, always talking 'bout other dancers. I hate it.

Jessica engages in some of the identity management practices for which she chastises other dancers. She constructs an exemplar and narratively distances herself from its deviant status. She tells us what "other girls" are like, she tells us gossip is harmful, and she distances herself from them by telling us what she is like. Jessica's typification of "other girls" was common. Most of the dancers interviewed joked that they talked behind each other's backs, wanted to know what others had said about them, and told us gossip about other dancers.

As deviance exemplars are constructed and narratively distance the self from deviance, they are used with the understanding that some dancers match the negative characteristics defined by the exemplar. Constructing deviance exemplars locates subjects on an emergent, multi-dimensional, non-cartesian map of identity. Male dancers use some of the same exemplars as female dancers use, as both groups are subject to discursive constraints and a negative identity. Exotic dancers create identity maps from the narratively shared knowledge of exotic dancing, and restructure that knowledge by avoiding locating their own identities at deviant map coordinates. Dancers locate themselves in social space by specifying, among other things, sleaze and immersion as exemplars.

THE SLEAZE EXEMPLAR

Dancers engage in biography work, specifically narrative resistance, by locating themselves relative to "sleaze." Sleaze is a deviance exemplar that serves to constitute a form of narrative resistance which helps map a dancer's claim to a location in social space. The type of exotic dancing a strip-teaser engages in can determine how she or he constructs her or his identity relative to sleaze. Most revue dancers remarked on how sleazy they think nude dancers are, which serves to narratively resist deviance by portraying themselves as less deviant in comparison. Garcia specifies this dimension of identity in his text:

> If you go all the way naked, which I never do, there is only so much you can do, offer to them. And from an exotic, appealing, sexy dancer, you become something that they are just looking at. What is this guy going to do now? Unless you can pull rabbits out of a hat or something—overkill.

Nina, a White revue dancer, also states, "I'll never go nude. I just can't." Garcia and Nina both believe they are less sleazy than other dancers because they don't undress completely.

Connor, a 19-year-old, White, female, nude dancer, expresses similar sentiments when sharing with us her experiences from when she first started stripping and was trying to figure out how she was supposed to dance in the private booths. She concludes, "When I first started working there, I sat there for ten minutes and watched the guys. And you see everything. And me, I never show everything." Even though Connor is a nude dancer, she specifies sleaze as an exemplar in a manner similar to revue and table dancers. She sets up nude dancers as the deviance exemplar and narratively resists the deviant identity by explaining that she is not like the typical nude dancer who exposes it all.

By specifying physical contact with customers as closer to sleaze relative to nudity, nude dancers use this exemplar differently from revue and table dancers. They assert that nude dancing is superior to topless or revue dancing because they are not touched by the audience except to receive tips. For example Madeline, a 20-year-old nude dancer, stated the following: "I would only work in a place where there is no contact involved." Ashley, a 36-year-old nude dancer, parrots Madeline when she says, "I feel like if they will pay me to look at me naked, they can't touch me, they can't screw me, I am safe."

Sometimes narrative resistance is practiced by establishing another dancer's behavior as an exemplar by locating it as sleazy and placing one's own conduct in opposition to that behavior. Stephanie, a 21-year-old nude dancer, illustrates this as she describes what goes on in a private dance booth:

> I have known some girls like that. They will bring vaseline, and jelly, but the extent of bringing things in there, sometimes I will bring ice in there. They are supposed to be simulating masturbation, and I don't do that.

Stephanie narratively constructs public masturbation as sleazy in order to narratively resist assigning to herself the deviance she attributes to the women who simulate masturbation. Her claims about her own behavior distance her from sleaze.

Madeline, a nude dancer, relayed a similar story:

> One girl asked me to do a dance with her in the private dance booth. And whenever you walk by the booth and she's doing a dance in there, you always hear a vibrator going off. That is so sleazy. I could not do that in front of somebody.

By disapproving of the girl who uses a vibrator, and claiming to be unable to use them in front of people herself, Madeline narratively resists what she considers to be "so sleazy" and distances herself from it. To make her point more explicit, Madeline went on to discuss a situation, which took place earlier in the evening before our interview:

> I don't know if you noticed it, but tonight there was a lot of tension because there was one girl that was out on stage and I couldn't believe it, and every girl I talked to was like, their faces just dropped. She grabbed the bars and flung her head down until it was almost on the floor exposing "the pink."

The phrase "the pink" refers to the labia and/or clitoris. Exposing the pink by lifting one's leg, spreading one's legs, or bending over is illegal and is considered by the dancers to be desperate and a way of "upping the ante." It one dancer does it, the customers will expect the other dancers to do it, or they won't tip. Furthermore, according to Madeline, "A girl like that gives all dancers a bad name." Not only does Madeline narratively distance herself from sleaze, but she also demonstrates an awareness of the implications of this dancer's behavior for the collective identity of dancers and distances the occupation from her also.

Hudson, a 23-year-old, White, male, revue dancer, uses a technique similar to Stephanie's and Madeline's when he talks about raunchy stage behavior: "Like a fake sixty-nine. I wouldn't do that on stage, but I have seen people do that." Hudson attributes a label of deviance to male dancers who perform acts such as a fake sixty-nine (pretending to engage in mutual oral sex), and then narratively resists the deviant label by stating that he could not behave that way.

Sleaze is also specified through the vocabularies of gender and race. It is taken to be common knowledge among female dancers that male dancers are sleazier. Kitty comments, "Guys get away with murder on stage. A woman would never do that stuff, wouldn't want to." Many other female dancers echo this sentiment. Only one of the 10 males interviewed, Ron, hints that he thinks women can be "sleazier" than men. He states, "Some women can be even more sleazier on stage than the most sleaziest man, but not usually."

The rest of the men are somewhat defensive about sleaze as they apply it to their own gender's participation in the occupation. Often, the sleaze exemplar is specified by male dancers in such a way as to distance themselves from the "sleaze" they believe typically applies to men in their field. Hollywood, for instance, talks about how he finds erections on stage to be objectionable:

> *Yeah, there was one guy that I danced with, he always got a hard-on while he was out there. But it was gross. ....I guess some girls would like it, but I guess most girls, the majority, thought it was disgusting.*

Likewise Hudson reported the following:

> *I wouldn't want to have an erection when I was dancing.... I think the girls would get turned off by that...a lot of them really grab for that area when you are up dancing close and stuff like that when you are up close to them, but I don't know if they would like it that far.*

Race, as a vocabulary, appears to intersect gender as a way to do biographical identity work and narratively resist the sleaze exemplar. It is taken to be common knowledge among Whites that African American male dancers are sleazier than all other dancers. The two African American male subjects did not speak of race in any manner when specifying the sleaze exemplar. When Rachel, a White female dancer, hears that Carol will interview a Black male revue dancer named Kareem, she feels obligated to issue this warning:

> *You gotta watch out for him. I don't think he will try anything, but he might. He likes blondes so, it ain't no big deal, just watch out for him. If you saw this guy on stage, actually all the Black guys are like this, they are so N-A-S-T-Y [spelled out]. Nasty. I know it sounds racist, but it's true.*

Ron makes a similar remark regarding Kareem as he discusses himself:

> *You need to come see me dance. When I do it, I do it for the ladies. I don't put it [his groin region] in their face. No chick likes that crap. And if they do, I ain't interested in spending too much time with them anyway. Now Kareem, he'll put it right up in their face. I watch their faces when he does that. I'm a professional and I say they don't like it. All the Black guys do that shit.*

Ron sets up Kareem and "Black guys" as the sleaze exemplar. He is White so he can distance himself from the sleaze attributed to male strippers by specifying his race. Ron elaborates on the intersection of the vocabularies of gender, race, and sleaze at another point in his interview. He remarked on three practices: "tying off" (tying something around the base of the penis after stimulating it to produce a tourniquet effect), "stuffing" (placing something in the groin region to produce the appearance of an erection), and injections (injecting a vasodilator into the penis to increase the blood flow and consequently the size). He explained: "Usually it's the Black guys doing it. No one needs a hard-on to dance. I get embarrassed when I spring one, and wait for it to go down if I can." Hollywood, as noted earlier, is similarly uncomfortable with men having erections on stage and stated, "I would never stick no needle in my dick." These practices, particularly the injections, are discussed in very hushed and conspiratorial tones. When Hudson is asked if he knows anyone who does things to enhance the appearance of their penises on stage, he commented, "Whites will sometimes tie off or stuff, but it's the Black guys that get radical. They inject. They have a reputation for having a big one to maintain."

No dancer specifies African American or Hispanic females as sleazy. The first author has heard White customers classify both racial groups as sleazier than Whites, however. Twice, male Hispanics were classified as sleazier or more vulgar, on average, than other dancers. Ron, when he learns Carol is to interview Garcia, commented the following:

> *He's a Spic, Cuban or something. Don't do his alone. No, do it alone, and if he tries anything with you call me, I'll set him straight, I'll kick his ass. In fact tell him at the start of the interview that I said I'd kick his ass if he tried anything. Then you'll be safe....*

Almost a page of transcription material covered this topic. The first author's subsequent experiences with both Kareem and Garcia were very positive. While Kareem was mildly flirtatious during his interview, like a couple of the White male dancers and one of the White female dancers, the first author always felt safe. Garcia was a graduate student living in campus married student housing with his wife and child. In both instances, the interviewer found nothing untoward in their conduct.

Sleaze, as an exemplar, forms one dimension of a working identity map where subjects may locate themselves based on who they are and the stocks of knowledge they have access to. By demarcating an identity for themselves relative to the sleaze exemplar, dancers do not reject the deviant stigma others apply to the occupation of striptease dancing as a whole. Indeed, both male and female dancers reinforce it by using it to narratively resist where they stand in relation to it. By practicing narrative resistance, however, dancers actively produce and reproduce an alternate stock of knowledge as an identity resource for themselves as individuals or as a group to draw upon. By exchanging this talk in backstage settings and reproducing it in an interview, dancers are jointly practicing identity as a form of resistance to mainstream society's definition of them—in this case, as sleazy. Sleaze, however, is not the only exemplar that dancers specify when mapping their identities.

THE IMMERSION EXEMPLAR

Another exemplar dancers appeal to when doing biography work involves describing the degree to which a dancer is immersed in the occupation. Total immersion in the occupation is viewed negatively (no dancer claimed to be totally immersed), so dancers narratively resist constructing identities for themselves which would define them as "too far into it." While they do not draw on medical frames like "rehabilitation" or "recovery," they do appeal to a vocabulary of getting "hooked" or "addicted" to the occupation, the money, or the excitement, as a way to specify immersion. Part-time dancers are more likely than full-time dancers to refer to this exemplar in their narratives.

Jarrod, a 28-year-old, Black, male striptease dancer who has danced on and off for 9 years, uses the vocabulary of addiction:

I could stop anytime, I could just get out of it at anytime, stop. I hope I don't sound like a dance-aholic, but...I'm not at the point of dancing that I have to do it. I don't depend on it for anything.

Helena also uses this vocabulary:

I'm fortunate that I turned out okay, because people, some people that I hung around with and the way my life was, you know, I'm surprised I'm not into drugs. I mean when I danced at Chèz Manique or Cat's, you get hooked on the money and you get hooked to the fun, and I really didn't get hooked and get pulled in.

When asked specifically why she did not get "pulled in," Helena answered the following:

I think I had more respect for myself and I think I had more, I cared more about things, about what happened in my life than a lot of them.

Helena used others that she "hung around with" as exemplars of who was too immersed in the occupation. She claimed they were "pulled in" while she was not. Describing how she respects herself, and how she cares about what happens to her, we can see her narratively anchoring herself on the identity map in such a way as to prevent her from seeing herself as "pulled in."

Others use this anchoring strategy more overtly to resist the exemplar of immersion. Rachel, a 25-year-old, uses her college and work experience as anchors which prevent her from being immersed too far. She distances herself from this exemplar by stating, "This isn't my life, that this is all I can do. I have my degrees, I'm managing the store now, I'm going to stay in retail. Once I leave [Townsville], I'm not going to do this anymore." Rachel speaks of her dancing as a temporary activity, thereby distancing herself from the total immersion that would be implied if it were a permanent career.

Jessica uses the immersion exemplar somewhat differently from Rachel:

I am going to stay in college, I will get a degree, and I will seek employment in another field, but I think having the ability to do this, it's something that is there in case, something to fall back on, and that makes me feel secure knowing I have that.

Jessica distances herself from the immersion exemplar when she claims that dancing is "something to fall back on," again offering the temporary nature of the activity to herself and us as evidence that she is not too immersed.

Claiming an intense personal relationship may also serve as a way to narratively resist immersion. Hollywood, a 36-year-old, White, male, revue and strip-o-gram dancer states, "My dad is real close, helps me keeps my head screwed on straight so I don't get into it any more like some of them do." Kitty, a White, female, revue and strip-o-gram dancer who claims to be 25 years old (others disputed this, claiming she was 27 or 28), similarly states, "We argue sometimes, we drive each other nuts, but my mom supports me, and she keeps me straight, so I don't get into any real trouble." Neither dancer claims to have activities which compete for their time and attention, but rather they claim a deep bond which serves to firmly anchor the self in such a way as to prevent total immersion.

Other exemplars presented themselves as resources for biographical work and narrative resistance such as attractiveness (who is too old, overweight, underweight, awkward, or ugly to dance), naturalness (how much does one depend on cosmetic treatments such as breast, pectoral, calf, or other implants, liposuction, hair coloring, and so forth), appropriate attitude (is the person in question too arrogant, vain, or conceited), as well as twenty other categories we noted. By using all of these themes, dancers are able to triangulate and map an identity for themselves through a very treacherous terrain which makes available less than perfect resources for accomplishing biographical work. Bit by bit, over time, through narrative resistance, alternative stocks of knowledge on the identity of dancers emerge, offering a small ray of hope that identity is a contextual matter

rather than a stagnant caricature which blankets all stripteasers regardless of their situations.

GENDER IN THE BIOGRAPHICAL WORK OF STRIPTEASERS

Our research reconstructs the academic stocks of knowledge on striptease dancers by applying the biographical work frame to their life histories. Instead of assuming a problem/pathology stance towards the occupation for women, but not men, the method of biography allows us to listen to both genders talk about themselves. By examining men and women within the same study, we found that men are subjected to discursive constraint and suffer from the consequences of a negative identity, similar to women.

Gender turned out to be a useful, if complex, consideration in biographical work. Both men and women narratively resisted discursive constraint, and specified the sleaze and immersion exemplars. However, men and women have access to different gendered tales of self which leads them to fashion different gendered versions of the deviance exemplars. The differences are subtle. For instance, the males are not as concerned as the females with seeming to be like prostitutes. The male dancers talk about not wanting to appear to be vulgar, raunchy, or sleazy to their female customers. The female dancers are more concerned with how other dancers perceive them. The female dancers are concerned about appearing too sleazy to the male customers only in contexts where it affects what the customers expect of other dancers, such as in the situation of "exposing the pink."

Other materials indicate that it is considered inappropriate for a man to focus too much attention on his appearance; to do so seems vain and thus feminine. Yet physical fitness, workout regimens, and pressure to "keep up with their looks" are all stressed more heavily in their life history interviews than in the female dancers' interviews.

Gender is also used as a biographical resource, a category on which dancers draw to construct deviance exemplars. Both female and male dancers in this study specify men as sleazier dancers than women, an idea which reflects mainstream conceptions about male and female sexuality in general. White males narratively resist some of the sleaze attributed to their gender by employing race as a biographical resource, another idea which reflects mainstream conceptions, this time in reference to African American male sexuality. The language of gender and race then, like the language of deviance, is used as a framing device which serves to map the identities of the striptease dancers in this study. By specifying sleaze, immersion, gender, and race as a few dimensions of identity, dancers are able to use the language of deviance to position themselves and anyone like themselves in a more advantageous place in social space.

NARRATIVE RESISTANCE AND BIOGRAPHICAL WORK

This article contributes to the social constructionist literature on deviance and deviant identities and implements a new theoretical framework (biographical work) within this tradition. By focusing on both males and females, this text has sought to remove certain stereotypes which may have operated in research in this area in the past. The theory of biographical work, applied specifically to alleviate a possible gender and deviance bias in the stripteaser literature, illuminated a specific pattern in the discourses of our subjects. These patterns, in turn, enabled us to develop the concepts of narrative resistance and deviance exemplars, thus expanding the applicability of biography work as a theory.

The use of narrative resistance, in particular deviance exemplars, is not restricted to stripteasers nor any group of people who engage in what might be considered "deviant behavior." Narrative resistance is a cultural universal. Everyone in their self talk sets up other individuals and/or groups as examples by which to compare themselves and triangulate identity. If one is a mother who works outside the home, she might say, "I wish I didn't have to work, but at least I make time for my kids, unlike Sally and Sue" or "I may not be the best father but at least I bring home my paycheck and check my kids' homework, unlike Bill and Steve."

By recognizing the generalizability of this strategy, then we come full circle to realize that both male and female striptease dancers, like everyone else, are engaged in the work of trying to make sense of their identities. The working mother is told she should be at home; the father is told he should do more for his kids; the striptease dancer is told stripping is wrong. All of these forms of discursive constraint are attempts at domination and control, either as an effort to constrain how a person chooses to self-identify or as an effort to change her or his behavior (become an at-home-mom, better dad, or stop dancing, and we won't label you). None of these subjects is forced to passively internalize a negative identity. To do so would create a problematic identity. By formulating and consulting an alternative stock of knowledge, subjects develop the resources to resist. The working mother talks with other mothers and taps into the story that as long as you make time for your children, you are still being a good mother. As more and more mothers work, these discourses circulate until finally being a working mother is not considered a problem by anyone anymore, unless you don't spend time with your children. Likewise with the father, the stripteaser, and everyone else. Through the process of biography work and narrative resistance we become the authors of our identities, charting for ourselves a place in social space which transforms negative discourses into more positive identity resources for ourselves and others to draw upon in the future.

REFERENCES

Berger, Peter, & Thomas Luckmann. 1966. *The Social Construction of Reality.* Garden City, NY: Doubleday.

Boles, Jacqueline, & Albeno P. Garbin. 1974. "The Strip Club and Stripper-Customer Patterns of Interaction." *Sociology and Social Research* 58:136–144.

Carey, Sandra H., Robert A. Petersen, & Louise K. Sharpe. 1974. "A Study of Recruitment and Socialization in Two Deviant Female Occupations." *Sociological Symposium* 11:11–24.

Chaftez, Janet S., & Anthony G. Dworkin. 1986. *Female Revolt: Women's Movements in World and Historical Perspective.* New York: Rowman & Allanheld.

Dressel, Paula L., & David M. Petersen. 1982a. "Gender Roles, Sexuality, and the Male Strip Show: The Structuring of Sexual Opportunity." *Sociological Focus* 15:151–162.

———. 1982b. "Becoming a Male Stripper: Recruitment, Socialization, and Ideological Development." *Work and Occupations* 15:151–162.

Enck, Graves E., & James D. Preston. 1988. "Counterfeit Intimacy: A Dramaturgical Analysis of an Erotic Performance." *Deviant Behavior* 9:369–381.

Glaser, Barney G., & Anselm L. Strauss. 1967. *The Discovery of Grounded Theory: Strategies for Qualitative Research.* Chicago: Aldine Publishing.

Gubrium, Jaber, James Holstein, & David R. Buckholdt. 1994. *Constructing the Lifecourse.* Dix Hills, NY: General Hall.

Gubrium, Jaber, & Robert Lynott. 1985. "Alzheimer's Disease as Biographical Work." Pp. 349–369 in *Social Bonds in Later Life,* edited by W. Peterson & J. Quadagno. Newbury Park, CA: Sage.

McCaghy, Charles H., & James K. Skipper. 1969. "Lesbian Behavior as an Adaptation to the Occupation of Stripping." *Social Problems* 17:262–270.

Miller, Gale. 1978. *Odd Jobs: The World of Deviant Work.* Englewood Cliffs, NJ: Prentice Hall.

Millman, Marcia. 1975. "She Did It All for Love: A Feminist View of the Sociology of Deviance." In *Another Voice: Feminist Perspectives on Social Life and Social Sciences,* edited by M. Millman & R. M. Kanter. New York: Anchor Books.

Peretti, Peter O., & Patrick O'Connor. 1989. "Effects of Incongruence Between the Perceived Self and the Ideal Self on Emotional Stability of Stripteasers." *Social Behavior and Personality* 17:81–92.

Petersen, David M., & Paula L. Dressel. 1982. "Equal Time for Women: Social Notes on the Male Strip Show." *Urban Life* 11:185–208.

Prus, Robert, & Styllianoss Irini. 1980. *Hookers, Rounders, and Desk Clerks.* Salem, WI: Sheffield Publishing Company.

Ronai, Carol R. 1997. "Discursive Constraint in the Narrated Identities of Childhood Sex Abuse Survivors." Pp. 123–136 in *Everyday Sexism in the Third Millennium,* edited by C. R. Ronai, B. Zsembik, and J. Feagin. New York: Routledge.

———. 1994. "Narrative Resistance to Deviance: Identity Management Among Strip-Tease Dancers. Pp. 195–213 in *Perspectives on Social Problems, Vol. 6,* edited by J. A. Holstein & G. Miller. Greenwich, CT: JAI Press.

———. 1992a. "Managing Aging in Young Adulthood: The Aging Table Dancer." *Journal of Aging Studies* 6:307–317.

———. 1992b. "The Reflexive Self Through Narrative: A Night in the Life of an Erotic Dancer/Researcher." Pp. 102–124 in *Investigating Subjectivity: Research on Lived Experience,* edited by C. Ellis & M. G. Flaherty. Newbury Park, CA: Sage.

Ronai, Carol R., & Carolyn Ellis. 1989. "Turn-Ons for Money: Interactional Strategies of the Table Dancer." *Journal of Contemporary Ethnography* 18:271–298.

Salutin, Marilyn. 1971. "Stripper Morality." *Transaction* 8:12–22.

Skipper, James K., & Charles H. McCaghy. 1970. "Stripteasers: The Anatomy and Career Contingencies of a Deviant Occupation." *Social Problems* 17:391–405.

———. 1971. "Stripteasing: A Sex Oriented Occupation." Pp. 275–296 in *The Sociology of Sex,* edited by J. Henslin. New York: Appleton Century Crofts.

Sundahl, Debi. 1987 "Stripper." Pp. 175–180 in *Sex Work: Writings by Women in the Sex Industry,* edited by F. Delacoste & P. Alexander. Pittsburgh, PA: Cleis Press.

Tewksbury, Richard. 1994. "Male Strippers: Men Objectifying Men." Pp. 168–181 in *Doing Women's Work: Men In Nontraditional Occupations,* edited by C. Williams. Newbury Park, CA: Sage.

Thompson, William E., & Jackie L. Harred. 1992. "Topless Dancers: Managing Stigma in a Deviant Occupation." *Deviant Behavior* 13:291–311.

Priests and Pedophilia

JAMES G. THOMSON, JOSEPH A. MAROLLA, and DAVID G. BROMLEY

People who violate the expectations of everyday life may have to answer for their misconduct. When deviant social acts are committed by a member of a formal organization, answers are required from both the person and his or her organization. The social status of the accused, the social definition of the actions, the degree of moral indignation those actions have aroused, and the prestige of the organization involved all bear heavily on the responses to an accusation.

James G. Thomson, Joseph A. Marolla, and David G. Bromley examine what happens when Catholic priests, persons of high moral rank, have been found to have engaged in "immoral" conduct. The stories priests tell about sex with young boys vary with the audience they address as well as with whether they offer these accounts before or after the fact. Before having sex with young boys, they make every effort to induce consent. After the fact, when talking with their superiors, they disclaim causing any harm. The power of their position relative to their young partners increases the appearance of mutual consent. And because accusations of pedophilia call into question the moral character of the church itself, the church claims either that it cannot screen every priest for personality disorders or that some priests have lost control over some very powerful impulses. The church also attempts to defend its moral reputation by attacking the accusers, by transferring the accused, and by controlling information about alleged immoral sexual acts between priests and young boys.

The priest abuse scandal in the Roman Catholic Church in the United States began to surface in 1983. Over the last decade the scandal has broadened, with a seemingly endless string of pedophilia cases involving scores of young children discovered and disclosed. In a number of instances priests have been criminally prosecuted and sentenced to long prison terms; others have been remanded for mental health treatment. Although sexual violations of various kinds have occurred across a number of religious groups (e.g., Jacobs 1989; Shupe 1995), what distinguishes the current Catholic cases analyzed here is that they involve sexual encounters between priests and children under the age of majority, often in their teen and preteen years. Most of the abuse has involved young boys, but there have been cases of abuse of young girls as well.[1] Scattered reports have surfaced of similar incidents involving clergy in other churches, but incidents involving non-Catholic clergy most often consist of extramarital affairs between adult women and ministers.

The child sexual abuse scandal constitutes an extreme case of deviance. The priests involved have violated their personal vows of celibacy and chastity; they have engaged in predatory homosexual activity in many cases, against which the Church they represent preaches; they have deliberately concealed the sexual violations that they committed; and they have violated the moral trust reposed in them by the Church, their fellow priests, and the families whose children they exploited. Most centrally to the analysis here, these priests have engaged in sexual activity with children (see Beal 1992; Provost 1992). Moral condemnation of pedophilia is virtually universal and impassioned, and efforts by individuals or groups to rationalize or defend such behavior meet strenuous resistance (de Young 1984, 1988, 1989). In addition to the nature of the acts themselves, the significance of these priests' actions is compounded by the status they occupy within the Catholic tradition. Priests are the immediate intermediaries between parishioners and the Church, trustees responsible for parishioners' spiritual lives and spiritual welfare.

DISCLAIMERS AND ACCOUNTS IN CONTEMPORARY PRIEST ABUSE CASES

...We examine the types of narratives priests construct in initiating sexual relationships with children and in explaining their conduct when the violations are exposed. Given the number and seriousness of norms that these priests are violating and their lofty moral standing, the ways they explain their conduct become an interesting sociological issue. We divide the narratives that priests and their spokespersons develop into two broad types. First, priests must formulate prospective interpretations, or *disclaimers,* for their behavior toward the children with whom they are sexually involved. These explanations are constructed within the perpetrator-victim relationship and are concealed from others by various means. Second, upon public exposure of the sexual relationships, priests and their spokespersons are compelled to offer retrospective interpretations, or *accounts,* for their conduct. As we look at both types of explanation and the relationship between them, we find that retrospective accounts are significantly influenced by and must be understood in the context of prospective disclaimers.

Not surprisingly the data on priest abuse cases are limited. Many local cases are not nationally reported, journalistic reports often are fragmentary or focus on issues other than defendant disclaimers and accounts, and the Catholic Church routinely has demanded sealed records as a precondition for out-of-court settlements. We gathered most of the narratives presented here from four recent books and 257 press reports on priest abuse cases. The most fruitful sources were books authored by journalists, which were based on cases that had reached a conclusion and contained considerable detail about events and explanations. In some cases, however, we find disclaimers and accounts in other sources, such as news conferences, trial testimonies, and victims' accounts. Journalistic narratives in particular are biased in favor of public statements that yield sensational stories; they systematically exclude stories that are handled privately or are more mundane and unexceptional. Given the nature of the sources, we must exercise caution in generalizing broadly from these data. At the same time, we have conducted an extensive review of scholarly and journalistic sources, which constitute virtually the only accessible data sources. We should also note that narratives constructed over a period of time typically are more complex than the analytic account categories employed here, and actors are likely to use multiple disclaimer and account types (Schoenbach 1990).

DISCLAIMERS

A disclaimer is "a verbal device employed to ward off and defeat in advance doubts and negative typifications which may result from intended conduct. Disclaimers seek to define forthcoming conduct as not relevant to the kind of identity challenge or re-typification for which it might ordinarily serve as the basis" (Hewitt and Stokes 1975, 3). Disclaimers, in other words, are offered to "cushion" an anticipated reaction when some behavior is about to be discovered. There are five types of disclaimers. Persons use *hedging* disclaimers when they have a tentative commitment to a forthcoming line of action and are uncertain about the probable response to their actions. In this circumstance they express willingness to consider and negotiate alternative perspectives. People use *credentialing* disclaimers when they are committed to a line of action that they know will be discrediting. They thus offer qualifications or credentials that legitimate the line of action they are proposing. Similarly, people use *sin license* disclaimers when they are committed to a line of action that they anticipate will evoke a negative response, but in this case they seek to depict a situation in which generally recognized rules may be suspended without discrediting themselves. People come up with *cognitive* disclaimers when they anticipate that others may doubt that there is a shared understanding of the "facts of the situation" on which they are operating; they use such disclaimers to reassure others of such agreement. Finally, people issue *appeals for the suspension of judgment* when they anticipate that their statements or actions may produce a negative emotional reaction. They ask others to suspend their response until the meaning of the line of action is clarified.

Virtually all of the explanations priests offered to children in the incidents we examined are *credentialing* disclaimers. In most cases their authoritative statements take the form of simply asserting divine approval for the proposed relationship. For example, "Sex is okay," a priest told one girl. "This is the way God would have it" (Burkett and Bruni 1993, 74). In some instances divine approval is paired with a stipulation that the relationship should remain secret: "Father Jay told the boy: 'This is between you and me. This is something special. God would approve'" (Burkett and Bruni 1993, 67). Children clearly are often shocked when priests first approach them. The credentialing disclaimers provide a means for moving beyond this disorientation and potential resistance. One victim recounts: "One day he went into the bedroom and all of a sudden he came out with his pants down around his knees and I freaked out...I was shakin'. He said, 'It's not wrong. God made the body to be beautiful—

for each of us to share it'" (Berry 1994, 128). Some episodes do involve considerably more planning and complex interpretations. One victim remembers that the priest organized the sexual encounters with him and another boy named Morris as therapeutic penance:

> *Ed's abuse began as a condition of absolution. The youth confessed to impure thoughts and to the sin of pride. Father Terrence directed him to learn self-control. The lesson was simple, Ed alleges: the priest would masturbate Morris, or lie on top of him rubbing their groins together, but would stop just shy of Ed's ejaculation. "Desensitization," Father Terrence called this penance. "No matter how you go to the altar, as a priest or to marry, this will help you," Ed remembers Father Terrence telling him. "You are special. You are pleasing to God. But you have a corruptible side you must learn to control." (Burkett and Bruni 1993, 76)*

In one case the priest employed a sin license. According to a December 12, 1993, story in the *Fort Wayne [Indiana] Journal-Gazette* by Ron French, "Shattered Trust: Pain Endures for Victim of Alleged Clergy Abuse": "'He'd talk about unconditional love,' Schrader [the victim] said. 'He said too many people love conditionally.' And so although Schrader was uncomfortable with the sexual relationship, he felt that 'it fit with what he [the priest] was saying about unconditional love,...if you're going to unconditionally love, you need to express it.'" Finally, in one incident credentialing was combined with a sin license disclaimer. In this case the priest not only asserts that his female partner has been chosen by God but also seeks to suspend the relevant normative context by asserting that he needs assistance because he is ignorant of sexual matters. "She recalled the beginning of the abuse...'I was told that I had been chosen by God to help him with his studies of sex because he was responsible for helping adults and he didn't know anything about it'" (Berry 1994, 128)

It is not surprising that credentialing disclaimers predominate in priests' constructions of sexual relationships to their youthful partners.

Proposing sexual relations and offering to negotiate the relationship, attempting to reach agreement on the nature of the situation in which they are involved, or asking the children to suspend judgment would each probably cause confusion or resistance that the priest would then have to surmount through some other disclaimer or line of action. The credentialing strategy places the priest firmly in control of the situation; it asserts a legitimate basis for the connection that then can be veiled from outside observation. That illicit sexual relationships with children have occurred in substantial numbers over a long period of time without being discovered outside the Church hierarchy suggests that this strategy has generally succeeded.

ACCOUNTS

Numerous typologies of accounts have been formulated (Sykes and Matza 1957; Schoenbach, 1980, 1990; Tedeschi and Reiss 1981; Semin and Manstead 1983). We base the analysis here on Scott and Lyman's widely used typology, which defines an account as "a statement made by a social actor to explain unanticipated or untoward behavior—whether the behavior is his own or that of others, and whether the proximate cause for the statement arises from the actor himself or from someone else" (1968, 46). Scott and Lyman divide accounts into two broad types, *excuses* and *justifications.* From their perspective, "An excuse is an admission that the act in question was bad, wrong, or inept, coupled with a denial of full responsibility. A justification is an admission of full responsibility for the act in question, coupled with a denial that it was wrongful" (1970, 93). Excuses thus are accounts constructed with the objective of mitigating the actor's responsibility for the act in question; justifications are intended to normalize the act in question.

JUSTIFICATIONS

Scott and Lyman define six types of justification. *Denial of injury* accounts construct events so as to minimize the negative and maximize the positive consequences of contested behavior. *Denial of victim* accounts define victims as deserving harm as a result of having injured the actor, being enemies of the actor, or holding membership in devalued groups. *Condemnation of condemners* accounts rationalize contested actions by comparing them to uncensored acts by others that are equal to or greater than the actor's own normative violations. *Appeal to loyalties* accounts deem contested conduct appropriate in terms of higher allegiances to which the actor is committed. *Sad tale* accounts reconstruct the actor's biography in highly disadvantaged terms that explain current behavior. Finally, *self-fulfillment* accounts lay claim to personal growth, health, or conscience as a legitimate rationale for contested conduct.

In the priest abuse cases we examined, almost every instance involved *denial of injury* accounts.[2] In one case a priest included in his account a statement referring to self-fulfillment. Father Ritter asserted his right to personal fulfillment, avowing that even divine disapproval would not override his right to pursue his own identity. He stated: "You know, I decided twenty years ago, if God didn't like me the way I was, that's His problem" (Sennott 1992, 30). However, this account differs markedly from virtually every other justificatory statement.

The priests or their spokespersons have employed several strategies to elevate the moral standing of the deviant behavior. One approach insists that the sexual contact is consensual. For example, a therapist/columnist specializing in treatment of priests accused of sexual abuse wrote in a Catholic magazine: "We are not involved with the dynamics of rape but with the far subtler dynamics of persuasion by a friend. As we speak to and about the victims we must be aware the child sometimes retains a loving memory of the offender" (Connors 1992). In this account the denial of injury is buttressed by characterizing the incident as involving persuasion rather than coercion and by further asserting that the child involved in fact harbors no hostility toward the priest.

In another account, journalist Jason Berry (1994, 11) records the statement of a diocesan vicar responsible for the conduct of priests. The vicar makes a comparable characterization of the sexual relationship as "misguided affection" but seeks to mitigate the damage by juxtaposing indiscretion or poor judgment in this incident with the catastrophic consequences for the priest's career. "The diocese had received a report some time ago, Larroque continued, terming it 'a case of misguided affection.... We're talking about ruining a man's career,' said Larroque, referring to the implication of charges against a priest."

A third strategy is to moderate claimsmaking by emphasizing the "extraordinary importance" of the work in which the priest and his colleagues are involved, a mission that should not be jeopardized by a single behavioral "failure": "It is probably better to say I failed. If I had to give a reason for my own personal failure it is probably hubris.... What happens to me, ladies and gentlemen, is not really very important. I decided long ago that I did not care about that. What happens to the kids is very important. The work we do here is of extraordinary importance" (Sennott 1992, 273). Justice for the victims and the vital mission of the institution thus are placed in opposition. Vigorously prosecuting the offender might cripple or destroy the institution, thereby sacrificing "the kids."

Finally, the harm involved in sexual abuse may be minimized by shifting the behavior to a category with at least subcultural legitimacy and by carefully distinguishing the traits of acceptable and unacceptable sexuality. For instance, in a legal statement one priest distinguishes between sexual intercourse and what he calls a "reserved embrace": "'I may have had a reserved embrace,' he admitted in a deposition in 1992....Sexual intercourse, he said, doesn't occur unless a man clutches a woman with passion and ejaculates into her. Yes, he had lain atop Susan. Yes, he put his penis in her vagina. But there was, 'no passion, no kissing, no nothing,' he said. And he had not ejaculated" (Burkett and Bruni 1993, 87–88).

What is most striking about justification accounts, of course, is their clustering in the denial of injury category. Other types of justification accounts apparently are unavailable or difficult to construct for this type of violation. Priests and their allies can hardly accuse the young boys with whom they have sexual liaisons of deserving harm. They would also be understandably reluctant to group themselves with the other categories of deviants with which comparisons are most likely to be drawn, such as incestuous fathers, sexual predators, and homosexuals. Likewise, given the high moral calling to which priests are pledged, it would be difficult to rationalize sexual relationships with children with an appeal to higher principles. Even were priests to make a case for the "sexual liberation" of children, they could not be the liberators. Given priests' pledge to the spiritual welfare of their parishioners and to sacrificial life-styles, self-fulfillment could not be accorded a higher priority than the welfare of children. Priests might conceivably reconstruct their biographies to explain their conduct, an accounting strategy often employed by psychotherapists accused of inappropriate sexual intimacy (Pogrebin, Poole, and Martinez 1992). However, since priests' personal lives are so completely enmeshed in the Church, such a strategy would almost inevitably involve an attack on the Church or admission of their own incompatibility with the priestly role. Priests seeking to mitigate claimsmaking against them seem to have few justification options beyond damage control. Asserting that the acts they have committed are not as heinous as public depictions of them in the media or prosecutorial rhetoric may be their best available option.

EXCUSES

Scott and Lyman identify four types of excuse accounts. *Accident* accounts seek to mitigate responsibility by asserting that the actor cannot control environmental events. Actors may misinterpret events, be unable to foresee impending events, become distracted, lack skills and abilities requisite to deal successfully with occurrences, or have insufficient time to respond. *Defeasibility* accounts aver impairment of mental capacity as a result of mental disorder, intoxication/addiction, or psychological duress. *Biological drives* accounts identify biological attributes such as sexual passion, sexual orientation, or criminogenic tendencies as the source of contested behavior. Finally, *scapegoating* accounts seek to shift responsibility for contested behavior to the participation, duress, or provocation of another actor.

Three types of excuse accounts dominate in the cases we examined. Accident accounts usually are presented by Church representatives with the objective of defending the Church rather than the individual priests. These accounts assert the impossibility of absolutely preventing individuals with psychological disorders from entering the priesthood. In some cases these errors are blamed on the absence of effective screening techniques. In this effort Church officials are supported by Church-affiliated clinicians responsible for treating offenders (e.g., Berry 1994, 208). For instance, the bishop of Baton Rouge blamed his ignorance on the priest's deliberate, skillful deception: "'My mistake,' said Frey, '[was] not being able to recognize the depth of [Gauthe's] mental illness. His personality was such that he skillfully masked his condition'" (Frey 1986).

A second type of excuse account is scapegoating, also largely employed by Church administrators. In these accounts Church officials imply, with varying degrees of specificity, that individuals or groups are using the abuse scandal for their own nefarious purposes. The issues of responsibility and harm are turned around, with the accused presented as a victim of a kind of conspiracy to discredit the offender. The controversy thus results not from the actions of the accused but from the evil intentions of named or unnamed enemies, calling the motives of the accusers into question. In some cases the alleged enemies remain anonymous. For example, an editorial in the *Lafayette [Indiana] Sunday Advertiser* for June 16, 1985, issued this advice under the headline "In the Gauthe Affair: The Catholic Church Is Not on Trial!": "Let's offer a special prayer for the resolution of the affair that has rocked the Acadiana community and ask the forgiveness of any unscrupulous individuals who for one reason or other attempt to blacken the reputation of our entire religious community."

Sometimes enemies are more clearly defined. In the now famous Covenant House case, one of Fr. Bruce Ritter's staff said to a reporter, "I think it was outrageous and disgusting for the District Attorney to outfit this kid with a wire to try to entrap Father Ritter" (Sennott 1992, 265).

Another strategy for scapegoating involves alleging that the charges against the Church are being pursued so vigorously precisely because of the Church's high moral standards. A letter from Pat Hayes to the editor of the *Springfield [Illinois] State Journal-Register* on December 13, 1993, published under the headline "Priests Should Not Be Stigmatized by the Few," blames the problem on the low moral character of the public in general and the mass media in particular: "[H]ow the media glorifies scandalous stories, but they do so because of the public's love affair with dirt....I have to wonder about the potential contagiousness of allegations, a contagiousness that is only being encouraged by sensationalistic media and a 'let's sue' atmosphere that is cheered on by some of the most ridiculous and inciteful advertising I've ever seen." Attacking the Church through the conduct of wayward priests becomes a cynical means for undermining its calls for moral standards to which the larger society does not wish to adhere: "Archbishop Daniel Pilarczyk [said:] 'I think our culture in general sees this as a chance to get a little bit even with the Church in the context of unpopular prophetic things the Church says about society. Maybe it's really a kind of implicit acknowledgment of the relevance that people, even unconsciously, find in the Church'" (Burkett and Bruni 1993, 199). In this account the vendetta is portrayed as part of a larger conflict, with the individuals accused merely victims of the Church's crusade to foster sexual morality. Condemnation of the priests helps undermine the Church as a bastion of morality.

In some instances Church spokespersons even question the motives of the victims making claims against the Church. A bishop wrote in a newspaper column: "[O]ne can ask: if the victims were adolescents, why did they go back to the same situation once there had been one 'pass' or suggestion? Were they cooperating in the matter, or were they true victims?" (Harris 1990, 16). However, in most instances accounts simply assert psychological disorder, often in rather perfunctory terms. This was the tack taken by North America's most notorious priest-pedophile, Fr. James Porter: His illness made him abuse a minimum of several hundred victims, many repeatedly (Burkett and Bruni 1993, 18). One source of defeasibility specified, which fits with current explanations for abusive behavior, is the priest's own abuse as a child: "A certain proportion of priests...abuse children not because they are sexually starved, but because their 'love-maps'— their objects of sexual desire—have been vandalized in childhood experiences of their own" (Greeley 1993, 45).

In these defeasibility accounts priests tend to emphasize the potency of their emotional feelings, which often become more powerful once they are expressed. One priest refers to the "enormous stress on him, which is why, he believes, his desires caught him so off guard. Horsing around with a parish altar boy for a Mass well done, he patted him on the rear.... The more he touched them, the harder it became to control his gestures. 'It opened up a hunger,' he says. "Now fantasy was not enough. It's like—how does a person go back to masturbation when he's had intercourse?'" (Burkett and Bruni 1993, 93). The offender's experience of desire is depicted as an inexorable progression from thought to physical satisfaction. The overpowering nature of the feelings and their growing strength are important in these accounts, for priests frequently abused a succession of children over an extended period of time. Loss of control may account for a single episode; a more elaborate accounting is necessary for extended abuse. The potency of his feelings becomes such an explanation to the extent that the priest is unable to resist them.

Church-affiliated professionals offer support for this interpretation. For example, in a professional paper both a canon and a civil lawyer use anecdotal evidence to argue that offenders have no control and therefore accrue a lower level of personal liability: "We are dealing with compulsive sexual habits which the priest may temporarily suspend in the face of legal or canonical pressure, but not in all instances. There are many examples wherein sexual abuse took place very soon after the confrontation between the priest and his Ordinary [bishop] had taken place. The priest must clearly be seen as one suffering from a psychiatric disorder that is beyond his ability to control" (Mouton and Doyle 1985). Making sexual abuse a psychological disorder offers the Church an explanation that relieves the individual priest of responsibility and avoids the stain on the Church's reputation that accompanies a moral interpretation (Freldson 1970). Thus to the extent that pedophilia is an undetectable disorder, this account reduces the responsibility of both priest and Church.

One more development of the defeasibility account mitigates priest responsibility even further. Using the medical model, Church psychiatrists separate behavior from character:

Diagnosing a person as a pedophile says something about the nature of his sexual desires and orientation. It says nothing about his temperament, or about traits of character (such as kindness vs cruelty, caring vs uncaring, sensitive vs insensitive, and so on). Thus a diagnosis of pedophilia does not necessarily mean that a person is lacking in conscience, diminished in intellectual capabilities, or somehow "characterologically flawed." One needs to evaluate independently the nature of an individual's sexual drives and interests, as opposed to what the person is like in terms of character, intellect, temperament, and other mental capacities. (Berlin and Krout 1986, 14)

Separating behavior from character is important to both the Church and the priest. The stigma for both is reduced if conduct rather than moral essence is at issue. The Church is less culpable for failing to detect behavioral disorders than for failing to recognize low moral character, and priests can be treated for specific disorders but not for flawed moral essence.

As with justification accounts, excuse accounts sometimes have several themes. For example, one priest who asserts long-term defensibility bordering on biological drives argues that the Church's structure caused his condition to manifest itself, mitigating his own guilt by transferring responsibility to the institution and his peers: "I sought that feeling out after that. I began to look for and depend upon affection from younger persons. There had been so many needs that had been unmet and so many disappointments and so many pains and so many rejections that it didn't matter.... After 20 years of parish life, I guess I felt that nobody gave a damn about me" (Burkett and Bruni 1993, 85).

Excuse accounts vary more than justification accounts. Accident and scapegoating accounts are employed primarily by Church officials who use them to defend the institution rather than individual priests. The Church improves its moral positioning by arguing that it cannot possibly detect every case of behavioral disorder, particularly when priests deliberately conceal such attributes, and by contending that opponents are using the few incidents that have escaped detection to discredit an institution that in fact is a moral exemplar. For their part, priests appear most likely to choose related biological and defeasibility accounts that attribute their conduct to loss of control. Where they offer more than perfunctory illness accounts, priests tend to emphasize a process of spiraling out of control after the initial transgression, which offers an interpretation that explains a pattern of long-term violation.

PRELIMINARY OBSERVATIONS

The analysis of narratives explaining priest sexual abuse led us to two general conclusions. First, we can better interpret narratives as a sequence than as separate elements. We have illustrated this point by exploring the relationship between prospective disclaimers and retrospective accounts. Second, we must examine narratives in their social structural context as well as their symbolic context. This dimension of narrative construction is not the focus of our analysis here, but we can offer some preliminary observations.

Developing the kind of explanatory narratives for behavior we examine here is an extended process that begins when the actor pursues a contested line of conduct. Most sociological research has focused on the account construction process. We believe that it is theoretically important to analyze both (1) the prospective explanations (disclaimers) through which actors initiate lines of action that may be contested and that may alter the actor's identity in a negative fashion and (2) the retrospective explanations (accounts) through which actors justify or excuse acts evaluated as deviant in an effort to minimize sanctions and defend personal identity. Whatever the ultimate sources of priests' motivation in initiating sexual relationships with minors, the evidence here indicates that priests find it important to assert a rationale and identity as central elements of the process.

Disclaimers largely cluster in the credentialing category. Priests draw on their spiritual authorization in most instances to legitimate the lines of action they are about to take. Particularly in dealing with children, this strategy maximizes the priest's capacity to orchestrate the interaction, reduces the necessity for more difficult, complex negotiation, and creates the basis for sealing off external disclosure. Virtually all priests select this solution as a way of asserting priestly authority, integrating the priestly role with conduct that norms define as incompatible with and violative of that role.

This type of disclaimer pattern arguably has clear links not only to the priests' behavioral objectives but also to a specific organizational context. Priests can employ the credentialing disclaimer in large measure because of their high moral/spiritual status. Devoted Catholics, particularly children, are unlikely to challenge their authoritative pronouncements. Further, the priest role is located within a religious organization that entrusts to priests' care the spiritual welfare of parishioners. In organizations granted trustee status, normative violations are adjudicated internally with limited, if any, external oversight (Bromley 1995). As findings from a number of priest abuse scandals make clear, Church officials were well aware of pedophile priests, deliberately concealed their identities and activities, and in a number of cases simply transferred priests out of one parish to a new, unsuspecting parish when sexual violations were discovered. That priests could use a credentialing disclaimer to initiate and sustain sexual relationships with a succession of youth over an extended period of time in the same and different locations becomes highly improbable outside of this structural context.

Justification accounts that diminish wrongfulness are considerably less common than excuse accounts. Where justifications are offered, they are almost invariably denial of injury accounts. Priests have little alternative but to attempt to mitigate the seriousness of their infractions by emphasizing the consensual nature of the sexual encounters; characterizing the behavior as misguided, an indiscretion, or reflecting poor judgment; or shifting the behavior to a less stigmatized category. Priests often incorporate into these accounts statements inviting comparison of the limited number and severity of the incidents to the vital larger mission of the Church or the priest. Such comparisons place the injury in a larger framework that tends to diminish relative harm and discourage prosecution that would unduly damage the priest or the Church. In short, priests concluded that damage control in the form of minimization of injury is their most viable course.

Excuse accounts are far more common than justifications as priests and their spokespersons acknowledge wrongfulness but deny culpability. Given the rapidly growing number of scandals and the frequent presence of numerous victim-witnesses offering corroborating testimony, neither priests nor the Church can easily refute the charges. Rather, institutional representatives seek to disavow responsibility through accident and scapegoating accounts. Both shift the focus of attention from the child to the Church as victim, in the first case accidentally and in the latter case as part of a deliberate campaign (both tend to infuriate victims and their families). Church officials offer an accident excuse account based on the impossibility of identifying psychologically disordered priests either because diagnostic procedures are fallible or because priests deliberately camouflage these personality characteristics. Alternatively, Church spokespersons contend that opponents paint a far grimmer portrait of Church untrustworthiness than a few individual violations warrant. In this version, the Church is being attacked precisely because of its principled character, which raises moral standards to a level that most individuals would prefer not to meet. Both the accident and scapegoating accounting strategies are premised on a "bad apples" theory that assumes the existence of few abuse cases. The Church has attempted to create this reality through an institutional strategy of not responding to victims and of private settlements that require the sealing of all records as a precondition. As the number of revelations has mounted and the concerted efforts by the Church to deny victim claims and conceal incidents come to light, both accounting strategies have become less tenable.

For their part, individual priests almost unanimously employ defeasibility accounts. There are scattered references to biological drives, but the primary theme is psychological disorder. These excuse accounts try to explain, first, having engaged in prohibited relationships at all but also the succession of illicit relationships over an extended period of time. One major problem that such defeasibility accounts face is that because priests consciously used their priestly authority (credentialing disclaimer) in initiating and sustaining sexual relationships with children, they need to account not only for a sexual encounter but also for a highly organized pattern of behavior and legitimation. This requires a stronger defeasibility claim than they might need to account for a single, momentary lapse. In essence these priests must argue that the planning and disclaiming in which they engaged are elements of the disorder, but this means pleading to a much more serious condition. Nonetheless, defeasibility accounts offer the best chance for priests to continue in their occupational/spiritual roles, for the issue becomes their behavior rather than their moral character, with at least a possibility of rehabilitation. The Church can also come to the defense of the priests for these same reasons.

The results of disclaimers and accounts we report here underline the significance of symbolic formulations in the organization of deviant behavior. Actors must prospectively construct motives and identities that permit them to engage in a deviant line of action, and they must do so in a way that minimizes the likelihood of resistance and stigmatization. Likewise, when violations are exposed, individuals are pressed to formulate accounts that will place their conduct in a symbolic context that minimizes sanctions and damage to individual identity. The data on priest sexual abuse presented here illustrate how explanations for action formulated at the prospective stage limit the degrees of freedom and shape the nature of accounts at the retrospective stage. Further progress in interpreting these symbolic strategies requires placing disclaimers and accounts in a relational context. In the case at hand, it is evident that major normative breaches are difficult to negotiate symbolically when violators are called to a final reckoning.

NOTES

1. Although we will probably never know the true extent of such activity, Sipe (1990) estimates that 2 percent of U.S. priests suffer from pedophilia and another 6 percent are attracted to older minor children.

2. This analysis focuses on priest-pedophile behavior. However, there have been cases of nuns engaging in similar activities, and they have resorted to comparable accounts.

REFERENCES

American Psychiatric Association. 1994. *Diagnostic and Statistical Manual of Mental Disorders,* 4th ed., rev. Washington, D.C.: American Psychiatric Association.

———. 1987. *Diagnostic and Statistical Manual of Mental Disorders,* 3rd ed. Washington, D.C.: American Psychiatric Association.

Beal, John. 1992. "Doing What One Can: Canon Law and Clerical Sexual Misconduct." *The Jurist* 52:642–683.

Berlin, Fred S., and Edgar Krout. 1986. "Pedophilia: Diagnostic Concepts." *American Journal of Forensic Psychiatry* 7 (1):13–30.

Berry, Jason. 1994. *Lead Us Not into Temptation: Catholic Priests and the Sexual Abuse of Children.* Garden City, N.Y.: Doubleday.

Bromley, David. 1995. "The Politics of Religious Apostasy." Paper presented at the annual meeting of the Society for the Scientific Study of Religion, St. Louis.

Burkett, Eleanor, and Frank Bruni. 1993. *Gospel of Shame: Children, Sexual Abuse, and the Catholic Church.* New York: Viking.

Connors, Canice. 1992. "Priests and Pedophilia: A Silence that Needs Breaking?" *America* 166 (May 9):400–401.

de Young, Mary. 1989. "The World According to NAMBLA: Accounting for Deviance." *Journal of Sociology and Social Welfare* 16 (1):111–126.

———. 1988. "The Indignant Page: Techniques of Neutralization in the Publications of Pedophile Organizations." *Child Abuse and Neglect* 12:583–591.

———. 1984. "Ethics and the 'Lunatic Fringe': The Case of Pedophile Organizations." *Human Organization* 43 (1):72–74.

Freidson, Eliot. 1970. *Profession of Medicine: A Study of the Sociology of Applied Knowledge.* Chicago: University of Chicago Press.

Frey, Gerard. 1986. "Bishop Denied Gauthe Cover-up, Won't Give up Job." *Lafayette [Ind.] Sunday Advertiser* (February 2). Quoted in Berry 1994, 145.

Greeley, Andrew. 1993. "A View from the Priesthood." *Newsweek* (August 16):45.

Hamilton, V. L. 1978. "Who Is Responsible? Toward a Social Psychology of Responsibility Attribution." *Social Psychology* 41:316–328.

Harris, Michael. 1990. *Unholy Orders: Tragedy at Mount Cashel.* New York: Viking.

Hewitt, John P., and Randall Stokes. 1975. "Disclaimers." *American Sociological Review* 40: 1–11.

Jacobs, Janet. 1989. *Divine Disenchantment: Deconverting from New Religions.* Bloomington: Indiana University Press.

Money, John. 1972. *Man and Woman, Boy and Girl.* Baltimore: Johns Hopkins University Press.

Mouton, F. Ray, and Thomas P. Doyle. 1985. *The Problem of Sexual Molestation by Roman Catholic Clergy: Meeting the Problem in a Comprehensive and Responsible Manner. Internal Report to the National Council of Catholic Bishops.* Washington, D.C.

Murphey, Michael. 1986. "Priest Faces Second Felony Charge." *Spokane Spokesman-Review* (March 4) as quoted in Berry 1994, 165.

Pogrebin, Mark, Eric Poole, and Amos Martinez. 1992. "Psychotherapists' Accounts of Their Professional Misdeeds." *Deviant Behavior* 13:229–252.

Provost, James. 1992. "Some Canonical Considerations Relative to Clerical Sexual Misconduct." *The Jurist* 52:615–641.

Schoenbach, Peter. 1990. *Account Episodes: The Management or Escalation of Conflict.* New York: Cambridge University Press.

———. 1980. "A Category System for Account Phases." *European Journal of Social Psychology* 10:195–280.

Scott, Marvin B., and Stanford M. Lyman. 1970. "Accounts, Deviance, and Social Order." In *Deviance and Respectability: The Social Construction of Moral Meanings,* edited by Jack Douglas. New York: Basic.

———. 1968. "Accounts." *American Sociological Review* 33 (1):46–62.

Semin, A. S., and S. R. Manstead. 1983. *The Accountability of Conduct: A Social Psychological Analysis.* New York: Academic.

Sennott, Charles M. 1992. *Broken Covenant.* New York: Simon and Schuster.

Shupe, Anson. 1995. *In the Name of All That's Holy: A Theory of Clergy Malfeasance.* Westport, Conn.: Praeger.

Sipe, A. W. Richard. 1991. *The Secret World: Sexuality and the Search for Celibacy.* New York: Brunner/Mazel.

Sykes, Gresham, and David Matza. 1957. "Techniques of Neutralization: A Theory of Delinquency." *American Sociological Review* 22:664–670.

Tedeschi, J. T., and M. Reiss. 1981. "Verbal Strategies in Impression Management." In *The Psychology of Ordinary Explanations of Social Behavior,* edited by Charles Antaki. New York: Academic.

CHAPTER 14

TRANSFORMING DEVIANT IDENTITY

Delabeling, Relabeling, and Alcoholics Anonymous

HARRISON M. TRICE and PAUL MICHAEL ROMAN

Over the course of time, deviance sometimes proves to be more punishing than rewarding. People whose deviance is self-destructive (for example, alcoholics, drug addicts, and mental patients) are especially apt to try to relinquish their deviant ways and identities. But terminating a deviant career is no easy matter. The conditions for successful transformation of a deviant identity are narrow and exacting. They include the development of a conventional lifestyle and identity, support from deviants and nondeviants alike, and opportunities to adopt conventional ways. Without these conditions, a transformation of deviant identity is less likely.

Harrison M. Trice and Paul Michael Roman argue that alcoholics stand much better chances of identity transformation than either drug addicts or mental patients. Heavy drinking is much closer to ordinary experience than behaviors of addicts and mental patients. Alcoholics Anonymous (A.A.) presents a simple picture of what causes alcoholism and some very practical means of recovery. A.A. members stop drinking, a visible sign of change. Then they redefine themselves as "sick," assume the repentant role, and take the label "arrested alcoholic." And then they begin to reclimb the social ladder as they reembrace the conventional sober and respectable ways of middle- and lower-middle-class citizens.

An increasing amount of research emphasis in social psychiatry in recent years has been placed upon the rehabilitation and return of former mental patients to "normal" community roles (Sussman, 1966). The concomitant rapid growth of community psychiatry as a psychiatric paradigm parallels this interest, with community psychiatry having as a primary concern the maintenance of the patient's statuses within the family and community throughout the treatment process so as to minimize problems of rehabilitation and "return" (Pasamanick *et al.,* 1967; Susser, 1968). Despite these emphases, successful "delabeling" or destigmatization of mental patients subsequent to treatment appears rare (Miller, 1965; Freeman and Simmons, 1963). It is the purpose of this paper to explore an apparent negative instance of this phenomenon, namely, a type of social processing which results in *successful* delabeling, wherein the stigmatized label is replaced with one that is socially acceptable.

Reprinted from "Delabeling, Relabeling, and Alcoholics Anonymous," *Social Problems* Vol. 17, No. 4 (Spring 1970), pp. 538–546, by permission of the Society for the Study of Social Problems and the authors. Copyright © 1970 by the Society for the Study of Social Problems.

The so-called labeling paradigm which has assumed prominence within the sociology of deviant behavior offers a valuable conceptualization of the development of deviant careers, many of which are apparently permanent (Scheff, 1966). In essence, labeling theory focuses upon the processes whereby a "primary deviant" becomes a "secondary deviant" (Lemert, 1951:75–76). Primary deviance may arise from myriad sources. The extent and nature of the social reaction to this behavior [are] a function of the deviant's reaction to his own behavior (Roman and Trice, 1969), the behavior's visibility, the power vested in the statuses of the deviant actor, and the normative parameters of tolerance for deviance that exist within the community. Primary deviance that is visible and exceeds the tolerance level of the community may bring the actor to the attention of mandated labelers such as psychiatrists, clinical psychologists, and social workers.

If these labelers see fit "officially" to classify the actor as a type of deviant, a labeling process occurs which eventuates in (1) self concept changes on the part of the actor and (2) changes in the definitions of him held by his immediate significant others, as well as the larger community. Behavior which occurs as a consequence of these new definitions is called secondary deviance. This behavior is substantively similar to the original primary deviance but has as its source the actor's revised self concept, as well as the revised social definition of him held in the community.

Previous research and theoretical literature appear to indicate that this process is irreversible, particularly in the cases of mental illness or so-called residual deviance (Miller, 1965; Myers and Bean, 1968). No systematic effort has been made to specify the social mechanisms which might operate to "return" the stigmatized secondary deviant to a "normal" and acceptable role in the community. In other words, delabeling and relabeling have received little attention as a consequence of the assumption that deviant careers are typically permanent.

Conceptually, there appear to be at least three ways whereby delabeling could successfully occur. First, organizations of deviants may develop which have the primary goal of changing the norms of the community or society, such that their originally offending behavior becomes acceptable (Sagarin, 1967). For example, organized groups of homosexuals have strongly urged that children be educated in the dual existence of homosexuality and heterosexuality as equally acceptable forms of behavior.

Secondly, it is possible that the mandated professionals and organizations who initially label deviant behavior and process the deviant through "treatment" may create highly visible and explicit "delabeling" or "status-return" ceremonies which constitute legitimized public pronouncements that the offending deviance has ceased and the actor is eligible for reentry into the community. Such ceremonies could presumably be the reverse of "status degradation" rituals (Garfinkel, 1956).

A third possible means is through the development of mutual aid organizations which encourage a return to strict conformity to the norms of the community as well as creating a stereotype which is socially acceptable. Exemplary of this strategy is Alcoholics Anonymous. Comprised of 14,150 local groups in the United States in 1967, this organization provides opportunities for alcoholics to join together in an effort to cease disruptive and deviant drinking behavior in order to set the stage for the resumption of normal occupational, marital, and community roles (Gellman, 1964).

The focus of this paper is the apparent success in delabeling that has occurred through the social processing of alcoholics through Alcoholics Anonymous and through alcoholics' participation in the A.A. subculture. The formulation is based chiefly on participant observation over the past 15 years in Alcoholics Anonymous and data from various of our studies of the social aspects of alcoholism and deviant drinking. These observations are supplemented by considerable contact with other "self-help" organizations. These experiences are recognized as inadequate substitutes for "hard" data; and the following points are best considered as exploratory hypotheses for further research.

THE "ALLERGY" CONCEPT

The chronic problem affecting the reacceptance into the community of former mental patients and other types of deviants is the attribution of such persons with taints of permanent "strangeness," "immorality," or "evil." A logical method for neutralizing such stigma is the promulgation of ideas or evidence that the undesirable behavior of these deviants stems from factors beyond their span of control and responsibility. In accord with Parsons' (1951) cogent analysis of the socially neutralizing effects of the "sick role," it appears that permanent stigmatization may be avoided if stereotypes of behavior disorders as forms of "illness" can be successfully diffused in the community.

Alcoholics Anonymous has since its inception attempted to serve as such a catalyst for the "delabeling" of its members through promulgating the "allergy concept" of alcohol addiction. Although not part of official A.A. literature, the allergy concept plays a prominent part in A.A. presentations to non-alcoholics as well as in the A.A. "line" that is used in "carrying the message" to non-member deviant drinkers. The substance of the allergy concept is that those who become alcoholics possess a physiological allergy to alcohol such that their addiction is predetermined even before they take their first drink. Stemming from the allergy concept is the label of "arrested alcoholic" which A.A. members place on themselves.

The significance of this concept is that it serves to diminish, both in the perceptions of the A.A. members and their immediate significant others, the alcoholic's responsibility for developing the behavior disorder. Furthermore, it serves to diminish the impression that a form of mental illness underlies alcohol abuse. In this vein, A.A. members are noted for their explicit denial of any association between alcoholism and psychopathology. As a basis for a "sick role" for alcoholics, the allergy concept effectively reduces blame upon one's *self* for the development of alcoholism.

Associated with this is a very visible attempt on the part of A.A. to associate itself with the medical profession. Numerous publications of the organization have dealt with physicians and A.A. and with physicians who are members of A.A. (["Doctors,"] 1968). Part of this may be related to the fact that one of the cofounders was a physician; and a current long-time leader is also a physician. In any event, the strong attempts to associate A.A. with the medical profession stand in contrast to the lack of such efforts to become associated with such professions as law, education, or the clergy.

Despite A.A.'s emphasis upon the allergy concept, it appears clear that a significant portion of the American public does not fully accept the notion that alcoholism and disruptive deviant drinking are the result of an "allergy" or other organic aberration. Many agencies associated with the treatment of alcohol-related problems have attempted to make "alcoholism is an illness" a major theme of mass educational efforts (Plaut, 1967). Yet in a study of 1,213 respondents, Mulford and Miller (1964) found that only 24 percent of the sample "accepted the illness concept without qualification." Sixty-five percent of the respondents regarded the alcoholic as "sick," but most qualified this judgment by adding that he was also "morally weak" or "weak-willed."

The motivation behind public agencies' efforts at promulgating the "illness" concept of behavior disorders to reduce the probability of temporary or permanent stigmatization was essentially upstaged by A.A. Nonetheless, the data indicate that acceptance of the "illness" notion by the general public is relatively low in the case of alcoholism and probably lower in the cases of other behavior disorders (cf. Nunnally, 1961). But the effort has not been totally without success. Thus it appears that A.A.'s allergy concept does set the stage for reacceptance of the alcoholic by part of the population. A more basic function may involve the operation of the A.A.

program itself; acceptance of the allergy concept by A.A. members reduces the felt need for "personality change" and may serve to raise diminished self-esteem.

Other than outright acceptance of the allergy or illness notion, there appear to be several characteristics of deviant drinking behavior which reduce the ambiguity of the decision to re-accept the deviant into the community after his deviance has ceased.

Unlike the ambiguous public definitions of the causes of other behavior disorders (Nunnally, 1961), the behaviors associated with alcohol addiction are viewed by the community as a direct consequence of the inappropriate use of alcohol. With the cessation of drinking behavior, the accompanying deviance is assumed to disappear. Thus, what is basically wrong with an alcoholic is that he drinks. In the case of other psychiatric disorders the issue of "what is wrong" is much less clear. This lack of clarity underlies Scheff's (1966) notion of psychiatric disorders as comprising "residual" or relatively unclassifiable forms of deviance. Thus the mentally ill, once labeled, acquire such vague but threatening stereotypes as "strange," "different," and "dangerous" (Nunnally, 1961). Since the signs of the disorder are vague in terms of cultural stereotypes, it is most difficult for the "recovered" mental patient to convince others that he is "cured."

It appears that one of the popular stereotypes of former psychiatric patients is that their apparent normality is a "coverup" for their continuing underlying symptoms. Thus, where the alcoholic is able to remove the cause of his deviance by ceasing drinking, such a convincing removal may be impossible in the case of the other addictions and "mental" disorders. Narcotic addiction represents an interesting middle ground between these two extremes, for the cultural stereotype of a person under the influence of drugs is relatively unclear, such that it may be relatively difficult for the former addict to convince others that he has truly removed the cause of his deviance. This points up the fact that deviant drinking and alcoholism are

continuous with behavior engaged in by the majority of the adult population, namely, "normal" drinking (Mulford, 1964). The fact that the deviant drinker and alcohol addict are simply carrying out a common and normative behavior to excess reduces the "mystery" of the alcoholic experience and creates relative confidence in the average citizen regarding his abilities to identify a truly "dry" alcoholic. Thus the relative clarity of the cultural stereotype regarding the causes of deviance accompanying alcohol abuse provides much better means for the alcoholic to claim he is no longer a deviant.

To summarize, A.A. promulgates the allergy concept both publicly and privately, but data clearly indicate that this factor alone does not account for the observed success at "reentry" achieved by A.A. members. Despite ambiguity in public definitions of the etiology of alcoholism, its continuity with "normal" drinking behavior results in greater public confidence in the ability to judge the results of a therapeutic program. An understanding of A.A.'s success becomes clearer when this phenomenon is coupled with the availability of the "repentant" role.

THE REPENTANT ROLE

A relatively well-structured status of the "repentant" is clearly extant in American cultural tradition. Upward mobility from poverty and the "log cabin" comprises a social type where the individual "makes good" for his background and the apparent lack of conformity to economic norms of his ancestors. Redemptive religion, emergent largely in American society, emphasizes that one can correct a moral lapse even of long duration by public admission of guilt and repentance (cf. Lang and Lang, 1960).

The A.A. member can assume this repentant role; and it may become a social vehicle whereby, through contrite and remorseful public expressions, substantiated by visibly reformed behavior in conformity to the norms of the community, a former deviant can enter a new role which is quite acceptable to society. The reacceptance may not be entirely complete, however, since the label of alcoholic is replaced with that of "arrested alcoholic"; as Gusfield (1967) has stated, the role comprises a social type of a "repentant deviant." The acceptance of the allergy concept by his significant others may well hasten his reacceptance, but the more important factor seems to be the relative clarity by which significant others can judge the deviant's claim to "normality." Ideally the repentant role is also available to the former mental patient; but as mentioned above, his inability to indicate clearly the removal of the symptoms of his former deviance typically blocks such an entry.

If alcohol is viewed in its historical context in American society, the repentant role has not been uniquely available to A.A. members. As an object of deep moral concern no single category of behavior (with the possible exception of sexual behavior) has been laden with such emotional intensity in American society. Organized social movements previous to A.A. institutionalized means by which repentants could control their use of alcohol. These were the Washingtonians, Catch-My-Pal, and Father Matthews movements in the late 1800's and early 1900's, which failed to gain widespread social acceptance. Thus not only is the repentant role uniquely available to the alcoholic at the present time, but Alcoholics Anonymous has been built on a previous tradition.

SKID ROW IMAGE AND SOCIAL MOBILITY

The major facet of Alcoholics Anonymous' construction of a repentant role is found in the "Skid Row image" and its basis for upward social mobility. A central theme in the "stories" of many A.A. members is that of downward mobility into Skid Row or near Skid Row situations. Research evidence suggests that members tend to come from the middle and lower middle classes (Trice, 1962; Straus and Bacon, 1951). Consequently a "story" of downward mobility illustrates the extent to which present members had drastically fallen from esteem on account of their drinking.

A.A. stories about "hitting bottom" and the many degradation ceremonies that they experienced in entering this fallen state act to legitimize their claims to downward mobility. Observation and limited evidence suggest that many of these stories are exaggerated to some degree and that a large proportion of A.A. members maintained at least partially stable status-sets throughout the addiction process. However, by the emphasis on downward mobility due to drinking, the social mobility "distance" traveled by the A.A. member is maximized in the stories. This clearly sets the stage for impressive "comeback accomplishments."

Moral values also play a role in this process. The stories latently emphasize the "hedonistic underworld" to which the A.A. member "traveled." His current status illustrates to others that he has rejected this hedonism and has clearly resubmitted himself to the normative controls and values of the dominant society, exemplified by his A.A. membership. The attempt to promulgate the "length of the mobility trip" is particularly marked in the numerous anonymous appearances that A.A. members make to tell their stories before school groups, college classes, church groups, and service clubs. The importance of these emphases may be indirectly supported by the finding that lower-class persons typically fail in their attempts to successfully affiliate with A.A., i.e., their social circumstances minimize the distance of the downward mobility trip (Trice and Roman, 1970; Trice, 1959).

A.A. AND AMERICAN VALUES

The "return" of the A.A. member to normal role performance through the culturally provided role of the repentant and through the implied social mobility which develops out of an emphasis upon the length of the mobility trip is given its meaning through tapping directly into certain major American value orientations.

Most importantly, members of Alcoholics Anonymous have regained self control and have employed that self control in bringing about their rehabilitation. Self control, particularly that which involves the avoidance of pleasure, is a valued mode of behavior deeply embedded in the American ethos (Williams, 1960). A.A. members have, in a sense, achieved success in their battle with alcohol and may be thought of in that way as being "self-made" in a society permeated by "a systematic moral orientation by which conduct is judged" (Williams, 1960:424). This illustration of self control lends itself to positive sanction by the community.

A.A. also exemplifies three other value orientations as they have been delineated by Williams: humanitarianism, emphases upon practicality, and suspicion of established authority (Williams, 1960:397–470). A definite tendency exists in this society to identify with the helpless, particularly those who are not responsible for their own afflictions.

A.A. taps into the value of efficiency and practicality through its pragmatism and forthright determination to "take action" about a problem. The organization pays little heed to theories about alcoholism and casts all of its literature in extremely practical language. Much emphasis is placed upon the simplicity of its tenets and the straightforward manner in which its processes proceed.

Its organizational pattern is highly congruous with the value, suspicion of vested authority. There is no national or international hierarchy of officers, and local groups maintain maximum autonomy. Within the local group, there are no established patterns of leadership, such that the organization proceeds on a basis which sometimes approaches anarchy. In any event, the informality and equalitarianism are marked features of the organization, which also tend to underline the self control possessed by individual members.

A.A.'s mode of delabeling and relabeling thus appears in a small degree to depend upon promulgation of an allergy concept of alcoholism which is accepted by some members of the general population. Of greater importance in this process is the effective contrivance of a repentant role. Emphasis upon the degradation and downward mo-

bility experienced during the development of alcoholism provides for the ascription of considerable self control to middle-class members, which in turn may enhance their prestige and "shore up" their return to "normality." The repentance process is grounded in and reinforced by the manner in which the A.A. program taps into several basic American value orientations.

A.A.'S LIMITATIONS

As mentioned above, A.A. affiliation by members of the lower social classes is frequently unsuccessful. This seems to stem from the middle-class orientation of most of the A.A. programs, from the fact that it requires certain forms of public confessions and intense interpersonal interaction which may run contrary to the images of masculinity held in the lower classes, as well as interpersonal competence.

Perhaps an equally significant limitation is a psychological selectivity in the affiliation process. A recent followup study of 378 hospitalized alcoholics, all of whom had been intensely exposed to A.A. during their treatment, revealed that those who successfully affiliated with A.A. upon their reentry into the community had personality features significantly different from those who did not affiliate (Trice and Roman, 1970). The successful affiliates were more guilt prone, sensitive to responsibility, more serious, and introspective. This appears to indicate a definite "readiness" for the adoption of the repentant role among successful affiliates. To a somewhat lesser extent, the affiliates possessed a greater degree of measured ego strength, affiliative needs, and group dependency, indicating a "fit" between the peculiar demands for intense interaction required for successful affiliation and the personalities of the successful affiliates. Earlier research also revealed a relatively high need for affiliation among A.A. affiliates as compared to those who were unsuccessful in the affiliation process (Trice, 1959).

These social class and personality factors definitely indicate the A.A. program is not effective for all alcoholics. Convincing entry into the repentant role, as well as successful interactional participation in the program, appear to require middle-class background and certain personality predispositions.

SUMMARY

In summary, we shall contrast the success of A.A. in its delabeling with that experienced by other self help groups designed for former drug addicts and mental patients (Wechsler, 1960; Landy and Singer, 1961). As pointed out above, the statuses of mental patients and narcotic addicts lack the causal clarity accompanying the role of alcoholic. It is most difficult for narcotic addicts and former mental patients to remove the stigma since there is little social clarity about the cessation of the primary deviant behavior. Just as there is no parallel in this respect, there is no parallel in other self-help organizations with the Skid Row image and the status-enhancing "mobility trip" that is afforded by this image. The primary deviant behaviors which lead to the label of drug addict or which eventuate in mental hospitalization are too far removed from ordinary social experience for easy acceptance of the former deviant to occur. These behaviors are a part of an underworld from which return is most difficult. On the other hand, Alcoholics Anonymous possesses, as a consequence of the nature of the disorder of alcoholism, its uniqueness as an organization, and the existence of certain value orientations within American society, a pattern of social processing whereby a labeled deviant can become "delabeled" as a stigmatized deviant and relabeled as a former and repentant deviant.

REFERENCES

"Doctors, Alcohol and A.A." 1968. *Alcoholics Anonymous Grapevine* (October).

Freeman, H. and O. Simmons. 1963. *The Mental Patient Comes Home.* New York: Wiley.

Garfinkel, H. 1956. "Conditions of Successful Degradation Ceremonies." *American Journal of Sociology,* 61 (March):420–424.

Gellman, I. 1964. *The Sober Alcoholic.* New Haven: College and University Press.

Gusfield, J. 1967. "Moral Passage: The Symbolic Process in Public Designations of Deviance." *Social Problems,* 15 (Winter):175–188.

Landy, D. and S. Singer. 1961. "The Social Organization and Culture of a Club for Former Mental Patients." *Human Relations,* 14 (January):31–40.

Lang, K. and G. Lang. 1960. "Decisions for Christ: Billy Graham in New York City." In M. Stein *et al.* (eds.), *Identity and Anxiety.* New York: The Free Press, pp. 415–427.

Lemert, E. 1951. *Social Pathology.* New York: McGraw-Hill.

Miller, D. 1965. *Worlds That Fail.* Sacramento: California Department of Mental Hygiene.

Mulford, H. 1964. "Drinking and Deviant Drinking, U.S.A. 1963." *Quarterly Journal of Studies on Alcohol,* 25 (December):634–650.

Mulford, H. and D. Miller. 1964. "Measuring Public Acceptance of the Alcoholic as a Sick Person." *Quarterly Journal of Studies on Alcohol,* 25 (June): 314–323.

Myers, J. and L. Bean. 1968. *A Decade Later.* New York: Wiley.

Nunnally, J. 1961. *Popular Conceptions of Mental Health.* New York: Holt, Rinehart and Winston.

Parsons, T. 1951. *The Social System.* Glencoe, Ill.: The Free Press.

Pasamanick, B. *et al.* 1967. *Schizophrenics in the Community.* New York: Appleton, Century, Crofts.

Plaut, T. 1967. *Alcohol Problems: A Report to the Nation.* New York: Oxford University Press.

Roman, P. and H. Trice (1969). "The Self Reaction: A Neglected Dimension of Labeling Theory." Presented at American Sociological Association Meetings, San Francisco.

Sagarin, E. 1967. "Voluntary Associations among Social Deviants." *Criminologica* 5 (January):8–22.

Scheff, T. 1966. *Being Mentally Ill.* Chicago: Aldine.

Straus, R. and S. Bacon. 1951. "Alcoholism and Social Stability." *Quarterly Journal of Studies on Alcohol,* 12 (June):231–260.

Susser, M. 1968. *Community Psychiatry.* New York: Random House.

Sussman, M. (ed.) 1966. *Sociology and Rehabilitation.* Washington: American Sociological Association.

Trice, H. 1959. "The Affiliation Motive and Readiness to Join Alcoholics Anonymous." *Quarterly*

Journal of Studies on Alcohol, 20 (September):313–320.

———. 1962. "The Job Behavior of Problem Drinkers." In D. Pittman and C. Snyder (eds.), *Society, Culture and Drinking Patterns.* New York: Wiley, pp. 493–510.

Trice, H. and P. Roman. 1970. "Sociopsychological Predictors of Successful Affiliation with Alcoholics Anonymous." *Social Psychiatry,* 5 (Winter):51–59.

Wechsler, H. 1960. "The Self-Help Organization in the Mental Health Field: Recovery, Inc." *Journal of Nervous and Mental Disease,* 130 (April):297–314.

Williams, R. 1960. *American Society.* New York: A. A. Knopf.

The Professional Ex-

J. DAVID BROWN

During their careers, deviants face changes in their life situation. Their opportunities for continued deviance increase while their chances to engage in conformist pursuits decrease. Conventional society has assigned them the master status of deviant and expects only continued violation from them, blocking their access to conformist life chances. Consequently, persons who seek to terminate their deviant careers confront social barriers to their social reintegration into conventional society. Three of those barriers are lack of practice in conventional roles, continued suspicion from conformists, and pressure from fellow deviants to return to the fold.

J. David Brown describes a "deviant" route to reintegration into conventional society. Substance abuse counselors, unlike conventional professional therapists, can draw upon their considerable personal experience with deviant substance use. Having "been there," they are more likely to establish rapport with their clients than are other professionals. Their past deviant identities provide accumulated social capital they can draw on when counseling substance users. In the process, they become role models in how to exit the career of deviant substance user.

This study explores the careers of professional ex-s, persons who have exited their deviant careers by replacing them with occupations in professional counseling. During their transformation professional ex-s utilize vestiges of their deviant identity to legitimate their past deviance and generate new careers as counselors.

Reprinted from "The Professional Ex-: An Alternative for Exiting the Deviant Career," *The Sociological Quarterly,* Vol. 32, No. 2, pp. 219–230, by permission of the publisher and the author. Copyright © 1991 by JAI Press, Inc.

Recent surveys document that approximately 72% of the professional counselors working in the over 10,000 U.S. substance abuse treatment centers are former substance abusers (NAADAC 1986; Sobel and Sobel 1987). This attests to the significance of the professional ex- phenomenon. Though not all ex-deviants become professional ex-s, such data clearly suggest that the majority of substance abuse counselors are professional ex-s.[1]

Since the inception of the notion of deviant career by Goffman (1961) and Becker (1963), research has identified, differentiated, and explicated the characteristics of specific deviant career stages (e.g., Adler and Adler 1983; Luckenbill and Best 1981; Meisenhelder 1977; Miller 1986; Shover 1983). The literature devoted to exiting deviance primarily addresses the process whereby individuals abandon their deviant behaviors, ideologies, and identities and replace them with more conventional lifestyles and identities (Irwin 1970; Lofland 1969; Meisenhelder 1977; Shover 1983). While some studies emphasize the role of authorities or associations of ex-deviants in this change (e.g., Livingston 1974; Lofland 1969; Volkman and Cressey 1963), others suggest that exiting deviance is a natural process contingent upon age-related, structural, and social psychological variables (Frazier 1976; Inciardi 1975; Irwin 1970; Meisenhelder 1977; Petersilia 1980; Shover 1983).

Although exiting deviance has been variously conceptualized, to date no one has considered that it might include adoption of a legitimate career premised upon an identity that embraces one's deviant history. Professional ex-s exemplify this mode of exiting deviance.

Ebaugh's (1988) model of role exit provides an initial framework for examining this alternative mode of exiting the deviant career. Her model suggests that former roles are never abandoned but, instead, carry over into new roles. I elaborate her position and contend that one's deviant identity is not an obstacle that must be abandoned prior to exiting or adopting a more conventional lifestyle. To the contrary, one's lingering deviant identity facilitates rather than inhibits the exiting process.

How I gathered data pertinent to exiting, my relationship to these data, and how my personal experiences with exiting deviance organize this article, follow. I then present a four stage model that outlines the basic contours of the professional ex-phenomenon. Finally I suggest how the professional ex- phenomenon represents an alternative interpretation of exiting deviance that generalizes to other forms of deviance....

Qualitative data were collected over a six month period of intensive interviews with 35

counselor ex-s employed in a variety of community, state, and private institutions that treat individuals with drug, alcohol, and/or eating disorder problems.[2]

These professional ex-s worked in diverse occupations prior to becoming substance abuse counselors. A partial list includes employment as accountants, managers, salespersons, nurses, educators, and business owners. Although they claimed to enter the counseling profession within two years of discharge from therapy, their decision to become counselors usually came within one year. On the average they had been counselors for four and one half years. Except one professional ex- who previously counseled learning disabled children, all claimed they had not seriously considered a counseling career before entering therapy.

THE EXIT PROCESS

Ebaugh (1988) contends that the experience of being an "ex" of one kind or another is common to most people in modern society. Emphasizing the sociological and psychological continuity of the ex phenomenon she states, "[I]t implies that interaction is based not only on current role definitions but, more important, past identities that somehow linger on and define how people see and present themselves in their present identities" (p. xiii). Ebaugh defines role exit as the "process of disengagement from a role that is central to one's self-identity and the reestablishment of an identity in a new role that takes into account one's ex-role" (p. 1).

Becoming a professional ex- is the outcome of a four stage process through which ex-s capitalize on the experience and vestiges of their deviant career in order to establish a new identity and role in a respectable organization. This process comprises emulation of one's therapist, the call to a counseling career, status-set realignment, and credentialization.

STAGE ONE: EMULATION OF ONE'S THERAPIST

The emotional and symbolic identification of these ex-s with their therapists during treatment, combined with the deep personal meanings they imputed to these relationships, was a compelling factor in their decisions to become counselors. Denzin (1987, pp. 61–62) identifies the therapeutic relationship's significance thus: "Through a process of identification and surrender (which may be altruistic), the alcoholic may merge her ego and her self in the experiences and the identity of the counselor. The group leader…is the group ego ideal, for he or she is a successful recovering alcoholic.… An emotional bond is thus formed with the group counselor.…"

Professional ex-s not only developed this emotional bond but additionally aspired to have the emotions and meanings once projected toward their therapists ascribed to them. An eating disorders counselor discussed her relationship with her therapist and her desire to be viewed in a similar way with these words:

My counselor taught me the ability to care about myself and other people. Before I met her I was literally insane. She was the one who showed me that I wasn't crazy. Now, I want to be the person who says, "No, you're not crazy!" I am the one, now, who is helping them to get free from the ignorance that has shrouded eating disorders.

Counselors enacted a powerfully charismatic role in professional ex-s' therapeutic transformation. Their "laying on of verbal hands" provided initial comfort and relief from the ravaging symptoms of disease. They came to represent what ex-s must do both spiritually and professionally for themselves. Substance abuse therapy symbolized the "sacred" quest for divine grace rather than the mere pursuit of mundane, worldly, or "profane" outcomes like abstinence or modification of substance use/abuse behaviors; counselors embodied the sacred outcome.

Professional ex-s claimed that their therapists were the most significant change agent in their transformation. "I am here today because there was one very influential counselor in my life who helped me to get sober. I owe it all to God and to him," one alcoholism counselor expressed. A her-

oin addiction counselor stated, "The best thing that ever happened in my life was meeting Sally [her counselor]. She literally saved my life. If it wasn't for her I'd still probably be out there shootin' up or else be in prison or, dead."

Subjects' recognition and identification of a leader's charismatic authority, as Weber (1968) notes, [are] decisive in validating that charisma and developing absolute trust and devotion. The special virtues and powers professional ex-s perceived in their counselors subsequently shaped their loyalty and devotion to the career.

Within the therapeutic relationship, professional ex-s perform a priestly function through which a cultural tradition passes from one generation to the next. While knowledge and wisdom pass downward (from professional ex- to patient), careers build upward (from patient to professional ex-). As the bearers of the cultural legacy of therapy, professional ex-s teach patients definitions of the situation they learned as patients. Indeed, part of the professional ex-mystique resides in once having been a patient (Bissell 1982). In this regard,

My counselor established her legitimacy with me the moment she disclosed the fact that she, too, was an alcoholic. She wasn't just telling me what to do, she was living her own advice. By the example she set, I felt hopeful that I could recover. As I reflect upon those experiences I cannot think of one patient ever asking me about where I received my professional training. At the same time, I cannot begin to count the numerous times that my patients have asked me if I was "recovering."

Similar to religious converts' salvation through a profoundly redemptive religious experience, professional ex-s' deep career commitment derives from a transforming therapeutic resocialization. As the previous examples suggest, salvation not only relates to a changed universe of discourse; it is also identified "with one's personal therapist."[3]

At this stage, professional ex-s trust in and devote themselves to their counselors' proselytizations as a promissory note for the future. The promise is redemption and salvation from the ever-present potential for self-destruction or relapse that looms in their mental horizon. An eating disorders counselor shared her insights in this way:

> I wouldn't have gotten so involved in eating disorders counseling if I had felt certain that my eating disorder was taken care of. I see myself in constant recovery. If I was so self-assured that I would never have the problem again there would probably be less of an emphasis on being involved in the field but I have found that helping others, as I was once helped, really helps me.

The substance abuse treatment center transforms from a mere "clinic" occupied by secularly credentialed professionals into a moral community of single believers. As Durkheim (1915) suggests, however, beliefs require rites and practices in order to sustain adherents' mental and emotional states.

STAGE TWO: THE CALL TO A COUNSELING CAREER

At this juncture, professional ex-s begin to turn the moral corner on their deviance. Behaviors previously declared morally reprehensible are increasingly understood within a new universe of discourse as symptoms of a much larger disease complex. This recognition represents one preliminary step toward grace. In order to emulate their therapist, however, professional ex-s realize they must dedicate themselves to an identity and lifestyle that ensure their own symptoms' permanent remission. One alcoholism counselor illustrated this point by stating:

> I can't have my life, my health, my family, my job, my friends, or anything, unless I take daily necessary steps to ensure my continued recovery. My program of recovery has to come first. Before I can go out there and help my patients I need to always make sure that my own house is in order.

As this suggests, a new world-view premised upon accepting the contingencies of one's illness while maintaining a constant vigilance over potentially recurring symptoms replaces deviant moral and social meanings. Professional ex-s' recognition of the need for constant vigilance is internalized as their moral mission from which their spiritual duty (a counseling career) follows as a natural next step.

Although professional ex-s no longer engage in substance abuse behaviors, they do not totally abandon deviant beliefs or identity. "Lest we become complacent and forget from whence we came," [was the way] one alcoholism counselor indicated the significance of remembering and embracing the past.

Professional ex-s' identification with their deviant past undergirds their professional, experiential, and moral differentiation from other professional colleagues. A heroin addiction counselor recounted how he still identified himself as an addict and deviant:

> My perspective and my affinity to my clients, particularly the harder core criminals, is far better than the professors and other doctors that I deal with here in my job. We're different and we really don't see things the same way at all. Our acceptance and understanding of these people's diseases, if you will, [are] much different. They haven't experienced it. They don't know these people at all. It takes more than knowing about something to be effective. I've been there and, in many respects, I will always be there.

In this way, other counselors' medical, psychiatric, or therapeutic skills are construed as part of the ordinary mundane world. As the quotation indicates, professional ex-s intentionally use their experiential past and therapeutic transformations to legitimate their entrance into and authority in counseling careers.

Professional ex-s embrace their deviant history and identity as an invaluable, therapeutic resource and feel compelled to continually reaffirm its validity in an institutional environmnent. Certainly, participating in "12 Step Programs"[4] without becoming counselors could help others but professional ex-s' call requires greater immersion than they provide. An alcoholism counselor reflected upon this need thus:

> For me, it was no longer sufficient to only participate "anonymously" in A.A. I wanted to surround myself with other spiritual and professional pilgrims devoted to receiving and imparting wisdom.

Towards patients, professional ex-s project a saintly aura and exemplify an "ideal recovery." Internalization of self-images previously ascribed to their therapist and now reaffirmed through an emotional and moral commitment to the counseling profession facilitate this ideation. Invariably, professional ex-s' counseling careers are in institutions professing treatment ideologies identical to what they were taught as patients. Becoming a professional ex- symbolizes a value elevated to a directing goal, whose pursuit predisposes them to interpret all ensuing experience in terms of relevance to it.

STAGE THREE: STATUS-SET REALIGNMENT

Professional ex-s' deep personal identification with their therapist provides an ego ideal to be emulated with regard to both recovery and career. They immerse themselves in what literally constitutes a "professional recovery career" that provides an institutional location to reciprocate their counselors' gift, immerse themselves in a new universe of discourse, and effectively lead novitiates to salvation. "I wouldn't be here today if it wasn't for all of the help I received in therapy. This is my way of paying some of those people back by helping those still in need," one alcoholism counselor related this.

Professional ex-s' identities assume a "master status" (Hughes 1945) that differs in one fundamental respect from others' experiencing therapeutic resocialization. Specifically, their transformed identities not only become the "most salient" in their "role identity hierarchy" (Stryker and Serpe 1982), but affect all other roles in their "status-sets" (Merton 1938). One alcoholism counselor reflected upon it this way:

> Maintaining a continued program of recovery is the most important thing in my life. Everything else is secondary. I've stopped socializing with my old friends who drink and have developed new recovering friends. I interact differently with my family. I used to work a lot of overtime but I told my old boss that overtime jeopardized my program. I finally began to realize that the job just didn't have anything to do with what I was really about. I felt alienated. Although I had been thinking about becoming a counselor ever since I went through treatment, I finally decided to pursue it.

Role realignment is facilitated by an alternative identity that redefines obligations associated with other, less significant, role identities. In the previous example, the strains of expectations associated with a former occupation fostered a role realignment consistent with a new self-image. This phenomenon closely resembles what Snow and Machalek (1983, p. 276) refer to as "embracement of a master role" that "is not merely a mask that is taken off or put on according to the situation.... Rather, it is central to nearly all situations...." An eating disorders counselor stated the need to align her career with her self-image, "I hid in my former profession, interacting little with people. As a counselor, I am personally maturing and taking responsibility rather than letting a company take care of me. I have a sense of purpose in this job that I never had before."

Financial remuneration is not a major consideration in the decision to become a professional ex-. The pure type of call, Weber (1968, p. 52) notes, "disdains and repudiates economic exploitation of the gifts of grace as a source of income...." Most professional ex-s earned more money in their previous jobs. For instance, one heroin addiction counselor stated:

> When I first got out of treatment, my wife and I started an accounting business. In our first year we cleared nearly sixty thousand dollars. The money was great and the business showed promise but something was missing. I missed being around other addicts and I knew I wanted to do more with my life along the lines of helping out people like me.

An additional factor contributing to professional ex-s' abandonment of their previous occupation is their recognition that a counseling career could resolve lingering self-doubts about their ability to remain abstinent. In this respect becoming a professional ex- allows "staying current" with their own recovery needs while continually reaffirming the severity of their illness. An eating disorders counselor explained:

I'm constantly in the process of repeating insights that I've had to my patients. I hear myself saying, to them, what I need to believe for myself. Being a therapist helps me to keep current with my own recovery. I feel that I am much less vulnerable to my disease in this environment. It's a way that I can keep myself honest. Always being around others with similar issues prevents me from ignoring my own addiction clues.

This example illustrates professional ex-s' use of their profession to secure self-compliance during times of self-doubt. While parroting the virtues of the program facilitates recognition that they, too, suffer from a disease, the professional ex- role, unlike their previous occupations, enables them to continue therapy indirectly.

Finally, the status the broader community ascribes to the professional ex- role encourages professional ex-s' abandonment of previous roles. Association with an institutional environment and an occupational role gives the professional ex- a new sense of place in the surrounding community, within which form new self-concepts and self-esteem, both in the immediate situation and in a broader temporal framework.

The internal validation of professional ex-s' new identity resides in their ability to successfully anticipate the behaviors and actions of relevant alters. Additionally, they secure validation by other members of the professional ex- community in a manner atypical for other recovering individuals. Affirmation by this reference community symbolizes validation by one's personal therapist and the therapeutic institution, as a heroin addiction counselor succinctly stated:

Becoming a counselor was a way to demonstrate my loyalty and devotion to helping others and myself. My successes in recovery, including being a counselor, would be seen by patients and those who helped me get sober. It was a return to treatment, for sure, but the major difference was that this time I returned victorious rather than defeated.

External validation, on the other hand, comes when others outside the therapeutic community accord legitimacy to the professional ex- role. In this regard, a heroin addiction counselor said:

I remember talking to this guy while I was standing in line for a movie. He asked me what I did for a living and I told him that I was a drug abuse counselor. He started asking me all these questions about the drug problem and what I thought the answers were. When we finally got up to the door of the theater he patted me on the back and said, "You're doing a wonderful job. Keep up the good work. I really admire you for what you're trying to do." It really felt good to have a stranger praise me.

Professional ex-s' counseling role informs the performance of all other roles, compelling them to abandon previous work they increasingly view as mundane and polluting. The next section demonstrates how this master role organizes the meanings associated with their professional counselor training.

STAGE FOUR: CREDENTIALIZATION

One characteristic typically distinguishing the professions from other occupations is specialized knowledge acquired at institutions of higher learning (Larson 1977; Parsons 1959; Ritzer and Walczak 1986, 1988). Although mastering esoteric knowledge and professional responsibilities in a therapeutic relationship serve as gatekeepers for entering the counseling profession, the moral and emotional essence of being a professional ex- involves much more.

Professional ex-s see themselves as their patients' champions. "Knowing what it's like" and the subsequent education and skills acquired in training legitimate claims to the "entitlements of their stigma" (Gusfield 1982), including professional status. Their monopoly of an abstruse body of knowledge and skill is realized through their emotionally lived history of shame and guilt as well as the hope and redemption secured through therapeutic transformation. Professional ex-s associate higher learning with their experiential history of deviance and the emotional context of therapy. Higher learning symbolizes rediscovery of a moral sense of worth and sacredness rather than credential acquisition. This distinction was clarified by an alcoholism counselor:

> Anymore, you need to have a degree before anybody will hire you. I entered counseling with a bachelor's but I eventually received my MSW about two years ago. I think the greatest benefit in having the formal training is that I have been able to more effectively utilize my personal alcoholism experiences with my patients. I feel that I have a gift to offer my patients which doesn't come from the classroom. It comes from being an alcoholic myself.

These entitlements allow professional ex-s to capitalize on their deviant identity in two ways: the existential and phenomenological dimensions of their lived experience of "having made their way from the darkness into the light" provide their experiential and professional *legitimacy* among patients, the community, and other professionals, as well as occupational *income*. "Where else could I go and put bulimic and alcoholic on my resume and get hired?" one counselor put it.

Professional ex-s generally eschew meta-perspective interpretations of the system in which they work. They desire a counseling method congruent with their fundamental universe of discourse and seek, primarily, to perpetuate this system (Peele 1989; Room 1972, 1976). The words of one educator at a local counselor training institute are germane:

> These people [professional ex-s]...are very fragile when they get here. Usually, they have only been in recovery for about a year. Anyone who challenges what they learned in therapy, or in their program of recovery [i.e., A.A., Narcotics Anonymous, Overeaters Anonymous]...is viewed as a threat. Although we try to change some of that while they're here with us, I still see my role here as one of an extended therapist rather than an educator.

Information challenging their beliefs about how they, and their patients, should enact the rites associated with recovery is condemned (Davies 1963; Pattison 1987; Roizen 1977). They view intellectual challenges to the disease concept as attacks on their personal program of recovery. In a Durkheimian sense, such challenges "profane" that which they hold "sacred."

Within the walls of these monasteries professional ex-s emulate their predecessors as one generation of healers passes on to the next an age old message of salvation. Although each new generation presents the path to enlightenment in somewhat different, contemporary terms, it is already well lit for those "becoming a professional ex-."

DISCUSSION

Focusing on their lived experiences and accounts, this study sketches the central contours of professional ex-s' distinctive exit process. More generally, it also endeavors to contribute to the existing literature on deviant careers.

An identity that embraces their deviant history and identity undergirds professional ex-s' careers. This exiting mode is the outcome of a four stage process enabling professional ex-s to capitalize on their deviant history. They do not "put it all behind them" in exchange for conventional lifestyles, values, beliefs, and identities. Rather, they use vestiges of their deviant biography as an explicit occupational strategy.

My research augments Ebaugh's (1988) outline of principles underlying role exit in three ways. First, her discussion suggests that people are unaware of these guiding principles. While this holds for many, professional ex-s' intentional rather than unintentional embracement of their deviant identity is the step by which they adopt a new role in the counseling profession. Second, Ebaugh states that significant others' negative reactions inhibit or interrupt exit. Among professional ex-s, however, such reactions are a crucial precursor to their exit mode. Finally, Ebaugh sees role exit as a voluntary, individually initiated process, enhanced by "seeking alternatives" through which to explore other roles. Professional ex-s, by contrast, are compelled into therapy. They do not look for this particular role. Rather, their alternatives are prescribed through their resocialization into a new identity.

Organizations in American society increasingly utilize professional ex-s in their social control efforts. For example, the state of Colorado uses prisoners to counsel delinquent youth. A preliminary, two year, follow-up study suggests that these prisoner-counselors show only 13% recidivism (Shiller 1988) and a substantial number want to return to college or enter careers as guidance counselors, probation officers, youth educators, or law enforcement consultants. Similarly, a local effort directed toward curbing gang violence, the Open Door Youth Gang Program, was developed by a professional ex- and uses former gang members as counselors, educators, and community relations personnel.

Further examination of the modes through which charismatic, albeit licensed and certified, groups generate professional ex- statuses is warranted. Although the examples just described differ from the professional ex-s examined earlier in this research in terms of therapeutic or "medicalized" resocialization, their similarities are even more striking. Central to them all is that a redemptive community provides a reference group whose moral and social standards are internalized. Professional ex- statuses are generated as individuals intentionally integrate and embrace rather than abandon their deviant biographies as a specific occupational strategy.

NOTES

1. Most individuals in substance abuse therapy do not become professional ex-s. Rather, they traverse a variety of paths not articulated here including (1) dropping out of treatment, (2) completing treatment but returning to substance use and/or abuse, and (3) remaining abstinent after treatment but feeling no compulsion to enter the counseling profession. Future research will explore the differences among persons by mode of exit. Here, however, analysis and description focus exclusively on individuals committed to the professional ex- role.

2. I conducted most interviews at the subject's work environment, face-to-face. One interview was with a focus group of 10 professional ex-s (Morgan 1988). Two interviews were in my office, one at my home, and one at a subject's home. I interviewed each individual one time for approximately one hour. Interviews were semistructured, with open-end questions designed to elicit responses related to feelings, thoughts, perceptions, reflections, and meanings concerning subjects' past deviance, factors facilitating their exit from deviance, and their counseling career.

3. I contend that significantly more professional ex-s pursue their careers due to therapeutic resocialization than to achieving sobriety/recovery exclusively through the 12 Step Program (e.g., A.A.). It is too early, however, to preclude that some may enter substance abuse counseling careers lacking any personal therapy. My experiences and my interviews with other professional ex-s suggest that very few professional ex-s enter the profession directly through their contacts with the 12 Step Program. The program's moral precepts—that "sobriety is a gift from God" that must be "given freely to others in order to assure that one may keep the gift"—would appear to discourage rather than encourage substance abuse counseling careers. Financial remuneration for assisting fellow substance abusers directly violates these precepts. Further, professional ex-s are commonly disparaged in A.A. circles as "two hatters" (cf. Denzin 1987). They are, therefore, not a positive reference group for individuals recovering exclusively through the 12 Step Program. Sober 12 Step members are more inclined to emulate their "sponsors" than pursue careers with no experiential referents or direct relevance to their recovery. Further data collection and analysis will examine these differences. Extant data, however, strongly indicate that therapeutic resocialization and a professional role model provide the

crucial link between deviant and substance abuse counseling careers.

4. "12 Step Program" refers to a variety of self-help groups (e.g., A.A., Narcotics Anonymous, Overeaters Anonymous) patterning their recovery model upon the original 12 Steps and 12 Traditions of A.A.

REFERENCES

Adler, Patricia, and Peter Adler. 1983. "Shifts and Oscillations in Deviant Careers: The Case of Upper-Level Drug Dealers and Smugglers." *Social Problems* 31:195–207.

Becker, Howard. 1963. *Outsiders: Studies in the Sociology of Deviance.* New York: Free Press.

Best, Joel, and David F. Luckenbill. 1962. *Organizing Deviance.* Englewood Cliffs, NJ: Prentice-Hall.

Bissell, LeClair. 1982. "Recovered Alcoholism Counselors." Pp. 810–817 in *Encyclopedic Handbook of Alcoholism,* edited by E. Mansell Pattison and Edward Kaufman. New York: Gardner.

Davies, D. L. 1963. "Normal Drinking in Recovered Alcoholic Addicts" (comments by various correspondents). *Quarterly Journal of Studies on Alcohol* 24:109–121, 321–332.

Denzin, Norman. 1987. *The Recovering Alcoholic.* Beverly Hills: Sage.

Durkheim, Emile. 1915. *The Elementary Forms of the Religious Life.* New York: Free Press.

Ebaugh, Helen Rose Fuchs. 1988. *Becoming an Ex: The Process of Role Exit.* Chicago: University of Chicago Press.

Frazier, Charles. 1976. *Theoretical Approaches to Deviance.* Columbus: Charles Merrill.

Goffman, Erving. 1961. *Asylums.* Garden City, NY: Anchor.

Gusfield, Joseph. 1982. "Deviance in the Welfare State: The Alcoholism Profession and the Entitlements of Stigma." *Research in Social Problems and Public Policy* 2:1–20.

Hughes, Everett. 1945. "Dilemmas and Contradictions of Status." *American Journal of Sociology* 50:353–359.

Inciardi, James. 1975. *Careers in Crime.* Chicago: Rand McNally.

Irwin, John. 1970. *The Felon.* Englewood Cliffs: Prentice-Hall.

Larson, Magali. 1977. *The Rise of Professionalism.* Berkeley: University of California Press.

Livingston, Jay. 1974. *Compulsive Gamblers.* New York: Harper and Row.

Lofland, John. 1969. *Deviance and Identity.* Englewood Cliffs, NJ: Prentice-Hall.

Luckenbill, David F., and Joel Best. 1981. "Careers in Deviance and Respectability: The Analogy's Limitations." *Social Problems* 29:197–206.

Meisenhelder, Thomas. 1977. "An Exploratory Study of Exiting from Criminal Careers." *Criminology* 15: 319–334.

Merton, Robert. 1938. *Social Theory and Social Structure.* Glencoe: Free Press.

Miller, Gale. 1986. "Conflict in Deviant Occupations." Pp. 373–401 in *Working: Conflict and Change,* 3rd ed., edited by George Ritzer and David Walczak. Englewood Cliffs: Prentice-Hall.

Morgan, David L. 1988. *Focus Groups as Qualitative Research.* Beverly Hills: Sage.

NAADAC. 1986. *Development of Model Professional Standards for Counselor Credentialing.* National Association of Alcoholism and Drug Abuse Counselors. Dubuque: Kendall-Hunt.

Parsons, Talcott. 1959. "Some Problems Confronting Sociology as a Profession." *American Sociological Review* 24:547–559.

Pattison, E. Mansell. 1987. "Whither Goals in the Treatment of Alcoholism." *Drugs and Society* 2/3: 153–171.

Peele, Stanton. 1989. *The Diseasing of America: Addiction Treatment Out of Control.* Toronto: Lexington.

Petersilia, Joan. 1980. "Criminal Career Research: A Review of Recent Evidence." Pp. 321–379 in *Crime and Justice: An Annual Review of Research,* vol. 2, edited by Norval Morris and Michael Tonry. Chicago: University of Chicago Press.

Ritzer, George, and David Walczak. 1986. *Working: Conflict and Change.* 3rd ed. Englewood Cliffs: Prentice-Hall.

———. 1988. "Rationalization and the Deprofessionalization of Physicians." *Social Forces* 67:1–22.

Roizen, Ron. 1977. "Comment on the Rand Report." *Quarterly Journal of Studies on Alcohol* 38: 170–178.

Room, Robin. 1972. "Drinking and Disease: Comment on the Alcoholist's Addiction." *Quarterly Journal of Studies on Alcohol* 33:1049–1059.

————. 1976. "Drunkenness and the Law: Comment on the Uniform Alcoholism Intoxication Treatment Act." *Quarterly Journal of Studies on Alcohol* 37:113–144.

Shiller, Gene. 1988. "A Preliminary Report on SHAPE-UP." Paper presented to the Colorado District Attorneys Council, Denver.

Shover, Neil. 1983. "The Later Stages of Ordinary Property Offenders' Careers." *Social Problems* 31: 208–218.

Snow, David, and Richard Machalek. 1983. "The Convert as a Social Type." Pp. 259–289 in *Sociological Theory 1983,* edited by Randall Collins. San Francisco: Jossey-Bass.

Sobell, Mark B., and Linda C. Sobell. 1987. "Conceptual Issues Regarding Goals in the Treatment of Alcohol Problems." *Drugs and Alcohol* 2/3:1–37.

Stryker, Sheldon, and Richard Serpe. 1982. "Commitment, Identity Salience, and Role Behavior: Theory and Research Example." Pp. 199–218 in *Personality, Roles, and Social Behavior,* edited by William Ickes and Eric S. Knowles. New York: Springer-Verlag.

Volkman, Rita, and Donald Cressey. 1963. "Differential Association and the Rehabilitation of Drug Addicts." *American Journal of Sociology* 69:129–142.

Weber, Max. 1968. *On Charisma and Institution Building.* Edited by S. N. Eisenstadt. Chicago: University of Chicago Press.

Medicalizing and Demedicalizing Hermaphroditism

MARTIN S. WEINBERG, COLIN J. WILLIAMS, and BO LAURENT

Numerous folk expressions that say, "once a…, always a…," attest to the many obstacles that social definitions of deviance place in the way of those who would seek to transform definitions of deviant identity. For the most part there exist just two traditional ways of accomplishing this kind of personal change. Some persons can change their deviant identity without the assistance of other persons or agencies of social control. Unknown numbers of alcoholics and drug addicts become abstainers, define themselves as nonusers, and forsake the company of users without any help from treatment agencies. Others make the transformation with the assistance of professional help, agencies of social control, and the like. In both instances, however, they reject their former self-definitions, statuses, and roles. In these cases, the transformation of personal identity requires renunciation of all previous ways of deviant thinking, feeling, and acting.

Since the late 1980s there have been a series of collective attempts to redefine deviant identities. Coalitions of persons, groups, organizations, and social movements have come into being that seek to redefine a specific deviant category. Here again there are two varieties of movements of redefinition: those staffed primarily by experts and those staffed primarily by the clients. Generally, what is at stake here is which group gains control over the right to define deviant identities. Medicalization is perhaps the best example of the case of experts winning the rights of social redefinition. Alcoholism, drug addiction, homosexuality (until 1973), and hyperkinesis are four instances of successful medicalization. Demedicalization refers to collective attempts by the clients of the institution of medicine to gain control of the right of self-definition. John Kitsuse has termed these attempts *tertiary* deviance. An example of successful demedicalization is the gay rights movement; one result of its efforts was the removal of homosexuality as a mental illness from the diagnostic manual of the American Psychiatric Association in 1973. Social movements staffed primarily by deviants can come into being, then, not to make changes in themselves, but rather to foster social change in their collective definition. They ask that the society accept them on their own terms rather than on the terms of social control experts.

Martin S. Weinberg, Colin J. Williams, and Bo Laurent direct attention to a recent social movement that calls into question the right of medical experts to control the definition of sexual identity at birth. Babies born with anomalous genitalia have been called hermaphrodites. Physicians insist upon almost immediate surgical repair whereby these infants will be assigned to either the female or the male sex. The authors show how an "intersex movement" has arisen among those who have been socially assigned to their public sexual definition by the medical profession and its use of surgery. They have described perhaps the most elemental example of a group of medical clients who are now fighting for the right of a social and personal sexual definition that is not a deviant or physically manufactured one.

The interactionist perspective on deviance has focused on the ways in which certain conditions and acts come to be conceptualized as deviant (Rubington and Weinberg, 1996). Thus, attention has centered on the activities of various persons or groups involved in this process (Best, 1995). One process—called the "medicalization of deviance" (Conrad and Schneider, 1980)—has been noteworthy for the controversy that has accompanied it. Two features underlie "medicalization" as defined by Riessman (1983:4): "First, certain behaviors or conditions are given medical meaning— that is, defined in terms of health and illness. Second, medical practice becomes a vehicle for eliminating or controlling problematic experiences that are defined as deviant."

To conceptualize deviance in this way is successful only to the extent that the behavior or condition can be construed as a medical pathology. Thus, we have the concept of mental illness as an exemplar with its own medical specialty (psychiatry), hospitals, and drug therapies (Szasz, 1970). In contrast, homosexuality, which was once viewed as an illness, had been demedicalized by the 1970s and was no longer considered an illness in the *Diagnostic and Statistical Manual* (DSM-III) of the American Psychiatric Association (Spector and Kitsuse, 1977; Bayer, 1981). In the 1990s, with the AIDS epidemic once again conjoining homosexuality and disease in some people's minds, there has been an attempt to remedicalize the behavior (Conrad and Schneider, 1992). A similar social contest characterizes alcoholism. A genetic cause is claimed, but has yet to be discovered. Nor does any germ or virus seem responsible. Indeed, alcoholism seems better treated outside of medical institutions (e.g., in self-help groups), making for a continued debate over its status as a medical problem (Appleton, 1995). This paper considers as a case study the current controversy surrounding the medicalization and demedicalization of hermaphroditism (being born with sexual organs that are not completely male or female).

As Conrad has pointed out (1975), medicalization can individualize a problem and locate it in the individual; demedicalization can lead away from individualizing a problem and situate it in the structure of society. Thus, we can ask what are the consequences of focusing on hermaphroditism as a problem in the individual's body as compared to being a problem in the social organization of society? This issue has produced two opposing groups. On one side are pediatric surgeons, urologists, endocrinologists, and associated personnel (e.g., psychologists and social workers) who work in medical settings like hospitals. To them hermaphroditism is a medical problem involving a surgical solution. This idea is supported by one group of academic sex researchers who believe in helping the individual adjust to society as it exists. They are supported by the majority of parents of hermaphrodites who want their child to grow up as a "normal" boy or girl, by some hermaphrodites, and by a society that resolutely insists on the division of human beings into two and only two sexes, male and female (cf. Kessler, 1990).

On the other side are some hermaphrodites, surgically altered in childhood to fit the male/female dichotomy, who have experienced negative consequences as a result. They oppose the conceptualization of this situation as a medical problem and have established an organization, the Intersex Society of North America (ISNA), to combat this view. Among their emerging allies are members of the transgender community (notably transsexuals, cross-dressers, and the like), and many academic sex researchers who believe society should change to accept individuals as they are. All on this side share a common stance: they question society's binary characterization of both sex and gender (cf. Bolin, 1996).

METHOD

Our methods for researching the opponents and proponents of medicalization are as follows. For the supporters of demedicalization, we have had a thorough knowledge of ISNA from its inception, as well as discussions with some 50 of the intersexuals associated with it and approximately ten parents. Our information also includes ISNA's newsletters, computer communications, and other correspondence. There have been discussions with the leaders and members of other organizations of intersexuals across the United States and in England, Germany, and Japan; attendance at the

Mount Sinai Symposia on Pediatric Plastic Surgery in 1996; and interviews with those who picketed the annual meetings of the American Academy of Pediatrics in 1997 and those who lobbied Congress in Washington, DC, to include cosmetic intersex genital surgeries in their legislation against clitorectomies. There have been conversations with sympathetic surgeons, pediatric urologists, gynecologists, endocrinologists, and counselors and with members of the transgender movement and sex researchers and social scientists studying gender. Finally, there has been a complete and careful review of all the literature from the viewpoint of various proponents.

As for the supporters of the medical view, our resources are not as vast but are equally thorough. In addition to conversations and written communications with them, media events and public airings of their viewpoint have been part of the database. They also have been observed in their discussions of the topic at medical meetings, and there have been personal discussions with the less famous as well as the more famous supporters. All their literature has been carefully read and analyzed.

THE MEDICAL VIEW

The term hermaphrodite has a long history with diverse meanings (cf. Fiedler, 1978). Its major interpreter has been the medical profession. Thus, hermaphroditism is given an anatomical definition, referring to individuals born with variant sexual anatomy. Furthermore, hermaphroditism may be caused by a variety of somatic factors (medical literature lists more than two dozen distinct etiologies; Migeon, Berkovitz, and Brown, 1994). As all these factors are caused by some body phenomenon, hermaphroditism is firmly placed within the purview of the medical profession. Even when *no* cause can be determined, a "large" clitoris or a "small" penis is considered problematic ("idiopathic") and surgically altered anyway.

Modern-day medical terminology reflects the late Victorian belief that gonads (ovaries or testes)

reveal a person's "true" sex (Dreger, 1995, 1997; Money, 1972). Thus, "true hermaphrodism" is restricted to individuals who possess a testis and an ovary, or testicular and ovarian tissue mixed in one or both gonads. This is contrasted with "pseudohermaphroditism" (which characterizes the vast majority of hermaphrodites): individuals with two ovaries and varying degrees of masculinized genitalia are labeled female pseudohermaphrodites; those with two testes and incompletely masculinized genitalia are labeled male pseudohermaphrodites.

External anatomical variations labeled hermaphroditic may also take the form of ambiguous genitalia. Most people labeled female have a small phallus that is called a clitoris; most people labeled male have a large phallus that is called a penis (which is simply the continuation in physical development of a clitoris). In medical discourse a phallus that lies between these endpoints is labeled ambiguous, and the person is considered an "intersexual" or "hermaphrodite." Ambiguities may also exist internally or as a discordance between the internal and external structures. For example, an individual who has a normal-appearing vulva but internally has testes also would be labeled hermaphroditic, as would a person who has a normal-appearing penis but internally has ovaries. "Hermaphrodite" then is not a well-defined category, and therefore a numerical assessment is problematic. The best estimate of the number of births where sex comes into question is 1 in 2,000 (Fausto-Sterling, [1996]).

The medical construction of the hermaphrodite usually begins at birth when routine sex assignment cannot be done purely on the inspection of the baby's genitalia. As a result the child may be subjected to a variety of medical investigations, such as chromosomal analysis, hormonal evaluation, and genitography. Test results may not be immediately available, yet there are pressures on medical personnel (especially from the parents) to make a decision as quickly as possible (Kessler, 1990).

Current theory also considers genital ambiguity to be both a medical and psychosocial emergency (Izquierdo and Glassberg, 1993) and requires

that sex assignment be made quickly in order to forestall family rejection, community stigmatization, and possible gender identity problems (cf. Meyer-Bahlburg, 1996). "We make it a social emergency by dragging the team in during the middle of the night," relates one prominent pediatric surgeon (Lee, 1994). Money counsels that it may be unwise at first to pronounce such a baby a boy or girl as such "nouns and pronouns convey certainty." Rather, to reassure the parents, it should be said the baby's sex is "indeterminant" or that the child has been born "sexually unfinished" (Money, 1968:46, 1994:67). But also, in speaking to parents, physicians assert that medical tests will reveal the "true" sex of the infant. This standard advice can be found throughout the medical literature; typical examples are Izquierdo and Glassberg (1993), Migeon, Berkovitz, and Brown (1994: 665).

Despite such uncertainty, physicians also understand that they do *choose* a sex. Kessler (1990) says this fact is conveyed in the terminology "sex assignment," the results of which are conveyed to the parents as the child's "true sex." She has also shown that in practice the fundamental criterion for assigning sex seems to be whether or not the infant has or can have (by surgery or androgen treatment) an "acceptable" penis. She quotes a pediatric endocrinologist: "[I]f the phallus is less than 2 centimeters long at birth and won't respond to androgen treatment, then it's made into a female" (1990:18). Indeed, physicians generally choose a sex according to the difficulty of surgery to normalize the genital appearance. "You can make a hole, but you can't build a pole," surgeons have been heard to quip (Hendricks, 1993), leading 90 percent of intersex cases to be assigned as female.

Also, for individuals who have an enlarged clitoris (exceeding one centimeter according to current protocols), Money's viewpoint (1968:93) has remained consistent, advocating surgery during infancy to remove parts of the clitoris. He argues (1994:94–95), "Despite the importance of the clitoris as a focus of erotic feeling, its removal does not *inevitably* abolish the capacity to reach orgasm" (our emphasis). Surgeons, however, concede their ignorance of the long-term outcome of such surgery. As stated in the literature: "[The] results of our study...do not guarantee normal adult sexual function" (Gearhart, Burnett, and Owen, 1995). "We cannot say that they will have orgasms when they are older" (Hendricks, 1993).

For hermaphrodites assigned male, genital surgery may be repeated many times in an attempt to fashion a "large enough" penis, with a closed urethra allowing standing urinary posture. One 13-year-old child had already had a half dozen surgeries (Hendricks, 1993); one article discussed 70 patients who had received an average of 5.5 surgeries, including one patient with 21 surgeries (Stecker et al., 1981).

SOCIAL MANAGEMENT

Specialist physicians overwhelmingly base their management of ambiguously sexed infants on Money's theories of gender (fieldwork data; Kessler, 1990:6). His belief is that all infants are gender neutral at birth; that an individual's gender identity is determined by the sex of rearing; and that the sex of rearing should be determined by the infant's genital appearance (i.e., assignment to male or female categories be done on the basis of whether an infant has or can have a socially acceptable penis or vagina). Hence it is important that such sex assignment be made as early as possible and be definitive so parents can socialize their children to the correct gender role. He does recognize the possibility of "mistakes" at first determination and allows for the possibility of "reannouncement." However, this should be done only once—it is meant to be forever.

Another major postulate of Money's theory is that there will be a period of time before an individual establishes a gender identity, before socialization "takes," as it were. Money argues that this critical period is limited: a given gender identity is analogous to imprinting in animals and is not subject to change after about two years of age even if the original assignment at birth was an error.

Since such change is viewed as being detrimental to the person's mental health, it is suggested that (through hormonal therapy and surgery) anatomy is best altered to fit gender identity. One case in particular, commonly known as the twin study (Money and Tucker, 1975:95), seems to support Money's ideas of genital primacy, critical period, and gender socialization. It was extensively reported—even appearing in *Time* magazine (January 8, 1973)—and has since reached textbook status in many disciplines. One of a pair of twin boys undergoing circumcision had his penis accidentally destroyed by cauterization. Using sex assignment logic from the theory of intersex management—if there is no functional penis make it into a female—the individual was surgically altered and reared as a girl. Theoretically this procedure resulted in a gender identity commensurate with the new genital configuration because all these things happened within the critical period. Nothing was reported by Money to suggest anything other than successful adjustment by the girl (by then in her mid-teens) and her family.

Genital surgery in infancy is not necessarily the end of medical intervention. As reported by our respondents and in the literature, at puberty especially, the individual may be confronted by alarming changes. For example, an individual raised as a boy may begin to grow breasts and menstruate, an individual raised as a girl may find her clitoris enlarging, and fail to menstruate. In such cases, Money's counseling technique assumes that the person's sexual identity will be congruent with the sex of rearing and that surgical and hormonal corrections will be made accordingly. Although he warns not to take this response for granted, the belief is that there are only two sexes, and that by surgery and/or hormonal treatment, the person will eventually find a home in one of them. As the child grows older, it is assumed the medical management will continue, especially if there are problems of social adjustment. Thus one technique is to provide the parents with a medical vocabulary as this "silences idle curiosity, for the idly curious hate to have their ignorance exposed" (Money, 1994:67). And, for problems that may emerge inside the family, there should be an available professional to talk to the child as the child gets older. This person may have to deal with parents who are "embarrassed, evasive, and, most important, unknowledgeable" (Money, 1994:68). Medical help and counseling, however, [were] the exception and not the rule for most intersexed persons we talked to. In general, they reported growing up in an atmosphere of secrecy and shame. Some reported feeling like "freaks," incapable of being loved; some said that they were "mutilated" and unable to be sexual. Most were angry that surgical decisions had been made without waiting until an age at which they could have been consulted.

Thus we see that social considerations play an important role in sex assignment and its social management in the form of cultural beliefs about sex, gender, and sexuality. These guiding notions rest on what Bolin (1996) has referred to as "the Western gender paradigm," which sees the existence of two (and only two) sexes, male and female, which determine two (and only two) genders, boys and men or girls and women. Thus the assumptions of medical personnel reinforce these cultural beliefs that there are only two sexes, that everyone has a discoverable "true" sex as one or the other, that genitals must match the assigned gender, and (though of less interest) that gender and sexual preference (heterosexual) eventually and normally will go together.

CHALLENGING THE MEDICAL VIEW

Until the 1990s hermaphroditism was very much a secret condition, known mainly to medical personnel and some social scientists, few, if any, of whom considered it anything but a problem to eradicate in those individuals unfortunate enough to suffer from it. That other perspectives could exist that might loosen hermaphroditism from the sole interpretation of medicine would not have been seriously entertained. But the 1990s saw the beginnings of attempts at demedicalization. These were part of a broader cultural shift that began in the late

1960s and early 1970s. At that time, the gay and women's movements challenged the whole notion of gender as an organizing device for social and personal life. Such movements were inexorably intertwined with academia, which gave more intellectual form to some of these ideas under the rubrics of social constructionism and postmodern thought, perspectives that became increasingly popular (Seidman, 1994b).

In this new view, gender roles are seen as social rather than biological units. Thus, they can be analyzed to show, for example, how social inequities between men and women operate; or that links that are taken for granted, such as that between gender and sexual preference, are the result of a socially sanctioned "compulsory heterosexuality" (Rich, 1980; Weinberg, Williams, and Pryor, 1994). The relativity of sex and gender categories is also demonstrated. In academia, historians showed the constructed nature of gender and sexuality over time (Foucault, 1980; Weeks, 1985); anthropologists, that binary notions of gender do not hold across cultures (Herdt, 1994a); and sociologists, the role of institutions in socially reproducing gender categories as a taken-for-granted reality (Garfinkel, 1967; Kessler and McKenna, 1978; Billings and Urban, 1982).

The interaction between inter- and extra-academic assaults on traditional notions of gender is also found in the queer movement and queer studies (Stein and Plummer, 1994; Seidman, 1994a). The first refers to a movement among younger homosexuals who reject the notion of a fixed and well-defined homosexual role. Seeing the connection between homosexuality and gender (gays and lesbians transgress gender expectations by choosing same-sex partners), they challenge such linkages. The movement also attracts other gender nonconformists, such as drag queens, and is sympathetic to the transgender community. In academia, queer theory acts as a guideline for such challenges to gender but goes further as it "calls into question obvious categories (man, woman, Latino, Jew, butch, femme), oppositions (man vs. woman, heterosexual vs. homosexual), or equations (gender = sex) upon which conventional notions of sexuality and identity rely" (Hennessy, 1993).

Totally outside of academia was the development of the transgender community. Early organizations of transvestites such as Virginia Prince's Society for the Second Self have allied with organized groups of transsexuals to create the "transgender" category, which is "a community term denoting kinship among those with gender-variant identities" (cf. Bolin, 1994). Their bone of contention is also with the traditional binary paradigm of gender, which sees anatomical sex as determining gender identity. Denying this simplistic view, this burgeoning movement creates new possibilities for gender blending and common cause with the queer movement as previously assumed assumptions fall by the wayside. For example, if anatomy and gender are rendered independent, then heterosexuality no longer can be considered natural unless procreation is considered the only reason for sex.

Hermaphroditism was a latecomer to these movements because it was considered a biological phenomenon. After all, hermaphrodites did have something "wrong" with their bodies, whereas transsexuals ostensibly did not. So why would anyone be upset by the medical establishment's efforts to help them? Also there seemed to be so few of them compared to other sexual minorities that their presence seemed unimportant to the gender-challenging movements.

Change began early with two studies that called John Money's theory into question. The first, known as the Dominican study (Imperato-McGinley et al., 1974), received attention in national news media such as *Newsweek* (November 26, 1979). Here, male pseudohermaphrodites who were assigned as girls at birth developed masculine characteristics at puberty and, despite their rearing as girls, were said to successfully change their gender identity to that of men. This finding challenged Money's theory that sex assignment and rearing determine gender identity and that gender identity change is impossible after about two years of age. Instead, it gave priority to

biological phenomena as producing gender identity. This study was contested on both theoretical and methodological grounds (Herdt, 1994b). For example, there is a term in these Dominican villages for such persons, indicating that discordant physical changes at puberty are expected, which casts doubt on the proposition that the children were reared unambiguously as girls. Money's theory thus remained relatively unscathed. The critical-period hypothesis in fact is vigorously reasserted in the second edition of *Sex Errors of the Body* (1994) in the form "nature/critical period/nurture" (Money, 1994:6). Sexual development must occur precisely on time, after which the outcome is immutable. The book, however, does not provide any (new) evidence for the existence of a critical period.

The next challenge occurred in 1982 when the biologically oriented sex researcher Milton Diamond was able to report on the fate of the male twin in Money's famous study and called into question the ease of transition to a female gender identity of the unfortunate cauterized twin (Diamond, 1982). He deplored the fact that treatment philosophies were based on this single case, and the general absence of follow-up studies to test Money's theory. Even though the BBC program (first aired in the United Kingdom in 1980) was later aired in the United States, and despite Diamond's reputation as a competent sex researcher, little notice seemed to be taken of the criticism at this time, and again Money's ideas survived more or less intact.

It was not until 1995 that the issue received more publicity, when at the annual meetings of the Society for the Scientific Study of Sexuality (SSSS), Diamond presented further data on this twin, now an adult. He said that throughout her life she refused to act like a "girl" and continually claimed to be a boy. Indeed, physically she did not look particularly female and refused to take feminizing hormones. Eventually she had a mastectomy and a phalloplasty (construction of a phallus) and married a woman. Diamond also recounted the refusal of the doctors at Hopkins to listen to the person's pleas that he was a "boy" and his resulting refusal to go to the hospital again after age 14. Diamond used this case to challenge the major postulates of Money's theory of gender, suggesting that individuals are not psychosexually neutral at birth, that psychosexual development is not determined by genital appearance, and that sex of rearing is not as important a determinant of gender identity as believed. When asked why this information had not influenced Money, he said Money insisted the twins had been "lost to follow-up." The second edition of *Sex Errors of the Body* (1994) makes no reference to the twin study with respect to Money's ideas on gender.

DEMEDICALIZING HERMAPHRODITISM

Challenges to the medical model of hermaphroditism did not have the effects that similar challenges had on the model of homosexuality. In the latter case the challenge was part of a wide and very successful civil rights program against demonstrable injustices experienced by many individual gays and lesbians.

This was not the case for the individual hermaphrodite. Lacking clear evidence of discrimination or of suffering from any injustice at all, what was the focus of their attention? And, there were no leaders, organizations, or potential members to articulate any dissatisfactions they may have had. Thus any social movement involving hermaphrodites did not seem a possibility in the 1990s. What type of problems could they face as a class of individuals, especially when it appeared that medical solutions existed for their plight? What reasons would they have for wanting to interact with other hermaphrodites? They were so socially disparate and unfocused in publicizing their social problem that collective efforts seemed doomed to failure.

But three factors help to account for the rise of an embryonic hermaphrodite movement. First, there was the continuing challenge to traditional notions of gender that we have discussed, especially the transgender movement in the early

1990s. Second, there was the technological ability to reach out to persons who have a similar interest yet are geographically isolated from one another. Such contacts were facilitated by the explosion of communication systems in the 1990s, especially the Internet, which allows for easy, anonymous communication between strangers through the computer. Thus like-minded people can organize themselves around a topic through bulletin boards, chatrooms, web home pages, e-mail, and the like.

Third, there was the appearance of a leader—who provided the type of leadership that a social movement requires. Herself a hermaphrodite, diagnosed as "male" at birth and raised as a male till a year and a half old, she subsequently was relabeled a "female" with an elongated clitoris. Her clitoris was removed and she was thereafter raised as female. Her surgery left her without a clitoris, labia minora, or orgasmic response, and a strong desire to discover how she ended up this way. This resulted in alienation from her family and frustration with the medical establishment. No social support was available from other hermaphrodites, and she found doctors whom she consulted to be evasive or obstructive. Others like her must exist, she reasoned, and perhaps had similar experiences, but there was nothing for them to rally around. Thus, in 1992, she moved to San Francisco (which she saw as a haven of tolerance) and within a year founded the Intersex Society of North America (ISNA) and its newsletter, *Hermaphrodites with Attitude* (*HWA*). Efforts since then have centered around publicizing ISNA's existence so that interested parties can get in touch, and using *HWA*'s pages to construct for intersexuals an agenda directed toward a clear target, dethroning the medical model of hermaphroditism. It seems the time was ripe, as groups with similar agendas arose independently during the same period in the United States[1] (Hermaphrodite Education and Listening Post), Britain (Androgen Insensitivity Syndrome Support Group), Japan (Hijra Nippon), Germany (Workgroup on Violence in Pediatrics and Gynecology), and New Zealand (Intersex Society of New Zealand).

ISNA'S CLAIMS

Based on our study of the organization and its literature, ISNA's position can be stated as follows. First, the term hermaphrodite is provisionally retained in order to connect with the cultural category into which persons with ambiguous genitalia have been placed. Fausto-Sterling (1993b), a developmental geneticist and adviser to the organization, sees this usage as important in order to facilitate communication with the medical community. However, ISNA also critiques the term because it reflects the Victorian belief that "true" sex resides in the gonads, a narrow, reproductively biased criterion. Additionally, the term (especially the distinction between true and pseudohermaphrodites) implies important differences between individuals who have similar problems produced by a variety of causes, thus dividing and isolating individuals with similar life experiences. For these reasons the name hermaphrodite is rarely used in practice by ISNA (the newsletter title being an exception) and has been replaced by terms like *intersexuals, intersexed persons, intersexual adults,* and *intersex* as nouns, and *intersexual* as the most common adjective (see also Money, 1994:37, who says, "A synonym for hermaphroditism is intersexuality," but makes no reference to ISNA). Reference is also made to the "intersex community" (as a subset of the transgender community, which is acknowledged as a model; *HWA,* spring 1995). One ISNA member writes: "Intersexed is a new self-label.... It seems to me that intersexed is a good, neutral, collective term that associates me with those who share my specific physical difference, and also with a larger group of people who have had to struggle with gender difference and have faced a gender rigid world, just as I have" (*HWA,* summer 1995).

The notion of intersexuality fits with the second pillar of ISNA's philosophy, the criticism of the Western gender paradigm with its binary framework. This is replaced by a conception of sexual differentiation as multidimensional—intersexuals fall between the ends of a male-female continuum with respect to one or more dimensions. Although this could produce an array of new gender categories, ISNA acknowledges the strength of the two-sex/gender model. It thus advocates that intersex children be raised as either boys or girls according to how comfortable the child feels with the particular designation and without the "normalizing" surgery that traditionally accompanies these choices.

The binary notion of sex creates the central problem for the intersexed person because it guides the medical model in assigning them to *either* the male or female sex and the imposition of cosmetic surgery. Surgery especially is challenged as a solution. For a start, there is no evidence that it is successful. Indeed, intersexuals interviewed present a litany of surgical horror stories. Here and in the letters ISNA receives from adult intersexuals there is no indication that they are typically either grateful or satisfied with their reconstructed genitals. To the criticism of a counseling psychologist who raises the possibility that ISNA could be dealing with a very unrepresentative sample of hermaphrodites (i.e., a small number of surgical failures), ISNA retorts that the stories have similar themes and, therefore, are believable (*HWA,* fall/winter 1995/1996). Also there is no mention of intersexed persons who are upset, not with the surgery per se, but because the results did not allow them to pass successfully as "normal." Be that as it may, what is true is the absence of follow-up data (especially comparing those who had surgery with those who did not) from the medical community, so that there is no evidence regarding how many the surgery benefits or evidence that refusal to subject one's child to it will result in psychological trauma and social maladjustment. For an emerging social movement, the message of surgical failure is focused enough to produce a rallying event of some importance.

It seems that in only a small number of cases do parents oppose the surgery recommended for their intersexed infants, and this fact provides ISNA's next objection—lack of informed consent. Treatment philosophy, as indicated, advocates early intervention, and it is impossible for an infant to provide informed consent. Even later, as a child or teenager, further surgery is often imposed to correct medical problems or "inadequate cosmetic results" resulting from earlier surgery.

ISNA asserts that the benefits of surgery have not been shown; rather, the potential for harm is demonstrated by the testimony of numerous ISNA members to us. To allow the individual to defer surgery until the child is old enough to understand what the options are challenges one part of the medical model (that surgery is beneficial), but also has more profound implications—that persons may wish to live *unaltered* in a social environment that is made to adapt to them rather than vice versa. (This approach, of course, dethrones the basic assumption of medicine—that the appearance of the genitalia should determine gender.) ISNA, moreover, has linked surgery on intersexed children to the issue of female genital mutilation found in Africa and the Middle East. This claim attacks the view that Western medical practice in this regard is operating at a more sophisticated level.

In addition to an agenda that reconstructs the meaning of hermaphroditism, ISNA functions as a support group for some of the hermaphrodites who share its views. For example, the sense of being deviant is a persistent theme among hermaphrodites who were interviewed. The realization that one is different sexually is reported by them to result in either living in public shame (being known about by persons outside of the immediate family, e.g., relatives, peers, neighbors) or with private guilt and anxiety (living with the knowledge that one could be unmasked; therefore avoiding intimate relationships and the like). The whole treatment ideology of early surgery is reframed by ISNA as primarily an attempt by the doctors to alleviate the *parents'* emotional distress and protect them from public shame, rather than necessarily being for the benefit of the intersexed child. Money (1994:66–67), as noted, realizes the shame that discovery may bring and recommends open announcement and the use of a medical vocabulary. But he says that parents should do so only if they are unable to geographically move and start life

anew. Such radical advice given by professionals to parents of intersexed infants highlights the deviance and stigma associated with hermaphroditism.

Although many persons seem to be convinced by ISNA's arguments, not all are swayed. John Money certainly does not accept their position, saying: "[Social constructionists] attack all medical and surgical interventions as unjustified meddling designed to force babies into fixed social molds of male and female, instead of allowing them to be a medically unmolested third sex" (1994:6). Attacking Fausto-Sterling (1993a), he says that one writer "has gone even to the extreme of proposing that there are five sexes" (1994:6). He finds all this irresponsible because without medical intervention many hermaphroditic babies would die. ISNA counters that genital morphology rarely has lethal consequences. And, though some intersexed babies with the genetic hormonal disorder congenital adrenal hyperplasia could die of shock without cortisone, ISNA says they are not suggesting that cortisone be withheld; only that the phallus not be surgically reduced. Money continues to argue that without immediate medical intervention children would grow up stigmatized. Again, ISNA counters by arguing that the source of stigma lies in social attitudes and the sex and gender structure of society and not the intersex body itself.

ISNA'S ACTIVISM

ISNA has not been content with merely presenting statements of its beliefs but has also organized itself as a protest group aiming attacks at individuals and organizations that directly support the medical model of hermaphroditism or indirectly hold traditional views of gender.

A deluge of e-mail messages has been sent by the organization, for example, on relevant research such as a study indicating poor outcomes of penile enlargement surgeries, criticizing the Defense of Marriage Act for its assumption of a fixed order of males and females, and celebrating Congress's outlawing of female genital cutting (ritual circumcision) in the United States, but noting its exclusion of intersexuals. One way in which ISNA's protests are demonstrated is the call for the picketing of former U.S. Surgeon General Joycelyn Elders. Elders, a pediatric endocrinologist, was contacted by ISNA but ignored attempts to reach her. One ISNA member challenged her at a public meeting, but she defended the traditional medical stance. ISNA now has asked its members to confront her at other public meetings whenever they can and is spreading news of her itinerary.

Following the model of the gay and lesbian challenge to the psychiatric profession over the definition of homosexuality in DSM-III (Bayer, 1981), ISNA attempted to organize a panel of intersexuals at the Mount Sinai Symposium on Pediatric Plastic Surgery to put forward their case. The director of the symposium refused this request. ISNA scheduled its own presentation nearby and was successful in getting two plastic surgeons, a psychiatrist, and a psychologist to join the panel despite hostility from most of the surgeons present.

ISNA also called for the picketing of the American Academy of Pediatrics [AAP], the first demonstration ever held by intersexed gender activists. They offered to meet with the head of the section on urology to discuss the changes that they would like to see in the model of treatment. The protest was jointly run by ISNA and the Transsexual Menace, and both groups were armed with flyers, banners, and posters. In response to the demonstration, however, the AAP released a statement reconfirming all the assertions of the medical model. Among its future strategies, ISNA plans to picket hospitals specializing in "managing" intersexed children in order to show that intersexuality is not rare; to oppose the assertion of doctors that all patients are satisfied with the surgical outcomes; to let parents know *before* surgery of the possible harm; and to increase their visibility so other intersexuals can find them.

DISCUSSION

What will become the outcome of this contest between two different views of hermaphroditism? Will hermaphroditism become demedicalized and take its place as a lifestyle issue among other conditions once considered pathological? The answer is presently impossible to give because the contest is in an early stage. It is also not clear what might constitute a victory for either side, or whether it is easy for participants to put themselves totally on one side or the other. How far away from the medical model is it possible to go before the medical metaphor is no longer relevant? And would a change in medical practices be satisfactory to ISNA even if the medical interpretation of hermaphroditism remained? Regardless of answers to these questions, what underlies the progress of ISNA so far?

First, it is made up of intersexed persons *themselves* who can contest medicine's assertions about how their lives have been affected by early surgical intervention. The mere existence of a public debate today over the management of intersexuality significantly undermines the medical claim to absolute authority and thus militates in ISNA's favor.

Second, it has been clever about its targets. Unable to be a grassroots organization building from the ground up, it has aimed at institutions and individuals who have great power in creating or sustaining social definitions of sex and gender. The current tactic to challenge former Surgeon General Joycelyn Elders is a good example of getting maximum publicity from minimum resources. And in the medical field ISNA has had an effect. The organization reports that it has approached the dean of Stanford University's medical school to consider including its concerns in the medical school's new curriculum. Such a change could be influential because this curriculum is likely to be adopted by other schools and because many of the school's graduates go into teaching. An article in the *Urology Times* (February 1997) featured a pediatric urologist who conceded that the protesters at the American Academy of Pediatrics have some truth in their message and that surgeons perhaps should rethink their philosophy for some early vaginal reconstructions. His opinion was reached after reviewing the disappointing outcome of a dozen cases of this procedure. The article concluded by noting that the questioning of early intervention is beginning to move into the mainstream, with the issue being featured in general-interest magazines. ISNA's success thus is a function of the groups it has targeted and the media selected.

Third, the medical profession and its allies are still so far the most important counterclaimant, although until recently their tactic has been to ignore ISNA's claims or to dismiss its members as "zealots." Nor have they been joined by any new groups. ISNA, however, has picked up important support from the academic world, and also from the gay and burgeoning transgender movements. Noting the possible negative consequences for intersexuals to come out publicly, ISNA has deliberately cultivated a network of non-intersexed advocates who enjoy high status and can speak in contexts where the intersexed are not allowed to (based on the medical profession's view that they cannot be objective). Feminist scholars, medical historians, anthropologists, and sex researchers have come to ISNA's aid. ISNA has also allied with Transsexual Menace and the National Gay and Lesbian Task Force, who have been willing to include intersex concerns as part of their political agenda. Allies are important because ISNA has not gained much through *nonconfrontational* interactions with the medical specialists who determine policy and actually carry out the surgeries on intersexed children. Another point is that intersexed persons currently cannot sue physicians because these doctors were following standard medical practice. As knowledge of negative surgical outcomes becomes more widespread, however, physicians will become more vulnerable to litigation, a powerful tool for ISNA if it could command

the resources to engage in prolonged legal battles. So, even though small in size, ISNA through its alliances has been able to spread its claims.

Fourth, these claims have been honed down to create a focus of attention: do not force genital conformity via surgery on children too young to consent, especially when it is accompanied by a management policy that involves secrecy and denial. This demand probably would not encounter as much public resistance as some other of ISNA's demands (e.g., that society recognize more than two sexes), since it refers to family decisions that affect "innocent children." However, the public may well empathize with parents who want to protect their children from an intersexed status.

Fifth, ISNA has been able to spread its message through different media—their own publication, *Hermaphrodites with Attitude,* presence on the Internet (through e-mail and their web page— http://www.isna.org), and face-to-face appearances, especially before professional groups, and even picketing such groups. An informative article on ISNA ran in the *New York Times* (February 4, 1996). And, as an indication of how important the leader has become, she was quoted again in the *New York Times* (March 14, 1997) in connection with Diamond and Sigmundson's (1997) published article on the Money twin (mentioned previously), a case that now has national recognition. These authors use the case to call for changes in the treatment of intersexed persons much as ISNA recommends. The leader is more sanguine in her reaction, believing that surgeons are unlikely to give up their medical interventions on the basis of this case. The article did mention that the debate about the medical treatment of intersexed children "has grown fierce" because of an "increasingly vocal group of intersexuals." She posted the article on the Internet, noting that it had been republished by many other newspapers, including the *Los Angeles Times, San Francisco Chronicle,* and *Chicago Tribune.* Lest ISNA supporters feel that this represented a wide acceptance of their position, she mentioned that the discussion of intersex had been omitted by some newspapers. Overall, ISNA has been able to address various audiences in ways that are effective.

Will an even wider acceptance of ISNA's claims depend on more intersexed persons joining the organization and providing money, skills, time, and organizing abilities? If it does, this may be an obstacle to ISNA's further success. How many intersexuals are there who see themselves through ISNA's eyes? For example, those who buy into the two-sex model may be upset with surgery only because they feel the results are inadequate for them to pass as "normal" males and females. Physicians claim (with little evidence) that most intersexed persons successfully treated as infants go on to merge into society and lead unremarkable lives; they refer to such grown patients as "formerly intersexed" (*HWA,* winter/spring, 1995/1996:6). If this is the case, it may limit ISNA's attempt to get such persons to adopt an identity consistent with its aims. ISNA has also been dependent, as mentioned, on one individual. (It is not a membership organization but is in touch with about 200 intersexuals and families.) It is by no means clear what the fate of her organization would be, should she falter. But with the independent genesis of several similar groups at about the same time, both in the United States and abroad, the movement seems to have become established. Further, the more success is achieved in making the public aware of its concerns, the more an environment exists in which future parents of intersexed children will be able to make choices other than surgery.

Does this issue have any wider implications, or is it just another case study of the "medicalization of deviance"? It serves both purposes. It is a case study, but it is important to see it also as part of a continuing social trend. ISNA's effort can be clearly located in what has been called the "politicization of deviance" (the political activism of so-called social deviants beginning in the 1960s in which they reject stigmatized identities and present their own conception of themselves to "normals"; Horowitz and Liebowitz, 1968; Kit-

suse, 1980). All the strategies used by these earlier groups (like the physically disabled and former mental patients) have been used by ISNA: *replacing an individual focus with a societal focus, advocating revolutionary change, and reformulating the discourse of their situation* (cf. Anspach, 1979). And within the intersex movement ISNA is the most socially active, urging political tactics on the more passive service-oriented or parent-dominated groups. Thus, those forces unleashed in the 1960s are shown through ISNA to still resonate. But why is it that claims by the "intersexed" are even being listened to today (regardless of whether they are accepted or not)? Certainly the historical moment is important. The contemporary concern with identities in academia and the popular media is providing an important backdrop. But there is perhaps a more specific lesson to be learned.

ISNA shows that the process of redefining deviance is not necessarily predicated on a mass movement. Often ignored by sociologists is the role played by the individual or small group (a focus often left to the historian or psychoanalyst) in favor of more general social processes. We cannot understand ISNA's situation, however, without such a consideration, and this topic has wider implications. One is that *any* individual today is much more important than in the past because of the technological resources available to her or him. It might not be far-fetched to argue that the reconstruction of deviance may increasingly involve an ISNA model as individuals make use of communication devices like the Internet and the camcorder to spread their message. Another implication is that not *all* individuals are equal in this regard: those who are most effective are those seen as having a very close connection to the issue. What we call "embodied claims" occur when a claim can be articulated through contact with an *actual person.* Such claims can run on a continuum from those with stigmata that are not immediately visible, like the hermaphrodite, to the immediately visible stigma of the terminal AIDS patient (cf. Scott and Morgan, 1993). In the former case the genitals need not be seen: the mere existence of a person willing to make such a claim is enough to be effective. In the latter case, the patient may be comatose, but the symptoms of Kaposi's sarcoma indicate a claim to a particular status.

To use a person who embodies the issue makes a claim more real because it is a real person who is standing there. And intersexed persons correspondingly plan to "march out of the endocrinology textbooks" (*HWA,* summer, 1995). This intention suggests another reason for part of ISNA's success. Intersexuals literally embody the contradictions and confusions of the sex and gender systems and stand before us as living testimony to the negative consequences of such abstractions. Thus, intersexuality is an embodied claim of great power: it does not need a cast of thousands to call into question some fundamental assumptions.

In conclusion, this paper is about people trying to change their social and personal identities as deviant. They have joined the ranks of those who do so by organizing a social movement to change society's views about their condition or behavior rather than by changing themselves to conform to society's norms. In the case of intersex persons, they must battle the very powerful medical profession that has controlled their definition and continues in its desire to maintain that control. While the intersex movement is small and far from a mass movement, in its early stages it is showing some success. Its progress may further suggest some modifications in the popular view of the conditions necessary for effective social movements: that such ventures need a lot of financial resources and widespread internal as well as external support—for example, money, a large number of constituents, and a large support base in the general population (Weitzer, 1991). The intersex movement does not have much in the way of such capital. The era of modern technology, however, makes access to people easier, so that today small movements may have greater success than they would have in the past. The question

that remains, though, is will the movement need to obtain larger amounts of social and financial capital to be fully successful, or will it proceed on the road to success simply by continuing in the manner in which it has been operating?

NOTE

1. The oldest support group for intersexed persons in the United States is the Turner Syndrome Society, established in 1987, which has a national organization serving thousands of members. ISNA's aims are wider and more political, seeking to challenge the medicalization of intersexuality itself.

REFERENCES

Anspach, Renee. 1979. "From Stigma to Identity Politics: Political Activism among the Physically Disabled and Former Mental Patients." *Social Science and Medicine* 13A:765–73.

Appleton, Lynn M. 1995. "Rethinking Medicalization: Alcoholism and Anomalies." In *Images of Issues: Typifying Contemporary Social Problems,* ed. J. Best, pp. 59–80. New York: Aldine De Gruyter.

Bayer, Ronald. 1981. *Homosexuality and American Psychiatry.* New York: Basic Books.

Best, Joel. 1995. *Images of Issues: Typifying Contemporary Social Problems.* New York: Aldine De Gruyter.

Billings, Dwight B., and Thomas Urban. 1982. "The Socio-Medical Construction of Transexualism: An Interpretation and Critique." *Social Problems* 25: 266–82.

Bolin, Anne. 1994. "Transcending and Transgendering: Male-to-Female Transexuals, Dichotomy and Diversity." In *Third Sex, Third Gender: Beyond Sexual Dimorphism in Culture and History,* ed. G. Herdt, pp. 447–85. New York: Zone Books.

Bolin, Anne. 1996. "Traversing Gender: Culture Context and Gender Practices." In *Gender Reversals,* ed. S. Ramet, pp. 22–59. New York: Routledge and Kegan Paul.

Conrad, Peter. 1975. "The Discovery of Hyperkinesis: Notes on the Medicalization of Deviant Behavior." *Social Problems* 23:12–21.

Conrad, Peter, and Joseph W. Schneider. 1980. *Deviance and Medicalization: From Badness to Sickness.* Philadelphia: Temple University Press.

Conrad, Peter, and Joseph W. Schneider. 1992. *Deviance and Medicalization: From Badness to Sickness,* 2nd ed. Philadelphia: Temple University Press.

Diamond, Milton. 1982. "Sexual Identity, Monozygotic Twins Reared in Discordant Sex Roles and a BBC Follow-up." *Archives of Sexual Behavior* 11: 181–86.

Diamond, Milton, and K. Sigmundson. 1997. "Sex Reassignment at Birth: A Long Term Review and Clinical Implications." *Archives of Pediatrics and Adolescent Medicine* 151: 298–304.

Dreger, Alice. 1995. "Doubtful Sex: Cases and Concepts of Hermaphroditism in France and Britain, 1868–1915." Ph.D thesis, Indiana University, Bloomington.

Dreger, Alice. 1997. "Hermaphrodites in Love: The Truth of the Gonads." In *Science and Homosexualities,* ed. Vernon Rosario, pp. 46–66. New York: Routledge.

Fausto-Sterling, Anne. 1993a. "The Five Sexes: Why Male and Female Are Not Enough." *The Sciences* 22:3 (March/April).

Fausto-Sterling, Anne. 1993b. Letter in *The Sciences.* 22:4 (July/August).

Fausto-Sterling, Anne. 1996. Personal communication, December.

Fiedler, Leslie. 1978. *Freaks: Myths and Images of the Secret Self.* New York: Simon and Schuster.

Foucault, Michel. 1980. *The History of Sexuality,* Vol. 1: *An Introduction.* New York: Random House, Vintage Books.

Garfinkel, Harold. 1967. *Studies in Ethnomethodology.* Englewood Cliffs, NJ: Prentice-Hall.

Gearhart, John P., Arthur Burnett, and Jeffrey Owen. 1995. "Measurement of Evoked Potentials during Feminizing Genitoplasty: Technique and Applications." *Journal of Urology* 153:486–487.

Hendricks, Melissa. 1993. "Is It a Boy or a Girl?" *Johns Hopkins Magazine,* November: 10–16.

Hennessey, Rosemary. 1993. "Queer Theory: A Review of the 'Differences' Special Issue and Wittig's *The Straight Mind.*" *Signs: Journal of Women in Culture and Society* 18:964.

Herdt, Gilbert. 1994a. *Third Sex, Third Gender: Beyond Sexual Dimorphism in Culture and History.* New York: Zone Books.

Herdt, Gilbert. 1994b. "Mistaken Sex: Culture, Biology, and the Third Sex in New Guinea." In *Third Sex, Third Gender: Beyond Sexual Dimorphism in Culture and History,* ed. Gilbert Herdt, pp. 419–46. New York: Zone Books.

Hermaphrodites with Attitude. 1995–96. San Francisco: Intersex Society of North America.

Horowitz, I., and M. Liebowitz. 1968. "Social Deviance and Political Marginality." *Social Problems* 15: 280–96.

Imperato-McGinley, J., L. Guerrero, T. Gautier, and R. E. Peterson. 1974. "Steroid 5 Alpha-reductase Deficiency in Man: An Inherited Form of Male Pseudohermaphroditism." *Science* 186:1213–15.

Izquierdo, Gerardo, and Kenneth I. Glassberg. 1993. "Gender Assignment and Gender Identity in Patients with Ambiguous Genitalia." *Urology* 42: 232–42.

Kessler, Suzanne J. 1990. "The Medical Construction of Gender: Case Management of Intersexed Infants." *Signs: Journal of Woman in Culture and Society* 16:3–26.

Kessler, Suzanne J., and Wendy McKenna. 1978. *Gender: An Ethnomethodological Approach.* Chicago: University of Chicago Press.

Kitsuse, John I. 1980. "Coming Out All Over: Deviants and the Politics of Social Problems." *Social Problems* 28:1–13.

Lee, Ellen Hyun-Ju. 1994. "Producing Sex: An Interdisciplinary Perspective on Sex Assignment Decisions for Intersexuals." In *Human Biology: Race and Gender.* Providence: Brown University.

Meyer-Bahlburg, Heino. 1996. "Gender Assignment from the Clinician's Perspective." Paper presented to the Society for the Scientific Study of Sexuality, San Francisco, August.

Migeon, Claude J., Gary D. Berkovitz, and Terry R. Brown. 1994. "Sexual Differentiation and Ambiguity." In *Wilkin's The Diagnosis and Treatment of Endocrine Disorders in Childhood and Adolescence,* ed. Michael S. Kappy, Robert M. Blizzard, and Claude J. Migeon, p. 1243. Springfield, IL: Charles C. Thomas.

Money, John. 1968. *Sex Errors of the Body: Dilemmas, Education, Counseling.* Baltimore: Johns Hopkins University Press.

Money, John. 1972. *Man & Woman, Boy & Girl: The Differentiation and Dimorphism of Gender Identity from Conception to Maturity.* Baltimore: Johns Hopkins University Press.

Money, John. 1994. *Sex Errors of the Body and Related Syndromes: A Guide to Counseling Children, Adolescents, and Their Families,* 2nd ed. Baltimore: Paul H. Brooks.

Money, John, and Patricia Tucker. 1975. *Sexual Signatures.* Boston: Little, Brown.

Rich, Adrienne. 1980. "Compulsory Heterosexuality and Lesbian Existence." *Signs: Journal of Women in Culture and Society* 5:631–60.

Riessman, Catherine K. 1983. "Women and Medicalization: A New Perspective." *Social Policy* 14: 3–18.

Rubington, Earl, and Martin S. Weinberg. 1996. *Deviance: The Interactionist Perspective,* 6th ed. Boston: Allyn and Bacon.

Scott, Sue, and David Morgan. 1993. *Body Matters: Essays on the Sociology of the Body.* Washington, DC: Falmer Press.

Seidman, Stephen. 1994a. "Symposium: Queer Theory/ Sociology: A Dialogue." *Sociological Theory* 12: 166–77.

Seidman, Stephen. 1994b. *Contested Knowledge: Social Theory in the Postmodern Era.* Cambridge, MA: Blackwell.

Spector, Malcolm, and John I. Kitsuse. 1977. *Constructing Social Problems.* Menlo Park, CA: Benjamin Cummings.

Stecker, John F., Charles E. Horton, Charles J. Devine, and John B. McCraw. 1981. "Hypospadias Cripples." *Urologic Clinics of North America: Symposium on Hypospadias* 8:539–44.

Stein, Arlene, and Ken Plummer. 1994. "I Can't Even Think Straight: Queer Theory and the Missing Sexual Revolution in Sociology." *Sociological Theory* 12:178–87.

Szasz, Thomas. 1970. *The Manufacture of Madness.* New York: Harper and Row.

Weeks, Jeffrey. 1985. *Sexuality and Its Discontents: Meanings, Myths, and Modern Sexualities.* London: Routledge and Kegan Paul.

Weinberg, Martin S., Colin J. Williams, and Douglas Pryor. 1994. *Dual Attraction: Understanding Bisexuality.* New York: Oxford University Press.

Weitzer, Ronald. 1991. "Prostitutes' Rights in the United States: The Failure of a Movement." *Sociological Quarterly* 32:23–41.